P9-DMM-112

SCARFACE
AND THE
UNTOUCHABLE

SCARFACE
AND THE
UNTOUCHABLE

AL CAPONE, ELIOT NESS,
AND THE BATTLE FOR
CHICAGO

MAX ALLAN COLLINS & A. BRAD SCHWARTZ

wm

WILLIAM MORROW
An Imprint of HarperCollinsPublishers

Page 675 constitutes an extension of this copyright page.

SCARFACE AND THE UNTOUCHABLE. Copyright © 2018 by Max Allan Collins and
A. Brad Schwartz. Excerpt from THE UNTOUCHABLE AND THE BUTCHER © 2019 by
Max Allan Collins and A. Brad Schwartz. All rights reserved. Printed in the
United States of America. No part of this book may be used or reproduced in
any manner whatsoever without written permission except in the case of brief
quotations embodied in critical articles and reviews. For information address
HarperCollins Publishers, 195 Broadway, New York, NY 10007.

P.S.™ is a trademark of HarperCollins Publishers.

HarperCollins books may be purchased for educational, business, or sales
promotional use. For information please email the Special Markets Department at
SPsales@harpercollins.com.

A hardcover edition of this book was published in 2018 by William Morrow, an
imprint of HarperCollins Publishers.

FIRST WILLIAM MORROW PAPERBACK EDITION PUBLISHED 2019.

DESIGNED BY WILLIAM RUOTO

Photo on page ii courtesy of Cleveland Public Library Photograph Collecton.
Map on page xxv courtesy of the Newberry Library.

The Library of Congress has catalogued a previous edition as follows:

Names: Collins, Max Allan, author. | Schwartz, A. Brad (Austin Bradley) author.
Title: Scarface and the untouchable : Al Capone, Eliot Ness, and the battle
   for Chicago / Max Allan Collins, A. Brad Schwartz.
Description: First Edition. | New York : William Morrow, 2018. | Includes index.
Identifiers: LCCN 2018024767| ISBN 9780062441942 (hardback) | ISBN
   9780062441959 (trade paperback)
Subjects: LCSH: Capone, Al, 1899–1947. | Ness, Eliot. |
   Gangsters—Illinois—Chicago—Biography. | Organized
   crime—Illinois—Chicago—History—20th century. | BISAC: TRUE CRIME /
   Organized Crime. | BIOGRAPHY & AUTOBIOGRAPHY / Criminals &
   Outlaws. | HISTORY / United States / 20th Century.
Classification: LCC HV6248.C37 C65 2018 | DDC 364.1092 [B]—dc23
   LC record available at https://lccn.loc.gov/2018024767

ISBN 978-0-06-244195-9 (pbk.)

19 20 21 22 23   DIX/LSC   10 9 8 7 6 5 4 3 2 1

In memory of

MICHAEL CORNELISON,

who brought Eliot Ness to life

CONTENTS

PART THREE: ON THE SPOT

There is something tragically wrong with a system of justice which can and does make criminals of honest men and can only convict gangsters and racketeers when they don't pay their income taxes.

—RAYMOND CHANDLER

Preface to the Paperback Edition

Eliot Ness appears in only one episode of the HBO series *Boardwalk Empire*, which memorably portrayed many of the major figures of the Prohibition era. In the fifth season's second episode, Ness (played by Jim True-Frost) gives a pompous speech to reporters, preening for the cameras as he vows to take down Al Capone. Meanwhile, Treasury agent Frank Wilson (played by Michael Countryman) passes silently behind him, ignored by the press, carrying one of the ledgers that will ultimately be used at Capone's trial.

In those few seconds, the scene encapsulates what most chroniclers of Chicago's gangsters have claimed for decades—that Ness and his Untouchables chased headlines and raided a few breweries here and there, while Wilson and the tax investigators did the real, painstaking detective work, building an airtight, escape-proof case against Capone. Far from the heroic gangbuster of television and film, Ness contributed nothing to the Capone investigation, while feeding his insatiable appetite for publicity by claiming credit for Wilson's sterling work—so say revisionist historians beginning in the early 1960s (in response to *The Untouchables* TV series) and continuing to this day.

But in researching *Scarface and the Untouchable*, we uncovered a wealth of primary source evidence contradicting this conventional wisdom. Not only was the income tax case against Capone weaker than Wilson's reputation suggests, but the work done by Ness and his Un-

touchables was far more significant than has been previously acknowledged. The headlines and raids were only a fraction of a sophisticated
and innovative investigation focused on proving Capone's place in a
vast bootlegging syndicate. To gather evidence of the scale and scope of
the Capone mob, the Untouchables pioneered practices used by federal
agents to this day.

We based our conclusions on federal files, court documents, press
accounts, and the recollections of several Untouchables—evidence
that, more often than not, looked at the Capone case from the outside or in retrospect—because precious few documents produced as
part of this investigation have survived. Shortly after publication of our
hardcover edition, however, a copy of the final case report summarizing Ness's work—apparently kept against Prohibition Bureau orders
by Lyle Chapman, the Untouchable who compiled it—turned up for
auction in the fall of 2018.

Before this important historical document was sold, we were able to
examine it at length. It confirms much of what we deduced about how
the Untouchables operated, while further debunking the way previous
writers have characterized Ness's investigation. We now know with certainty that the brewery raids so damaging to Capone's cash flow were
secondary to the team's building a conspiracy case that could have seriously crippled the Chicago Outfit had it ever gone to trial. Why this
case was never prosecuted, as you will see, had little to do with Ness
himself, and much to do with the politics of going after America's most
famous and powerful criminal.

When the Untouchables weren't raiding breweries or tailing beer
trucks, they interviewed more than six hundred witnesses, compiled
countless pieces of evidence, traced vehicle registrations and bank records, consulted with handwriting experts, and in under twenty months
tied Capone and dozens of others to a decade-long bootleg conspiracy.
This unseen detective work, alluded to throughout our book but never
fully explored, comes into stark relief when the investigation is viewed
from within.

Access to this document allowed us to make a handful of small changes and corrections throughout the text, in places where the public record failed to conform with this privately held information. But we have made no substantial revisions, because the case report does not contradict our narrative of the Capone investigation. If anything, it places exclamation points where before we could only offer periods and question marks.

Instead, we have chosen to include excerpts from the document in the P.S. section at the end of this edition, so that readers can see for themselves exactly what these agents accomplished. Popular culture remembers Ness and the Untouchables largely for refusing bribes and busting through the doors of illegal breweries, while revisionist historians have gone out of their way to discredit the team's work as trivial press puffery. Neither portrait tells the true, full story. We hope to have finally balanced the scales of justice for these legendary—but real, and humanly flawed—crime fighters.

M.A.C. and A.B.S.
February 2019

Introduction

UNTOUCHABLE TRUTH

by Max Allan Collins

On Monday night, April 20, 1959, the first of a two-part TV presentation called "The Untouchables" appeared on *Westinghouse Desilu Playhouse.* I was eleven years old, watching in Muscatine, Iowa, and I was dumbstruck. The next day, all the kids—well, the boys, anyway—were talking about this hardhitting crime show, the fact-based story of federal agent Eliot Ness and his band of incorruptible lawmen, taking on the Al Capone gang during Prohibition.

Me, I was bowled over by how much it tallied with my obsession (which had started at age six) with Chester Gould's *Dick Tracy,* particularly reprints of 1930s and '40s comic strips. When the concluding "Untouchables" episode aired, finally presenting Al Capone on camera (after the prior week's crafty cliffhanger), I was struck by how much Capone resembled the '30s *Tracy* villain, Big Boy.

I could hardly have imagined that less than twenty years later, I'd be writing the legendary *Dick Tracy* strip and hearing Chester Gould confirm my suspicions that detective Tracy had been based on Ness and the Untouchables—a fact still little noted or known.

That was the beginning of my interest in true crime in general and

Eliot Ness specifically. I immediately read Ness's memoir, *The Untouch-ables* (1957), cowritten by sportswriter Oscar Fraley, as well as Fraley's follow-up, *4 Against the Mob* (1961), about Ness's later law enforcement career in Cleveland, Ohio.

The Ness-Fraley book has largely been dismissed as a fabrication, but one of our many discoveries while researching this book has been to confirm how surprisingly accurate it was. Fraley built his narrative on a decidedly nonboastful, fairly short memoir by Ness, amplifying it with newspaper and magazine accounts. But the ghostwriter paid no heed to chronology, and events appeared in what struck Fraley as the most effective order. Ness protested to no avail, taken out by a heart attack at fifty-four, before publication of the work that would make him far more famous dead than he'd been alive.

Fraley's readable if creatively rearranged account led to a backlash among Ness's contemporaries in law enforcement as well as Chicago journalists, building him (inaccurately) into a glory hound. The enor-mously successful TV series spawned by the *Desilu Playhouse* two-parter did Ness's real-life reputation no favors, either.

Ironically, the original two-part film (released theatrically as *The Scarface Mob*) was the most accurate presentation on film Eliot Ness and the Untouchables have ever received. Director Phil Karlson was a master at true-crime noir, with *The Phenix City Story* (1955) behind him and *Walking Tall* (1973) ahead of him (with its similar glorifica-tion of real-life lawman Buford Pusser).

Featuring Hollywood star Robert Stack as a grimly charismatic Ness, the "Untouchables" two-parter boasted a semidocumentary style, Roaring Twenties nostalgia, and fast, violent action, with '30s media star Walter Winchell's rat-a-tat-tat narration perhaps the masterstroke.

A much-fictionalized Chicago mob was amplified by similarly fan-ciful episodes with Ness taking on such real-life criminals as Vincent "Mad Dog" Coll, Dutch Schultz, Waxey Gordon, Legs Diamond, and Lucky Luciano. J. Edgar Hoover, never a fan of the real Ness, objected so much to the Untouchable's latter-day fame that he insisted the producers credit the FBI's work at the end of the Ma Barker episode. Capone himself (with Neville Brand reappearing) was again featured only in the two-part episode, "The Big Train."

The only other two-part *The Untouchables* episode, "The Unhired Assassin," was loosely based on the assassination of Mayor Anton Cermak. That event also became the subject of my detective novel *True Detective* (1983).

In the late '70s, while teaching mystery fiction at a community college, I happened to notice *The Maltese Falcon*'s 1929 copyright—the year of the St. Valentine's Day Massacre. That meant Sam Spade and Al Capone were contemporaries—instead of Philip Marlowe meeting an Al Capone type, Al Capone could meet a Philip Marlowe type.

In 1981, I set out to write a period private eye story around a real crime—the Cermak assassination. I sought the help of George Hagenauer, a Chicagoan whose knowledge of the city and its mob history was considerable. I said to George, "My private eye, offended by the rampant graft, will quit the Chicago PD." When he stopped laughing, George said, "Max, don't you know? You get on the PD *for* the rampant graft!" In that exchange, Nathan Heller was born.

Ever since, George has been my primary research associate on the Heller novels, as well as many other historical thrillers. With Heller, the approach is to research a famous unsolved (or controversially solved) crime, and when I'm ready to write the definitive work on the subject, I write a private eye novel instead.

Early on I had the idea of making Eliot Ness the honest law enforcement contact for my somewhat shady PI—every private eye has a cop pal, after all. But I'd read in Fraley that Ness and the Untouchables had disbanded after Capone went to prison, with Ness gone from Chicago by 1933. The mandate of my novel was authenticity, so I abandoned the notion of using him.

And then he turned up in the research! Ness was right there on the scene, after two corrupt cops attempted the assassination of Frank Nitti. And into *True Detective* he went. Ness appears in a number of subsequent Heller novels as well, in particular *The Million-Dollar Wound* (1986), *Stolen Away* (1991), and *Angel in Black* (2001).

In 1986 I was asked by an editor to spin Ness off into his own novels—a good opportunity to explore his little-written-about years as public safety director in Cleveland. George and I made several trips to that city and explored the locations of potential Ness novels, from the castle-like boathouse on Clifton Lagoon, where Eliot lived, to the dreary Kingsbury Run gully, where the serial-killing Mad Butcher pursued his homeless prey.

Our research took us to the Cleveland Public Library, the City Hall Municipal Reference Library, and the Case Western Reserve Society, where the Ness papers reside. I expected to be disappointed. Noted mob expert Hank Messick's *The Silent Syndicate* (1967) explored the Cleveland mob while disparaging Ness's gangbusting role.

So when I found in the Case Western Reserve card catalog (remember those?) an entry saying, "Eliot Ness Scrapbook," I held out little hope. We'd already been there all afternoon but asked to see the scrapbook anyway. A civil servant slogged off dutifully to answer our request.

Near closing, the civil servant returned, pushing a hand truck laden with perhaps half a dozen huge scrapbooks, each many inches thick and large enough for a newspaper front page of the era to be pasted in. George and I exchanged the same kind of dumbstruck look the original "Untouchables" broadcast had generated in me.

Actually exploring this treasure-trove find—apparently the last person to use the scrapbooks had been Oscar Fraley—meant returning the next day, and the next, and many more after that. Examining such items as Ness's eyeglasses and a signed photo, I alerted the staff that this material should not be handed out to the general public, and soon Case Western had put the scrapbooks on microfilm.

Among that material were postcards sent from a mental institution to Eliot Ness by the Mad Butcher of Kingsbury Run. Eerily, the front of one postcard depicted Neville Brand, insane and ranting, clutching prison bars, in a still from *Riot in Cell Block 11* (1954)—years before Brand would be Al Capone on *The Untouchables*.

My four Ness-in-Cleveland novels—*The Dark City* (1987), *Butcher's Dozen* (1988), *Bullet Proof* (1989), and *Murder by the Numbers* (1993)—were followed in 2004 by a play, *Eliot Ness: An Untouchable Life*. A one-man show performed by my late friend Michael Cornelison, *Untouchable Life* became a film of the same name in 2005, airing on a number of PBS stations.

I had written the play, and then filmed it, in part because I wanted to go on record with my version of Ness's life. The research George and I did, particularly on *Butcher's Dozen* (the first book-length work on the Kingsbury Run slayer), had been plundered without credit by other novelists and graphic novelists, and by nonfiction writers, who apparently felt that not acknowledging my work was fine because it was "fiction."

I also wanted to address aspects of director Brian De Palma's 1987 film, *The Untouchables*. De Palma is a director I admire, and the film is well-made and entertaining. The screenplay is another matter. David Mamet certainly created a memorable speech for Sean Connery—"You wanna get Capone? Here's how you get him. He pulls a knife, you pull a gun," and so on.

But the historical inanities—*inaccuracies* doesn't cover it—are unforgivable. I have no trouble with liberties being taken with historical material for dramatic purposes. But having Mounties chase rumrunners in a country where rum is legal? Depicting a trial where a jury is changed midstream? Showing Eliot Ness tossing Frank Nitti off a building? The screenwriter displays a lack of respect not just for history but for his audience.

Untouchable Life attracted a high school student from Michigan to the Des Moines Playhouse to see Michael Cornelison perform as Eliot Ness. A. Brad Schwartz had been a *Dick Tracy* fan since around five years of age, having been exposed to the film of that name (on which I was a creative consultant and wrote the movie tie-in novel).

Just past age eleven—and this may sound very familiar—Brad saw a movie called *The Untouchables*, recommended by his mother as being "like *Dick Tracy* but real-life." He became enamored with that film, which led him to my work, including *Road to Perdition*, a graphic novel in which Eliot Ness appears. Brad was fifteen the summer he came to Des Moines for the play *Untouchable Life*, going to the premiere of the film in Rock Island, Illinois, in February 2005.

Somewhere along the way we got to know each other, and—while his college thesis evolved into the Orson Welles book, *Broadcast Hysteria* (2015)—he suggested we collaborate on a biography of Eliot Ness. I'd had several editors suggest the same, but I felt *Untouchable Life* was my last word on the subject.

Apparently I was wrong.

The project morphed into a dual biography of Capone and Ness. For a good long while, we hoped to follow Ness through to the end of his days, but eventually Chicago became the focus. For now.

We hope to set the record straight on any number of things. The inaccurate and unfair portrayal of Ness is one; the glorification of Al Capone is another. Jonathan Eig, in his *Get Capone* (2010), is guilty of both, particularly in trying to clear the mobster of the infamous baseball bat murders and the St. Valentine's Day Massacre.

For the former, Eig claims the baseball bat story dates only to 1975 when we have the basics in the *Chicago Tribune* and the *New York Times* within two days of the murders, and Capone wielding the bat himself in print within a year of the event. For the latter, Eig ignores ballistics evidence, eyewitness testimony, and a credible confession in favor of a convoluted theory based on a single error-ridden letter to the FBI.

Deirdre Bair, in her book *Al Capone: His Life, Legacy, and Legend* (2016), collaborates with Capone family members to present a portrait of a loving husband and father. Typically, Bair disparages Ness, claiming he made "sure the press was there to take his photograph as he struck heroic poses over gallons of illegal booze being smashed to pieces and going down the drains and into the sewers."

No such pictures exist.

A handful of diligent researchers—among them Rebecca McFarland, Paul Heimel, and Scott Leeson Sroka—have endeavored to shed light on the real Ness and his accomplishments. But even self-proclaimed Ness defender Douglas Perry—in *Eliot Ness: The Rise and Fall of an American Hero* (2014)—lingers on sordid details of Ness's supposed womanizing and drinking, with little in the historical record to back him up.

Filmmakers Ken Burns and Lynn Novick use Eig as a source for their documentary *Prohibition* (2011), Novick insisting, "Eliot Ness had nothing to do with catching Al Capone. . . . he wrote a book in which he just made stuff up."

By dismissing Ness's work, Eig and others seek to shift the spotlight to the Treasury agents who compiled the tax evasion case against Capone—in particular lead investigator Frank J. Wilson and his boss, Elmer L. Irey. The public has all but forgotten these men, a fact their admirers seem to blame on Ness.

For example, Gary Alford of the IRS—singing the praises of tax investigators—told the *New York Times,* "They don't write movies about Frank Wilson building the [Capone] tax case."

Only they did—*The Undercover Man* (1949), directed by B-movie master Joseph H. Lewis of *Gun Crazy* fame. Starring Glenn Ford as "Frank Warren," the film—which plays like a dry run for the *Untouchables* TV series—was based on Frank Wilson's self-aggrandizing article in *Collier's* magazine in 1947 (a hardcover book followed in 1965). Wilson made a boatload of money off the film—he literally bought a boat.

Elmer Irey wrote (or a ghostwriter did, as had been the case with Wilson) his own puffed-up work, *The Tax Dodgers* (1948), taking credit for busting up the Capone mob. Irey also filmed a crime-does-not-pay opening scene for *T-Men* (1947); one wonders if he realized that Chicago gangster Johnny Rosselli was an uncredited producer on the picture, with a 10 percent piece of the action.

Neither Frank J. Wilson nor Elmer Irey even mention Eliot Ness in their respective memoirs. Read this book and see if you think that was fair. Add to that the treatment Al Capone got from the federal government, as well as the questionable conduct of the much-lauded Judge James Herbert Wilkerson.

In trying to set the record straight, we have used decades of Collins-Hagenauer research, including published sources—newspapers, books, and long-forgotten true-crime magazines—as well as newly uncovered archival documents and federal files obtained through numerous Freedom of Information Act requests. Trips have been made to libraries, archives, and personal collections in a dozen states as well as the District of Columbia, including the office of the Cook County Medical Examiner.

Coauthor Schwartz has combed through the personnel files of the Untouchables in the historic archives at the ATF's D.C. headquarters. Brad also made a trip to the small Pennsylvania town where Eliot Ness died, speaking with the last people with living memories of the man. He also spoke with the son of one Untouchable and the grandson of another, and spent an afternoon exploring Ness's old South Side neighborhood, later visiting Capone's Miami mansion.

A few notes about the pages ahead. Al Capone's famous successor is known in the popular media and most books as Frank Nitti, but the name he used was Frank Nitto. We have honored that, though when the Nitti usage turns up in a quote, we spare you the "*sic*." We also use "Jack Guzik," as Nitto's fellow gangster was known to his associates and family, although some media quotes will retain the more commonly seen "Jake." Similarly I have taken the liberty of correcting minor spelling, grammar, and usage errors in quotes from newspapers and magazines of the day.

We do not use the Ness-Fraley book, *The Untouchables*, except where verified by multiple sources, with the occasional exception of drawing upon Ness's state of mind in relation to certain incidents.

Neither of our subjects has really gotten a fair shake from history. Our hope is to balance the scales of justice on their behalf. Telling the story of Capone and Ness accurately is our goal—not only is truth stranger than fiction, in this case it's even more compelling than the many lies and exaggerations visited on both.

Organized Crime in 1920s Chicago

Touhy Gang
(headquarters in
Des Plaines)

Dion O'Banion/
Bugs Moran
Gang

LAKE
MICHIGAN

Guilfoyle Gang
(with Capone)

St Valentine's Day Massacre
at Heyer's Garage (Feb. 14, 1929)

Maddox
"Circus" Gang
(with Capone)

Aiello

O'Banion's Shop

Klondike
O'Donnell Gang

Murray

LOOP

Genna Bros

Druggan
Lake Gang

Lexington Hotel
Four Deuces
Metropole Hotel

Hawthorne
Hotel

CICERO

Capone's headquarters
at various times

Hawthorne
Race
Track

Capone's
Brothels

STICKNEY

Saltis
Gang

Ralph
Sheldon
Gang

De Courseys

McGeoghegan

Spike
O'Donnell
Gang

Capone's
Home

Torrio's
Home

CITY LIMITS

Lake
Calumet

BURNHAM

Torrio/Capone syndicate
Independent gangs
Disputed areas
Gang hangouts

Suburbs shown were sites of
Torrio/Capone operations

Devon Ave

Irving Park Rd

North Ave

22nd St

Garfield Blvd

79th St

95th St

147th St

Sibley Blvd

Harlem Ave

Cicero Ave

Western St

Halsted St

State St

Archer Ave

Archer Rd

Stony Island Ave

South Chicago Ave

Torrence Ave

N

TWO MILES

© 2004 The Newberry Library

Rogues' Gallery

CAPONE FAMILY

Alphonse "Scarface Al" Capone

Mary Josephine "Mae"
Capone

Ralph "Bottles" Capone

Frank Capone

Charles Fischetti

CHICAGO OUTFIT AND ALLIES

John Torrio

James "Diamond Jim" Colosimo

Frankie Yale

Frank "The Enforcer" Nitto

Jack "Greasy Thumb" Guzik

"Machine Gun" Jack McGurn

Frankie Rio

Albert Anselmi

John Scalise

Tony Lombardo

Mike "de Pike" Heitler

Dr. Kenneth Phillips

E. J. "Artful Eddie" O'Hare

THE AMERICAN BOYS

Gus Winkeler

Fred "Killer" Burke

Fred Goetz

CHICAGO HEIGHTS MOB

Lorenzo Juliano

Joe Martino

NORTH SIDE GANG

Dean O'Banion

Hymie Weiss

Vincent "Schemer" Drucci

George "Bugs" Moran

Joe Aiello

Jack Zuta

THE TERRIBLE GENNAS

"Bloody" Angelo Genna

Mike Genna

Anthony Genna

Pete Genna

POLITICIANS AND PRESS

Mayor William Hale
"Big Bill" Thompson

Mayor Anton J. Cermak

William McSwiggin

Robert E. Crowe

Jake Lingle

BUREAU OF PROHIBITION

Eliot Ness

Alexander G. Jamie

Albert M. Nabers

Edna Stahle Ness

E. C. Yellowley

George E. Golding

THE UNTOUCHABLES

Lyle B. Chapman

Bernard V. "Barney" Cloonan

William J. Gardner

Martin J. Lahart

Joseph D. Leeson

Paul W. Robsky

S. Maurice Seager

Robert D. Sterling

Warren E. Stutzman

SECRET SIX

Robert Isham Randolph

Samuel Insull

Julius Rosenwald

Shirley Kub

DEPARTMENT OF JUSTICE

George E. Q. Johnson

Assistant Attorney
General Mabel Walker
Willebrandt

Assistant Attorney
General G. A. Youngquist

Judge James H.
Wilkerson

William J. Froelich

Dwight H. Green

Jacob Grossman

Samuel Clawson

Attorney General
William D. Mitchell

J. Edgar Hoover

Melvin Purvis

INTELLIGENCE UNIT

Elmer Irey

Frank Wilson

Arthur P. Madden

LAWMEN AND ALLIES

President Herbert
Hoover

Pat Roche

LeRoy Gilbert

August Vollmer

SCARFACE
AND THE
UNTOUCHABLE

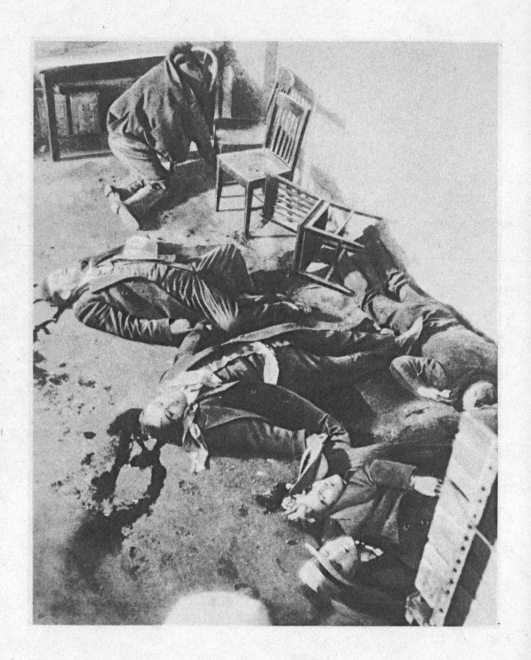

2122 North Clark Street—February 14, 1929. *(Authors' Collection)*

Prologue:
St. Valentine's Day

On a frigid February morning in 1929, gangsters gathered in a garage on Chicago's North Side, waiting for their boss.

Outside, a bitter wind pelted pedestrians with a faint dusting of snow. The garage—a narrow, one-story structure squeezed between two buildings on North Clark Street—offered shelter but no furnace. Most of the men kept their heavy overcoats on, or huddled around a pot of brewing coffee. A single dangling bulb gave off just enough light to cast a stark glow over a few trucks and cars, each registered to a fictitious address.

Nine years had passed since the start of national Prohibition, the benefits of which the men in this garage had reaped. They wore tailored overcoats over custom-made suits, jeweled stickpins on brightly colored neckties, silk shirts, and diamond rings. Most had fat wads of cash in their pockets and pistols under their arms.

Three were hardened gunmen, enforcers for the North Side mob controlling this part of Chicago. Two handled business tasks—one a financial wizard and the gang's reputed "brains," the other a speakeasy owner and labor racketeer. A sixth, a former safecracker, was employed by the gang as a $50-a-week mechanic—he wore only coveralls, and probably worked under one of the vehicles as the rest assembled. The seventh wore a carnation in his button hole—a thrill-seeking optician with no known criminal record who hung out with gangsters and bragged he could have anybody he didn't like killed.

Just past 10:30, two armed raiders burst in through the back door. The gangsters might have felt a momentary surge of adrenaline—after years of open warfare on Chicago's streets, they had every reason to expect retaliation from South Side rivals. But a glance at the invaders quelled their fear.

The blue-uniformed pair announced themselves as cops. The North Side gang had things well worked out with ranking members of the Chicago police. A raid like this was just a nuisance, a sham conducted by a department of unparalleled corruption. It wasn't like any of them would ever serve time for violating the most unpopular law in the history of the United States.

The bluecoats brandished a shotgun and lined men up facing the wall. The gangsters, and the optician and coverall-clad mechanic, raised their hands and offered no resistance as one officer patted them down and took their weapons. A snub-nosed .38 clattered to the floor, nobody bothering to pick it up.

Then the uniformed pair ushered in two men in long, heavy overcoats, from under which they produced two Thompson submachine guns. Perhaps the weapons were handed off to the uniformed "officers"; but more likely the new arrivals held on to the guns themselves. Either way, the tommy guns were raised and leveled at the backs of the seven men leaned against a cold brick wall.

One weapon was equipped with a twenty-round stick magazine, the other a fifty-round drum that wound up like a watch. Each contained .45-caliber pistol bullets, weighty rounds with a relatively slow muzzle velocity, losing much of their power flying through the air. Being shot by a .45, even multiple times, did not necessarily mean instant death.

But the Thompson could fire six hundred rounds every minute, and when the first tommy gun opened fire, all fifty of its rounds were spent within five seconds.

The harsh chatter of machine-gun fire filled the tight space as the gunman raked his Thompson back and forth, huge jets of flame leaping from the muzzle, strobing the garage as a hail of .45s caught the gangsters first in the heads, then across their backs. The shooter had to fight to keep control of the weapon, pulling down on its front grip as the movement of its heavy bolt—snapping back and forth ten times a second—pushed the barrel up toward the ceiling.

At such close range, the bullets shredded flesh, snapped bone, mutilated viscera, and spurted hot blood onto the cold concrete floor. Some slugs passed through their targets and pounded into the brick wall, shattering into fragments and ricocheting back into the dying men. The victims spun violently and fell—on their backs, on their faces, one slumping over a chair. A shotgun barked, and a burst of buckshot caught the optician in the back as he dropped.

When the tommy gun's last spent shells rattled to the floor, the air was dense with smoke and a mist of blood and brain matter.

Some, perhaps most, victims were taking their time dying, writhing and moaning as their lifeblood seeped out. But their killers were in a hurry. They had held the second Thompson in reserve, should the often-unreliable drum mag of the first fail to fire properly. Once that drum had been emptied, the man holding the backup tommy stepped forward and fired into the men on the floor. The mechanic caught a bullet in the head, but must have still been moving, because whoever held the shotgun finished him, firing directly into his face. The charge obliterated the left side of his forehead, spilling his brains onto the cement, what remained of his eye sinking back into its shattered socket.

The gunfire attracted only scant attention outside the garage. A witness later testified he mistook the chatter for a car backfiring. But men in heavy overcoats exiting with their hands up, held at gunpoint by two apparent uniformed cops, indicated a routine bootlegging arrest—business as usual in Prohibition-era Chicago. The quartet piled into a big black Cadillac and sped off into the snowy city.

The entire operation had taken no more than five minutes.

Prompted by a suspicious housewife, a neighbor forced his way into the garage and walked into a scene out of Dante's *Inferno*. Gun smoke still hung thick and heavy, but not concealing the seven bodies sprawled against the back wall, blood coursing down a central drain. Nearby, a survivor howled—a big German shepherd straining at a rope tied to a truck. Highball, the dead mechanic's dog, appeared to be the only living thing in the room.

But one man was moving, crawling through puddles of scarlet in a hopeless bid for the door. Frank Gusenberg, younger brother of the dead man bent over a chair in the corner, had been shot fourteen times. Police arrived and took him to a nearby hospital, where Gusenberg refused to identify his killers, saying only that the raiders were dressed like cops. He died around 1:30 P.M., after defiantly telling police, "Nobody shot me."

The garage on North Clark Street soon filled with police, reporters, and photographers. Many had seen their fair share of violence, but never such sickening carnage.

The *Chicago Daily News* described "the circle of yellow lamplight, where six things that were men are sprawled." A *Chicago Evening American* reporter, after walking around the room, remarked, "I've got more brains on my feet than I have in my head."

What the newsmen couldn't describe, the cameramen captured, their gruesome photographs pushing the limits of what the newspapers dared print. The next day's *Chicago Tribune* tried to shelter its readers from the horrific slaughter by covering the corpses with cartoonish images. The *Chicago Herald and Examiner,* however, forced its readers to view the carnage, a huge photo of the only slightly touched-up bodies next to a story beginning: "Chicago gangsters graduated yesterday from murder to massacre."

On February 14, 1929, gangland sent Chicago a very bloody valentine. Like the unlucky, bullet-and-buckshot-riddled optician, many Chicagoans took a perverse pride in their city's reputation for gangsterism and corruption. They enjoyed the bootleg liquor organized crime was happy to supply, and to the citizenry—the police included—an occasional murdered gangster or two seemed a fair trade.

But the calculated brutality of the massacre shocked the nation, and far exceeded what even the most jaded Chicagoans might shrug off. Bootleggers seemed suddenly less like daring outlaws breaking a stupidly unfair law, and more like bloodthirsty killers. Many gangsters fled the city, temporarily at least, for fear of a police crackdown.

The most notorious of gangland leaders, a celebrity criminal like none the world had seen before, was not even in Chicago that icy February morning. But he would return from a sunny vacation to a city turned cold and far less hospitable.

No one was ever charged, much less convicted, for committing the so-called St. Valentine's Day Massacre. But almost immediately everyone in Chicago seemed to know who had given the order. Police fingers pointed at the South Side gangsters who had been at war with the North Siders since the early 1920s.

Prominent among the accusers was George "Bugs" Moran, the North Side mob leader whose tardiness spared him the grisly fate of his cronies. Over the preceding few years, several Moran allies had been wiped out with the same careful planning and brutal efficiency that characterized the massacre.

Now the word got around that Moran blamed his South Side rivals for these killings as well. As he was said to have put it, "Only one gang kills like that—the Capone gang."

At the very hour of the St. Valentine's Day Massacre, Alphonse Gabriel Capone was in Miami, Florida, answering questions in the Dade County Courthouse about his financial transactions and alleged underworld connections.

As a stenographer established a beyond-any-doubt alibi for his whereabouts, Capone flatly denied ever being a bootlegger. What was he, then? A onetime antiques dealer turned professional gambler, whose losses at the racetrack far outstripped his meager winnings. How he managed to pay those debts—or to afford a $40,000 house on Miami's

Palm Island, a custom-built armored limousine, and $7,000 in tailored suits, pajamas, and silk underwear—remained between him and his wallet.

Though originally from Brooklyn, Capone embodied the ethos of his adopted hometown. As one observer said in 1931, "No one is ashamed of anything in Chicago," which was "too big, too busy, too powerful. . . . [It] is gorgeous and it is awful."

Al Capone fit right in. Hefty and powerful, an inch or two under six feet, he threw around more than two hundred pounds of fat and muscle. Every feature of his broad, expressive face seemed too large—big eyes under thick eyebrows, wide nose over fat lips, thick cheeks and bulbous chin, a visage encouraging caricature.

He wore his wealth literally on his sleeve by way of brightly colored, custom-tailored suits in every shade from sober blue to bright yellow. His trademark pearl-gray fedoras and fat, expensive cigars would soon be copied in films and comic strips, and by lesser gangsters. Where most criminals lurked in the shadows, Capone embraced the spotlight, becoming (as *Harper's* put it in 1931) "one of the central figures of our time."

This was a man whose hunger for more of everything—power, pleasure, publicity—drove him from the slums of his boyhood to the pinnacle of luxury. A conservative estimate placed Capone's net worth in 1929 at $20 million, or more than $280 million by early twenty-first-century standards. But he cared little for dollars and cents.

Georgette Winkeler, wife of one presumed St. Valentine's assassin, wrote Capone "had no regard for money except as a business necessity and a personal convenience." He spent freely, tipped extravagantly, and gave generously, handing out $100 bills to kids to "go buy some ice cream."

Like many a mobster, Capone maintained his power through fear. In 1926, famed Chicago attorney Clarence Darrow said the illicit nature of bootlegging made violence and intimidation inevitable.

"The business pays very well," Darrow said, "but it is outside the law and they can't go to court . . . so they naturally shoot."

And Capone would not hesitate to pull the trigger. Stories of his capacity for violence—firing into a man's face four times in a bar full of witnesses, or bludgeoning three men to the edge of death with a baseball bat—served the same purpose, partly fabricated or not. That fearsome reputation was essential to cement his place in Chicago's gangland.

Yet some part of Al Capone desperately wanted to be liked, even admired, and he took pains to put up a respectable front. As an up-and-coming hood, he saw how his mentor, Johnny Torrio, lived the life of an honest businessman, even a gentleman, while thriving off vice and crime.

"Everybody calls me a racketeer," Capone supposedly said. "I call myself a business man. When I sell liquor, it's bootlegging. When my patrons serve it on a silver tray on the Lake Shore Drive, it's hospitality."

Capone was a man perfectly fitted to his times. He rose to prominence when Americans were idolizing the great captains of industry—the Rockefellers, the Carnegies, the Fords—and for a while Capone assumed an unlikely place in that pantheon. The public knew Capone had killed, by proxy if not always in person, yet that seemed only to add to his roguish appeal.

As W. R. Burnett, author of the seminal gangster novel *Little Caesar,* observed in 1930, "Capone is no monster. Far from it. He is merely a thoroughly ruthless individual, who had acumen enough to take advantage of a very unusual situation."

Capone's ability to murder at a distance made him easier to accept. He offered himself up as a flamboyant character, known affectionately as "the Big Fellow," while staying aloof from the evil done in his name. The public could look at him the way they might a lion in a zoo—a colorful killer, safely domesticated, if not yet behind bars.

His true self seemed always to hover just out of view. He tried to have press photographers take his picture from the right side, so the camera wouldn't capture the thin white lines across his left cheek that had earned him his hated nickname: "Scarface."

Those scars, a memento of his rough-and-tumble bouncer days in New York, Capone did his best to minimize—shaving three times a day, using talcum powder, turning down hat brims on the left side to keep his torn cheek in shadow. He would claim a bayonet had sliced his face during battle in the Great War, though he never actually served. But like the violence defining his career, the scars remained a part of him, famous and impossible to conceal.

On that Valentine's Day in 1929, Capone seemed at the height of his power. He effectively controlled Chicago's city government and had his chief gangland rivals beaten back. Whether by accident or design, the Clark Street massacre wiped out Capone's last major opponent by shattering what remained of the North Side mob. Many observers considered Capone the undisputed king of Chicago, and he had only just turned thirty years old.

But he remained a victim of his own success. His meteoric rise to power and fame had trapped him in a kind of purgatory—"the most-shot-at man in America," according to his first biographer. Surrounded by bodyguards, slipping from hideout to safe house, he seemed always on the lookout for another assassination attempt. After years of fighting to stay on top—to say nothing of fighting to stay alive—he'd grown tired and weary. He frequently announced a desire to retire, and probably spoke the truth—not that he ever could achieve that goal.

"Once in the racket, you're in it for life," Capone supposedly said in 1931. "Your past holds you in it. . . . If I could go to Florida and live quietly with my family for the rest of my days, I'd be the happiest man alive. But no such peaceful life is in the cards for me."

And yet Capone's exit would arrive sooner than he might have expected. The event cementing his hold on the city also set the stage for his downfall—although Capone would never be tried for the St. Valentine's Day Massacre, the court of public opinion would convict him, the media behind his national celebrity turning against him.

After the stock market crash that October, resentment grew over Capone's conspicuous wealth. With a quarter of Americans out of work, the new U.S. president became desperate for a victory . . . and the possibility of one presented itself in taking down the nation's most famous bootlegger.

In their search for a hero to fight that battle, the government and the media would pluck from obscurity a federal agent four years younger than Capone—a scrupulously honest man in America's most dishonest city, working in the most corrupt law enforcement agency in the nation's history.

This ideal G-man, with a growing record of arrests, convictions, and daring undercover work, had a dislike of guns and violence, preferring to leave his service revolver behind even when on duty. Those who met him but had never seen him in action usually found it hard to envision him going on raids or tussling with gangsters.

He was not lacking in courage or conviction; as one friend put it, "I have never known a man who lived by a stricter code." But in person he seemed remarkably mild-mannered, passive, even shy. He had an easy smile and a good sense of humor, but was recalled by that same friend as "extremely modest and introverted," a person "who could get lost in a crowd of two people."

Yet serving as an officer of the law built up his self-confidence; having the authority of the federal government behind him gave the young G-man an inner strength he perhaps couldn't muster on his own. Eliot Ness did not believe in Prohibition but felt it should be respected. Moreover, he understood the true danger of the ill-advised dry law was the power and influence it gave to organized criminals like Al Capone.

Physically, they were polar opposites—Capone, big and imposing; Ness, slim and retiring. Where Capone outfitted himself flashily, Ness dressed with professional care, his brown hair parted neatly down the middle. Even as a Prohibition agent he had a collegiate look, with a boyish, lightly freckled face and the broad shoulders of a student athlete.

Still, his gray-blue eyes could turn cold in an instant. Ness "immediately strikes one as 'all business,' then smiles and winks," wrote one

Chicago reporter, "as if the fact that he is merely acting in a role is just between you and him."

And yet their backgrounds were more alike than either might ever have known. Both were first-generation Americans, sons of immigrant fathers who worked as bakers in the old country. Once in America, Capone's papa chose a new trade, barbering, while Ness's remained a baker, yet both fathers went on to build successful independent businesses in their adopted land.

While Capone and Ness had similar role models in their fathers, each learned very different lessons. Ness was proud to be the son of a man "who never cheated anyone out of a nickel." Capone embraced a career in crime, the life of a struggling honest businessman not for him.

Capone and Ness shared a certain ambition, each with an impulse to turn his chosen field into a fully modern profession. While Capone applied the methods of corporate business to organized crime, Ness worked to elevate the role of the police officer in American society, urging the adoption of new technologies and scientific techniques.

Both men were willing to work hard to succeed, each in his own way—with energy, charisma, and recklessness, the assets of their remarkable youth. Capone became the head of a multi-million-dollar criminal syndicate at age twenty-six, while Ness at twenty-seven took charge of the federal squad tasked with bringing Capone down.

In the Untouchable Eliot Ness, fate and the federal government had found the perfect foil for Scarface Al.

The central irony of the now-legendary struggle between Ness and Capone is how little direct contact the two men had—one phone call, and a single face-to-face meeting when, in 1932, the convicted Capone was put on the Dixie Flyer to the federal penitentiary in Atlanta.

And yet they continue to do battle, each locked in the other's terrible embrace, like Holmes and Moriarty on the cliff's edge over Reichenbach Falls.

PART ONE

PRAIRIE AVENUE BOYS

"Diamond Jim" Colosimo with Dale Winter (top) and following his murder (bottom), May 11, 1920. *(Authors' Collection)*

One

1895–1920

Over the years, many would claim (falsely) that Al Capone had been an immigrant, as if they wanted to disown one of America's most notorious native-born sons. But Capone himself insisted on setting the record straight.

"I'm no foreigner," he would say. "I'm as good an American as any man. My parents were American-born and so was I."

In this, as he so often did, Capone specialized in half-truths.

When Gabriele Capone moved his family from Italy to a better life in America, he chose a place called Brooklyn. Perhaps he'd been warned of New York's overcrowded ghettoes with their rotten wooden firetraps, where cholera or typhus drove the rich from the city while corpses of the poor littered the Lower East Side. A father relocating his brood might well want to avoid crime-ridden streets where an immigrant's meager daily wage could wind up in a mugger's grasp.

But in 1895, Brooklyn was rife with opportunity. The Brooklyn Bridge, an engineering marvel known worldwide, had been finished in 1883. The ever-growing City of Brooklyn was annexing other towns and cities in Kings County, with talk in the air of one great emerging metropolitan area. Clearly opportunities existed in Brooklyn that did not in Gabriele's home region.

Gabriele was born in 1865 in small-town Angri, southwest of Naples, on the edge of Salerno province in the shadow of Mount Vesuvius. Unlike many of his countrymen, he was literate, training outside the oral traditions of his village, working as a baker (pasta-making a specialty) and a lithographer. He married Theresa Raiola in 1891, their son Vincenzo (James) arriving the next year. And in 1895—with second son Raffaele (Ralph) also in tow and Theresa pregnant with Salvatore (Frank)—the family made its way across the Atlantic.

At first, they continued to pronounce their surname phonetically—*Caponi*—though that would soon change. Classified at Ellis Island as Italian, the Capones were more rudely branded as "dagos" or "wops"— low-class, unintelligent southern Italians, disposed to crime.

Thousands of Italians came to Brooklyn before the Great War, a world bordered by factories on the north and warehouses on the south, its streets mingling neighbors and kin from Campanian and Calabrian villages among bright flowers and holy imagery and sublime cooking smells. On front stoops, mothers with babies at their bosoms would oversee armies of kids in the street, while neighbors sat in sunshine and shared gossip and letters from home.

However poor the inhabitants of a tenement, a certain joy and exuberance might be found—in the Union Street marionette theater, perhaps, or a festival like the feast of the patron saint or the Assumption of Our Lady, electric-bulb-lined arches lighting up the night as statues of saints were paraded, until fireworks and explosions pronounced the proceedings at a joyful end.

But those who had known Italy were soon confronted by a generation not so tied to heritage, who studied English and spoke in the language of the streets. America, even Brooklyn itself, was their world, a world that bred restlessness in its youth.

In the neighborhoods near the Navy Yard, from Red Hook to Greenpoint, Old and New World ways came together and sometimes clashed. Here the Capone family settled, an area dominated by defense spending, relatively immune to economic recessions.

Seagulls soared above, offering a constant, cawing reminder of the nearby Atlantic. But the fresh sea air was tainted by a caustic bouquet of oil, fumes, and rot. Sailors and shipbuilders came in droves, bringing with them a wealth of gambling, prostitution, and saloons—on Sands Street, chippies prowled and dancehall girls pranced, while tattoo parlors thrived on drunken bad decisions, and cheap whiskey was often laced by the Mickey Finn that led to a mugging.

A summer's day might bring the stench rolling in from the Gowanus Canal, a nasty gash in the marsh-like landscape, its murky green-brown waters hungry for rusty vessels, dead machinery covered in funereal snarls of green, nature in a particularly ironic mood. The canal attracted a legion of lawbreakers, who often made it home to a special kind of swimmer—a floating corpse, bloated and ripe.

The Capone family's two-room flat had a single potbelly stove and no running water, with access to an outhouse. Theresa now had three little children to care for—cooking, warmth, and bathing required hauling up water, coal, or wood. A fourth child came on January 17, 1899. Baptized without a godfather, he was given the Latin name Alphonsus, though he would be known by its English equivalent: Alphonse Capone.

To support his growing family while saving to start his own business, Gabriel (his name Americanized now) toiled as a manual laborer, baker, and grocery clerk before taking up barbering. The shipyards made a ready market for Gabriel's scissors and razors, with many workers and sailors passing through—the same clientele who frequented brothels, gambling joints, and saloons. While less congested and safer than New York's East Side slums, the Navy Yard soon revealed itself as a dicey place to raise a family.

Tall, handsome Gabriel Capone made friends with ease. His literacy helped him stand out among his countrymen, who often addressed him as "Don." Theresa soon had nine children: Erminio (Mimi) came along in 1901; Umberto (Albert) in 1906; Amadoe (Matthew) in 1908; Erminia in 1910 (dying the same year); and, finally, in 1912, dark-haired Mafalda, who developed a particularly close relationship with Al. The Don's children, however, were not free from discrimination and ethnic conflict.

The active young Capone boys fled their two-room flat, making the street their major playground. On the street and in school, name-calling could escalate into violence, teachers thrashing students and debasing them racially. Children united along ethnic lines, often with older kids, forming surrogate families that taught survival.

Smoking started in primary school, crap games under a street-corner gaslight around age eight or nine. Sex had to wait for high school and a mature twelve. Childhood pursuits like flying a kite off a rooftop had their place, as did swimming in the East River, though a kid got no more than three lessons before he drowned. The Fourth of July meant single-shot pistols, a bargain at a quarter, and Election Day was about nicking barrels and boxes for the big fire—didn't matter who won, if the fire burned high and bright.

An older youth, Francesco (Frank) Nitto, his family also from Angri, lived near the Capones at two Navy Street addresses within half a mile of Al's family. Typically, Nitto dropped out during the seventh grade, age fourteen. The close proximity of their homes suggests the short, feisty Nitto knew the Capone boys—at least the older ones, James, Frank, and Ralph.

The whole family needed to work not only to survive but to improve their lot, one economic unit with everyone pitching in. Theresa would bake bread and the older boys would sell it on the street. The brothers hawked newspapers and shined shoes—low-income kids following their honest father's lead. Of course, dishonesty could also help support the family—stealing food, clothing, and other necessities from pushcarts or stores.

Gabriel became a citizen in 1906, making his wife and children citizens as well. He moved the family to Garfield Place in Park Slope, and opened his own shop in the building where they lived. Young Nitto, working as a barber years later in Chicago, listed Brooklyn as the site of his professional training. He and his family moved from Navy Street to

Garfield Place, even closer to the Capones, where Frank likely learned barbering from Gabriel.

The oldest Capone boy—Vincenzo, called James—became fascinated with the romanticized dime-novel West and the lure of wide-open spaces away from crowded, crime-ridden streets. Gabriel arranged a job for his oldest son caring for horses in rural Staten Island, a world and a ferry ride away. Finally, in 1907, an opportunity arose for James to work with horses, traveling with a touring circus.

James bid his little brother good-bye at the Staten Island Ferry, not to return for decades, his exit saving him from the life of crime consuming many of his brothers. Influenced by movie idol William S. Hart—whose last name he assumed—James came to work in various law enforcement capacities out west, including Prohibition agent. The oldest son leaving home, however, meant more than just family heartache, but a loss of income.

The family's new, more predominantly Italian neighborhood bordered Irish Red Hook and a Sicilian enclave, where turf wars among youth gangs often broke out. The corner of Broadway and Flushing, near a saloon, became young Capone's territory, shared with racetrack touts, bookies, and drug dealers. From there and other such notorious corners, kid gangs cheerfully terrorized Jewish neighborhoods, turning over pushcarts and milk cans, yanking on the beards of old men, and busting out random windows.

Frank Nitto, more than a decade Al's senior, emerged as a leader among the young toughs. He adopted Capone as a mascot for his gang—the Boys of Navy Street. Even as an eight-year-old, Capone had proven himself a born fighter, and the teenaged Nitto trusted him enough to have him join the group in battle.

For some time, local Irish roughnecks had been harassing the Italian women of Capone's neighborhood—first by coming up behind them and lifting up their skirts, and later graduating to property destruction and theft. These brazen assaults demanded a response, and Nitto took it upon himself to deliver it.

The task of broadcasting Nitto's message fell to young Capone, then about eight. Nitto's boys lifted a washtub from one of the women they were planning to defend—they would get it back to her before her next batch of laundry—and strapped it to Al's chest. With stick in hand, he became the group's drummer boy, leading their march into enemy territory. As they arrived outside an Irish bar, they drew their rivals out with a mocking chant: *"We are the Boys of Navy Street—Touch us if you dare!"*

The Irish emerged to do battle, but they proved no match for Nitto's crew. Capone, probably younger than any other combatant, stayed right in the thick of it—urging his allies on by rapping the washtub and keeping up the chant. When police arrived to break up the scuffle, the Irish had been walloped—and the Boys of Navy Street had vanished, scurrying away over the rooftops.

For Nitto, this was a rare instance of fighting in the open. In later years, he would prefer to do battle in the shadows, catching his targets off guard. For Capone, on the other hand, this scrap set the tone for his future criminal career. He couldn't help but announce himself by breaking the law loud and proud, and he always liked to be seen fighting for something larger than himself—whether for his family, his business, or the neighborhood women.

Perception mattered to Al Capone. He would soon meet a mentor whose lifestyle proved what Capone always seemed desperate to believe—that one didn't have to be a thug in order to be a gangster.

Near the Capone home, the John Torrio Association, from its second-floor window, wielded great influence over the Italian gangs. Torrio, perhaps New York's most improbable criminal leader, was among its most prosperous.

In a field where size, strength, and brute force ruled, Torrio was short, soft, and nonviolent. An elementary school dropout, he was one smart crook, who—in a world where gang leaders battled to the top—boasted he never fired a gun. Others fought his wars, his strategic expertise making young toughs rich by ghetto standards.

As a teen on New York City's Lower East Side, Torrio didn't join gangs; instead, he organized them, moving them into grown up criminal activities. His James Street Boys committed the usual petty larceny but also worked with Tammany Hall, the New York City political machine, to help steal elections. Torrio's political influence expanded his criminal activities into gambling and prostitution, as he formed relationships with the likes of budding gangsters Charles "Lucky" Luciano, Ciro Terranova, and Frankie Uale. Soon Torrio joined Uale across the river in Brooklyn, where racketeering flourished.

Born Frank Ioele (Yo-A-Lee) in Calabria, Italy, plump and of medium height, Uale was a tough street fighter who rose fast in the Five Points ranks. Like Torrio, he moved from traditional gang activities into new areas, including prostitution and unionism. Unlike Torrio, Uale was known for violence, ready to kill an opponent or beat an underling, even his own brother.

At age eight, Al Capone moved into the neighborhood near Torrio's office. The avuncular little gangster regularly used local boys to run errands, at first innocuous ones, then—if they proved trustworthy—making payoffs and delivering contraband. It's likely Al ran such errands, beginning a relationship with Torrio that lasted for decades.

To navigate the turbulent world into which he had been born, young Al had little choice but to join a street gang. For those hardcore street kids, such gangs served "as a training school," one resident remembered, prepping them for more serious forms of crime. While the Irish were scrappy kids up for any fight, and tough Jewish youths worked hard at defending themselves, the Italians earned a reputation for preferring blades and bullets over fisticuffs and street-corner diplomacy. Still, most kid gang members would come to be solid citizens, going into business or on to higher education. The others would graduate from crap games, stealing, and truancy into organized crime, armed robbery, and incarceration.

At his father's suggestion, the teenaged Al set up a shoeshine box under a large clock on a busy street. By chance, the spot proved the perfect place to observe the workings of a protection racket run by local godfather Don Batista Balsamo.

After watching Balsamo's men extort money from neighborhood businessmen, Capone decided to try it himself. He built a small crew of youths who could serve as muscle—among them his cousin Charlie Fischetti—and had them shake down his fellow shoeshine boys. The racket started small but grew to such an extent Balsamo's men took notice and put a stop to it.

Yet at home, Al Capone was a polite, dutiful son, bringing money and food to his family, thanks to his secret life as a thief and errand boy for gangsters. The praise from his family, especially his mother, inadvertently propelled him toward a life of crime.

In the sixth grade, when a teacher at P.S. 133 struck him for insubordination, the fourteen-year-old Al supposedly struck her right back. He never set foot inside the school again, or perhaps he just dropped out to work and help support his family.

Bigger and stronger now, on his way to a burly but nimble five foot ten, Al developed into an outstanding pool player; he was also capable of knocking a man out with a single blow. By his midteens, he was affiliated with the South Brooklyn Rippers and later the Forty Thieves Juniors, the latter with ties to Torrio's friend Uale, who by now was diversifying into loan-sharking, the protection racket, and even a line of cigars.

Uale decided to mimic the profitable College Inn near Coney Island with his own Harvard Inn, which he operated under the assumed last name Yale. For this, Yale needed men who were more than simple street-gang thugs—young Al Capone, six years Frank's junior, had the necessary skills. Tough and strong, capable of violence but affable and well liked, Al would matriculate as a bouncer-cum-bartender at the Harvard Inn.

The Harvard Inn was no nightclub for college students—its customers were dockworkers and low-life criminals, and sometimes their

families and friends. Capone kept busy maintaining order and keeping the clientele's glasses brimming; a show-off pastime of the young
bartender, when business was slow, was shooting at beer bottles and
shearing off their necks. But much as he admired and imitated the
superficially slick Yale, he still had plenty to learn.

On a sultry evening in 1917, Frank Galluccio drifted into the Harvard Inn with his girl on one arm and his sister on the other. Pretty
little sis in her clingy dress caught Al's attention, and he brushed near
her when she was swaying by, but his sly comments got no response.

Capone tried something more direct: "You got a nice ass, honey,
and I mean it as a compliment. Believe me."

The grinning gorilla broadcasting this crass remark was too much.
Galluccio demanded an apology. Capone, realizing he'd overstepped,
approached the table, ready to calm things down.

Galluccio was slight—five feet six and under 150 pounds—but a
street tough, a small-time criminal, and already drunk. Capone tow-
ered over him, bigger, wider, obviously stronger. But Galluccio leapt
forward with a knife, cutting three quick slashes down Capone's left
cheek—a long one four inches down, two smaller ones along his left
jaw and on his throat.

As Capone reeled, Galluccio hurriedly collected the girls and bolted.
No one bothered taking pursuit; everyone's attention was on stopping
Al's bleeding and getting him to a hospital. Thirty stitches closed his
wounds but left scars that would become his unwanted calling card.

Later, Yale settled both Capone and Galluccio down, and no follow-up mayhem occurred. Eventually, on occasional New York trips,
Capone would hire as a bodyguard the man who disfigured him.
Maybe Al learned playing it cool only got you killed—better to take
out the other guy first.

Why get killed over some skirt, anyway? Sex was readily available
in the streets, and at the Harvard Inn and the Brooklyn brothels where
he collected for Yale. In the process, Capone contracted the disease he
dealt with the rest of his life.

Even as he was consorting with prostitutes and loose women, young Al
was on the lookout for a life's partner. Mary Josephine Coughlin was
a lovely dark-haired Irish girl from Red Hook, a nicer part of Brooklyn where rows of well-tended houses sported windows with lace curtains. Two years older, Mae (as everyone called her) lived with her
sisters and widowed mother; a breadwinner now, she held a clerical
post at the box factory where Al worked days while helping Yale out
nights.

Mae's apple cheeks, arresting green eyes, and wavy brown hair immediately seized Al's attention. Her musical laugh and broad, winsome
smile—made all the more prominent by a marked overbite—gave her
a singular beauty, and her personality seemed remarkably in tune with
his. Like Al, Mae enjoyed having a good time, going out dancing and
drinking with friends.

She possessed a definite independence, her burgeoning romance
with Capone crossing several cultural boundaries. Irish girls tradi-
tionally married older men, while Italian boys usually chose younger
brides, making the twenty-year-old Mae an unusual partner for the
eighteen-year-old Capone.

Perhaps the love affair began at the factory, or at one of the dance
halls where young people socialized across ethnic lines. The pair dressed
stylishly, though Mae was tasteful and Al gaudy. While Al's second job
might have been a mystery to her, he was clearly striving to be more
than a box- or paper-cutter.

Dancing became a favorite pastime for the couple, and Al was surprisingly graceful. Daniel Fuchs, Capone's Navy Yard contemporary,
reported Al was "something of a nonentity, affable, soft of speech and
even mediocre in everything but dancing." Yet Al and Mae shared a
strong physical attraction, and the couple wound up after hours in back
at the box factory. Soon Mae got pregnant.

Al wanted to marry this smiling, plucky Irish girl, but Mae's mother rejected him. To the Irish, Italians were "colored"—this despite both groups being Catholic and often spurned by white Protestants.

As Mae's pregnancy progressed, Al made frequent visits when her mother wasn't around. When Mae could no longer work, Al helped her family out, gradually building relationships with Mae's brothers and sisters. But her mother remained unmoved.

Mae gave birth December 4, 1918, to a sickly, two months premature boy, Albert Francis Capone—"Sonny" would deal with the side effects of congenital syphilis all his life. With Mae insisting on keeping the baby, her mother gave in, and on December 30, 1918, at the bride's neighborhood church, Alphonse Capone and Mary "Mae" Coughlin were married.

After the devastation of the 1871 fire, Chicago reinvented itself as it rebuilt. City leaders made sure the new technology of the railroads converged with the ships that moved among the Great Lakes. Already a major slaughterhouse for the cattle that grazed in the plains to the west and south, the center of the Near South Side was one large barnyard of animals waiting for the knife. Here the urban east met the Wild West. Unlike New York, Chicago had miles of adjacent prairies, and its leaders were expanding the city at an amazing rate by the end of the 1800s.

As a gateway to the west, Chicago's downtown in the prefire days always had a large transient male population of pioneers, cowhands, and prospectors passing through to make their fortunes farther west. A major industry developed downtown to profit off these visitors by offering gambling, drink, and women, as well as outright theft. The grafters who ran the downtown gambling joints, saloons, and brothels had a lot of votes, resulting in Chicago being underpoliced for all of the nineteenth century. Crime became one of the city's major industries.

As the manager of several boxers, Johnny Torrio visited Chicago many times. He almost certainly met James "Diamond Jim" Colosimo, a major political player in Chicago's First Ward, home to a sprawling red-light district just outside the Loop, Chicago's downtown business district. By 1909, with gang wars heating up in Brooklyn, Torrio had made the move to Chicago, and by 1914 he was Colosimo's right-hand man.

For all his wealth and influence, Colosimo yearned for respectability and recognition as a successful man of business. He opened a posh café called Colosimo's at Twenty-First Street and Wabash, while a short block away at 2222 South Wabash, the Four Deuces, his four-story house of gambling and prostitution, ran wide-open under Torrio's watch.

That left Diamond Jim to focus his energies on his restaurant, including its entertainment, particularly Dale Winter, an attractive, blue-eyed thrush who wore an air of virtue despite a figure-hugging white gown, its bosom bedecked with a red rose. Even as he paid her top dollar, Colosimo lavished Dale with furs and jewelry, seeing in her the respectable good girl of his dreams. He decided in 1919 to divorce his wife, a brothel madam. But while Colosimo busied himself with his new love and the diamonds that studded his clothes and filled his pockets, outside events began to reshape his fate.

For more than a century, a growing coalition of moralists and progressives had worked to abolish alcohol from American life. Their reasons varied greatly, from the misguided to the pernicious. Advocates for women's rights, who knew all too well the damage liquor could do to a family, found themselves allied with immigrant-hating nativists, who sought to exterminate the saloon not so much because it might gobble up a breadwinner's paycheck but because it represented an outpost of a foreign culture.

Yet they all agreed alcohol was inherently a vile and treacherous substance, which inevitably dragged all drinkers down the road to debauchery and despair. Take away the opportunity to drink, and Americans would become healthier in body and soul, morally upright and mentally sound.

In 1919—after decades of lobbying and grassroots organizing, of rewriting textbooks and federal law—the drys finally won the chance to put their ideas to the test. That year saw the passage of the Eighteenth Amendment to the Constitution, making illegal "the manufacture, sale, or transportation of intoxicating liquors" inside the borders of the United States. Consumption and purchase of alcoholic beverages, however, remained legal. The new law gave Americans exactly one year to bid farewell to the bottle; it would go into effect at midnight on January 17, 1920.

Prohibitionists heralded this new dry era as a day of salvation, the moment when Americans would exchange freedom to imbibe for liberty from crime and vice. In Norfolk, Virginia, the evangelist Billy Sunday presided over an elaborate funeral for booze, attended by a crowd of ten thousand. "Heaven rejoices," Sunday told the Demon Rum. "The devil is your only mourner."

Most Chicagoans gave that notion a Bronx cheer. The city, which later voted five to one to stay wet, wasted little time in defying the dry law. Less than an hour after Prohibition took effect, six masked men stole a shipment of "medicinal" liquor from a Chicago rail yard. Within minutes, four barrels of booze were looted from a warehouse in another part of town, while a group of bandits hijacked a truckload of whiskey elsewhere in the city.

That same day Al Capone turned twenty-one.

Alcohol was a key component of the Colosimo operation—which comprised not only the precious café but his suburban roadhouses, where prostitution was on the menu. Pop-eyed pimp Jack Guzik, a Torrio crony, learned of a brewery at Twentieth and Wabash available for sale, cheap, and hit Colosimo up for a loan. The jowly Guzik had a head for business—he saw a rich future in bootlegging and left his brothers to run the family brothel business.

Torrio also saw the kind of money to be made from Prohibition—like prostitution, something was now illegal that large numbers of people desired. Police payoffs could easily be expanded to booze—Torrio just needed the means to brew and store the stuff.

Brewers who wanted to sell out, or go into business with bootleggers willing to distribute the banned product, were eager to talk. That Colosimo's restaurant was no First Ward dive, but a high-hat nightclub attracting both upper-class society and the better-behaved denizens of the underworld, helped facilitate negotiations.

But Diamond Jim Colosimo had no interest in across-the-board bootlegging. All he wanted from Torrio was a supply for their operations, while other Chicago gangs were entering the racket, servicing a whole new market, more lucrative even than brothels. Neighborhoods often railed against the latter, but what Chicago neighborhood didn't want its saloons back?

On March 31, 1920, Colosimo was granted a divorce from his wife, Victoria, who netted $50,000. Johnny Torrio frowned on this. During the day, Torrio traded in corruption and sins of the flesh; but by night he was the faithful husband of his loving wife, Anna. The couple maintained a quiet middle-class life at home, listening to the Victrola and playing card games. Divorce just wasn't done.

On April 17, Colosimo and Dale Winter wed in Southern Indiana at a hotel-casino. Victoria took her generous divorce settlement and married a Neapolitan grocer-cum-bartender in California. Back in Chicago, Colosimo nestled Dale in his mansion on nearby Vernon Avenue, and returned to his happy life. He had everything—money, a lovely, gifted new wife, and an ever-growing prominence in high society.

On May 11, Torrio called Colosimo with word two trucks loaded down with fine whiskey would roll up at 4:00 P.M.—Colosimo himself had to be there to seal the deal. Diamond Jim left before four to go to the café, a .38-caliber revolver in his pocket. He took his standard tour of the facility, checking on various staff members, then went out to the lobby to wait for the delivery.

Two shots exploded the silence.

Colosimo dropped facedown on the floor, blood spilling from his skull, dead long before the doctor and police came. The murder was close-up, a bullet in the head, leaving powder burns. With his diamond ring, loaded revolver, and $120 on him, the motive could hardly be robbery.

Suspicion settled on spurned ex-spouse Victoria, though she was across the country at the time; still, she had underworld contacts—by divorcing his wife, Colosimo had provided the perfect smoke-screen motive for his own murder.

A funny fact emerged: Torrio's old pal Frankie Yale was in the city that day. A stranger in Chicago, he made the ideal torpedo to remove Colosimo and do Torrio a favor, while laying the groundwork for a lucrative trade in alcohol between the East Coast and the Midwest. Yet despite matching a witness description, Yale was never charged.

Colosimo's passing established the pattern for lavish gangster funerals to come, with judges, elected officials, and criminals marching in procession behind a hearse festooned with thousands of dollars' worth of flowers.

But Diamond Jim was soon forgotten, even if the café bearing his name continued for decades. A $10,000 payment to Frankie Yale bought Torrio a criminal operation worth millions, clearing the way for expansion into large-scale bootlegging.

In 1919, the Italians in Brooklyn were battling the Irish for control over the docks. Al Capone stepped into a poor choice of waterfront tavern, running into a profanely insulting Mick, whom he promptly beat to a pulp.

The cops could be bought, but the Irish mobsters wanted blood— Al's. The throttled victim worked for mobster Dinny Meehan, whose minions were on the lookout for a burly young brawler with some distinctive scars. Frankie Yale likely arranged a job in Chicago for young Capone with Torrio, who needed trustworthy men, expanding his influence after Colosimo's murder—perhaps Johnny even remembered a plump kid who ran errands back in the day.

Avoiding an accelerating gang war in Brooklyn, young Capone headed west. He could hardly imagine that even more violence awaited him.

He would already be in Chicago when, on November 14, 1920, his father died of heart failure at the pool hall where Gabriel and his son had so often played. With the family losing its main source of income, Al now had his mother and siblings to support halfway back across the country.

Money needed to be made.

Alexander Jamie early in his federal career (top). Young Eliot Ness (left) with Jamie's son, Wallace (bottom). *(Top: National Archives. Bottom: Cleveland Press Collection, Cleveland State University.)*

Two

1850–1923

Eliot Ness considered himself "the thrifty and industrious son of thrifty and industrious parents," immigrants who had made it into the American upper middle class. Not rich but far from poor, they raised their son with love but firmly—for those who played fair, they taught the boy, the land of opportunity worked as advertised.

"What I now appreciate most about my father," Ness said, "is the way he took the time to give me quiet lectures separating right from wrong. He made sure I recognized the importance of hard work, honesty, and compassion."

The Ness surname came from the farm near Ålvundfjord in Norway where Eliot's father, Peder Johnsen Ness, was born out of wedlock on March 31, 1850. Norwegian surnames in those days derived from where you lived: Peder Johnsen Ness meant "Peder, son of John, who lives on Ness farm."

Peder grew up in a pastoral world of striking beauty, rich meadows and craggy peaks hugging the edges of fjords, the deep, icy seawater fingers carved into the coast by ancient glaciers. But the boy's early years were marked by tragedy—his carpenter father died when Peder was seven, his mother taken by pneumonia when he was thirteen.

Work became Peder's salvation. From the beginning, he was tireless and meticulous, apprenticing as a baker at sixteen, mastering his craft in three and a half years. Peder spent his twenties plying his trade in and around the Norwegian capital city of Christiania (Oslo), saving for a ticket to America. On April 22, 1881—less than a month after his thirty-first birthday—he set sail for the States, never to return.

When he arrived at Castle Garden at the southern tip of Manhattan, Peder had just fifty Norwegian kroner in his pocket. There's no reason to suppose he knew anyone in America, and he couldn't speak the language. Not that Peder expected America to welcome him with open arms. He shared the attitude of another Norwegian immigrant, who wrote home saying, "There are better and more numerous chances for young men here than in Norway . . . [but] one must work, for here nothing may be had for nothing."

Peder knew all about hard work, which had brought him this far, and he knew his future depended on it. Marking his break with the old country, he Anglicized his first name to "Peter" and set out for the Midwest. In all likelihood, Peter had his sights set on Chicago: work was plentiful in the factories and stockyards of the South Side, its skies filled with grime, its air thick with the stench of slaughter. The city was growing with the hunger of an unruly child: a baker could do well feeding that appetite.

But first Peter needed capital. In McGregor, Iowa, a bustling little Mississippi River town, he got a job in a lumberyard. Two years of labor and thrift earned him enough for a move to South Chicago.

Peter established himself in a small community on Chicago's far southern outskirts called Kensington—the last stop on the Illinois Central, where rail-riding hoboes hopped off, giving it the nickname "Bumtown." "Little more than a swamp," as one local paper put it, Kensington was a cluster of boardinghouses and saloons around a rail yard with scant to recommend itself to an aspiring baker. The roads were rutted, muddy, and often impassable, especially for the heavy wagons used by wholesale bakers.

Three bakeries in the area had failed before Peter got there, one owned by another Norwegian who welcomed an offer to buy—a risky but shrewd investment for a near-penniless immigrant. Still, Peter could see Kensington was changing.

In 1881, industrialist George Pullman opened a new factory just across the tracks from Kensington to build his famous railroad sleeper cars. Around the facility, he created a rigidly structured "model town" designed as a kind of workers' utopia. Wrapped in the trappings of wealth, employees supposedly wouldn't feel the "discontent and desire for change" that gave birth to labor unions.

Stately brick homes lined clean, orderly streets, the modern marvels of gas lighting and indoor plumbing standard. The town—also called Pullman—was a self-interested social experiment, an attempt to mass-produce workers as "elevated and refined" as the cars they made. For its founder and namesake, the operation just made sense—as a "strictly business proposition."

Pullman selected this spot for its isolation on the low prairie, away from Chicago's "evil influences." Other than Kensington, the only other settlement in the area was Roseland, a well-established Dutch farming town dating to when Chicago was a frontier fort. The sudden influx of workers swelled both communities, turning "Bumtown" into boomtown.

The town of Pullman had no saloons, and the Dutch kept a tight rein on drinking in Roseland, so Kensington became the place where workers went to "raise hell." Saloons sprang up like poisoned mushrooms. Saturday night was Pullman's payday, the "busy season" in Kensington, when police could count on twenty arrests for drunken brawling. George Pullman hadn't escaped the "evil influences" of the big city—he'd brought them south.

"Leave the well-paved, well-sewered, and well-cleaned streets of [Pullman]," a rabble-rousing reverend wrote, and you'd find "the half-hid-out streets of Kensington, with its open sewers, its piles of decaying vegetation, its pools of stagnant water, its ill-ventilated and tumbledown tenements, its scores of liquor shops and houses of doubtful character."

Yet many workers preferred living in Kensington and Roseland, where they weren't forced to hide their ethnic identities behind uniform brick facades. Those who lived in Pullman could never own their own homes; everyone paid rent to the company. Without notice, Pullman inspectors could invade a worker's home and redecorate, automatically taking the cost from wages.

And if residents weren't living up to Pullman's standards, they could be kicked out on ten days' notice. The company also charged for the use of the only church, which no congregations could afford, leaving the house of God largely vacant.

"The company care nothing for our souls," the employees would say, in hushed tones. "They only want to get as much work as possible out of our bodies."

But for Peter Ness, Pullman's nightmarish utopia was a dream of opportunity. The sale of meats and groceries was restricted to the Market House at the center of town, where Peter secured a stall to sell his bread. The punishing $40-a-month rent meant access to a captive audience of roughly eight thousand people.

Before long, Peter's business outgrew the small stand, and in July 1885 he and a partner built their own wholesale bakery at 373 East Kensington Avenue. The brick and stone structure, with "Peter Ness" written high and proud, might have seemed bigger than their business could support, but the neighborhood was bound to grow into it. Peter bet on the future in another way, too, leaving plenty of space upstairs for a family.

That same summer, twenty-one-year-old Emma King boarded a ship in Norway and retraced Peter's journey to Chicago. Her father, an English engineer, helped build Norway's first railroad; her mother was a Norwegian dressmaker. Emma grew up in small-town Ullensaker, Peter's last Norwegian place of residence. Almost certainly they had known each other; someone in America, presumably Peter, paid for Emma's ticket to the States. They married on April 2, 1886, when Peter was thirty-six and Emma twenty-two. Six months later, they had their first child, Clara. In the next few years, three more would follow— Effie, Nora, and Charles.

Peter became a U.S. citizen in 1889, while his business prospered thanks largely to its prime location. With Kensington to the south, Roseland to the west, and Pullman to the east, the Ness bakery sat at the intersection of three expanding communities bursting with steady paychecks and mouths to feed. Business was so good that by 1892, Peter and his partner opened a second bakery in South Chicago.

Then disaster struck—early one January morning in 1893, the Kensington bakery caught fire. The Nesses, still living upstairs—their youngest, Charles, not yet two—managed to escape the burning building unharmed. But two firefighters were buried under a collapsing wall, one killed instantly, the other badly injured. The fire consumed four buildings on that block, causing tens of thousands of dollars in damage.

"The origin of the fire is not known," wrote the *Chicago Tribune*, "but the starting point is supposed to have been Baker Ness' oven." Peter estimated his own losses at $3,000.

Peter didn't take long to rebuild, and soon had the Kensington bakery up and running again. As the year wore on, however, things only got worse, as a series of bank failures and business collapses threw the country into a depression.

The Pullman Company slashed wages and laid off thousands, yet George Pullman refused to lower rents. That winter found many starving families unable to heat their beautiful rented homes. Workers began to meet across the tracks in Kensington, away from prying company eyes, talking about organizing and collective bargaining—exactly what Pullman had built "his town" to avoid.

Peter Ness didn't go in for that kind of talk, but he hated seeing his neighbors suffer due to Pullman's intransigence. A year after his business and home were burned out, Peter gave free bread to families who couldn't afford it, and never asked to be paid back.

On May 11, 1894, after Pullman refused one last time to raise wages and lower rents, his workers walked out. Kensington became the front line in a battle that would change the course of the American labor movement. Down the block from the Ness bakery, at Turner Hall, strikers met to hear young labor leader Eugene Debs inveigh against "the paternalism of Pullman."

In June, the American Railway Union announced a boycott of all railroads handling Pullman cars, bringing much of the country screeching to a halt. Trains could no longer deliver mail and food into Chicago; prices shot up. The strike divided the city—you were either with workers or management.

Peter Ness chose workers.

Always a believer in a fair day's pay for an honest day's work, he couldn't fault his neighbors for demanding as much from their employer. Nor had he forgotten he owed his success—his foothold in America—to the people who made up this community. He gave strikers his support by feeding them for free. Many others did the same, donating food, money, and medical care, allowing workers to hold out much longer than Pullman expected.

But once the strike stopped the mail, making it a federal matter, President Grover Cleveland sent in troops, and riots broke out. Mobs destroyed hundreds of thousands of dollars' worth of railroad equipment, while the grounds of the previous year's World's Fair—the "White City" that had dazzled millions of visitors—went up in flames. Two thousand federal troops, and scores more police and militiamen, finally brought the chaos to an end.

The strike was a calamitous defeat for organized labor. Workers gradually returned to the town of Pullman, by now officially part of Chicago, but they never forgot their anger. When George Pullman died in 1897, his will wisely stipulated his grave be lined with asphalt, concrete, and steel, to protect his remains from vengeful employees.

But while Pullman's actions damned his memory forever on the South Side, Peter's generosity made the baker one of the community's most respected citizens. Perhaps he was too soft a touch, loaning money to those in need and never seeking repayment. His "reputation for integrity and philanthropy," as one local biographer put it, was "unexcelled by that of any citizen of that suburb."

The turn of the century found Peter and Emma still living above the Kensington bakery with four children and several live-in servants. Peter turned fifty that year but worked as hard as ever, closely overseeing the work of his eight employees and five bakery wagons. In November, Emma turned thirty-seven; their children ranged in age from nine to fourteen. Any new additions to the family would likely be after the girls reached marriageable age.

But three years later, on April 19, 1903, Emma gave birth to a fifth and final child, a son, in the flat above the bakery. The Nesses named the boy after Victorian novelist George Eliot, probably never realizing this was the pen name of Mary Ann Evans.

Peter insisted his son would have no middle name, despite friends arguing for "at least a middle initial." Customarily, in Norway, a child would bear his or her father's first name as a patronymic—Johnsen, in Peter's case, marked him as the son of John. Tradition dictated his son's middle name be Peterson.

But the Nesses were Americans now, and their child would bear a simple, American name: Eliot Ness.

Technically, Eliot Ness was the native Chicagoan and Al Capone the transplant, but the former's upbringing made him the outsider. Chicago fit Capone like his fine silk underwear, Brooklyn preparing him well for life in the bustling, brawling Loop and the rough-and-tumble South Side. But Roseland and Kensington were an enclave apart, separated from the city by miles of undeveloped prairie, operating by a very different set of rules.

Ness grew up in a neighborhood in transition—moving, like the rest of the country, from an agrarian past into an industrial future. Farmland still dotted the area and many streets remained unpaved, even as heavy industry increasingly moved in. Just a few blocks from the Ness bakery sat the Sherwin Williams paint factory. Every day of his childhood, Eliot's nostrils experienced a mingling of the sweet smell of baking bread and the toxic fumes of brewing paint.

Kensington remained the place where locals went to get decent food and drink, serving as a release valve for its buttoned-down neighbors. But sleepy, stolid Roseland—a community proud of its "pretty homes and well-kept lawns"—grew to dominate the area, its Dutch influence keeping things tame.

Local police were, by Chicago standards, honest and competent; people generally respected law and order. The moralistic influence of the Dutch Reformed Church, which filtered into the schools and every aspect of community life, discouraged vice.

Industrialization brought with it plenty of immigrants—like Capone, Ness grew up surrounded by diversity. His family lived in a largely Italian area of Kensington, apart from the Norwegian enclave in West Pullman, and young Eliot would hang around the bakery with the sons of Italian immigrants. Workers who came to Roseland and Kensington had often been recruited for their skills, and those who wanted jobs could get them. With little incentive to make a living outside the law, street gangs and juvenile delinquency were rarities.

In his 1929 study of organized crime in Chicago, sociologist John Landesco perfectly captured the gulf between Al Capone and Eliot Ness.

"The good citizen has grown up in an atmosphere of obedience to law and of respect for it," Landesco wrote. "The gangster has lived his life in a region of lawbreaking, of graft, and of 'fixing.' That is the reason why the good citizen and the gangster have never been able to understand each other. They have been reared in two different worlds."

Many who grew up in the heart of the city also learned to navigate boundaries of class, race, and crime—shifting their personalities to fit their surroundings. Capone excelled at this: much of his appeal came from his contradictory capacities for great kindness and extreme cruelty . . . the murderer who gave generously to charity.

Ness, meanwhile, grew up the son of a respected man in a tightly knit, circumscribed community, much more like a small town than a big city. He never learned to wear a false face so blithely as Capone.

Even as an infant, Eliot was remarkably well-behaved.

"He was so terribly good he never got a spanking," Emma Ness recalled. "I never saw a baby like him."

He grew into a blue-eyed, freckle-faced kid with a shaggy head of brown hair and a good sense of humor. He was bookish but loved the outdoors, passing many afternoons in the Palmer Park playground a few blocks north of the bakery.

As the youngest member of the household by more than a decade, Ness spent much of his youth around adults, and he grew up closest to his mother. Her influence, and that of his three sisters, left its mark on his personality. Somewhat sensitive, he was "a good listener among older members of the family," as a brother-in-law recalled, and preferred the company of girls to boys, always bowing out of playing war or other masculine games.

If Ness cared what others thought, he didn't show it—a quiet loner, he was never one to assert himself socially. At Pullman Elementary and Calumet Junior High, the clean-cut, well-scrubbed kid dressed nicely and didn't bother trying to fit in. Some kids took this for arrogance—"like he thought he was better than everybody else," one classmate recalled— and tried to put him down with the nickname "Elegant Mess."

But in truth, this shyness was mixed with a kind of proud self-reliance. Young Eliot had "a mind and a will all his own," his mother said. Although some would later accuse him of being a Boy Scout, he never joined. He preferred going his own way.

He also liked to work. Practically from the day he was old enough for a paper route, Ness took every odd job he could find, helping out in the bakery, too, frequently tending to the twenty-seven horses that pulled his father's wagons. The afternoons and evenings in the bakery, learning its ins and outs, were precious to the boy, because it meant quality time with his father.

Eliot said his father "never had a lot to say, but when he did speak, I knew it was something worth listening to." He did regret not seeing his father "all that much," and wished he'd gotten to know him better.

Although the bakery stole Ness's real father away, a surrogate appeared in the form of Alexander Gleig Jamie—an imposing, six-foot Scotsman whose hawk nose and piercing gaze were seemingly on loan from Sherlock Holmes. Jamie would have a lasting influence on Ness's character and career, a mentor guiding him much as Johnny Torrio did Capone.

Like Torrio, Jamie was born abroad in 1882, emigrating from Sterling, Scotland, to the United States as a child. He grew up in Pullman, attended school there, and clerked for the company for seven years, internalizing the ethos of that company town. Honest, dependable, hardworking, Jamie shared with Peter Ness the immigrant's determination to make good in America.

But for Jamie, hard work alone was not enough. He was, at heart, a political operator, who made sure to ingratiate himself with those worth knowing. He joined the right organizations, cultivated the right friendships, and never hesitated to pull the right strings. Unlike Peter Ness, Jamie sympathized not at all with the plight of the workingman. He aspired to management.

In October 1907, when Eliot was four years old, Jamie married the eldest Ness daughter, Clara. Two years later, the couple had a son, Wallace Ness Jamie, and moved in with the Nesses on Kensington Avenue. At that time, Peter's business was "in a precarious condition," Jamie recalled.

The losses on stale bread had made wholesaling too costly, forcing Peter to focus on the more profitable retail market. He hired Jamie to manage his Kensington bakery, and together they helped get the business back on a more stable footing. Jamie now had more than twenty bakers to supervise, but always found time for his young brother-in-law, Eliot.

Ness, in turn, grew up much closer to his nephew Wallace, six years his junior, than to his actual siblings. He took it upon himself to protect Wally, teaching him how to defend himself against bullies.

Ness soon became known around the neighborhood as a protector willing to stop older kids from picking on younger ones. One neighbor recalled Ness taking care of two brothers after their father was injured at the Pullman plant. They had no one to look out for them, so Eliot stepped in, even offering to help pay the bills, though the brothers wouldn't take his money. By appointing himself the guardian of those smaller and weaker than he was, Ness had found a way around his shyness—he could be liked and respected by the neighborhood kids without really being one of them.

Religion, too, set the Nesses apart from the larger community. Life in Roseland centered on its churches, many dating back fifty years or more to the first Dutch settlement. But the Nesses were Christian Scientists, a new sect arriving in the area only in the 1890s, following reports of miraculous healings in West Pullman.

For the faithful, such healings proved diseases were imaginary, according to founder Mary Baker Eddy, an erroneous manifestation of the human mind. Our true nature, like God's, was perfection. These ideas inspired suspicion and disdain among many Americans, and no doubt raised a few eyebrows among the Nesses' conservative, church-going neighbors. Roseland's Christian Scientists didn't even have their own building until 1912, meeting for services in public meeting halls or each other's homes.

Eliot didn't stay with the faith very long, but he never quite shook Eddy's ideas about disease. Sickness was something he powered through and tried to ignore, as if he could just will it away.

But such stoicism was of little use when young Eliot came down with rheumatic fever, a terrifying infection resulting from untreated strep throat or scarlet fever. His joints became painfully inflamed, with lumps developing under his skin. If the infection had passed to his brain, his hands, feet, and face would have begun to jerk and twitch. Almost certainly, he experienced chest pains and shortness of breath as the disease attacked his heart.

Ness survived, but at great cost. The disease scarred the valves of his heart, forcing it to pump harder to keep him alive. The damage would not be detected for many years, but this added stress shortened Ness's life just as surely as syphilis did Capone's.

By 1910, Peter's business had grown into an impressive operation, employing twenty-four bakers, ten wagon drivers (each with his own team of horses), and nine shop clerks. Besides the original Kensington bakery, Peter now operated two storefronts on Michigan Avenue and contracted with a third independent operator to sell his goods exclusively.

"Every morning and afternoon," said the *Calumet Index,* "there is a fresh output of bread, biscuit[s], buns and rolls delivered to all the stores," one of which sat in the shadow of the Peoples Store, the South Side's answer to Marshall Field's. This was prime real estate—Chicago's largest, most bustling business district outside the Loop, known locally as "the Avenue," and Peter must have done a tremendous walk-in business.

Peter prided himself on running a clean, modern shop using only the finest ingredients and hiring only the best people, right down to the "hustling young salesladies" behind the counter. At their height, the Ness bakeries took in about $150,000 in gross annual sales.

This remarkable American success story, however, did not last. The rapid growth of the business left Eliot's father vulnerable to overextension—losing just one of his outlets could bring the whole chain crashing down. And this appears to be exactly what happened in 1917. The expansion of the Peoples Store and a bakers' strike are likely culprits. In any event, Peter lost control of his business. And because the family still lived above the Kensington bakery, they might have briefly lost their home.

Peter was in his late sixties; after more than thirty years of hard work, almost everything he'd built was swept away. But life had taught him early on how cruel fate can be, and he took the loss in stride—he had Eliot, fourteen, and Charles, twenty-six, to rely on. With their help, Peter soon established a new bakery. Eliot had spent a previous summer working a gas oven in a radiator plant, and he used what he'd learned to build his father's new oven.

Still, the family's finances remained tight. When the Nesses moved to a new house, they took in boarders, fellow Norwegians. Eliot now had to pay all his own expenses, and he fell into a succession of odd jobs—timekeeping for Pullman, checking gas meters, painting autos, whatever it took. The backbreaking work of dipping radiators gave him upper-body strength, packing a surprising amount of power into his slim frame.

When America entered the Great War in April 1917, Ness took time out from high school to work at a munitions factory in West Pullman. He didn't stay out of the classroom long, his parents having drilled in him the importance of a good education. Always an individualist, Ness hated the compulsory military training at Christian Fenger High School, yet he proved proficient, and managed to keep his grades up at the same time.

Alexander Jamie, meanwhile, left Peter's employ shortly before the business collapsed, returning to the Pullman Company, this time as an investigator—or an undercover man, as he put it. Memories of the 1894 strike remained fresh, and the company sought to keep tabs on its workforce in order to prevent another revolt. Jamie spent eight months traveling, "securing data as to the honesty of employees," keeping his ears open for any information helpful to the company.

He also joined the American Protective League, a vigilante group formed in Chicago. Its members carried "Secret Service" badges and raided anyone they suspected of pro-German sympathies—draft dodgers, socialists, and immigrants. Their mission went hand-in-hand with Jamie's work for Pullman.

The job kept Jamie on the road—some fifty thousand miles in under a year—which soon put a strain on his marriage. Clara prevailed on her husband to find work closer to home, which he soon did. His investigative experience, and especially his membership with the American Protective League, made him an attractive candidate for a young federal agency seeking new men: the Bureau of Investigation of the Department of Justice, later known as the FBI.

The Bureau, when Jamie joined, employed only about three hundred agents in fifty-four offices across the country, but it grew rapidly after the war amid a wave of anticommunist paranoia. In 1919, bombings and riots rocked the country; the newly formed Soviet Union's loud calls for global revolution made Bolshevism seem an imminent threat. Under Attorney General A. Mitchell Palmer, the Bureau cracked down on any suspected anarchist or communist, rounding up thousands of innocents in the notorious Palmer Raids. Directing the drive was Palmer's young assistant, twenty-four-year-old John Edgar Hoover.

Except for one notable case of election fraud, Jamie's time with the Bureau was hardly glamorous—he pursued leftist agitators, white-collar criminals, and interstate pimps. Yet to teenage Eliot Ness, Jamie's new career was an inspiration.

In between school and work, Ness had discovered Sherlock Holmes. Those stories, still pouring at the time from the pen of Sir Arthur Conan Doyle, were a veritable textbook of modern crime solving, introducing Ness and millions of other readers to fingerprinting, ballistics, toxicology, and other forensic sciences well before they became standard in the American detective's toolkit. In whatever idle moments he could spare, Ness dreamed of following his brother-in-law into the profession and becoming a real-life Holmes. But those remained little more than fantasies while his family struggled its way back to prosperity.

In June 1920, Ness graduated from Fenger High with excellent grades. He had grown into a handsome young man with a serious cast, approaching six feet. Fellow students, when asked what stood out about Eliot, remarked on his sense of calm. Behind that placid mask was an engaging personality few got the chance to see. "Although he has a store of wit," Ness's senior yearbook observed, "he's very shy in using it."

Peter and Emma dreamed of having their son go off to college, but instead Eliot decided to enter the workforce. His father was seventy, his mother a few years shy of sixty. Their seventeen-year-old son, unwilling to be a burden on them, had every reason to want to strike out on his own. And besides, with only a grammar school education, his brother-in-law had managed to become a federal agent. Soon Ness secured a painting job at a company where Jamie had once worked.

Peter was appalled, and made sure Eliot knew it.

"He said he hadn't worked day and night so that his youngest son would be a failure," Ness recalled, "and have to work just as hard [as he did]."

The father had crossed an ocean to find opportunity for himself and his children, and feared Eliot wouldn't amount to anything. First a man needed an education, and only then could he "set his own course."

Ness listened respectfully but kept his painting job. Yet his father's words ate away at him through the fall and winter of 1920.

"One day," Emma later told a reporter, "Eliot came home from work with a new suit and a suitcase. He announced he had already enrolled in the University of Chicago because he 'didn't want to get into a rut without a higher education.'" Signing up on his own, without telling anyone, was entirely typical of headstrong young Eliot.

By then, the Nesses lived at 10811 South Prairie Avenue, a narrow brick building made up of two stacked apartments—one of innumerable such "two-flats" lining the leafy streets of Roseland. Far to the north, between Sixteenth Street and Twenty-Second Street, Prairie was known as "the richest half-dozen block[s] in Chicago," where tycoons like George Pullman and Marshall Field built their mansions. This far south, Prairie was a humbler street, "a refuge to which the tired business man may repair," according to Chicago reporter Fred Pasley.

But in 1923—while Ness still lived with his parents on Prairie, commuting every day to the University of Chicago—a different kind of tycoon moved into a modest but comfortable red brick two-flat at 7244 South Prairie, five miles up the road from the Nesses.

Indeed, little distinguished it from the Ness house: the two were mirror images. But in a few years, 7244 South Prairie would be world famous, a hub of activity, with police and reporters camped out around the clock.

Al Capone had moved in on the Ness family's street.

7244 South Prairie Avenue. *(Authors' Collection)*

Three

1920–1925

Al Capone's new two-flat at 7244 South Prairie Avenue was a large building of the era, each floor a separate apartment with three bedrooms, built on a double lot. Far more spacious than anything they'd known in Brooklyn, the new house initially housed Al's mother, his wife, his son, and two of his siblings. Most had a room to themselves or shared with one loved one, a major improvement from Brooklyn days, and an arrangement perfect for a large extended family reflecting the close Italian *famiglia* ideal.

Al and his brothers did not operate openly in their new neighborhood, Park Manor, not with cops living on the same block. That legal presence was not considered security by the family, whose house was already protected by basement windows with iron bars. Capone commuted to work at Johnny Torrio's Four Deuces in the Levee district, taking another step up from the lower-class dives of the crowded ethnic neighborhoods he'd known in Brooklyn.

Chicago's Levee—just south of downtown, running along State and Dearborn Streets near several train stations—made a perfect location for a red-light district, for visitors and residents alike. A few blocks east, nearer the lake and its parks, were the mansions of the Prairie Avenue District. Many of the rich were no strangers to the Levee. The Four Deuces and Colosimo's on Wabash bordered the better Near North

Side sections and its swank hotels and classy restaurants. Al Capone was well schooled in the hypocritical sexual tastes of the middle and upper classes while working for Torrio at the Four Deuces, where prostitutes often served the captains of industry.

While he began as a Four Deuces pitchman, enticing men to gamble or philander, Capone's duties and income swiftly grew. This reflected the personable young man's powers in business management, but also Torrio's rapidly expanding bootlegging. More than a million citizens in greater Chicago had lost easy access to liquor, and while homemade wine and beer were an option for some, hordes of thirsty customers remained.

Torrio envisioned a citywide coalition of alky cookers, brewers, and suppliers—graft on a countywide scale, with set markets for gangs and organized distribution of capital and supplies, linked with local gambling and prostitution.

He began with his own organization, which would come to be known as the Chicago Outfit. The infrastructure supporting Colosimo's brothels around the county now became the spine of an illegal booze distribution system. Long-trusted Levee veterans were recruited, like veteran pimp Jack Guzik, now Johnny's bookkeeper and payoff man.

The other dependable source was relatives—Al's brother Ralph left passable pay in New York for better money in Chicago, and soon was joined by brother Frank, and their cousins, Charles, Rocco, and Joseph Fischetti. Al could assign his brothers critical tasks, the three siblings often living together, and—with the Fischettis—their slice of the Outfit began to feel like a family business.

Ralph started in distribution, where he picked up the nickname "Bottles" for his ability to encourage tavernkeepers to buy Capone product. He eventually organized a legitimate enterprise for the Chicago Outfit—the sale and distribution of near beer and soft drinks used as mixers. He also was proficient at managing nightspots, brothels, and gambling dens.

Tall, with dark curly hair, fastidious Frank—who had no truck with "broads"—drew dangerous whispers regarding his sexual orientation. A skilled, charming front man, out in the community making contacts and sales, Frank was nonetheless a behind-the-scenes player who would rather negotiate than strong-arm, displaying a political sensibility at first eluding Al.

Cicero journalist Robert St. John wrote that the more famous Capone "had a strong hero worship for his older brother. [Al] would have liked to have the poise, the air of a gentleman, the appearance of good breeding which Frank had."

Al spoke, some time later, of the new family venture.

"We had to make a living," he said. "I was younger then than I am now, and I thought I needed more. I didn't believe in prohibiting people from getting the things they wanted. I thought Prohibition an unjust law and I still do. Somehow I just naturally drifted into the racket. And I guess I'm here to stay until the law is repealed."

Management challenges accompanied the Outfit's burgeoning new business. Teenage ghetto gangs fed fresh talent into the organization, while other new recruits were honest laborers put out of work by Prohibition. Brewmasters and others involved in the liquor industry had two options: learn a new trade or go into bootlegging.

The Outfit mingled investments from criminal gangs and upper-class private partners, its operation staffed heavily by thugs and hardened criminals. Torrio had the unique ability to manage an enterprise of that scale while maintaining authority and respect.

Facilitating all this was Chicago's mayor, William Hale Thompson, a crook with the common touch. He called himself "Big Bill the Builder," because he loved taking credit for massive construction projects.

"Winning the election feeds his ego," noted one observer. "He takes a boyish delight in playing with crowds and getting his picture taken. But more fundamental than that, he has a mania for building lasting monuments to William Hale Thompson."

Big Bill connected well to society's lowest classes, courting African-Americans and interacting with the underworld. To curry favor among the large number of German voters, his campaign had even attacked the British. Thompson preached reform and promised newly enfranchised women he'd place "a mother" on the Board of Education. Colorful and amiable, Big Bill promised every special interest the moon, made an issue of his opponent's Catholicism, and won one of the largest pluralities in Chicago history.

Of course, his campaign pledges were for the most part forgotten. Nonetheless, in 1919, a scandal-ridden Thompson was narrowly reelected, thanks in part to the African-American vote. And with the recent passage of Prohibition, Thompson's reelection guaranteed a wide-open town—the Torrio organization and the Levee supported the mayor vigorously, knowing reelection meant a free ride (well, not free) for the Outfit's bootlegging and vice empire.

Now important enough to need a front, Capone set up an antiques shop within the Four Deuces building. His "Alphonse Capone" business cards announced no hours, and the storefront window displayed a bookshelf bearing a prominent Bible.

Good Book or not, in January 1921 Capone had his first documented face-off with Chicago law, who brought him in for operating a brothel and handling slot machines. A guilty plea got him a fine of $150 and $110 in court costs; Capone covered up for Torrio and showed his loyalty and commitment to the organization.

Al's low profile was next disrupted in the early morning hours of August 30, 1922, when his car collided with a taxi, leaving the driver in need of an ambulance. An inebriated Al leapt out, brandishing a deputy sheriff's badge and a revolver, threatening to shoot an accusing witness.

Booked at Central Station as Alfred Caponi, "alleged owner of the 'Four Deuces,'" he faced charges in Harrison Street Court for carrying a concealed weapon, driving under the influence, and assault with an automobile. Capone told the arresting officer he'd get him fired and did his best to intimidate the prosecutors with claims of "pull."

"I'll fix this thing so easy you won't know how it's done," he crowed. He was escorted for a brief stay in the lockup before being bailed out.

The charges were dropped while Capone sobered up—this was the First Ward and Torrio's territory. But the incident indicated street thug Al Capone had not yet matured into a business executive, despite the calming influence of brother Frank and mentor Torrio.

Meanwhile, Torrio added to his staff another ex-Brooklynite: the Capones' old neighbor, Frank Nitto. At just over five feet, dapper and well groomed, Nitto did not have to work his way up—the unlicensed barber, who floated shop to shop, already had a reputation as a reliable fence. Stolen jewelry fit naturally with Nitto's barbering, enabling him to develop neighborhood relationships, including one with Alex Greenberg, a bootlegger–loan shark crony of Torrio's.

Nitto started out keeping track of receipts, intimidating wayward barkeeps, and adding new customers. In Chicago's slums, goons and killers were a dime a dozen, but crooks with business acumen like Torrio, Jack Guzik, and the three Capone brothers were uncommon. Nitto easily entered their ranks.

Johnny Torrio's operation continued to grow. The unlikely little godfather's vision was a synchronized system, each bootlegger with an explicit territory and a means of taking care of payoffs. The system worked fine for a while, but some in the bootlegging game had their own ideas.

Like many Prohibition-era crooks, Charles Dean O'Banion saw the dry law as his shortcut to respectability. He started off as a burglar and safecracker before graduating into hijacking illicit-booze shipments. Although he never quite shook his appetite for hands-on crime, he—like Torrio—realized the federal government's folly had opened the door to bigger and better things.

As O'Banion explained to his close confederate, Hymie Weiss: "We're big business without high hats."

So O'Banion began dressing the part, clothing his athletic frame in finely tailored suits—always tasteful, never flashy—and keeping his small hands carefully manicured. He also branched out into legitimate business, including a North Side flower shop across from Holy Name Cathedral. There he indulged his love of all things floral, moving about with the lurching gait he'd acquired after a youthful collision with a streetcar. He specialized in gangland funerals.

O'Banion "could twist a sheaf of roses into a wreath or chaplet so deftly as not to let fall a single petal," wrote Fred Pasley, Capone's first biographer.

But even among his flowers, O'Banion never went unarmed: his suits contained special pockets for three guns.

"His round Irish face wore an habitual grin," Pasley wrote. "His fathomless blue eyes, wide and unblinking, stared at all comers with a candor fixed and impenetrable."

This cheerful front belied the quick trigger finger of someone who could swing wildly from childish silliness to dispassionate violence and back again. O'Banion told a Chicago journalist about the time a car backfired as the florist walked across a downtown bridge.

"I didn't know what it was," O'Banion admitted. "I took a pop at the only guy I saw."

When O'Banion read the man he'd shot was in the hospital, he sent him a few cigars.

Some claimed O'Banion had killed eight men; the chief of police put his tally at no less than twenty-five. To Pasley, this incorrigible rebel lashed out at the constraints of civilization "like a man in a crowded street-car seeking elbow-room." That anarchic attitude made him a threat to the peaceful criminal empire that Torrio hoped to build.

O'Banion—rich from bootlegging, but still blowing safes—was backed up by an improbable bunch. Louis Alterie was a self-styled cowboy who dressed the role; Vincent "Schemer" Drucci, in priestly drag, propositioned women as they walked by; George "Bugs" Moran was saner than his nickname but not by much; and crafty Pole Earl "Hymie" Weiss displayed a proclivity for violence. Together this rogues' gallery ran a surprisingly stable bootlegging setup on the North Side, if occasionally sidetracked by any easy score that came along.

The Sicilian Genna family provided a buffer between O'Banion and Torrio—six brothers controlling countless Italian and Sicilian alky cookers on the Near West Side—but trusted few outside their clan. On the Near South Side, Frankie McErlane was an unbalanced alcoholic prone to brutality.

Any bootlegging peace meant stage-managing this diverse ethnic brew of criminal personalities into something cohesive. The goal, of course, was avoiding open warfare, encouraging bootlegging gangs to pool their resources, while the Thompson administration enabled organized graft.

Torrio knew he had to keep public opinion on the Outfit's side. But police corruption meant lax enforcement of other crimes—a cop taking in $25 a week for ignoring Prohibition laws, or working after hours as a guard outside a brewery, was less motivated to look into house burglaries or street muggings. A public happily looking the other way on violations of bootlegging laws got suddenly alert when a drunken gangster ran down a pedestrian, or a drive-by shooting endangered innocent bystanders.

And then, in 1923, Mayor Thompson, bogged down in scandals, declined to run again. A Democrat, former judge William E. Dever—campaigning to clean up Chicago—won by more than a hundred thousand votes. The new mayor replaced all key positions with competent leadership, including a new police chief.

With a reform administration in power in Chicago, Torrio turned to the suburbs. Like many a tycoon, he had the "cash register mind," as one judge described it, to spot new markets. Automobiles had opened up fresh vice territories—where city dwellers once had to go to their local red-light district, they now had the means to head out into the country, patronizing brothels and roadhouses in environs where fewer police meant fewer payoffs.

Locals didn't always welcome the arrival of gangsters and prostitutes, but that was where Capone and his brothers came in. Under Torrio's direction, they began a hostile takeover of the suburbs, spreading Chicago's corruption west, like a growing stain.

An early target was Forest View, a village founded by a lawyer from Chicago as a haven for veterans of the Great War. When the founder, also the town's police magistrate, learned Capone and his brother Ralph hoped to build a hotel in the area, he welcomed their arrival.

"It looked like a good chance to improve our village," he said, adding he knew nothing of the Capones. But as soon as he got a look at the parade of hoods and prostitutes, the city father sought to turn them away, shrugging off a threat from Ralph Capone as a joke.

Soon after, a pair of armed men showed up before dawn at the man's home, and escorted him to the town hall, where seven goons awaited to beat him with gun butts and, when he fell to the floor, kick him repeatedly. Bleeding and dazed, he knelt and pleaded for his life. They told him to get out of their town.

"I moved," the founder said. So did nearly two dozen other respectable citizens of the village, similarly beaten and driven off.

Capone's gang took over the government and built a massive brothel, the Maple Inn, housing sixty prostitutes and bringing in roughly $5,000 a week. Thanks in part to its presence, the once-peaceful village of Forest View earned a new name—"Caponeville."

The Outfit's approach in Cicero, an industrial town half an hour outside Chicago, was somewhat different. Many of its fifty-some thousand inhabitants were Bohemian by birth or extraction, and liked to have a beer after work, no matter what the Constitution said. They did not, however, want wide-open vice in their town, though a local slot machine racket did quite well under police protection.

Torrio made no attempt to pay off the local authorities. Instead, he "brought an automobile load or two of painted women," as the *Tribune* described them, and set up a brothel on Roosevelt Road. Police quickly shut it down, even tossing furniture through its windows, then raided the next Torrio brothel as well. Torrio responded by having the Cook County sheriff round up all of Cicero's slot machines.

"Then Torrio made it known that if he couldn't have prostitutes," the *Tribune* reported, "nobody else could have slot machines."

Eventually, the gangsters and the locals came to an arrangement—the Outfit could sell its beer in town, but the brothels would stay in Forest

Park and other suburbs. The interlopers also took over Cicero's casinos by partnering with the local racketeers, offering protection for a hefty cut.

As his base of operations, Capone chose the town's biggest inn, the Hawthorne Hotel, and had its windows outfitted with bulletproof shutters. Next door he set up the Outfit's premier gambling den, the Hawthorne Smoke Shop, whose handbook alone brought in a staggering $50,000 daily.

But Capone had a grander vision for Cicero than simply milking it for cash. Robert St. John, the editor of the town's muckraking young newspaper, recalled learning of a meeting Al and Frank Capone held for their handpicked candidates for the Town Board. After one man complained about his meager municipal salary, Al unloaded a profanity-laced tirade, berating the corrupt officials for their lack of vision.

"Why don't you make Cicero a real town?" he supposedly said. "Improve it! Fancy it up! . . . Pave the streets with cement! Make the dump an up-to-date place!"

The paving job proved exceedingly expensive, costing ten or twenty thousand dollars per city block, and the Capones set up a system of providing kickbacks to contractors, costing the taxpayers even more.

Back in Chicago, Torrio's peacemaking efforts between bootlegging factions were going bust. Gang warfare between his allies and vicious South Side bootlegger Edward "Spike" O'Donnell raised the new mayor's ire. Oddly, the mayor himself was opposed to Prohibition but abhorred the violence it engendered. If he cleaned up the breweries, he thought, the violence would wither away.

This theory did not bear out.

In the meantime, an overzealous, publicity-happy Prohibition agent got himself banished to the hinterlands, where he promptly raided John Torrio's West Hammond, Indiana, brewery. This involved a $2,500 fine and shuttering the brewery for a year, not a big deal in the scheme of things—Torrio pleaded not guilty. The courts were choked with Prohibition cases, and his trial would not come up for months.

While Torrio was busy, Capone was dealing with Cicero, aided by brothers Ralph and Frank. Mayor Dever's Chicago victory moved Cicero Democrats to run a reform slate against longtime mayor Joseph Klenha, under whom various casinos and taverns flourished. Capone backed Klenha's candidacy to keep Cicero secure for Outfit operations, assigning brother Frank to make sure Klenha won.

Frank began with leaflets and threats, but intimidation soon escalated into violence. The Democratic clerk running for election was roughed up; on Election Day, poll workers were beaten or kidnapped as thugs flooded in, set on insuring everyone voting did so for the current His Honor.

When news of these outrages reached him, Mayor Dever found a judge to deputize a squad of Chicago police as the court's special agents. Soon plainclothes detectives in an unmarked car were stopping across from the Twenty-Second Street and Cicero Avenue polls, where Al's brother Frank, his cousin Charlie Fischetti, and another Outfit soldier stood watch. Nearby, at the Hawthorne plant of the Western Electric Company, twenty thousand–some workers were streaming out into a rainy, chill afternoon, though the arriving police from Chicago seemed unconcerned about witnesses.

Apparently Frank shot at the plainclothes officers, who returned fire, plugging Al's big brother through the heart, while Fischetti ran into a field to surrender. The other thug was wounded on the run.

Some said Frank drew but didn't fire, others that he didn't draw at all, but the officers produced Frank's gun with three empty chambers. In any event, Frank probably did not know these men arriving in an unmarked sedan were plainclothes police.

Al Capone won the Cicero war, carrying Klenha to victory, but lost a beloved brother.

The wake and funeral were held at the home on Prairie Avenue, the silver coffin's lavish floral displays purchased from O'Banion's flower shop. A one-hundred-car cortege with fifteen bearing flowers— Capone unshaven in the old country mourning manner—was almost as elaborate as Colosimo's.

Frank's killing struck Al a terrible blow. At twenty-five, Al was still at an age where a man feels immortal. That was over. And whatever rage and frustration followed, however deep his desire for revenge, young Capone could do nothing. Johnny Torrio would not sanction Al becoming a cop killer.

On May 8, 1924, in a Levee bar, Jack Guzik waddled past Joe Howard, a minor hood who'd lately been hijacking liquor trucks. The well-lit Howard hit Guzik up for a loan and got promptly refused. Annoyed, the hijacker thrashed the portly panderer.

Guzik ran to Al Capone, who had a low tolerance for hijackers, much less any who went around pummeling Outfit staffers. Al would take care of it. He found Howard at Heinie Jacob's tavern near the Four Deuces.

Howard said, "Hello, Al."

Irate, Capone ignored any social niceties, demanding to know why Howard had clobbered Guzik, to which the drunken hijacker replied, "Go back to your girls, you dago pimp!"

Al did not appreciate being called a pimp, even though he ran brothels, and took umbrage. He clutched Howard's shirtfront with one hand and filled his other with a gun. He fired six times, sending four bullets into Howard's head and another two in a shoulder. Then Capone stormed out, leaving Howard on the floor, floating in a sea of blood.

Annoying Al Capone so soon after he'd lost his favorite brother proved ill-advised. While demonstrating a soon-to-be-celebrated hot head, Capone had sent a message—those who risked their lives hauling Outfit beer were under his protection, and hijackers targeting a Torrio shipment might want to reconsider.

Just ask Joe Howard.

By the time witnesses were brought in for the inquest, memories had changed and another patron present on that murderous night simply disappeared. Al, in hiding for a month or so, hadn't attended the inquest, either. He showed up after the fact, though, at the Cottage Grove Police Station.

"I hear the police are looking for me," he said.

When told he was suspected of murder, Capone said, "Who, me? Why, I'm a respectable business man. I'm a second-hand furniture dealer. I'm no gangster. I don't know this fellow Torrio. I haven't anything to do with the Four Deuces. Anyway, I was out of town the day Howard was bumped off."

The so-called Beer Wars would soon follow, with Torrio asked to mediate the conflict between the Genna family and Dean O'Banion. The latter became convinced the Italians were conspiring against him, and hatched a scheme to get rid of Torrio without firing a shot.

O'Banion offered to sell the would-be mediator his share of the Sieben Brewery on the Near North Side, claiming he planned to retire with his missus to Colorado, leaving Torrio to deal with the Gennas. Johnny agreed and paid O'Banion hundreds of thousands in cash. But O'Banion knew, courtesy of a police tip-off, a raid on the brewery was in store for May 19.

Before dawn that morning, several carloads of gun-toting gangsters converged at the Sieben Brewery on North Larrabee Street—a sprawling complex, complete with beer garden, topped by a squat brick tower. With them were Torrio and O'Banion, who oversaw the loading of several hundred beer barrels onto a small fleet of trucks. Meanwhile, out of sight, armed sentries were being taken into custody.

Then thirty cops descended on the brewery, sending bootleggers scurrying. While all around were losing their heads, O'Banion kept his, even saying hello to one officer and suggesting another had earned a raise. He calmly advised the workers to give up without a fight.

Torrio knew he'd been had: he'd paid all that dough for a brewery about to be shuttered. He would face jail time on this, his second bust, while O'Banion, looking at his first offense, could pay the fine with Torrio's own money. The obvious setup was enough to convince the normally peaceable Torrio his Irish rival had to go.

O'Banion's flower shop was well located in the Gold Coast of the Near North Side, across from Holy Name Cathedral and its wealth of weddings and funerals. The Irishman co-owned the shop, which he relished running. When not facing a judge, cracking a safe, or bashing a rival senseless, he was helping wealthy women select floral arrangements or providing young gents with just the right corsage for their best girl, pistols ever present in specially designed pockets.

On November 10, as the shop was busy dealing with dozens of orders for the latest gang-related wake and funeral, three men came in around noon to pick up their purchases. O'Banion emerged to greet familiar faces and extend a hand, instructing his assistant to go in back. Fifteen minutes later the assistant behind his closed door heard gunshots.

Five bullets shook the florist, hitting him in the head, chest, and neck, with another splintering display-case glass behind which roses burned as red as the blood O'Banion now lay sprawled in. The gunmen scrambled out the front, knocking down three teenage boys. O'Banion's staff, hearing the shots, had fled out the backroom door.

Suspects were not in short supply—O'Banion was linked with a half dozen or more murders. Capone and Torrio had already been around to buy flowers that week and were given a pass. Anyway, the underworld code of silence meant no one would ever be caught. Twenty-some cars made up the long procession to O'Banion's grave; there was no lack of flowers.

John Torrio was off dealing with his bootlegging charges when, just before Christmas, the Four Deuces was finally padlocked. Alphonse Capone, antique furniture dealer, had moved his office a few blocks away—the door now bore a new name and an even unlikelier profession: *Dr. Ryan, M.D.*

Less than two weeks into 1925, "Doctor Ryan's" car made an unscheduled early-morning stop. A cold dawn had awaited the driver and his passengers after some all-night partying. Now, at Fifty-Fifth and State, they found themselves nosed to the curb by a sedan, their vehicle promptly perforated with pistol bullets and peppered with shotgun blasts—"everything but the kitchen stove," a weathered police sergeant would report.

In the car were Al's cousin Charlie Fischetti, an Outfit bodyguard, and the ganglord's chauffeur, who got a nonfatal back wound, as well as two others who escaped unharmed. Al was not present. Nonetheless, shortly thereafter Capone paid $20,000 for a custom Cadillac outfitted with armor plating and bulletproof glass.

Staying alive meant living under constant guard. A crowd of armed bodyguards would now surround Capone, tall enough to tower over him and thick enough to be human shields. As he walked, they slowly scanned the area for threats.

"For Al's protection, [his] men wear bullet-proof vests," reported the *New Yorker*. "Nothing smaller than a fieldpiece could penetrate his double-walled fortress of meat."

Even the bulletproof Cadillac was not enough to keep Capone entirely safe; he rode about town in a convoy with a scout car in front and another packed with gunmen in the rear. At restaurants, he sat where he could see the door and duck out if need be. He avoided open windows, living behind curtains and shutters, and divided much of his time between well-fortified hideouts and the homes of friends—usually fellow Italians, connected to the Outfit but not always overtly.

"You fear death every moment," he would say in 1929. "Worse than death, you fear the rats of the game, who would run and tell the police if you didn't satisfy them with favors. I never was able to leave my home without a bodyguard. . . . I haven't had peace of mind in years."

Johnny Torrio might have been wise to be schooled by his pupil.

Thirteen days after the assassination attempt on Capone, Torrio—on parole and awaiting sentencing for the brewery bust—returned from shopping with his wife, Anna, to his apartment at 7011 South Clyde in the South Shore neighborhood near Jackson Park. Driving was Capone's chauffeur's brother. Anna emerged and started for the door. Johnny trailed after with an armful of packages as two men came running at him from a parked Cadillac.

O'Banion's vengeance-thirsting partner, Hymie Weiss, gripped a ready shotgun, "Bugs" Moran a .45 automatic. The driver, out to help Torrio with his packages, caught a bullet in the leg while Johnny sprinted toward the apartment.

Moran's slug ripped into Johnny's arm, sending him spinning, scattering packages, giving Weiss a clear shot. Weiss's shotgun blasted, chewing into Torrio's neck, chest, and stomach. Torrio crumpled, leaking blood from five major wounds. Moran rushed over and thrust his gun at Johnny's head, but the weapon was empty.

As Moran reloaded, the driver of the Caddy honked—a van was rounding the corner. Time to scram before witnesses got close enough to identify them.

Torrio looked to be dead or dying, just bloody meat in a winter topcoat. But an ambulance tried anyway, conveying the gang boss to Jackson Park Hospital, where Capone came and stayed until his mentor miraculously made it through.

A young witness tagged Moran as one of the would-be assassins, but Mr. and Mrs. Torrio weren't interested in identifying anyone, and soon the case was dropped. Other solutions would be found.

On February 9, shaken but alive, Torrio paid the $5,000 fine and took new if temporary residence in Lake County Jail—where the sheriff could keep him away from the city's maelstrom of violence.

In March, Capone came to the jail at Torrio's bidding. With his lawyers present, Johnny turned his operations over to his protégé—nightclubs, casinos, brothels, breweries. Wealthy and alive—and no doubt wanting to stay that way—the former boss would receive a percentage of profits, available to consult as needed . . . but at a safe distance. Al might not have been surprised—Torrio had fled gang violence before—though perhaps had not expected the complete control Johnny ceded him.

Capone had gone to the jailhouse confab as an ex-pimp and mob enforcer. He left as head of perhaps the most powerful and profitable criminal enterprise in the world. Spring was just around the corner, and Al Capone was twenty-six years old.

Eliot Ness's Treasury Department credentials. *(Carolyn Wallace, ATF photographer / Bureau of Alcohol, Tobacco, Firearms and Explosives)*

Four

1925-1926

Under Torrio and Capone, sleepy little Cicero transformed, its once peaceful, prosperous streets now lined with speakeasies and gambling joints.

Local government became an arm of the Outfit. In one editorial, the *Chicago Tribune* argued Cicero had effectively seceded from the United States and become "The Free Kingdom of Torrio."

"Nearly all the activities conducted under Torrio's administration are against the law," the *Tribune* wrote. "It is said that the majority of the citizens do not care for this but cannot do anything about it."

Once Capone took over from his mentor, he maintained his powerful hold with a thuggish brutality found mainly in fascist dictatorships. His men broke up one town meeting by slugging a trustee, while Capone himself punished the mayor for disobedience, shoving him down the City Hall front steps, kicking him while a police officer watched.

Efforts were made to cover up such brazen violence, but Cicero soon became known around the country—and eventually abroad—for its system of gangster governance.

"If you are in doubt when you pass from Chicago to Cicero, use your nose," a Chicago saying went. "If you smell gunpowder, you're in Cicero."

By the spring of 1925, most of Capone's opposition had been driven out of Cicero or silenced, with one prominent exception—newspaper editor Robert St. John. Distinguished, trimly mustached, St. John— just twenty-three—had cofounded the *Cicero Tribune* three years earlier.

He'd viewed Capone's rise with righteous indignation, while acknowledging certain inherent talents. The gangster "had great executive and organizational ability," enough to rise to the top of a major corporation in other circumstances. Or, St. John later wrote, Capone "might have wound up as a Hitler or a Mussolini, for he had that ruthlessness typical of a dictator in disposing of his opposition."

St. John dedicated his newspaper to exposing the sleaze and corruption unleashed in Cicero. No saint himself, the editor went undercover as a john at a Capone brothel, paying for a prostitute's time and then convincing her to tell her story. He moved room to room, gathering material from various fallen angels.

The grim, industrial nature of the place moved St. John to write, "Here in this place on the edge of Cicero, Scarface Al Capone had taken sordidness and made Big Business of it."

The Outfit initially responded to St. John's work via various forms of harassment, threatening and bribing his reporters, and convincing advertisers to stop buying space. They also used their hold on local government, the *Cicero Tribune* receiving scant help from city officials in compiling the most basic material for news stories. Those businesses still advertising in the paper could suffer a sudden hike in property taxes.

Yet Capone refrained from attacking St. John directly, claiming to like and respect newspapermen. As St. John wrote, Capone "knew that [the press] too, had to supply a thirsty public with the strong drink it demanded."

On April 6, 1925, the journalist caught sight of a scuffle in the street outside his office. Four gangsters with a grudge, led by Ralph Capone, leapt out of a car and attacked a policeman, beating and kicking him, until he managed to flee into a store.

St. John mistook this for a holdup, rushing down to try to stop it. He carried a deputy policeman's badge, but the gangsters beat him unconscious, anyway.

That same day, in neighboring Berwyn, a car pulled up beside St. John's brother, Archer, and its passengers opened fire. Then a brace of hoods got out, dragged Archer—wounded in the arm—into the vehicle, and sped off.

Archer also ran an upstart newspaper, the *Berwyn Tribune,* railing against local corruption. The paper planned a special Election Day edition attacking the current mayoral administration and revealing Capone's efforts to seize power. Without their editor, the *Berwyn Tribune* couldn't go forward with their exposé, but it ultimately didn't matter—the mayor lost anyway, and Archer was released, after being held captive for forty-eight hours.

Meanwhile, brother Robert lay in the hospital, recovering from injuries courtesy of Ralph and his thugs. When he went to pay his bill, it had been taken care of.

"He was rather dark-complexioned," the cashier said of the man who'd covered the *Cicero Tribune* publisher's hospitalization, "about your height but much huskier, and he was very well dressed, all in blue, with a diamond stickpin. He didn't give his name. Just said he was a friend of yours." The mystery man also "had a scar on his left cheek."

This attempt to buy St. John off only infuriated the publisher further. He went to the local police chief to swear out warrants against Ralph and the other attackers, but was told to forget it. Al Capone, the chief claimed, had taken a liking to the young journalist, but still wouldn't hesitate to kill him.

When St. John refused to cooperate, the chief told him to come back the next morning. When he did, the chief directed him to his office, where the editor was soon joined by Al Capone.

The gangster offered his hand; St. John refused it.

"I'm an all-right guy, St. John, whatever they say," Capone insisted. "Sure I got a racket. So's everybody."

Capone said he'd like to promote his businesses with full-page ads in the *Chicago Tribune*, only with brothels and casinos that was impossible.

But the *Cicero Tribune* put stories about him, Capone said, "right on the front page and I get my advertising for free. Why should I get sore?"

He produced what St. John later described as "the biggest roll of bills I've ever seen," all hundreds. Then Capone began counting them off, listing the various inconveniences St. John had suffered—time away from the office, missing hat, ruined clothes.

St. John considered the stack of cash. Capone had charmed him, and he had to admit at least some of what the gangster said made sense.

Then St. John turned and walked out silently, slamming the door behind him.

Capone couldn't pay the newspaperman off, but he could buy him out—or, at least, his paper. Sometime after his meeting with the gangster, St. John learned Capone had acquired a controlling interest in the *Cicero Tribune*.

Through an emissary, Capone said St. John could stay in charge and collect the paper's profits; his difficulties with advertisers and local government would vanish. But the gang, of course, would have a say in what he wrote.

St. John left town, integrity intact. He would not return for some sixty years, until TV personality Geraldo Rivera brought him back to share his memories before the opening of a supposed "vault" beneath Capone's old headquarters.

While Capone took the reins of Torrio's crime combine, Eliot Ness prepared to embark on his own business career.

But as a senior at the University of Chicago, studying business administration and political science, he lacked any drive for the commercial path. His grades, though respectable, had slipped since Fenger

High. A restless, adventurous soul, he couldn't stand "the monotony of an office" and came to dread the prospect of a life spent balancing books or trading stocks.

In this, he was far from alone. The pointless chaos of the Great War had raised a generation hell-bent on escaping the mundane, Victorian rhythm of their parents' lives.

The Lost Generation, as historian Frederick Lewis Allen put it, embraced "the eat-drink-and-be-merry-for-tomorrow-we-die spirit" the doughboys had brought back from the trenches. Women were wearing makeup and smoking cigarettes, hemlines retreating toward their knees like a losing army. Men welcomed females into social drinking, a formerly all-male preserve Prohibition had invaded.

College students of both sexes reveled in newfound freedom, scorning classes for sports, dances, and "petting parties." With parents paying their tuition, these kids had plenty of money to fund fast cars, sharp clothes, and endless parties, the latter fueled by pricey bootleg liquor.

Unlike many of his peers, who were flush with disposable income, Eliot had to work his way through school, a steady series of jobs devouring much of his free time. He worked as a checker for the Pullman Company, where his boss later told a proud Emma Ness that Eliot "could always count on a job anytime he wanted it." Later he kept books for a real estate firm on South Michigan Avenue, not far from the resurrected Ness bakery where he worked part-time.

His campus reporter position with the *Chicago Herald and Examiner* gave him a glimpse of the hardboiled, fast-talking world of Chicago journalism. His fellow reporters, Ben Hecht and Charles MacArthur, would soon immortalize this environment in their classic play *The Front Page*.

Yet somehow Ness found time for extracurricular activities. He had a passion for athletics, and enrolled at the University of Chicago in part to watch the Maroons play football at Stagg Field. He joined the varsity tennis squad, playing obsessively until nobody in his circle could beat him.

He also pledged a fraternity, Sigma Alpha Epsilon, though he'd never before been much of a joiner. Fraternities dominated campus life in the 1920s, setting trends, serving as gatekeepers, and keeping track of who was who. For a shy student like Ness, Sigma Alpha built confidence and social status. And, of course, frat parties were the best place to meet eligible young women, at mixers open to a privileged few—members of the "right" fraternities and sororities. The Greeks taught each other how to dance, what "lines" to deploy, and which women were "too fast." Frat culture shaped Ness's lifetime attitude toward women. Socially, he enjoyed an easy intimacy with the opposite sex—he knew how to flatter, how to flirt.

"Eliot had a tremendous line," recalled Marion Hopwood Kelly, a friend's wife. "He was one of the most attractive men I have ever seen or known."

But Ness struggled to push past flirtation into any serious relationship. He remained closed off, something of a traditionalist—marriage, kids, those were the goal. And he picked up a frat boy's suspicion of "loose" women—not that it stopped him from encouraging feminine attention.

Ness "had the girls swooning," recalled fraternity brother Armand Bollaert. "We used to double-date, and we used to have some very interesting escapades."

Ness's calm, steady, "almost priestly" demeanor didn't fit the frenetic Jazz Age beat.

"He wasn't handsome or flashy," Kelly recalled, "but women were drawn to him. Sometimes I think it was because they wanted to mother him."

The conventional wisdom of Prohibition held that "girls simply won't go out with the boys who haven't got flasks to offer," but Ness apparently didn't need one. "He didn't drink at all," Bollaert asserted, although Eliot didn't begrudge those who did.

This was unusual at a time when, as the University of Chicago's student handbook observed, "In order to be collegiate, one must drink."

But as the son of Christian Scientists, their church allied with the Prohibition movement, Ness had almost certainly grown up in a liquor-free home.

Ness received his bachelor's degree on June 16, 1925, arming himself to enter the world of business. Whether deliberate or instinctive, he put himself on an alternate career path.

He took up the martial art of jiu-jitsu because, he told a friend, "I liked it." He spent hours on the police department's firing range, working to become a crack shot. The young man who had once bowed out of playing war still disliked guns, and always would. But he hated the gangsters who used them—cowards who shot their victims in the back.

Ness seemed to be emulating his childhood hero, Sherlock Holmes, that master of "the Japanese system of wrestling" known as "baritsu," who could write the Queen's initials on the wall with a revolver.

Closer to home, Eliot had another role model, encouraging his interest in police work, right beside him on the pistol range. No detective was needed to deduce that Alexander Jamie was grooming his brother-in-law to become his brother-in-arms.

Since joining the Bureau of Investigation in 1918, Jamie had made himself indispensable to the Chicago office. He knew the city, building a strong network of informants. Unlike his energetic young brother-in-law, however, Jamie preferred desk work to fieldwork and virtually took over the office—assigning cases, monitoring reports, and dealing with personnel.

This didn't sit well with J. Edgar Hoover, who sent him back into the field. Yet Jamie kept his sights set on becoming the Chicago office's special agent in charge, and clearly had his young brother-in-law in mind for second in command.

But Jamie surely knew the Bureau wouldn't hire someone fresh out of school, whose knowledge of detective work came largely from the pages of mystery stories. As Jamie himself had done back in 1917, Eliot needed to find a job in the private sector to boost his qualifications.

Ness became an investigator for the Retail Credit Company, which proved the perfect place to learn the basics of detective work. He chased credit "skippers," learning to trace individuals who didn't want to be found. He also prepared credit reports from a variety of sources to weigh the trustworthiness of each person or firm.

J. P. MacDowell, manager of the Retail Credit office in Chicago, remembered Ness as "a bright, energetic, clean-cut young man" who "had the respect of those working with him." MacDowell said the company "regretted losing" him, but it's doubtful Ness felt the same way.

He longed for a job offering a little more action, and he hung around for only a year, the minimum needed to build his résumé. But that delay was all it took to destroy his chances of joining the Bureau, as by then his brother-in-law had managed to run afoul of J. Edgar Hoover.

That September, Hoover picked Jamie and several other agents for "a special assignment" in Washington, D.C., and ordered them to report to the capital immediately. This, Hoover stressed, was not a transfer, but temporary duty lasting "two months or four months or even longer."

The other agents, scattered across the country, quickly obeyed, but Jamie refused—he and his wife had put down roots in their city. They'd built a home, they both had jobs, and couldn't simply pack up and leave. Jamie had spent years constructing a political network in Chicago, and he had no intention of starting all over again in D.C.

For Hoover, this was rank insubordination, and the director demanded his agent's resignation. Jamie complied, but started rounding up "certain influential friends" in business and politics who could put pressure on the attorney general, Hoover's boss. Pulling strings had always worked for Jamie before.

Hoover, on the job for less than eighteen months and still reshaping the Bureau, wanted men immune to political influence, who understood "efficiency and obedience to discipline" were their only means of getting ahead. To him, Jamie's brand of politicking was a cancer that would destroy the Bureau if not eradicated.

Hoover intended to make an example of Jamie, and told the assistant attorney general "that there is no prospect of [Jamie's] reinstatement because of his refusal to obey the orders of the Bureau."

Jamie didn't stay unemployed for long, knowing exactly where to take his G-man skills. The Treasury Department's Prohibition Unit was fighting a losing battle to purge itself of corrupt and inept agents, some offices losing as much as 30 percent of their men.

With a desperate need for new recruits, the Unit could hardly turn down an applicant who, as Jamie's immediate supervisor described him, was "absolutely honest, capable, dependable, trustworthy, loyal, with much ability, and very efficient." And so on January 18, 1926, Jamie joined the Prohibition Unit. By the end of the year, he'd become assistant Prohibition administrator for Illinois, Indiana, and Wisconsin.

Still, the new position was a definite step down. Prohibition agents were reviled and distrusted throughout the country, "a corps of undisguised scoundrels with badges," as H. L. Mencken put it. Everyone knew the Prohibition boys locked up only small-timers—the poor, minorities, immigrants—while killers walked the streets and swells flouted the law.

It was understood, too, that the Unit's halfhearted raids did nothing to stop the flood of poisoned liquor leaving drinkers blind, palsied, and lying dead in the streets. The gangsters, it was said, only shot each other; but trigger-happy Prohibition agents opened fire at the slightest provocation.

By Prohibition's end, according to one writer, dry agents had killed at least "twenty-three innocent, definitely non-gangster citizens" in Chicago alone, with not one such death resulting in a murder conviction. Facetious motorists took to driving around with a rear window sticker: DON'T SHOOT—I AM NOT A BOOTLEGGER.

That Ness would even consider joining such a disreputable outfit speaks volumes about the bond he'd formed with his brother-in-law. But like Jamie, Ness had ambition, and law enforcement offered him a path.

"I looked around me after a little while," Ness said, "and decided there really wouldn't be much competition in that field."

As an honest, well-educated professional, he would stand tall among the blundering grafters filling the Prohibition Unit. If he did good work, stayed true to his principles, and kept close to Jamie, he could count on quick advancement. Plus, the job offered something of the excitement he'd always craved.

Ness left the Retail Credit Company in August 1926 and took his oath of office as a Prohibition agent that same month, at a starting salary of $2,500 a year.

When Ness broke the news to his parents, Peter and Emma couldn't fathom why their son, with his brains and work ethic, would devote himself to a dirty profession like law enforcement.

Ness merely replied, "Someone has to do it."

But, Emma said, "So many of them are dishonest men."

"Not me," Eliot said. "If there's anything you've taught me, Mother, it's to be honest."

But Ness should have listened to her. His first week on the force, he told his more experienced partner, Ted Kuhn, about an illicit distillery.

"He couldn't wait to make an arrest," Kuhn recalled. "He thought it would have some kind of domino effect and scare away all the other moonshiners."

In his excitement, Ness had blabbed his discovery to other, less trustworthy agents. When Kuhn found that out, he knew right away the bust would never happen.

But he encouraged Ness to get a warrant anyway, because the kid had a lot to learn about how things worked in Chicago. And when the pair showed up to raid the place, the still had, unsurprisingly, disappeared.

The incident taught Ness a valuable lesson. His nearest enemies weren't the bootleggers, but the corrupt cops and feds who took their money. If he wanted to succeed, he'd have to keep his mouth shut. He would play his cards close to the vest from now on.

"I'll say this for him," Kuhn remarked of Ness, "he was a fast learner."

Capone hiding his scars from the press, mid-1920s.

(Cleveland Public Library Photograph Collection)

Five

1925–1926

As a young hoodlum, Capone treated reporters with open hostility, and when confronted by a camera, he'd either hide his face or attack the photographer. Then an editor at the *Chicago Evening American* advised him to stop behaving like a common thug.

"You're a public figure," the newspaperman said, "and you ought to act like it."

Soon, Capone became the most accessible of gangsters, making public appearances, giving lengthy interviews, and—provided the cameras couldn't capture his scars—allowing himself to be photographed. He had an intuitive understanding of how the press could help him, not just by advertising his businesses but also by shaping how the public saw him.

He worked to project in the press the image of a businessman doing what anyone else would do in his place. Caught by the *Herald and Examiner* in his Prairie Avenue home, wearing a "gaudy pink apron" and holding "a pan of spaghetti," he seemed human—never mind he never actually cooked.

"I violate the Prohibition law, sure," Capone said. "Who doesn't? The only difference is I take more chances than the man who drinks a cocktail before dinner and a flock of highballs after it."

Not really—the Eighteenth Amendment had not outlawed drinking or buying alcohol, just its manufacture and sale. Still, Al's seeming honesty about his activities came off disarmingly, particularly in a two-faced town like Chicago.

"There's one thing worse than a crook, I think, and that is a crooked man in a big political job," Capone said. "A man who pretends he's enforcing the law and is really making dough out of somebody breaking it."

From implied bribery, Capone moved on to homicide. "What does a man think about when he's killing another man in a gang war?" he asked. "Maybe it means killing a man who'd kill you if he saw you first. Maybe, it means killing a man in defense of your business—the way you make the money to take care of your wife and child."

But Capone wasn't always so polished or articulate. Backed in a corner, he could prove chillingly nasty.

On May 16, 1925, a young reverend from Berwyn named Henry C. Hoover arranged to have deputy sheriffs raid Capone's big Cicero casino, the Hawthorne Smoke Shop. Shortly after raiders burst in, Capone arrived wearing pajamas and an overcoat, unshaven and surly. Rarely rising before noon, he'd been summoned from bed at the hotel next door. When he tried to force his way inside, a real estate broker turned deputy blocked his way.

"What do you think this is," the broker asked, "a party?"

"It ought to be *my* party," Capone snarled. "I own the place."

The broker took a harder look at Capone, saw the long scar, and bid him, "Come on in."

Another raider brought Capone upstairs, where the men were dismantling and carting off gaming equipment. Capone claimed he was being picked on, then said ominously, "This is the last raid you will ever make."

Reverend Hoover watched the man in pajamas clean out the cash register and asked him who he was.

"Al Brown," Capone shot back, invoking his preferred alias, "if that is good enough for you."

"Muttering and grumbling, Capone went out," the reverend recalled, "and disappeared down the stairs. Some time later . . . he reappeared, neatly dressed and shaven and clothed in an entirely different spirit."

"Reverend," he asked, "can't we get together?"

"What do you mean, Mr. Capone?"

"I give to churches," Capone said, "and I give to charity . . . if you will let up on me in Cicero, I will withdraw from Stickney."

The reverend was unmoved. "The only understanding, Mr. Capone, that you and I can ever have is that you must obey the law or get out of the western suburbs."

But Capone's earlier threat had been a promise: as they left the Hawthorne Smoke Shop, the raiders were attacked and beaten. The broker who'd let Capone inside suffered a broken nose. A few days later, another raider was shot when four thugs surprised him at home. He survived, but took no further interest in Al Capone's affairs.

Reverend Hoover and his men had gone on their last Capone raid.

That same spring, Al Capone, now the head of a multi-million-dollar criminal empire, found himself in the midst of a multifaction gang war. O'Banion's unpredictable partner Hymie Weiss was tied up in a bootlegging case that would send him temporarily to jail. Spike O'Donnell was still acting up on the South Side, and the Gennas on the West Side remained a real problem.

In 1925, "the Terrible Gennas" were, in the words of contemporary writer Edward Dean Sullivan, "overdressed, boastful, reeking with money and strutting for their countrymen." Capone had done business with them—"though they were about as serviceable as a litter of wildcats"—because they controlled a most profitable and powerful bootleg operation, worth some $5 million.

Thousands of Genna stills were tucked away among the tenements of Little Italy, tended by residents who received a princely $15 a day for their trouble. The generous wages built in these poor immigrants a strong allegiance to those who paid them well and bailed them out of trouble.

The Gennas could easily afford the expense, because their toxic liquor—which reportedly could cause blindness, insanity, and death— raked in $350,000 in gross sales every month. Their product's nasty bite matched the character of the Gennas themselves, whose religious devotion never seemed to stay their hands from killing.

"Bloody" Angelo, the brother handling enforcement, earned a fearsome reputation among West Side Italians. To maintain their hold on power, the Gennas paid police off handsomely, and employed the most coldly efficient killers in the city. Clannish and territorial, they were the antithesis of Capone's open and inclusive Outfit.

When volatile Angelo Genna took over the politically powerful Unione Siciliana, the non-Sicilian Capone had his influence over the Near West Side greatly reduced. The fraternal organization—with some forty thousand members in Chicago alone—was key to Capone's ability to both sway honest Sicilian-Americans and control the area's illicit, profitable activities, namely bootlegging. Wresting control of the Unione Siciliana from the Gennas would buy for Capone the loyalty of a community.

And Capone held two advantages over the Gennas. First, the brothers had many enemies, with Hymie Weiss blaming them for complicity in O'Banion's death. And Weiss was, in author Sullivan's words, "the most energetic dynamo of revenge Chicago gangland ever knew," fearless in part because he'd been diagnosed with cancer in 1924.

Second, Capone had added a new enforcer-bodyguard, Vicenzo Gibaldi, a Sicilian with the unlikely alias Jack McGurn, who bore a vengeance-fueled hatred against the Gennas for killing his stepfather over a bootlegging beef while Jack was still a teen. Still, McGurn's training as a boxer and pro-level golfer gave him a focus and discipline not found in many street punks.

The newly wed Angelo Genna and his bride were living outside

Little Italy in a hotel on O'Banion turf. Angelo's post-wedding hope was to buy a place in fashionable Oak Park, among the many strikingly modern homes built by Frank Lloyd Wright and away from the brutal inner city.

On May 26, 1925, flush with cash to purchase property, Angelo tooled his flashy roadster along Ogden Avenue toward the West Side. An engine roared as a sedan caught up alongside and a shotgun started blasting. Genna pulled a revolver and emptied it at his attackers, then swerved into a lamppost. The sedan drew up and perforated "Bloody" Angelo further, splintering his spine. At the hospital, he bid his bride good-bye before making a final getaway.

The Gennas and the cops agreed the North Side mob, now run by wildman Hymie Weiss, was responsible. Others theorized Capone had launched the attack, knowing the blame for a shooting in O'Banion territory would be misdirected. Typically, no one was charged.

Angelo Genna's funeral was the usual gangster spectacle—high-priced coffin, endless flowers, burial in Mount Carmel Cemetery—with the added touch that the wreckage of Angelo's bullet-punctured roadster got towed in the procession. Angelo was buried not far from O'Banion, as were so many of the gangster enemies who wound up in the same cemetery's unconsecrated ghetto.

The Gennas sought immediate revenge, Mike Genna enlisting his favorite torpedoes, the inseparable Albert Anselmi and John Scalise. Dubbed the "Murder Twins," Scalise was tall and slim while Anselmi was short and stocky. Born in Sicily, the ruthless pair had become Mafia assassins in the old country until murder raps sent them scurrying to America.

"They were abnormal and unaccountable men without nerves, emotion, or heart," wrote one gangland observer. "They looked upon murder as routine day labor."

Reportedly, Scalise and Anselmi imported the Sicilian practice of rubbing garlic on their bullets to create gangrenous wounds. It didn't really work, but it soon became a habit among Chicago killers.

Early on June 13, Mike and his Murder Twins, trolling the Near South Side for O'Banion gangsters, were seen heading south on Western Avenue by police in an unmarked car, which took chase. The Genna crew raced down Western, only spurring the cops on. Braking suddenly when a truck started across the next intersection, the car spun, winding up with its tail jumping the curb, right fender crunched against a lamppost in a terrible echo of Angelo's demise.

The Genna driver bolted, but the Twins and Genna himself got behind the wrecked car, the police skidding to a stop and piling out to be greeted by gunfire. The police driver and another officer went down dead while the other two officers shot back, one taking a shotgun blast to the chest that, incredibly, didn't kill him. Seventy bullets peppered the police car; one punctured Genna's ride.

The Twins and Mike fled but were pursued, the latter turning to fire a now-empty shotgun and getting a bullet in the leg for his trouble. Genna hobbled bloodily away, firing a handgun as he went, then scrambled into a basement to hide. Two more cops joined the pursuing officer, following a trail of blood to Genna in his hideaway, where life was oozing out of him, an artery severed.

Anselmi and Scalise were grabbed as they fled on a streetcar. At their booking for murder, they were dragged in badly battered (having "resisted arrest"), lucky to be breathing at all after a cop-killing bust.

On July 8, Anthony Genna went for a morning walk and was shot five times in the back. On his deathbed, he fingered an ex-Genna henchman now working for the Capone-affiliated Chicago Heights gang.

That was enough to encourage brothers Sam, Jim, and Pete Genna to leave town. This would seem to open the door for a Capone stooge to head the Unione Siciliana, but instead a Genna enforcer pronounced himself new president. His term was short, however, ending in a hail of gunfire delivered by Jack McGurn and another hood at a barbershop on Roosevelt Road.

McGurn had taken his vengeance on the Gennas, and Capone could now install his own man as head of the Unione Siciliana.

After almost two years, three trials, and thousands in defense money, Anselmi and Scalise would be acquitted for killing the two policemen, earning a big celebratory shindig from Al Capone.

Why Capone was so devoted to the pair remains a mystery. Perhaps they had supplied him with inside dope while working for the Gennas. And of course he knew how useful they could be—hitmen didn't come more ruthless.

A triumphant Al decided to spend Christmas 1925 with his family in Brooklyn.

He said, "I guess [Mae] didn't know what she was letting herself in for when she married me. I was just a nice little boy that grew up with her in Brooklyn, and she was a sweet little Irish kid who took me for better or for worse."

Asked what he wanted his son to grow up to be, Al said, "A brave man who can look anyone in the eye and stand his ground no matter what comes. I like a man with nerve—even if he's on the other end of a gun fight." Changing course, Capone said, "I don't want him to be a bootlegger or a reformer, either. I'd rather like him to be a professional man, a doctor, lawyer, or a business man."

What did Capone want his son to think of his papa? "I want him to know that I loved him enough to risk my life to work for him. . . . I expect him to repay me by playing the game straight."

Christmas wasn't the only reason for the family trip—Capone had two other agendas, starting with getting his son to New York for surgery for a mastoid infection imperiling the child's hearing.

"I had three doctors there," Capone said, "and they told me that operations of that kind were about a fifty-fifty chance." His offer of $100,000, which he bragged about to the press, was declined in favor of the standard $1,000 fee. The operation saved Sonny's life but took a toll on his hearing.

"It was Christmas Eve when my wife and I were sent home to get some sleep," Capone said. "We found her folks trimming the Christmas tree for her little nieces and nephews and it broke us all up."

This Norman Rockwell scene was interrupted the evening of Christmas Day by a friend of Capone's dropping by to ask him "to go around the corner to his place to have a glass of beer." Al added, "My wife told me to go; it'd do me good."

Capone's friend's "place" was the notorious Adonis Social Club, a seedy speakeasy with a cigarette girl and a ragtime piano player with a songbird on the side, enlisted for the occasion of Frankie Yale's holiday party. Orange bunting draped the club, shaky lettering wishing a MERRY CHRISTMAS AND HAPPY NEW YEAR.

Capone with two bodyguards—including Frank Galluccio, provider of Al's famous scars—ambled in to pay Yale their respects. Center floor, in a chandelier's muted glow, was a table Capone and his men strolled past without occupying. Al and his boys took seats here and there in the shadows.

The party showed no sign of losing steam by a little before 2:00 A.M., when six men drifted in—White Hand members, the Irish answer to the Italian Black Hand—with whom Yale had long been at odds. Their leader, Richard "Peg Leg" Lonergan, brazenly, if stiffly, traversed the dance floor.

Already well lubricated, Lonergan and his men strolled over to the only open table, the one under the chandelier. Once the unwanted guests had settled themselves, somebody hit the lights, with only the overhead fixture still going to highlight the White Hander table. Shots came from everywhere, tables overturning, silverware clattering, glasses and dishes shattering.

The White Hand leader, a toothpick still clenched in his teeth, wobbled on his wooden leg, then hit the floor a corpse; another Irish guest dropped, dead before he landed. Two more scattered for the door, then two wounded confederates, the last out leaving a scarlet trail to the gutter.

Yale had been warned Lonergan intended to show up for the annual get-together and then attack. Some nonlocal faces would be needed to help turn the Irish ambush into an Italian one. Capone, with a trip already planned to do his fatherly duty, had agreed to participate, pleased to pay Frankie Yale back for various homicidal favors.

Of course, Capone's version of the proceedings differed, retaining the sanitized slant of him going innocently to his friend's "place" for a holiday beer.

"And we were no sooner in there," Capone said, "than the door opens and six fellows come in and start shooting. . . . In the excitement two of them were killed and one of my fellows was shot in the leg. And I spent the Christmas holidays in jail and the next week after that, too, and my poor wife had to carry the weight of the two of us."

Local cops took Capone and six others into custody. Wiped-clean weapons, dead Irish gangsters, and a gunfight in the dark added up to self-defense. Charges were dropped.

Waxing sentimental about his family to the press—even in the aftermath of a massacre—was partly publicity. Nonetheless, Al was the kind of man who called home every day, wherever he was, to speak to his sister, mother, and wife, when he woke up at noon or at dinnertime.

Mafalda would snatch up the receiver and immediately hand it off to Theresa, irritating Mae, sometimes to the point where—when she finally got her turn—her husband had to kid her back into a better humor.

Sonny's condition improved following his operation, even as the boy's mother began suffering symptoms of an advanced case of syphilis. At her physician's urging, she sought treatment at the Mayo Clinic, despite fears that the newspapers might get wind. In pre-penicillin days, little could be done; the disease would flare up again.

Although Mae's husband knew of the diagnosis, he seems to have taken little notice for his own well-being. He apparently did not seek treatment, having displayed no outward symptoms for many years. Anyway, enemy bullets posed a much more pressing threat.

But the disease would work on Capone in dangerously subtle ways. Once syphilis enters the brain, it begins to affect its victim's personality. The sufferer's mood can swing rapidly from gregariousness to open hostility; he may develop an explosive temper and an obsession with sex, while behaving in ways that seem both curiously distracted and melodramatic—heightening tendencies Capone already possessed.

Back in the city, a special Santa's bag of Christmas gifts had arrived— the Capone gang's very own supply of Bergmann submachine guns. The weapons, German surplus from the Great War, were delivered to the Cicero PD for Outfit soldiers to pick up.

A gangland arms race had begun the previous fall, when Capone's competitors adopted a new tool: the Thompson submachine gun. Newer and lighter than the Bergmanns, the tommy gun took some getting used to. When its fully automatic chatter first echoed in Chicago, the gunman missed his target and left police puzzling over how one weapon could leave so many bullet holes.

"That's the gun!" Capone said. "It's got it over a sawed-off shotgun like the shotgun has it over an automatic." His men, unwilling to lag behind their rivals, ordered three Thompsons in February.

The tommy gun was streamlined, compact, and devilishly easy to use. Light enough to carry yet heavy enough to absorb its own recoil, the Thompson was surprisingly gentle on its user, hardly kicking when fired—"the deadliest weapon, pound for pound," *Time* magazine declared, "ever devised by man."

Born of the Great War, this "trench broom" meant to help American doughboys sweep their way across Europe. But the conflict ended too soon for the Thompson to take part, and many of the fifteen thousand guns in circulation by 1929 ended up in private hands. Because the weapon was so new, few laws governed its sale. Legally purchasing a tommy gun in Chicago, in those days, was easier than acquiring a handgun.

The new year found recent recruit Jack McGurn—who would earn the nickname "Machine Gun" for his prowess with a Thompson—gladly knocking off former Genna gunmen. Over two weeks, McGurn dispatched three ex-Genna hoods in a succession of well-executed executions, narrowly escaping death himself on March 29 while fleeing four gunmen down an alley, his hat the only casualty.

When the West Side mob of William "Klondike" O'Donnell (no relation to South Side bootlegger Spike) tried to horn in on Cicero, Capone unleashed McGurn, who struck at a top O'Donnell gunman picking up his girl at her beauty shop. McGurn nosed a Thompson out a car window and unloaded a one-hundred-round drum, destroying everything in the shop except its human inhabitants, who ducked below the "Chicago lightning."

A few nights later, an informant pointed Capone to the Pony Inn, a speakeasy on Roosevelt Road where O'Donnell and his boys were imbibing. As the happy group stumbled out with plans for barhopping, five sedans thundered up. This time the Thompsons didn't miss: three of the O'Donnell party were hit, two dying at once, another staggering to a tree where he expired. The other three—O'Donnell himself included—somehow avoided injury.

The carnage would have serious ramifications. One of two bullet-ridden bodies proved to be William H. McSwiggin, bespectacled twenty-seven-year-old star prosecutor.

Dubbed "Little Mac" and "the Hanging Prosecutor," McSwiggin had scored seven convictions over the past ten months. A Chicago policeman's son and a favorite of the press, McSwiggin's successes helped reelect his boss, State's Attorney Robert Crowe.

"We are going to get at the bottom of this," Crowe said, offering a hefty reward. "I am going to root out the booze and gang killings . . . if we have to use all the peace officers in Cook County on the one task."

Mayor Dever's police chief promised to put every available man on the case, and issued a warrant for Capone's arrest. Meanwhile, the papers hammered at two questions: "Who killed McSwiggin?" and "Why?"

Task forces, courtesy of the state's attorney and the Chicago PD, shuttered every speak and vice operation in and out of sight, bleeding the Outfit of as much as a million dollars.

In Forest View, the once-quiet suburb now called Caponeville, vigilantes targeted the massive Outfit brothel known variously as the Maple Inn and the Stockade. They descended on the morning of May 30, overpowering a watchman before setting fires throughout the building. Firefighters arrived from Berwyn but did nothing more than stand back and watch the conflagration.

According to the *Tribune,* Capt. John Stege, considered by many a rare honest Chicago cop of the era, "said no attempts would be made to find the vigilantes." He hoped they would burn down a lot more joints as tough as the Stockade—it was easier than trying to obtain injunctions.

Capone, who had never intended to kill McSwiggin, could only stand back like the Forest View firefighters and watch his empire burn.

McSwiggin was at a speakeasy for investigative purposes, some said. That claim fell apart when the bar's owner identified McSwiggin as a regular who'd known the O'Donnell mob members since childhood. Their respectable friend partying with gangsters conveyed a nod-and-a-wink assurance that the prosecutor and his pals would not likely raid the speaks they themselves frequented.

Also, the press finally noticed, the colorful murderers McSwiggin had put away were not mobsters, while shortly before his death he unsuccessfully prosecuted the Murder Twins, Anselmi and Scalise. Added to that, one companion slain at the Pony Inn had been a defendant in a murder case Little Mac had lost.

State's Attorney Crowe was up against it—his election had been aided by the bootlegging gangs agreeing to cut back on violence until Crowe was voted in. Now, with his star prosecutor tainted, Crowe looked bought and paid for.

The time had come to go after Capone, the likely culprit, who had not only organized the attack but apparently manned one of the Thompsons himself.

"Scarface Al Brown, whose real name is Caponi [*sic*]," the *Chicago Tribune* reported, "was the machine gunner who shot and killed William H. McSwiggin . . . according to the best information elicited by State's Attorney Crowe . . . and Deputy Chief Stege of the detective bureau last night."

The *Tribune* found a witness who "was in a restaurant in Cicero on last Tuesday evening at 7 o'clock and saw Al Brown, his brother, and two or three other men in hasty and agitated conversation," which was followed by Capone going to a panel in the wall and taking out a machine gun. The thugs with Capone took pistols from the compartment and the group rushed out, shortly before the McSwiggin killing.

The state's attorney's office and the Detective Bureau believed "Capone in person led the slayers of McSwiggin. It has become known that five automobiles carrying nearly thirty gangsters, all armed with weapons ranging from pistols to machine guns, were used in the triple killing."

Whether he'd led the attack or not, Capone took to heart a lesson: the brazen McSwiggin killing had riled the citizenry. In particular, cops, angered by one of their own dying, were as dangerous as any mobsters—look what had happened to Al's brother Frank, who had suffered virtual police assassination. To succeed in his chosen field, Capone needed the public on his side—but such wanton violence would inevitably turn them against him.

Capone sought shelter in the southern suburb of Chicago Heights, at the home of bootlegger Dominic Roberto. Some years before, Roberto's wife—a nightclub singer who performed as Rio Burke—had encountered a drunk, obnoxious Capone at a picnic.

Now Rio could only marvel at the change she saw in Capone. Hiding out in her home, he dressed in silk suits and took great care with his appearance. If anything, he seemed subdued, rarely laughing or smiling, "all business."

Perhaps the McSwiggin mess had chastened him.

After eight days with Roberto and Rio, Capone switched hideouts, fleeing at night to the suburb of Freeport, where another family of Capones—no relation—had previously sheltered him. Raphael, the patriarch, had shadowy Outfit ties; the gang hid a set of ledgers in his home, and Al would frequently come by to go over them.

Raphael always made a point of criticizing Al's drinking, womanizing, and brutish behavior. So far, Al had brushed his criticism aside, but Raphael could no longer contain himself. When Al entered his Freeport home after the McSwiggin murder, Raphael greeted him silently, beating him with a cane.

Al's bodyguards made a move to stop the attack, but Capone held up a hand.

Next Capone traveled two hundred miles to a place where he could truly feel safe: Lansing, Michigan. Once again, he hid out among a family of Italian-Americans whose patriarch had once worked for the Outfit.

Thanks to an arrangement with local police, Capone could walk freely around the city, soon becoming known in the Italian-American enclave. Al bought presents and ice cream for kids, financed at least one wedding, and lavished huge tips on a teenage errand boy. And, like Rio Burke, locals marveled at his quiet, gentlemanly manner.

"Capone was not loud, flashy, and coarse," recalled the daughter of the family who'd taken him in. "Capone had class. More than that, he had grace."

But a cloud of violence and fear surrounded him still, as did the armed bodyguards who followed him everywhere.

Capone spent much of the summer in a cabin on Round Lake, just outside town. He would read, hole up with his latest mistress, and indulge his love of swimming. On the Fourth of July, he paid for a huge fireworks show and performed as its master of ceremonies.

"He'd be out on the end of the dock, acting just like a little kid," recalled the man who, as a teenager, had served as Capone's gofer.

He would also remember Capone's sadness one evening as they walked home from a movie theater and passed a house where a family was sitting down to dinner. Capone wished he could do the same— enjoy a quiet meal with his wife and son in front of an open window with no thought of gunfire.

He warned his young companion not to get involved in the criminal life.

"If you do," Al said, "and I'm alive, I'll personally kill you."

The more time he spent in Lansing, the more Capone spoke of retiring from crime, of staying in Michigan or fleeing to Canada.

But he must have known he could never leave that life, not completely. He would turn himself in for McSwiggin's murder, figuring he had little chance of being convicted. He would show Chicago he had nothing to hide—that his racket was no worse than anybody else's.

He would offer himself up as a public figure, legitimizing his business by force of personality, if not by law. And he would work to make peace, resorting to war only if necessary, so he and his family could escape the threat of death.

Ness (second from right) poses with liquor seized from Pullman porters, alongside E. C. Yellowley, Frank White, and Alexander Jamie (left to right), August 1927. *(Bureau of Alcohol, Tobacco, Firearms and Explosives)*

Six

1926–1927

Sgt. Anthony McSwiggin, the dead prosecutor's father, was determined to see his son's killer brought to justice. Talk of McSwiggin's brothers in blue being trigger-happy was in the air.

To avoid the Chicago police, who might hold him for their own brand of questioning, Capone made an arrangement with State's Attorney Crowe to meet federal agents at the Illinois-Indiana border on July 28, 1926.

"I think the time is ripe for me to prove my innocence of the charges that have been made against me," he told reporters, insisting he had nothing to do with killing "my friend McSwiggin."

Capone handled the press with ease, seeming anything but the ogre he'd been made out to be. *Of course* Al hadn't killed McSwiggin.

"I liked the kid," he said, then added an offhand bombshell: "I paid him plenty and I got what I was paying for."

Police confirmed Al could not have snatched a machine gun from a hidden compartment at the Hawthorne Hotel, because they'd searched the place and found no secret cabinets behind trick panels.

But Sergeant McSwiggin remained fixed upon avenging his murdered son. Some said the detective worked out a deal with friends on the force, who brought Capone to a room where McSwiggin could shoot him in private, without fear of prosecution. Others claimed the elder McSwiggin confronted Capone at the Hawthorne Hotel. When McSwiggin accused him of murder, Capone handed him his own pistol.

"If you think I did it," Capone said, "shoot me."

Whoever told the tale, the payoff was always the same. As one gangster put it, Sergeant McSwiggin "was just too decent a guy to shoot a man, even Capone, in cold blood."

Information about prosecutor McSwiggin's double life spilled out of the grand juries and other sources, revealing no martyr, rather the accomplice of his crooked drinking pals.

After a night in stir, Capone was back reestablishing his realm. The task at hand was handling the North Siders, now led by the unstable Hymie Weiss, released from prison. "Weiss, the Pole, was the antithesis of Capone, the Neapolitan," Fred Pasley wrote, "unemotional, of a cold ferocity that made him a dread figure to both friend and foe. He was a combination of brain and brute and said to be the only man Capone ever really feared."

In July, one of Capone's chauffeurs was kidnapped, tortured, and killed, then left to rot in a southwest suburban cistern. Whether for vengeance or self-protection, Capone knew Weiss and his key minions had to go.

The following week, Hymie Weiss and second-in-command Vincent Drucci exited the Congress Hotel and sauntered south on Michigan Avenue to make a cash payoff to a ward boss. The major business district at the south end of Chicago's Loop surely seemed safe for a morning walk . . . before the skidding of tires and report of a gun. Weiss hugged the pavement, pedestrians scattering, as two gunmen scrambled from a car. Drucci took cover behind a mailbox and blasted back. A police car squealed up and the getaway car tore off, stranding the two gunmen. The fevered Drucci jumped onto a running board to commandeer a car and give chase, but was mobbed by cops.

One captured shooter proved to be a Capone enforcer who Drucci refused to ID. Five days later, again on Michigan Avenue, Weiss and Drucci would survive a similar attack.

Gang violence in the bustling Loop business district was previously unheard of. Such dirty business was reserved for in and around speaks and gambling dens, not where tourists and businessmen got in the line of fire. And as the bullets kept flying where they shouldn't have flown, those businessmen would soon demand protection—for themselves, and for their city's bottom line.

On the afternoon of September 20, 1926, Al Capone was enjoying coffee with his bodyguard, Frankie Rio, in the restaurant on the ground floor of the Hawthorne Hotel, his Cicero headquarters. The restaurant was especially busy, thanks to that day's horse races, with parked cars lining the street outside.

The hustle and bustle was blotted out as a sedan sped by, a Thompson firing wildly out of the back. Capone and Rio ducked, along with everyone else, and somehow nobody was hurt. Rio assessed the scene— confirming the bullets had done no damage. Had the gun been aiming away from the building?

"It's a stall, boss, to get you out," Rio said. "The real stuff hasn't started."

Meanwhile, Outfit member Paul Ricca, about to enter the restaurant, spotted a second suspicious vehicle approaching, and caught a slug in the arm as he called out the alarm.

Another sedan was rolling past now, a tommy gun blazing from its back window, this time taking aim at the restaurant—bullets ripping through parked cars, shattering windows, tearing apart wood-paneled walls, and turning ceramic plates and mugs into powder.

More sedans followed, over half a dozen, each with a tommy gun pouring lead into the wrecked restaurant. Then a car stopped and a man in brown overalls got out, clutching a Thompson with a hundred-round drum, which he emptied with the precision of a master craftsman, raking the weapon back and forth. The men in the car behind him kept lookout, shotguns ready at the hint of movement.

The final gunner got back in the car, which joined the caravan heading in the general direction of Chicago.

The North Side gangsters had fired an estimated thousand bullets into the Hawthorne Hotel and thirty-five cars parked out front. Weiss, Drucci, and Moran had left nothing to chance, yet still they had failed.

Four bystanders were injured in the tommy gun fusillade, including a mother and her son visiting from Louisiana; Capone and Rio escaped unscathed. Ricca, the only Outfit soldier wounded, won the Big Fellow's gratitude and a promotion to the front office.

"A machine gun was used to shoot up the Hawthorne Hotel a few days ago, and they can't blame that on me," Capone told the press. "Why, I'm still paying owners of automobiles parked in front for the damage done to their cars in that raid, and I am trying to save the eye of the poor innocent woman they wounded sitting in a car in front."

Capone paid for the damage done to the café, too.

Once again, the ganglord used the press to his advantage. If he could position himself as better than the other guys—or, in the case of McSwiggin, reduce them to his level—he could retain some measure of public sympathy.

In private, he planned retaliation. Unlike Weiss's attack on the Hawthorne, a surgical strike was called for. Al would remember McSwiggin's death and the dangers of collateral damage.

"The Big Fellow," an Outfit soldier explained, "never wants any innocent bystanders hurt."

In early October, Capone assembled a peace conference at the Hotel Sherman, sending Tony Lombardo of the Unione Siciliana as his representative. Weiss had a demand: the two men who'd attacked him on Michigan Avenue must be turned over.

"I wouldn't do that to a yellow dog," Capone told Lombardo.

Giving up a pair of expendable types might seem a fair trade for a bootlegging alliance, but who of Capone's men would put their lives on the line for him after he turned over two of his own for execution?

So the war would go on. Weiss was the one man whose death would slow or stop the conflict. But the last thing PR-savvy Capone wanted was more bullet storms on city streets. The hit had to be well-planned and sudden.

He handed the task to Frank Nitto.

Weiss still maintained O'Banion's old office above the State Street flower shop. Holy Name Cathedral, the mammoth limestone seat of Chicago's archdiocese, consumed the opposite block. But in a rooming house at 740 North State, to the north, a second-floor apartment had a view on the street.

On October 11, around 4:00 P.M., Weiss, his lawyer, driver, bodyguard, and a politico pulled into a parking lot catercorner from the flower shop, just south of Holy Name Cathedral. Weiss and his business associates were lost in conversation; the others may have slowly scanned the street, alleys, and doorways, including the church, before starting across. No one looked to the heavens, however, from which rained down machine-gun rounds and shotgun bursts. Weiss's bodyguard collected seven slugs while Weiss took ten, lurching to the sidewalk and falling, never regaining consciousness.

The machine-gun nest hustled the rest of the Weiss party along, wounding them all, bullets careening off the cathedral's cornerstone, obliterating letters from its inscription.

The police rushed the room at 740 North State and found three shotgun shells, thirty-five machine-gun shells, and plenty of cigarette butts near two window chairs. The gunmen had taken care to zero in on their targets and keep pedestrians out of the line of fire. Nitto had planned the job well.

Virtually every cop in Chicago believed Capone had ordered the hit. In response, Capone did something unusual for a gangster but typical of "other notables of the news," as the *Tribune* put it—he called a press conference.

To receive reporters, Capone used a drably furnished Hawthorne Hotel room to downplay his financial status. In slippers but no jacket, trademark cigar in his teeth, Capone appeared relaxed, despite—or perhaps because of—the fifteen bodyguards standing by.

"I'm sorry Weiss was killed," Capone said, after handing out cigars and drinks. "But I didn't have anything to do with it. I telephoned the Detective Bureau I'd come in if they wanted me and they told me they didn't want me. I knew I'd be blamed for it, but why should I kill Weiss?"

"He was supposed to be your rival," one reporter pointed out, "for control of all the gangs of Cook County."

Capone ignored the question, instead launching into a whitewashed version of his life, with no reference to his ventures in vice and gambling, though frankly admitting his involvement in the "beer racket." He went back to his boyhood in Brooklyn, insisting both he and his parents were American born.

"I have to laugh at the way those hoodlums squawk that I'm a foreigner. . . . You can count on the fingers of one hand the foreigners I've got with me here," Capone said.

He gave his version of the Beer Wars, in which he and Torrio were earnest peacekeepers while the North Siders were incorrigible troublemakers.

"I'll tell them why I want peace," Capone said, "because I don't want to break the hearts of the people that love me. . . . Especially I don't want to die in the street, punctured with machine-gun fire."

Capone blamed his adversaries for all the bloodshed. He had "tried since the first pistol was drawn in this fight to show them that there's enough business for all of us without killing each other like animals in the street."

He even spared a thought for Weiss's grieving mother. "I know that sweet old lady. . . . When Hymie was in business with us, many's the night I slept in his house and ate at his table. Why didn't he use some sense and keep out of this shooting stuff?"

The Weiss funeral, with its few hundred attendees, was small by gangster norms. Weiss—never without his rosary—was, like O'Banion, refused Catholic rites and interred in unsanctified ground without a final Mass.

Finally, well into October, a major peace conference took place, most likely at the Hotel Sherman across from City Hall and a major haunt of fixers, politicos, and lobbyists. Bugs Moran was against North Siders attending, but Drucci forced the issue and both appeared.

Past clashes were to be forgotten, future differences resolved nonviolently, the old Torrio borders restored. To Capone's benefit, the original pact hadn't included his Cicero holdings, his interests already furthered by the removal of the Gennas.

"Here they sat," Fred Pasley wrote, "partitioning Chicago and Cook County into trade areas, covenanting against society and the law, and going about it with the assurance of a group of directors of United States Steel or Standard Oil transacting routine matters."

The gang leaders, who a short time before had been trying to kill each other, retired to a bacchanal of drinking and laughter, dubbed the "feast of ghouls" by the press. According to Pasley, Capone was now "the John D. Rockefeller of some 20,000 anti-Volstead filling-stations. He was sitting on top of the bootleg world" from the Loop to Cicero, and east to Indiana.

Flush with victory, Capone gushed to a *Herald and Examiner* reporter, "I believe it's peace to stay. . . . I know I won't break it and I don't think they will. I feel like a kid I'm so happy. When the meeting was over I called up my wife and told her. She cried so she couldn't talk to me."

Capone added, with a straight face, "I'm going home to sleep now after I have a couple of beers. That's my celebration. I don't drink as a rule, but the lid's off tonight."

The man who lent his name to the dry law was, like its most famous enforcer, the son of two Norwegian immigrants. Congressman Andrew J. Volstead of Minnesota was not a die-hard dry but firmly believed laws held the power to regulate morality. He put his faith to the test with a bill designed to give teeth to the Eighteenth Amendment—the National Prohibition Act. Passed over a presidential veto in 1919, it would forever be known by the name of its sponsor: the Volstead Act.

Most Prohibitionists gave little thought to actually enforcing the dry law. Getting it into the Constitution was all that mattered; certainly good, ordinary Americans would never willingly violate their nation's sacred charter.

But Volstead knew his namesake would be dead on arrival without strong, effective enforcement. To that end, his Act set up the Prohibition Unit, empowering it to go after bootleggers. Prohibition agents were exempted from civil service requirements, making them essentially political appointees. By giving themselves the power to handpick these agents, the drys hoped to make sure only true believers fought the war on liquor.

Politicians flooded the Unit with their faithful supporters, a crew of hacks, sycophants, and outright criminals who bore little love for the law they would supposedly enforce.

Soon after taking office, Mabel Walker Willebrandt, the assistant attorney general in charge of Prohibition cases, discovered "that hundreds of prohibition agents had been appointed through political pull and were as devoid of honesty and integrity as the bootlegging fraternity."

Those agents not actively colluding with gangsters were often hopelessly inept, unqualified to carry a badge, much less a gun. A more perfect engine of corruption than the Prohibition Unit could scarcely have been designed. Rather than protecting the Eighteenth Amendment, the Volstead Act had virtually doomed it to failure.

Congress compounded the problem by drastically underfunding the Unit. Prohibition agents made less than garbage collectors, earning what amounted to a starvation wage in bigger cities like New York and Chicago.

And, as the late, selectively lamented Dean O'Banion once observed, "Gold badges look swell, but you can't eat 'em."

Yet agents making roughly $2,500 a year were seen wearing diamond rings and riding around in chauffeured cars. These upholders of law and order rarely raided a Chicago speakeasy without warning the owner.

"When the cops and the Prohibition agents come here after hours all the time to get drunk," remarked one saloon keeper, "why, of course, they go along with us."

Something akin to the later Internal Affairs Divisions of modern law enforcement agencies seemed called for. The task of policing these couple of thousand Prohibition agents fell to the Treasury Department's Intelligence Unit, a team of thirty-nine men under the command of Elmer Lincoln Irey.

A soft-spoken man who began his career as a post office stenographer, Irey had taken the job thinking he would spend his time going after tax evaders. Instead, the Prohibition Unit all but drowned him in an endless tide of corruption and criminality. From January 1920 until February 1926, more than 750 Prohibition agents resigned under charges of extortion, insubordination, theft, and worse—a rate of more than two a week. Many more never got caught.

"As I think back upon Prohibition enforcement," Irey wrote, "I am astonished that so many agents did remain honest. Certainly they, and the law they were enforcing, were held in high contempt across the land."

One such honest agent—stationed in Chicago, of all places—was E. C. Yellowley, the Prohibition administrator for Illinois, Indiana, and Wisconsin. Yellowley had turned down an assignment in balmy California and requested a transfer to Chicago, just in time for winter, because he wanted to take the fight to the bootleggers. And he was absolutely incorruptible, having once refused a $250,000 bribe to protect an illicit still. With Eliot Ness's brother-in-law Alexander Jamie as his second-in-command, Yellowley made a valiant effort to combat Chicago's drinking problem.

But this "rip snortin' enforcer" (as the *Tribune* dubbed him) proved no match for a city with thousands of speakeasies, a place where cops regularly hired themselves out to guard liquor shipments and bars operated in the county building and the Board of Education. This was Chicago, where the police chief offered booze to journalists, and a politician could declare, "I drink as much and as often as I can, in order to lessen the supply!" The Loop was littered with more gin joints than Yellowley had Prohibition agents in his entire district.

In the late spring of 1927, Special Agent Pat Roche of Elmer Irey's Intelligence Unit tipped Jamie off to a huge South Side brewery at 70 East Thirty-First Street. Roche received the intelligence from a mechanic who worked nearby, but when Jamie sent agents to interview the witness, the men reported they didn't buy his story. The next morning, the mechanic saw a huge beer truck rumble into the suspected brewery and called Jamie's office to report it. Unknown to the informant, Jamie wasn't in that day.

Within half an hour, two Prohibition agents arrived, questioned the mechanic, and tailed the beer truck when it drove off. Then George Howlett, a major player in Capone's beer racket, approached the informant, claiming to be a prohibition agent.

"You appear to be a pretty decent fellow," Howlett said. "There are some big people connected with the operations carried on in that building, and there are a number of officials in the Prohibition office on the payroll . . . I will put you on for $75 a week, and all you will have to do will be to keep your mouth shut."

The mechanic accepted a $20 down payment and reported the bribe to Roche, who immediately telephoned Yellowley and Jamie; they had never received the informant's call. Yellowley asked the Intelligence Unit to carry on the investigation—his men weren't up to the job.

Roche and another special agent, Clarence Converse, staked out the brewery and kept track of everyone who came and went. They also discovered that the Prohibition agents the mechanic had seen were really members of what the feds were still calling "the 'Al Caponi' alias 'Al Brown' gang." The license plate numbers of cars parked outside confirmed a Capone operation.

Early on the morning of June 8, 1927, Roche and Converse led several Prohibition agents—among them Eliot Ness's partner, Ted Kuhn—in a raid on the brewery. The place was empty; someone had tipped off the workers. But the agents did seize the brewing equipment.

Hoping to track down the phony Prohibition agents, the real ones continued to investigate and soon found an even larger brewery nearby, at 217 East Thirtieth Street. The agents knew the place would be alerted if they told the Prohibition office of their discovery. Instead, they would lie in wait.

After several weeks of surveillance, on August 5, the special agents noticed Capone cars prowling the neighborhood. A motorcycle cop and squad of police cars also swept the area, apparently making sure the coast was clear.

Then a ten-ton truck laden with beer barrels backed out of the brewery. Posing as corrupt Prohibition agents, Roche and Converse seized the truck. One bootlegger told them "the brewery was owned by Al Brown, that he was a good fellow, and that he would go and see a man right away who would fix everything with us."

The special agents let him go, but when he hadn't returned after forty-five minutes, they arrested the other three. Only then did they call the Prohibition office.

The impressive raid, the district's largest in years, resulted in the seizure of a massive brewery capable, the feds reported, "of putting out at least 200 barrels of beer a day," costing Capone a minimum of $100,000.

But Yellowley, in no uncertain terms, told the special agents he didn't want the Intelligence Unit making Prohibition raids, as having the tax investigators do his job for him reflected badly on his office. Roche and Converse explained the bootleggers obviously had a connection in Yellowley's office sharing any contemplated raids.

Yellowley wasn't having any. The official who turned down fabulous gangster bribes was susceptible to pride, refusing to let the Intelligence Unit pursue the case. Roche and Converse reluctantly gave up their hunt for Capone's mole in the Prohibition office.

By now, the drys had to admit the only way to fix the Prohibition Unit was to scrap the whole venal, blood-soaked mess and try again.

Congress had tried and failed to pass a bill replacing the Unit with a new Bureau of Prohibition. When that bill finally became law in March 1927, every Prohibition agent had to take a civil service test. Current agents, and anyone seeking to join their ranks, now faced stricter qualifications. The tests did weed out some of the worst offenders, while others managed to hang on through political influence. And the stringent new standards wound up disqualifying many competent agents.

Eliot Ness was among those nearly thrown out. To become or remain a Prohibition agent, applicants now had to be at least twenty-five years old. But when the new rules went into effect that April, Ness was just turning twenty-four.

This man so noted in history for his honesty appears to have added a year to his age—claiming to be born in 1902, not 1903, in order to make the cut. This was easy enough to do; he had been born at home, leaving no official record of his birth. If Eliot Ness's true age had been discovered, he'd have been barred from government service and possibly prosecuted. Of course, in the miasma of misconduct pervading the Prohibition Bureau, the infraction may have seemed relatively minor to Ness.

Almost certainly, Eliot's brother-in-law encouraged him to lie about his age, and—as the second-highest ranking man in the office—could ensure he wouldn't be caught.

Ness would have to keep up the fiction for the remainder of his federal service—the stakes growing higher as his career advanced. For the moment, though, the job remained a game Ness played gladly. More than anything, he loved going on raids. He savored the rush of kicking down a door and throwing himself over the threshold, never knowing what was on the other side. A desk job couldn't compete, he said, because "there certainly is a thrill in pitting your wits against others'."

This thrill-seeking, game-playing attitude helped give Eliot's early raids the flavor of schoolboy pranks, or an elaborate round of cops and robbers, where one couldn't always tell which was which.

In the fall of 1926, Ness broke up a bootleg ring supplying students of the University of Illinois. To obtain the necessary evidence, he went undercover, enrolling as a graduate student.

The following April, Ness and another agent, Frank L. White, staked out a roadhouse in Lyons, just west of Capone's stronghold in Cicero. They saw a truck drive up to deliver two barrels of beer and quickly got on either side of the man behind the wheel.

"You can't arrest me," the driver declared. "I'm the chief of police."

He was telling the truth. The agents apprehended him anyway.

The very next week, Ness and White made headlines yet again for a daring bit of undercover work. Disguised as "Kentucky colonels who owned racing stables," they visited four gin joints in Aurora on race day, gathering evidence so Jamie could raid each place.

The disguises may have been unnecessary, but they did add a certain flair—something out of the Sherlock Holmes stories young Eliot had so loved.

And since Ness and White were essentially barhopping on the government's dime, they might as well enjoy themselves.

Prohibition agents built cases by "making buys"—patronizing speakeasies, often over a period of several days, and recording what they ordered. Some went far above and beyond the call of duty, one agent claiming to have consumed "seven hundred glasses of alcohol and seven hundred glasses of moonshine whisky" in fourteen days.

The Bureau required its men to be drinkers on the job and abstainers off the clock. Alcoholism became a serious if ironic occupational hazard.

If Ness had never taken a drink before, he certainly did now, in the line of duty . . . and found that he liked it. His friends and colleagues insisted he didn't drink socially during Prohibition. But Ness already displayed hallmarks of an addictive personality as an adrenaline junkie, workaholic, and compulsive risk taker, hungry for thrills.

Ness's drive earned the admiration of E. C. Yellowley, who remembered the young agent as "always on the job and an extremely hard worker." When Ness and White busted a pair of Pullman porters bringing Canadian liquor in on trains bound from Detroit, Yellowley made sure the press got the story. A photographer captured the seized bottles in a carefully arranged tableau, with Ness, White, and Yellowley posing like hunters with their trophies, Jamie at Ness's side.

The porters had smuggled an estimated forty cases of whiskey and champagne into the city every day before Ness and White shut them down—a significant leak, to be sure, but one Chicago would hardly miss. The bust and its attendant publicity made something of a sideshow, designed to demonstrate Yellowley's boys were on the job.

Ness's work remained largely unglamorous, and not at all newsworthy, chiefly rousting penny-ante bootleggers caught with cans of liquor in their cars or stills in their basements. Such cases joined tens of thousands of others clogging court dockets around the country.

Desperate judges, overcome by the onslaught, gladly gave out fines in exchange for pleas of guilty, fixing the plea bargain as a standard part of American courtroom practice. Bootleggers who could afford a fine were back on the street in no time; those too poor to pay went to jail. Either way, the booze kept flowing, as did money into Capone's pockets.

Ness had no illusions about Prohibition—the public didn't believe in it, and to "legislate against human nature," as he put it, was pointless. After one raid south of the city, he called up his fraternity brothers and invited them to help dispose of the evidence. Ness didn't partake, according to his friend Armand Bollaert.

"But nevertheless, he was looking out for our best interests," Bollaert said.

Or perhaps Ness felt since his frat brothers were going to drink anyway, they might as well get their booze direct from the government, and not subsidize a bootlegger.

Money, Ness knew, was a far more corrosive substance than alcohol. And thanks to Prohibition, the love of it was eating away at the workings of government. Rather than trying to dry up the city, Ness sought to attack the sources of that money—the gangs sullying Chicago and its politics.

But, surrounded by graft, hemmed in by corruption, Ness often felt powerless—like a "white knight on a broken-down horse," as one friend put it. Eliot hated it when people assumed he was on the take like any other agent. He seethed at how the bootleg barons remained, in their way, untouchable. Every arrest he made only drove home the futility.

But those early arrests brought Ness to the attention of a powerful man who shared his frustrations: Chicago's new federal prosecutor.

A slight, taciturn man of fifty-three with a wild graying mane, George E. Q. Johnson looked, some said, like a poet. Chess master was more like it—a crusader who went about his job, grimly unemotional. When the new federal prosecutor spoke about organized crime—"crime with riches"—he would fix the listener with an icy stare, his brow hard over wire-frame glasses, his voice reedy through clenched teeth.

Johnson despised gangsters, considering them "human in form only," but perhaps hated corrupt officials more.

"I don't take the least credit to myself for refusing money," he told the *Tribune*. "It merely had no attraction for me."

Ness and Johnson had a lot in common. Both were sons of Scandinavian immigrants, taught by their fathers to prize hard work and honesty above all else. Johnson, too, was christened without a middle name, but had adopted two middle initials—the "E" for Emerson, after his father's literary hero, Ralph Waldo Emerson; the "Q" only there, he wryly noted, to help you find "which George E. Johnson in Chicago you are looking for."

Like Ness, Johnson was ambivalent about Prohibition, but believed the law, no matter its flaws, had to be enforced.

"If you are going to rid the city of crime you must take crime without any process of selection," he explained. "You will have to root it up wherever you find it and shake its roots out to the glare of pitiless publicity."

Johnson came from a hardscrabble Iowa farm, but got his start as a lawyer in Roseland. His law office sat just down the street from one of the Ness bakeries, and he knew Peter Ness well enough to have met the young Eliot.

In 1927, after Johnson's appointment as U.S. attorney for the Northern District of Illinois, the prosecutor encountered a grown-up Eliot Ness, who he found to be "a very intelligent investigator . . . courageous and a hard worker." The only flaw in Ness's character Johnson could discern "was that he was perhaps too suspicious of everyone and reluctant at times to trust even those working with him."

Overall, Johnson would remember Ness as "one of the best prohibition agents in the service"—making the youthful agent especially valuable, given what Johnson was planning. For while Ness was making his bones rousting nickel-and-dimers, Johnson had studied up on the big shots.

He dispatched a journalist to comb through newspapers to build an index of Chicago's gangs, allowing him to chart their operations and seek out weak spots. He kept the project to himself, telling the press he would speak "only with indictments and verdicts."

But as Capone's power grew, so did Johnson's anger. He hated these gangsters, despised them for their arrogance—their attempts to pass themselves off as legitimate businessmen turned his stomach.

When the time was right, the prosecutor intended to rip them out of the city like the weeds he knew they were. And the gardener he'd put in charge would be a young man from his own neck of the woods.

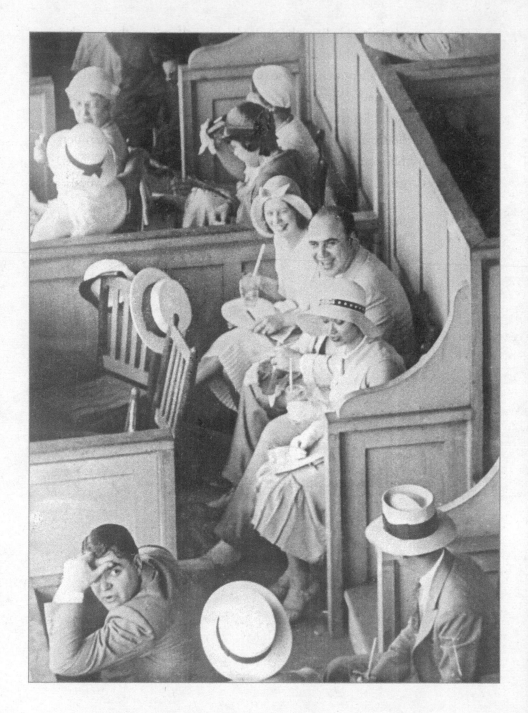

Capone with Mae (on his right) at the races. *(Mary Evans Picture Library)*

Seven

1927

_____

Following the treaty negotiated at the Hotel Sherman, the Outfit's trucks could haul beer openly through the city without risking arrest or a hijacking. Al Capone whittled his retinue of bodyguards down to one, and seemed delighted with his newfound freedom.

It's "just like the old days," he told a reporter from the *Herald and Examiner*. "They stay on the North Side, and I stay in Cicero and if we meet on the street we say 'hello' and shake hands. Better, ain't it?"

Capone emphasized how peace had benefited the lives of his wife and son. "The reason I wanted to stop all that [violence] was because I couldn't stand hearing my little kid asking why I didn't stay home," he said. "I had been living at the Hawthorne Inn for fourteen months. He was with his mother way out on the South Side."

Capone went on, "He's been sick for three years—mastoid infection and operations one right after another—and I've got to stay here to take care of him and his mother. If it wasn't for him, I'd have said: 'To hell with you fellows. We'll shoot it out!'"

A rumor went around that Capone planned to quit and leave for Europe. On January 23, a reporter found Capone dressed for housework and holding a pot of spaghetti at the front door of his South Prairie Avenue house.

"I positively have retired," the gangster said, before going back inside. "I am out of the booze racket and I wish the papers would let me alone."

But after an official with the Cook County highway police took credit for kicking Capone out of Cicero, the ganglord went to the *Herald and Examiner* and said nobody had driven him out. "I have merely transferred my headquarters. . . . I'm not leaving Chicago. I'm a business man and I've got plenty to keep me here."

Al explained that he'd left Cicero's Hawthorne Hotel because, "I found that my business took in a bigger area than it used to, and I needed a central headquarters."

Quietly Capone set up operations in Chicago at the Hotel Metropole at Twenty-Third and Michigan, near the now-padlocked Four Deuces. Al took a corner suite with a view on his South Side kingdom. Portraits of George Washington, Big Bill Thompson, and Abraham Lincoln supervised from a nearby wall.

Capone soon occupied most of the seven-story hotel, which provided lodging (for gunmen and their molls), a gymnasium, and administrative offices. The Metropole lobby brimmed with young men in loud suits swollen with shoulder holsters. For many Capone hoods, the criminal life was rarely exciting; mostly it was one long wait for their next assignment.

But orders were slow to come. Even at the height of the Beer Wars, gunmen were mostly defensive, a hoodlum purgatory on the lobby floor protecting the heavenly corporate offices above; other thugs lingered outside breweries and on trucks, discouraging hijackers. Such gunmen were paid big for little; the gym was available to keep them in shape and alert.

Chicago's mayor since 1923, William Dever had brought strong management to the city and reduced the many debts accumulated under the prior administration's mismanagement, though his efforts to contain deficit spending were often overruled by the City Council. Yet he had managed to build considerable infrastructure and had laid the foundation for the planned World's Fair.

Nonetheless Dever faced a serious challenge in 1927 from a buffoon who shouted "America First" as he ranted against the King of England. Many Chicagoans considered Big Bill Thompson an embarrassment—on a recent campaign appearance, the eccentric once-and-future mayor had brought along a birdcage with two rats named for an opponent and a ward boss. But voters knew he represented a wide-open town—any "frivolous" concerns about Thompson's competence were left to the eggheads who wrote books and read the news.

Thompson knew just how to capitalize on this populist sentiment. He appeared at campaign rallies carefully choreographed to present him as the "friend of the plain people," and told voters to beware a host of enemies—from the universities to the newspapers to the elite outsiders angling to run the city.

"Yes, they lie about Bill Thompson . . . ," he would say, "but they rob you . . . everybody robs you! . . . They call you low-brows and hoodlums . . . they call me that, too. . . . We low-brows got to stick together. . . . Look who's against us!"

Thompson's posturing as a common man was insultingly ironic; he came from a wealthy family while his opponent had worked his way up from slaving in a tannery. Yet that mattered little to the voters, in part because Dever's failed campaign against crime helped turn the city against him. Closures of speakeasies and gambling joints, and overzealous police raids on homes where alcohol was cooked, only added to Dever's unpopularity. The mayor's old slogan—"Dever and decency"—now got him more laughs than support.

"Away with decency," the voters would reply, "give us our beer!"

Dever also suffered from an inability to raise the kind of campaign funds Thompson could easily get from bootleggers, speakeasy proprietors, and gamblers.

"The Dever administration," Thompson declared, "has made one of the greatest records in Chicago's history for closing up business."

By "business," Thompson meant the illicit variety; Mayor Dever hadn't shut down any legal establishments.

"When I'm elected," Thompson went on, "we will not only reopen places these people have closed, but we'll open ten thousand new ones."

Thompson's promise of ten thousand new speakeasies reached its intended audience—Al Capone, who threw his support (at least $100,000 worth) behind Big Bill.

On April 5, 1927, Thompson beat Dever by more than eighty-three thousand votes. For a Chicago election, things were relatively quiet—a couple of bombings, two election judges kidnapped, a dozen voters harassed. The only fatality happened the day before—Vincent "Schemer" Drucci, killed when he resisted cops who picked him up on a roust, a Capone enemy gone without Outfit involvement. On the negative side, Bugs Moran, nicknamed "the Devil" by the Capone crowd, rose to chief of the North Side mob.

Thompson took office on April 11, promising to "give the old town the greatest ride for prosperity she ever had!" The ride began when Thompson rehired the corrupt police chief Dever had fired, with an order to throw the crooks "out in ninety days!" In fact, Thompson chose one of those crooks—Capone crony Daniel Serritella—as Chicago's new city sealer. Ostensibly in charge of protecting consumers by checking scales, Serritella was really a fixer with an office in City Hall easily accessible to aldermen and others. He'd performed much the same role during the campaign, ferrying money from Capone to Big Bill.

The rest of the country viewed Thompson's reelection as a new low for Chicago. The city had chosen as its mayor a "political blunderbuss," in the words of one journalist—"indolent, ignorant of public issues, inefficient as an administrator, incapable of making a respectable argument, reckless in his campaign methods and electioneering oratory, inclined to think evil of those who are not in agreement or sympathy with him, and congenitally demagogical."

Many saw Thompson as a product of the special cocktail of corruption and bluster that animated local life.

"They was trying to beat Bill with the better-element vote," observed the humorist Will Rogers. "The trouble with Chicago is that there ain't much better element."

But others recognized Big Bill as the symptom of a deeper rot permeating the country—"a striking example," wrote the *Indianapolis Star,* "of the potency of demagoguery and appeals to prejudice in American elections."

For one sociologist, writing in *Century Magazine,* Thompson's victory proved that democracy itself had failed—not just in Chicago, but in any major metropolis.

"The people were not fooled," he wrote. "They knew that a vote for Thompson was a vote for Thompson and the 'boys.'"

The old, open form of government—"the kind of democracy visioned by Thomas Jefferson"—had given way to cabals of crooks, grafters, and party bosses who cut their deals behind closed doors.

"That is essentially what has come to power with Thompson," this sociologist wrote. "His election is the triumph of the gang."

By that standard, Capone should have had little to worry about. The peace agreement had mostly held, and with Thompson now in the mayor's office, enough money was rolling in to keep the gangs happy and decrease the violence.

Still, for some—like Joseph Aiello, heading up another Sicilian clan in the old Genna territory—there was no such thing as "enough money." Capone's control of the Unione Siciliana had prevented Aiello from taking over the Genna alcohol racket in its entirety. So Aiello—who resembled Eddie Cantor minus the comedy—offered $35,000 to the chef at Capone's favorite restaurant, "Diamond Joe" Esposito's Bella Napoli Café, to poison their famous customer's soup.

The chef—figuring there was scant likelihood of both serving that dish and living to enjoy Aiello's tip—warned Capone.

Next Aiello put a $50,000 price tag on Capone's head, intended to attract out-of-town torpedoes. But Al had contacts and informants far and wide. Led by Gus Winkeler, former members of the Egan's Rats gang out of St. Louis would prove to be effective Capone allies in the Aiello attacks.

Lanky Winkeler, a graduate of teen street gangs, had been an ambulance driver in the Great War, racing through flying bullets and falling shells. In peacetime, he found work in St. Louis as a top-notch getaway driver. Winkeler and two other ex-Rats, fellow veterans Robert Carey and Raymond Nugent, were among the best at the ransom racket in the Midwest. Snatching a bootlegger, gangster, or gambler was a popular hustle during Prohibition. Kidnapping—not yet a federal crime, the targets unlikely to go to the law—could bring in several thousand dollars.

Winkeler first floated into Capone's orbit after his crew kidnapped Detroit gambler Henry Wertheimer. They drove their captive to Chicago and hid him away in a North Side apartment, then sat back and waited for a payoff call from Wertheimer's associates. But the call they got was from Al Capone himself, who ordered the kidnappers to the Hawthorne Hotel. Winkeler figured fleeing would be fatal, and persuaded his accomplices to go along with Capone's summons—their only option.

"Al Capone is a swell fellow," Gus later reported to his wife. "He talked to us like a Dutch uncle trying to show us we were in the wrong racket and couldn't last long at it. He told us snatching was a rotten business and begged us to quit. Then he set up the drinks and took us to a swell feed."

Winkeler's two cronies got drunk. Capone might have had them killed, but instead filled their pockets with cash, while a quite sober Winkeler passed. Capone drew Gus to one side, encouraging him to give up the "bum" snatch game and come see him for real work. The ganglord had a genuine dislike of kidnapping, built on fears for his family and coworkers. But Egan's Rats were known for their toughness, and Capone—in the face of Aiello and other challenges—could use guys like that. Wertheimer was let go and Winkeler went on staff with the Outfit.

Gus liked that Capone was a guy who kept his nose clean. Maybe he could do the same. After all, among the gamblers and bookies, Al was known as "a square shooter," a man who always paid his debts, however exorbitant.

"If he gives you his word," the racetrack crowd said of Capone, "you can believe him."

And if you did right by Al, it was understood, he would go to the wall for you; but if you crossed him, well, that's why he needed men like Gus Winkeler on call.

In late May 1927, Antonio Torchio came by train from New York City to Chicago, drawn to town for a try at the Aiello gang's open contract on Al Capone. Heading on foot from Union Station to Little Italy, taking in these impressive new surroundings, the Sicilian heard a click behind him followed by thunder as Capone enforcer Jack McGurn's bullet traveled through his brain. Four more followed, but Antonio heard and felt nothing.

A few days later, a big black sedan pulled up in front of 473 West Division—the Aiello family bakery. Working inside that evening were Joe Aiello's brothers Dominick and Tony and three employees. When a tommy gun noisily chewed at the building, two drums' worth of bullets flying, everybody hit the deck. Cakes were decorated with bullets, furniture went to pieces, and a player piano gave out not music but the crunch of splintering wood.

Tony and a baker suffered serious wounds, surviving what was apparently intended as a warning. But Joe Aiello only stepped up his drive to kill Capone, this time enlisting a crony, Lawrence LaPresta, who on the first of June took two sawed-off shotgun barrels in the back courtesy of McGurn. Had Capone dispatched McGurn to preemptively take out any Aiello gunmen, or had the torpedo taken it upon himself to make a brutal point? Either way, in a month and a half, McGurn gunned down another seven. Brought in on one murder, McGurn walked away—insufficient evidence.

With the press making noise about a new mob war, Capone gave McGurn a rest and brought his bought-and-paid-for cops in off the bench. A raid on the Rex Hotel on North Ashland nabbed five gunmen with rifles and ammunition who, after backroom interrogation, gave up their boss. Joe Aiello was arrested, but he remained unworried—his contacts would bail him out.

With Aiello snug in his cell, several taxis rolled up outside the Detective Bureau. A dozen husky Capone gunmen piled out like combat soldiers from military vehicles. Nine armed thugs circled the block while Louis Campagna and two others stood out front, one hood transferring an automatic pistol from a shoulder holster to his side overcoat pocket. This caught police attention, and before any siege could be laid on by the gangsters, Campagna and the two hoods were rounded up, the rest scurrying off into the night.

Short, heavyset, oval faced, with thinning hair and thick dark eyebrows, Campagna was another ex-Brooklynite who might have known Al in early young-gang years. "Little New York," as Louis was known, was an ex–bank robber, ex-con, and successful Outfit enforcer, much valued by Capone.

The trio of hoods was taken to the cellblock where Aiello watched in horror. Campagna whispered to Joe in Sicilian (a language distinct from Italian), "You're dead, friend, you're dead. You won't get up to the end of the street still walking."

Aiello whimpered, "Give me fourteen days and I'll sell my stores, house, and everything and quit Chicago for good. Can't we settle this? Think of my wife and my baby."

"You started this," Campagna snarled back. "We'll end it. You're as good as dead."

Aiello pleaded for police protection, but on release got escorted only as far as a cab. Within hours he had gathered his family and taken the train to New Jersey.

Capone claimed he was happy to let Aiello settle his affairs and go, always glad to avoid bloodshed.

"But I'm going to protect myself," he said. "When someone strikes at me, I will strike back."

After ducking assassination attempts for six months, Al Capone was now viewed as a liability by Big Bill Thompson, of all people. The most corrupt mayor in Chicago's history—an astonishing accomplishment in itself—was running for president.

And even a buffoon like Thompson knew Capone, the top criminal in a city now world famous for crime, was attracting the wrong kind of national attention. The Aiello clashes only ramped that up. Now anybody affiliated with the Outfit faced police harassment and arrest, with Al himself constantly tailed by the law.

Capone's growing notoriety weighed heavily on his wife and son.

"Can't something be done to protect this innocent and inoffensive child?" Mae pleaded to the *Herald and Examiner* in mid-December. "Every day [Sonny] comes home crying. His schoolmates tease him and abuse him, all because of what has been said and printed about his father."

Soon Al was holding court from his bulletproofed desk chair, needing a shave but decked out in hunting togs—as worn by wealthy types who shopped at Marshall Field's, not the average hunter in Wisconsin's north woods.

"I'm leaving for St. Petersburg, Florida, tomorrow," he told reporters. "Let the worthy citizens of Chicago get their liquor the best they can. I'm sick of the job—it's a thankless one and full of grief. I don't know when I'll get back, if ever. But it won't be until after the holidays, anyway."

He'd given the best years of his life to the public, providing pleasures and showing them a good time.

"And all I get is abuse," he said, "the existence of a hunted man. I'm called a killer."

Then his tone grew sarcastic. "Well, tell the folks I'm going away now. I guess murder will stop. There won't be any more booze. You won't be able to find a crap game, even, let alone a roulette wheel or a faro game."

He claimed that 99 percent of Chicago's adults drank and gambled. "I've tried to serve them decent liquor and square games. But I'm not appreciated."

Then he brightened. "Say, the coppers won't have to lay all the gang murders on me now. Maybe they'll find a new hero for the headlines. It would be a shame, wouldn't it, if while I was away they would forget about me and find a new gangland chief?"

While Capone's complaints were as sincere as they were hypocritical, he was also doing Mayor Thompson a favor and the police, too, who could brag about driving Capone out of Chicago. Of course, with Frank Nitto running things, bootlegging, gambling, and prostitution would experience no shortage of customers.

The trip to St. Petersburg—where Johnny Torrio had a place— never happened. Instead, Al, his family, and two bodyguards journeyed to Los Angeles. On their two-day stay, the Capones never left the Biltmore Hotel grounds, before getting cast out by the L.A. police and put on the train back to Chicago. Los Angeles was mounting its own tough-on-crime campaign.

Capone whined to the *Los Angeles Times,* "Why should everybody in this town pick on me? I wasn't going to do anything here. . . . We are tourists and I thought that you folks liked tourists."

Back in Chicago, the police were talking tough again.

"Despite the cold wave," the chief told the *Herald and Examiner,* "my men are prepared to make Chicago too hot for Capone."

Even the Metropole, Capone's headquarters, claimed his rooms had all been rented out.

"It's pretty tough," Al told a reporter, "when a citizen with an unblemished record must be hounded from his home by the very policemen whose salaries are paid, at least in part, from the victim's pocket. You might say that every policeman in Chicago gets some of his bread and butter from the taxes I pay. And yet they want to throw me in jail—for nothing."

This had to sting Capone, with so many police on his payroll, although with the Thompson crowd unfriendly now, Outfit graft was said to be down. Why pay to be harassed?

Then Capone announced: "I'm going back to Chicago. Nobody can stop me. I have a right to be there. I have property there. I have a family there. They can't keep me out of Chicago unless they shoot me through the head."

His mood turned combative. "I've never done anything wrong," he said. "Nobody can prove that I ever did anything wrong. They arrest me, they search me, they lock me up, they charge me with all the crimes there are, and when they get me into court I find that the only charge they dare to book against me is disorderly conduct."

Nonetheless, Capone had arranged for his brother Ralph to collect him in Joliet to bypass any problems at the Chicago station.

But when Ralph arrived an hour early, with four men carrying pistols and shotguns, police placed all five under arrest; and their presence immediately told local authorities Ralph's brother would soon arrive.

When Al got off the train in Joliet, he walked right "into the arms of the entire police force of that city," the *Herald and Examiner* reported. The local police chief and a captain stood waiting to greet him.

"You're Al Capone," the captain said.

"Pleased to meet you," Capone replied.

The chief personally frisked Capone, finding nearly $3,000 in cash on his person as well as two guns.

"You may want some ammunition, too," Capone said, as he handed over a few excess magazines.

Police confiscated seven other guns and more hefty bankrolls from Capone's bodyguards, then locked the gangsters up at the local jail. Capone took offense at having to share his cell with two strangers. According to the *Tribune*, they "made too much noise and were too long unshaven to suit the fastidious taste of Capone."

Al paid both of his cellmates' fines—for a grand total of $23—so he could enjoy some privacy.

While he waited for his lawyers to post bail, Capone remained magnanimous.

"When I come back for my trial," he told the *Tribune*, "I am going to make a good big donation to the worthy charities of Joliet. I'm not mad at anybody."

But his resolve remained firm. As he prepared to leave Joliet, a reporter asked him for a forwarding address.

"I am going to my home in Chicago," Capone declared.

When he finally arrived at South Prairie Avenue, after a celebratory stopover in Chicago Heights, harassment at the hands of police continued. The police chief stationed twelve detectives around the house, with orders to nab Capone if he walked out, or any other gangsters should they walk in.

"I wouldn't invade his mother's home to arrest him," said the chief of detectives. "Anyway, we haven't any specific charge against him. But—if he is seen on the street, my men have instructions to pick him up and take him to jail."

And so Al Capone hunkered down to spend Christmas on Prairie Avenue, surrounded by police. Business interests, he told the press, would keep him in the city for the foreseeable future.

"Besides," he added, "I like Chicago. It's my home and I pay taxes here. I'm not a gangster, I'm a real estate broker."

Meanwhile, Big Bill Thompson's cross-country travels had gone almost as poorly as Capone's. As with Al, Big Bill found few outside his city to be on his side, his "America First" message bombing as badly as his birdcage humor. He slunk back to Chicago, his presidential candidacy a bust.

On December 22, 1927, Capone went back to Joliet and pleaded guilty for carrying a concealed weapon. He paid in cash the fines and court costs for himself and his men, casually peeling a thousand-dollar bill and six hundreds off his ever-present roll. The clerk offered him $10.20 in change, but Capone refused it.

"Please take that down to the Salvation Army Santa Claus on the corner," he said. "Tell him it's a Christmas present from Al Capone."

Ness (behind wheel) with unidentified agents, late 1920s.

(Cleveland Public Library Photograph Collection)

Eight

Spring–Summer 1928

On March 29, 1928, twelve men invaded a speakeasy on South State Street, carrying "shotguns, pistols, rifles, sledge hammers and at least one machine gun," according to the *Tribune*, bursting in through three separate entrances, demanding patrons "stick 'em up!"

The apparent robbery sent thirty-five-year-old customer William Beatty fleeing with his wife, but before the couple could make it to the street, one invader opened fire. The bullet caught Beatty in the back, cutting through his chest and shattering his pocket watch. Other raiders dragged the wounded man inside, forcing him to stand with his arms up, a shotgun buried in his stomach, while they proceeded to harass his wife.

These men were not gangsters but a special squad of Prohibition agents sent from Washington at Chicago prosecutor George E. Q. Johnson's request. Johnson had gone to D.C. the previous fall to ask for fresh investigators—outsiders, men untouched by mob influence, who could expose the corrupt ties between bootleggers and Prohibition agents.

The Bureau had sent him chubby-faced George Elias Golding, thirty-eight, who despite his owlish eyeglasses, considered himself a "hardboiled" New York copper. After Beatty's shooting, the press took to wryly nicknaming the federal man just that: "Hardboiled" Golding.

Golding's men were special agents, a new group independent of the regular Prohibition force. Rather than going after small, local bootleggers, they tackled conspiracy cases against large-scale violators, specifically gangsters like Capone.

Ideally, these were investigators suited to building cases carefully and quietly over many months, able to weave fine strands of evidence into a tapestry that wouldn't tear in court. Unfortunately for Johnson and the city of Chicago, Hardboiled Golding was no such investigator.

Formerly of Elmer Irey's Intelligence Unit, Golding—who considered himself "a fighter"—loved to throw his weight around. But he also took offense easily and refused any duty that affronted his sense of virility. In Cleveland, he once arrested a police officer who stopped him for jaywalking.

Golding pleaded guilty to his reputation as impulsive when requesting a Prohibition Bureau job, but insisted, "The fact cannot be denied that I obtained results."

Results, yes—convictions, no. His habit of failing to show up in court when his cases went to trial guaranteed they would fall apart and exasperate his colleagues.

"His raids are spectacular and his prosecutions fall into a vacuum," wrote a Rhode Island newspaper after Hardboiled blew into town, labeling his record "a striking illustration of prohibition as a farce."

Hardboiled arrived in Chicago in January 1928 and managed to keep himself and his men undercover for over two months. The squad also did its best to keep a lid on the Beatty shooting, placing a guard on their victim's hospital room and barring any press or police. But Beatty turned out to be a municipal court bailiff, and the state charged his shooter with assault to commit murder. The agent holed up in the Federal Building for days, like a gangster gone to ground.

Golding refused to cooperate with police, claiming Beatty had fired first, and that his men "had to shoot back in self-defense." The special agents conveniently found a revolver across the street, which they declared belonged to the bailiff, a gun that had not been fired recently.

The matter would be settled in-house, Golding insisted, saying, "I don't care what the police want to know."

"If there is any law in the United States, these quick-trigger men from Washington don't represent it," the police commissioner told the press. "They may be able to get away with their shootings in other cities and tell the police to go to hell, but they're in Chicago now."

Of course, plenty of gangsters had gotten away with worse in Chicago, but the city held Prohibition agents to a much higher standard.

Golding remained on the attack. Now that his men were in the open, they descended on Chicago, smashing up speakeasies and stills, brandishing pistols and shotguns, and vaulting over furniture like they were bank robbers. Such legal niceties as obtaining search warrants were of little interest, their cases in court invariably proving flimsy. But convictions seemed beside the point—this was harassment.

In their drive to dry up the city, Golding and his men took on the thuggish tactics of the gangsters they sought to destroy. Chicago had flaunted federal law for too long, and these special agents intended to beat it into submission.

As an ordinary, run-of-the-mill Prohibition agent, Eliot Ness remained on the sidelines as Golding tormented the city. But as tensions grew between local officials and the federal government, Ness suddenly found himself drafted onto the controversial squad.

Once again, he had Alexander Jamie to thank for his promotion. When the Civil Service Commission deemed Jamie too inexperienced to keep his post as assistant Prohibition administrator, Eliot's brother-in-law typically turned to his network of contacts to lobby for an exemption. His most important ally was George Johnson, who saw Jamie as a key asset in the effort to clean up Chicago.

"I have been very much impressed by [Jamie's] character and integrity in my official dealings with him," Prosecutor Johnson wrote Prohibition Commissioner James Doran that March.

To accommodate Johnson, Doran transferred Jamie to the special agent squad, which kept him on the force in a position of influence while eliminating any civil service issues. Visiting Chicago that spring, Doran asked Golding to bring Jamie onboard, which meant also taking on Ness.

Golding was glad for the additional manpower—the Chicago Division could use more special agents. Jamie joined the unit in May 1928, Eliot following in June.

That same month, twenty-one-year-old Edna Stahle reported for duty as Golding's new stenographer. A petite brunette with deep blue eyes and a teardrop face, Edna had worked for the Prohibition Bureau since 1925, mostly in its Legal Division. Somewhere along the way, she crossed paths with Ness, likely recognizing him from her old neighborhood, where they'd gone to the same elementary school.

Both were serious, self-conscious, and somewhat withdrawn. Even more than the solitary Ness, Edna liked to wall herself off from the outside world. She would shut her eyes as she rode around on an old bicycle, enjoying the wind whipping through her hair.

She felt drawn to the dashing young agent, so courageous and effortlessly charming. And about the time Ness joined Golding's unit, she requested her own transfer there. Perhaps she wanted to be closer to him.

She could hardly avoid Eliot on the top floor of the Transportation Building, south of the Loop, where the special agents had their offices. Working as Golding's secretary meant taking dictation from other special agents, Ness included. And it was no secret she'd managed to catch his eye.

Another woman who worked in the office recalled a weekend that summer when the Prohibition Bureau secretaries got away to a rented cottage on Lake Michigan. They brought with them some bootleg liquor. Unannounced, Eliot appeared, and in his presence the girls "were afraid to break out the booze, since he was just the type who might arrest them."

Except of course he wouldn't, not with Edna there.

Even so, Ness took his time working up the courage to ask Edna out. The gossip around the office was she had another beau, a spiffy dresser among Golding's top special agents. But there was never any real contest.

When Ness finally asked her out, Edna later said, she knew right away she wanted to spend her life with him.

Several new recruits joined the special agent squad around the same time as Eliot Ness. They, too, were young, honest, competent men who took their responsibilities seriously.

Unlike Ness, most were new to the Prohibition Bureau. This left them unspoiled by the agency's patronage and politicking. Among them Ness would find a handful of dedicated and trustworthy allies. Several would stick with him all the way through his war on Capone.

Ness formed a close bond with Martin J. Lahart, twenty-nine, Chicago-born son of immigrant parents. Ladies' man Lahart had blue eyes, wavy brown hair, and a square jaw like screen and magazine detectives. Before joining the Prohibition Bureau, Lahart had been a Pinkerton operative and a post office clerk, a job he found so dull he signed on as a special agent just to escape. The agent oozed personality, pegged by a future boss as a "tiresome and repetitive talker."

But Ness, quiet and reserved, enjoyed this "tall, happy Irishman." And Lahart appreciated the low-key Ness, who struck him "as a kind, conscientious, and considerate man." They got along like gin and tonic.

Ness and Lahart shared an offbeat sense of humor. In July 1928, after hearing liquor was for sale inside the Shakespeare Avenue police station, Ness brought Lahart and another agent in as phony prisoners and locked them up. Once Ness had left, the undercover men got a hapless janitor to sell them moonshine. After getting sprung, the agents brought this evidence to Golding.

"Let us raid the raiders," Golding declared, before marching in and seizing several bottles from the cops. Both Ness and Golding would forever relish the irony of getting a search warrant for a police station.

The bust had the same prankish quality as Ness's earlier work. At heart, he remained a daring young college boy, playing detective. But with the promotion to special agent came new risks and new adversaries. That same summer, Ness got roped into his first major investigation, an attempt to break up a violent bootleg conspiracy south of the city.

He now faced real gangsters, men he couldn't treat flippantly if he wanted to stay alive. But he blazed ahead as before, with all the brashness of youth, heedless or unaware of the danger he faced. He wouldn't realize how much the game had changed until it was almost too late.

"This," Ness wrote, "is where my connection with the Mafia began."

The case had its roots in Kensington, Ness's old neighborhood, with Frank Basile, a young bootlegger. Born in 1901 to Italian immigrants, Basile lived just half a mile from the first Ness bakery. He and Eliot, only two years apart in age, may well have known each other as boys. Prohibition took them down very different paths, on opposites sides of a law neither had any reason to believe in.

Basile's friends called him "Burt," but many knew the big, imposing man—at six foot, more than two hundred pounds—simply as "Fat."

"No door could stand up against his fist or foot," Ness recalled.

That Basile spoke fluent Italian he kept to himself; with the light skin and fair hair of northern Italians, he could easily hide his ethnicity. By posing as an Irishman, or just another American, he could listen in when other Italians whispered supposedly secret conversations.

After the dry law took effect, nineteen-year-old Basile became an "alky cooker" in Kensington. He soon partnered with Lorenzo Juliano, a Sicilian immigrant in Roseland and a rising star in the liquor business. Dead-eyed and rotund, the pencil-mustached Juliano had been a grocer before Prohibition, but nonetheless brought a cold, cruel efficiency to his new profession. Forming an alliance with Capone—a personal friend—Juliano helped the Outfit expand its bootleg empire south, until it covered a swath of territory from Kankakee to Kensington.

The center of this massive operation was Chicago Heights, a factory town about thirteen miles south of Kensington and thirty miles south of Chicago proper. The city hadn't developed into the manufacturing hub its fathers envisioned, but it had become a bootleg powerhouse, stills dotting the flat, wet, industrial landscape like black squares on a chessboard. From farmers growing grapes, to plumbers building stills, to grandmothers cooking up white lightning for special occasions, everyone in the Heights seemed to have some stake in the liquor business.

The Outfit had a long, profitable relationship with the Heights, dating back to 1920. A rival Sicilian crew had moved in during the first half of the decade, seeking to take over the city's bootleg operations. But a trio of Capone allies killed them off in the bloody summer of 1926, becoming the local kingpins, with Capone ruler by proxy. The Heights became Al's safe haven when things got too hot in Chicago. Riding through town in his bulletproof Cadillac, he would toss silver dollars out the window for kids to scoop up.

Juliano ensured liquor cooked in the suburbs flowed north, without interruption, into Chicago's thirsty speakeasies. He soon became known as a brutal enforcer who brooked no disloyalty. In the fall of 1927, one bootlegger passed trade secrets to a housewife he'd been sleeping with. She had sold the information to government agents, who used it to raid several of Juliano's stills. Juliano had both lovers killed.

That same year, Basile managed to get on Juliano's bad side after a violent quarrel. Juliano, just to close out the partnership, gave Schemer Drucci $5,000 to finish Basile off; but the cops killed Drucci first. Basile's luck ran out soon after, when he greased the palm of a rare honest Prohibition agent, who ran him in on bribery charges. Facing a year in jail, Basile turned state's evidence, linking Juliano to at least twelve bombings and eight murders, including the dead lovers in the Heights.

Basile's testimony offered George Johnson and the special agents their first line of attack against Capone's southern flank. With Juliano lying low, Johnson—with a single conspiracy case for the Kensington–Chicago Heights liquor racket in the works—ordered Golding to find him. The special agents fanned out in the spring of 1928, searching several of Juliano's haunts without success.

In early April, Pat Roche of the Intelligence Unit tracked the gangster down, but Juliano held up under questioning. Meanwhile the gangster's fifteen-year-old daughter defended her father. He never slapped her, she told the *Tribune*. This seemed insufficient praise, but so was what the government had on him. The agents let Juliano go.

Basile, now a marked man, signed on with the government as an informant and a chauffeur. For $5 a day plus gas money, he ferried Prohibition agents around the South Side in a massive Cadillac that had been impounded in a liquor raid. This dangerous duty brought Basile back into the territory of the very men he'd betrayed. And while gangsters generally considered it bad business to murder federal agents, federal informants enjoyed no such protection. Basile, just turning twenty-seven, with a wife and two children, a third on the way, had no choice—if he wanted to stay out of prison, and keep his family fed, he had to play along with the government until his parole ran out.

Johnson didn't have to wait long for another shot at Chicago Heights.

In the late spring of '28, after Golding and his special agents seized a suburban still, they "were immediately approached," as Ness told the story, "by a representative of the Mafia." John Giannoni, a small, slim mobster wearing "a diamond stickpin about the size of a lump of sugar," served as the gang's paymaster. He offered Golding a hefty reward to forget about the still.

Giannoni had the local cops and the regular Prohibition force on his payroll, but what about these new feds who spouted incorruptibility? Would Golding live up to his bluster, or was he just another crooked cop looking for a bigger handout? The paymaster decided to find out.

And for once, Golding played it cool, sensing an opportunity to work his way into the bootleggers' confidence, agreeing to the payoff. Back in Chicago, he conferred with George Johnson and laid the groundwork for an undercover operation. They tapped Donald L. Kooken, "a rather short, stocky chap," as Ness recalled, who "was an expert shot, and fearless, and spoke with a slow, quiet, Indiana drawl."

On June 18, Golding and Kooken traveled to Calumet City for a meeting with four Heights bootleggers. There the special agents accepted a payoff of $75—the first link in their chain of evidence.

Over the next few weeks, Kooken built a relationship with Giannoni and other gang members, showing more interest in making money than pulling raids. The bootleggers were happy to oblige, paying Kooken two additional bribes of $100 each. Kooken made sure a different special agent witnessed each payoff—the more men who could testify, the stronger the conspiracy case. He stayed alert for details of the gang's operations, where they had their stills, who they sold to, and who they paid off.

For the third such meeting, Kooken chose Ness as his latest witness. The young man brought a fresh pair of eyes, but also something more important—local knowledge. Ness knew the territory in a way the Indiana-born Kooken didn't.

Also along was drawling Georgian Albert M. Nabers, a new recruit on the squad. Nabers had lied about his age to fight in the Great War and lost a big toe for his trouble, earning him the memorable nick-name "Nine Toed." With keen eyes under thick slashes of eyebrow, hair slicked back in gleaming waves, and pouting lips above a stubby chin, he had the look of a silver-screen gangster.

On July 7, Basile and the special agents piled into their confiscated Cadillac and took off for the Heights. Heavy summer storm clouds loomed as they rolled into the grimy little town of twenty-five thousand, "spotted with numerous saloons, abandoned houses, barns and garages." They pulled up to the corner of Seventeenth Street and East End Avenue in front of the Monroe Hotel. A saloon known as the Cozy Corner occupied the ground floor, where bootleggers from Illinois, Iowa, and Missouri would drop off liquor destined for Chicago speakeasies.

"They would leave their cars with the bartender," Ness recalled, "and the cars would be driven away by members of the Chicago Heights alcohol mob. The drivers from out of town would stay at the bar, drinking, or avail themselves of what the brothel located on the second and third floors had to offer."

When the special agents walked into the Cozy Corner, the first thing they saw was a uniformed policeman at the bar. Kooken approached the bartender and explained who they were. Right away, the bartender fixed them a round and went to fetch Giannoni. The feds downed their cocktails before moseying into the back. When Giannoni showed up, he brought with him a short, swarthy man with a thick Italian accent. This was Joe Martino, head of the local chapter of the Unione Siciliana.

Martino was the lone survivor of the Sicilian gang that failed to take over the Heights. Although Capone's men killed off his partners, they'd let Martino live because of his position with the Unione, whose control Capone so badly needed. Also, over the years, Martino had built valuable relationships with local law enforcement.

Whenever the cops knocked over a still in the area, Martino was the fixer who made things right. This made him an absolute prize for Ness and the special agents—a single crook who knew all the corrupt officials in the Heights.

The special agents and the bootleggers had another round of drinks and got to talking. Giannoni remained wary—a gangster first and foremost, he knew better than to let his guard down. Martino, on the other hand, was a businessman, even a community leader, willing to open up. Already under indictment for a bootleg conspiracy in another suburb, his place in the underworld precarious, Martino needed allies. He came on genial, eager to make friends with federal men who might help save his neck.

Ness, Nabers, and Kooken did their best to get on his good side and draw him in. They pressed to discover the extent of bootlegging in the Heights, making it clear the more liquor the gang produced, the bigger bribe they expected. Martino should share the locations of the "right" stills—why pay to protect any alky cookers who weren't part of his organization?

Martino took the bait. If he didn't have to worry about federal raids, he could run his business in the open, raking in more profits than ever. Readily, he agreed to tell the feds anything they wanted to know. Even Giannoni was convinced, delighted to have the special agents on his payroll, the local law enforcement situation seemingly all sewn up. As a down payment, the gangsters handed over $300.

Ness, Nabers, and Kooken returned to Chicago, marking the payoff and turning it over at George Johnson's office. They now had Giannoni and Martino cold on bribery, but still hoped to make a much bigger case. They would bide their time and see how many others they could snare.

Soon, with Basile at the wheel, Martino was riding around the Heights with the agents like a gushing tour guide, showing them var-

ious stills and even introducing them to the operators. These bootleggers weren't quite as friendly as their boss, eyeing Ness and his partners
suspiciously. But once Martino made his introductions, they willingly
shook hands with the federal men. In the process, they practically
signed their names to the growing list of liquor crimes that would form
the basis of an indictment.

Basile warned the special agents to stay on their guard—the rest
of the gang wouldn't be quite so easily fooled. Nor could the feds
expect their badges to keep them safe—sure, gangsters rarely killed
honest cops, but Ness, Nabers, and Kooken had stepped over the line,
taking the syndicate's money. If the agents went back on their deal,
they'd be seen as traitors, and Basile knew all about what gangsters
did to traitors.

But the special agents kept building their case. And they soon came
up with another ruse to burrow deeper into the gang's operations. One
autumn night, the agents began searching the area around Calumet
City for alky-cooking plants. As always, they relied, literally, on their
noses: fermenting mash gave off a familiar stench. As they drew close
to the source, they saw they were being tailed. They left town and tried
again the next night, with the same result, two cars picking up their
trail almost immediately.

Evidently, the bootleggers posted lookouts and followed any un-
familiar cars getting too close. If the special agents kept up their
search, they'd blow their cover. Basile drove them to a saloon, where
they kept up appearances, throwing down some drinks before leaving
town.

The next night, they changed tactics. Shabbily dressed, the special
agents came in by a back road, hid the Cadillac, split up, and sneaked
past the lookouts on foot. Then they combed the area, prowling
through the darkness as the powerful odor of mash led them to eighteen more stills scattered throughout Calumet City.

These bootleggers operated within Heights mob territory but didn't pay tribute to the Outfit or the special agents. The feds carefully noted the location of each still and saved their notes for search warrants when the time was right for raids. When the agents returned to the Heights a day or two later, they went right to the Cozy Corner and asked for Giannoni.

"We told him that we had located quite a number of stills," Ness recalled, "and asked him what he wanted us to do about it."

If Ness could get them all together in one room, he'd have proof of a conspiracy. He suggested Giannoni round up the still owners for a meeting with the feds. Giannoni agreed and set a conference for a couple of days later at a saloon in East Chicago.

Kooken had moved on to another case, leaving the younger men in charge. On the day of the meeting, Basile drove Ness and Nabers to the saloon on State Street, in an area notorious for its gin mills and strip joints. The bar's tall, husky owner welcomed them into the back room, where they found Giannoni and half a dozen suspicious still owners. Off to one side sat a dark, gloomy gangster in a silk shirt. The special agents took little notice of him.

Ness, Nabers, and Basile sat around a table with the bootleggers, who tried to probe how much they knew. The feds assured them everything would be all right, for the right price. They insisted on a hefty bribe, one the gangsters would try to haggle down. The actual amount didn't matter, since the special agents would turn the cash over to their superiors. The idea was to spark a debate—the more they negotiated, the more the gangsters might let slip about their organization.

Ness, more experienced than Nabers, took the lead. He became "the main objector and the hungry one," insisting on a weekly payoff of about $500. Giannoni and the bootleggers balked at such a stiff sum, stirring up a heated argument. Ness carefully steered the conversation toward how many cops the gang paid off. But he overplayed his hand.

"If you don't take the money," Giannoni said, "we can handle this in another way."

Ness knew exactly what that meant. Still, he held firm, fully embracing the role of a dirty cop. He had learned in previous undercover work to play his part to the hilt. Only he had misjudged these ruthless men.

The bootleggers conferred among themselves in hushed tones, some taking the special agents for the spies they were. These feds already knew too much; they needed to be taken care of right away. As the whispering went on, the silk-shirted gangster deliberately sidled up right behind Ness. So far the slick gangster had taken in the conversation in silence. Now he spoke to Giannoni in Italian.

Basile leaned over to Ness.

"The silk-shirted Italian," he whispered, "has just asked 'Johnny' whether or not he should let you have the knife in the back."

Basile's tone convinced Ness the threat was real. He sat frozen, blood pumping, fear washing over him.

"I felt young and alone at that minute," he recalled of a rare time when he ever truly feared for his life on the job, with no choice but to sit tight and wait for the blade.

Basile was coiled to throw himself at the killer if he made any move, while Nabers eyed the gangster grimly, fingering a pistol in his pocket, all but daring the man to try something.

Giannoni watched in alarm as the standoff developed. He had every reason to distrust these feds, but a bloodbath was the last thing he wanted. Finally he raised a hand and called off the killer. The group agreed on a one-time payoff of $100 per still.

The special agents accepted with thanks, then—Nabers keeping the gangsters covered—headed quickly out to their Cadillac. They sped out of the Heights, shudders of relief broken by dark laughter.

To a man like Basile—already living on borrowed time—the little band had come much too close to meeting the kind of end these Heights gangsters would not hesitate to provide. Basile warned Ness and Nabers to wrap up their case and get out while they could. But the agents knew it wasn't that simple.

They still had work to do.

The front gate (top) and bathhouse (bottom) of Capone's Palm Island mansion, Miami Beach, Florida. *(Top: Authors' Collection. Bottom: Cleveland Public Library Photograph Collection.)*

Nine

Winter 1927–Summer 1928

"In December of 1927," wrote Chicago journalist Fred Pasley, "a looker-on at the Chicago scene would have concluded that Al Capone was pretty comfortably ensconced, pretty well content with himself and the world . . . master of all he surveyed."

Less than three years after taking over the Outfit, Capone had made Torrio's vision of a cooperative, corporate-style underworld a reality. A government estimate found the Capone organization took in $105 million a year. Most of that money—some $60 million—came from bootlegging, the rest from gambling, vice, and various other rackets.

"No accurate estimate is possible as to the amount Capone was pocketing," Pasley wrote in 1930, "but those in his confidence have put it at $30,000,000."

Capone spent as if his financial resources were endless, gambling compulsively, throwing away small fortunes on races and crap games. Although he should have had the benefit of insider information, he lost consistently, and when he did win, he would either gamble the money away or spend it on a good time.

In 1927, the ganglord said he'd lost a million and more on the horses in the past two years. And, he said, "if someone handed me another million, I'd put it right on the nose of some horse that looked good to me."

Within a couple years, he would tell reporter Alfred "Jake" Lingle of the *Tribune* he'd blown about $7.5 million since arriving in Chicago. Another estimate put Capone's gambling losses at around $10 million. But Capone never stayed depressed about such figures for long.

"The winnings did not interest Capone," Pasley wrote. "It was the excitement. He was a gambling addict."

Plenty of other Americans chased the same compulsion at the tail end of the Roaring Twenties, as the frenzy of speculation on Wall Street pushed the country to the peak of prosperity, on paper. But Capone refused to play that game: he considered the stock market "a racket."

He had plenty of other ways to blow his money. Sometimes Capone and his entourage would take over a speakeasy, paying off the manager to lock up the joint before declaring, "This is our night." Over the course of the evening, Al and his pals might run up a tab of as much as $5,000.

"Every nightclub you went to," recalled a former dancer with the Ziegfeld Follies, "you saw Al with about two other men and three women at the table."

Capone always appeared impeccably dressed and "very much of a gentleman," taking childish delight in being the center of attention. A more skeptical observer described him as "really a bigger boob than any small towner who comes in from the sticks to do Chicago in one night."

Often he would hold court as politicians came to pay their respects like vassals to their feudal lord, the gangster considering himself "big business" as he ordered more champagne. "Capone likes that sort of thing," wrote one Chicago journalist.

Capone loved music, too, particularly opera, with a passion for Giuseppe Verdi, *Rigoletto, Il Trovatore,* and especially *Aida.* Attending the theater on opening night became a ritual, requiring as many as eight seats for his bodyguard retinue, whose eyes were everywhere but on stage.

One theatergoer complained about sitting right behind Capone "in the direct line of fire." The manager could only sympathize—he didn't like having the gangsters around, but they bought the best seats.

Capone also drank in jazz, lavishly tipping musicians, who regarded him as a source of fun, excitement, and cash.

His speakeasies catered almost exclusively to whites, but he opened the stages to premier jazz talent, showcasing Chicago's best black musicians. These illicit bars—particularly brother Ralph's Cotton Club in Cicero—featured the likes of trumpet legend Louis Armstrong, who remembered Al as a "nice little cute fat boy."

But Capone's belief that anyone could be bought led him to treat black performers as something akin to property. When he assigned two bodyguards for famed pianist Earl Hines, the implication was the African-American musician "belonged" to the Outfit.

Another time, Capone asked black clarinetist Johnny Dodds to play a particular tune. When Dodds admitted he didn't know it, the Big Fellow tore a $100 bill in two and stuck one half in the musician's pocket.

"Nigger," he said, "you better learn it for next time."

One January night, four hoodlums kidnapped pianist Fats Waller, sticking a gun in his stomach and hustling him into an automobile. They brought the terrified musician to a party, showed him a piano, and told him to start playing. Waller did so, soon realizing this was a birthday revel for Capone—the gangster was a fan, and the boys had delivered Fats as a present.

Waller "swung it so hard, Capone kept him there several days, shoving hundred-dollar bills into his pocket per every request played, and keeping his glass filled with vintage champagne."

In late 1927, singer-comedian Joe E. Lewis left his gig at the Green Mill nightclub for a more lucrative engagement. Capone enforcer Jack McGurn, who owned a sizable stake in the Mill, threatened "to take

[Lewis] for a ride" if he didn't change his mind. But the comic brushed him off.

Soon, Lewis was beaten in his hotel room by three armed invaders, his skull cracked by a pistol butt. His assailants sliced his jaw up to the ear, and carved bloody gashes in his neck and scalp, leaving Lewis unable to speak, brain damage robbing him of the ability to read or write.

Eventually Lewis recovered and resumed performing, thanks to Capone. The gangster kept Lewis afloat with a gift of $10,000, even offering to help the comedian open his own cabaret.

"Why the hell didn't you come to me when you had your trouble?" Capone asked Lewis. "I'd have straightened things out."

Future actor-director Orson Welles, who hung around Chicago's theaters as a student in the late 1920s, said Capone and other gangsters made a special effort to ingratiate themselves with stage performers.

"Capone used to take four rows at the opening night of every play in Chicago and come backstage and see everybody," Welles said. "They were horrible people—I never thought they were glamorous or interesting or anything—but there they were, part of the scene, and so one got to know them."

Famed vaudevillian Harry Richman recalled being so terrified having Capone in the front row, he almost didn't go on. Afterward, Capone came backstage and embraced the performer, saying, "Richman, you're the greatest!"

The entertainer joined Capone at a party, and—after considerable champagne—Richman found himself enthralled: "It was hard for me to believe that this man had been responsible for all the horrible things I'd heard about him."

Many people who encountered Capone in a nightclub or a speakeasy felt the same. They met a man so unlike the demon in the papers they couldn't help but be disarmed. Fred Pasley described the social Capone as "a fervent handshaker, with an agreeable, well-nigh ingratiating smile, baring a gleaming expanse of dental ivory; a facile conversationalist; fluent as to topics of the turf, the ring, the stage, the gridiron, and the baseball field . . . generous—lavishly so, if the heart that beat beneath the automatic harnessed athwart the left armpit were touched."

Stories abounded of Capone's generosity, like the Christmas baskets handed out to girls who went to school with his sister, Mafalda. A damp and disheveled newsboy once approached Capone on a rainy night and got twenty bucks for his remaining papers. People told tales of going to Capone after robberies, only to have their property returned intact.

To Capone's defenders—a growing legion of admirers Pasley and others christened "Capone fans"—such stories proved the gangster's inherent decency.

A socialite spoke of Capone "with tears in her eyes," novelist Mary Borden wrote. Borden fully expected "the hungry and ragged" recipients of Capone's generosity to, "with a catch of the throat, mumble the maudlin words, 'Good-hearted Al,'" but seeing "the petted and pampered daughters of Chicago's old families . . . moved to tears by the . . . bootlegger's big heart" left her deeply unsettled.

Capone could afford to throw money around. Comedian Milton Berle told of shaking Al's hand after a performance, only to come away with a palm full of hundred-dollar bills. Berle demurred, claiming he didn't need the money.

"I don't need it either," Capone replied.

"Everybody was making money," recalled a musician who played in his clubs. "And it was because of Al Capone. . . . Plenty work, plenty money, plenty girls, plenty this and plenty of that. And everybody was happy."

Away from his wife and Prairie Avenue, Capone continued to chase other women, including prostitutes, some in their teens. Taking pains not to be seen or photographed with them was Al's idea of protecting Mae's feelings.

But after he took up with a platinum-blonde lover, Mae responded by dyeing her hair the same shade. Capone first saw her new look on an infrequent visit home for Sunday dinner. Mrs. Capone meant to silently humiliate him before the rest of the family, but he only complimented her. She continued to bleach her hair until old age.

"Those who have known Capone for years grant him qualities—a few—that would be acceptable in anyone," Chicago journalist Edward Dean Sullivan wrote. "He has concentration and executive ability which many possessors of better trained minds might envy. He is not petty. He is generous, foolishly so. He is intensely loyal. He has a good memory and is appreciative. He talks little, but when he has uttered a few sounds you have heard something.

"The rest of him," Sullivan said, "is yours for a nickel."

In the mid-1920s, Al and Ralph Capone purchased a secluded property near a lake in northern Wisconsin. They sank over a quarter of a million in the place, converting an old house into a well-fortified compound where Al could swim under the watchful eye of a guard tower. But in winter months, Capone looked south.

At considerable expense, he rented a house in Miami Beach for his family and bodyguards. The vacationing owners had no idea "Al Brown" was Capone until a shipboard radio news dispatch revealed it. The couple spent their winter worried about what would be left of their lovely home, picturing broken furniture, shattered china, ruined objets d'art, and bullet-riddled walls.

The couple returned to find their home its usual beautiful self, contents undamaged. In the cabinets, however, dozens of new sterling sets and chinaware awaited. The only annoyance was a $500 phone bill. A few days later a slim, attractive blonde, dressed rather simply, arrived in an expensive motorcar, to drop off a thousand-dollar bill to take care of the phone charge, telling them to keep the change.

Capone also rented a high-priced office suite in downtown Miami atop the Hotel Ponce De Leon, getting to know its manager, Parker Henderson Jr., twenty-four, son of a former mayor. Capone impressed the young man as the rare celebrity who wasn't full of himself.

Soon, the young hotel manager was gambling and drinking alongside his famous tenant, and running his errands, including picking up (and cashing) money orders from Chicago for "Albert Costa." Parker now sported a diamond-studded belt buckle, a gift the gangster gave his closest pals.

Miami, with its dog tracks and barely concealed casinos, was much to Al's liking—his wife and child enjoying the outdoors, the climate almost Mediterranean. With those who sought to kill him far away, he could at last sit back and enjoy the fruits of his hard work, like any respectable man of business.

Florida might also provide the solution to a long-brewing concern. On Prairie Avenue, Al's mother, Theresa, played matriarch, doing all the cooking and taking charge of housework while Mae tended to Sonny. Because of the boy's ailments—and security issues—he was schooled at home till the seventh grade. The friction between Mae and Theresa became unbearable, with Capone's spoiled sister Mafalda adding to the stress. Mae and Sonny needed their own place, and Miami seemed the answer.

But the City Council and local newspaper were troubled by the idea of Al Capone becoming a Miamian. Only the mayor, a real estate agent, could see the advantage of pumping Chicago money into a city suffering the aftermath of a destructive hurricane and a land boom gone bust.

In January 1928, Capone paid a visit to the police chief, arriving quietly without his usual bodyguards.

"Let's lay the cards on the table," he said. "You know who I am and where I come from. Do I stay or must I get out?"

The chief said, "You can stay as long as you behave yourself."

"I'll stay," Capone replied, "as long as I'm treated as a human being."

After this meeting, Al held an off-the-cuff press conference: "I've been hounded and pushed around for days. . . . All I have to say is that I'm orderly. Talk about Chicago gang stuff is just bunk."

Miami, Capone said, was "the garden of America, the sunny Italy of the new world, where life is good and abundant, where happiness is to be had even by the poorest. I am going to build or buy a home here and I believe many of my friends will also join me. . . . If I am invited, I will join the Rotary Club."

With the help of Parker Henderson and the real-estate-agent mayor, Capone went house hunting. They led him to man-made Palm Island and one of many boom-era mansions—93 Palm Avenue, built by Clarence Busch of St. Louis's Anheuser-Busch.

Through Henderson, in Mae's name, Capone met the $40,000 asking price. Secluded, secure, the mansion had fourteen rooms and a wide enclosed porch on a 300-by-100-foot plot in the shade of a dozen royal palms. The stucco Spanish-style compound included a gatehouse bridging the driveway.

The public howled—not only was Capone moving in, the mayor had been his realtor! Al reached for his wallet, contributing to local causes and political campaigns. That helped settle the rumbling.

But when representatives from the local Community Chest refused his thousand-dollar donation, due to "very general and wide-spread opposition," the newly minted Miamian was dismayed.

"I wanted a home," Capone said. "I bought one. And what happens? They tell me I'm not wanted. Yet they take my money. The merchants take it. The grocer takes it. The builders take it."

Meanwhile, police kept the Palm Island place under surveillance, recording license plate numbers.

"They threaten to arrest every member of my family that they can find," Capone complained. "What do they want me to do? Get an airplane and live up in the clouds?"

The mansion, or "Palm Island," became a shared project for Al and Mae. Capone spent more than $100,000 adding a swimming pool—largest in the state—outbuildings, and security features, including a concrete fence. Mae lavishly furnished the house with gilded replicas of Louis XIV furniture and expensive trinkets. An oil portrait of Al and Sonny in the living room testified to Capone's love for his boy, as did the cabin cruiser, *Sonny and Ralphie*, docked at the house, taking its name from the sons of Capone and his brother Ralph.

Still, Miami offered its own enticements. At the races, Capone found another mistress, whose black hair soon became platinum blonde. He plied her with gifts and money, made sure never to be photographed with her; but Mae almost certainly knew.

That seems to have been all right with Mrs. Capone, who had chosen to end any sexual relationship with her husband, her syphilis seemingly subsiding. They still shared a bed on those rare occasions when they slept under the same roof, which was as far as their physical intimacy went.

The purchase of the Palm Island property represented a shift in the couple's relationship. Mae and Sonny would stay in Florida year-round, while Al divided his time among Chicago, Miami, and various hideouts. She would always love her husband, but Mae's disappointment with him was clear.

"Your father broke my heart," she would say to their son. "Don't you break my heart, too. Don't do anything like what he did."

Back in Chicago, a rising tide of violence announced the approaching election of April 10, 1928. The city had seen plenty of campaign bloodshed before, but the brazenness of these attacks—and the repeated use of small round bombs, nicknamed "pineapples"—now captured international attention, branding this the "Pineapple Primary."

Though neither man was running for reelection, Mayor Thompson's slate faced a primary challenge from Republican reformer Charles S. Deneen's candidates, backed by racketeer-restaurateur Diamond Joe

Esposito, who saw Deneen's anti-Capone crusade as a means to seize the Outfit throne. Al of course lined up on Thompson's side, which had taken the first blows when the homes of the city controller and commissioner of public service were hit with explosive "pineapples."

The Capone forces retaliated by bombing the home of Judge John A. Swanson—the Deneen-backed rival to State's Attorney Robert Crowe—and Deneen's home itself. These bombings followed the funeral of Esposito, who—after ignoring Capone's death threats— got himself peppered with bullets and buckshot. The Chicago police stayed mostly on the sidelines, though clergymen across the city spent the weekend before the election urging their congregations to vote for reform.

"Ours is a government of bombs and bums, of grafters and corrupt politicians," declared one rabbi. A United States senator from Nebraska publicly suggested deploying the Marines in Chicago "to protect American property."

The violence reached its peak on Election Day, with the murder of one reform candidate—an African-American attorney who had served his country in the Great War, shotgunned at least a dozen times. But the voters, twice the anticipated turnout, sided with Deneen's slate, all three of his candidates winning. And the terrible publicity generated by the Pineapple Primary effectively crippled the Thompson machine, leaving Big Bill an emotional wreck.

"He drank constantly," reported his biographers, "gabbled hysterically and spoke irrationally, stared through rheumy eyes at men he had known for years and called them by wrong names, raged against enemies who had long ago faded out of politics." Nevertheless, Thompson refused to resign—as he'd threatened to do if his allies lost—and settled in for his remaining three years in office.

The election of reformer Swanson as state's attorney over Crowe indicated an unexpected—even miraculous—shift in public opinion against crime and corruption.

"The political revolution in Chicago came as a surprise to most political observers," wrote the *New York Times*. "They had thought the city was disgraced, but not ashamed."

Yet even this upset victory could do little to rehabilitate Chicago's image. Newspapers carried the results as far away as Paris, where *Le Journal* remarked that "the good city of Chicago, which . . . enjoys a world-wide reputation as the great center of the meat industry, has developed a new form of slaughter, heretofore limited to the stockyards. It is human lives in which the world's sausage metropolis is now specializing."

That slaughter would only grow more savage, more coldly efficient, thanks to someone Capone added to his staff around this time: Fred Burke, a strong, tall, former farm boy from Kansas. Born Thomas Camp, Burke raised hell with the likes of fellow Egan's Rat Gus Winkeler, joining him in the snatch racket as well as pulling robberies and killing on contract. After a bloody run-in with the Purple Gang in Detroit, Burke at Winkeler's suggestion signed on with Capone.

Burke joined the assassination squad Capone dubbed his "American Boys"—Italians tended to refer to anyone not from the Old Country as "Americans"—who as non-Chicagoans were unknown to Al's enemies. The squad also included ex-Rats Bob Carey and Ray Nugent, Winkeler's former partners in the snatch racket, and Fred Goetz, a college-educated, good-looking lunatic who was not the pride of his respectable family.

This group came together at a convenient time, as Capone faced a tough, even heartbreaking situation. For roughly a year, shipments from his boyhood mentor Frankie Yale had been hijacked left and right. While Canadian smuggling was an Outfit mainstay, the East Coast was the gateway to high-quality overseas liquor. But a Brooklyn friend of Capone's warned him Yale was stealing his own booze en route to Chicago. Soon after, that friend fell victim to a drive-by shooting.

This obvious treachery enraged Capone, his fury overwhelming whatever regard he had left for Yale. And the Brooklyn mobster's list of sins didn't end there. As head of the national Unione Siciliana, Yale proved suspiciously uncooperative in helping Capone gain control— even backing Al's mortal enemy, Joe Aiello. A Sicilian torpedo from Yale's New York had been an early entry in the Aiello sweepstakes to kill Capone. And what about the fleeing Aiellos settling in nearby New Jersey? Rumor had it Yale welcomed Joe to New York, where he could plot his takeover of the Chicago Unione.

Capone's American Boys were as unknown in New York as in Chicago, making them the perfect weapon. Winkeler, Goetz, and Burke were dispatched with the regrettable task of killing Al's first real boss, his onetime role model, Frankie Yale.

Louis "Little New York" Campagna escorted them around Brooklyn's Italian area. The boys had bought a car in Tennessee, while Capone pal Parker Henderson purchased several handguns and stowed them in a Ponce de Leon hotel room for pick-up.

On July 1, Yale received a phone call at his Brooklyn speakeasy, the Sunrise Café—his wife was sick and needed him at home. He headed there in his Capone-style bulletproofed Lincoln, soon realizing he was being followed. He made no effort to evade the tail until he made a sharp turn onto residential Forty-Fourth, where his pursuers let loose their firepower in what was now a high-speed chase.

The Lincoln's windows were rolled down, so the bulletproofed vehicle was scant help for Yale. He swerved onto the sidewalk, kids and moms fleeing before the Lincoln crashed against the front steps of a home. The pursuing car pulled up and Burke piled out. Capone's dead mentor, trapped behind the wheel, was beyond objecting as the .45 drilled bullets into him.

Everything about the killing seemed to signal Chicago. Police discovered the hitmen's car a few blocks away and found it laden with firepower—a shotgun, two pistols, and a tommy gun. This made Yale the Thompson's first New York casualty, and those weapons weren't called "Chicago typewriters" for nothing. If that weren't enough, the anonymous murderers had unintentionally further signed their work by making several long distance calls home to their women. Capone, incensed by this lapse in judgment, kept Burke, Goetz, and Winkeler on call nevertheless.

A month or so after suffering the loss of his mentor, Capone received a visit from a prominent community leader, attorney Frank Loesch. Balding, beetle browed, with an overripe banana of a nose, the seventy-seven-year-old Loesch had seen Chicago at its best and its worst. He'd been in love with the city since 1871 when he saw it consumed by fire. Ever since, he'd made himself Chicago's protector, a Christian warrior fighting the forces of evil; he admired the way Mussolini had chased the Mafia out of Italy, desperately wanting something similar for Chicago.

Loesch had been a member of the Board of Education, vice president of the Historical Society, and president of the prestigious Union League Club. He was also president of the Chicago Crime Commission, formed in 1919 by the Chamber of Commerce to decrease crime, advance policing, and inform the citizenry.

The business community was hoping to mount a world's fair, its success dependent upon attracting a million visitors to Chicago. But international headlines were depicting Chicago as the crime capital of the world, and the Pineapple Primary with its murder and bombings had added a new dimension to Chicago's image of anarchy. Instead of a magnet for commerce and tourism, Chicago had become, in the words of one Arkansas newspaper, "America's worst advertisement."

Too often people were frankly afraid to visit the now infamous city—and those who did often came to see Al Capone. At hotels from Boston to Richmond and everywhere in between, the clerks all greeted one Chicago journalist with some variation of the same phrase: "Well, I see you got out alive!"

Even across the Atlantic, people knew to steer clear. One young businessman traveling through Italy and France that spring "heard evil remarks about Chicago" wherever he went.

"Judging from the reports in the papers," he told the *Tribune*, "a European who had never visited our city would think every Chicagoan took his life in his hands when he stepped out of doors."

Repairing such a vile reputation would not be easy, but Loesch took it upon himself to do the impossible—even if it meant seeking help from the man most responsible for tarnishing the city's image.

Capone had recently shifted from the Hotel Metropole to more expansive offices at the nearby Lexington Hotel. The gray-haired, distinguished Loesch strode chin up through the lobby, past huddling hoods, hard young men with hard old eyes, watching, watching. More hoodlums were waiting on the fourth floor as he made his way to suite 430, crossed the parquet floor with its inlaid "A.C.," and entered the executive office where he would ask a favor of the man he wanted so badly to depose.

Half a dozen more guards were positioned around the room. Loesch noted three oil portraits on the side wall over a fireplace—Washington, Thompson, Lincoln—then sat at the massive mahogany desk across from the equally massive Capone. The gangster's powerful body had a swollen look, no doubt the effect of rich meals and late-night partygoing.

Gracious, hospitable, Capone asked his guest if he'd like a drink, which was declined. Loesch quickly got down to business, expressing his concern about the upcoming election for state's attorney and various important city and county offices. He asked Capone how long he expected to beat the law and the gun. Capone replied that while he would always beat the law, he expected his demise some day at the business end of a shotgun.

"But they'll only get me when I'm not looking," he added.

"I am here to ask you to help in one thing," Loesch said. "I want you to keep your damned Italian hoodlums out of the election this coming fall."

Capone didn't reply at first, then said, "I'll help."

The gangster went on: "I'll have the cops send over the squad cars the night before election and jug all the hoodlums and keep 'em in the cooler until the polls close."

"I can tell you it was a grateful handshake that I gave Mr. Capone at this proposition," Loesch said, adding, "It turned out to be the squarest and most successful Election Day that Chicago ever had in forty years. There was not one complaint, not one election fraud, not one threat of trouble all day."

But granting the Crime Commission this wish cost Capone nothing. His slate of candidates had all lost in the primary. He might not even have intended to try to influence the election with so little at stake.

Chicago's most respected attorney marched out past well-tailored hoodlums whose shoulder-holstered weapons barely bulged. Such young men might have been soldiers in the legion of the unemployed, or in that army of menials manning mops or hauling crates. The general they served had brought them up from the bottom, even if they were nowhere near the top. The twenty-nine-year-old captain of industry on the fourth floor ran the city, not gray-haired old men like Loesch.

Amid all the plotting and attempts on his life, Al Capone sought safety and relaxation on the fairway. Since the mid-1920s, he'd made regular visits to a golf course in Burnham, a southern suburb on the Indiana border. There he would play a few holes with the likes of Jack Guzik, Jack McGurn, and Johnny Patton, Burnham's "boy mayor," a longtime Outfit stooge.

Capone loved the game, and stunk at it.

"He could drive the ball half a mile," recalled his caddy, "but he always hooked it, and he couldn't putt for beans."

The gangsters gambled on every green, black holes consuming more squandered money.

Capone grew to like his caddy, a young boy from Burnham who endeared himself to the ganglord by cheating for him without being asked. Whenever Capone lost his ball, as he did frequently, the caddy would produce another and drop it on the ground without being seen.

"Nobody had ever treated me or my family with such kindness," the caddy recalled. Only later did he learn Capone was romancing his teenaged sister, even expressing a dubious willingness to leave Mae for her.

Still, the caddy's admiration for Capone remained strong. Once he asked to join the Outfit "and carry a gun like the other guys," but Capone told him to forget it.

"You might get hurt," he said. "Most guys in my line of business do. So stay just like you are, OK?"

Capone proved himself right one Saturday morning in September 1928, after playing a round of golf with Mayor Patton. Though Capone didn't always carry a gun, he had one on him now: a .45-caliber pistol tucked in his pants pocket. As he and Patton got into a car, the gun went off into Capone's groin.

"The bullet plowed down through the fleshy part of his right leg," wrote the *Tribune*, "narrowly missed the abdomen and then imbedded [*sic*] itself in his left leg." Somewhere along the way, it tore a hole in Capone's scrotum.

Patton rushed the wounded gangster to a nearby hospital, where Capone checked in under an assumed name. His bodyguards, Louis Campagna among them, soon filled four rooms around Capone's while their boss underwent treatment.

The *Trib* put the story on the front page, though the exact nature of Capone's injury remained hush-hush. Despite the location of the wound and the large caliber of the weapon, Capone apparently managed to avoid any long-term damage, back on his feet within a week, dancing for a reporter just to prove he was all right.

Perhaps even more humiliating than the public embarrassment had been Mae's visits to his hospital room, when she'd berated him for his carelessness—and, perhaps, for the teenage mistress she knew he'd taken up with in Burnham.

Plenty of gangsters had tried and failed to shoot Capone, only to have the gangster do it himself, in the most undignified way possible. Yet Capone's ability to brush off such an intimate injury only added to the aura of invincibility surrounding him in the late 1920s.

This would be the only time that a bullet ever pierced his skin—proof, if any were needed, of who his worst enemy really was.

Top: Prohibition Bureau raid on Chicago Heights, January 6, 1929. Bottom: Lorenzo Juliano's body as it was found on June 20, 1930. *(Authors' Collection)*

Ten

August 1928–January 1929

"Hardboiled" George Golding, special agent in charge, continued to wield his men like Cossacks. When Golding wanted a car, he simply confiscated one, which he outfitted with an ear-splitting siren to speed around the Loop, daring the cops to try to stop him.

Alexander Jamie watched Golding's antics with growing concern. Jamie had gone from a leader in Chicago's Prohibition office to a lackey in Golding's "reign of terror," as the press called it. If that weren't enough, he'd taken a significant pay cut. Jamie considered himself an administrator, not a field agent, his raiding days supposedly behind him. Surely, he thought, he could do a better job than the cowboy in charge.

The assistant commissioner of Prohibition, Alf Oftedal, sympathized with Jamie's frustrations and urged Golding to treat this experienced investigating officer with respect.

"If you deal with him tactfully," Oftedal wrote to Golding, "I believe he will come to realize . . . that [he] is not in fact demoted, but is now in a position to conduct investigational work that is really worthwhile."

But Golding wanted men ready to wield axes, not push paper. To him, Jamie was "lazy" and a "sort of Bolsheviki," more interested in politics than his job.

As a feud brewed between the two men, Jamie's grumbling grew louder. Golding's tactics were ineffective, he said—harassing petty offenders, not major bootleggers. Jamie contemplated pulling strings to get Golding's job, and when Hardboiled found out, he banished Jamie to St. Paul.

But Jamie kept angling for leadership back in Chicago. And if he couldn't unseat Golding, maybe he could topple his old boss, Prohibition Administrator E. C. Yellowley.

Yellowley had been one of Jamie's staunchest backers, choosing him for the post of assistant administrator back in 1926, describing him as "a very fine fellow . . . absolutely loyal."

But shortly after joining the special agent squad, Jamie had closed a case involving an industrial alcohol plant that diverted its product into bootlegging. Its owner kept a "little black book" of everyone he bribed, including thirty Prohibition agents. The entire business seemed to depend on systemic corruption within Yellowley's office.

When that information made the papers, Yellowley accused Jamie of leaking it. Jamie vigorously denied doing any such thing, and his superiors in Washington took him at his word. Although Yellowley managed to hold on to his job, he never forgave Jamie.

On August 21, Golding's men burst into an office in the City Hall Square Building, in the heart of the Loop. They were looking for the distribution center of a liquor smuggling ring, but hadn't bothered getting a warrant. A visitor to the office, Merle Adams, thirty-six, punched the nearest fed and dashed out, making a break for the stairway.

He didn't get far. Arthur Franklin, twenty-six, on the job for about three months, ran after Adams, gun in hand. Witnesses said the agent appeared "in a frenzy." He opened fire just as Adams reached the top of the stairs. Adams crumpled and tumbled down with a bullet hole through his torso "the size of a dime" on entry and an exit wound "the size of a lemon." Adams survived only because the slug had glanced off a rib, missing major organs.

Office workers dove for cover and clambered under their desks. Franklin ran back into the office, screaming, "I got him! I got him!" Another agent went to check, found the wounded man still moving, blackjacked him a few times, then dragged him back into the office. When police showed up, the special agents told them to stay away. They were even rougher with the press.

"Get out," they ordered, threatening to smash cameras and faces alike. Federal officials claimed the shooting was justified—Adams had resisted arrest, assaulted an officer, and given authorities a false name. The *Tribune* identified him as "a grape juice salesman"—code for bootlegger.

But when police examined Adams's wounds, they found he'd been shot with a so-called dumdum—a lethal round with a crease carved in its nose, to ensure the bullet would expand and break apart inside the body.

"Dumdums are often used in killing big game, such as bears," observed one firearms expert, "[because] they cause death quickly by profuse bleeding." Using them on a human being was "monstrous," and such bullets were even banned from the battlefield. Gangsters made notorious use of them! What were they doing in a federal agent's service revolver?

Within a week, the Treasury Department promised to break up the squad, transferring Golding and his more zealous agents out of Chicago. But Hardboiled went right on battling bootleggers in Philadelphia and elsewhere. Back in the Loop, the Prohibition Bureau began looking for a less controversial special agent in charge.

Alexander Jamie put himself up for the job, again pleading his case to George E. Q. Johnson, who called the commissioner of Prohibition. The squad, Johnson believed, needed the leadership of "a Chicago man" who knew his way around the city. After some political infighting, including objections from both Yellowley and Golding, Jamie became the Chicago office's de facto special agent in charge, which the Bureau made official on November 30.

Another year and a half would pass before Golding's arrogance caught up with him. In July 1930, with Golding stationed in Albany, New York, all the female employees in his office walked out, claiming he'd tried to force himself on each of them. Over the next few weeks, five other women came forward. Among them was Edna Stahle, who told investigators Golding had "succeeded in kissing and embracing her in spite of her objection" back in 1928, when they both worked in the Chicago office.

Ever the fighter, Golding denied the charges and did everything he could to slander his accusers. In a florid, fifty-nine-page memo, he declared himself the victim of a huge conspiracy, promising to "fight until the last" to clear his name. His superiors were unconvinced.

"It is impossible to believe that the eight female employees who are witnesses against Mr. Golding," wrote one official, "and who are located in five different cities of the country, have entered into a conspiracy and perjured themselves in order to have Mr. Golding dismissed from the Service."

On October 18, 1930, Golding's tumultuous federal career finally reached its overdue end with his dismissal from the Prohibition Bureau.

Before becoming special agent in charge, Jamie had never risen higher than second in command. Now he could finally make his mark, as the federal war on crime gathered momentum. In Chicago Heights, for example, his brother-in-law's undercover investigation had begun to turn bloody.

Word had gotten around that Eliot Ness "was on the take." He kept up the masquerade, waiting for more leads to pour in. In mid-November, after several Prohibition agents seized a still on the Near

West Side, a bootlegger from Melrose Park offered Ness a payoff to make the case go away.

Ness made sure to check with his superiors, who ordered him to accept the bribe as part of a growing web of evidence that bootleggers in the southern and western suburbs were all part of one big criminal conspiracy, with Chicago—and Al Capone—at its center.

Back in the Heights, Joe Martino was boasting about the great deal he'd cut with the feds. Special Agent Don Kooken, he said, was just "one of the boys," and a good man to have in their pockets. But Kooken was already appearing before a secret grand jury, testifying about his dealings with the Heights mob.

The special agents got warrants to raid the eighteen stills uncovered in Calumet City, but didn't have enough men to hit all at once. This left no choice but to borrow a few regular Prohibition agents. Ness didn't trust these men for a second, knowing the crooked ones would tip off the bootleggers at the earliest opportunity.

So they arranged to meet in Chicago and broke up into small groups, each with a special agent in command. They kept the locations of stills secret until the last moment, after which they didn't let the borrowed raiders out of their sight. The busts were successful, netting several bootleggers, considerable equipment, and great quantities of alcohol.

On November 27, the grand jury indicted Giannoni and Martino on bribery charges, the former managing to evade arrest, the latter putting up no resistance. Ness went with federal marshals to arrest Martino at home, where the bootlegger meekly tossed a handgun to the floor. Ness felt a twinge of pity for a man clearly scared out of his wits. Martino, posting a $10,000 bond, was on the street that night.

Federal officials probably assumed they could use the bribery indictment to pressure Martino into turning state's evidence. The fixer knew all about the crooked ties between government officials and Heights gangsters, information the special agents badly needed.

But Martino kept his mouth shut. More than the old code of omertà, this was simple self-preservation—he knew his partners would silence him at even the slightest hint of cooperation. To stay alive, he had to prove that he could still be trusted, even at the risk of going to jail.

But it was already too late for Joe Martino. After all that bragging about his close relationship with special agents, the gang didn't care whether he was an informer or just plain stupid. Either way, he had to go.

Two days after his arraignment—on a cloudy, snowy afternoon—Martino stood outside his saloon on East Sixteenth Street, hands in pockets. He didn't see the assailant come up behind him, raise a revolver, and fire several times. Dumdum bullets smashed through Martino's skull, pulping his face the way a propeller churns water. The fixer dropped to the pavement, his hands still in his pockets.

The killer expected a getaway car to pull up and spirit him away, but none came. He sprinted down East Sixteenth Street, shooting wildly at anyone who got too close, and disappeared down an alley. Only then did a pair of cars cruise past Martino's corpse, apparently looking for their confederate. Each vehicle paused at the curb, then sped off.

The operation reeked of haste and desperation. The killer had acted in broad daylight, before several witnesses, practically within sight of a police station, his escape nearly botched. This slapdash killing convinced police the Heights mob was running scared. Still, Martino's secrets had died with him.

A *Chicago Heights Star* reporter found Martino's corpse "lying on the sidewalk, its head trailing blood. . . . Scores of curious spectators . . . gathered about, silent and impassive."

From Martino's home, just across the street, came his wife and seven-year-old son. Mrs. Martino stood silent for a moment, then collapsed with a scream, while her son knelt by his father's corpse, hugging it, wailing. By the time police arrived, both were drenched in the dead man's blood.

"That," Ness wrote, "was the end for Joe Martino."

Martino's death set off a cycle of slaughter threatening to derail the entire investigation. George Johnson and his assistants had already begun bringing witnesses before the grand jury for a conspiracy indictment aimed at cleaning up the Heights. But now they found themselves in a race to get testifiers to court before the gangsters could wipe them out.

One key witness was thirty-five-year-old LeRoy Gilbert, police chief of South Chicago Heights, a different municipality with cleaner cops than the Heights. A slight man with a carefully trimmed mustache, Gilbert had worked closely with Johnson's office to break up the local liquor racket. The chief had befriended a pair of bootleggers by promising to "get them out of trouble" following an arrest. Then he testified against them, and was slated to return to the grand jury two days later, when prosecutors expected him to give further damning testimony.

The night before his court date, Gilbert relaxed with his wife in the living room of their bungalow. Sitting in an easy chair, reading the newspaper, his back to the window, his head outlined by a reading lamp, he made a perfect target.

Outside, two killers hurried up to the window, feet crunching softly in the snow. They climbed up on a lattice outside his window, rested the barrels of a pair of sawed-off shotguns on the sill, and opened fire.

Three blasts ripped Gilbert's head open. A stray slug caught his wife in the hand, nearly severing a finger. Gilbert's thirteen-year-old daughter rushed into the room to find her father nearly decapitated and her wounded mother crawling toward the kitchen.

Citizens, including the dead man's brother-in-law, formed an impromptu posse. But they only succeeded in shooting up a couple of cars not wanting to stop for a mob of armed strangers—in one vehicle, a twenty-two-year-old Canadian typesetter got drilled through the forehead while riding home after visiting his fiancée.

Chicago officials reacted with horror to the utter breakdown of law and order in the Heights. With the police chief's death, the gangsters had crossed a line—Gilbert was an honest officer of the law, hence off-limits. Yet the Heights mob murdered him in cold blood at home, in front of his family. Suddenly, no one was safe, especially not Ness and the other government agents still working in the Heights.

The next major witness was Ness's driver and informant, Frank Basile, who had just received a $90 bonus from the Prohibition Bureau for his help in locating stills. On December 11, Johnson brought him before the grand jury to testify about his long history with the South Side rum ring. Basile's testimony was the linchpin of the government's case. With it, Johnson said, they had everything they needed for an indictment. The prosecutor left Basile with an order not to go anywhere by himself.

Early the next morning, Ness got a phone call from Don Kooken to come at once to the Kensington Police Station. The cops had a body, found at dawn on the far South Side—perhaps the agents might be able to identify it. With a growing sense of dread, Ness traveled to the squat, brick fortress sitting a couple blocks from his father's first bakery. Next door was Doty's Funeral Home, where police had taken the corpse. Ness hated such places, particularly the smell. But he went in with Kooken, and the mortician escorted them into the back room and lifted the sheet.

Frank Basile looked back at Ness blankly with his remaining eye.

Basile had been taken for a ride—picked up on his way home from a card game and driven to a vacant lot. His killers shot him repeatedly in the face. Basile's bulldog had been with him, and they shot it, too.

Ness liked to think his years as a federal agent had hardened him. But here was someone he'd known and trusted, laid out on a slab with much of his face blown away. More than just an informer or a wheel-man, Basile had been a comrade, a friend—and if not for Basile, Ness might have been knifed back at that East Chicago saloon. Eliot would have been stretched out, cold and lifeless, not this young father of three, going straight for the first time.

Prosecutor Johnson's case suffered a major setback with the loss of this key witness. But, most distressing, one of their own had been slain—Basile was a federal man in everything but name.

"The challenge to the government is clear-cut and definite," Johnson told the press. "The time has come for action—to bring every possible force to bear and bring Basile's murderers to justice."

Ness threw himself into the hunt. The prime suspect was the man Basile's testimony most definitely damned—Lorenzo Juliano. But even if Juliano had ordered Basile's murder, surely someone else had pulled the trigger. Police found a notebook in Basile's coat pocket and used it to piece together his movements in the days and hours before his death. Within a week, they had a promising suspect—Tony Feltrin, forty-two, a known Juliano associate.

Police arrested Feltrin and offered him a deal: Give up Juliano, and receive lenience in court. But Feltrin refused to talk and got locked up in the Kensington Police Station. His stay was brief. On December 19, he was found dead in his cell, hanging from his necktie.

That Feltrin would be left in a cell with only his necktie for company seems unlikely. But in those days, murder suspects cheated the official hangman with suspicious regularity. If Feltrin didn't kill himself, "suicide" was a convenient way to cover up an interrogation gone wrong—or for a crooked cop to fill an Outfit contract. Either way, on a cold, cloudy Christmas Eve, the grave took Tony Feltrin.

But the evidence against the hanged man convinced Ness that Basile had been avenged, in some manner at least, and the young agent went back to building the case against the men who had ordered his friend's murder.

"In Chicago Heights," Ness wrote, "the heat was on."

The special agents hit back by raiding the Cozy Corner, with Ness's pal Marty Lahart in the lead. Lahart burst in carrying a sawed-off shotgun, and announced a federal bust. Immediately, as Ness recalled, "four revolvers and one shotgun hit the floor." Miraculously, none went off.

As the other agents rounded up patrons, Lahart gathered discarded firearms, shoving the revolvers in his belt and holding the shotgun in his free hand. Then he charged upstairs.

Instead of finding gangsters on the upper floors, Lahart discovered prostitutes in various stages of undress, less than impressed with this flustered federal agent.

"Look who's here," one remarked. "Tom Mix!"

This rare flash of humor brightened the otherwise tense circumstances—Ness and the other special agents might be ambushed at any moment.

"We always traveled with sawed-off shotguns . . . ," Ness recalled, "and when we went into a restaurant, we always took a corner table as the danger of our undertaking was becoming more imminent."

Even so, Eliot Ness remained cool. Friends and coworkers marveled at his ability to keep spookily calm, considering him fearless. He wasn't, really—he just kept his fear bottled up like the rest of his emotions, biting his fingernails and picking at the skin on his thumb until there wasn't any left.

The sun broke through on December 28, bringing the temperature up above freezing. That day Ness rode through the Heights in the confiscated Cadillac with handsome Al Nabers at the wheel, flush with confidence as their case approached its conclusion.

Then they became aware of being followed—"a flashy new car," as Ness described it, stayed on their tail for a couple blocks. Nabers hit the gas. The other car did likewise. Nabers slowed down. So did the other car, careful not to overtake them.

Ness told Nabers to make a quick turn down a narrow side street, which he did, sliding through the intersection and parking the car diagonally so it would block the road. When their tail came around the corner, he had no choice but to stop to avoid hitting the Cadillac.

Ness and Nabers sprang out, guns drawn. They ordered the other driver, a heavyset Italian, to get out. Ness restrained the man, frisking him for a weapon while Nabers covered him with a shotgun. Then they searched his car, where Ness found a revolver with the serial number filed off, its chamber full of dumdum bullets.

"This was a killer's gun," Ness knew, lethal and untraceable, meant to be emptied into a victim and dropped next to his body. Neither Ness nor Nabers recognized its owner—his name proved to be Mike Picchi—but they had no doubt as to his profession.

"This gun," Ness wrote, "was obviously meant for us."

The special agents took Picchi to the Kensington Police Station and booked him. Then they drove a few blocks north to 11015 South Park Avenue, the sturdy brick home where Ness, by now a twenty-five-year-old federal agent, still lived with his parents.

The Nesses had recently moved from the house on South Prairie to this larger one with its own garage and yard, sitting across the street from the expansive campus of Pullman Tech High School. Peter Ness's business was once again on firm footing.

Nabers was a frequent visitor, often staying overnight when work on the South Side ran late. That evening, he joined the family for dinner. Emma Ness seemed not to mind such intrusions, but she couldn't hide the toll her son's job took on her.

Eliot recalled her staying up late, waiting for him to come home from his latest stakeout, fussing over him before he left in the morning. She clearly feared he would be "killed by those murderers," as she put it. Her son put on a brave face, trying never to bring his job home.

Around dinnertime, Ness got a call from an informant, a bootlegger who'd been trying to get in touch for days, desperate to deliver urgent information he couldn't give over the phone. He'd visited the South Prairie house looking for Ness, but found the family gone. He'd only been able to track Ness down because Peter and Emma held on to their old telephone number.

Somewhat reluctantly, Ness gave the informant their new address and told him to come right over. The bootlegger did so—while buying corn sugar in the Heights, he said, he overheard two Italians plotting to kill Ness. One instructed the other to use dumdum bullets. Now Ness had no doubt the mob wanted him dead.

They might try again, soon. Chief Gilbert had died in his home, his family in the line of fire. Ness couldn't abide the thought of something similar happening under his parents' roof. He reached out to the local police captain for a round-the-clock guard on the South Park Avenue house.

Then, doing his best not to alarm his folks, he moved out and got a room with Nabers, in another part of town. He wouldn't allow himself to see Peter and Emma until this whole thing blew over.

Ness also stopped seeing Edna Stahle, his increasingly steady girl-friend, though he couldn't cut her out of his life completely—she was Jamie's confidential secretary, at the very center of the special agents' activities, preparing their reports, recording witness testimony, taking tips from informants. She also kept track of the position of every agent in the field, meaning she knew exactly where Ness was as he probed the underworld of Chicago Heights.

For her sake, if not his own, Ness had every reason to wrap this case up.

As the New Year dawned, conservative estimates put the death toll in the Heights gang war at sixty. This, according to the *Herald and Examiner,* earned the town "the strange distinction of having the highest per capita murder rate of any city in the United States." Newspapers declared the Heights "a center of lawlessness" and "the municipal sanctuary for killers and bootleggers."

Local leaders decried their community hijacked by the criminal class. "The good name of a good city has been sacrificed on an altar of bloodthirsty racketeering and money-mad politics," said the *Chicago Heights Star,* whose offices had been bombed the previous summer. They believed "the bad work can probably never be undone."

But George Johnson was determined to try. On January 5, he received the final report on the special agents' investigation, listing the names and addresses of conspirators—everything the prosecutor needed for warrants. That afternoon, he met in secret with the recently elected Cook County prosecutor, John Swanson, to plot a large-scale invasion. Once they'd decided on a course of action, Swanson put in a call to William F. Russell, Chicago's new police commissioner.

"May I have ten squads of police tonight?" Swanson asked.

"Twenty, if you like," Russell replied.

The next morning, before sunrise, Ness met the raiders at the corner of Ninety-Fifth Street and South Park Avenue, north of his parents' home. After several rainy days, a cold snap had hit Chicago. The temperature hung around freezing, streets and piles of snow ice-crusted. Fifteen special agents waited in the predawn darkness with ten U.S. marshals and a handful of state's attorney's investigators. Then twelve squads of Chicago police showed up—around one hundred officers in all, ignorant of the task ahead.

The federal men broke the cops into separate units and deputized them all, giving them temporary authority to work outside the city. Each squad had an address to visit and a warrant to serve; no one was told where the others were headed. They took off in one long convoy, cars weighed down with shotguns, rifles, and machine guns.

Just as dawn broke, they reached the Heights and split up, fanning out toward their assigned targets. Once there, they would wait till the prearranged time to go in and bust down doors, rounding up the gangsters before they could resist.

The plan hinged on first striking one unlikely location: Chicago Heights City Hall. The building doubled as headquarters for the police department, which remained under the tight control of local mobsters. The raiders knew these officers would sound the alarm as soon as they got wind. For successful raids, they had to shut the cops down first.

That task fell to John Stege, deputy commissioner of the Chicago Police Department. A bespectacled bulldog with silvery hair and a no-nonsense manner, Stege breezed into City Hall at 5:00 A.M. and marched up to the desk sergeant.

"Where are the keys to this joint?" he demanded.

His bluster bowled over the officer, who gave up the keys. Only then did the desk man bother asking why.

"We're running the place for a while," Stege said.

The sergeant's eyes bugged out.

"We'll need all the room you have in a few minutes," Stege said. How were they fixed for cells?

Before the sergeant could reply, Stege went to check for himself, finding three women in one and ordering them out. When the desk sergeant complained, Stege locked him up in their place.

Then his detectives flooded into the building, rounding up all the other officers, including the local chief of police, putting them in jail as well. As the morning wore on and more policemen reported for duty, they quickly found themselves behind bars, too.

Meanwhile, the gutting of Chicago Heights had begun. Federal agents and police broke into the homes of twenty-five suspects, arresting them all in under an hour. Most gave themselves up. Some, assuming the heavily armed invaders were mob killers, seemed relieved to be arrested. A few made a break for it, firing off potshots before dashing into the street, where raiders outran them. No one was hurt, but frightened neighbors hid and called police, demanding to know what was happening. The officers commandeering City Hall assured them everything was fine.

"There would be a lot of emotion at the separation of the women and children from their men," Ness recalled, never quite understanding how a killer could ever be kind to anyone. Breaking the law was one thing, taking a life quite another. Frank Basile's family had loved him, too.

Each home housed a small arsenal—rifles, shotguns, revolvers, and hundreds of rounds of ammunition. Police emerged with weapons stacked like cordwood, knees buckling. Long lines of arrested men wearing caps and heavy overcoats, downcast faces hidden from photographers, marched into paddy wagons and rode down to City Hall. Searched during booking, nondescript suspects gave up thick bankrolls and diamond rings.

The raiders were confident they'd rounded up the men responsible for the deaths of Martino, Gilbert, Basile, and many others. They paraded Ness's would-be murderer, Mike Picchi, before the prisoners, to see if his presence sparked the slightest reaction, believing him to have pulled the trigger on Martino. Picchi remained tight-lipped and impassive, while the arrested men said they'd never seen him before.

"Their silence," Jamie told the press, "smacks of the Mafia."

Federal officials remained in charge of Chicago Heights into the night, trusting local cops only with routine tasks. Feds kept an eye on the homes of city leaders, too, should any corrupt officials try to escape. Meanwhile, the prosecutors, including a jubilant John Swanson, examined evidence uncovered in the raids.

"We are anxious to find the fellows higher up," Swanson told the *Chicago Daily News,* adding with a smile, "I don't know who they are, but I have my suspicions."

The grand jury handed down a sweeping conspiracy indictment in May, declaring that since January 1925, the Heights mob had operated seventy-five stills and manufactured at least three million gallons of illegal alcohol. Among the eighty-one defendants were the gang's key local leaders, as well as two former police chiefs. No less than fifty-five were convicted, though many pleaded guilty in exchange for light fines. Federal officials had cleaned up Chicago Heights in the short term, but the Outfit would remain deeply enmeshed for years to come.

Included on the list of conspirators was John Giannoni. The payoff man for the Heights mob escaped the massive raid but remained a fugitive until July, when federal agents arrested him at a saloon in Gary, Indiana. Facing bribery charges in addition to a bootleg indictment, Giannoni pleaded guilty and received eighteen months.

Lorenzo Juliano also managed to avoid the Heights cleanup—on June 20, 1930, his battered, bullet-riddled body turned up in an abandoned car near Blue Island, south of Chicago. His killers were never caught or identified, but his death may have given Frank Basile's family some measure of satisfaction.

The most imporant discovery of the Heights raids, however, had little to do with bootlegging. The raiders hit the home of Oliver J. Ellis, owner of a roadhouse just north of town. Unlike the other arrested men, Ellis lived on a country estate behind a tall iron fence. In his garage, investigators found an abundance of liquor and four hundred–some neatly stacked slot machines. They smashed them with axes and sledgehammers, keeping three for evidence.

But the real treasures were financial records. A ledger documented income from each slot machine, adding up to about $725,000 a year. A bankbook made out to a mysterious "J. Lazarus" pointed to a First State Bank account in Chicago Heights, leading to a wealth of canceled checks and deposit sheets documenting a massive influx of cash. This money had been parceled out to Ellis and four others.

Questioned by Jamie and others, Ellis admitted he was the collector for booze and gambling profits in the Heights. He even confirmed those profits were "split five ways," one share his, but refused to say who got the other four. His most damning admission came as an afterthought.

Had he paid any tax on this income?

No, he had not.

Ellis probably felt he had nothing to hide. That the government could collect taxes on illegal income had only recently been decided. When the federal income tax became permanent in 1913, Congress restricted it solely to "lawful" revenue. But this changed in 1921; after bootlegging became big business, Congress deleted the word *lawful* from the Revenue Act. The Supreme Court affirmed it in 1927—now every American who earned an illegal income in excess of $1,000 a year was also guilty of failing to pay his or her taxes.

To make a tax evasion case, however, the government needed absolute proof a defendant had earned income—bank slips, ledgers, check stubs. Showing he or she spent too much money, without visible legal means of support, was not enough. And criminal enterprises such as bootlegging, gambling, and prostitution tended to be cash businesses, leaving no money trail.

By admitting he'd never paid taxes, Ellis unwittingly gave Elmer Irey's Intelligence Unit their entrée. They scoured his bank records, collating each check, documenting where all that booze and slot machine money had gone. Those checks bore some very familiar names, among them Jack Guzik and Frank Nitto.

But the investigators found one individual they couldn't track down—a Mr. James Carson, who cashed a check dated June 27, 1928, in the amount of $2,130.

Carson's account at the Pinkert State Bank in Cicero, Illinois, had recently been closed out. The bank claimed not to know his whereabouts. But Intelligence Unit agents Archie Martin and Nels Tessem, looking over the bank's records, discovered Carson had opened his account on the same day a Mr. James Costello Jr. closed out his. Both accounts had contained identical amounts of money.

Convinced Carson and Costello were one and the same, the agents traced Costello's account to another bank customer with a bland name, whose individual deposits were mostly multiples of $55—the wholesale price of a barrel of beer in Chicago. Three more such customers led to a familiar name.

Ralph Capone.

The taxmen already had a history with Ralph.

Back in 1926, tax agent Eddie Waters had gone to various Chicago mob figures and urged them to pay their taxes. Bottles Capone took him up on it and declared a pitifully small income.

Then Ralph refused to pay the $4,086.25 he owed—instead offering $1,000, all (he said) he could afford. He dickered for the next few years, gradually upping his offer to cover the full tax debt but never agreeing to pay the interest and penalties.

By then it was too late. Thanks to Ellis, the government now had proof that Ralph (under the name James Carter) had $25,000 in the bank on the same day he offered them $1,000. In the years since, he'd amassed more than $1.8 million.

The Intelligence Unit had enough to slam a cell door on Ralph, but now they set their sights higher. They'd opened an investigation into brother Al in October 1928, but found nothing—no checks, no bank accounts, no tax returns, no receipts. As far as the taxmen were concerned, Scarface Capone was a ghost. But the evidence seized in the Jamie-Ness Heights raids had given them their first wedge into his organization.

Who knew what they might find if they kept digging?

PART TWO

CITIZEN CAPONE

Top: The St. Valentine's Day Massacre, February 14, 1929. Bottom: Capone, about a week later, with boxer Jack Sharkey in Miami. *(Top: Library of Congress. Bottom: Cleveland Public Library Photograph Collection.)*

Eleven

January–March 1929

By 1929, Al Capone—elementary school dropout, shoeshine boy, newsie, street tough, whorehouse tout—was the unofficial face of Chicago.

Take the arrival two years earlier of Italian dictator Benito Mussolini's "round-the-world flyer and good-will emissary," as reported by Fred Pasley. Landing on Lake Michigan, rolling in at Grant Park, aviator Francesco de Pinedo was greeted by waving flags, cheering citizens, and city dignitaries, the latter including one Alphonse Capone—among the first to shake the honored visitor's hand. The police department had sought Al's presence to quell threatened anti-Fascist demonstrations.

The city's most notorious gangster was now an official greeter and peacekeeper.

On a given workday, the Outfit leader could be found behind several layers of bodyguards in his office, suite 430 of the Lexington Hotel, his mahogany desk nestled in the curve of a bay window with four large views of Michigan Avenue. At any time, Capone might get up from his chair—expensive, hand-carved, with a towering, bulletproofed back—and look out with field glasses over the South Side he ruled. Crimson curtains ringed the windows, matching the red and gold plaster on the walls.

The décor ran to ostentatious displays of wealth and masculinity, from the beautiful Chinese chest and cuckoo clock to hunting and fishing trophies, including the mounted head of a moose. One visitor noted Abraham Lincoln memorabilia, including a bronze paperweight of the Lincoln Memorial and a framed facsimile of the Gettysburg Address. On Capone's desk sat stacks of mail, a gilded inkstand, and nine telephones. Coat off, attention divided between a host of tasks, Capone looked as much the captain of industry as any member of the Chicago Association of Commerce. He was taking pains to clean up his speech, and questioned one editor, politely, of his paper's habit of alluding to him as "Scarface."

"Does your newspaper consider it fair play," he asked, "to refer to a physical disfigurement every time it mentions my name?"

"The man was right," the editor admitted. "I just had not thought of it before."

As Capone assumed an air of legitimacy, so did his organization. He began pushing the Outfit toward greater diversification, realizing— unlike the wets and drys—Prohibition would not last forever. He saw particular potential in labor racketeering—taking control of a union and then bilking its members.

For years, a powerful protection racket had strangled Chicago's laundry business, setting high prices enforced through beatings and bombings. After failing to break the racket in court, Morris Becker, owner of a chain of cleaning and dyeing establishments, appealed to a higher authority: Al Capone.

The gangster partnered with Becker to form a new corporation, Sanitary Cleaning Shops, Inc., ensuring no racketeers would ever try to extort them. Capone's end was $25,000 a year.

"I have no need of the police or of the Employers' Association now," Becker told the press. "I now have the best protection in the world." And Capone could now truthfully claim to be "in the cleaning business."

As always, he treated his partner fairly. But Becker was a businessman, like Capone—the gangster showed less respect for the men of organized labor.

Meeting with union leaders in his office, Al would provide a drink and a smoke, before offering himself as a silent partner—for half the dues and command of the treasury. Labor officials who agreed got to keep their well-paid positions; those who refused faced threats, bombings, and intimidation.

Capone soon controlled the unions, from coal truck drivers who kept the city warm in winter to elevator operators who allowed workers to reach their offices in Chicago's many skyscrapers. The town could not afford to see such workers walk out, and so the Outfit could—and did—extort a fortune in strike insurance.

The ganglord's mercenary attitude toward unions reflected a dim view of the labor movement, which he saw as just another racket—a scheme to prevent workers from enjoying the freedom to sell their labor.

"The members," he said, "will always vote for the loudest talker, the guy who promises the most in the way of more pork chops. You give it to them with one hand and you take it away with the other. As long as their take-home pay is higher this year than it was last year, they don't care how much you take from them in the way of dues."

Maintaining control of a union often meant silencing the opposition, violently if necessary.

"You either buy these wiseacres off by giving them jobs on the union payroll at good salaries," Capone told a *Tribune* reporter, "or you scare them off. If they don't scare, you take them in the alley. When they get out of the hospital, if they still want to squawk, you get rid of them."

The Unione Siciliana (recently renamed the Italo American National Union) continued to give Capone problems. Al's handpicked local president was shot in the head on a rush-hour sidewalk in the Loop, leaving an opening for a candidate selected by Joey Aiello. Aiello had been dodging Capone hitmen while nursing his own need for revenge since the recent killing of his uncle. But Aiello's pick for president got taken out by shotgun.

Then the Capone Outfit placed one Pasqualino "Patsy" Lolordo in the presidential post—the kind of job that can get a guy killed in his own parlor, which is what happened to the well-named Patsy. Mrs. Lolordo tentatively identified Joe Aiello as one of the killers until she was convinced to honor the code of silence.

Meanwhile, Capone was at Palm Island enjoying another Christmas season, leaving Frank Nitto in charge back home. Al had succeeded in elevating Joseph "Hop Toad" Giunta to the top of the Chicago Unione Siciliana, giving Giunta the Murder Twins, Anselmi and Scalise, as bodyguards.

But Capone rarely saw the need for violence, finding bribery to be a much more effective tool. Another journalist summed up Capone's philosophy: "Why kill a man when you can buy him so cheap? You learn his price—and you pay it."

A rival Capone couldn't seem to buy off, portly gangster George "Bugs" Moran, still headed up the North Side mob. Moran's criminal record stretched back to his teens—horse theft. Never one to shrink from a fight, Moran bore a prominent scar on his neck from a knife slash in 1917, the same summer Capone got his own scars. Like Capone, Moran sought to conceal his disfigurement, but his efforts—bundling up in a scarf or hiding behind high collars—succeeded better than his rival's.

With his reputation for brawn over brains, and a full, fleshy face with its cleft chin, the dark-haired Moran struck some as dour, even morose. But he also had a broad smile and a sharp sense of humor, echoing his old boss, Dean O'Banion. Moran once complimented a Chicago judge's "beautiful diamond ring."

"If it's snatched some night, promise you won't go hunting me," Bugs quipped. "I'm telling you now I'm innocent."

Yet like O'Banion, Moran "could go berserk when provoked," one relative recalled—hence the nickname "Bugs." The deaths of his partners—beginning with mentor O'Banion—had led Moran to focus his fury on Capone, rarely calling the gangster by name, preferring "the Beast" or "the Behemoth." He derided Capone as a glorified pimp—always a sore spot for Al—and branded him a coward for not fighting his own gun battles, as Moran so often had.

"The Beast uses his muscle men to peddle rotgut alcohol and green beer," Moran said. "I'm a legitimate salesman of good beer and pure whiskey. He trusts nobody and suspects everybody. He always has guards. I travel around with a couple of pals. The Behemoth can't sleep nights. If you ask me, he's on the dope. Me, I don't even need an aspirin."

Capone never took kindly to criticism, though Moran's jibes bothered him less than the North Sider's constant efforts to undermine him. Moran had recently offered aid and comfort to Capone's chief rival, Joe Aiello.

"Any enemy of the Beast," Bugs would say, "is my pal."

As long as Moran drew breath, Capone had reason to fear, his goal of consolidating Chicago's underworld remaining just out of reach.

In the fall of 1928, Al gathered his closest associates at a lodge in northern Wisconsin, not far from the lakeside Capone compound near Couderay. They spent a couple of weeks enjoying a nice vacation and debating how to kill Bugs Moran. Attending were Gus Winkeler, Fred Goetz, Louis Campagna, and Fred Burke, several of whom numbered among their host's American Boys, the hit squad used sparingly on key projects like the murder of Frankie Yale. Their relative anonymity was critical as the North Siders knew many of Capone's inner circle—Moran's man Pete Gusenberg, for example, had made several attempts on Jack McGurn.

They decided upon a carefully staged assassination, to be carried out by Burke, Winkeler, Goetz, Bob Carey, and Ray Nugent. As with the Hymie Weiss murder, they planned to employ lookouts to keep watch on Moran's frequent meeting place, the S-M-C Cartage Company at 2122 North Clark Street, to chart his daily routine; but unlike the hit on Weiss, the lookouts would not do the shooting. The assassins would be "police"—Fred Burke had used a fake cop routine before in other crimes. Moran, and anybody unlucky enough to be with him, would be taken out not on the street but inside the garage, as Capone never wanted innocent bystanders hurt.

Back in Chicago, Capone assigned the job to Frank Nitto, who had Frankie Rio acquire the cars, weapons, and police uniforms. Nitto's careful staging of the Hymie Weiss hit, which one observer termed "gangland's most perfect execution," helped secure him a trusted place in the organization, though his rise rubbed some gang members the wrong way.

One Capone associate felt Nitto "always acted kind of snotty, like he was in charge." Another complained, "What had [Nitto] ever done, except push a few punks around and shoot some guys in the back?" Yet Nitto's talent for taking care of dirty work while keeping his own hands spotlessly clean would soon earn him the status of the Outfit's second in command, as well as an imposing and durable nickname: "the Enforcer."

Gus Winkeler's wife, Georgette, described the effect of seeing the police uniforms before she knew how they'd be used.

"Goetz enjoyed his costume," she recalled, "and strutted about the house imitating a policeman making a raid. He lowered his voice, talked out of one corner of his mouth, and impersonated several officers he knew, much to Gus's amusement."

Later, when Georgette learned just how Gus and his associates had employed those uniforms, she threw a newspaper in her husband's face and ran to her bedroom, "too sick with horror to shed tears."

Legend has it that Capone's men laid a trap for Moran by offering him the chance to buy a hijacked shipment of whiskey. But the men in the garage that morning included top Moran associates, not hired hands there to unload a liquor truck, hardly dressed for manual labor.

Moran's son, seven years old at the time, said his father received a phone call from an informant shortly before the massacre. Perhaps the Outfit passed along a tip about a traitor in the North Side gang or some other threat to the organization, alarming Moran enough to call a meeting of his "board of directors" for Thursday, February 14, 1929.

Moran showed up late, delayed by a haircut that took longer than expected. The six men he was planning to meet—along with their optician pal—arrived well ahead. And unfortunately for Capone, one bore a striking resemblance to Moran himself. The lookouts, believing they'd seen their target enter the garage, gave the signal. When Moran approached, he saw what he thought were policemen exiting the garage, their guns trained on two guys whose faces he did not know. Moran hadn't heard the gunfire, but he had sense enough to slip into a nearby building.

The assassins' careful planning had worked too well—the ruse they'd devised to trick Moran actually wound up saving his life.

On the typically sunshiny Miami morning of February 14, 1929, Al Capone arrived at the Dade County Courthouse, fresh from a brief Bahamian vacation and far from the blustery thirteen-degree Chicago weather. Outfit matters were in the good hands of Frank Nitto, Jack Guzik, brother Ralph, and various handpicked others. Al and Mae were looking forward to celebrating Valentine's Day in their newly redecorated home.

That would come after Al dealt with the latest harassment by Florida authorities, calling on Dade County Solicitor Robert Taylor; also on hand was New York Assistant D.A. Louis Goldstein, looking into the death of Frankie Yale. The latter investigation went nowhere, since Capone hadn't even been in New York at the time.

More evidence had come to light linking Chicago and/or Miami to the Yale murder. The discarded tommy gun had come from a Chicago gun dealer, with the handguns tracked to Capone's young Miami friend, Parker Henderson; neither professed to know how the weapons got into the hands of killers in New York. Henderson had just stored the guns in a hotel room, but they had vanished when he came back for them.

Anyway, Frankie Yale was one of Al's oldest friends—Capone wanting anything but the best for him was nonsense.

Asked about his business, Capone said, "I am a gambler. I play the racehorses."

"Besides gambling, you're a bootlegger, aren't you?"

"No, I never was a bootlegger."

He denied using the name Al Brown, as well as A. Costa, whose money orders Parker Henderson had gathered.

"You didn't receive any money by Western Union from Chicago?"

Capone couldn't recall, but as for funds he'd received while in Florida, "all of it comes from Chicago." Gambling income.

After the meeting, a *Miami Herald* reporter asked when Capone planned to return to Chicago.

"I am not going back," Al said, "as I am having a pretty good time in Miami."

Capone may not have known the Valentine's Day hit had already gone down, or that Moran had skipped the party. No calls from Chicago had gone out or come in during recent days, to avoid any phone traces. Rumor had it one of the participants, Ray "Crane Neck" Nugent, went to Palm Island to personally deliver the bad news.

"Capone," reported one federal agent, "was very much incensed . . . presumably because [Nugent's] going there might tend to connect Capone with the killing."

Nugent would eventually be arrested in Florida for a crime committed up north. After Capone paid his $10,000 bond, Crane Neck disappeared. According to federal sources, the Outfit left his body in the Everglades—perhaps for supplying his saloon with beer from their competitors. Certainly Nugent's conduct after the massacre proved this American Boy couldn't be trusted to follow orders.

Finding out his men had missed their target seems not to have soured Capone's mood, at least publicly. On Saturday evening, two days after the killings, he threw another lavish party at his Palm Island estate. Playing host to roughly eighty people, mostly strangers, "Capone entertained with the prodigality of a Medici and the wistful pride of a small boy," according to the *Los Angeles Times*.

Yet behind the gangster's frequent smiles, the reporter noticed "something harried about him." Capone seemed skittish as a deer, rarely sitting, and "anxious only to please those who accepted his hospitality." As always, he betrayed a need to surround himself with people.

" 'Scarface' led the way around his place with pride," wrote the *Times*. "His guests agreed that he had done things in a big way."

For Bugs Moran, the St. Valentine's Day Massacre brought back a very familiar kind of pain. He'd been with Hymie Weiss when they learned of Dean O'Banion's death; Weiss had keeled over at the news, so shocked he could barely speak, mumbling only, "Everything I have is gone." Now Weiss was dead, and Schemer Drucci, too, with seven bloody corpses stretched out on the floor of 2122 North Clark Street.

When Moran learned just how close he'd come to ending up alongside his slaughtered men, his grief got the better of him. He escaped to the suburbs and checked into a hospital, where he hid out for days, laid up with shock. Once he felt well enough to leave, he fled the country—first to Canada, then France.

The same day Moran left the hospital, Capone gave a jovial interview to the United Press, joking about the fearsome reputation that sent Moran scurrying to safety.

"If I were as bad as I'm reported to be," Capone said, "I'd be afraid of myself."

The gangster chuckled at that, but then grew serious, his resentment bleeding through.

"I think it is absolutely unfair to tie me up with every gun explosion in Chicago," he said.

Moran had done just that; newspapers were already pinning the massacre on the "Capone mob." Speaking to the *Herald and Examiner* by long-distance telephone, Capone denied the charge without losing his sense of humor.

"That fellow Moran isn't called Bugs for nothing," Capone said. "He's crazy if he thinks I had anything to do with that killing. I don't know anything about that shooting, and I don't care."

But he certainly reaped the benefits. Beyond causing the deaths of a garage mechanic and an optician, the St. Valentine's Day Massacre had sapped the strength of the North Side gang—eliminating three deadly gunmen, a key union racketeer, and a dog-track rival of Capone's. Moran's mob would never be the same, and more reasonable North Side gangsters soon would help Capone increase his scope of operations.

Yet even though the massacre had succeeded despite its own failures, Capone remained in a precarious position. By knocking Bugs Moran out of the arena, Capone became the city's reigning gangster— and also its greatest shame. Chicago's editorial pages, always offended by the local lawlessness, went into hysterics, crying out for a civic savior.

"The mass murder on the North Side has sounded an alarm like a call to arms," wrote the *Herald and Examiner*. "Every true Chicagoan should rise to the defense of this city against disloyal traitors in the public service who have betrayed it."

The *Tribune* reflected on the absurdity of the city's inability to solve even a single gang murder. The motive for each crime seemed obvious, yet the proof remained elusive—at least to the police.

"The Moriarties of detective fiction are plenty and realistic," observed the *Tribune*. "Sherlock Holmes remains imbedded in legend."

With city government paralyzed by corruption and apathy, the *Tribune* wanted to know if anyone would—or even could—stand up to the gangsters who seemed so untouchable.

"The butchering of seven men by open daylight attack," they wrote, "raises the test question for Chicago: Is it helpless?"

When the massacre first hit the papers, Capone was not yet a focus of inquiry. Some thought real police had done the murders. Other possibilities were a hijacking gone awry or vengeance for the murders of various Unione Siciliana presidents.

With neighborhood help, the police quickly found the lookout posts. A hunt was launched for Jack McGurn, who was holed up in a downtown hotel room not far from a suite rented by the task force investigating the slaughter.

McGurn was in the midst of a protracted Valentine's Day frolic with his latest sweetie, Louise Rolfe. He might have been a Hollywood actor with his slicked-down hair and slim build; his blonde lover had already hit Hollywood and missed, before turning showgirl to provide for her daughter. The press called her McGurn's "Blonde Alibi"—a genuine alibi at that, since Jack was for once innocent of a crime.

On February 22, a garage in back of 1723 Wood Street erupted in flames, while an Italian-looking man, his face badly scorched, fled the scene. After the fire department put out the blaze, police found a partially disassembled black Cadillac tallying with the one used in the massacre. Evidently, the burned man had been chopping it up with an acetylene torch—"a little bit each day . . . so it would never appear as a mute witness," said the *Tribune*—until he unwittingly hit the fuel pump, full of gasoline. In one corner of the garage, police discovered a discarded siren.

The ranking officer on the scene alerted headquarters: "The murder car has been found."

The singed fugitive was identified as a gangster who ran a café with another mobster—an Outfit-affiliated former Egan's Rat, like Fred Burke and Gus Winkeler. Moving from one mob connection to another eventually drew attention to Capone. Another of the fake cop cars—a Peerless touring job—blew up five days later, this time on purpose. McGurn was captured on the same day and charged with the murders, as were several other Capone gunmen, including Anselmi and Scalise. They all walked.

To date no one had bothered to talk to Capone.

"We may find reason to change our minds on the matter," Deputy Police Commissioner Stege told the *Tribune,* "but as things now stand, we don't want to talk to Capone at all. He was in Florida at the time of the Clark Street murders."

That same month, U.S. Attorney George E. Q. Johnson subpoenaed Capone about bootlegging in Chicago Heights—a direct result of the raid Ness and other federal agents had pulled off in January.

A deputy federal marshal and an Intelligence Unit special agent went to Capone's Palm Island home to deliver the subpoena, only to be told no one there knew "anybody by that name." The special agent threatened to find some way of serving the subpoena in public, rather than affording Capone the courtesy of receiving it privately. From inside the house, someone called, "Here I am, boys, come in."

Capone received them on the porch, wearing "a brown camel hair coat typical of Florida" over silk shirt and tie, his light-toned pants a match for his shoes. As the marshal read the subpoena, Capone listened politely, then asked what was required of him. The marshal told him he would have to testify in Chicago.

"He was pleasant and affable to us," the special agent recalled, "and treated us, I thought, very gentlemanly."

Capone seemed the very picture of health. But earlier in the year he had suffered a serious bout with influenza; Sonny had picked it up at school and passed it on to his parents. On January 13, not long after the feds raided the Heights, Al was fighting a 104.5-degree fever.

This prompted a call to a local doctor, Kenneth Phillips, who visited Palm Island and found Capone's bedroom packed with people "sitting with their hands posed—I presume praying—when I came in." The doctor diagnosed Capone with bronchial pneumonia, wiring the family physician in Chicago that the condition was "not serious," despite a persistent cough.

By early February, Capone was well enough to make regular visits to the Hialeah Race Track, take a daylong plane trip to the Bahamas, and board a ship for a few days in Nassau.

The day he received his subpoena, Capone attended a prizefight in Miami Beach, sitting beside Jack Dempsey to watch Jack Sharkey and William Stribling battle it out. Mae, in a purple dress and a fur, made a rare public appearance with her husband at the fight.

Within a few days Al's mood darkened, thanks to the summons.

"I am sick of being accused of everything that happens," he said. "I am out of the racket and I am entitled to a chance to stay away and live my own life."

Dr. Phillips lived in fear of the Capone brothers—Ralph, in particular—and didn't need much convincing to declare his patient too sick to travel. On March 5, Phillips swore out an affidavit—Capone had been bedridden with pneumonia for six weeks since January 13, with no mention of Bahamian trips and other activities. Capone "has not fully recovered," Phillips swore, and the change of temperature in Chicago might very well kill him.

Capone's lawyers brought the affidavit before Judge James H. Wilkerson and asked for a forty-day delay. Reluctantly, the judge gave them eight, postponing the hearing until March 20.

Prosecutor Johnson saw through the claims in Phillips's affidavit, recognizing an opportunity to lock Capone up on a federal contempt-of-court charge. He asked the Chicago office of the Intelligence Unit to look into proving the affidavit false, but they concluded they lacked the authority to make an investigation.

So Johnson reached out to Assistant Attorney General Mabel Walker Willebrandt, asking the Justice Department to step in.

Willebrandt forwarded Johnson's request to J. Edgar Hoover. "As a personal matter of very great importance to me," she wrote, "I wish you would look into this Al Capone affidavit . . . so that we can punish Capone and the Doctor for contempt. May I rely upon you to do so secretly and soon?"

Hoover wasted no time putting agents on the case. Although he would later display a curious reluctance to battle organized crime, Hoover recognized a potential coup for his young Bureau of Investigation. Disproving the affidavit would take little effort—newspapers had printed photos of the supposedly sick Capone at the Sharkey-Stribling fight—while allowing J. Edgar to take credit as the lawman who'd finally gotten the goods on America's most notorious gangster.

But even an investigation this simple would take time. Capone's grand jury appearance would be the perfect opportunity to arrest him on contempt charges; after that, he might disappear again. Even before Hoover's Bureau could begin its work, the gangster had already made the trip up north for his court date.

On the evening of March 19, scheduled to testify the next day, Capone holed up in an Indiana suburb, informing the press he would appear at the Federal Building as scheduled. The gangster knew he was sought in connection with "the four or five hundred murders I'm supposed to have had a hand in and didn't." George Johnson's office responded by promising to treat Capone "like the hoodlum that he is."

As Capone strode toward the Federal Building, police held back traffic while crowds followed Pied Piper–like, "bankers and brokers, stenographers and office boys," the *Herald and Examiner* said. Capone seemed indifferent, never tipping his pearl-gray fedora, though he did wave to cops and plainclothes dicks he recognized, and in the anteroom to the grand jury chambers gave an autograph to a fan, proving to some he could write.

The press was aware Capone was here to be asked about "certain racketeering, alky cooking, bootlegging and killing in and about Chicago Heights," due to the work of Jamie, Ness, and other Prohibition agents.

"It's a bum rap," Capone told reporters. "I don't know anything about Chicago Heights and if I did, I forgot it, see?"

Arriving at 9:30 A.M., taking lunch at noon, he wasn't called till two. When the grand jury adjourned at four, with an order for him to return the following Tuesday, Capone rushed to the U.S. attorney's office to get fee cards entitling him to a nickel a mile for the Miami trip and five bucks a day for testifying. His impaired health "seemed entirely mended," reported the *Herald and Examiner*. "In fact, he's a little bit rotund."

"I ought to go into vaudeville," Capone said. "Look at the crowd I get."

But he didn't like it up in Chicago, where he seemed to be regarded as a freak.

"Down in Florida they leave me alone," he said. "I go swimming when I want to. I go to the races when I want to. I do whatever I want to."

In Florida, Bureau of Investigation agents were seeking to prove just that, gathering sworn statements from witnesses about the supposedly sick-in-bed Capone's presence at the Hialeah Race Track. On the case just two days, Hoover's agents reported "beyond a doubt" Dr. Phillips's affidavit "was wholly and materially false."

The day before Capone was scheduled to return to the grand jury, Johnson asked Willebrandt to rush him the results of the Bureau's investigation.

"It may become difficult to hold [Capone] here longer on the subpoena," Johnson wrote, "and if there is a possible basis for filing an information for contempt, I would like to have the information on hand."

The feds arranged to postpone Capone's testimony for another day, sparking whispers around the Federal Building: "something was up." Unnamed "friends" of Capone told the *Tribune* they feared the grand jurors might try to probe Capone's possible income tax liability—from the question of his palatial Palm Island home to his possible take from Cicero dog tracks to his involvement in the cleaning and dyeing business. These obvious lines of income, the *Tribune* reported, "might be defined as Al's current weakness."

On March 27, Capone emerged with a smile from the grand jury room after another hour of testimony, perhaps relieved he'd dodged the income tax issue. But his good spirits disappeared when someone stepped forward to read him a warrant for contempt of court, technically placing him under arrest.

Johnson had sworn out the warrant personally, accusing Capone of "willfully, corruptly, knowingly, falsely and contemptuously" giving an affidavit that was "untrue and false."

"This is a disgrace!" Capone barked, before regaining his composure. Someone took him to the office of the chief clerk to post a $5,000 bond.

"That's easy," Capone said with a laugh.

After handing over his bond, Capone flashed the press another smile and said, "See you later, boys," before a retinue of lawmen escorted him out.

The press treated the contempt charge as a major victory for law and order. Much credit went to Willebrandt, the *Washington Post* saying "a feminine hand of the law" had caught Capone in its grasp.

Only Johnson acknowledged the work done by Hoover's Bureau of Investigation. "Permit me to say," Johnson wrote to Hoover, "that I appreciate very highly your cooperation in this matter and the prompt and efficient manner in which it was handled."

Hoover replied, "It has been a pleasure to be of service in this matter as in all other cases which are referred to the Bureau for investigation." Then he sat back to let Johnson do the work.

As a victory, the contempt charge left much to be desired. At most, Capone would face a prison term of one year and a thousand-dollar fine. But even so, the feds had drawn first blood—among them young Eliot Ness, a major player in the Chicago Heights investigation. And more was soon to come, as Capone picked up a powerful new enemy living in a palatial house six hundred miles away.

A White House.

Top: Calvin Goddard inspecting revolver barrel. Bottom: Leonarde Keeler and his lie detector. *(Top: Smithsonian Institution Archives. Image #SIA2007-0458. Bottom: Authors' Collection.)*

Twelve

February–October 1929

Across the turquoise waters of Biscayne Bay, barely a mile from Al Capone's Miami villa, sat the beachfront mansion of J. C. Penney. The department store magnate wasn't home on St. Valentine's Day in 1929—he'd lent the place to a distinguished guest whose very presence might raise its value. The esteemed visitor divided his days between meetings and fishing trips, riding off on a houseboat far down into the Keys, where no one—not the press, not even his bodyguards—could find Herbert Hoover, on this last, brief idyll before moving into the White House.

Hoover was no one's idea of a master politician. Stiff in public, frigid in private, he had the "sour, puckered face of a bilious baby," one observer noted. Still, he projected confidence and competence, his cold, impersonal manner fitting the new mechanized age. Automobiles, washing machines, and vacuum cleaners had reshaped American life, speeding it up, streamlining it, making it run more smoothly. The new president pledged to do the same for government.

"We were in a mood for magic," a journalist wrote. "We had summoned a great engineer to solve our problems for us; now we sat back comfortably and confidently to watch our problems being solved."

Hoover had built his career on working such miracles. A great humanitarian, an able administrator, an efficiency expert, he was also a self-made millionaire, an orphan who'd risen out of poverty. He was among the first American politicians to embrace public relations, promoting himself as a rags-to-riches hero, a "superman" who could fix any problem.

Privately Hoover worried his campaign had overpromised. At J. C. Penney's mansion, just before the St. Valentine's Day Massacre, Hoover remarked, "If some unprecedented calamity should come upon the nation . . . I would be sacrificed to the unreasoning disappointment of a people who expected too much."

At the close of the Roaring Twenties, the country's future seemed bright. Hoover preached the creed of American individualism, believing the United States offered opportunities for anyone.

"If a man has not made a million dollars by the time he is forty," Hoover said, "he is not worth much."

With the stock market soaring and business booming, few would argue. Such optimism carried Hoover to a landslide victory in 1928. But the president-elect didn't need to look farther than his own vacation spot to know the good times couldn't last.

A speculative mania gripped Miami earlier in the decade, as investors rushed to buy up overpriced land in the vain hope they might sell it for a profit. Their confidence came from little more than wild optimism and self-delusion—and the "inordinate desire," as one economist put it, "to get rich quickly with a minimum of physical effort." The bubble inevitably burst, leaving financial ruin and great swaths of undeveloped land in its wake, but somehow the country's faith in the future remained unshaken.

Investors kept chasing the same golden dreams in other markets— driven on, this economist wrote, by "the conviction that God intended the American middle class to be rich." After all, hadn't they learned from example, the two men Miami made such improbable neighbors: Herbert Hoover and Al Capone?

Some said Hoover was incensed when the papers printed side-by-side photos of the Penney mansion where he was staying and Capone's Florida place, which the *Miami Daily News* called Al's "Summer White House." Others claimed the president-elect had encountered Capone in a Miami hotel lobby only to lose his admiring crowd to the gangster. The most famous tale, courtesy of a Chicago journalist, was of a night when the boisterous noise of a Capone party carried over the water to the Penney mansion. When Hoover sent a message asking for quiet, Capone wrote back, "Go to hell." Then and there, Hoover vowed to see the bootlegger in jail.

No evidence supports any of this. That winter, Hoover saw only a general breakdown of law and order in America—clogged courts, overcrowded prisons, and defendants who could buy and cheat their way out of jail.

On March 4, in a driving rainstorm, Herbert Clark Hoover took his oath of office before a dripping, shivering crowd of fifty thousand. Then he delivered his inaugural address, the first to be broadcast over the new medium of radio . . . and the first to mention crime.

"Justice must not fail because the agencies of enforcement are either delinquent or inefficiently organized," Hoover said. "To consider these evils, to find their remedy, is the most sore necessity of our times."

The president proposed forming a commission to look into crime, lawlessness, and the problem of Prohibition—both how to enforce it and how to make people abide by it. Apart from the corrupt and ineffective Prohibition Bureau, law enforcement still remained a mostly local affair, with J. Edgar Hoover's infant Bureau of Investigation still limited in size and authority. For the first time, a chief executive had taken an interest in policing at every level—federal, state, and local.

Three years earlier, Charles Dawes, the previous vice president, had called upon Congress to investigate the "shocking conditions" in his hometown of Chicago. Speaking for concerned Cook County businessmen, Dawes declared that local government had given way to a "supergovernment" controlled by organized crime. The city couldn't count on its police and politicians; it needed federal help.

But Dawes spoke before a conservative Congress that considered crime a local issue. Senator Hiram Johnson of California called any such federal inquiry "a subversion of the fundamental principle of local self-government."

The nation's newspapers agreed. "The rest of the country," wrote the *Indianapolis News*, "will hardly expect the Government to turn out the Army and Navy for Chicago."

The new president, however, took a much more activist view. On April 8, Hoover sent a memo to Treasury Secretary Andrew Mellon and Attorney General William D. Mitchell, outlining his ideas for Prohibition enforcement.

That "large operations in illicit liquor" were widely distributing their product appeared obvious. "It seems obvious also," Hoover wrote, "that the most important area for enforcement of the 18th Amendment should be directed toward these larger rings and conspiracies."

Hoover proposed the creation of a "special corps of attorneys in the Department of Justice . . . who would have as [their] own investigating staff special delegates from the Prohibition Bureau." These agents would work as small, elite squads, handpicked for their honesty and effectiveness, to build conspiracy cases against large gangs—a blueprint for what would eventually become the Untouchables.

The special agent force offered many candidates for such teams, but Mellon went a step further. A die-hard opponent of Prohibition, he'd long sought to remove Treasury from any role in its enforcement. Seeing this as an opportunity to dump the whole mess on the attorney general, Mellon suggested "the ultimate transfer of the Bureau of Prohibition to the Department of Justice."

But that was a much bigger feat, requiring an act of Congress, and it would have to wait.

On April 14, the president met with Col. Robert R. McCormick, the eccentric, imperious publisher of the *Chicago Tribune*. Like Mellon, McCormick was a Republican who despised the dry law, and he used his time with Hoover to enumerate its failures. The Prohibition Bureau was wasting time with petty violators and ignoring the gangsters shooting up the city.

"They're not touching Al Capone," McCormick said.

"Who is Al Capone?" the president asked.

February 15, 1929, Cook County's new coroner, Herman Bundesen, convened an inquest before a "Blue Ribbon" panel of six jurors—local business leaders, a prominent attorney, two masters in chancery, and the dean of the law school at Loyola University. A crime as outrageous as yesterday's mob massacre, Bundesen believed, deserved investigation by men whose judgment was above reproach—the city's better element had finally had its fill of gangland rule.

Over the bullet-riddled bodies of the dead men, Bundesen swore his jurors in, then led them through the gruesome facts, taking them to the garage on North Clark Street, its floors still bloody.

He staged a reenactment, plainclothes detectives pointing shotguns at other cops lined up against the pockmarked wall. Intently watching, the jurors in their tailored suits might have been a board of directors. Even the sole survivor of the crime—the murdered mechanic's police dog, Highball—howled on cue. Press photographers captured all this great theater.

At the inquest, when a police detective spoke of seventy spent slugs and shells taken at the scene, jury foreman Bert Massee asked why those bullets had been preserved. The rifling inside each gun barrel, the detective explained, left unique marks on the bullets passing through, allowing a trained investigator to match bullets to the guns firing them. But, the detective admitted, the Chicago PD had neither the money nor the know-how to do that.

Massee, vice president of the Colgate-Palmolive-Peet Company, found this unacceptable. He asked around about this new science called ballistics, and learned its leading light was Maj. Calvin Hooker Goddard, a consultant whose hefty fees the city couldn't afford. Massee and another juror brought him in at their own expense.

Slight, dour, with pince-nez glasses and a weak chin, Goddard looked more like a priest than a detective. Trained as a physician, a veteran of the Great War, he had long been fascinated by firearms. In 1925, he abandoned his medical career to join the newly minted Bureau of Forensic Ballistics. Its founder, Charles Waite, was a former investigator who'd seen an innocent man convicted on spurious "expert" firearms testimony. This injustice inspired Waite to devote his life to creating a scientific standard for ballistics evidence.

"By such methods we are supplanting 'expert opinion' with facts," Goddard wrote. "Our goal is that innocent men shall not be sent to their deaths, nor guilty men acquitted, by testimony unsubstantiated by the facts of exact science."

The two men based their work on a simple principle—"that no two objects, either of God's or man's fabrication," as Goddard put it, "are ever identical in detail."

Even mass-produced gun parts carry their own idiosyncrasies, they realized. As a gunmaker's tools wear down, unique markings are left on every part they fashion—the bullet sliding down the barrel, the primer struck by the firing pin, and the cartridge thrown back against the breech, all retaining a microscopic imprint.

"These irregularities leave their marks," Goddard wrote, "the same ones each time . . . and they constitute, to all intents and purposes, a fingerprint of that particular barrel. It can never be exactly reproduced, any more than can the fingerprint of a human being." With a newly developed comparison microscope, Goddard could examine two bullets side by side and prove whether or not they had come from the same gun.

When Goddard arrived in Chicago from New York, the coroner

presented him with all seventy spent slugs and shells from the Clark Street garage. Goddard had never seen so much evidence. These rounds had been fired in under a minute, witnesses testified. Although they were of the type designed for .45-caliber Colt pistols, the sheer number of bullets indicated a Thompson.

Goddard minutely examined each shell and slug, systematically ruling out every other weapon using this kind of ammo. Only the Thompson matched. The killers had used two tommy guns, the expert could tell—one firing twenty rounds (almost certainly from a single magazine), and another using a fifty-round drum.

To find the killers, Goddard would have to find their weapons. And because witnesses had seen blue-uniformed men and squad cars at the scene, many still suspected police had committed the crime. So Goddard requested all the Thompsons and several shotguns owned by police departments in and around Chicago.

Without his own lab in the city, Goddard did most of his test-firing in Massee's basement, shooting into cotton-filled wastebaskets so he could recover undamaged slugs. And he didn't limit himself to the types of guns used in the massacre—he tested forty-one weapons seized by police and seventy-four bullets taken from the bodies of people killed in Chicago's gang war. Taking the bullets back to New York, he compared them with those in evidence.

On April 13, Goddard presented his findings to the coroner's jury, stating definitively no Chicago police Thompsons or shotguns had been used in the Clark Street massacre. Goddard hadn't exonerated the cops, but confirmed the killers' masquerade. The major also testified he'd solved a handful of other gang killings, tying the bullets taken from three victims to a single firearm owned by one suspect.

The press hailed Goddard's work, while Bundesen declared ballistics the greatest crime-fighting discovery since fingerprinting, whose "systematic application" could help "check the slaughter" in Chicago. But Goddard knew more was required.

"The city needs men who know about handwriting and typewriting," he said, testifying on April 19, "and who can just about tell the height, weight, age, sex, speed and mental condition from a person's footprints. You also need a highly trained toxicologist—someone who can analyze stains and determine if they are bloodstains and whether the blood is human or not; who can analyze soil residues; tell from the dust on a man's shoes whether he was in the part of Cook County he claimed to have been in."

Such full-scale crime labs were scattered throughout Europe, but nothing like them existed in the United States. Massee offered to fund a "Scientific Crime Detection Laboratory" in Chicago—not part of the police department, but rather a nonprofit corporation "outside the pale of politics and divorced from all petty and narrow influences." The dean of the Northwestern University law school offered the facility a home on campus. Massee tapped Goddard to run it.

"We had no precedent to go upon," Goddard recalled. That summer, he visited thirteen European cities with crime labs "at least sixty years" ahead of the United States in every respect but one.

"In general," Goddard wrote, "European methods of bullet identification are hopelessly antiquated."

But the ballistics expert knew much was to be learned from his continental colleagues. He returned intent upon building a lab that would rival those in Europe.

The Clark Street massacre was never far from Goddard's mind. Every so often, Bundesen would send him another suspected Thompson to test, but none matched. Goddard remained confident he could identify the right guns . . . if police ever found them.

While Northwestern staked its claim on the future of forensics, the University of Chicago announced its own program in police reform. Not content to give cops better tools, they intended to give the country better cops. The new department would offer advanced criminology courses, drawing upon research ranging from law and medicine to psychiatry and anthropology. Chicago would be their laboratory, a training ground for a new kind of policeman. Among the first to sign up was Eliot Ness.

Eliot's life had quieted down in the months since Chicago Heights. He had resumed seeing Edna Stahle, still Alexander Jamie's secretary, their romance growing steadily while their work lives remained entwined. When they were together, her mask of shyness dropped to reveal a refined, sophisticated, and sparkling personality.

One night that summer, Ness took Edna to a fancy restaurant and popped the question. They married on August 9, 1929, a month before Edna's twenty-third birthday, in a civil ceremony as quiet and private as the bride and groom.

Eliot and Edna moved into a residential hotel at 6811 Paxton Avenue, just south of Jackson Park, a respectable, upscale neighborhood a few blocks away from where Johnny Torrio had been shot four years earlier. Like the Torrios, the Nesses kept mostly to themselves. Their landlord remembered Eliot as a quiet tenant who "never discussed his affairs with anyone."

Neither did Edna. She hated the spotlight, staying in the background as her husband rose to prominence. Eliot, for his own reasons, would never talk much about their time together. Their mutual silence cloaks much of their relationship.

But with married life came new priorities. A month after the wedding, Ness signed up for a correspondence course in law. Off duty, he'd come home to write papers on contracts, torts, and agency—all civil matters, not the criminal law he dealt with at work. Newly married, perhaps planning to start a family, Ness had every reason to consider a career that did not include getting shot at.

Then came the University of Chicago's program in police administration. Ness joined the first class with a handful of other Prohibition agents, among them his old partner, Don Kooken—Alexander Jamie no doubt sending his top men to see what they could pick up and bring back.

Jamie's son, Wallace, though still an undergrad, also took the course. A sensitive soul and lover of literature, Wallace longed to be a crimefighter like his uncle Eliot. More than ever, he and Ness looked like brothers, better suited to a classroom than a crime scene.

Their professor was August Vollmer, fifty-three, police chief on leave from Berkeley, California. Tall, strong, with piercing gray eyes on a cinder block head, Vollmer hid gregarious charm behind his flinty facade. Ness surely knew of the world-famous law enforcement pioneer—at Berkeley, Vollmer had created the nation's first truly modern police force.

Twenty years before Massee and Goddard, Vollmer's cops were solving crimes using bloodstains, soil, and fibers. His department's firsts included putting officers on bicycles (and later in squad cars), forming a police training school, employing two-way radios, and making systematic use of crime statistics.

The aggressive interrogation of suspects—the so-called third degree—was, Vollmer told his officers, "an admission of stupidity and ignorance and brutality." He forbade them to "strike any person, particularly a prisoner, except in extreme self-defense." At Berkeley, he encouraged two protégés, John Larson and Leonarde Keeler, to develop a more humane, "scientific" alternative to backroom interrogations—the lie detector.

Vollmer sought to redefine what it meant to be a cop. Police work in those days was a low-skill, low-wage occupation. Men got on the force through political pull, promoted by shaking the right hands and busting the right heads. Berkeley offered an entirely different system: well-trained, scientifically literate "college cops," hired and promoted on merit. Though, like Capone, Vollmer's schooling ended at the sixth grade, he dreamed of a day when every police officer would have a college degree. He believed his system could work anywhere, and made his case in the press, feeding reporters exciting stories in exchange for coverage.

Vollmer didn't mince words about his colleagues, referring to the San Francisco Police Department as a "bunch of morons." Half of Chicago's cops, he told the *Tribune*, were "stupid" with "no business being policemen." He abhorred racism, campaigned against the death penalty, and opposed police crackdowns on political radicals.

"If the communists have arguments that are sufficiently convincing," he wrote, "why shouldn't we listen to them?" Beating and locking them up would only "make martyrs out of a lot of dumbbells."

Vollmer saw the dry law as a destructive distraction crafted by zealots with little understanding of the real world. He made open visits to speakeasies, and was critical of bans on gambling, drugs, or prostitution, which he saw as public health problems, not police matters.

"The eradication of drug addiction by short jail sentences," he wrote in 1936, "has proved a futile effort."

In class, Vollmer was passionate and entertaining, bringing in professional criminals for guest lectures, somehow charming them into speaking before a room full of cops. He had a rare gift for inspiring students, building relationships lasting for years. Ness became one of his most ardent disciples.

The young agent also picked up his mentor's fascination with the scientists who, as Vollmer put it, were "out-Sherlocking the old Sherlock Holmes of fiction." Ness began hanging around the Northwestern crime lab, eager to learn. One chemist recalled him dropping by at all hours and staying late into the night—"always smiling, but very earnest about his work."

Ness got to know Calvin Goddard, who gladly taught him the basics of ballistics; he also took an interest in the lie detector and befriended its inventors, John Larson and Leonarde Keeler. Keeler was a college dropout about Ness's age, recently hired by the crime lab to perfect his polygraph. A whiz kid and a promoter, Keeler hoped the device might one day make juries obsolete.

But Larson, famed as America's only Ph.D. policeman, had less faith in his invention's unerring accuracy. While the Prohibition Bureau might find the device useful for getting leads out of suspects, Larson told Ness, lawyers would tear apart prosecutors trying to use it in court. Nevertheless, Ness soon began bringing in gangsters he arrested for a spin on the new machine.

Well-read college boy Ness had always been an odd man out in the Prohibition Bureau. Jamie had protected him so far, but Ness would never be the glad-hander his brother-in-law was. Vollmer gave Eliot a new aspiration—being a cop in the way that other men were doctors or lawyers . . . a true *professional*.

"Merely arresting the offender and sending him to jail," Vollmer said, "is like pouring water into a sieve."

Instead, the teacher saw a role for policemen as social engineers, addressing crime's root causes.

"Common sense teaches us that the time to begin crime prevention is in the formative part of the child's life," Vollmer argued.

These ideas transformed Ness's thinking about policing, giving him an alternative to the more cynical brand of law enforcement practiced by his brother-in-law. In Vollmer, Ness had found another surrogate father he seemed eager to please. Jamie had set him on his path, but Vollmer became his role model.

Not given to writing letters or openly expressing affection, Ness did both for his most important teacher.

"I feel, and for many years have felt," Ness wrote to Vollmer in 1935, "that my connection with you at the University of Chicago was one of the most beneficial things in my life."

In mid-September, Alexander Jamie sneaked out of the city after receiving an urgent phone call from Washington, D.C. The press soon got wind Jamie was in the capital for a secret meeting with George E. Q. Johnson and top Prohibition Bureau officials. Those in the know speculated he would soon replace E. C. Yellowley as Chicago's Prohibition administrator.

Johnson had lost his patience with Yellowley, whose office all but ignored the prosecutor's urging to go after the city's gangsters. Instead, Yellowley and his agents doggedly pursued innumerable small fry, only making Johnson's life worse. Already the prosecutor faced a backlog of hundreds of criminal cases, many pending for a year or more, lacking enough judges to hear them all. Yellowley's only success had been Chicago Heights, which Jamie and his special agents had cleaned up on their own, with Ness in the lead.

Now the press speculated that Johnson wanted Jamie to head a similar cleanup in Chicago. Instead, the Prohibition Bureau held on to Yellowley and kept Jamie in his current job, proudly announcing an "intensive" new campaign against Chicago's bootleg barons, which Jamie and Yellowley would carry out together. Unwilling to "warn the enemy in advance," they refused to say more. Asked for comment, prosecutor Johnson spoke vaguely of the "harmonious" arrangement the Bureau had worked out.

"A greater effort will be made to reach the sources of the bootleggers' supply," he said, "and get at the revenue which finances the organized gangs."

He had told the truth, but not the whole truth.

Cutting off Capone's cash flow was a lofty goal, but Yellowley's Prohibition agents remained much too dysfunctional to ever make that happen. Federal officials would pursue another line of attack that, for the moment, remained top secret.

Members of the Treasury and Justice Departments had met to discuss plans for income tax prosecutions against various Chicago gangsters. With the bank records seized after the Heights raids, they now had solid leads on three of the Outfit's four senior partners— Ralph "Bottles" Capone, Frank Nitto, and Jack Guzik. The fourth, Al Capone, remained the ultimate prize, but they still had nothing on him.

They decided to work their way up the chain. Ralph would be first to go. The taxmen had the most evidence against him, and he'd unwittingly set himself up by lying about his income and falsely pleading poverty. That meant the feds could charge him not just with tax evasion but fraud.

The government needed an airtight case. Although the Supreme Court had ruled illegal income taxable, no one had ever tried to convict a gangster—a suspected murderer, pimp, and who knew what else— for not paying taxes. If the feds couldn't lock Bottles up on tax charges, they'd have no hope of convicting his brother Al.

They arrested Ralph in the most public way possible. On October 8, he arrived at Chicago Stadium with tickets to a prizefight, dressed to the nines. On the way to his front-row seat, he was stopped by two rumpled, portly men—a United States marshal and a special agent with the Intelligence Unit, carrying an arrest warrant. Bottles made a fuss, but they hauled him off anyway and brought him to the Federal Building, where George Johnson was waiting.

Johnson and his assistants questioned Ralph into the night. The gangster took on a haughty, indifferent attitude—these civil servants were stupid! After asking permission to smoke, Ralph lit up a cigar and laid a few others on the table. He invited the federal men to help themselves. No one did.

Bottles clearly had no understanding of the charges. Without his lawyer present, he assumed the feds wanted him on liquor violations, and when they asked about his numerous bank accounts, under various assumed names, he freely admitted they were his. That was all gambling money, he claimed, not booze money. Definitely not booze money.

But to the taxmen, the source didn't matter. Income was income. Clarence Converse, the arresting Intelligence Unit agent, took careful notes, keeping his busy hands under the table.

Ralph answered all their questions, then found it was too late to raise his $50,000 bail. Couldn't he stay the night in a hotel and post bond in the morning? The federal men refused. But Al Capone's brother hadn't lost his confidence.

"Well," Ralph crowed, "you don't have anything on me."

"Only enough to send you to the penitentiary," Johnson said.

Feted by Capone at what was supposed to be an honor banquet, Joe Guinta, John Scalise and. Albert Anselmi, imported Mafiosi, (left to right) were suddenly denounced as Aiello double-crossers and slain with baseball bats in the hands of Scarface Al himself. An artist has recreated the scene.

Top: Capone's baseball bat attack on Joe Giunta, Albert Anselmi, and John Scalise (left to right), as illustrated by the December 1932 issue of *Startling Detective Adventures*. Bottom: Capone (center) with Enoch "Nucky" Johnson (second from right) on the Atlantic City boardwalk, May 1929. *(Top: Authors' Collection. Bottom: Brinks38200 via Wikimedia Commons, licensed under CC BY-SA 3.0.)*

Thirteen

May–October 1929

Just before dawn on May 8, 1929, two patrol cops came upon a Cadillac parked with its lights off on the outskirts of Hammond, Indiana. This bleak stretch of prairie near the Pennsylvania railroad and the Illinois border might have been the perfect getaway for a pair of backseat lovers, but when the cops got close enough to look under the blanket in back of the car, their flashlight revealed two dead men, bathed in blood.

The unloved couple was Capone triggerman John Scalise and new Unione Siciliana president Joseph "Hop Toad" Giunta. After alerting local officials, the cops combed the area and found Albert Anselmi's equally bullet-ridden, battered body flung farther out on the road.

The Murder Twins had lived up to their nickname, but not in the way Scalise and Anselmi might have liked.

At the Hammond morgue, Chicago police captain John Stege and Cook County coroner Herman Bundesen were on hand to witness the autopsy. Each victim was shot numerous times, both .45- and .38-caliber slugs present. Judging by the trajectory, the three had all been seated when slain. The bullets were gathered for Calvin Goddard's ballistics lab.

Scalise and Anselmi would be shipped to Sicily for burial, but Giunta wound up in Mount Carmel Cemetery, in a tuxedo and dancing pumps.

——————

Not long after the grisly discovery, the authorities heard a story on the gangland grapevine fleshing out reports "from Sicilian sources" in both the *Tribune* and the *New York Times*.

Seemed the Murder Twins had been planning an Outfit takeover, in concert with Joe Aiello, so that Giunta could rule the Unione Siciliana without Capone as puppet master. A crony of the recently killed Yale, Giunta was popular with Sicilians, a twenty-two-year-old sharpie and jazz-mad dancer who mixed well, both socially and in business. With Aiello's backing and the Twins' firepower, Giunta was going places.

Scalise had gotten similarly full of himself. A trusted Capone bodyguard now, he was sending big money home to Sicily, dressing loudly, and swaggering around, basking in his killer reputation. Sure of his hold on Giunta, he boasted, "I am the most powerful man in Chicago."

The Murder Twins had been seen meeting regularly with Aiello in a Division Street joint. Wary now of the strutting pair, Frankie Rio, Capone's top bodyguard, faked an argument with the boss in their presence. Convinced he'd turned on Capone, the Twins brought Rio in on the plot to take over the Outfit.

Shortly thereafter, a banquet was announced to take place outside Hammond at the Plantation, a Torrio joint. All the Outfit insiders would be on hand to applaud the rise of Giunta to the presidency of the Unione—Capone himself had invited the three guests of honor.

The vice resort-cabaret was closed that night for the private party, exterior lighting dimmed to discourage locals looking for a good time. Armed guards made sure the guests weren't disturbed. When the Twins and Hop Toad arrived, they were escorted to a banquet room in back where twenty or more Outfit guys were already seated, though Capone was not yet present. Scalise, Anselmi, and Giunta received warm, back-slapping greetings in both Italian and English, then were given center-table seats of honor. Corks were popped, toasts made. Platters of spaghetti and chicken came, the guests eating with gluttonous glee, sharing wisecracks and wine with good friends.

Finally, Capone arrived and, as if a judge had entered a courtroom, everyone rose. He sat and ate heartily, his honored guests on either side. He conversed with the three men of the hour, smiling, friendly, if overanimated. Behind him a clutch of bodyguards stood—perhaps they would dine later.

When the table had been cleared of dishes, a bodyguard strode to the doors, locking them with a sound not unlike a gun cocking. The ganglord rose. He bowed to his guests of honor, who smiled up at him.

Then Capone said, "This is the way we deal with traitors."

A bodyguard handed Capone a baseball bat, which he gripped in hands as powerful as Babe Ruth's. While the stunned conspirators, still seated, were held at gunpoint, the boss began with Scalise, crushing his skull. Red streamed down the man's face like a cracked egg. The screams of the two brave gunmen awaiting their turns were cut off, one at a time, by similar blows, first Anselmi, then Giunta.

Capone worked them over for a while, then—none of the men dead, each clinging to consciousness—they were turned over to the waiting clutch of bodyguards, who blasted away.

Scalise tried to protect his face with a hand that got its little finger shot off; another bullet took out an eye, another broke his jaw. The other two received similar treatment, and all three sat shivering in their chairs, not from fear but pounding gunfire.

So goes the story, with variations but chilling similarities.

The tale reached the ears of police and the press not long after, and appeared in print at least twice within a year. Although details varied, this was the underworld consensus, and—significantly—the narrative as Capone's Outfit wanted it told.

Whether or not the baseball bat story is true—and that the Murder Twins and Hop Toad were battered and shot to death after a nice meal is incontestable—it added to Capone's power by sowing fear throughout the underworld.

"Those who work *with* me are afraid of nothing," Capone told *Liberty* magazine. "Those who work *for* me are kept faithful, not so much because of their pay as because they know what might be done with them if they broke faith."

Like getting beaten with a baseball bat and riddled with bullets.

As one gang associate put it, "The word spread out among the boys. It made [Capone] a man to be afraid of. A lot of tough guys who were running a few speaks or going with a wildcat brewery or some other money-maker began getting chills in the spine."

Capone crony George Meyer reported the cold-blooded beginnings of the plan.

"I was in an office and Capone came in with Nitti and Joe Fischetti," he said.

They began talking and Meyer got up to go, thinking the big boys wanted privacy. Al told Meyer to stick around.

"You're gonna know about it anyway," he said.

The banquet was Nitto's idea, including the touch of making the three conspirators the guests of honor: first, hearty good fellowship, putting the trio at ease, and then the horror and its sweet, terrible irony. Again Nitto had quietly planned one of the high-profile killings behind Capone's bloodthirsty reputation—the Hymie Weiss hit, the St. Valentine's Day Massacre, and now the baseball bat murders.

Meyer stood guard outside the banquet hall while the murders took place.

"We frisked everyone going in as usual," he said, including taking the honored guests' weapons.

A fellow Outfit guy told Meyer, "Capone got so worked up they thought he had a heart attack."

By literally bloodying his own hands, Capone hadn't just sent a message about the price of disloyalty. According to one relative, he'd felt the need to personally punish Scalise and Anselmi for targeting his family.

"They were going to blow up the house on Prairie Avenue on a Sunday," Ralph Capone told his granddaughter, Deirdre, "when we were all there having dinner. They felt they could pull it off because they were insiders and the bodyguards wouldn't suspect them. . . . If they had pulled it off, Grandma Capone, Aunt Maffie, your father . . . all of us would have been killed.

"When Al heard this," Ralph said, "he went berserk. I have never seen him that mad. He was like a wild man."

The murder of the Murder Twins made headlines as far away as New York, where the *Times* noted that Chicago had now seen forty gang slayings so far this year—"an average of more than one a week." The paper quoted John Stege's prediction that the killings would lead to "a serious attempt on the part of the Moran gang, especially the Aiello faction of it, to wipe out the leaders of the Capone gang, including Capone himself."

Al knew just how much danger he faced, skipping town right after the murders. With Frank Nitto and Jack Guzik, he'd gone to Atlantic City for a gangster convention hosted by Enoch "Nucky" Johnson himself.

The freewheeling town on the New Jersey shore offered beaches and boardwalks, restaurants and carnival attractions. Also available were prostitutes, gambling, and booze, the city a major off-loading port for liquor smuggling. Nucky Johnson made it all possible.

Looking like a banker, Nucky was both political boss and racketeer, and a perfect host for the conference. Law enforcement was just one of many things this fixer among fixers controlled in Atlantic City, guaranteeing no interference from the authorities.

The peace conference took place in the President Hotel and lasted three days. Capone's account of the meeting portrayed him as instrumental in restoring "co-operation in the ranks of Chicago's beer-running syndicates." In "sumptuous quarters," men from the various Chicago gangs discussed how to share their notorious city's liquor business without resorting to so much killing.

"We all agreed . . . to sign on the dotted line," the *New York Times* reported Capone saying, "bury the past and forget warfare in the future, for the general good of all concerned." Capone implied he'd called the peace summit.

But the real instigator was New York slot machine czar Frank Costello, who believed organized crime should be run like any other business, with a minimum of violence. Costello represented a rising generation of racketeers who saw the value of nationwide cooperation.

Borders were already being crossed. Outfit guys like Ralph Capone were operating in Wisconsin, while Capone and Torrio lived part-time in Florida where the Outfit controlled dog and horse racetracks. Expansion without sparking new conflict was a top priority.

Intentionally or not, the groundwork was being laid for a national crime syndicate—not one big organization, but interlocking ones. Cooperation among mobsters was the future, to Costello and Johnny Torrio, among others—better to make more money expanding markets than waste it on warfare.

Such conflicts brought down the heat, as the Capone-directed killing of Yale in Brooklyn and the homegrown St. Valentine's Day Massacre demonstrated. Torrio did not want to see his share of the Outfit's profits diminished by such stupidity. And by the spring of 1929, Costello had decided Capone must be reined in.

Costello discussed the matter with Torrio and up-and-coming New York mobster Charles "Lucky" Luciano. Together the trio devised a plan to clip Capone's wings by giving him what he always claimed to want: peace.

Invitations went out to Chicago gang figures, with New York

mobsters and Unione members such as Torrio, Costello, and Luciano also attending, perhaps as mediators. Bugs Moran, still on the run in France, was absent; but Joe Aiello and other North Siders showed up, along with representatives from the city's smaller bootleg gangs.

The ensuing treaty involved the consolidation of all the Chicago gangs into a single syndicate under Torrio's control. Each boss would keep his territory, but the profits, after expenses, would go into a pool to be divided between the "Big Four"—Capone, Moran, Aiello, and Torrio. The syndicate's books would be audited monthly.

Above all, the gangsters agreed to settle disputes peacefully, stipulating an end to killing, disagreements settled by "an executive committee." Past grievances, and violence, were to be forgotten.

The Atlantic City agreement did hold, in the short term. For about a year, Chicago's underworld enjoyed relative peace. Outfit members entered joint business ventures with onetime North Side rivals. Gang leaders talked things out over dinners and poker. But years of warfare, peaking on St. Valentine's Day, had badly fractured the North Side gang, and its gradual collapse would doom the accord.

For Capone himself, the agreement meant peace at a serious cost—ceding considerable authority to Torrio and giving up several rackets. Even worse, he had to accept the installation of Joe Aiello as head of Chicago's Unione Siciliana. Aiello had been the puppet master behind Joe Giunta, masterminding the failed coup that got "Hop Toad" killed along with Scalise and Anselmi. The Atlantic City agreement cut out the middleman, giving Capone's mortal enemy what he'd always wanted—direct control of the Unione.

That Capone would give his rivals so much indicated his hold on the Outfit had begun to wane.

"Capone is not the real leader," a Chicago businessman, once connected with the gang, told the *Herald and Examiner*. "Torrio never really let loose his grip."

According to the *Tribune,* such major Capone partners as Jack

Guzik and Frank Nitto "have made it known that they weren't at all pleased at the way Scarface was living in Florida while they dug for dollars in Chicago." Such rumblings had given Capone "the idea of recouping his dwindling fortunes through peace." Guzik would take a leading role in the operations of the new syndicate.

Capone appeared to accept the new arrangement gladly. "I want peace and I am willing to live and let live," he said.

But according to the *Tribune,* the "peace conference broke up in a row when 'Scarface' refused to 'retire' or to come through with a large share of his fortune. He was told by rival gang leaders that if he showed up in New York he would 'get his head blown off' and that the minute he appeared in Chicago he would be 'on the spot.' "

Torrio likely had a heart-to-heart with Al. The killings of the Murder Twins and especially of Unione Siciliana president Joe Giunta would spur "a good many hotheads [to go] after Capone's scalp," as crime reporter George Murray wrote. Threats continued to flow from Bugs Moran and his camp, and Joe Aiello reaffirmed his $50,000 open contract on the Big Fellow.

For somebody as hot as Capone then was, Torrio advised, prison was "the safest place in the world." Hell, Johnny's own jailhouse stay had been a much-needed vacation.

Al saw the sense in his mentor's advice. Anselmi and Scalise were trusted employees—if they'd turned against him, who might betray him next? And of course the ganglord was facing contempt-of-court charges in the Heights business. A cool-off visit to stir might delay legal actions, and maybe allow his lawyers to work out a deal.

The Capone women were told the idea of a sojourn behind bars was Al's, and believed the plan had been in place before the Atlantic City trip. But Capone did not call Mae in Miami until the last moment, describing the proposed jail time as an effort to keep him safe. Almost certainly, he didn't expect to be gone long, but he would soon discover that the near-total influence he enjoyed in Chicago did not extend to other cities.

Or perhaps his trusted mentor had intentionally given him bad advice. After trying to rein Capone in at Atlantic City, maybe Torrio felt more was needed to protect the organization. Getting Capone out of the way, if only for a while, might have been Torrio's next attempt to bridle his notorious protégé for the sake of his own bottom line.

Capone and his bodyguard Frank Rio supposedly had car trouble near Camden, New Jersey, on their post-conference ride back to Chicago. After catching a local train into Philadelphia, they got 9:05 P.M. reservations on the Pennsylvania Railroad, but had some time to kill. They went to a detective-versus-gangster movie, *Voice of the City*, where two plainclothes detectives spotted the famous real-life gangster.

"You're 'Scarface' Capone," one said, grabbing Capone by the arm.

"My name's Al Brown," Capone replied. "Call me 'Capone' if you want to. Who are you?"

The detectives displayed their badges and Capone promptly handed over a .38 pistol. So did Rio.

Those looking on would never guess both officers already knew Al Capone personally. They'd been to his Florida home, where their host gifted them Sharkey-Stribling fight tickets. The obviously prearranged arrest, however, had undoubtedly involved paying the detectives off with more than ringside seats.

In Illinois, where a weapons charge required a warrant, Capone and his pistol-packing retinue were never arrested for carrying. The Philadelphia police, currently facing a grand jury investigation into departmental corruption, could pride themselves on one-upping their Chicago brothers in blue. Capone praised their professionalism when he met the city's public safety director, Lemuel B. Schofield.

Schofield reported having a "most interesting talk on racketeering in the United States with Capone," who was "a serious man" speaking "quietly and in a gentlemanly manner."

Al's attitude was in sharp contrast to his bodyguard, Rio, who was snarling like a movie tough guy: "Give me a mouthpiece and I'll talk."

Capone lifted a manicured hand and said, "Listen, boy—you are my friend and have been a faithful bodyguard, but I'll do the talking."

The prisoner told Director Schofield about the peace conference in Atlantic City. Fearing this arrest meant he wouldn't be home for a while, he wanted "the boys" back home to know about it.

"I've been trying to get out of the racket for two years," Capone said, "but I couldn't do it. Once in, you're always in. . . . You fear death and worse than death; you fear the parasites of the game, the rats who would run to the police if you didn't constantly satisfy them with money."

Schofield asked Capone what it felt like, knowing death waited around every corner.

"I've been in the racket long enough," Capone said, "to realize that a man in my game must take the breaks, the fortunes of war. Three of my friends [Scalise, Anselmi, and Giunta] were killed in Chicago last week. That certainly doesn't get you peace of mind."

Presumably Capone said this with a straight face.

At the arraignment on May 17, the courtroom was packed not only with spectators but armed detectives. Indictments were read, the defendants declining to plead. The judge gave Capone and Rio thirty minutes to meet with their attorneys. At noon, court was reconvened and the attorneys approached the bench, conferring for fifteen minutes with the judge. Capone joked with spectators, who asked about his massive diamond ring; he told them it was eleven and a half carats.

Someone called out, "Worth about $50,000, isn't it?"

"You made a good guess!" Capone cheerfully replied.

At the bench, Capone's counsel said the defendants would plead guilty.

"All right," the judge said. "Each of the prisoners is sentenced to one year's imprisonment."

Hearing he'd received the maximum term for his offense, Capone no longer seemed so cheerful. He'd clearly expected a shorter sentence—most offenders paid a fine; none got more than ninety days—but no one had secured the judge's cooperation.

"Al figured on taking a rap," one Outfit associate remarked, "and he took a kayo."

Capone accepted his defeat philosophically, telling a guard as they left the courtroom, "It's the breaks, kid. It's the breaks."

The ganglord removed the diamond ring and handed it off to his attorney, with orders to give it to Ralph. This perhaps indicated Ralph would be in charge of the Outfit, although Nitto and Torrio bore the real power.

Capone was taken to Moyamensing Prison, where he figured to do his time, but within a day was transferred to Holmesburg Prison, a county facility near the Delaware River in northeast Philadelphia. Built in 1896, its cellblocks planned for six hundred prisoners but home to almost three times that, Holmesburg was notoriously inhospitable. Lighting sneaked in through tiny, filthy skylights, the concrete-over-brick-walled cells freezing in winter and roasting in summer. Shortly before Capone's arrival, prisoners had rioted over the execrable food and sadistic guards.

Frank Nitto visited almost immediately. Frustrated by the long sentence, Capone instructed the Enforcer to get their lawyers working on a way out. But the Outfit's offer of a $50,000 fee to any lawyer who could arrange Capone's freedom got nowhere. Nor did a bribe of the same amount move the Philadelphia district attorney. Capone found another use for his money by contributing $1,000 to a local children's hospital.

"I've got a kid myself," Capone said, "and I'm always interested in helping out other kids. Only, I make the one provision that my contribution be sent in anonymous. Otherwise people will think I'm making a grandstand play and they wouldn't understand it."

Capone's words, and the details of his donation, inevitably found their way into the Philadelphia newspapers, but they failed to win him any reduction of sentence.

In early June, Capone was allowed an interview with a reporter. With his hair sheared off, and wearing a white cotton shirt and baggy blue-gray pants, the gangster cut "a sinister figure."

Capone, clearly disliking prison life, claimed he hadn't chosen to live in a cell. "The stories that I was running away from anybody are all wrong," he said. But he refused to say much more, because "the less I say for publication the quicker the public will forget me.

"You see," the talkative gangster added, "I want to get out of here. If the public is constantly reminded that I am still in jail it will be that much worse for me."

Some observers began to doubt whether Capone had truly arranged for his own arrest, since he obviously wanted out now. But another convict offered his own explanation to a reporter from the *Philadelphia Public Ledger*.

"Jail," he said, "seems a heap different . . . when you're on the outside looking in from what it seems on the inside looking out. Maybe Capone decided he would just as soon take them chances on his life being free than living this here life. I would."

Still, Capone found some enjoyment in Holmesburg. The *Philadelphia Record* reported he and Frankie Rio joined the prison baseball team. Capone became their " 'star' pitcher," though the *Record* said nothing about his skill with a bat.

Capone's time at Holmesburg ended early on the morning of August 8. Prison officials spirited him away while the other inmates ate breakfast, under such secrecy that not even their superiors knew he'd gone. By the time they found out, Capone was already ensconced in Eastern State Penitentiary, a century-old prison just north of downtown Philadelphia.

Officially, Capone had been transferred to relieve the overcrowding at Holmesburg. But the *New York Times* reported a more pressing need to get him out quickly. Other prisoners had grown so jealous of Capone's regular parade of visitors that "an atmosphere of unrest and uneasiness" soon filled the prison. When "the threats and murmurings" grew sufficiently serious, Capone was sent to Eastern State.

"Perhaps Capone will be safer here than at Holmesburg," said Herbert Smith, the prison's notoriously "hardboiled" warden.

Eastern State appeared just as tough as its warden—a stone castle complete with turrets and battlements, entered by a single arched gate missing only a drawbridge and moat. But this medieval exterior concealed a rare luxury for a prison of its time: a thoroughly modern hospital offering everything from X-rays to cosmetic surgery.

Capone ended up there soon after arriving; the prison's intake procedure involved both vaccines and a blood test. The results of that test are not known, but they probably revealed one or more of the sexually transmitted diseases—syphilis and gonorrhea—that plagued Capone throughout his life.

Shortly thereafter, Capone underwent minor surgery, apparently a circumcision. At the time, some doctors believed the procedure might treat or prevent venereal disease, which explains why Capone would be circumcised as an adult. But if this is the case, it didn't work; Capone couldn't shake his syphilis so easily.

The operation caused a minor stir in prison, as virtually every inmate asked Warden Smith whether Capone would be okay. Smith received numerous phone calls from Chicago, too—including from Capone's sister, Mafalda, who called as soon as the operation had ended. Upon learning her brother would be all right, Mafalda sighed, "I'm glad," and hung up.

While recovering from the procedure, Capone settled into his cell, which was near the front gate in the prison's "Park Avenue" block. The cell was a little larger than normal, its arched ceiling boasting twin slotted skylights while most had only one. The cement floor, one reporter noted, was obscured by the "soft colors and luxurious texture" of a fine rug. The walls were hung with framed, "tasteful paintings," the cell basking in a desk lamp's glow, the desk itself fine polished wood. The easy chair, reading lamp, wardrobe, chest of drawers, and bed fitted with a fine mattress did not seem to be standard prison issue. Nor were the silk underthings worn under the variety of casual clothes and suits. Pleasant music could be heard emanating from a cabinet radio said to be a $500 model.

The press made much of Capone's "cheery and homelike" cell; the prisoner said he found it "very comfortable." Yet Capone had to share a cell built for one inmate with another man, and both enjoyed a level of luxury not unheard of in Eastern State. A previous prisoner had paid for the paintings on the walls, and Capone bought his radio from the earlier inhabitants of the cell.

"It is by no means the most luxuriously furnished cell in the prison," wrote the *Philadelphia Record*. "There are others that are more sumptuous."

Warden Smith wanted the public to understand that Capone received no special treatment. He showed the *Record* the rugs on Capone's floor, saying they were prison made, cost ninety cents apiece, and could be had by any well-behaved inmate.

"This man, called a gangster, comes here to me as just another prisoner," Smith said. "I'm not interested in his past—I'm more interested in his behavior here. He has proved an ideal prisoner, and anyone who behaves gets the breaks."

For Al Capone, those "breaks" reportedly included long-distance telephone calls, using the warden's office for business meetings and attorney conferences, and receiving regular visits from Nitto, Guzik, and brother Ralph. Mae came by train in a coach compartment, as did Theresa and Mafalda, on the rare times they braved the long distance. Al's wife made sure he didn't have to eat prison fare, and several of Philadelphia's many Italian restaurants were only too pleased to deliver regularly to the great man, who gained weight on his prison stay.

Thanks to Warden Smith's willingness to let his famous guest use his office, Al made his regular phone calls to Mae on Palm Island and his mother and sister on Prairie Avenue. He and Smith became pals— now and then Al would be driven to the warden's house for a home-cooked meal.

In front of one reporter, the warden asked Capone whether he had the run of the prison. Capone laughed.

"That *is* funny," he said. "Let me say right here and now that I'm satisfied here, but if I'm getting away with anything I want to know it."

Despite Capone's incarceration, the ravenous press kept him in the headlines. News stories reported his choice not to go to church and his pick of the Cubs to win the World Series. When the prison doctors prepared to amputate the arm of an inmate who suffered a gunshot wound, Capone reportedly urged them to save the limb however they could.

"If it takes money," Capone said, "I'll be glad to bear whatever expense there is."

And the man who made a fortune off prostitution shared his views on the opposite sex.

"The trouble with women of today," Capone told the *Public Ledger*, "is that they get interested in too many things outside of their home. A woman's home and children mean the real happiness to her. If she would stay there, the world would have much less to worry about the modern woman."

One reporter found Capone reading a biography of Napoleon, wearing the "silver-rimmed spectacles" cameras almost never saw. Capone claimed the French emperor was his childhood hero, and viewed the life of this "great little guy" through the prism of his own profession.

"I'll have to hand it to Napoleon as the world's greatest racketeer," Capone said. "But . . . he didn't know when to quit and had to get back in the racket. He simply put himself on the spot. That made it easy for the other gang to take him, and they were no dumbbells. If he had lived in Chicago it would have been a sawed-off shotgun Waterloo for him. He didn't wind up in a ditch as a coroner's case, but they took him for a one-way ride to St. Helena, which was about as tough a break."

The reporter showed Capone an article by Chicago gangland observer Edward Dean Sullivan, which claimed the Outfit took in $70 million a year.

"That shouldn't be published," Capone said. "It's a pack of lies, and I'm going to start trouble just as sure as you're born."

Then Capone's self-pity came roaring back.

"Why can't I be left alone?" he asked. "I'm a prisoner now, and I mean to make the best of it."

He even gave up his efforts to win his freedom, having failed six different times, and settled in to wait for the end of his term. But when that time came, he would leave Eastern State into a world far different from the one he'd left.

On Thursday, October 24, 1929, the "blue-sky, big money era" making Capone a household name came to an abrupt but inevitable end. The confidence and optimism that had pushed the stock market to new heights gave way to terror as panicked speculators thronged Wall Street, selling everything they had for whatever they could get.

"The total losses," reported the following day's *New York Times,* "cannot be accurately calculated. . . . However, they were staggering, running into billions of dollars."

Telegraph wires carried the chaos to Chicago, ticker tape machines pouring the bad news into the city's financial center. Investors looked on, stunned, as all their wealth vanished into so much paper.

"If this goes on much longer," someone said, "there won't be a stock market left."

To Herbert Hoover, the cause of the crisis seemed obvious. For years, Hoover had watched "the growing tide of speculation" with deepening concern, rightly fearing catastrophe. But his attempts to tame Wall Street had failed, and the president could only criticize the men whose greed had brought the economy to ruin.

"There are crimes," Hoover wrote, "far worse than murder for which men should be reviled and punished."

The nation's foremost criminal, no fan of bankers or the stock market, would certainly have agreed. Almost immediately, Capone seemed to realize the shocked nation would be looking for a scapegoat. When news of the collapse penetrated the stone walls of Eastern State Penitentiary, Capone happened to be in conference with a Republican congressman, Benjamin Golder.

"Listen, Ben," Capone said, "if those newspaper guys ask you about the stock market crash, tell them I deny absolutely that I am responsible."

Top: Ralph Capone and his attorneys. Bottom: Herbert Hoover (second from left) and his cabinet playing "Hoover-Ball" on the White House lawn. *(Top: Authors' Collection. Bottom: National Archives.)*

Fourteen

December 1929–March 1930

Fred Burke had bigger things to worry about than the collapse of the American economy: he had been widely pegged as a St. Valentine's Day Massacre machine gunner. And for good reason, since police knew of his propensity for pulling jobs in a police uniform. Also, a Clark Street witness had seen a man missing a telltale front tooth, just like Burke, driving a police car that turned out not to be one. Tried in absentia by the press, Capone's chief American Boy earned a new nickname—"Killer" Burke.

After a few months' vacation in northern Minnesota, bug-eyed Burke holed up in a charming bungalow in Stevensville, Michigan, just south of St. Joseph. Perched on a hill at the edge of Lake Michigan, surrounded by apple and cherry orchards, St. Joseph was a favorite getaway for Chicago businessmen and gangsters. Jack Guzik and Capone bodyguards Louis Campagna and Phil D'Andrea all had homes in the area.

Burke arrived in September, tail end of tourist season, and started throwing money around, saying he was a wealthy oilman. Some neighbors bought that, while others took him for a bootlegger, not that they minded. He had $320,000 in stolen bonds to live off and a new moll for company. Life was good.

But Georgette Winkeler, wife of massacre coconspirator Gus Winkeler, said Burke "was a victim of shattered nerves." And the more strained his nerves, the more dangerous he became.

On December 14, 1929, Burke got into a fender bender outside St. Joseph. A local cop hopped on Burke's running board and ordered him to the police station. Burke, returning from an evening of drinking, pulled a .45 and shot the officer three times, then sped off. A few miles down the road, he wrecked his car, but somehow managed to escape by carjacking his way out of town. Back in St. Joseph, the twenty-five-year-old officer died on the operating table.

Police followed Burke's trail back to the house in Stevensville, where he'd abandoned his latest girl. They also found stolen bonds and a huge cache of weaponry—two high-powered rifles, a shotgun, seven semi-automatic pistols, more than a thousand rounds of ammunition, and a pair of Thompson submachine guns. Fingerprints taken off a salt-shaker confirmed the supposed well-heeled oilman was Killer Burke.

The St. Joseph authorities brought Burke's Thompsons to Calvin Goddard in Chicago. Emptying the guns, Goddard noted the same brand of bullets used in the massacre. "The very presence of these cartridges was in itself a highly significant feature," Goddard wrote, "since . . . this vintage had been on the market for but a short period and had not been distributed since July, 1928."

Next, Goddard reloaded the weapons and fired them into his cotton-stuffed wastebasket. "I made long and careful comparisons of the shells and bullets recovered in this test with those from the garage," the ballistics expert reported. "The result . . . the two guns found in the Burke home were those that had been used in the massacre."

The coroner and his jury named Burke as the only known suspect in the massacre. Impressed, the New York police commissioner sent Goddard a bullet taken from the late Frankie Yale, dispatched back in '28 by three of Capone's killers. Goddard compared the slug to rounds fired from Burke's Thompsons, and they matched, linking two of the past decade's most notorious gang murders.

For Chicago's coroner, the ballistics expert's work marked "the turning point in police methods in the United States." Even with Burke still on the lam, the case was closed. Goddard couldn't ask for a better advertisement for his new crime lab.

The law finally caught up with Burke in March 1931. He'd grown a mustache and undergone plastic surgery making him look "imbecilic" and "insipid," in Georgette Winkeler's view. But a wannabe detective in Missouri recognized Killer anyway, from his picture in *True Detective* magazine, and led police to Burke in the home he shared with his new wife, a farmer's daughter.

Burke took the law for killers in cop drag, availing themselves of his own trademark disguise.

"What are you going to do," he demanded, "take me for a ride?"

Then seeing their squad cars—*actual* squad cars—he cracked a relieved smile. Asked by a reporter if he'd been in on the St. Valentine's Day Massacre, Burke didn't bite.

"Get a spiritualist and go into a dark room and hold hands," he said. "Maybe you'll find out."

No seance was needed—the evidence spoke from beyond the grave. The St. Joseph cop's murder took precedence, and Burke stood trial in Michigan. He pleaded guilty, received a life sentence, and died at the Marquette Branch Prison on July 10, 1940, never copping to the Clark Street killings.

Like an earthquake, the St. Valentine's Day Massacre had shaken the city of Chicago, transforming its criminal landscape. Now, thanks to Burke, a distant aftershock had claimed the life of a policeman a hundred miles away. More and more, the city seemed a nexus of violence.

"A real Goddamned crazy place," Lucky Luciano reportedly said of Chicago. "Nobody's safe on the street."

Civic leaders fretted about their city's reputation, and not just for reasons of pride—insurance rates climbed and investors stayed away. And as the mob moved deeper into labor racketeering, extorting money through threats of strikes or property damage, they increasingly hurt legitimate commerce. By early 1930, Capone had become more than a civic shame—he was bad for business.

CHICAGO IS NOT ALL GUNMEN, declared a headline in London's *Daily Mail,* above an article designed to reassure even the most terrified tourist.

"City of dreadful reputation," the piece began, "whose business men wear bullet-proof vests and cower in fear at the explosion of an automobile tyre. Is this a caricature or a reality?"

The article replied with a caricature of its own—a gentle jaunt about town, from the well-policed northern suburbs to the beaches where children played unattended, their wealthy parents unafraid of kidnappers.

"To the law-abiding Chicagoan . . . crime would be something remote and far removed were it not that such killings have injured the name of his city," the *Daily Mail* said.

But restoring the city's good name would take more than a few puff pieces. The city fathers began planning a grand world's fair, the Century of Progress Exposition, timed for 1937 and Chicago's centennial—an opportunity to wipe the gangsters from the headlines and place Chicago at the forefront of science and industry. After the stock market crash, civic leaders clung to the fair like a lifeline, even moving it to 1933, in hopes it would bring the economic boost their city so sorely needed.

But Capone threatened to derail it all.

"Unless gang rule is wiped out in Chicago before the Century of Progress exposition," one observer noted, "there will be no visitors here in 1933, for the simple reason that people will be too scared to come."

And yet the business elite remained aloof. The St. Valentine's Day Massacre had been shocking enough to prompt a meeting of the Chicago Association of Commerce, the businessmen's organization dedicated to burnishing the city's image. Even that notorious crime couldn't spur them to action—if the gangsters wanted to kill each other, so much the better. Anyway, the boosters argued, the crime situation wasn't as severe as the press painted it. Statistically, Chicago was only seventeenth in the nation for violent crime.

Then, on February 5, 1930, two gunmen opened fire on the leafy campus of the University of Chicago, near the construction site for a new hospital, two bullets dropping foreman Philip Meagher, one nearly severing his spine. He survived and Chicago barely noticed the incident, having grown used to gunfire on its streets.

Both Meagher and his boss, Harrison B. Barnard, belonged to the Association of Commerce. The next day, Barnard visited the group's new president, Robert Isham Randolph, forty-six, and laid blame for the crime on labor racketeers—the shooting was a declaration of war on the business community.

Barnard had come to the right man. Tall and lean, Randolph always appeared a bit sickly, his baggy gray eyes hidden in deep, dark sockets. But he was energetic and charismatic, quick to smile, and solid as a tombstone. More than one reporter noted the Sherlock Holmes resemblance, the high forehead and hooked nose.

Some called him Bob, others "the Colonel." He had served in the World War and, as a civil engineer, built bridges and redirected rivers. The Association elected him president in January 1930, to do for their organization what that other great engineer, Herbert Hoover, would for the country. Now, like Hoover, Randolph was on a collision course with gangsters, agreeing with Barnard—they had to retaliate.

Two days after the Meagher shooting, Randolph declared "a war on crime which will continue as long as I am president of the Association of Commerce." He met with State's Attorney John Swanson, who helped plan the raid on Chicago Heights, to inquire why the prosecutor had failed to make more inroads against organized crime. Swanson said his investigators couldn't build strong cases because their names were on the public payroll, leaving them open to bribes and intimidation.

If the businessmen wanted to help, they should fund an off-the-books squad of detectives—"a real secret service in which the operatives are not known, perhaps not even known to each other," free to uncover the evidence Swanson's men could not. With that kind of backing, the state's attorney believed he could put any gangster in jail.

Randolph embraced the idea of a private spy service with himself as its commanding officer. He called a special meeting of the Association of Commerce and laid out the plan; after two hours, Chicago's wealthiest men remained unconvinced.

"Oh, the situation may not be so bad as you picture it, Colonel," one remarked. "Suppose we wait until the mob really does something that will arouse the entire citizenry of Chicago, something really terrible."

Apparently only the death of someone in this room would spur civic action. Randolph, with an ironic smile, declined the honor of becoming a martyr to gangster bullets.

Then one attendee stood, white-haired with a drooping mustache and pince-nez glasses. Probably the richest man present, Samuel Insull owned a network of utility companies valued at $3 billion. Recently he'd poured a fortune into erecting the "tallest opera building in the world," which opened six days after the stock market crash.

Insull said the situation was already "bad enough" and agreed to back Randolph's plan, adding, "you can put me down for ten per cent of any amount of money you want to raise."

This show of support came from a man who displayed a thirst for power and a gift for corruption rivaling any gangster's (he'd once hired bodyguards from Capone). Insull's financial empire was essentially a pyramid scheme of holding companies propped up by manipulated stocks and catastrophic debt; he shamelessly purchased politicians, keeping one United States senator on a monthly retainer.

With Insull's golden blessing, Randolph's plan could not fail. Other members of the association kicked in large sums, $25,000 or more.

On February 8, Randolph announced formation of a "Citizens' Committee for the Prevention and Punishment of Crime," declaring no one would be safe from its prying eyes.

"If our information shows that the police should be hit, then the police will be hit," Randolph said, not exempting the legislature, either. "And we're going to keep on working until we have dragged the city out of the mire."

How many, the *Chicago Daily News* asked, were on the committee?

"There may be a hundred—or there may be six," Randolph said, "but in any event it obviously would be wrong to announce who they are." The *News* reporter ran with Randolph's figure, giving the committee its catchy nickname: the Secret Six.

Members, besides Randolph and Insull, included philanthropist Julius Rosenwald, Western Electric vice president C. L. Rice, phone company executive William Rufus Abbott, and stockbroker George E. Paddock. That indeed made six, but building contractor Harrison Barnard, who'd put the plan in motion, lent his support as well; and several members of the Chicago Crime Commission also took part, among them Frank Loesch.

Randolph claimed the Six had bottomless financial resources. "If the needed sum be $1,000,000 or $2,000,000 or $5,000,000," he wrote, "the business men of Chicago will furnish it." But the gathering Depression had a chilling effect even on this affluent crew, putting a crimp in Randolph's fund-raising. He would later estimate his total budget more conservatively at $350,000.

Most of the Six were Protestants; two were Sons of the American Revolution. Randolph was as close as Chicago came to old money, with roots stretching back to Virginia in the 1600s. His ancestors had lived next door to George Washington, and his family lent its name to Randolph Street in the Loop. As an upstanding native Chicagoan, Randolph took great offense at Capone—that "dirty, vicious killer"— becoming the face of his city.

"He doesn't belong to us," Randolph insisted, pointing out that Capone was a New Yorker born and bred.

But when Randolph called the gangster a "dago bootlegger," or referred to one of his own operatives as "a little 'Red' wop," he revealed his distaste for more than just Capone's Brooklyn background. Frank

Loesch, described by one observer as "a xenophobic bigot," made this explicit.

"The real Americans are not gangsters," claimed the man who not long ago asked Capone for a favor. "Recent immigrants and the first generation of Jews and Italians are the chief offenders, with the Jews furnishing the brains and the Italians the brawn."

Men like Randolph objected not only to Capone's illicit business, or to the threat he posed to their aboveboard ones, but to his very identity—the presence of this first-generation Italian-American in *their* city, *their* country.

Randolph remained the front man of the Secret Six, its only known member and chief booster. He denied the Six were in any way vigilantes. "We didn't choose to get into this," he said, "but we were forced into it. . . . We will resort to no extralegal methods and any talk of vigilants [*sic*] is ridiculous."

But at times he admitted his men employed "all sorts of devious and extra-legal means of securing information" because they were "forced to fight fire with fire"—a civilized alternative to lynch law, a release valve for the pent-up frustrations of a city sick and tired of slaughter.

"Even now," Randolph said in 1931, "it wouldn't take much effort to arouse the American Legion in Chicago to go down to Cicero one night and burn the place up and string the gangsters up on telegraph poles."

The Secret Six's original purpose was to hunt down the men who shot Meagher, but that fell quickly by the wayside. Their unnamed and unnumbered operatives began gathering all kinds of intelligence, offering rewards, paying off tipsters, even tapping phone lines.

"We wasted a lot of money," Randolph admitted, "because our best information was purchased from stool pigeons."

Their biggest operation seems to have been setting up a working speakeasy in Cicero as a listening post. The project cost about $12,000, but lasted only five or six months before the proprietor they hired skipped town. Whatever they learned they passed on to the authorities, especially John Swanson and George E. Q. Johnson. Those prosecutors—

understaffed, underfunded, and overworked—welcomed the help, and publicly aligned themselves with the Six. But desperation had driven them into a dangerous experiment, one they'd come to regret.

Randolph promoted the Six at every opportunity, writing, lecturing, liberally consenting to interviews. He seized upon the dramatic potency of its nickname to inflate the group into a fearsome intelligence agency that had the city's gangsters running scared. His claims didn't impress Chicago's hard-bitten reporters, but Randolph knew the real battle for Chicago's future lay with the American people.

"Give us the benefit of the doubt," he implored non-Chicagoans. "I assure you that when you come to Chicago . . . for the Century of Progress Exposition, you needn't bring a bodyguard with you. If you are timid, I will give you an escort from the Secret Six."

With the tax case against Ralph Capone coming up in the spring, George Johnson prepared a new line of attack. Bottles, as his nickname suggested, handled the Outfit's main source of revenue—beer distribution.

"Take their money away," Johnson told the *Tribune,* "and they dry up like a weed that has been cut down."

In early 1930, Alexander Jamie sent his special agents into Cicero to find out where Ralph got his booze. Jamie's right-hand man, Eliot Ness, led the charge.

Joining Ness were two other special agents who'd worked on the Heights case—bright, buoyant Marty Lahart and thirty-nine-year-old Samuel M. Seager.

Lahart's opposite in almost every way, the lanky, long-faced Seager served with distinction in the Great War, slogging through mud, rain, and heavy fire as his artillery company chased the Germans across France. Wounded in action, he never fully recovered. Back in the States, Seager—known by his middle name, Maurice—worked as a chiropractor and a prison guard before joining the Prohibition Bureau in June 1928.

Memories of death row, and perhaps the war, plagued Seager, giving him a perpetually downbeat cast. As an investigator, he was steadfast, dependable, and as sober as the driest dry. His only weakness, as far as Ness could tell, was a serious fear of germs that all but paralyzed him whenever he entered a hotel bathroom.

The special agents focused on three of Ralph's Cicero nightspots—the Cotton Club, the Greyhound Inn, and the Montmartre Café. These popular "whoopee" joints, known for some of the best jazz in Chicago, hired mostly African-American musicians but catered exclusively to whites. Bottles ran them with an iron fist.

"Ralph was always hitting porters and slapping people around," a musician recalled. "He wasn't very likable, as Al was. I never had any problems with Ralph, but you could see what he would do if some girl got out of line."

Each club had a round-the-clock, heavily armed guard. Pianist Luis Kutner remembered running into those watchdogs during a visit to the Greyhound with an unknown young singer. Chicago made Bing Crosby nervous, and what they found at the Greyhound didn't exactly put him at ease—Capone's "boys patrolling the streets armed to the teeth like a small army."

Crosby got out of the limousine and saw all the machine-gun-toting mugs and asked Kutner, "Is this a jazz joint or World War Two?"

Mounting a direct assault on any of Ralph's joints would be a waste of time—the next night, it would be doing business again. The clubs were more valuable open, anyway—as an information source.

Although Al got credit as an organizational wizard, Bottles kept things running behind the scenes, and—like any other business exec—couldn't do his job without the telephone. He spent much of each day taking orders, supervising distribution, and fielding customer complaints. Ness, Lahart, and Seager would turn that against him.

Wiretapping had been legalized only two years before, when the Supreme Court upheld the conviction of a Seattle bootlegger on wiretap evidence. The Court gave law enforcement permission to tap any phone line they wished, without asking for a warrant. And the feds wouldn't hesitate to use this new weapon against gangsters.

Ness's investigation hinged on wiretapping the Montmartre Café at 4835 West Twenty-Second Street. Despite the unassuming plain brick storefront with its large windows, and a neon sign inviting visitors to DINE and DANCE, the Montmartre served as Ralph's main headquarters. If the special agents could tap its phone line, they'd have a direct line into the clearinghouse for local liquor traffic.

Ness, Lahart, and Seager rented a basement apartment three blocks away, on the same phone circuit as the café. Now all they had to do was find the terminal box and link their line to Ralph's. But once they found it, they realized putting in a tap would be all but impossible.

The junction box sat high on a telephone pole behind the café in the alley, which Capone's gunmen patrolled at all hours. To make the tap, a lineman would have to scale the pole, open the box, and rack the entire board, checking each and every line.

The 150 lines weren't labeled; finding the right one took listening in for a voice the lineman recognized. Someone from the Prohibition Bureau would have to call the Montmartre and chat with whoever answered long enough for the tapper to find the right line. All the while, the lineman would be hanging there, an easy target for a tommy-gun-toting thug. The operation would simply take too much time—no one could climb up, make the tap, and get out fast enough to avoid being spotted.

"In desperation," Ness recalled, "I got my Cadillac touring car out, took down the top, and put my four biggest special agents in the car"—hoping the mob would mistake them for rival gangsters. Eliot's audacious plan was to have them drive around the café as slowly and suspiciously as possible, drawing the armed guards away from the alley.

That should give Ness and the lineman an opening to sneak in the alley and tap the wire. At a prearranged time, Ness's secretary would call the café and try to strike up a conversation with one of Ralph's men. By then, the lineman would have to be up the pole, ready to find her voice. If the guards didn't take the bait, if the secretary couldn't keep some guy on the line, if the lineman got to the box too late . . . the plan would fail.

And if Ness and his man were still in the alley when the guards came back, they just might end up dead.

One afternoon, probably in January or early February, the carload of special agents began conspicuously circling the block around the Montmartre in plain view of the pearl-hat hoods. Braving a Chicago winter in their open-topped car, they could hardly not be noticed by the gangsters. Ness waited and watched from afar, hoping the guards would fall for the ruse, but nothing. . . .

Finally, after about ten minutes, the hoods hopped in their own car and tailed the agents at a safe distance. Ness and the lineman rushed down the alley. The secretary would be calling any moment—every second lost raised their chance of discovery. The lineman, in a pair of climbing spikes, wrapped a leather strap around the pole and began clambering up. Ness remained at the base of the pole, eyes darting from the man above to the mouth of the alley, hand on the .38 in his topcoat pocket. But what good would a revolver do against a Thompson submachine gun?

Minutes crawled past. Ness kept checking his watch, counting seconds that felt like hours. Yet again, he glanced up at the man still searching for the right line.

"Suddenly he gave me the high sign that he had found it," Ness recalled. "The bridge was made and the telephone tap on the Cicero headquarters of the mob established."

The lineman shut the junction box and clambered down the pole. He and Ness hurried away.

"This tap was kept alive for many, many months," Ness recalled, "and we learned a great deal about the operations and personnel of the gang through it."

The rest of the investigation would be less nail-biting. After securing taps on Ralph's other Cicero operations, the special agents spent weeks at their respective listening posts, waiting by the phone. They passed the time as best they could till the phone started to buzz, a call coming in on one of Ralph's lines. Then they'd grab a pencil and listen in, jotting on a yellow legal pad. They processed hundreds of calls, many idle chatter. Ness, eager for action, chafed at being stuck in a Cicero basement apartment. But the more they listened, the more they learned about the Outfit's vast liquor racket.

Meanwhile, the Intelligence Unit kept running down leads from the records seized in Chicago Heights. Nels Tessem traced a $1,000 check made out to Frank Nitto back to the Schiff Trust and Savings Bank, where he found evidence of $742,887.81 in untaxed income. Nitto had made most of that money before 1927, with the three-year statute of limitations about to expire on March 15.

Shortly before the clock ran out, Johnson won a secret indictment against Nitto for income tax evasion. Somehow, the Enforcer got word and disappeared before the feds could arrest him. But Nitto's life, like Ralph's, had just become considerably more complicated.

Weekdays at seven A.M., as the nation's capital stirred, anyone passing by the White House would hear strange sounds from the south lawn—the voices of fifty- and sixty-year-old men, calling out like kids on a playground, laughing, shouting. The most powerful men in Washington—Herbert Hoover and his cabinet—were delighting in a new game the press called "Hoover-ball."

The paunchy commander in chief, not one to exercise for its own sake, enjoyed tossing around a six-pound sphere with his "Medicine Ball Cabinet." But between whoops of joy came weightier, decidedly joyless subjects, as even on the playing field, Hoover could not escape the economic blight sweeping across the country.

On Hoover's watch, the United States was transforming, and not for the better. Long lines of shabbily dressed men, overcoats tattered, fedoras battered, faces haggard, haunted city streets. Some sought shelter in boxcars, quickly renamed "Hoover Pullmans." Others inhabited metropolises of tarpaper shacks springing up in public parks, and empty lots, and on the outskirts of town—"Hoovervilles."

Chicago's own Hooverville appeared later that year, on the edge of Grant Park. The residents practiced what their mayor called "a sort of communistic government," sharing whatever they had and scrounging for sustenance amid the trash bins of nearby hotels. They even put up crudely lettered street signs; the mayor lived "at the corner of Prosperity Road and Easy Street," according to the *New York Times*.

"Building construction may be at a standstill elsewhere," he said, "but down here everything is booming."

The president, once renowned as a great humanitarian, seemed not to know what to make of it. Unwilling to give federal aid to the starving, he wrote, as if to explain the situation, that many citizens "left their jobs for the more profitable one of selling apples."

The deeper the Depression grew, the further Hoover divorced himself from reality. The day after the stock market crashed, Hoover proclaimed, "The fundamental business of the country . . . is on a sound and prosperous basis." Four months later, he assured the nation "that the worst effects of the crash" would pass within sixty days. In June 1930, he told a group of concerned citizens, "Gentlemen, you have come sixty days too late. The Depression is over."

The dour president spoke of prosperity, but no one could afford to buy it. One advisor wrote Hoover that summer, "I am sure that under present conditions you could not carry the election [today]. The public, generally speaking and without regard to party, thinks the administration to date has been a failure."

Hoover had come into office with the reputation of a man who could achieve almost anything; now his administration seemed capable of nothing. To turn things around, Hoover needed to show the American people that their government still worked; he had to prove that this onetime wonder worker could still achieve what seemed impossible.

Before the crash, Hoover had put in motion his program to reform the criminal justice system. His administration tapped the biggest names in law enforcement—among them August Vollmer and Frank Loesch—to serve on a national commission. Chaired by a former attorney general, the Wickersham Commission delivered its preliminary report on October 28, 1929—Black Monday, the day before the climax of the stock market crash. They kept on throughout the crisis, searching for meaningful solutions to the problems of Prohibition.

On March 15, Hoover welcomed commission member Frank Loesch to the White House. Loesch explained how crime had infected every level of his city—gangsters owning the cops and courts, the governor helpless. Only federal intervention could restore the city's ability to govern itself.

Loesch, of course, was hardly the first to make this argument. Only now, with his political future evaporating, did the president take a serious interest. And the media hysteria surrounding Capone's imminent release from prison in Pennsylvania finally pushed the president into action—he could not tolerate having such a flagrant criminal paraded before the public as a celebrity. Hoover knew convicting Capone would mean "much more than just sending a gangster to jail." Like the president himself, Capone had become a symbol of government ineptitude and incompetence, and the breakdown of the rule of law.

Hoover had always believed "the very essence of freedom is obedience to law; that liberty itself has but one foundation, and that is in the law." By this logic, Capone and his kind posed a direct threat to the American way of life. So did breadlines and the shantytowns, of course, but Hoover wasn't about to use his power to feed the hungry. He would, however, call up every legal means at his disposal to crack down on the country's most notorious ganglord. And he would do it to send a message—law still reigned supreme in the United States.

One day that spring, not long after his meeting with Loesch, the president brought a new issue to the Hoover-ball field. Every morning came a constant refrain, repeated until the members of his Medicine Ball Cabinet came to dread it: "Have you got Capone yet?"

Capone with Capt. John Stege, March 21, 1930. *(Author's Collection)*

Fifteen

December 1929–April 1930

Clerking in the library at Eastern State Penitentiary, Al Capone made a model prisoner. He stayed popular with his fellow cons, buying Christmas baskets for their families and supporting the arts and crafts program—sending $1,000 worth of fancy boxes, cigarette cases, wooden ships, and carved figurines as Christmas gifts to Outfit soldiers and friends. He saved one mother and her eight children from eviction by sending $200. Another woman accepted Capone's money to pay her hospital bills, but politely declined his offer of a job for her husband.

"I cannot estimate the money he has given away," said the prison board doctor who took out Al's tonsils. "Of course, we cannot inquire where he gets it."

Capone found a kind of freedom in custody, for once living without fear of "the lights going out." As one reporter put it, "He had peace of mind. He could sleep nights."

Reminded he had five bucks and a new suit coming on leaving prison, Capone said with a laugh he had ten new suits already. "Each one cost more than $100," he told a *Herald and Examiner* reporter, "and I don't owe any tailor bills."

Al had hoped to be out sooner, but wound up serving ten months with two months off for good behavior, finally set to leave on March 17. With hundreds of gawkers and reporters amassing outside the prison gate, Warden Herbert Smith was not about to let his model prisoner's ten uneventful months conclude as a press circus. A Philadelphia paper had made a headline story out of triggermen supposedly waiting to rub out the notorious ex-con—a high-profile murder could be terribly embarrassing to a warden.

So, on March 16, Capone and Frankie Rio were driven past the throngs in an unmarked car to another, newer facility, where the next day they were secretly released. Crowds milling overnight at Eastern State pen were outraged when they heard, accusing the warden of a payoff.

"You get the hell out of here," the warden told them, "and stay out."

Among those incensed was reporter Jake Lingle, a legman for the *Chicago Tribune*. Lingle had a singular, scoop-making relationship with both the Outfit and police, and his paper expected him to keep track of his friend, Capone. Yet the gangster left him holding the bag—literally, as Lingle waited for hours outside the prison with only his suitcase for company.

Back in Chicago, a miffed Lingle called Ralph Capone, who swore not to know Al's whereabouts. Really, Al was down the block in Cicero, at the Western Hotel—the renamed Hawthorne—on a bender, celebrating his release. Eliot Ness recalled his wiretap picking up Capone gunmen begging Ralph to come over and deal with his out-of-control brother.

Once sober, Capone set up a meeting with Captain John Stege of the Detective Bureau. Soon smiling businessman Al was wading with his counsel through sightseers and press in the headquarters lobby at Eleventh and State.

A reporter hurled a question on a new subject: "Did you pay your income tax this year? . . . You got out on March 17, two days after the last day to file your tax statement."

Capone's smile seemed to say he had.

Stege greeted the gangster by ordering him taken under police escort to the Federal Building. There, prosecutor George E. Q. Johnson said he wasn't yet prepared to take Capone into custody. Seemed State's

Attorney Swanson was not in, nor was his assistant and chief investigator, Pat Roche.

Hauled back to the Detective Bureau, Capone was questioned without press present. An account of the questions and answers was later provided by Stege and Assistant State's Attorney Harry Ditchburne.

Ditchburne asked Capone about the murders of those "seven Moran fellows" on Valentine's Day.

"I was in Florida then," Capone said.

"Yes," Stege said, "and you were in Florida, too, when Frank Yale was murdered in New York."

Capone said nothing.

After Ditchburne asked him again about both the massacre and the Yale murder, Capone replied, "I'm not as bad as I'm painted. . . . I get blamed for everything that goes on here, but I had nothing to do with any of the things you talk about."

Ditchburne said Capone's name was "synonymous with a large gang," assumed to be behind the murders in question.

Capone said he wasn't responsible for what others did.

"We have to protect the public," the assistant state's attorney said, "and such fellows as you must go. There used to be a time when we wouldn't have a hundred murders in ten years, but since you gangsters have been at war, we have had three hundred murders a year."

Stege put in: "That's why we are going to drive you out of town."

"But you haven't any right to arrest him," Capone's attorney objected, "unless you have evidence of some crime against him. You, Mr. Ditchburne, as a lawyer, know the police can't do that."

Ditchburne said, "I'm not interested in protecting Capone. If Capone feels that he is being arrested wrongfully he has his remedy. He can sue for false arrest."

Stege told Capone and his lawyer to go ahead and sue him—other gangsters had tried that and failed.

"I don't want to sue anybody," Capone insisted. "All I want is not to be arrested if I come downtown."

"You're out of luck," Stege replied. "Your day is done. How soon are you going to get out of town?"

Capone said he wanted to go to Florida sometime next week. "I don't know when I have to go to the federal court for trial on the contempt case."

Stege said, "I've given you notice now. You can go because no one wants to put a complaint against you today. But next time, you go into the lockup. . . . Be on your way."

Capone's attorney said, "Lenin and Trotsky and others rebelled against that kind of treatment."

Stege said, "I hope Capone goes to Russia."

But instead Capone went to his Lexington suite, to once again sit behind the massive mahogany desk with George Washington, Big Bill Thompson, and Abe Lincoln staring down approvingly. There he met with the *Tribune*'s Genevieve Forbes Herrick.

He told her he'd been imprisoned in "the City of Brotherly Love" not for carrying a gun, but because his name was Capone. His celebrity had cost him dearly. While he was inside, the Supreme Court ignored his writ of relief—would they have done that if he was "John Smith from Oshkosh"?

Then he pressed a buzzer and a young gent came in. "Please ask my wife and sister to come here," Capone told him.

Soon two women came in—willowy Mae Capone, pudgy Mafalda. Introductions were made, pleasantries exchanged, before the two women withdrew in "swirls of blue chiffon."

"Did you notice my wife's hair?" Capone asked the reporter, who said she had, calling it "lustrous and fluffy."

"No," Capone said. "I mean the streak of gray. She's only twenty-eight, and she's got gray hair, just worrying over things here in Chicago."

Mae was a month shy of thirty-three.

"Say, I'm only thirty-one," Capone went on, "and I've been blamed for crimes that happened as far back as the Chicago fire."

He complained of the "bum rap" blaming him for the Yale

murder—he'd been in his attorney's office at the time, "an iron-clad alibi." All he wanted to do was mind his own business, wind up his affairs in Chicago, and leave for his home in Miami.

When the reporter suggested Miami didn't seem particularly anxious to have him back, Capone laughed. "There's been a change of administrations since I was there last," he said. "The brother of one of the officials owns a paper there that's losing a thousand dollars a day. Naturally, they got to make news. . . . They got to sell papers."

As soon as Capone left the Eastern State pen, the Hoover administra-tion set out to put him back behind bars. On March 18, G. Aaron Youngquist, the mustachioed Swede who'd replaced Mabel Walker Willebrandt as assistant attorney general, began making noise about getting Capone indicted. First, he called the commissioner of Prohibition, who reported their agents had yet to find any evidence linking Capone to the liquor racket. Then he phoned George Johnson, who said beyond the contempt-of-court case, his office had yet to make any inroads.

"The difficulty seems to lie in the fact that Capone keeps himself two or three or four times removed from the actual operations," Youngquist observed. "In that situation it is almost impossible to procure evidence unless his henchmen will talk—and they won't."

While Youngquist made his calls, Assistant Secretary of the Treasury Walter Hope ordered a complete audit of Capone's tax history. The commissioner of Internal Revenue said Capone didn't have much *to* audit—he never filed a return—and while the Intelligence Unit had investigated him a year and a half ago, they'd found nothing to use in court. Much progress had been made toward jailing Ralph Capone (about to go on trial for tax evasion), Frank Nitto (in hiding from similar charges), and Jack Guzik (soon to face his own indictment); but Big Al remained out of reach.

That same day, the order "to proceed vigorously with the investigation of Al Capone" arrived at the office of Arthur P. Madden, special agent in charge of the Intelligence Unit in Chicago. Madden, who had long hoped to build a tax evasion case against Capone, met with Johnson and assistant prosecutor Dwight H. Green to draw up a plan of action. Madden knew the commissioner of Internal Revenue and the attorney general were interested in the Capone case. And word was the White House had "a desire to see it brought to an early conclusion."

But Madden also knew they couldn't wrap this case up quickly. Capone, he told a colleague, had "prepared himself for almost every contingency."

Nor could they expect any of Capone's partners to turn state's evidence. Ralph would never betray his brother, and Nitto, as Madden observed, "is the type of individual who would submit to a sentence of ten years in the penitentiary before he would inform on any of his associates."

To build a case, Madden needed a paper trail. So far, his men hadn't found one, with little hope they ever would.

From the earliest days of the income tax, Treasury had made a policy of not prosecuting evaders who admitted their mistakes and agreed to pay up. Elmer Irey himself had started this practice, believing "Treasury's prime function is to collect money for Uncle Sam, not to catch crooks." If Capone moved to settle, precedent said the case should stay out of court.

But, as Irey freely admitted, this was "custom, not law." Nothing would prevent the feds from prosecuting Capone if he admitted, in a settlement offer, he hadn't paid his taxes.

Capone seemed willing to take that chance. The indictments against Ralph, Nitto, and other gangsters had left him deeply concerned and desperate to settle. So he tried to do what he always did—smooth problems over with money—as if the government were just waiting for a payoff, like everybody else.

While in prison, Capone retained the services of Johnny Torrio's tax lawyer, Lawrence P. Mattingly. Soon after Capone's release, Mattingly reached out to the Intelligence Unit, hinting his client would happily pay any tax debt If the government promised not to prosecute.

Once again, Capone was demanding the government treat him like just another businessman. Internal Revenue had settled with scores of other tax cheats. Why not him?

Of course the feds had no intention of settling; they wanted Capone in jail. And now they had him in a bind—he could decide not to settle, and risk investigators finding evidence of his income. Or he could keep trying to cut a deal.

The only way Mattingly could dispose of the case was to file returns. But in doing so, he would be furnishing evidence the government could use in prosecuting Capone for delinquency.

By holding out the promise of clemency, the tax men were luring Capone right into a prison cell.

Capone met with the feds in Chicago on April 17.

Before the stenographer began taking notes, C. W. Herrick, head of the Chicago Internal Revenue office, advised Capone "any statement you make here will naturally be the subject of such investigation and verification as we can make; that is, in the nature of income or anything of that sort."

Herrick wrapped up with, "And I think it is only fair to you to say that any statements which are made here, which could be used against you, would probably be used. I want you to know your rights."

At that moment Capone and Mattingly should have found the door. Mattingly did say he wouldn't allow Capone to testify in a way that might imply criminal activity. But after Herrick's statement, anything spoken of substance would indeed contribute to the ongoing investigation.

Still, Capone gave little away, frequently deferring to his attorney.

Herrick asked, "How long, Mr. Capone, have you enjoyed a large income?"

Capone said, "I never had much of an income, a large income."

"I will state it a little differently—an income that might be taxable?"

"I would rather let my lawyer answer that question."

Capone did admit to contributing some currency when Mae bought the Florida place, but said he used only cash day to day, with no checking account, no business, no property. This was essentially an admission of income during the time in question.

Once Capone and the government steno had left the room, Mattingly told the tax men, "Mr. Capone owes some tax, and Mr. Capone wants to pay it."

This off-the-record appeal only offered further proof of his client's guilt—dealing openly with the feds just dug Capone in deeper.

The attorney suggested Uncle Sam act promptly, because right now Mr. Capone was in a position to pay. Of course, the government had an entirely different idea of how he might pay.

On March 22, film star Adolphe Menjou stopped briefly in Chicago on his way from France to Los Angeles. With only a few hours to spend in town, Menjou had one item on his itinerary.

"Where can I find Al Capone?" he asked.

The actor might have been directed to one of the tour buses taking sightseers past Capone's old haunts in Cicero.

Two days later, paving the way for Gandhi and Stalin, Capone made the cover of *Time* magazine, the first American mobster to do so. The honor was somewhat lessened by the caption inserting *"Scarface"* between *Alphonse* and *Capone*.

"No desperado of the old school is 'Scarface Al,' plundering or murdering for the savage joy of crime," *Time* reported. "He is, in his own phrase, 'a business man' who wears clean linen, rides in a Lincoln car, leaves acts of violence to his hirelings. He has an eleven-year-old son noted for his gentlemanly manners." *Time* balanced Capone's domesticity with his career, minus the carnage. Al was credited with forging peace at Atlantic City, and the article closed with an allusion to his Florida problems.

On March 19, the governor of that state, Doyle E. Carlton, banished Capone. Police departments and sheriff's offices got the order, some by telegram: "Arrest [Capone] promptly if he comes your way and escort him to State borders with instructions not to return."

"And all I've ever done in Miami," Capone once said, "was to spend my money there."

He also turned his Palm Island manse into an Outfit clubhouse with the welcome mat out for crooks, making him unpopular with certain neighbors. The more proper sector of society did not appreciate Capone's men, their wild parties, wild women, and fishing expeditions where rods replaced rod-and-reels. Even so, the outgoing Capone mixed well with elements of the Miami social set—the slick hustlers and smiling grifters who'd always been part of the city's rise from the swamps. And local businesses—especially casinos—had no problem in these Depression times with a high roller like Capone.

As the *Miami Daily News* put it, "Our people have favored a liberal policy for winter months," tourists enjoying the city's wide-open gambling and illegal liquor.

But the pressure came less from blue noses and more from the corrupt likes of political fixers and newspaper publishers who preferred local sellers of sin to outsiders like the Italian Capone. Fear that Chicago gangsters would take over was understandable if largely unfounded—Capone's investments in Miami vice were minor, including interests in local speakeasies, an Everglades casino, and the Miami Beach Kennel Club.

The remedy to this paranoia was a campaign encouraging Capone to leave Florida. So the day after the governor's wire to the state's sheriffs, a raid seemed in order.

The sheriff, several of his deputies, and the county prosecutor himself all came loaded for bear, but no one was home except the caretaker.

Some whiskey, wine, and champagne bottles clearly intended for home use were seized; five people staying at the estate were off swimming. The returning bathers were arrested, including Capone brothers Ralph and Albert, and Jack McGurn, no machine gun in sight. Charges were later dismissed, though a fine was paid on the liquor.

When a petition from Miami Beach protested "the invasion of Al Capone," a neighbor on Palm Island stood up in the gangster's defense. "Al Capone's the best protection we can have on Palm Island," he said. "As long as he's here there'll be no trouble."

On March 22, the Capone attorneys won a temporary restraining order protecting their client from arrest for just being in Florida. The governor wasn't having any: "He may for a time wrap about himself the technicalities of the law, but he will not establish headquarters in Florida."

Capone, arriving in Miami on April 20, told the press, "I have no interest in politics, either in Chicago or Miami. I am here for the rest I think I deserve, and all I ask is to be left alone. I have done nothing in violation of the law in Miami and I will not."

On April 22, the local state's attorney sued to padlock the Palm Island estate as a public nuisance—"the scene of repeated liquor law violations . . . frequented by law violators . . . habitual loafers, illegal dealers in liquor, and gamblers."

Accompanied by Mae, Sonny, and brother Albert, Capone came to court on April 26 to contest the padlock petition.

"Capone is charged with no crime," his attorney argued. "He is not under indictment and has a perfect right to live in Florida."

"It is no crime for rattlesnakes to live," replied the prosecutor, "but if you were to keep rattlesnakes in your backyard where they would be dangerous to your children and your neighbors, they should be exterminated."

In later proceedings, the state's attorney would argue Capone's "reign of terror" in Miami had negatively impacted property values.

While his attorneys fought for him in court, Al took a Havana getaway with *Chicago Evening American* editor Harry Read, brothers Albert and John, his doctor, a lawyer, and two bodyguards. At the Sevilla Biltmore, some of the entourage signed the register with false names, though impudently Capone did not. They spent their first day in a third-floor suite, handing out $5 tips to waiters, barbers, and manicurists, before indulging in the pleasures of Cuba.

Back in Miami by early May, Capone, his brother John, a visiting Chicago alderman, and a bodyguard decided to take in a matinee of a Fu Manchu movie starring Warner Oland. But as they drove toward the theater, they encountered two police detectives ordered to arrest Capone on sight.

Al asked to see their warrant, but the cops didn't have one. Instead, they took the whole entourage to the station, where the ganglord asked to call his lawyers. The police refused. Capone tried to win their sympathy by falling back on a familiar lie—that he'd served in the Great War.

"I was in the army, too," the police chief told him. "Don't talk to me. Shut up."

Al insisted his brother be released, and demanded a receipt for his valuables; neither request was granted. According to Capone, Director of Public Safety Samuel D. McCreary ordered the police chief to file the gangster's things "in the shit house." Then McCreary took their guest to a windowless cell and told him he would be arrested whenever he showed his face in Miami.

"I asked him even if my mother and wife and kid was there would he pick me up," Capone recalled, "and he said he would. I said, 'If you was me what would you do?' He said, 'I would not want to be you.'"

The safety director ordered the prisoner be kept isolated, prevented from contacting anyone, and denied food and blankets.

"I wonder how he would feel," Capone huffed, "without no blankets."

When lawyers arrived to spring him, things got physical. The police, under orders to search anyone visiting Capone, sent one attorney fleeing the station, chasing him down the block before hauling him back for a frisk. The circus finally ended in court with the judge tossing out the charges.

But Capone's attorneys failed to get an injunction requiring a warrant for any arrest of Al Capone, the judge preferring to rule on any such violations as they came. And the violations came, all right.

On May 13, the day after a grand jury report blamed him for dragging their city down to Chicago's level, Capone and three companions were arrested at a boxing match and jailed overnight, where after some huffing and puffing Al settled in to play cards with his cellmates.

On May 19, at another boxing match, he was arrested for the third time in ten days, getting off on a $100 bond.

Back in Miami, Capone's lawyers charged Director of Public Safety McCreary with false imprisonment for the May jailing. The judge told McCreary if this harassment continued, he would toss the director in jail.

Elsewhere, the Miami city commissioners were harassing Capone as well, coming up with a new law defining an illegal vagrant as anyone "having some visible means of support acquired by unlawful or illegal means or methods."

Capone himself did his best to appear normal—a legitimate businessman, a family man. He and his boy really did have a warm, loving relationship, with father-and-son fishing trips, afternoons swimming and loafing around the pool, evenings playing board games, listening to music, while Mae sat by quietly approving.

When his son's Miami schoolmates begged for a swim in the family's Palm Island pool, Al and Mae—with written parental permissions—entertained fifty of Sonny's friends.

"The lawns were decorated," the *Chicago Tribune* reported, "and fried chicken, cake, soda pop, balloons and noise makers were provided the youngsters, who spent the afternoon splashing in the pool and romping over the terraces."

Perhaps the success of the swimming party inspired Capone to mount a banquet (sans baseball bats) for a select fifty of Miami society. His chef, formerly of Colosimo's, put on a sumptuous spread, portraying the host not as a beast but a gourmand. The number of invitations accepted to the evening of dining and music was not made public, nor the guest list itself, and those who attended weren't talking.

On June 10, a judge heard the prosecution's pathetic case as to why Capone should be denied access to his own home. Seemed guests had been served alcohol—not a crime under Prohibition. Another prosecution witness, the president of a major Miami department store (who'd apparently attended the recent banquet), said he too had seen alcohol served. Also, some of the guests were not entirely sober. Imagine!

The department store magnate said some of Capone's associates had asked his help breaking their boss into polite society. But the witness—also president of the local country club—admitted Capone was not welcome among Miami's upper crust. The members at his club wouldn't even discuss the matter.

"Why not?" asked Capone's attorney.

"It wouldn't do," the witness replied. "He is what we call a gangster."

Capone clearly took great offense at this, sitting forward, muttering to himself.

Other witnesses described Capone as a risk to their community—armed men patrolled the gangster's estate.

"He harbors people who are dangerous to us," said a local real estate developer. "I want to live in peace and quiet, not among gangsters."

On June 14, the judge dismissed the case. But similar courtroom harassment would continue.

Yet Capone never lost his affection for his southern home.

"I like Florida," he said. "I like it here because it's different. I want a home for my people. I want a place for my mother, my wife, my boy . . . and my friends. Why shouldn't a fellow have a place where he can go when he's tired?"

Even after convincing President Hoover to bring the full might of the federal government down on Capone, Frank Loesch had lost none of his determination to personally make life miserable for Chicago's gangsters. He took particular offense at known criminals walking the streets of his city without fear of arrest and conceived a means of bringing their liberty to an end.

In April, Loesch asked Col. Henry Barrett Chamberlin—the Crime Commission's gaunt, aristocratic operating director—for "a list of the outstanding hoodlums" who were known, but unproven, murderers.

Chamberlin came up with one hundred or so names, which Loesch whittled down to twenty-eight. Naturally, Capone made the list, as did his brother Ralph, Jack Guzik, Frankie Rio, and Jack McGurn. So did two of Capone's biggest rivals, Joe Aiello and Bugs Moran, though the latter had already passed the peak of his power. Yet Loesch left off some of the prime movers in Chicago's gang scene—notably Frank Nitto, whose influence in the Outfit continued to grow.

On April 23, Loesch sent his list to George Johnson, State's Attorney John Swanson, and other Chicago officials. He outlined all the ways these gangsters could be harassed—from arrest, raids, and deportations to publishing their home addresses and investigating their income tax.

"The purpose," Loesch said, "is to keep the light of publicity shining on Chicago's most notorious gangsters," to subject them to "constant observation" by law enforcement, and discourage "law abiding citizens" from "dealing with those who are constantly in conflict with the law."

Chamberlin put the matter bluntly to the *Herald and Examiner*: "Gangsters must be made to understand Chicago will not tolerate them. This plan will do that. We'll arrest them and jail them and subject them to expenses for counsel until they're so sick of it they will leave."

But to win the kind of publicity Loesch and Chamberlin hoped for, the Crime Commission needed something catchy the newspapers couldn't resist. Several lackluster phrases were floated. Finally the *Tribune* hit the bull's-eye with its banner headline of April 24: LIST 28 AS "PUBLIC ENEMIES."

The *New York Times* ran an almost identical headline that same day—soon the one-two punch would be drummed into the American psyche.

"The phrase 'public enemies' caught the popular fancy at once," one gangland observer wrote. Newspapers ran with it; books and movies turned it into a national catchphrase. And all that publicity gave these gangsters the wrong kind of celebrity.

No one suffered more from the bad press than Capone, who'd taken such pains to project himself as the public's friend, servant of anybody who wanted a good time. "I never heard of anyone being forced to go to a place to have some fun," Capone said. "I have read in the newspapers, though, of bank cashiers being put in cars, with pistols stuck in their slats, and taken to the bank, where they had to open the vault for the fellow with the gun."

Al wondered if taking a drink was really worse than robbing a bank.

But the "public enemies" list did away with any distinction between outlaws and gangsters. "Public enemy" became indelibly linked with Capone, and the Crime Commission kept up the heat by doing everything they could to tarnish his reputation.

They cast Capone as the enemy of the very public he always claimed to serve. And not just any enemy, but the one who outshone them all. "Capone is the most dangerous, the most resourceful, the most cruel, the most menacing, the most conscienceless of any criminal of modern times," Chamberlin said. "He has contributed more to besmirch the fair name of Chicago than any man living or dead."

Initially, the "public enemies" list was not numbered or ranked. The *Tribune* printed it in alphabetical order, while the *Herald and Examiner,* bowing to Capone's celebrity, put him first. Soon the *Trib* began calling him "the chief public enemy" and "the No. 1 public enemy."

Over time, the phrase would revise itself into an enduring nickname for the gangster, rivaling even "Scarface." Unlike that hated sobriquet, this new designation demanded action, casting Capone as an all-American villain who cried out for someone to take him down. Other crooks would assume the mantle in later years, but Capone would be the first—and most notorious—"Public Enemy Number One."

State Street in the Loop, 1930. *(Library of Congress)*

Sixteen

March–June 1930

Through the winter and into the spring, raids by police and State's Attorney John Swanson choked the flow of liquor into Chicago.

"Beer deliveries have fallen off almost 90 percent," a reporter revealed shortly before Capone's release from the Pennsylvania pen. "The hard liquor business is in almost as bad a condition." The impact of the Depression on many Capone customers added to the downturn.

"Capone," the reporter wrote, "will return to find his business just about paying expenses."

Eliot Ness and the other special agents keeping tabs on the wiretaps in Cicero heard plenty of proof the Outfit was short on booze. The bootleggers knew their phones might be tapped, so much of the time they stayed vague about their product, referring simply to "bum stuff" or "good stuff." But they couldn't hide the fact they rarely had enough stuff, good or bad, to meet demand.

"Have you got any? . . . Are you going to have any or not?" asked a bootlegger named Vic, in a conversation Maurice Seager recorded on February 24.

"I don't know yet," the other man said.

When Vic called back later, a different bootlegger, Dutch, picked up the phone. Ness had taken over the listening post, and he heard Vic complain about his lot in life.

"I'm in a swell spot now," Vic said.

"Why," Dutch asked, "what's the matter?"

"My joints ain't working and somebody else is making all the dough. . . . I ought to have my head examined."

"Well, you'll smarten up some day."

Monitoring these taps brought Ness into a strange intimacy with the men he hunted. Listening in on the Montmartre line, Ness heard one gangster brag to another about a gang rape.

"Well," Ness recalled the man saying, "we settled Miss High-Hat's hash last night. She wouldn't go for so-and-so, would she? Well eighteen of us showed her how wrong she was."

This conversation stuck in Ness's memory for the rest of his life, helping shape his understanding of the criminal mind.

"The criminal, you see, has time on his hands," Ness explained. "He hasn't respect for one kind of law—be it gambling or bootlegging—and he won't have respect eventually for any kind of law."

At other times, the bootleggers spoke like working stiffs, complaining about customers and bosses, joking about drunken escapades, hinting they'd like a new career. They spoke in insider lingo, coded or nearly so, which the agents sometimes struggled to interpret.

Yet guns and liquor filtered easily into their talk, the way butchers speak of cleavers and meat. Even plotting violence, they could be remarkably banal.

Maurice Seager recorded a conversation between Dutch and a man named Pete.

"Say, Dutch," Pete asked, "I want to collect a bill in East St. Louis, have you got anyone there?"

"I might have, how much is it?"

"Thirty-eight hundred—it's not a legitimate bill, you know, the guy is a businessman, he sells what we do."

"Will I get $800 if I get it?"

"Yes," Pete assured him, "if you get the guy here, we will make him pay."

"All right, when you get here, we will talk about it."

Then Pete casually switched the conversation to weapons. "Say," he asked, "have you got the little one there?"

"No, Little Mike took it. I let him."

"I mean the sawed-off one."

"Yes, I know, Little Mike has it."

"What have you got?"

"My own, the one I always carry."

Other wiretapped conversations revealed the tight links between crime and politics.

One bootlegger asked another to "help their man who is running for Congress." Ness recalled hearing gangsters discuss two candidates for office, one a reform candidate, the other a well-known Capone ally. The reformer, Ness learned, was secretly working with the Outfit. No matter who won the election, Capone couldn't lose.

Nor would the Big Fellow suffer much from the latest spate of raids. The hardship fell mostly on low-level suppliers, while corruption kept their bosses well insulated.

One afternoon, as Marty Lahart listened in on the Greyhound Inn line, someone delivered a whispered warning of an impending raid: "The state's attorney is on the way."

Lahart hurried to the club as cars pulled away just before the raiders arrived. Didn't take much of a detective to figure out the Outfit had a leak in the state's attorney's office, or that Swanson's raids wouldn't drive Capone out of business anytime soon.

Even with all this heat, Ralph had little sympathy for men who couldn't deliver. On March 11, shortly after 11:00 P.M., "Barnback" phoned Ralph's office in search of product.

"Say, I'm out of beer and got a party here," Barnback said. "I need some right away."

"All right," Ralph's man replied, "I'll go right away."

"Make it snappy. I'm all out."

Fifteen minutes later, Ralph's man called Barnback. "Say, I was going out for some beer," he said, "but [Bottles] don't want to let me go. He's raising hell."

Before Barnback could respond, Ralph grabbed the phone. "Say, what's the matter with you fellows?" he demanded. "Can't you take care of that place?"

"Let me explain."

"Explain nothing."

"Goldie had the ticket, but he was off today."

They were speaking in bootlegger code, but Ralph's nastiness needed no translation.

"You're not going to get it," he snarled.

"Let me explain, Ralph."

But Ralph had already hung up.

Barnback kept trying till 1:00 A.M., getting nowhere with Ralph, who was still "raising hell," according to his man. The product-needy caller's problem remained unsolved, but the special agents had solved theirs—the boss was on record admitting his role in an illegal enterprise. The transcript went into their growing conspiracy file.

They also listened in as Bottles spoke with his lawyer, George Murdock, about the impending tax trial. As an afterthought, Ralph asked Murdock to help "fix up" that year's tax returns. If nothing else, Al's brother had finally learned the importance of paying Uncle Sam his slice.

Still, when Judge James H. Wilkerson brought him to trial on April 9, Ralph felt shocked, even ambushed.

"This is Jim," a voice said, in a call Seager overheard that evening. "Did you see what they did to Ralph?"

"Why no," said a feminine voice. "Was he hurt?"

"Oh no, in court, they double-crossed him," the caller said. "It was supposed to be all fixed up and they pulled a jury on him this morning." In gangster-speak, *jury* might have been a concealed weapon.

"Why, the rotten skunks."

"He is liable to get from three to ten years and a $10,000 fine."

"Isn't that a shame."

Murdock's rather lame defense insisted his client rushed to pay his back taxes as soon as illegal income became taxable—seemed as a "poor race-horse man," Ralph couldn't afford to settle up. The life of a gambler, after all, came with constant financial upheaval.

The prosecutors brought in reams of evidence attesting to Ralph's wealth. They ran through all the checks, deposit slips, and aliases the Intelligence Unit had uncovered. Witnesses testified Ralph sold beer—real beer, not the watered-down legal stuff he peddled mostly as a cover. Workmen wheeled piled bank records into the courtroom on hand trucks.

"What are those?" Judge Wilkerson asked, as another hand truck rolled in.

"More records," a prosecutor said.

The end came April 25. After two and a half hours, the jury found Ralph guilty on all counts. Bottles had finally surpassed his brother, becoming the first Chicago gangster ever convicted on tax charges. Shaken by the verdict, he strained to smile as he left the courtroom.

Federal officials rejoiced. Assistant Treasury Secretary Walter Hope forwarded a clipping on the conviction to President Hoover: "The enclosed represents a little progress even though the chief offender still goes unapprehended." At a press conference not long after, Hoover said his administration planned to use Ralph's conviction as the springboard to "reach" his more notorious brother.

Meanwhile, Youngquist kept pestering George Johnson to go after Capone, but Johnson refused to be rushed—he had "many lengthy cases" he refused to compromise, and Capone had been delayed accordingly. To speed things up and clear the backlog, Johnson asked the Justice Department to send more judges. That wasn't what Youngquist wanted to hear, and he made sure the president knew the delay wasn't his fault.

"I impressed upon [Johnson] the one big job was to convict Al Capone for violation of the law," Youngquist told Hoover, adding, "I wanted you to know we are keeping after it."

Despite a clogged caseload, Johnson wasn't finished with Ralph. By early May, Alexander Jamie and the special agents had linked Bottles to a massive international smuggling plot.

Most Canadian booze came into the country by truck or boat, but the Capones had adopted a new vehicle, the airplane. Six times a week, their men flew cases of Johnnie Walker and Old Smuggler, worth $50 in Canada, from Windsor, Ontario, to an airfield near Cicero. When the planes touched down, the liquor's value doubled. The Outfit had smuggled in about fourteen thousand cases over the past eight months, with a street value of $1.4 million. Then they cut the liquor with pure alcohol and artificial flavors, stretching profits even further. They may also have been smuggling drugs by air.

Jamie raided the Cotton Club and Greyhound Inn in the early morning hours of May 8. First the special agents hit the Cotton Club, well-dressed patrons packing the place as the feds stormed in, creating chaos. But the lawmen left the customers alone, arresting only employees and seizing some important-looking records.

The raiders moved on to the Greyhound Inn, where they arrested a waiter and a bartender. Ralph was conspicuously absent, but his attorney called Jamie later that day and promised to bring his client in for arraignment.

Just hours after Bottles left the Federal Building, the special agents struck again. This time Ness led his own raid on the Cotton Club, hitting it at its peak capacity. Club manager Percy Haller, arrested in the earlier raid, lost his patience. As Ness picked up a highball and went to pour it into an evidence bottle, Haller knocked the glass out of his hand, and got taken in for resisting a federal officer and obstruction of justice.

On May 28, the grand jury handed down indictments against Ralph, Haller, and seven associates, including a doorman at the Cotton Club known only as "Rasputin," on conspiracy to violate the Volstead Act. Under the newly enacted Jones Law, mandating stiffer sentences for Prohibition violations, Ralph faced five years in prison and a $10,000 fine.

But these cases would never go to trial. From Johnson's point of view, the potential result wasn't worth the Herculean effort. Until he got his wish for more judges, he had to think carefully about where to invest precious time and resources.

Johnson already had Ralph on tax charges, and the chances of convicting him again seemed slim—juries rarely found anyone guilty of bootlegging. And with the Hoover administration clamoring to bag Ralph's younger brother, harassing the gangsters and exposing their secrets seemed enough—for now.

With these parallel investigations into Ralph's affairs, Johnson had developed the strategy he would use against Capone. While the Intelligence Unit worked to build another tax case, Jamie's special agents would smash the Outfit's breweries and distilleries, bedeviling the gang and drying up its income.

Jamie's men would also gather evidence for more liquor conspiracy cases, because whether investigators could hang a tax evasion charge on Capone remained to be seen. Ralph had left no shortage of evidence of tax fraud, but his brother had been much more careful. Johnson needed to keep his options open.

In mid-June, Judge Wilkerson sentenced Ralph Capone to three years in prison and a $10,000 fine. Bottles got out on bond, pending appeal.

As the marshals led him away, someone heard Al's brother remark, "I don't understand this at all."

He'd sounded tougher on the phone, pushing underlings around.

"There is nothing of much interest to report in connection with the Al Capone investigation," Art Madden, special agent in charge of the Chicago Intelligence Unit, wrote to Elmer Irey shortly after Ralph's conviction.

Madden had a hunch Capone took a share of the proceeds from the Hawthorne Kennel Club, a Cicero dog-racing track, but couldn't prove it. Profits from the track passed through the Roosevelt Finance Company, a money-laundering operation run by Frank Nitto's old associate, Alex Greenberg. After that, the trail grew muddy.

"As a matter of fact," Madden wrote, "there is fairly convincing proof that substantial sums were paid to Frank Nitto, who is one of the principals in the Capone organization." To gather more evidence, Madden intended to question "the head of the dog track, a man named O'Hare," who had "already been before the Grand Jury." Madden advised "a more determined effort" be made against this O'Hare.

The special agent didn't know it yet, but he'd found the lead that would break the case wide open. The man he knew as the "head of the dog track" was Edgar Joseph O'Hare, a fast-talking, clean-living lawyer from St. Louis. Charming, cultured, and athletic, O'Hare was a family man who doted on his only son, Edward, nicknamed "Butch."

As an attorney, O'Hare had come to control the patent on the mechanical rabbit used in dog races, soon growing wealthy licensing the device to racetracks. His success caught the eye of the Outfit, which liked dog racing because it was easy to fix. All they had to do was overfeed the dogs they wanted to lose.

The Outfit opened its own track in Cicero near one run by O'Hare, without paying for use of his rabbit, hoping to run him out of business. The spunky lawyer threatened legal action.

"If I can't operate in Chicago," he warned the gangsters, "then nobody can."

Capone, perhaps impressed by the entrepreneur's pluck, offered a partnership. O'Hare accepted, Nitto working out the deal. They'd all earn a fortune, but O'Hare made a show of scorning his partners. "You can make money through business associations with gangsters," he claimed, "and you will run no risk if you don't associate personally with them. Keep it on a business basis and there's nothing to fear."

To his daughter, O'Hare declared, "I have never accepted so much as a bottle of beer from the gangsters with whom I must do business because one cannot accept anything, no matter how small. . . . If you do, they have you."

Despite his lily-white front, O'Hare was no angel. An exceedingly sharp slickster, he possessed an unmatched talent for finding holes in the law, earning the nicknames "Fast Eddie" and "Artful Eddie."

He also had a history of double-crossing his friends. In the early 1920s, O'Hare partnered with George Remus, the nation's most successful bootlegger, in purchasing a Jack Daniel's distillery in St. Louis. Remus doled out whiskey "for medicinal purposes," while secretly diverting much of it into the illegal beverage market—essentially stealing from himself.

But "Artful Eddie" did him one better. While Remus was in prison, O'Hare siphoned off some thirty thousand gallons of his partner's whiskey and sold it to bootleggers in New York and Chicago, filling the emptied barrels with water. Remus learned of this when O'Hare was indicted on Prohibition charges, and his testimony helped get "Fast Eddie" convicted in 1926.

True to his nickname, O'Hare squirmed out of serving time, paying Remus $250,000 for the looted liquor, after which Remus withdrew his testimony, winning O'Hare a reversal on appeal. Then O'Hare reportedly cut Remus in on the profits from Capone's dog track.

Madden and the Intelligence Unit tried unsuccessfully to trace those profits back to Capone.

Then on May 9, Madden informed Irey about government securities the Roosevelt Finance Company had passed through to Capone. Madden was convinced O'Hare was the source—prove that, and they had the makings of a case against Capone, a real paper trail to big income the Big Fellow paid no tax on.

But before the tax men could act, a pair claiming to be government agents raided the Roosevelt Finance Company and seized all important records. Then the "agents" disappeared, taking with them evidence crucial to the government's case, and any hope of linking Capone to that line of income.

Undeterred, Madden focused squarely on O'Hare, telling Irey he wanted to look into the lawyer's tax situation. Irey met with his superiors, who found this lead promising enough to put their best investigator on the case—Frank John Wilson, forty-two, special agent with the Intelligence Unit out of Baltimore.

Wilson had already worked in Chicago, building tax cases against bootleggers Terry Druggan and Frankie Lake. On a recent visit, he'd helped comb through Ralph Capone's bank records, and sat in on a meeting with Mattingly discussing brother Al's tax situation.

Irey knew this agent—relentless and determined, as cold and gray as a January day—was the only person who could follow the money from O'Hare to Capone. "Wilson fears nothing that walks," Irey wrote, nor did tedium deter him: "He will sit quietly looking at books eighteen hours a day, seven days a week, forever, if he wants to find something in those books."

Wilson's doggedness sprang from the frustration of failed ambition. His father had been a cop, and Frank wanted nothing more than to be one, too. But, severely nearsighted, he couldn't be trusted with a gun—bad eyes bounced him out of the army, and during the Great War he'd settled for working as an investigator with Herbert Hoover's Food Administration.

Did Wilson feel the need to compensate—to be tougher, rougher, and stronger than anyone on the battlefield? Perhaps. In the Intelligence Unit, his ruthlessness, and not just his financial acumen, set him apart. One colleague said, if so assigned, "Wilson would investigate his own grandmother." A crook who had the misfortune of crossing Wilson's path said the investigator "sweats ice water."

Yet the balding, bespectacled, somewhat stocky Wilson might have been an insurance salesman. He spoke stiffly in flat, nasal tones and smoked cheap cigars, shrouding himself in a foul haze. When he threatened to use his "regulation forty-five," he meant the forty-fifth volume of Internal Revenue regulations, not his sidearm.

Wilson knew how to break men down psychologically—to bru-

talize them not with fists, but with facts. And he never let up till he
got what he wanted. Seeing Wilson in action, Adela Rogers St. Johns
wrote, "A year—ten years—twenty years—you would never be safe,
never be out of reach. . . . You could no more shake him nor reflect
upon his honesty or his sureness of his facts than you could melt a
glacier with a blow torch."

Wilson took charge of the Capone tax case in late May, after arriving in Chicago with his wife, Judith. He made sure she had no idea
why they were in town.

"There are some things you can tell a woman," Wilson wrote, typically for his era, "and some things you can't."

Not wanting to worry her—or, worse, have her drag him back to
Baltimore—he lied about the case, saying only that he'd been ordered
to start "investigating some politicians."

Then Wilson set out to get the lay of the land. Early on he learned
that Alfred "Jake" Lingle, a crime reporter for the *Tribune,* knew more
about the Outfit's operations than just about anyone outside the organization. It was said Lingle counted Capone as a personal friend—
though at present the two were on the outs. Wilson sensed a potentially
valuable informant. In early June, he met with an attorney and an editor at the *Tribune,* who offered to put him in touch with the legman.

Wilson had his first major lead.

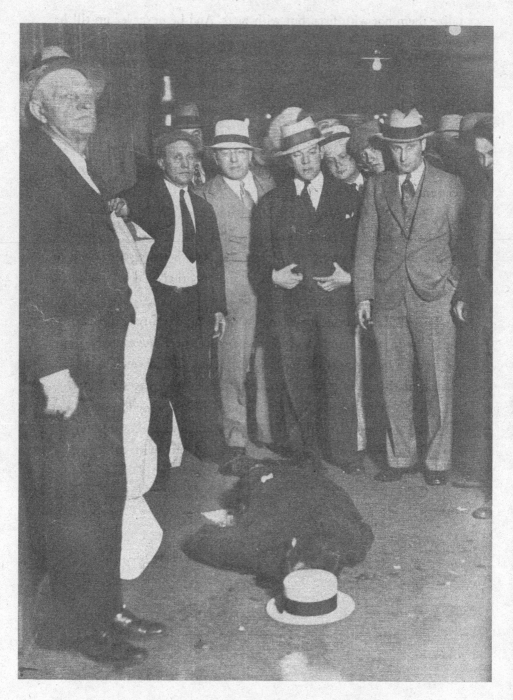

Jake Lingle's final scoop, June 9, 1930. *(Authors' Collection)*

Seventeen

June–August 1930

Chicago's train stations were often grand, but not Randolph Street Station, where the Illinois Central Railroad joined commuter lines to the South Side and working-class suburbs where the Outfit provided beer, gambling, and women.

To access Randolph Street Station, you disappeared down a wide stairwell outside Chicago's main Public Library, a splendid stone edifice with marble interiors—but the reading material chosen by commuters more likely came from the large newsstand nearby. This was where, on June 9, 1930, *Tribune* reporter Jake Lingle, thirty-eight, on his way to catch an early afternoon train, paused to make a selection from rival papers, racing forms, and pulp magazines.

A former street kid with an elementary school education, reporter Lingle never wrote a word for publication—that was left to rewrite men. From a childhood friendship with beat cop Bill Russell, Jake picked up an easy way with police and their subculture, which proved invaluable as he worked his way up from office boy to budding crime reporter. He would drop by station houses and trade cheap cigars for tips.

"He knew all the coppers by their first names," Fred Pasley wrote. "He spent his spare time among them. He played penny-ante with them. He went to their wakes and funerals; their weddings and christenings."

As his closeness with the police grew, so did an acquaintance with "that nether stratum of society, the underworld." Lingle met these tough boys in cells and poolrooms and speaks, on good terms with many, including the bosses. They became an inside source of gangland gossip.

Once on a streetcar with his fiancée, he was jostled and knew right away his wallet was gone; but he also knew just what West Madison Street bar to go to, to retrieve it.

He retained a street kid's charm throughout his *Tribune* career, his moon face wearing a persistent grin pierced by an ever-present cigar (now in the three-for-half-a-dollar range). Yet the eyes in the boyish face of this thickset man were as old and tired as time. His curly hair thinning, his complexion dark, cheeks rosy—well tailored, well manicured, well barbered—this was a newspaperman as skeptical and vaguely sinister as any Hecht and MacArthur would serve up in *The Front Page*.

Unlike many crime-beat reporters, he didn't carry a gun and held the drinking to an occasional beer. But in one word—*"Yeaaah?"*—he could serve up a lifetime of cynicism. Still, most considered him a friendly sort, bighearted, even generous. As writer Walter Noble Burns put it, "Just a happy-go-lucky, roughneck West Side kid."

Shortly before he picked up a racing form at the newsstand outside the train station stairs, Lingle took a late breakfast at the Hotel Sherman coffee shop, where in the hotel lobby he spoke to a police sergeant.

"I am being tailed," Lingle told his friend.

The sergeant looked around, saw no apparent hoodlums, and shrugged it off.

As Lingle was about to head down the stairs to the train station, someone from a roadster at the curb called out, "Play Hy Schneider in the third race!"

Lingle turned and said, "I've got him!" and started his descent.

Had this seemingly friendly exchange been the way to confirm the reporter's identity?

Like so many others this time of day, Jake's destination was the Washington Park racetrack in the far south suburbs, via the 1:30 P.M. express. There he could mix business and pleasure, hobnobbing with crooks and politicos, picking up leads. In the tunnel under Michigan Avenue emptying into the station's low-ceilinged underground chamber, Jake was already checking his racing form, oblivious to two men who'd also paused at the newsstand. The pair—a tall, boater-hatted blond and a shorter, darker guy—hustled down the stairs and closed in on Lingle.

The blond shoved a revolver behind Lingle's head and squeezed off a round. Jake didn't live long enough to hear the echo. The reporter who never wrote anything belly-flopped to the concrete, his latest cigar gripped between his lips, racing form like a hymnal in both hands, head spilling blood and brains.

The blond paused, flung the Colt .38 snub-nose by the body, and about-faced to a side tunnel leading up to Michigan Avenue. The short, dark man kept going straight ahead. The shot reverberated through the tunnel, hundreds hearing it, but only a few near enough to see Lingle drop and the assassin depart. Two witnesses took chase, following the blond up the stairs to the street, where they saw him dash through the bustling intersection at Randolph and Michigan, dodging traffic.

Someone yelled, "Catch him!" to a traffic cop, who joined the pursuit as the shooter cut down an alley, dropping a gray silk glove, which was all the cop caught up with.

Quickly to the scene came Outfit favorite Capt. Daniel "Tubbo" Gilbert, Commissioner of Detectives John Stege, and Police Commissioner William Russell. The latter had stayed Lingle's close friend since beat cop days; "Jake's like a son to me," the chief often said. Seeing his pal on the cement with the inside of his head leaking out must have shaken Russell. Some said Lingle helped Russell land his job, that the reporter's influence with the chief had—in the words of Edward Dean Sullivan—made a lowly legman "a major power in the underworld."

At the morgue, when the coroner searched the body, only $65 was found. Seemed a *Trib* reporter had taken fourteen C-notes from Jake's pocket to get to the widow Lingle . . . but also to protect the paper's rep from so suspiciously thick a bankroll.

"The meaning of this murder is plain," stated a *Tribune* editorial, ignoring or unaware of that early danger sign. "It was committed in reprisal and in an attempt at intimidation." The paper declared war: "There will be casualties, but that is to be expected. . . . Justice will make a fight or it will abdicate."

The *Herald and Examiner* briefly forgot their rivalry with the *Trib* to close ranks. The day after the murder, a huge photo of Lingle ran on the *Examiner*'s front page under a bold headline: REPORTER KILLED BY GUNMAN: CAPONE GANGSTER ACCUSED. They considered the crime "a new high point in ruthless outlawry," and called on Chicago to finally bring an end to the lawlessness that had blackened its name from coast to coast.

"This city is in a state of political corruption that will not cure itself," the editorial continued. "It can only get worse unless decent Chicagoans take matters in hand, insist upon honesty and efficiency from men elected to office and in the police department, or throw the crooked incompetents out."

The city was all but numb to gangland shootings—Lingle's murder was the eleventh in ten days. But gangsters were expected to kill their own, not journalists. To the papers, a line had been crossed—the Fourth Estate itself was suddenly a target, and that would not do.

Both the *Tribune* and the *Herald and Examiner* offered rewards of $25,000 for information leading to the killer's capture. The *Chicago Evening Post* offered an additional $5,000, and civic groups kicked in more, for a grand total of $55,750—an astronomical sum in the early days of the Depression.

Tribune publisher Col. Robert R. McCormick viewed the murder as a reprisal for his paper's strong anticrime stance. Never mind that McCormick had no idea who Lingle was. "A *Tribune* man had been killed," Fred Pasley wrote, "and [McCormick] was putting the vast resources of the *Tribune* into action not only to solve the murder, but to expose to public view that pyramid of crime and its hookup."

Discreetly, McCormick followed the Secret Six's lead and got in touch with State's Attorney John Swanson, offering to bankroll the investigation. McCormick funded independent prosecutor Charles Rathbun and lead investigator Pat Roche. Collaboration between various reward-posting papers proved short-lived, as did withholding news about the investigation until Swanson released it, so as not to jeopardize the investigation.

The press did agree that Commissioner Russell should be removed from the police investigation. Russell resigned as chief but retained his rank of captain, becoming commissioner in charge of the Detective Bureau, replacing a transferred Stege. Though less visible to the public, Russell remained actively involved with the Lingle inquiry.

Echoing the McSwiggin case, the "martyred reporter" story fell apart fast. Lingle was shown to be "a $65-a-week legman" who somehow made $60,000 a year. He had a home on the West Side, a summer place in Indiana, and a room at the Stevens Hotel. He was driven around in a chauffeured Lincoln, bet hundreds on horse races, and shared a speculative brokerage account with former chief Russell.

More and more, Jake Lingle seemed like something out of Damon Runyon. "A prize specimen of the era," Pasley called him, someone claiming he'd "fixed the price of beer" in Chicago, and had won the label "unofficial chief of police." He had mingled with millionaires and high-ranking Illinois politicians, and sported a diamond-decorated belt buckle given to him by a special pal.

"A Christmas present," Al Capone said of the ostentatious gift. "Jake was a dear friend of mine." The relationship was no surprise—Capone biographer Pasley believed "Lingle's multifarious activities included the post of liaison man for Capone."

The legman had been seen attending boxing matches with Al and the boys, hanging around the Hawthorne Hotel, and as a guest at the Palm Island estate. Providing police protection to Capone's rival gangs at a high price for low return, Lingle got on the wrong side of Moran and the North Siders.

But the friendship between Capone and Lingle had showed signs of fraying in recent years. Back when Al had been imprisoned for two days in the McSwiggin inquiry, the Big Fellow's meals were delivered exclusively by the trusted Lingle. Then the reporter took advantage, going to Al's personal tailor and charging four or five suits at a crack to his pal. And Jake's failure to provide police protection for the dog tracks he'd advised Capone to invest in may have cost the gangster a cool million.

If Capone's good feelings for Lingle had dimmed, so did the *Tribune*'s, whose attitude toward their fallen brother had changed noticeably by June 30.

"Alfred Lingle now takes on a different character," an editorial said, "one in which he was unknown to the management of the *Tribune* when he was alive. He is dead and cannot defend himself, but many facts now revealed must be accepted as eloquent against him."

The editorial granted Lingle's inability to write stories, but noted his skill at gathering information from police circles, while finding him entwined in a world of politics and crimes "undreamed of" by the great newspaper.

Nonetheless, the stand of the *Tribune* was firm: "That he is not a soldier dead in the discharge of duty is unfortunate considering that he is dead . . . [but] of no consequence to an inquiry determined to discover why he was killed, by whom killed and with what attendant circumstances." Not a soldier, then, but a reporter—defined by Hecht and MacArthur in *The Front Page* as "a cross between a bootlegger and a whore."

Eliot Ness's movements in the first part of 1930 remain largely obscure, yet it's clear he was doing plenty.

When he wasn't raiding Ralph's Cotton Club, he kept working in the shadows—monitoring the wiretaps on the Montmartre and other Outfit hot spots, gathering evidence and biding his time. The waiting came to an end on June 12, 1930—the same day Jake Lingle was laid to rest in a gangster-worthy coffin of silver and bronze—when Ness made his first direct hit on Al Capone.

The sign out front identified the garage at 2108 South Wabash as an auto parts supplier, but Alexander Jamie suspected a major Capone brewery. Spring rain dampened the pavement as Jamie led Ness and the other special agents around back, under the clattering tracks of the L, armed with a search warrant.

When the agents tried to enter through the rear, they ran into a pair of heavy steel doors, barred shut. Half an hour later they had crowbarred and sledge-hammered their way in, which of course gave anyone inside ample time to escape. The only arrest was a probable lookout.

Inside, the special agents found one of the largest Capone breweries ever raided in Chicago—fifty thousand gallons of beer in wooden barrels waiting for speakeasy delivery. Massive fermenting vats, filled to the brim, held 150,000 gallons of foamy brew still in the process of cooking.

The feds estimated the brewery turned out a hundred barrels a day. At the going rate of $55 per, Jamie, Ness, and company had cost Capone more than $38,000 in weekly revenue, to say nothing of the seized equipment and product. George E. Q. Johnson declared it the opening salvo in his campaign of economic warfare against Capone.

But Jamie wasn't content with simply shutting the place down—he seized ledgers and records, as well as canceled checks bearing the name of a suspected Capone henchman who now ran Colosimo's restaurant. This evidence, Jamie told the *Tribune,* might seed a conspiracy case linking Capone to the brewery.

Jamie had good reason to feel confident. His men had secretly secured a wiretap on Capone's headquarters in the Lexington Hotel, just around the block from the raided brewery.

As they listened, the special agents heard Frankie Rio, Jack McGurn, and the Guziks discussing the beer trade, referring constantly to "Snorky"—a slang term meaning "stylish" or "up-to-date" in a teasing yet affectionate way. This, they gathered, was Capone's nickname among the Outfit's elite, which he much preferred to the despised "Scarface."

The same day as the Wabash raid, the tap picked up evidence of a conference between "Snorky" and four top bootleggers, perhaps to discuss the loss of their brewery. This—the only meeting of Capone's inner circle the feds ever became privy to—gave the special agents their first concrete proof linking Capone to the beer business.

Ness would long remember the special agents' struggle to batter their way inside that garage. The next time he raided a Capone brewery, he wouldn't let steel doors slow him down.

That same summer, Ness got caught up in the hunt for Jake Lingle's killer, thanks to his acquaintance with Lt. Col. Calvin Goddard. The ballistics expert, now ensconced at Northwestern, had restored the filed-off serial number on the murder weapon using the same chemical process he'd applied to a St. Valentine's Day tommy gun.

This helped police identify the revolver as one of six sold by Peter von Frantzius, the dealer who'd supplied the Thompsons used at the massacre. The purchaser was a former North Sider who joined up with the Capones, Frank Foster (real name Ferdinand Bruna).

"This town is getting too hot for me," Foster told his friends, shortly after the Lingle murder. "I'm going to lam."

And he did.

Ness had crossed paths with Foster weeks before Lingle died. Cruising past the Lexington Hotel with Marty Lahart, Ness spotted Foster and another suspicious character—both wearing the pearl-gray hats of the Capone crowd—drive off, with Foster at the wheel. The special agents tailed the gangsters, who quickly made them and tried to shake them. Ness and Lahart forced the car to the side of the road, then ordered Foster to get out and stand for a frisk, finding a snub-nosed .38.

After running Foster in on a concealed-weapon charge, Ness brought the gun to the Northwestern Crime Lab, where Calvin Goddard gave him a basic lesson in ballistics. The Colonel fired Foster's gun into a cotton-filled wastebasket, then showed Ness how he might compare the spent bullet to one found at a crime scene. Goddard filed the slug away with scores of other test bullets, should Foster's gun ever turn up as evidence, while Ness took the weapon itself back to his Transportation Building office and locked it in a file cabinet.

Later that summer, Ness received a call from Pat Roche, former Intelligence Unit man now working as a state's attorney investigator on publisher McCormick's dime. Roche explained the gun Ness confiscated came from the same batch of six as the Lingle murder weapon, and asked Ness to hang on to it.

Ness checked to make sure the gun was still where he'd left it. But when he opened the drawer he saw the revolver was missing.

Searching the cabinet for the gun, unsuccessfully, he discovered carelessly arranged papers—had someone been rifling through the special agents' files? Ness suspected the Capone Outfit, but gangsters need not have invaded the Transportation Building to make the search— someone in the office might have taken a bribe, even one of their select squad of special agents.

In any case, the gun was gone.

Ness felt a growing sense of dread—had he inadvertently provided the weapon for Lingle's murder?

Then he remembered the test bullet fired at Northwestern—and dashed to the crime lab to ask if Goddard had held on to it. Goddard said yes, and brought the Foster slug out; he sat down at his comparison microscope, examining it alongside the one taken from Lingle's skull.

When Goddard determined the bullets had been fired from two different weapons, the news felt to Ness like an eleventh-hour acquittal. He would long remember this moment as "one of the most graphic and emphatic examples of the newly developed ballistics science."

In July, Foster turned up in Los Angeles, where he was arrested and extradited back to Chicago. Although he didn't fit eyewitness descriptions of the shooter—Foster was short and dark, the killer tall and blond—he matched the likely accomplice. But he refused to say what he'd done with the guns purchased from von Frantzius, and the authorities could produce nothing else tying him to the crime. Some observers believed they weren't trying very hard.

In June 1931, after several continuances, Foster's case was dismissed for lack of evidence.

Meanwhile, Pat Roche and his men were at work.

They interviewed eyewitnesses and gathered good descriptions of the shooter; they tracked down the car whose passengers had hailed Lingle with a betting tip, and who turned out to be racing fans, not mobsters.

Lingle's Capone belt buckle directed Roche to the North Side, despite rumbles of the Jake-and-Al friendship turning rocky. Of course, the Outfit might have known that Special Agent Frank Wilson was looking to interview the reporter, which kept Capone himself in the running.

But the prime suspects remained the North Siders, bolstered by an anonymous tip labor racketeer James "Red" Forsythe was involved. A dragnet was set up to find the elusive Forsythe; an anonymous informant claimed crafty Nitto had hired Forsythe to get rid of the legman and tag the North Side for it. And another tip vaguely implicated Grover Dullard, a North Side gambler associated with Bugs Moran, the Aiellos, and prostitution czar Jack Zuta.

Pudgy little Zuta was reigning vice boss and business manager of the Moran-Aiello alliance, though Bugs disliked the glorified pimp. Just the same, Zuta took over for Moran and Joe Aiello, both of whom had gone into out-of-state hiding after the Lingle shooting.

To Walter Noble Burns, Jack Zuta was "a noisome, slime-bred creature, utterly conscienceless, but suave, unctuously ingratiating and plausible . . . depraved and soulless . . . a rat, a poltroon, and a traitor who would not hesitate, if cornered, to turn on his friends and betray them to save his own life."

But Fred Pasley, also obviously no fan, gave Zuta credit as having "a shrewder mind than the run of the mill criminals," considered by some the "brains" of the Moran bunch.

And ruling for Moran in absentia laid the Lingle hit at his feet—of the top three in the North Side mob, only Zuta was around to take credit or blame. Fear that the glorified pimp couldn't hold up under police grilling—that he would "spill his guts"—meant his own boys were as likely to hit him as the Capone Outfit.

Roche was eyeing Zuta, too, prompted by several recent clashes between Lingle and North Siders—the reporter had double-crossed Moran-connected gamblers, pocketing fifty grand for a bogus dogtrack authorization. And the Biltmore Athletic Club—where among the exercises undertaken were shuffling cards and tossing dice—had been raided by Roche himself, despite the Unofficial Chief of Police getting paid for protection. Also, Jake had insisted on a raise of his take from 10 to 50 percent on Moran's posh, popular Sheridan Wave Tournament Club, post–St. Valentine's Day. When he didn't get it, he made sure the club couldn't reopen.

On June 30, Chicago police captured Jack Zuta in his apartment, hauling him down to police headquarters on the Near South Side.

"I'll be killed the minute I leave this building," he immediately insisted. "Don't stand around looking sleepy! Do you cops want me killed? . . . My God, I'm a goner—I know it."

Even surrounded by blue uniforms, Zuta stayed away from windows, and requested a cell facing no other building. The vice lord, his latest moll, and two cronies—Leona Bernstein, Albert Bratz, and Solly Vision—were held on a disorderly conduct charge overnight, and questioned the next day by Roche and others. When they were let out on bail at 10:25 P.M., Jack demanded passage to a "safe spot."

Lt. George Barker, the stocky plainclothes head of the bomb squad, said he would take the Zuta party to where they could easily get transportation to their North Side turf. They all piled into Barker's Pontiac and headed north on State.

Zuta, his two cronies, and the moll got comfortable as Barker drove into the Loop, State Street nearly a ghost town. At Quincy Street, a dark-colored sedan surged up behind them. Zuta yelled, "Here they come! It's all over now. They'll get us sure," and ducked down to the floor.

The vice lord's pal Solly, in the front seat, clambered over and down next to Jack, a rather ungentlemanly move leaving Leona and Bratz to shrink into the corners of the otherwise exposed backseat. The sedan came up on the driver's side, three men in it, one stepping out on the running board wearing a flashy Panama hat, a flower in his lapel, a tan suit with creased trousers—and a shoulder holster, from which he drew a .45 automatic.

The snappy dresser fired seven rounds into the back of the car. A buddy in the sedan's backseat began emptying his pistol as well, and the sedan's driver—steering one-handed—started firing off rounds, too.

Barker yanked his emergency brake, leapt out, and began blasting away with his revolver. A single cop against three hoodlums, he stood like a Wild West gunfighter in the street and gave it back to them. The hoods had figured their surprise attack would take Zuta down with little trouble, but the detective's unanticipated response shook them. The driver hit the pedal and the sedan roared off.

Barker got behind the wheel, laughing as he said, "I'll bet I winged them," but he was talking to himself: Zuta and his cronies had taken off on foot.

As the cop drove after the gunmen's sedan, the hoods unleashed a new gadget: their car had a rigged exhaust that laid down a smoke-screen. Barker kept on their tail nevertheless, but his car soon sputtered to a halt, its fuel tank punctured by a stray bullet, letting the gunmen escape.

In the melee, two bystanders caught bullets—a streetcar driver, fatally, and a night watchman on the way to work, his arm clipped.

Like his boss Moran, Zuta went into hiding, forfeiting his bond. Had the vice monger's allies made a preemptive strike, knowing Jack would likely fold up and squeal? Or had Capone been avenging the death of his pal Jake Lingle?

Pat Roche was certain of one thing.

"If we can learn from Zuta who was shooting at him," he said, "we may have the solution of the Lingle murder."

In mid-July, at 1:00 A.M., *St. Louis Star* reporter Harry T. Brundidge—due to testify in Chicago about his exposé of crooked Chicago newspapermen—interviewed Al Capone on the sun porch at Palm Island.

Capone slipped an arm around the reporter's shoulder.

"Listen, Harry," Al said. "I like your face. Let me give you a hot tip. Lay off Chicago and the money-hungry reporters."

When the reporter asked why, the ganglord explained: "I mean they'll make a monkey out of you before you get through. No matter what dope you have to give that grand jury, the boys will prove you're a liar and a faker."

The reporter found Capone friendly, chatty, and something of a big, overgrown kid. He also considered Public Enemy Number One an intelligent subject with "a dark, kindly face, big sparkling eyes," the trademark scar only adding to his bearing. If you didn't know better, Brundidge wrote, you might think him "as harmless as a big St. Bernard dog."

Earlier that evening, the reporter had arrived unannounced outside the big iron gates of the Capone estate, where a tough-looking guard said Capone was out, meeting with his attorneys. When would he get back? Brundidge asked. A shrug.

The reporter sat on the grass and waited. When Capone's big black limo finally pulled up, the gangster got out and, after Brundidge introduced himself, said pleasantly, "This is a surprise. Come on in."

Now, as they spoke on the sun porch, moonlight glimmering on Biscayne Bay, Capone asked, "What brings you here?"

"I thought I would ask you who killed Lingle."

"Why ask me? The Chicago police know who killed him."

"Was Jake your friend?"

"Yes, up to the very day he died."

"Did you have a row with him?"

"Absolutely not."

"It is said you fell out with him because he failed to split profits from handbooks."

"Bunk. The handbook racket hasn't been really organized in Chicago for more than two years, and anyone who says it is doesn't know Chicago."

The reporter asked why Capone, on his release from the Pennsylvania pen, hadn't given his friend Lingle the inside story. Capone responded dismissively, as if he didn't remember the incident.

Brundidge asked, "What about Jake's diamond belt buckle?"

"I gave it to him."

"Do you mind stating what it cost?"

"Two hundred and fifty dollars."

"Why did you give it to him?"

"He was my friend."

Asked about Lingle's involvement in various rackets, Capone shrugged, but in his opinion newspapermen should be working against the rackets, not backing them. And he should know—he'd had "plenty" on his payroll.

The impromptu host escorted his uninvited guest around the house and grounds—swimming pool, bathhouse, private pier, boathouse, speedboat, luxurious cruiser. The two wandered through the well-tended grounds by a coral grotto, surrounded by many trees, flowers, and ferns.

Capone spoke of his love for the area, and how he'd refused to be chased out by "a little clique," or harassing police. He claimed to be "out of all rackets," intending to make Miami his home, going to Chicago only now and then.

The tour extended to the seventeen-room house, "tastefully appointed" under Capone's personal direction—no mention of Mae's role. Capone walked the reporter out, past the gates to a sedan the host had provided for the ride back to the hotel.

After publication of the mostly flattering article, Capone called the more controversial revelations "deliberate lies," including such tidbits as the Chicago police knowing who killed Lingle and Scarface's boast of having "plenty of newspapermen on his payroll."

Brundidge stood behind his story.

Twilight was easing into night outside the Lake View Hotel, a resort and roadhouse on Upper Nemahbin Lake near Delafield, Wisconsin, twenty-five miles from Milwaukee. Inside all was bright and cheery, as young couples danced to player piano music, courtesy of one nickel after another being dropped into the slot.

He was a pudgy, pasty-faced character with the kind of rectangular, hooded-eyed face that looks depressed even when it smiles. But he was a snappy dresser, in a brightly banded straw hat, silk shirt, four-in-hand tie, and tweeds. Despite his naturally solemn mug, Mr. Goodman—at the resort for three weeks now—seemed genial and, well, nice.

None of the several dozen dancing couples would guess Mr. Goodman was Jack Zuta, chicken-hearted prostitution czar. And Mr. Goodman did not suspect his life of crime and sin was about to catch up with him, by way of two cars pulling up outside.

Five men got out, while the drivers remained with their rides. They trooped single file into the bar carrying assorted weapons—a tommy gun, two sawed-offs, a pair of pistols. Moving into the bright world of the adjacent dance hall, they didn't see Zuta at first, his back to them as he dropped one last nickel into its slot.

A peppy new tune started up—"Good for You, Bad for Me"—the couples swinging to the occasion. Zuta turned to beam at these fun kids and, looking across a sea of youth, saw a row of gunmen.

Zuta was a natural runner, but fear froze him, his face blister white, his eyes wild. The young dancers scattered while the party of five crowded in. The machine gun impolitely burped bullets, punctuated by the coughing of sawed-off shotguns and the blurts of revolver fire, gun barrels issuing flame and smoke and slugs.

Zuta fell on his face, dead but not dead enough for one gunman, who walked over to the splayed corpse and fired twice into its head.

The gangsters fled in an automobile with stolen Chicago plates.

In the weeks ahead, Goddard would link some of the Lake View Hotel bullets to the Capone gang. And the Roche investigation would become a comedy of errors, when their Lingle suspect, Foster—thought to be the accomplice, not the shooter—was identified as the killer by a traffic cop prone to hallucinations from a head injury.

But Roche had also raided a North Side mob business office, just two blocks north of Lingle's Tribune Tower newsroom, and turned up a set of ledgers for Moran's and Zuta's operations. These and Zuta's own files would document police and political corruption better than ever before. Still, while Roche relished the dirt he now had on dozens of bent officials, he was no closer in locating the man who pulled the trigger on Lingle.

On the night Zuta was so thoroughly killed, Al Capone returned to Chicago to play host to one hundred close friends at the Hawthorne Hotel in Cicero. On the business side, he was back to assess the damage of various federal raids in June and July, courtesy of Roche, Johnson, Jamie, and Ness.

But perhaps Al also intended to underscore having done what the local law could not: avenge his friend Jake Lingle's death.

Frank Nitto (center) with Pat Roche (far left) after Nitto's arrest, October 31, 1930.
(Abraham Lincoln Presidential Library & Museum [ALPLM])

Eighteen

June–October 1930

With Jake Lingle's execution, tax investigator Frank Wilson lost more than a potential informant—his chances of getting anyone else to talk died, too. If the mob could kill Lingle, no one in their orbit was safe.

"Every witness we needed was dumb as an oyster when it came to talking about Capone," Wilson said. "They were a hundred times more afraid of being killed by Capone guns than they were of having to serve a prison term for perjury."

Wilson reached out to Chicago reporters for assistance, to no avail. In St. Louis, he called on an old friend, John T. Rogers of the *St. Louis Post-Dispatch*. Like Lingle, Rogers worked both sides of the crime beat, with a knack for making friends with unsavory characters. Every Christmas, cards and gifts filled Rogers's mailbox.

"The whores and hoodlums always remember me!" he'd say.

Rogers owed Wilson a favor for helping expose a corrupt judge for a Pulitzer Prize–winning story. Now Wilson badly needed to talk to E. J. O'Hare, still seeking to prove Capone's taxable income by linking him to Hawthorne Kennel Club profits. Rogers knew O'Hare, head of that dog track, from covering the Jack Daniel's distillery trial back in '25, after "Fast Eddie" cheated George Remus. With his *Post-Dispatch* editor's blessing, Rogers agreed to serve as intermediary between Wilson and O'Hare.

In June, Wilson returned to St. Louis for a meeting with Rogers and O'Hare. Fearful of getting "knocked off," the glib lawyer agreed to speak only confidentially. Then O'Hare admitted he'd incorporated the dog track in 1927 with Capone, Jack Guzik, Frank Nitto, and Johnny Patton.

These names had appeared on stock certificates, but Capone and Nitto had theirs struck off, after word of the deal got out. Wilson reported back to Washington, certain Capone "received a big cut of the proceeds from the track." But after scouring the operation's books, he found no proof of "unreported income of the Hawthorne Kennel Club." Once again, a dead end.

Maybe the lead hadn't panned out, but its source certainly did. Despite fears of reprisal, O'Hare had no problem passing along secrets of the Outfit's operations, soon becoming Wilson's most trusted informant.

"I saw my undercover man, Eddie, infrequently," Wilson wrote, "but I was in almost constant touch with John Rogers. . . . When there was a missing link in a puzzle, I slipped the word to John." The St. Louis reporter would meet secretly with Wilson and say, "Eddie said here's the answer. . . ."

Wilson considered O'Hare a naïve businessman in over his head who wanted out. "He didn't then realize that he was in the gang for keeps," Wilson wrote of O'Hare, "and could not drop out if he wanted to. . . . I thoroughly sympathized with Eddie as I fully realized the serious predicament into which he unconsciously had been enticed."

More than anything else, O'Hare feared his son, Butch, might follow him into the gambling business. Butch had a wild streak his father hoped to tame with military school. O'Hare often told his daughters, "If we have a war, Butch will become an admiral; if not, I fear he will become nothing." Wilson felt O'Hare's concern over his son's future had convinced him to turn on Capone.

But "Artful Eddie" was not the innocent he'd sold himself to be— O'Hare understood what he was getting into with the Outfit, and had no intention of getting out. He also knew the feds had enough evidence from the dog track to send him away on his own income tax rap. Maybe Wilson used that as leverage; maybe he didn't have to.

O'Hare figured to stay out of jail by cooperating. But he also had another agenda, one to which Wilson seemed oblivious—the federal drive to get Capone had brought unwanted attention to the entire Outfit. Raids, arrests, indictments, and screaming headlines were cutting into everybody's bottom line—including O'Hare's.

Like Chicago's legitimate businessmen—and their private police force, the Secret Six—O'Hare knew Capone and his notoriety were bad for business. That made O'Hare eager to give the feds the prize they sought—the Big Fellow—in hopes they might lay off everybody else. He would have to act fast, with the tax men swinging through the Outfit like a wrecking ball.

Next up was Jack Guzik. Though filing tax returns since 1927, Guzik declared an income well below his actual take. The Intelligence Unit, digging through the records at Pinkert State Bank, uncovered tens of thousands of dollars in cashier's checks purchased by one "J. C. Dunbar."

Guzik endorsed many of these checks. To prove this represented taxable income, the agents had to identify its source, finding Dunbar and getting him to testify. But so far, they had no leads. "Dunbar" was clearly an alias. But for whom?

Probably with O'Hare's help, Wilson identified "Dunbar" as Fred Ries, cashier for several Capone-controlled Cicero gambling joints. A handwriting sample, compared with the cashier's checks, confirmed Ries filled them out. But Guzik and his brother-in-law, Louis Lipschultz, had spirited the cashier away for safekeeping. Then, in late August, Wilson learned from a postal inspector that Lipschultz sent a certified letter to Ries, with money and instructions to flee to California. Wilson and Nels Tessem followed the letter to St. Louis. As soon as Ries got his mail, the tax men served him a subpoena.

Bald, with thick eyebrows on a long, sour face, Ries telegraphed his hatred of cops with a beady-eyed glare.

"When we questioned him regarding his employment in the gambling establishments in Cicero," Wilson recalled, "he cleverly denied any knowledge of the facts which could be used by the government as evidence against Al Capone, Jack Guzik or other principals in that organization."

Wilson and Tessem, wary of Ries again slipping their grip, held the cashier as a material witness. They returned him to Illinois and locked him up at the Danville county jail under a $15,000 bond, keeping his location a secret so the Outfit couldn't bail him out to save or kill him.

Eventually Ries opened up, outlining in detail his work at a Cicero casino known variously as the Hawthorne Smoke Shop and the Ship—each Dunbar check represented a day's gambling profits, over and above the $10,000 "bank" kept on hand. Jack Guzik had instructed Ries to give these profits to Bobby Barton, Guzik's driver, collector, and all-around stooge.

Simply handing over bags of cash might risk theft, Ries decided, and instead bought cashier's checks under various assumed names. Cash, of course, would have left no trace, whereas checks left a paper trail leading right back to Guzik, arrested on income tax evasion on September 30.

Federal agents shuffled Ries from Milwaukee to Highland Park, working to keep him alive till the trial. While Ries's testimony heavily implicated Guzik, Capone remained untouched. Ries said he'd seen Al around the casino a few times; he'd heard that Capone, his brother Ralph, and Frank Nitto made up the syndicate running the place. But such hearsay was inadmissible, and—unlike Guzik—the others never dealt directly with Ries, at least as far as he was willing to admit.

One night in September, Frank Wilson took stock of how he'd spent his summer. Holed up in his cramped, claustrophobic office, he laid out all the evidence he and his men gathered in their hunt for Capone.

"By midnight I had decided that it amounted to just about nothing," Wilson recalled, "and was ready to go home."

Wearily, he gathered up the papers to put them away, but the file cabinet was locked, and he couldn't find a key. Tired, impatient, cranky, he found an unlocked cabinet in a nearby storeroom and opened it, looking to leave his papers and sort it all out tomorrow.

"As I was doing this I uncovered a ledger," Wilson wrote. "It had been lying there in that file for about five years and the label on it didn't mean a thing to me. But curiosity made me open it."

He flipped through the dusty book, taking in the headings. On one page, he saw payments to "Town," "Ralph," "Pete," "Frank," "J & A," "Lew," and "D." His breathing grew faster—the ledger appeared to document the profits of a major gambling house, nearly $600,000 from 1924 to 1926. But the raid took place in the suburbs, an unlikely site for a casino that size.

Then he spotted a simple notation: "Frank paid $17,500 for Al." Wilson felt certain that "Al" was Al Capone.

"As soon as I looked inside that book," Wilson said, "I knew we had our case."

Proving it would be another matter. The ledger, dating to the McSwiggin murder crackdown, had been misfiled. The book bore no identifying marks, not where it came from nor what it represented. Nowhere did the name "Capone" appear. To use it in court, Wilson would have to trace the ledger to its source, and the person or persons who'd filled it out.

Handwriting from three individuals was apparent. During their investigation, the Intelligence Unit gathered script samples from several members of the Outfit, which they compared to the ledger, searching for matches. They found two—both Hawthorne Smoke Shop employees. But the bulk of the entries, apparently made by the casino's bookkeeper, remained unidentified.

Wilson turned to E. J. O'Hare, who said the Smoke Shop books were kept by a meek little man named Leslie A. Shumway. The two had a history—Shumway and O'Hare had been indicted back in 1929 for allegedly conspiring to give perjured testimony about local dog tracks. The agent already had a handwriting sample from Shumway not matching any ledger entries.

But Shumway's script was in pencil, while the book had been filled out in ink—perhaps when Shumway used a pen, his handwriting differed. Wilson got hold of something Shumway wrote in ink, and compared it to the ledger—a perfect match.

He set out to find the bookkeeper.

On October 31, the Intelligence Unit traced Frank Nitto to an apartment in Berwyn. Nitto had grown a mustache, not enough of a Halloween disguise to keep Pat Roche from making him and putting on the cuffs. The arrest brought Nitto into a limelight he'd always worked to avoid. A reporter in court called him "a velvet glove over an iron hand," with "no suggestion of the grim name—the Enforcer—he won in the Capone organization."

If the government had understood Nitto's importance in the Outfit—his relative anonymity having served him well—George E. Q. Johnson might have been less receptive to a plea bargain. The prosecutor, overworked and understaffed, doubted the strength of his case; he remained focused on nailing his bigger and flashier target—Capone. Ultimately he agreed to an eighteen-month sentence, with the possibility of parole in as little as a year, if Nitto met certain conditions.

This included the gangster promising to turn his back on both Chicago and the rackets, to start a "useful life," though how that might be enforced remained unclear. Nitto agreed, taking a guilty plea in late December. By not fighting, he had won the shortest prison sentence of any Capone gangster convicted of tax evasion. He announced his victory to the press.

"I have never committed a crime of moral turpitude," he lied. "I have never done anything that is condemned by society as morally wrong. I didn't pay income taxes because the laws were not clear. But if society demands a penalty from me, I am glad to pay it."

Less than three weeks after Nitto's arrest, Jack Guzik, too, was found guilty of income tax evasion. Apparently unmoved by the verdict, "Greasy Thumb" got out on bond to await appeal. But the speed of his conviction—under two months since his arrest—sent tremors through the underworld.

"When the witnesses we needed saw those leaders of the Capone organization getting knocked off in rapid-fire order," Frank Wilson said, "it began to dawn upon them that the United States Government meant business and that Capone, perhaps, after all was up against something he couldn't beat this time. He'd failed to fix it for the fellows closest to him."

But to get anyone else to talk, the tax men had to protect star witness Fred Ries. Federal agents bounced him from hotel to hotel, under constant armed guard. The Secret Six paid him $10 a day, but Ries grew stir-crazy, his mood foul. Life on the run didn't agree with him. The feds feared they might lose his cooperation before Capone went to trial—didn't Ries understand if he walked out, he'd be dead?

That spring, Wilson visited Robert Isham Randolph to ask if the Secret Six might help get Ries out of the country for a while, and soon Ries was booked on a round-trip voyage to Montevideo, Uruguay.

That way the Six would keep Ries safe and happy until they needed him again—an all-expenses paid vacation, and early forerunner of the Federal Witness Protection Program.

As Frank Wilson chased down every lead, Capone kept pressing for a settlement.

His attorney, Lawrence Mattingly, negotiated with the tax men throughout the spring and summer of 1930. On September 20, Mattingly visited Revenue Agent Louis H. Wilson (no relation to Frank) to seal the deal.

"Mr. Mattingly . . . said it was very difficult to get the facts and figures together," Louis Wilson recalled. "He took some papers out of his inside coat pocket and in turning them over he would look out the window and talk very slowly, deliberately. Finally he threw the papers over to me. . . . 'This is the best we can do. Mr. Capone is willing to pay the tax on these figures.' "

Mattingly hemmed and hawed, indicating he knew the risk: He was handing over evidence that could be used against his client in court. But this still seemed Capone's best bet to stay out of prison. The letter roughly sketched the gangster's financial situation and business history: before 1925, when Torrio turned over Outfit control, Capone had earned no more than $75 a week, not enough to owe any income tax. Since then, as a full financial partner, he'd received one-sixth of the gang's total profits.

Mattingly said Capone's "taxable income for the years 1925 and 1926 might fairly be fixed at not to exceed $26,000 and $40,000 respectively, and for the years 1928 and 1929 not to exceed $100,000 per year."

The government knew this assessment was ridiculous. Capone's "sources of income are known to us," one Internal Revenue official said. "We believe he could cash in for $20,000,000. But where has he hidden it? Our men get so far, then they find themselves in blind alleys. . . . We get leads that look good, but don't materialize."

Now they had a solid starting point. To convict Capone of a felony, they had to show he knew about his tax debt and willfully chose not to pay it by hiding money from the government. The Mattingly letter proved the first point—the gangster could no longer claim ignorance; his lawyer had admitted, in writing, Capone received taxable income.

And if the feds could establish Capone earned *more* money than the sums in the letter—that he'd lied—they'd have him on the second point. Just like Jack Guzik, Capone had badly miscalculated. By trying to pay his taxes, he'd given the feds a foundation upon which to build their case.

Yet Capone still seemed convinced he could buy his way out. In November, Commissioner of Internal Revenue David Burnet had a visit from Chicago lawyer Harry Curtis, son of the vice president of the United States. If Burnet's bureau would drop any and all investigations of Chicago gangsters, the racketeers would pay "at least $3,500,000" to wipe away their tax debts.

Burnet didn't accept the offer, nor did he when Lawrence Mattingly visited some time later with what some might call a settlement, and others a bribe.

"I have been informed," Burnet wrote, "that approaches have been made from time to time to various Federal officials in Chicago in the interest of these gangsters with a view to having their cases settled in other than a regular manner."

In October, Pat Roche decided to take his sixteen-man squad and go on the offensive—if the Capone Outfit felt the heat, maybe they'd turn over the Lingle shooter, most likely a member of a rival gang. Wielding sledge, ax, and crowbar, Roche and his wrecking crew raided gambling joints, bordellos, and speaks in Chicago and the suburbs, arresting one and all, capturing ledgers and other evidence.

Roche's boss, State's Attorney Rathbun, exhumed dormant charges against known gangsters and rounded up parole violators. Sky-high bail, courtesy of Judge John H. Lyle, kept hoods behind bars till their court date. This put certain key Outfit players temporarily out of commission.

Judge Lyle was launching his own attack on Capone. Pompous, self-righteous, Lyle hated gangsters almost as much as he loved publicity. At Roche's urging, the judge cooked up a scheme to use an old vagrancy law—defining vagrants as anyone not "lawfully provid[ing] for themselves," and/or who frequented "houses of ill fame, gaming houses, or tippling shops."

"I had within me a warm, tingling sense of satisfaction as I reviewed the possibilities in the law in the case of . . . Al Capone," Lyle wrote. "If Capone, arrested on a vagrancy warrant, declined to answer questions he would automatically fail to disprove the allegations. I could find him guilty of vagrancy and fine him $200."

If Capone tried to pay a fine, he'd have to tell where the money came from, which if he told the truth meant criminal charges, and if he lied meant perjury. Failing to pay the fine could send him to the workhouse.

What sounded good in theory flopped in practice. A fleet of squad cars went out in an effort to round up names on the "Public Enemies" list, serving up but a single warrant for a "vagabond" already in custody on an unrelated charge. In the coming weeks, names from that list did appear before the judge—including Ralph Capone and the Guzik brothers—who received a severe scolding from the bench before getting out on bond.

Capone himself avoided Judge Lyle's roust by staying outside the city limits. In late September, a Chicago Crime Commission investigator reported Capone and six of his bodyguards had attended a high school football game in Cicero. Two police officers paid the gangsters no heed, despite whispers of "There's Al Capone" rippling through the stands.

Escaping both winter cold and official heat, Capone hid out in Miami. Lyle's ire grew—he would send Capone to the chair for the murders of Colosimo and Joe Howard, should he ever get the "reptile" before his bench. Lyle had never been much for respecting civil liberties, routinely setting obscenely high bail.

The Illinois Supreme Court, finding Lyle's use of the vagrancy statute unconstitutional, said, "It sought to punish an individual for what he was reputed to be, regardless of what he actually did." Still, Capone kept getting hit on all sides—Prohibition agents hitting his speaks and breweries, Roche raiding brothels and gambling joints, and the Intelligence Unit building their tax case, right down to an inventory of the Big Fellow's silk underwear.

In late October, as *Tribune* reporter John Boettiger reported, a "wealthy businessman" approached Roche and his boss Rathbun with a message: Al Capone wanted a meet. This intermediary from the world of business may well have been the ubiquitous E. J. O'Hare; Boettiger took pains to conceal the man's identity. Neither Roche nor Rathbun was interested. Pressed for a meeting, the state's attorney finally agreed to send a representative to hear Capone out.

The businessman led the representative to a suburban home "surrounded by old elms and beautifully landscaped"—O'Hare was dividing his time between Chicago and St. Louis—and ushered him into a drawing room, where Capone awaited. They shook hands and sat by a fireplace, the businessman leaving them to it.

"Here's what I want to tell you," Capone said, "and I won't be long about it. I can't stand the gaff of these raids and pinches. If it's going to keep up, I'll have to pack up and get out of Chicago."

The representative told Capone there would be no letup, that things remained hot since the Lingle murder.

Capone said, "Well, I didn't kill Jake Lingle, did I?"

"We don't know who killed him."

"Why didn't you ask me? Maybe I can find out for you."

"Maybe you can."

Capone shifted in the easy chair's deep cushions. "I know none of my fellows did it. I liked Lingle, and certainly I didn't have any reason to kill him."

He offered a possible motive. "I have heard that Lingle was involved in the attempts of the North Side gangsters to open a dog track in the [Chicago] Stadium . . . that Lingle was asked by the Zuta crowd to see to it that the police and the state's attorney would not bother them, and that Lingle was paid $30,000."

When "the Zuta crowd" got shut down in their effort, Capone said, "they blamed Jake Lingle, and I think that's why he was pushed."

Pushed—underworld lingo for "killed."

"But I don't know who they used to do the job," Capone insisted. "It must have been some fellow from out of town. I'll try to find out."

The representative said Capone could do that if he wanted to, but it wouldn't help him with Roche.

Capone said nothing for a while, then claimed he'd been approached by Bugs Moran and the North Side gang to make peace.

"[Moran] wants to join up with me," Capone said, "and maybe I can trade off with him for a bit of information on the Lingle murder. I might take him in, if he will tell who killed Jake."

Capone would succeed in ending the North vs. South Side war by buying Moran out, but Aiello wouldn't go so quietly.

The ganglord said when he had the name of Lingle's killer, he'd send it through the businessman connection who was again on hand to drive the representative out of this nice neighborhood from which the Big Fellow would no doubt soon depart, Judge Lyle's vagrancy charge still looming.

The representative reported back to Rathbun and Roche, who had their doubts about Capone's offer, with nothing to do but wait for developments.

And continue raiding.

A few days later, another of Capone's problems walked briskly out of an apartment building on North Kolmar Avenue, apparently on his way to grab a train out of town. Before he got to the waiting cab at the curb, machine-gun fire pelted Joe Aiello from a second-story perch across the way.

The mortally wounded Aiello stumbled into a courtyard, out of the line of fire, only he wasn't, really: another tommy gun above showered down more burning metal projectiles. Fifty-nine bullets, a pound's worth, had solved another Capone problem.

The hit, recalling the Hymie Weiss job engineered by Frank Nitto, took careful planning. Aiello, hiding out in a business associate's apartment, had not shown his face for two weeks. Almost that long, in a pair of machine-gun nests—on either side of the street—killers had been on round-the-clock watch. The hit suggested Nitto's careful planning— even the path of Aiello's flight had been predicted.

Five men quickly left their perches—getaway cars, and the night, were waiting.

Capone's soup kitchen at 935 South State Street. *(Top: National Archives. Bottom: Library of Congress.)*

Nineteen

November–December 1930

For several weeks, whoever might be responsible for the charitable endeavor on South State Street remained a mystery—no Salvation Army officer present, no representative of any relief agency supervising. The "keen-cyed, silent men" in charge said nothing beyond inviting the unfortunate in for what the banner above the vacant store's entry promised: FREE SOUP, COFFEE AND DOUGHNUTS TO THE UNEMPLOYED.

"Today it became known," the *Chicago Evening Post* reported, in a puff piece posing as investigative journalism, "that Chicago's public benefactor is no other than Chicago's foremost 'public enemy,' the notorious Al ('Scarface') Capone. The king of gangsters cast in a new role."

Finally, a bent-nose greeter to the homeless and jobless confirmed this, talking "out of the side of his mouth in the approved gangster fashion." Tight-lipped the hood wasn't: "Nobody else was doing it, and Mr. Capone couldn't stand it seeing so many poor fellows dying of starvation. . . . Somebody had to do something about it, so he opened up this place. Pretty nifty, isn't it?"

Maybe not nifty, but certainly serviceable—half a dozen long, linoleum-covered tables with benches, the kitchen clean and the counter offering a noon lunch of fresh white bread, vegetable soup and coffee. Three meals a day were served, according to the *Evening Post,* "at a cost of $2,100" a week.

Much as he might have enjoyed this good publicity, Capone could not afford a visit to the gratis eating establishment—he remained out of town, ducking Judge Lyle's vagrancy warrant. But Ralph promoted the venture.

"My brother," Bottles announced, "is feeding three thousand unemployed a day."

"If machines are going to take jobs away from the worker," Al would say, "then he will need to find something else to do. Perhaps he'll get back to the soil. But we must care for him during the period of change."

The soup kitchen chiefly served those who camped out in Grant Park to the east, or under the tracks at the Dearborn and La Salle Street stations to the west. Some could still afford rooms at the YMCA Hotel on Wabash, or in flophouses around the neighborhood. This was the mean world where the South Loop bumped against the old Levee district.

Newsreel cameramen visited the storefront on a cold and windy day, capturing sweeping shots of the long line of men waiting to get in. Then the news crew ventured inside to interview those fortunate enough to grab a seat. One said he'd had his "first real meal in days, thanks to Mr. Capone's hospitality." Others praised the quality of the food, with one going so far as to call it the best soup he'd ever had.

"It wasn't for our friend Al Capone-ee-oh . . . we wouldn't eat!" declared a patron who appeared to have rustled up money earlier for alcoholic sustenance. Another remarked as he stood outside, "Look at what Capone is doing for these poor guys. He's doing all this himself."

That last point was debatable. Court testimony would reveal Capone and his political cronies had leaned on local merchants for donations of food and other goods. Al then gave the stuff away through his soup kitchen, passing it off as his own charity, with perhaps a few crusts of bread remaining on his dime.

This conspicuous if disingenuous display of benevolence bought Capone a great deal of public good will, which would linger for years. One Chicago Heights resident in 1980 thanked God for Al Capone.

"At that time I was seventeen," he said, "with nowhere to go. . . . My folks lost everything, and their ten children had to fend for themselves. I found Mr. Capone's soup line. At least I didn't starve."

But the spectacle deeply disturbed a *Harper's* magazine writer, who recalled standing outside the soup kitchen while flipping through a souvenir book printed up for tourists, featuring ghastly photos of the city's most notorious gangland murders.

She sensed "a connection between the two lots of men, those who stood shivering outside the soup kitchen and those who . . . lay sprawled on the bare boards of matchbox rooms or crouched in the corners of taxis with their heads bashed in. For Al Capone is an ambidextrous giant, who kills with one hand and feeds with the other."

After a few weeks, Capone turned the operation over to United Charities. But the experience of (briefly) running the soup kitchen convinced him real money was to be made . . . selling milk.

"You gotta have a product that everybody needs every day," he would say. "We don't have it in booze. . . . But with milk! Every family every day wants it on the table."

By the following spring, the Outfit had begun establishing its own dairy business, which in later years would come to control a large portion of the Chicago milk market. While forcing its competitors out of business, it got the city to adopt higher quality standards and date labels for dairy products—though Capone, and his supposed concern for Chicago's milk-drinking children, would retroactively get the credit.

As Al would often remark to his close associates, "Do you guys know there's a bigger markup in fresh milk than there is in alcohol? Honest to God, we've been in the wrong racket right along."

Shortly before the soup kitchen sprang up on South State Street, Judge Lyle received an urgent message from an emissary of Capone's, labor leader Tommy Maloy.

They met after hours at a Loop restaurant, where Maloy made an enticing offer "straight from the Big Fellow." Capone, Maloy said, would be willing to fly back to Chicago and turn himself in on the vagrancy charge. Al would even plead guilty, if Lyle would only give him a small fine.

"Then," Maloy said, "he'll make an announcement in court. He'll ask for ten days to clean up his affairs. And then he'll promise to leave Chicago and never come back."

This, Capone hoped, would settle his legal problems. The tax men were having difficulty building a case against him—maybe Irey and Wilson would declare victory and let him off with a fine.

Capone made sure to sweeten the deal, knowing the Republican judge would be running for reelection in a very Democratic season—he offered Lyle a campaign contribution of $10,000. The judge was contemplating running for mayor as well. In next year's Republican primary, Lyle could brand himself the man who'd chased Scarface out of Chicago.

But Lyle hated the "public enemies" too much to even consider the offer. Not about to let Capone dictate the terms of his own surrender, the judge refused to wipe away all of Capone's crimes with a small fine and a sentence of exile, telling Maloy he'd throw the book at Capone the moment he turned himself in. Not surprisingly, the gangster chose to keep his distance.

Meanwhile, Capone kept up back-channel communications with Pat Roche and his investigators hunting Jake Lingle's killer. The businessman emissary assured Roche's representative the Big Fellow was working on the case but hadn't yet come up with anything.

The businessman claimed Capone had made inquiries throughout the Chicago underworld, employing fifty men to do so, but the killer was apparently hiding out of town. Or maybe he'd been rubbed out himself.

Then, in early November, the businessman (who might have been E. J. O'Hare) met with Roche's representative and nervously said, "Al wants to know if you will take the Lingle killer dead."

This question—or was it an offer?—came to Pat Roche and his boss, Charles Rathbun, six weary months into their search for Lingle's killer. But they sent their businessman intermediary back with a message: "You can tell Capone that we know he has been bluffing and that he can go to hell."

Roche was not about to sign someone's death warrant—anyway, he couldn't prosecute a corpse. Capone was either a dead end or, worse, behind the killing—stalling and misleading the investigation. Ultimately, employing a somewhat questionable undercover investigator, Roche had a hand in serving up Leo V. Brothers as the assassin.

Brothers was either the real shooter, or a patsy playing along—out of fear or for money or both—to help shut down the bothersome investigation. Brothers was reportedly enlisted by the ever-crafty Frank Nitto on Capone's behalf. A small-time union racketeer from St. Louis, Brothers had come to Chicago eighteen months before to duck a murder inquiry. He claimed to have no memory of where he was the day Lingle was shot.

Several eyewitnesses disagreed. With no visible means of support, Brothers was represented by four high-priced criminal lawyers, including John Dillinger's future defender, Louis Piquett. Eight witnesses identified Brothers as the fleeing accomplice; seven did not. He received a fourteen-year sentence for a death-penalty crime, serving only eight, with partnerships in two mobbed-up businesses waiting on his release.

Capone almost certainly fixed the trial. But had he ordered Lingle's death? Or had the late Jack Zuta been responsible, perhaps doing Joe Aiello's bidding, or maybe Moran's?

Either way, the guilt or innocence of Leo Brothers seemed strangely irrelevant.

———

In mid-November, Eddie O'Hare reached out to his pal John Rogers, the St. Louis reporter, requesting an urgent meeting in Springfield. When Rogers arrived, he found O'Hare and an unnamed "gang associate," who told them Capone's offer to turn over the Lingle killer's corpse had been discussed at a meeting of top Outfit leaders.

When Jack Guzik objected, Capone had laughingly revealed it as a blind to win Roche's trust. It seemed Al had imported five torpedoes from New York to kill Roche, George Johnson, Art Madden, and Frank Wilson. When all those officials turned up dead, Capone felt he'd be free of suspicion because he'd been helping Roche.

O'Hare couldn't name or even describe the imported killers, but somehow knew the men would be driving a blue sedan with New York plates. The St. Louis reporter brought the story to Johnson, Madden, and Wilson at the Federal Building in Chicago. The three alleged targets accepted a police guard while Wilson hurriedly moved his wife into a new hotel, without telling her their lives might be in danger. One Intelligence Unit agent wanted to round up Capone and "shoot him on the spot."

But not everyone took the threat so seriously. Roche confirmed Capone had offered to serve up the Lingle shooter, which the investigator had refused, proving that O'Hare's tale had a basis in truth. Still, Roche had his doubts.

"It seemed too bizarre, too unreal," the *Tribune* reported, "too much like a movie thriller, to be true."

Then a trusted tipster called a *Trib* reporter who knew his voice but not his name, and said "a carload of gangsters from New York" had come to town "to kill some big shots here." The informer didn't mention Johnson, Wilson, or the other known targets, but did specifically name Judge John Lyle, the vagrancy-warrant king.

"They're tough birds, and one of them is known as 'Max the

Strong,'" the tipster said. "There's five of them and they're ridin' in a Chevrolet sedan."

When the reporter asked when and where the killing would take place, the tipster hung up.

Federal and state investigators fanned out across Chicago, searching for the blue Chevrolet and seeking to put Capone in handcuffs. In the early morning hours of November 30, they raided several Capone hideouts in Cicero and Berwyn.

Judge Lyle himself took part in the raid on a Cicero apartment, filling the address in on the warrant by flashlight. Then the raiders burst in, front and back, with drawn guns. Finding no one home, they did discover a plethora of fancy pajamas and other clothing, all with the monogram "AC."

Other raids turned up more clothes with the same initials, but no sign of Capone or the shadowy killers. One of Roche's investigators reportedly earned $500 calling Capone, warning him "that a posse had been organized to get him and for the good of his health he had better get out of town quick."

Intelligence Unit agent Art Madden had been spoiling for a fight with Scarface for years. Now he called Johnny Torrio to the Federal Building and laid down the law.

"You tell Capone," he said, "that if those five New York killers are not out of town by night, I'll go after Capone with two guns!"

Coolheaded as always, Torrio left and came back two hours later.

"The men have been gone an hour," he said.

No one ever saw the elusive blue Chevy. Word came back to the feds, probably from O'Hare, that Capone had called off the killers and returned to Miami.

Federal officials decided not to pursue the story any further. Guzik's conviction and Nitto's arrest proved the Outfit wasn't all-powerful, but Wilson and others felt this alleged murder plot would build the gangsters back up.

The feds kept the story under wraps until, in late April 1931, the *Tribune* published a detailed account including everything but Rogers's and O'Hare's names. The piece left Wilson "much disgusted."

"By that breach of confidence the lives of our informants may be in jeopardy," Wilson wrote Irey, "and our chances of obtaining further help from this source may be eliminated."

That same day, Wilson's wife, Judith, also saw the *Trib* story. For the first time, she understood why her husband had come to Chicago, and that he had been lying to her for months. She didn't take it well. At the office, Wilson got a phone call from another agent's wife, asking Frank to go home immediately and comfort Judith.

"No," Wilson said. "It's best she fights it out alone."

No one ever saw the blue Chevrolet or the killers inside it; no concrete proof of their existence ever came to light. The descriptions given by O'Hare and the anonymous tipster are sufficiently detailed to seem credible, yet vague enough to ensure the feds would never find the car.

By telling Madden the killers had taken a powder, Torrio may simply have been trying to defuse the situation. Or did he know the truth? That the hitmen and their Chevy didn't exist?

What if the anonymous *Tribune* tipster had been O'Hare himself? But how exactly could O'Hare have learned about the killers in the first place? The Capone crowd was a tight-lipped bunch, especially when it came to murder. Of course, the tipster could have been the unnamed gang "associate" who had accompanied O'Hare to Springfield. . . .

Americans in those days ranted about placing Chicago under martial law, of dragging gangsters before military courts or just shooting them on sight. The cold-blooded murders of a judge, a prosecutor, and three federal agents could very well have kicked off such a crackdown. Just the rumor was enough to send armed men bursting through the doors of Capone's hideouts, ready to shoot the ganglord on sight.

"A theory held by one set of investigators," the *Tribune* reported, "was that O'Hare invented the story of Capone's threats in the hope that the government would seize Capone at once and that in the raid on his stronghold the gang czar might be killed."

The feds took O'Hare's five-hitmen story seriously only because it contained a piece of privileged information—Capone's offer to turn over Lingle's killer—which they knew from Roche to be true. O'Hare, the probable liaison between Roche's representative and Capone, may very well have fabricated that "information" in the first place.

But "Artful Eddie" was a businessman, not a gangster—plotting to topple the Big Fellow would be exceedingly dangerous, if not suicidal. Perhaps he was doing someone else's bidding—someone who could fill the leadership vacuum Capone would leave behind. This individual or a confederate might have been the third man who met with O'Hare and Rogers, the "gang associate" who backed up his unbelievable claims.

O'Hare, and perhaps others in the Outfit, already considered Capone a liability. This mad murder plot only seemed to confirm the need for the Big Fellow to go. Or had it been concocted for that very reason—to remove Al Capone from the throne?

The tax men, it seemed, had a valuable and extremely unlikely ally within the Outfit, sharing—for his own particular reasons—their goal of toppling Capone.

As the year neared its close, with Al Capone not in prison, the Hoover administration began to lose its patience with George E. Q. Johnson. The president kept close tabs on the Capone case, receiving regular updates from Treasury, urging them to keep after the mob kingpin. But the Justice Department, which had recently absorbed the Prohibition Bureau, could show little in the way of progress.

Attorney General William Mitchell and his assistant, G. A. Youngquist, couldn't understand why Johnson still hadn't prosecuted Capone for contempt of court, where they stood a solid chance of convicting him right away. Johnson wasn't really dragging his feet—he merely remained as careful and methodical as ever. He would not take action until he had everything in order.

And he would not settle for a lesser case simply to score political points, when he could get Capone on bigger charges.

"Yes, George E. Q. is slower than the Second Coming," Senator Charles Deneen observed, "but he grinds and grinds and grinds all the time."

Johnson's bosses, sick of waiting, pushed him to grind faster. Everybody knew Capone was violating federal laws, Mitchell told Youngquist that fall, and whenever "a chance appears to convict him, not a minute should be lost." The attorney general even suggested taking the contempt case out of Johnson's hands and trying Capone in Florida, where his doctor had sworn out the false affidavit.

"A Florida jury would make short work of him," Mitchell insisted, "if given a fair chance."

But the attorney general chose another way of spurring Johnson to action. Back in July, after the Prohibition Bureau jumped from Treasury to Justice, President Hoover had dredged up his old plan for attacking bootleg gangs with small, elite squads of Prohibition agents.

"I think it would hearten the situation a good deal," Hoover wrote Mitchell, "if we could revive this idea and make such an organized staff under some special attorney."

Mitchell embraced the plan, and in September sent William J. Froelich, a twenty-nine-year-old special U.S. attorney from Omaha, to organize just such a flying squad in Chicago. This didn't sit well with George Johnson. In a lengthy memo to Mitchell, he made it clear he didn't want or need this young interloper showing him how to do his job.

Johnson demanded the right to choose the investigators working on the Capone case, citing a need for absolute secrecy. Mitchell wouldn't change his mind about Froelich, but agreed to the latter point. Johnson would also help select the head of this new special squad.

The natural candidate was Alexander Jamie, who had directed the

Bureau's anti-Capone efforts so far. But Robert Isham Randolph was lobbying to get Jamie as chief investigator for the Secret Six. Jamie's wartime work for the American Protective League—the private spy service set up by Chicago businessmen—made him uniquely qualified, and most of all, Randolph respected his integrity.

"Thousand dollar bills were floating around like autumn leaves in the bootleg racket," Randolph wrote, "and it was a great temptation to law enforcement officers to pick them up, but Jamie had the reputation of being fearless and incorruptible."

To get his man, Randolph reached out directly to President Hoover, winning Jamie a leave of absence from his federal job. Jamie left the Bureau on October 30, taking his first assistant, Don Kooken, with him to the Secret Six. Edna Ness followed a week later, resigning from the Prohibition Bureau to keep working as Jamie's secretary.

Her departure eliminated a potential conflict of interest—Eliot could now succeed Jamie as special agent in charge, without having to fire his own wife. On October 22, Jamie recommended his brother-in-law for the post.

"Mr. Ness is known to you personally," Jamie wrote to the director of Prohibition, "as is also his reputation for honesty and ability to hold such a position. Should you see fit to appoint him . . . I am sure that it would meet with the approval of United States Attorney George E. Q. Johnson and Col. Robert Isham Randolph . . . and would be considered advantageous to the Chicago program."

Jamie's memo hints at a plan for a coordinated attack on Capone, one combining the efforts of the Secret Six and the special agents—and one in which Ness would play a major role. But the Prohibition Bureau prized seniority over strategy, and went instead with W. E. Bennett, former head of the special agents in Jacksonville, Florida.

Soon after, the question of picking a leader for Froelich's squad came up. Jamie again pushed for Ness, getting Randolph to pressure Johnson on Eliot's behalf. Not that Johnson needed much convincing—he knew Ness and trusted him. With Jamie running the Secret Six, and

Ness leading this squad of special agents, Johnson could step up his economic attacks on Capone, finally getting the results the White House wanted.

New boss Froelich didn't have a history with Ness, but he admired the young man's record. All that Ness had done so far—from his undercover work and raiding in the Heights to his studies under August Vollmer and his wiretapping of Ralph Capone—had prepared him well.

One day in late November, Johnson ordered Ness to meet with Froelich. Pleased when he got the news, Ness didn't expect a leadership position. He would gladly have settled for just making it onto the squad.

But when he met with Froelich, the tall, barrel-chested young lawyer offered him the top spot. Ness would lead a small team in a direct assault on the Outfit's main sources of income, smashing its breweries and distilleries and gathering evidence linking Capone to the liquor racket.

Eliot's agents would work outside the Prohibition Bureau, serving instead as part of the U.S. attorney's office. Although Ness would report directly to Johnson and Froelich, the choice of personnel would be his—and his alone.

Whether he knew it or not, Ness had waited his entire career for just such an opportunity. Finally, he could slough off the corruption, incompetence, and apathy dragging him down with the rest of the Prohibition Bureau, and show Chicago what he could do. By the finish of his meeting with Froelich, Eliot Ness was the lead Prohibition investigator on the Capone case.

He was twenty-seven years old.

PART THREE

ON THE SPOT

Eliot Ness's Justice Department credentials. *(Carolyn Wallace, ATF photographer / Bureau of Alcohol, Tobacco, Firearms and Explosives)*

Twenty

December 1930–February 1931

On Monday, December 8, 1930, Eliot Ness reported for duty as head of the new Capone squad.

With him were two others from the Chicago Prohibition office—Maurice Seager, the slab-faced special agent with whom Ness had served in Cicero, and E. A. Moore, a "special employee" who had yet to pass his civil service test. That same day, George E. Q. Johnson requested transfers for four more agents stationed in other cities: Ulric H. Berard, Lyle B. Chapman, William J. Gardner, and Joseph D. Leeson.

When they arrived in Chicago, Ness would have six men at his command, each making no more than $3,000 a year. Together, they would take on a multi-million-dollar criminal enterprise employing some two thousand people.

"If this group . . . were to make a dent where 250 Prohibition Agents and quite a few thousand police had not," Ness recalled, "a different kind of game would have to be played."

Ness had combed through the Prohibition Bureau's personnel files, searching for agents who fit August Vollmer's ideal of a proper policeman: hardboiled yet scholarly, streetwise yet scientific. Though he was himself a married man, Ness wanted young, courageous men without wives and children to support.

And he needed specialists of various kinds—experts in wiretapping, tailing cars, shadowing suspects, and painstaking paperwork. Above all, each candidate had to be ready and able to resist massive bribes.

But Ness could find few men fitting all these criteria. Each agent he selected was more than thirty years old; two were in their forties, and at least three had wives. A few had serious character flaws.

Still, Ness was in no position to be choosy—he had to make do with what the Bureau could spare, which forced him to compromise. Left with imperfect materials, he built an imperfect team, one that would take time to refine.

Joe Leeson was thirty-two, married with three children, but everything else about him fit Ness's ideal agent. Born in Indiana, Leeson was soft-spoken and reserved, a face in the crowd despite his blue eyes and reddish brown hair. In just two years with the Prohibition Bureau, Leeson had racked up an enviable record, proving his integrity and ability.

"Mr. Leeson has been one of the best agents that has ever worked under my direction in the Detroit office," his superior gushed that winter. "He has been a hardworking, conscientious agent and he at all times gave the best that was in him in the interest of the Government."

A natural undercover man, Leeson won fame throughout the Bureau for his talents as a driver. When tailing a suspect, he could snake through traffic, slipping between other cars while keeping himself well hidden. He didn't play the stock market, didn't gamble, and didn't buy things he couldn't afford—he had never even opened a bank account. In short, Ness could trust him. And he probably came highly recommended: Leeson's brother-in-law was Don Kooken, Ness's partner on the Chicago Heights case.

Ness also sought the services of a "pencil detective," someone who could decipher documents seized in raids and find the hidden clues that would lead to Capone. For this he chose Lyle Bishop Chapman—"L.B.," to his friends—a forty-year-old special agent from Los Angeles who'd been serving in Indianapolis.

Tall, handsome, his slicked-back brown hair graying at the temples, the blue-eyed Chapman had a deep, booming voice that "hits you like a bass drum," as one reporter wrote. On paper, Chapman—who had studied chemistry and played football at Colgate University—seemed exactly the kind of brainy yet brawny crimefighter Ness sought.

Before joining the Prohibition Bureau, Chapman had worked for the Intelligence Unit, learning how to build complex cases out of minute financial details. As a Prohibition agent, he kept a scrapbook on known bootleggers—"a veritable registry of rum runners," according to the *Los Angeles Times*—that he used time and again to win convictions.

"It goes without saying that Mr. Chapman is a very intelligent and capable investigator," a superior of his observed, "when he wishes to apply himself diligently to his work."

That, as Ness would soon discover, was precisely Chapman's problem—he treated being a special agent like a nine-to-five job. When an undercover assignment kept him out late, he moaned and griped, demanding time off to catch up on his sleep.

One special agent claimed other agents didn't want to work with Chapman—L.B., despite his obvious abilities, was lazy. The man needed to get it "out of his head that all the women in the country are crazy about him," and that "somebody is always abusing him."

Chapman routinely asked for raises in pay, leading one official to suspect, "He is inclined to live beyond his means, and, therefore, finds himself in almost continual financial embarrassment." Both traits should have disqualified him from the Capone squad. But Ness needed Chapman's pen-and-pencil prowess.

Why Ness chose William Jennings Gardner is less clear. The forty-five-year-old regular Prohibition agent, then stationed in Syracuse, New York, had also played college football. At a strapping six foot one and nearly two hundred pounds, he brought much-needed muscle to the team.

But Gardner's record with the Prohibition Bureau, where he'd served off and on since 1926, offered little to recommend him. Superiors found him "quite lacking in initiative" and displaying no "investigative turn of mind." He had resigned or been dropped from the service multiple times, once because of an anonymous letter accusing him of corruption.

His turbulent home life, and his fractious marriage to a Michigan heiress, kept intruding into his career. Mrs. Gardner didn't like her husband's work. After resigning from the Bureau over trouble at home, his return to the job prompted "one 'Hellacious' fight" that set the stage for the couple's second divorce.

The son of a white Civil War veteran and a Chippewa woman, Gardner had received his education in Pennsylvania at the Carlisle Indian Industrial School—a radical, experimental boarding school founded on the belief that Native Americans could survive only if they left their culture far behind.

"Kill the Indian," went the founder's motto, "save the man."

Carlisle cut its students' hair, forced them to speak English, and kept them from their families for years at a time, all with the goal of making them white in everything but skin color. As an adult, Gardner worked to keep up this paleface facade, making a point of dressing well, sometimes wearing a matinee-idol mustache. But nothing could hide the copper-toned skin of his mother's side of the family.

The school's football team achieved national fame in the early 1900s. At a time when the game was muddy, bloody, and often deadly, Carlisle elevated the sport, introducing such innovations as the forward pass, revolutionizing the game. Gardner became one of their star players—a powerhouse runner, nimble, determined, unstoppable.

His coach recalled one game where Gardner, after having "his leg wrenched and his jaw broken . . . played on the finish without telling me a word about it, afraid I would send in a substitute." Knute Rockne wrote Gardner's "down-the-field play . . . was as fine as I've ever seen—a thing of beauty."

Gardner would never recapture the glory of his football days. His life after Carlisle was a series of promising opportunities going nowhere. He was accepted to West Point but didn't attend. He earned a law degree and practiced for several years, but the Great War put his legal career on hold.

He served with distinction on the Western Front, but a mustard gas attack left him hospitalized for a year, his lungs blistered, burned, and permanently damaged. When Gardner got out, he tried to resume his law practice, but gave up after poor health forced him to seek a kinder climate. Eventually, like many a failure and reject, he wound up with the Prohibition Bureau.

Ness and Gardner had briefly served together in 1928, as members of George "Hardboiled" Golding's squad in Chicago. Gardner had proven himself a willing soldier, even taking part in the disastrous raid when special agents shot bailiff William Beatty.

"We are quite busy showing these natives that the law of the land is supreme," Gardner wrote to Washington after the raid. "Some of them are hard to convince."

That Gardner took pride in subduing hostile "natives" on behalf of his government suggests Carlisle's influence.

Alexander Jamie thought highly of Gardner, and may have suggested him for the Capone squad. But Gardner was no longer the man he'd been, his body beaten and battered on the gridiron and poisoned in the trenches, his very identity broken down and reshaped.

By late December, the four additional agents had all assembled in Chicago. The Detroit office resisted having to give up Leeson, but no one raised objections to losing Chapman or Gardner. George E. Q. Johnson secured the men their own office on the fifth floor of the Transportation Building, away from the rest of the special agents and files already breached at least once.

Maurice Seager, serving as Ness's second in command, wrote his family on December 28, saying the Prohibition Bureau kept the team well supplied and armed to the teeth. Their three Cadillacs, he reported, were loaded down with a police radio, bulletproof windows, armor plating, and a full complement of weapons—machine guns, sawed-off shotguns, handguns, and grenades.

The men were hard-bitten and "ready to go at any time," Seager said with obvious pride. He and his fellow agents saw their "share of blood & broken bones every day," which served to "relieve the monotony of life somewhat."

But not everyone felt so gung-ho.

"I remember my knees shook like jelly when I got the orders telling me what was up," Lyle Chapman recalled. "Frankly, I pondered how to get out of it."

Meeting Ness calmed Chapman's fears somewhat, but the pencil man wouldn't stop searching for an escape route.

Like the tax investigators, Ness's agents faced the nearly insurmountable challenge of proving the obvious—everyone knew Capone was a bootlegger; he'd admitted as much in the press. But charging him with liquor crimes seemed all but hopeless, thanks to holes in the dry law big enough to drive a beer truck through.

The Eighteenth Amendment prohibited exactly three things: the manufacture of beverage alcohol, the transportation of beverage alcohol, and the sale of beverage alcohol. But Capone had carefully insulated himself, never operating his own stills, tending his own bars, or making his own deliveries.

And unlike brother Ralph, Al knew not to discuss booze orders over tapped phone lines.

So, rather than go after Capone directly, Ness and his team would focus on exposing his organization. Thanks to the Bureau's Lexington Hotel wiretap, they already knew of a strategy meeting Capone attended in June 1930 with the top brass in the beer business: Joe "Shrinking Violet" Fusco, Bert Delaney, and George Howlett.

Fusco directly managed the brewing, sale, and delivery of every beer barrel the Outfit sold. Delaney specialized in finding buildings to house illicit breweries or distilleries. Howlett signed the leases for each operation, acting as flamboyant front man, living the life of a socialite, supposedly in the printing business. Nobody asked too many questions about garages and warehouses he rented in out of the-way parts of town.

The special agents stood a good chance of getting hard evidence against Fusco, Delaney, and Howlett. And if they could prove these lieutenants had taken a direct hand in bootlegging, they could use the Lexington Hotel meeting to tie Capone in, building a bridge between the gangster and his crimes.

That meant charging Capone with *conspiring* to violate the Prohibition law, rather than simply violating it. He would face a maximum of two years in prison, as opposed to five for each Prohibition offense. But with the limited legal tools at their disposal, this was the best Ness's squad could hope for.

By early January, the special agents were tapping the phone lines of every Capone haunt they could locate. One such target, a sugar warehouse and distribution center, sat across an alley from the Institute for Juvenile Research, where Ness's old friend (and co-inventor of the lie detector) John Larson worked.

Ness showed up one Saturday afternoon with an electrician, hoping to tap the line on the sugar building and use Larson's lab as a listening post. This turned out to be technically impossible, and Ness had to abandon the notion. But before he could leave, he got an urgent phone call—someone had seen two men drive up to the sugar building in a truck carrying a prisoner, bound, gagged, and bleeding from the mouth.

Ness hung up and looked at Larson.

"Doc," he asked, calm, quiet, "got a rod?"

"Hell, no," Larson said.

Ness turned to the only other man in the lab, one of Larson's fellow scientists.

"Jim," Ness asked, "got a rod?"

"No, sir."

Ness avoided carrying a weapon whenever he could.

"They won't be so quick to shoot at you," he believed, "if they know you can't shoot back."

A diplomat at heart, he preferred having adversaries underestimate him, lulling them into inaction. Pulling a gun said he'd lost control of the situation.

But going on a raid with only a pair of unarmed scientists as backup was another thing entirely.

Still, Ness didn't hesitate. "Let's go," he said.

He led Larson and Jim across the alley into the sugar building. They found two men leaning against piled sacks of sugar, looking like gangsters, not warehouse workers. A hand thrust deep in his pocket, feigning a revolver, Ness kept them covered with his pointing finger—or was it a rare instance of the Untouchable actually packing heat? The two scientists did their best to follow suit, pointing their hidden fingers like gun barrels as well.

The apparent gangsters decided not to call Ness's bluff, putting up no resistance as the raiders searched the building—no trace of the tied-up prisoner.

Larson recalled feeling suspicious when he saw some pigeons flying about, as if their roost had just been disturbed. Years later, when the building was demolished, excavators discovered what Larson called "an underground 'death to rats' chamber"—apparently the final destination for the man Ness tried to save.

The squad found more success elsewhere. Ness hoped to tap Capone's sales office phones, in a hotel on the South Side. Once again, the building presented technical problems making a wiretap impossible.

But this time, Ness decided to find a way of convincing the mob to move where the special agents could easily listen in. He got word to the gang his men were keeping tabs on the sales office; if they looked out the window at a certain time, they'd see federal agents taking down license plate numbers.

"I, of course, made good on this promise," Ness wrote. "The following three days my men were around the hotel doing a lot of conspicuous note taking."

The Outfit reacted just as Ness had hoped, by moving the office to the second floor of a garage, where they could drive right inside the building and keep their cars, and their work, hidden. But not from Eliot Ness.

"In a short period of time I had those telephones tapped," Ness recalled, "and after a time it became almost impossible for them to deliver beer without a good risk of being knocked off by us."

Ness kept his superiors apprised of the squad's work.

"After experiencing great difficulty," he wrote to Washington on January 20, "we have been able to secure telephone taps covering the various headquarters' spots of the Capone gang and are in a favorable strategical [sic] position to obtain considerable information relative to their workings as soon as operations begin again."

Wiretaps revealed the gang had gone temporarily underground.

"At the present time several forces are brought into play in Chicago," Ness wrote, "and the operations of the Capone syndicate have for the last few days been absolutely stopped."

Capone himself remained on the run, trying to dodge his contempt-of-court charge. From the phone taps Ness knew "Snorky" had briefly stopped in Chicago to redraw the bounds of his empire, but had since disappeared. The squad stayed glued to the taps for any hints to his location.

But even as they made progress, the unit began to fray. Ulric Berard left the squad almost immediately, for unknown reasons. E. A. Moore apparently failed his civil service test, despite receiving study help from Ness, and also had to be dropped. Subpoenas dragged Leeson and Chapman away from Chicago for weeks at a time, with Chapman traveling all the way to Seattle.

"Mr. Seager and myself have been greatly handicapped owing to the fact that our small number of men has been drawn upon by court subpoenas," Ness wrote Washington in a plea for more manpower.

Dwight Avis, chief of the Special Agency Division, sympathized with Ness, and sent a few agents on a temporary basis. "I am also endeavoring to find an agent or two to assign permanently to you," Avis wrote.

But with courts in session around the country, and too few special agents to go around, the prospects for help on the Capone case seemed slim.

Then, in mid-January, came the sudden disappearance of William Gardner. He had requested thirty days' leave soon after arriving in Chicago, claiming an attack of chronic bronchitis going back to being gassed in Europe.

Ness had passed Gardner's request on to William Froelich, who turned it down. On January 18, Gardner called Seager and threatened to resign if he didn't get his leave. Soon after, without another word to the office, he vanished.

"Mr. Gardner recently was paid over $3000.00 army pay, which was past due," Ness wrote Avis, "and his wife's uncle recently died, I understand, leaving her a large fortune, so I assume that Agent Gardner feels he is no longer dependent upon his position in the Bureau of Prohibition."

This was hardly the first time Gardner had gone AWOL, Avis replied.

On February 2, Ness got a newly minted special agent to replace the absent Gardner—Warren E. Stutzman, thirty-one, a former police officer from Pennsylvania. Blue-eyed, bald, with a lampshade mustache, Stutzman had—much like Gardner—bounced in and out of the Bureau for years before becoming a special agent.

Stutzman was outgoing and energetic, a tireless investigator who never let go of a lead, even if it led him down the wrong path. One superior described him as "an untrained hunting dog" who "invariably would go off at a tangent on matters not pertaining to his assignment."

While nothing in Stutzman's record indicated outright corruption, he was constantly borrowing money from his coworkers, asking how other agents made do on such a meager salary. This struck some as suspicious. The agent was "not lacking in forwardness and brass," George Golding wrote in 1929, "and is given to making, what I would call, ungentlemanly remarks."

But Eliot couldn't possibly have known his newest team member had a dark secret he'd managed to conceal from the Bureau, which could blow up the entire investigation—Stutzman was a convicted felon. During the Great War, "a youthful drunken escapade" got the seventeen-year-old Stutzman court-martialed for robbery, desertion, and larceny.

Sentenced to ten years, Stutzman served only a fraction of his time before returning to duty. But his conviction, if uncovered, would make him worse than useless as a federal agent, "because of the possibility of attacks by defense counsel based on his criminal record," a Treasury official noted. Every piece of evidence Stutzman touched was potentially contaminated by his past.

Ness also almost lost the pencil detective, so crucial to building a conspiracy case. Chapman seized on the subpoena summoning him to Seattle, asking for a transfer back to Los Angeles. Since he was already on the West Coast, Chapman argued, why not save the government the cost of traveling back to Chicago? His friends and family also sent letters to their senator and congressman, urging them to reach out to the Bureau on L.B.'s behalf.

Avis remained unmoved.

"Climatic conditions on the Coast," he wrote, "and other general conditions prevailing there are not conducive to inspiring a man who is not already so inclined to produce more work, or work longer hours."

He ordered Chapman back to Chicago. Meanwhile, Avis's boss, the director of Prohibition, noted in Chapman's file the agent's attempt "to use political pressure" to get out of an important assignment. Ness would soon get his pencil detective back, but he couldn't fix Chapman's attitude so easily.

To shore up the crumbling squad, Ness recruited agents from the Chicago office, starting with Bernard Vincent "Barney" Cloonan, thirty-four, a burly, blue-eyed, brown-haired Chicagoan with a no-nonsense demeanor. Only recently promoted to special agent, Cloonan had experience finding stills and breweries and following paper trails back to their owners, his work supplementing the sometimes-unreliable Chapman's.

More help came from Thomas J. Friel, a skinny special agent and former Pennsylvania state trooper. Friel, thirty-eight, unmarried, had the perfect background, taking law courses from the same correspondence school as Ness and working to build conspiracy cases under Alexander Jamie. He was also terribly shy around women, something Marty Lahart—who also joined the squad around this time—ribbed him about unmercifully.

Even Bill Gardner returned. He had gone to San Diego with his wife and young daughter, seeking relief for his ailing lungs. When Gardner finally checked in with Ness and learned no one knew what had happened to him, he rushed back to Chicago and showed up, ready to carry on as if he'd never left.

Ness told his wandering agent to call Washington; if it was all right with them, he could stay. Gardner then spoke to someone in the home office, who raised no objections, if Ness gave the okay. But rather than getting Ness's approval, Gardner simply slipped into a bureaucratic dead zone, keeping his job because no one had fired him. He didn't stay long—after spending three more weeks on the Capone case, Gardner resigned and returned to California.

Gardner would eventually bounce back to the Bureau, though never again serve on Ness's squad. When Prohibition began to wind down, Gardner's mediocre record made him among the first agents dropped.

He spiraled into alcoholism, living off various family members till he wore out his welcome and went back to the bottle. The marriage that kept upending his career eventually collapsed. He died in Arizona in June 1965, having lived long enough to see his brief, five-week stint on the Capone squad become the basis for a central character on the popular *Untouchables* TV series.

Ness left little record of his struggle to hold his squad together. Though modest by nature, he tended to cover up his own embarrassments and never dwelled on his mistakes, at least not publicly. He would later paint the team as a well-oiled machine, harmonious from the start—not just comrades but friends, even brothers.

More likely, they were simply men doing a job, one that didn't seem all that remarkable at the time. But as he looked over the complex structure of the Outfit, and saw how the man at the top kept everything under control, Ness had to admit a certain admiration for his nemesis.

"Capone was a natural," Ness said. "He could organize and he had appeal; men fell in behind him." Had Capone played it straight, Ness believed, the ganglord could have been a major figure in legitimate business.

This perhaps gave Capone too much credit—Al had inherited Torrio's Outfit almost fully formed, while Ness had to build his team from scratch. And yet, when it came to being a leader and convincing his men to fall in behind him, Ness still had much to learn.

Elsewhere in Chicago, Frank Wilson kept searching for bookkeeper Les-lie Shumway, the one man who could tie the Hawthorne Smoke Shop ledger to Capone. But Wilson was running out of time, if he wasn't already too late.

Federal courts had yet to decide whether income tax evasion fell under a six-year statute of limitations or one lasting only three years. A case working its way through the courts in Boston would soon settle the matter—if a judge ruled the shorter statute applied, the Hawthorne ledger would be inadmissible, covering as it did income from 1924 to 1926.

Even if the longer rule won out, the ledger was perilously close to its expiration date. To charge Capone with tax evasion in 1924, federal officials had to win an indictment before March 15, 1931. And without Capone's bookkeeper, they had nothing to present before a grand jury.

About a month before deadline, Wilson got word through "underground channels"—probably Eddie O'Hare—Shumway could be found in Florida, Wilson's favorite vacation spot. He went down to Miami with O'Hare's reporter pal John Rogers, and squeezed in a day of fishing on the Gulf Stream before locating Shumway at his place of employment, a Capone-connected dog track. Figuring the man would flee if approached directly, Wilson had another agent serve him a subpoena from a fictitious business, the "White Steel Company."

When the bookkeeper said he'd never heard of the firm, the agent spoke casually of a probable mix-up, but advised he appear anyway and expect to be excused. Shumway took this advice, walking right into Wilson's trap.

"Once we had Shumway where we wanted him," Wilson said, "we showed him the records."

Wilson leaned hard on the timid little bookkeeper, threatening to let the gang know the feds had located him. Surely, the agent said, the syndicate would not hesitate to silence a potential witness, and leave Shumway's poor wife a widow.

"It took some time," Wilson recalled, "but we finally convinced Shumway that Capone's day was done and that he had better come clean."

On February 18, Shumway signed a sworn statement identifying the ledger as the business record he'd kept at the Hawthorne Smoke Shop. Apart from the club's managers, "the only other person whom I recognized as an owner of the business and from whom I took orders relating to the business was Mr. Alphonse Capone."

Now, Wilson had all he needed to secure an indictment. He secretly spirited Shumway to Chicago and brought him before the grand jury. On March 13, two days before deadline, the grand jury returned a secret indictment charging Capone with evading his income tax in 1924.

But the case against the gangster remained incomplete. Federal officials won the indictment "not because there was enough evidence available," Assistant Attorney General Youngquist wrote, "but because the statute of limitations was about to run for the year in question, 1924."

This gave the government a reprieve, but only a brief one. Sooner or later, Capone would learn of the indictment, and the feds would lose the element of surprise. If word of the charges got out, George Johnson knew potential witnesses would clam up, destroying any chance for a second indictment.

So Wilson kept gathering testimony. Once he had enough, the investigation would go public.

Having just managed to corral his own unit, Ness now found himself racing against the tax men to avoid losing his shot at Capone.

Capone leaving court after his contempt-of-court trial, February 27, 1931. *(Cleveland Public Library Photograph Collection)*

Twenty-One

December 1930–February 1931

Al Capone's imperious eighteen-year-old sister, Mafalda, had always been important to him. She loved him deeply, too, although she would sometimes chafe at the damage his notoriety did to her.

"Who," she often complained, "would dare to risk dating Al Capone's little sister?"

The answer could be found in her brother's circle of business associates—John J. Maritote, brother of another "public enemy." They'd been childhood sweethearts, Mafalda said, though Maritote—a twenty-three-year-old whose eyebrows overwhelmed his otherwise handsome face—currently had a different woman in his life. He took out his marriage certificate with transparent reluctance, remarking, "I've hardly seen the girl in a year."

Capone arranged the wedding to shore up his own power, gangland observers said, like the head of a royal family in the Middle Ages, barely consulting the couple. Still, Mafalda apparently welcomed this solution to her dating woes, and the groom's qualms were eased by a $50,000 dowry and the gift of a home from the bride's big brother.

The wedding took place at St. Mary's Church in Cicero on December 14 before a packed sanctuary of "the elect of the alky aristocracy," as the *Tribune* put it. The only "untoward event" was the arrest of five armed bodyguards by uninvited party pooper Pat Roche. Despite a snowstorm, local rubberneckers swarmed the edges of the red carpet to the church doors while Cicero police dealt with heavy traffic; schoolchildren crawled under the ropes beneath the canopy, chased away by the police before trying again.

From the silk top hat of Ralph Capone, who gave the bride away, to the soft white leather shoes of the little flower girl, the afternoon event was a perfect, perfectly normal North Shore wedding—ushers in tuxes, bridesmaids in pink taffeta, matrons of honor (Mae, and Ralph's slim blonde wife) in silver-edged chiffon. In ivory satin, Mafalda, pretty and plump, beamed next to her uncomfortable soulmate. The reception would showcase a wedding cake that cost more than two thousand Depression dollars.

Apart from actual romance, the wedding had everything, except the older brother who arranged it—Al Capone stayed behind at Palm Island. Though Cicero was outside Chicago police jurisdiction, Capone was still ducking Judge Lyle's vagrancy warrant, and likely didn't want to subject Mafalda and other relatives to increased press attention.

Missing the event would be painful for a man so devoted to his family. Despite the comforts of Miami, Capone remained indignant about his expulsion from his adopted hometown, unloading his frustrations to sympathetic journalists a few days after Christmas.

Washington Herald editor Eleanor Patterson—who stopped "on an impulse" at Capone's home on Palm Island—was granted a surprisingly frank interview.

Patterson found her famous host a "kindly, hospitable man, proud of his estate," though she remarked his famous scar was "like the welt from the lash of a whip."

"Come in," he told her, a bodyguard nearby. "Let me show you around."

The iron gates clanked behind her. Capone escorted her through his garden and back to the swimming pool and two-story bathhouse with its second-floor diving board extending over the pool. Smartly dressed young bodyguards lurked in the shadows. In the sunshine, she got her first real eyeful of her host.

"He has the neck and shoulders of a wrestler," she reported. "One of those prodigious Italians, thick-chested, close to six feet tall. The muscles of his arms stretched the sleeves of his light brown suit, so that it seemed to be cut too small for him."

But she couldn't look him in his "ice-gray, ice-cold eyes," any more than she could a tiger's.

As they strolled, Capone groused about not "getting a square deal" from society or law enforcement.

"I don't interfere with big business," he said. "None of the big business guys can say I ever took a dollar from 'em. Why, I done a favor for one of the big newspapers in the country when they was up against it."

He was referring to strikebreaking activities he'd provided for the *Tribune,* owned by Patterson's cousin, Robert McCormick.

"And what do I get for doing 'em a favor?" he asked, adding, "I only want to do business, you understand, with my own class. Why can't they let me alone? . . . I don't interfere with their racket."

He said the government was framing him back home—both the tax charge and the vagrancy beef.

Patterson asked why he wanted to return to Chicago, anyway. Had he considered living in Italy?

"What should I live in Italy for?" Capone was no Italian; he'd been born in Brooklyn. "My family, my wife, my kid, my racket—they're all in Chicago."

Not really—Mae and Sonny were Florida residents now.

He walked the reporter to the sun porch, "furnished in excellent taste." Open doors onto the living room revealed more loitering bodyguards, smoking, reading. In a nearby corner, cotton snow surrounded a brightly decorated Christmas tree under whose branches Sonny's toys could be glimpsed, including child-sized golf clubs. Patterson and her host sat at a glass-topped table. Lemonade was served.

That was when she noticed Capone's half-clenched hands.

"Enormous," she wrote. "Powerful enough to tackle—well, most anything, although superficially soft from lack of exposure, and highly manicured."

Capone sat impassively, like an intense, if nervous Buddha. But when she suggested he'd gone into prison out of fear, he bristled.

"Oh, you think I'm afraid? I'll show you how afraid I was."

As he spoke of how hard he'd worked to get out of prison, he began to talk "very fast and for the first time with a tinge of foreign accent. You sensed again the terrific tension hidden behind the deliberate gestures and stolid face."

"And where did I go when I got out of jail?" Capone went on defensively. "Just to show you how much afraid I was. First thing I did, I went back to Chicago, didn't I? And believe me, I'm going back there now!"

From this "flash of real hate and rage," Patterson knew she'd hit a nerve. "The one thing every gangster fears most is fear," she wrote. "One sign of weakness, one second of faltering and his own wolf pack is upon him, tearing at his throat."

This show of temper indicated Capone—normally so cool with the press—was starting to have trouble controlling himself. Stress? Syphilis?

Around this time, Capone played host to another famous journalist. Gossip columnist Walter Winchell was in Miami when a mutual friend asked if he would like to visit Palm Island. Winchell arrived to find Capone and "three huskies" playing cards. The boss sat facing the door, as he always did; when Winchell entered, the three men vanished at Capone's unspoken command.

Winchell was impressed with Capone's size—not just his hands, but his whole form. He also took note of a large automatic pistol on the card table.

"Here you are playing a game of cards with your friends," Winchell said, "but you keep a gun handy."

"I have no friends," Capone shot back.

This from a man who'd conspicuously palled around with entertainers and politicians. But those relationships were based on Capone's ability to supply money and booze. Like many a celebrity, Al found himself surrounded yet always alone.

Capone spoke about his upcoming contempt-of-court trial, heaping scorn on his physician, Kenneth Phillips, though the doctor had stood by the affidavit claiming Capone was too ill to go to Chicago. Al insisted he'd been "so sick I fell down a whole flight of stairs!"

But Phillips, he said, recanted after trying to chisel Capone with a huge bill, which his patient only partly paid.

"So he told the Government that I was never sick," the ganglord said—adding, with a heavy sigh, "Anybody I have wined and dined right in my own house crossed me."

The prospect of another jail term loomed large to Capone, yet Winchell could see that, in a way, the gangster was already imprisoned.

Capone did what he could to help Big Bill Thompson beat back a primary challenge from John Lyle. The judge, claiming Capone contributed as much as $150,000 to Thompson's campaign, asked voters what kind of influence that money bought. He even brandished a machine gun in one speech.

"The real issue in this campaign," Lyle said, "is not whether I shall be elected or whether Thompson shall be elected, but whether Al Capone is to be authorized to rule Chicago again through the medium of a dummy in the Mayor's office."

On primary day, February 24, Lyle predicted he'd "take the city by a majority of 150,000 votes"—the same margin Thompson expected for himself. Both were overly optimistic, though in a crowded field, Thompson won by almost 68,000 votes, less than 47 percent of the total.

"The majority of the Republican vote was against him," said the *Tribune,* "but its distribution made it ineffective. Judge Lyle could have been nominated if he had been given a clear field against the mayor, whose acts and character are condemned by the majority of voters in his own party."

Weakened but unbowed, Thompson would go on to face Democrat Anton J. Cermak in the general election.

"The chance of escaping four more years of political depravity in the city hall," wrote the *Trib*, "is contained in the Democratic ticket."

But Thompson's opponent was no reformer—for years, Anton Cermak opposed Prohibition and pocketed graft as a state legislator, alderman, and Cook County Board president. Born in Bohemia, Tony grew up in Braidwood, Illinois, where he worked in a coal mine; in Chicago, he was a railroad brakeman and horse-drawn streetcar driver, then set up a hauling business before winning election as state representative in 1902.

A hard worker and ready fighter for his constituents, Cermak maneuvered well in county government, moving up the Democratic ladder. The Bohemians were a comparatively small ethnic group; but Tony, working with other voting blocs, saw his influence grow—and his wealth, from graft and payoffs.

Cermak, roughhewn but pragmatic, won with 58 percent, thanks in part to Lyle voters who liked the Bohemian's tough anticrime talk. Finished in Chicago politics, Thompson slunk off to retirement and irrelevance. The *Tribune* bade him good riddance.

"For Chicago," they wrote, "Thompson has meant filth, corruption, obscenity, idiocy and bankruptcy. He has given the city an international reputation for moronic buffoonery, barbaric crime, triumphant hoodlumism, unchecked graft, and a dejected citizenship. . . . He made Chicago a byword of the collapse of American civilization."

As his hold on city government slipped away, Capone focused on his upcoming contempt-of-court trial. Nearly two years had passed since the ganglord ducked a federal subpoena to testify about the massive Jamie-Ness raid on Chicago Heights, but George E. Q. Johnson had waited until other lines of attack against the gangster—the tax and Prohibition investigations—were well under way.

Finally, the trial was set for February 25, the day after the primary, in the courtroom of sixty-one-year-old James Herbert Wilkerson, who had overseen Ralph Capone's prosecution for tax fraud.

Wilkerson, in nearly ten years on the bench, earned a reputation as every gangster's worst enemy. Once, in a fit of "righteous wrath," he locked up the Cook County sheriff for letting two bootleggers run free.

On the first day of the trial, the Federal Building swarmed with cops, plainclothes detectives, deputy sheriffs, lawyers, bailiffs, reporters, Secret Service ops, gangsters in their best business attire, and—as the *Chicago Daily News* put it—"people who had nothing much to do." Outside, squad cars circled the block with sirens screaming while spectators worked at not "being trodden underfoot."

On the sixth floor, a two-desk roadblock supervised by Secret Service agents and marshals examined the credentials of all seeking passage. Certain would-be attendees were singled out for a frisk, while rejects scrambled to the railings of other floors to lean over and catch a look at the Great Man as he crossed the rotunda.

Arriving early at the Adams Street entrance, Capone was heavier than on his last courtroom appearance, yet he moved gracefully through the crowd to dart up the stairs, looking prosperous and businesslike in his trademark pearl-gray fedora. No bodyguards in sight but with cops fore and aft, he laughed off requests to pause and pose.

As he arranged his 235 pounds into a counsel's table chair, he seemed to the *Trib* to have "the complacency of a milk-fattened shoat lolling in a mud puddle." But they also commented on his sartorial splendor: "A platinum watch chain, studded with diamonds, crossed his waistcoat, and pearl-gray spats and a white silk handkerchief in his coat pocket set off his rich, blue suit."

Like Kris Kringle in *Miracle on 34th Street,* Capone had fan mail delivered to him in court, including a pink, perfumed letter he perused with a chuckle.

He chatted up reporters about the Florida weather, the Depression, and an upcoming heavyweight bout. The *Chicago Daily News* caught him taking in the courtroom's "white marble walls, its dull gold ceiling and ornaments and the preamble to the constitution in Roman letters above the door."

Al cheerfully answered the reporters' more pertinent questions. Why had he failed to show at the grand jury in March 1929?

"It's on the up and up that I was sick," he said. "I came up here when I was able to travel. I don't mind seeing grand juries. I do everything I can to help them."

Asked whether he'd come by train, plane, or car, Capone smiled and said, "Oh, I just got here." Between handshakes with reporters, feds, and cops, Capone claimed he hadn't wasted money on Thompson's campaign, and had dismissive words for Judge Lyle, who "tried to make a campaign issue out of me, but the public answered him."

The difference between him and Lyle, Capone said, was that Lyle "spent thousands of dollars trying to get into office, while I'm spending thousands to feed people."

This he said while fingering his ornate diamond-studded watch chain and wearing a ring with a single massive diamond.

Capone planned to stay around Chicago a while, because the winter was a mild one. "I've been asked if I have come home to write my autobiography. . . . The last bid I had was $2,000,000—that included moving-picture rights, serial rights and book rights. But I'm not going into the literary business. That would be cutting in on the work of the boys who are writing about me."

Still, Capone was critical of a recent book about him—probably Fred Pasley's *Al Capone: The Biography of a Self-Made Man* (1930).

"I don't belong in this book any more than I belong in a book by Horatio Alger," he said. "I guess maybe I could write a better one, but that sort of stuff isn't my line."

Al also said he wasn't interested in going into motion pictures, though he'd seen an article saying he was.

"Can you fancy that? Well, anyway, I'm not going into the movies. I'm no Mary Pickford."

The entire trial hinged on Dr. Kenneth Phillips's sworn affidavit of March 5, 1929, saying Capone "for six weeks was confined to his bed . . . and has been out of his bed for only ten days," or roughly since the last week of February.

But thanks to legwork by J. Edgar Hoover's Bureau of Investigation, the government witnesses would show Capone had been up and about as early as mid-January. Three policemen testified they'd seen him at the Hialeah racetrack that month; one recalled the gangster tipped him $10, as if he were a valet.

A pilot swore he'd flown Capone to the Bahamas on February 2 in a plane with an open cockpit—tough for a man down with pneumonia. Six days later, witnesses said, Capone returned to the Bahamas by ship.

The secretary for the Dade County solicitor told of Capone testifying on St. Valentine's Day, and appearing "to be in good health," unlike the North Siders getting gunned down in a garage that very hour.

When Capone rose from his counsel table for the noon recess, police detectives approached.

"Get your hat and coat," one said.

They'd come to serve Capone with Judge Lyle's vagrancy warrant, "dog-eared and frayed in the pockets of many officers 'looking' for him," said the *Herald and Examiner*. Capone made no protest and followed the cops out.

Hustled into an elevator by a brace of detectives and deputy marshals, Capone was taken to a waiting squad car in a basement tunnel. Soon he was ushered into the Detective Bureau, where chaos reigned. Watching from fire escapes and in windows across the way, scores of young women screamed as if a movie idol had wandered into view. Dozens of cops, newshounds, and photogs swarmed the office as a grinning Capone took it all in.

Capone's attorney caught up with his client and immediately had the vagrancy warrant served by the detective squad. When Al probed a pocket, the cops ducked reflexively, but what he withdrew was a $10,000 real-estate bond—appropriate for a real-estate dealer, the occupation given in response to the vagrancy charge.

The bond did not preclude booking Capone, who denied his "public enemy" status as he was fingerprinted, a first for him in Chicago.

That taken care of, Capone returned to the Federal Building for the afternoon session, leaving under heavy police guard. The escort came courtesy of the police commissioner, who told the *Tribune,* "We don't want Capone killed in Chicago."

Capone received the same royal treatment on the second day, but the circus atmosphere had died down. Most people eager to get a look at the Big Fellow had been satisfied the day before.

But one "girl reporter," as the newspapers described her, approached Capone timidly before the proceedings began. The defendant got up and bowed gallantly.

"I wanted to ask you a question," the young woman said, "but I am so flustered I can't remember what it was."

Al gave her an indulgent smile.

Then she remembered. "I wanted to ask you what you think of the American girl."

"Why," he replied, "I think you're beautiful."

Despite the evidence steadily piling up against him, Capone remained relentlessly cheerful, telling reporters he'd probably take the stand in his own defense.

But his lawyers talked him out of it—questioning on cross-examination could drift into areas where their client would be uncomfortable. And Capone probably didn't need much convincing after he saw how the judge and the lead prosecutor teamed up to dismantle Dr. Phillips.

The unfortunate physician—a bespectacled, meek-looking man with a trim mustache—found himself caught between his fear of the Capones and the might of Uncle Sam. As the first defense witness, he was to describe Capone's illness, and explain its severity.

On cross-examination, however, Wilkerson and the prosecutor took turns pressing Phillips on claims in his affidavit, forcing him to admit to some misstatements while trying to squirm out of others.

Why, Wilkerson asked, had Phillips told Capone's Chicago doctor the illness was "not serious," if the situation was in fact dire?

"I didn't want any more emotion stirred up than was necessary," Phillips said.

Wilkerson pressed on: "When you used the expression 'confined to bed' in the affidavit, you thought that taking airplane rides, steamer cruises and visits to the race track might be included in the 'confinement'?"

"I didn't mean that."

"But when you said 'confined to bed,' you didn't exactly mean that?"

"That is right."

Phillips tried to walk back this apparent lie by claiming "confined to bed" didn't necessarily mean bedridden.

" 'Confined to bed' means that the patient couldn't work or perform the usual duties of a well man," he explained. "Of course, he could be carried to his automobile and taken for a ride."

That unleashed a wave of courtroom laughter.

Eventually, Phillips had to admit he'd never read, much less written, the affidavit. He'd simply signed the statement Capone's lawyer dictated.

Two nurses who treated Capone did better, maintaining their patient's illness had been serious. But they'd stopped treating him in late January, well before the period in question. The meager defense put forward by Capone's attorneys collapsed.

Yet the defendant kept his cool, looking on "with an attitude," said the *Herald and Examiner*, "ranging from jocularity to boredom."

During the closing arguments, Capone chewed gum, his jaw grinding to a halt as the prosecutor railed against him. Wilkerson let the state make its case without interruption, but frequently broke in on Capone's lawyer, who grew so flustered he started referring to his client as "Capone-y."

This was not a jury trial; Wilkerson was the only one the lawyers needed to convince, and his attitude clearly telegraphed the verdict.

The defendant's self-satisfied demeanor eroded. According to the *Herald and Examiner,* "Capone leaned nervously forward in his chair, his face alert for the first time during the trial."

Even with the conclusion obvious, most observers expected Wilkerson to take some time deliberating. But the judge launched into his summary while Capone, dressed in what the *Tribune* called "a flashy brown suit," listened nervously, squirming in his chair.

Wilkerson dismissed Phillips's affidavit as "glaringly false," labeling Capone's disregard for the subpoena a threat to the entire judiciary. The federal court, he said, "is to be respected, it is to be obeyed. . . . In no other way may the Courts operate."

Then came the verdict: "Upon the record as it stands here there is nothing for the Court to do except to adjudge the respondent guilty of contempt of Court . . . and as punishment for the contempt the respondent will be committed to the County Jail of Cook County for the period of six months."

Six little months? In the county jail? Capone went back to chewing his gum. The deal only got sweeter as Wilkerson continued the case for thirty days to permit an appeal, and let the defendant go on a $5,000 bond.

Capone seemed to sense he had scant chance of reversing Wilkerson's verdict.

"If the judge thinks it's correct, he ought to know," Capone remarked. "You can't overrule the judge." But he flashed a smile to a press photographer as he left the Federal Building. Capone knew he wouldn't see the inside of a cell till summer at the earliest, and could easily run his business from within the confines of Cook County Jail.

The federal government had won its first victory against Public Enemy Number One, but the light sentence only revealed Uncle Sam's impotence.

A *Herald and Examiner* editorial noted Capone's delight, and said Chicago would "have to do more than slap its enemies on the wrist. That is a foolish thing to do to an enemy who carries a six-shooter."

Perhaps to counteract such complaints, George Johnson's office leaked rumors, saying, "Income tax investigators are completing the network of evidence which will result in the indictment of Capone." The *Tribune* went on: "If Mr. Johnson maintains the '100 per cent' standard of successful convictions thus far achieved, Capone is regarded as a certainty for Leavenworth penitentiary."

This didn't sit well with J. Edgar Hoover, whose agents deserved credit for gathering evidence leading to Capone's first federal conviction. Admittedly, the case had not required much investigating, and the meager penalty seemed to fit the level of work Hoover's men had put in.

But the Bureau of Investigation could still truthfully claim to have gotten Capone, and Hoover hated all the good press going to Johnson. When the special agent in charge of the Bureau's Chicago office passed along Johnson's thanks, the director scribbled his frustration at the bottom of the memo.

"The U.S. Attorney's enthusiasm now is rather annoying," Hoover wrote. "It has taken us nearly two years to force him to bring this matter to an issue."

Two days later, when Hoover saw a glowing profile of Johnson in the *Washington Evening Star*, his anger boiled.

"Well of all the bunk, this takes the prize," Hoover wrote of the two years Johnson took to try Capone. "Now he basks in the sunlight of the effort which he did everything to avoid."

Soon Judge Lyle's legendary vagrancy charge, also gathering dust, came to naught.

On April 3, a well-dressed Capone—gray suit, gray-striped navy tie, pearl-gray fedora—returned to court to hear Judge Frank M. Padden dismiss the case. The prosecutor had been directed to bring in a complaint signed by a policeman acquainted with the defendant—*any* policeman.

None could be found.

"Couldn't you find a single copper?" the judge asked.

The prosecutor admitted as much.

———

In February 1931, Robert Isham Randolph, head of the Secret Six, accepted an invitation to meet with his nemesis, Al Capone.

At the Lexington Hotel, in the back way and up a freight elevator, Randolph went through door after door, past thug after thug, until he was ushered into Capone's suite.

Coming around his enormous desk, a smiling Capone extended his hand, saying, "Hell, Colonel, I'd know you anywhere—you look just like your pictures."

Shaking his host's hand, Randolph said, "Hell, Al, I'd never have recognized you—you are much bigger than you appear to be in photographs."

Surprised not to be searched, Randolph handed over his .45 automatic to Capone as if in offering. Then he asked to use the phone, saying he wanted to tell his wife, fearful of this meeting, that "everything is OK."

"Women are like that," Capone said, and walked him to a private phone in an adjacent room. On Randolph's return, glasses of "good beer" were waiting. The two men sat.

"Colonel, what are you trying to do to me?"

"Put you out of business."

"Why do you want to do that?"

"We want to clean up Chicago, put a stop to these killings and gang rule here."

"Colonel, I don't understand you. You knock over my breweries, bust up my booze rackets, raid my gambling houses and tap my telephone wires, but yet you're not a reformer, not a dry. Just what are you after?"

Randolph chuckled. "Maybe we are just campaigning to lower the price and improve the quality."

"Listen, Colonel—you're putting me out of business. Even with beer selling at $55 a barrel, we didn't make a nickel last week. Do you know what will happen if you put me out of business?"

Capone told Randolph about the nearly two hundred men on the Outfit payroll—many ex-convicts, but respectable workingmen now. Put out of work, those men would almost certainly return to a life of crime.

Capone offered to make a deal with the colonel.

"If the Secret Six will lay off of my beer, booze, and gambling rackets," he said, "I'll police this town for you. I'll clean it up. There won't be a stickup, a murder, nor a poke [pocketbook] grabbed in Cook County."

Randolph declined.

The .45 was returned to him, on his way out.

"So even respectable people carry those things?" Capone asked him with a laugh. "No hard feelings?" he added, as they shook hands.

"No hard feelings," his guest said.

Randolph was not worried about being taken for a ride anywhere but back to his office. He felt that—"barring stick-ups, of course"— gangsters killed only each other, and the corruptibles with whom they were in bed. Crooked reporter Jake Lingle, for example, had been killed in public as a warning. The colonel felt his own protection came from the spotlight of the press and his "sincerity of purpose."

Capone, who largely confirmed Randolph's account of their meeting to the *Tribune,* was frustrated his offer had been rejected. He would have stopped bombings of local companies and factories, among other crimes, in exchange for being allowed to peacefully run his beer business.

"I laid my cards on the table and asked him to lay his," Capone reflected. "Well? What do you think I got?"

Ness in 1931. *(Cleveland Public Library Photograph Collection)*

Twenty-Two

February–May 1931

Capone's empire rested on a frothy foundation of beer. His product may have been "lousy," as one competitor described it—weak, green, and hurriedly brewed—but it sold.

A Secret Six investigation revealed Capone moved about a hundred thousand barrels of beer per week, enough to fill 25 million pints—or six for every resident of Cook County. Each barrel cost less than $3 to make and sold for $55, netting the Outfit a gross weekly profit of $5.2 million.

"Of course, that's absurd," Capone told the *Tribune*. "Why, I don't believe there is that much beer in the United States."

But with this immense income came tremendous overhead. To slake Chicago's thirst, the Outfit needed breweries, large and hard to find; a fleet of vehicles, from delivery trucks to glass-lined tankers; and a legion of tradesmen earning regular salaries as brewers, coopers, drivers, and armed guards.

And they had to pay off countless cops—of the $52 profit the gang made from each barrel, the Secret Six estimated $20 wound up paying off police, Prohibition agents, and other officials, a staggering $2 million weekly.

The beer trade had done more to corrupt local government and empower the criminal class than any other vice, turning gangsters into industrialists and police into their employees. By early 1931, Robert Isham Randolph and others were lobbying for a change in the Volstead Act, to legalize the sale of beer without another constitutional amendment. Even if hard liquor remained outlawed, damming up this torrent of illicit revenue would deal a death blow to criminal syndicates like Capone's.

Eliot Ness agreed but wouldn't wait around for a change in the law.

"We had to . . . find a vulnerable point," Ness reflected. "We decided on the breweries because their product is bulky and because they have the toughest transport problem."

The breweries also evidenced the greatest capital investment and biggest income generator. By shutting them down, Ness hoped to dry up that foamy $2 million weekly "slush fund" for bribes. If Capone couldn't make his regular payoffs, then police would stop protecting his rackets, making them that much easier to find and destroy.

And the more Ness's men cut into the Outfit's bottom line, the more the gang would struggle to pay its salaried employees—money was the glue holding the syndicate together, without which it would splinter, perhaps even turn on itself.

"Kill the revenue," Alexander Jamie said, "and you kill the gang."

Ness wasn't content with shuttering each operation. He wanted to catch the brewers in the act, adding their names to his conspiracy case and locking them up, even briefly, to further stretch the gang's resources. Locating each brewery required weeks of agents working slowly and carefully so as not to blow their cover. They soon learned saloons received deliveries every Friday, stocking up for weekend business. All Ness's men had to do, in theory, was wait for trucks to arrive and then follow them back to their source.

But the Outfit had ways of keeping its breweries well hidden. One night, the special agents tailed a beer truck from a Cicero speakeasy to a nearby garage. After forty-eight hours, the truck hadn't moved, stashed there to cool off, leaving their pursuers at a dead end.

Then the agents tried pulling over a truck fully loaded with beer and interrogating its driver. But the trucker had picked up the barrels at a spot far from the brewery. That way, if he fell into federal hands, the trucker wouldn't know anything to hurt Capone.

Ness's agents examined financial records, seeking to trace the purchases of brewing vats. But the gang had covered its tracks too well. Then it came to Ness—the Outfit *must* use the same barrels over and over again. They made a shell game of shuffling trucks and drivers around, confusing anyone who tried to follow their movements. But if the special agents could keep their eyes on the kegs, they'd eventually find the breweries that filled them. . . .

Ness ordered Maurice Seager and ace driver Joe Leeson to camp out at a large saloon south of the Loop. They arrived around 9:00 P.M., just when business would start to heat up, and watched the alley. As the hours crawled past and the beer flowed, empty kegs piled up out back.

Then, around 2:00 A.M., two men drove up and loaded the used barrels into a truck. Leeson and Seager followed them around the South Side, the trucks making more pickups before hauling their cargo to an old industrial building near Comiskey Park. Fearful of being spotted, the special agents sped off, then returned to rent rooms nearby.

"We, of course," Ness wrote, "thought at last we had located a Capone brewery."

But they hadn't. Leeson and Seager had stumbled onto a plant where used barrels were washed and steam-cleaned before being refilled—the Capone mob had adopted modern hygienic practices. Instead of a single brewery, the agents had discovered something much better—a wellspring that, with care, might lead to several more targets.

Over the next few days, Leeson and Seager watched truck after truck leave the barrel-cleaning plant, each guarded by two pearl-hatted gangsters in "a souped-up Ford coupe." After years of working without interference, the guards had grown complacent, no longer watching their backs.

Still, the special agents took no chances, tailing the coupe a few blocks at a time, then picking up the trail when another convoy rumbled by the same spot the next day. Leeson and Seager made their careful way to another cooling-off garage, across the street from a vacant lot, where the agents took up watch, crouching in the high grass into the small hours of the morning.

They saw the trucks driven out around 3:00 A.M., then tailed the convoy on foot. A truck pulled into 1642 South Cicero Avenue, a squat garage with an arched roof a short distance from the cooling-off point.

Confident they'd finally found a brewery, Ness put a round-the-clock watch on the Cicero garage. His men reported two trucks carrying empty barrels showed up every day around 4:30 P.M. The vehicles exited forty or forty-five minutes later, riding a lot lower. Ness laid plans for a raid, set for early morning when he knew brewers would be on duty.

Sports fan Ness designed the operation like a football play. Two cars would roll up to the brewery and cover all exits. Then, sixty seconds later, more agents would come in through the front door. Anyone trying to flee would run into the arms of the waiting men. Ness gathered Chapman, Lesson, Seager, Stutzman, and two more special agents, plus a rookie member of the regular Prohibition force named McCabe, whom Ness picked up himself. The mousy young man made a poor fit among the brawny Capone squad.

Shortly before dawn on March 25, the raiders gathered in a rented room and received their assignments. They set out for Cicero in a convoy of two cars and a big, heavy truck that could cart off whatever they seized. A block or so from the brewery, they stopped, awaiting 5:00 A.M.—zero hour.

Several agents went to the truck and grabbed ladders with muffled tips, to scale the roof. The two cars drove off to take their prearranged places near the exits. Ness and the rest rumbled up to the building in their truck, getting out with guns drawn. Trying to force their way in through the front, they discovered the big double doors would not give.

With the other agents in place and time slipping away, Ness's men

had to think fast—quickly, they decided to use their truck as a battering ram. The driver climbed in, and backed into the entrance.

"The doors fell with a great loud clap," Ness recalled, "and at that
moment my heart sank. There was no brewery!"

Instead, he saw a large, vacant space.

But this was just a "false face," designed to fool would-be raiders,
the far wall painted black, making the place look empty. The special
agents rushed over, found another set of doors, and forced through
them. They came upon a red truck that looked like a moving van, its
engine running, as if recently abandoned.

In fact, a special attachment to the motor was pumping wort, the raw
material fermented into beer, from a 3,000-gallon tank inside the truck
through a hose and into a massive vat hidden deeper inside the building.

The special agents smashed in yet another set of doors and finally
found the actual brewery.

Three workers stood rooted, too stunned to move, the federal agents
arresting them without a shot fired.

The fresh, yeasty scent of brew in their nostrils, the agents saw,
everywhere they looked, "genuine Capone beer"—31,800 gallons in
fourteen enormous vats and five large cooling tanks. Sixty barrels sat
ready for delivery. All told, the raid cost Capone $100,000 in seized
equipment, trucks, and product, robbing him of a brewery capable of
turning out one hundred barrels of beer a day.

The setup matched the brewery Ness had seen at 2108 South Wabash. Evidently, the Outfit ran their plants like franchise operations.
Among the arrested men was Steve Swoboda, the gang's top brewmas-
ter, who oversaw production at several breweries. The special agents
emptied Swoboda's pockets and examined his personal effects, searching unsuccessfully for anything tying him to Capone.

Then, after an inventory and taking some samples of beer for evidence, they smashed the vats and broke up the barrels, creating what
the *Evening American* called "an amber flood that would bring tears to

the eyes of any beer lover." Thick, frothy waves coursed over the floor like knee-high snowdrifts.

Riding high off his victory, Ness headed back to the Transportation Building to meet with Colonel John F. J. Herbert, chief of the regular Prohibition force. Ness intended to thank Herbert for the loan of his men, but the colonel only gave him an accusatory stare.

"What did you do to him?" Herbert asked, referring to the rookie agent Ness had taken along.

McCabe had come in before Ness arrived, ready to turn in his badge and gun.

"If the job is anything like *that*," the rookie had said, "I'm through!"

Ness couldn't possibly relate. The raid had given him the kind of rush he always craved, and the sight of those brewers, staring dumbly at the agents as they stormed in, tickled his peculiar sense of humor.

"It's funny, I think, when you back up a truck to a brewery door and smash it in," Ness said. "And then find some individuals inside that you hadn't expected."

Eliot—who was only just getting started—would make many such discoveries in the months ahead.

Less than a week after the Cicero raid, Ness welcomed a new agent onto the squad—Robert D. Sterling, forty-eight and the oldest on the team, after more than a decade with the Prohibition Bureau. His record of building conspiracy cases, including one against a sacramental-wine racket, surely appealed to Ness. But when it came to busting mobsters and other violent violators, Sterling had little to offer.

"He is not a criminal investigator nor will he ever be," Dwight Avis wrote. "My impression is that he dislikes criminal investigative work and suffers from personal fear," particularly when gangsters were in play. Sterling would last only three weeks on the Capone squad.

Now that they were moving from investigation into action, Ness needed a different breed—aggressive, take-charge raiders sharing or even exceeding his own thirst for excitement. Just in time, the perfect pair of agents arrived, skilled investigators who'd cut their teeth chasing moonshiners.

Ness had been after Paul Wenzel Robsky for some time. Robsky, thirty-three—high forehead, intense gray eyes, and full lips—lacked investigative experience but made up for it in brass, his appetite for danger running deep. He had been a pilot in the Great War, signing up as a Prohibition agent in South Carolina because "it might be interesting and exciting." Thanks largely to Robsky's own recklessness, the job more than lived up to expectations.

One time Robsky tried to stop two fleeing bootleggers by throwing himself onto the roof of their car, only to have them both bail out with him still hanging on. Thrown from the out-of-control auto as it barreled down a mountain, Robsky got away with a broken ankle. The driver, less lucky, fractured his skull and, Robsky recalled, "was never right in the head again."

Arriving in Chicago in early April for "a temporary detail," Robsky found his new boss "nervous and tense, sort of collegiate looking, a nice guy doing a job." The newest squad member spent his nights on stakeout or bent over a phone receiver, listening to Outfit members talk about "Snorky." Never did he feel the same rush he'd felt while breaking up hillbilly stills.

But he did good work, and Ness soon made his temporary assignment a permanent one.

The other new arrival was Marion Andrew Rockwell King, twenty-seven, a lean Virginian who joined up April 14, the only team member younger (by two months) than Ness. Energetic, fearless, he had a talent for undercover work.

"He is young, dependable and hard-working," wrote the commissioner of Prohibition in early 1930, "and is the type of employee the Bureau seeks."

Like Robsky, King came on a temporary appointment, which Ness arranged to make permanent in May. With King on board, the team reached its full ten-man strength; Ness finally had the flying squad he'd envisioned since December.

He also prepared to deploy a new weapon, something Leeson and Lyle Chapman devised on his orders. Since their truck had served so well as an impromptu bulldozer, Ness hoped to keep using it to bust down brewery doors. But he knew the vehicle couldn't take such repeated abuse without modifications, and suggested protecting its radiator with a heavy steel bumper mounted on the front.

Chapman designed the attachment; Leeson, once a welder, probably constructed it, creating a flat, horizontal battering ram out of old streetcar rails. These reinforcements may not have been much to look at, but they enabled the truck to plow headlong into a brewery instead of backing in.

The agents kept up their barrel-cleaning plant surveillance on the South Side. Following the barrel trucks grew more difficult as the guards realized they might be tailed. Ness's men had to tail the trucks on parallel streets, or somehow manage to get ahead of the gangsters and watch them in their rearview mirrors.

Eventually, these barrel convoys led the team to an apparently vacant warehouse at 3136 South Wabash Avenue—THE OLD RELIABLE TRUCKING COMPANY, according to the sign out front. But the special agents detected a familiar faint aroma and took up watch, to see if the Outfit would tip its hand.

One night, with Ness and four other agents parked across the street, a barrel truck pulled up, a convoy car right behind. Without warning, four other cars appeared, each with two men inside. The gangsters got out and surrounded the special agents. Ness and his men sat poised to go for their guns.

Then one man stepped forward—Bert Delaney, Capone's buildings manager. After ordering his boys to stand down, Delaney approached Ness, eager to make a deal.

"How much you guys want?" Delaney asked. How about $600? "No? Two grand, then . . ."

Ness remained stony-faced and silent.

"All right," Delaney said, "you guys set your own price."

"You haven't got enough money," Ness said, and drove off.

The squad hit the warehouse at daybreak on April 11. As before, Ness sent his men to cover all six exits. Several agents grabbed ladders off the juggernaut truck and climbed onto the roof, where they waited by the fire escapes. Wearing a leather football helmet, Ness took his place inside the truck and gave the signal. The driver shifted into low gear and rumbled ahead, then plowed through the front doors, wood splintering like breaking bones, the impact shuddering through the truck.

As the raiders burst in, a dozen shrieking alarm bells went off. While their partners used axes to hack into the other entrances, the special agents in the truck smashed through two more pairs of heavy doors before finding a working brewery.

Agents Lahart, Leeson, Robsky, Seager, and Stutzman, Ness wrote, "were on the necks of five operators in less time than it takes to tell it."

A few brewers tried to flee out the roof, only to run into more agents waiting to nab them. One arrested man was Steve Swoboda, out on bail after the Cicero raid. Another was Frank Conti, a top Capone lackey. Ness would arrest both again.

Agents led the brewers away for questioning, pressing for any connections to Capone. Other squad members took stock of everything they'd seized, then destroyed it. With fourteen 2,500-gallon vats, five 1,800-gallon cooling tanks, and more than 40,000 gallons of beer, the brewery was the largest found in Chicago since Jamie's raid the previous June.

The plant could produce 180 barrels a day, Ness estimated, set up very recently, probably to replace the Cicero brewery. Mothballs lay strewn about, and an electric ventilation system purred, in a vain attempt to hide the stench of brewing beer. The Outfit had invested $25,000, only to lose it after four or five days.

An informant warned Ness the gang might try to recoup. He ordered his men to spare several big vats, then made a show of leaving the brewery unguarded. Agents took up concealed spots. The next morning, they spied four cars cruising, searching for threats. Satisfied the coast was clear, the cars took up lookout positions.

Then four men nonchalantly let themselves into the brewery and began loading a large vat onto a truck. The special agents dashed across the street as the lookouts honked their horns like mad. But the feds moved too fast, arresting four men, Bert Delaney among them.

A few days later, the team turned up where the mob might least expect them—Chicago Heights. Ness had unfinished business there—in the two years since he and Jamie shut it down, the Heights had regressed. The special agents drove around like old times, letting their noses lead them to stills in three houses on the same block. They crashed into each, arresting five men and destroying tens of thousands of gallons of liquor. Ness told reporters these raids would help shore up the conspiracy case he'd built back in 1929.

"We secured convictions against fifty-six men in this neighborhood last year," he said. "We were just checking up today."

Local authorities seemed amazed to find bootleggers in their midst.

"I can't understand it," said the Heights police chief. "These fellows must have just slipped in. We've been keeping an awfully close check on things out here."

Ness planned to make sure of that.

"I'll be back," he promised.

Sometime that spring, a young man showed up at Ness's office looking for a job. Millions like him haunted American office buildings in those Depression days, shuffling from rejection to rejection as their savings bled out like a slow wound.

Ness gave the young man a hearing, only to learn the potential recruit had no investigative experience, lacked education, and boasted no special qualifications. He could bring nothing of value to the Capone squad, unless he had some connection to the gang.

"The Kid," as Ness called him, offered precisely that—he said he could get a job through Jack Guzik and report back whatever he learned.

"I told him he would be taking a great chance," Ness wrote, "but if he were accepted by the mob, I would have some assignments for him."

A few days later, the Kid returned, having made contact with the Outfit through a "mouthpiece" of Capone's. The attorney had warned the Kid the gang knew about his meeting with Ness, and "that the Government would use him and throw him out like an old shoe when they were through."

But Capone's men wouldn't pass up the chance to get a double agent on Ness's squad—if the Kid signed on, the gang would happily pay him to report Ness's movements.

Eliot remained suspicious. "I couldn't understand why the young man wanted to play such a dangerous game," he recalled. The Kid batted such doubts away by explaining he needed money, and an exciting job, to impress his wife, a striptease dancer. More likely, the Outfit had sent him in the first place, hoping to plant someone on Ness's staff.

Either way, Ness saw the value in having a double agent of his own. He could use the Kid to feed misinformation to the mob, taking care they never learned anything that could hurt his own squad.

Ness also knew he was placing his informant in a risky position. Pass along too many bad tips, and the Kid wouldn't outlive his nickname. Ness didn't relish playing games with someone else's life; he didn't want another Frank Basile on his conscience. He told the Kid "the job would be extremely dangerous and of short duration."

And the Kid would have to open a Postal Savings Bank account, from time to time showing Ness enough of a cash balance to support fleeing if need be. The Kid readily agreed, becoming Ness's man inside the Outfit.

From the Kid's reports, Ness learned of the gang's growing determination to do something about his Capone squad. The Kid passed along a message: If Ness quit raiding breweries, he could expect to see two crisp, clean $1,000 bills resting on his desk each and every Monday morning.

"This was a pretty good sum of money," Ness recalled, "considering that they would pay me weekly a large part of what the government was paying me per year."

Ness had recently received a $900 raise, giving him an annual salary of $3,800. And he was lucky to have it, as the Depression rolled on with no end in sight. In Chicago the following spring, one social worker would report seeing "a crowd of some fifty men fighting over a barrel of garbage which had been set outside the back door of a restaurant. American citizens fighting for scraps of food like animals!"

In that desperate climate, the Capone mob was offering Eliot Ness the best kind of security—$104,000 a year just to look the other way, the modern equivalent of $1.5 million.

"The offer, of course, was not considered," Ness wrote.

The gang zeroed in on his men. One frigid night, Seager cruised along Wabash with Lahart riding shotgun. They were tailing a truck from the "barrel wash" plant, plowing through a fierce wind in their aging Essex auto.

"We were about two blocks behind," Lahart recalled, "trying to look like just another car on the street. But they had 'trailers' of their own. . . . One of them must have spotted us."

A car zoomed up and a package came flying through the window, landing right in Lahart's lap.

For a panic-stricken moment, Lahart thought he had a hand grenade between his legs. Instead, he found a packet full of cash. By then, the Capone car had sped on, but Seager hit the gas and caught up, throwing the bribe back in the driver's face.

Capone's men tried the same tactic on Paul Robsky, tossing an envelope of thousand-dollar bills into his car. Robsky couldn't manage to hurl it back, so he turned it over to the district attorney's office. On a separate occasion, Robsky said, "two of us were told we would be put on the payroll for $1,000 a week if we played ball." The agents didn't, much to the gangsters' surprise.

"They told us that 'everyone here in Chicago gets along good with each other,'" Robsky recalled. "'Why not you?'"

For one thing, most of Ness's men weren't from Chicago, where getting a badge usually required political connections or a flat-out bribe. The city's police force offered men from working-class, immigrant communities a chance at advancement—if they stayed in the good graces of their local ward boss. Otherwise, they'd never rise to the rank of captain or inspector, where a man could enrich himself through payoffs.

Ness's men, even the local ones, hadn't signed on for the graft.

"They're working guys with families . . . ," says Scott Sroka, grandson of Joe Leeson. "None of these guys were in it to get rich."

Instead, they wanted an exciting career, and a shot at the American Dream. They were in for the long haul—grabbing a quick bribe simply wasn't worth it.

Leeson, for example, didn't have much education, but he'd worked his way up from an Indiana farm with skills and drive. He would be hard-pressed, in the midst of the Depression, to find another job offering him a better future.

Ness had chosen men who shared not only his midwestern faith in hard work and public service, but his ambition. Although they still dressed like workingmen, they were professionals, making a career out of law enforcement. Wads of cash offered by slick-suited gangsters, Sroka says, probably insulted them.

Even Lyle Chapman, who had a taste for fine clothes, refused to fill his pockets with payoffs. Many times when Chapman was on stakeout, a Capone thug would appear out of nowhere and offer him a bribe.

"Oh, we'd take the money," Chapman said, "but turn it over as evidence and then smash another brewery."

Having learned bribery got them nowhere, the gang turned to harassment, following the agents at all hours and loitering outside their homes, hoping to throw a scare into them and their families. Chapman, with Ness along, had to speed to his girlfriend's apartment more than once after she called saying "hoods were outside and she was scared."

The Outfit put Ness under constant surveillance. Death threats came in by mail and over the phone, warning Ness he would be castrated, shot, and left lying in a ditch. According to Lahart, Ness heard from "time to time" that hitmen were gunning for him, but while the danger seemed real, the bullets failed to fly.

When he left his Paxton Avenue apartment for a Sunday morning stroll, Ness noticed a suspicious character watching him, always staying a block behind but following at every turn. This was probably the private detective the Outfit had hired to shadow him and dig into his background, searching for anything the gang might use to scare him off the case.

And the investigator hit pay dirt. In looking over Ness's civil service record, he noticed the birth date on the federal forms didn't match Ness's college records. Ness, the detective realized, had lied about his age to keep his job. And the Outfit could prove it.

The Kid brought this news to Ness as if it were a friendly warning.

"They have information that you got your job under false pretenses," the Kid said. "Wouldn't that go pretty hard against you on the witness stand?"

But if Ness was at all concerned, he didn't show it. The gang proceeded to file a complaint with the Civil Service Commission, hoping to get Ness dismissed. No soap.

The squad kept up their own investigations. One agent devoted himself to tracking purchase records of all "suspicious looking automobiles and trucks" and made a list of vehicles linked to the Capone mob. If a squad member chanced to spot one, he'd follow it. Soon the team knew every Capone truck and driver by sight.

One such truck crossed the paths of two agents in the early morning hours of May 11. They spotted it at the corner of Wabash Avenue and Twenty-Second Street, a block from the Lexington Hotel. Its side bore the name of the Acme Seamless Tube Company, a lame attempt at camouflage.

The bootleggers must have spotted their tail, because they took off, heading north. The agents gave chase. A convoy car carrying two gangsters fell in beside them and kept swerving into their path, trying to run them off the road, nearly succeeding.

The truck plunged into the heart of the Loop, weaving up back alleys and down side streets in a vain attempt to shake the feds, finally pulling into an alley between Wells and La Salle. Two men jumped out, the driver leaping onto the running board of the convoy car, which sped away, out of the agents' reach. But his passenger, Frank Uva, didn't move fast enough. Ness's men quickly collared him, confiscating the truck and its eleven barrels of beer.

The gang responded to the loss of one vehicle by stealing another— sometime in late May, Ness's car vanished. A few days later, the vehicle was found on the street, stripped. Ness picked up the remains and somehow got it back in working order, but made the mistake of parking it outside his apartment. When he got up to go to work, he found the car missing its front wheels. He told the *Herald and Examiner* "thieves were stealing his automobile on the installment plan."

And they wouldn't stop trying—Ness's car disappeared again some time later, as did Marty Lahart's and that of another special agent working the Capone case.

Thieves also penetrated the agents' offices, rifling their files and stealing evidence. A check on the Transportation Building's phone lines revealed two wiretaps on Ness's office. The agents used this as another opportunity to feed the gang misinformation.

As the case got closer to a grand jury, Ness decided to move their work where he felt it would be safe—the marble-and-granite edifice of the First National Bank at Dearborn and Madison. Ness rented "a large safety deposit box" on the ground floor and stashed everything they'd gathered inside. The vault became the unit's second office; Chapman and the other agents went there to do all their paperwork.

Ness's pencil detective had begun to link various parts of the beer business into one giant web, with a scar-faced spider at its center. From the Intelligence Unit, Chapman got records of money orders showing Capone had received large sums from George Howlett and Joe Fusco, two top men in the bootleg racket.

Chapman also traced the serial number of a truck seized at the Wabash Avenue brewery and found Fusco purchased it back in 1927. At that time, Fusco turned in an older truck once registered to Capone under his favorite alias, "Al Brown," which had been repeatedly seized hauling beer.

Now the squad could demonstrate Capone had taken a hand in transporting illicit alcohol, one of the three acts outlawed by the Eighteenth Amendment—a tenuous link, but proof connecting Capone to a crime. No other investigator could boast as much—not even the tax men, with their circumstantial case. Organizing and distilling all these documents would take time, however, and Chapman—never the speediest or most dedicated worker—had little to spare.

The Capone case turned Ness's men into outsiders. By refusing to take the mob's money, they opened themselves to constant harassment—threats and thefts, attempted bribes, and profane insults. They reminded Charles Schwarz, Ness's friend on the *Chicago Daily News,* of India's "untouchables," the men, women, and children trapped at the bottom of the Hindu caste system.

India's untouchables lived as outcasts, scorned by nearly everyone. Even their shadows were seen as unclean. Barred from normal society, unable to enter temples or schools, they retreated into the night and did the dirty work no one else would do—everything from killing animals to hauling human waste. They had recently made headlines in America because of Mahatma Gandhi's efforts to improve their lot in life.

Schwarz's paper ran its first article about Ness's men just a few columns away from a story about Gandhi. Perhaps that's what gave him the idea. Or maybe it was hearing how Lahart and Seager threw that wad of cash back at Capone's men. Lahart recalled seeing a newsman in Ness's office when he reported the bribe to his boss.

"I remember telling him, 'This will show them they can't touch us,'" Lahart said.

Impressed by the squad's resistance to bribes, Schwarz began calling them Chicago's "untouchables."

The name appealed to Ness's dry Nordic sense of humor. He had learned about India's untouchables in a University of Chicago history course, and saw a certain parallel in how the underworld treated his men.

But George Johnson considered the name a badge of honor—a mark of incorruptibility. These men couldn't be bought, influenced, or scared off.

No one could touch them.

Ness might have used the term as a joke, but Johnson picked it up and ran. Like the phrase *Secret Six,* this was newspaper bait—a dramatic, irresistible title turning this small squad into something big.

For all their successes, they still remained a motley, imperfect crew. But at least on paper, they could be a symbol of the honest, dedicated, and fearless law enforcement Chicago so sorely needed.

Before long, Johnson would make sure the entire country knew the Capone squad by its new name: the Untouchables.

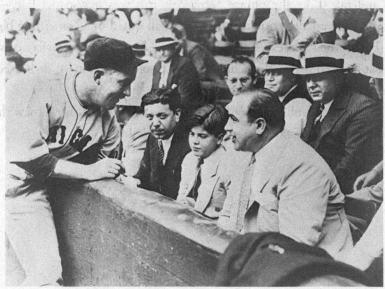

Capone on Palm Island (top) and with Sonny, in 1931, receiving a signed baseball from Gabby Hartnett of the Chicago Cubs (bottom). *(Library of Congress)*

Twenty-Three

Spring–Summer 1931

Al Capone never commented publicly on the work of Eliot Ness's Untouchables, but he certainly knew about their raids, and probably approved the attempted bribes and threats. That was how he liked to deal with reformers and principled lawmen.

"I got nothing against the honest cop on the beat," Capone said. "Most of them you can't buy. So you just have them transferred someplace where they can't do you any harm. But don't even talk to me about the honor of police captains or judges. If they couldn't be bought, they wouldn't have the jobs."

Capone and Ness had in common a hatred of corrupt officials, if for different reasons.

"A crook is a crook," Capone said, "and there's something healthy about his frankness in the matter. But a guy who pretends he is enforcing the law and steals on his authority is a swell snake. The worst type of these punks is the big politician, who gives about half his time to covering up so that no one will know he's a thief."

When he should've been focused on the federal men working to put him in jail, Capone instead became obsessively annoyed with his treatment by the media. Over the past two years, Capone had been the subject of numerous books, including narrative histories of Chicago gangland, a rambling biography by a local journalist, and magazines depicting the Beer Wars carnage. Then came the emerging medium of sound motion pictures.

Gossip columnist Louella Parsons, who encountered Capone more than once, witnessed his transformation into celluloid myth.

"It has always stayed vividly in my mind that there was something almost sleepy in Al Capone's voice," she wrote, "a hushed undertone, such as a man uses in a library or a sickroom. . . . Later, on the screen, I am sure that all our top movie gangsters, Edward G. Robinson, Jimmy Cagney, Humphrey Bogart, et al., copied this vocal characteristic of Capone's."

Capone had offers to join them in the movies, but he always refused. "It's foolish to talk about it," he said.

He already got movie-star-sized bags of fan mail—up to two thousand letters each week—many asking for handouts. A good share came from overseas, in languages he could not read.

Capone showed one to a journalist, who translated a Berlin woman's sob story, pleading for money. An English woman sought only a small favor—to have some quarrelsome neighbors killed. She even offered to pay his passage to London.

"Even over there I'm known as a gorilla," Capone griped.

Any other gangster facing federal indictment would have known not to talk to the press. But Capone couldn't help venting to a reporter from *Variety,* trade journal of the film industry, about "the flock of books, stories, articles and interviews written by guys, all of whom claim to know me personally. You can put me on record as saying I don't know any of 'em. Furthermore, I've never authorized any book or story about me."

Still, Capone professed a love for the movies, saying he enjoyed private screenings. Gangster films made him laugh.

Another reporter asked Capone about a *Real Detective* magazine article saying he was an imposter, the real Al Capone having been murdered. The gangster had a good laugh about it.

"So now I'm a 'phoney,' am I?" he said. "It's the funniest thing I've ever read. . . . Wait until my wife finds out that someone switched husbands on her."

Despite Capone's openness with the press, he didn't let reporters get too close—as *Chicago Daily News* literary editor Howard Vincent O'Brien found out. Seeking intimate access to Capone, O'Brien arranged through a Secret Six detective to have lunch with Jack Guzik at a Madison Street speakeasy.

After ordering tomato juice, the genial Guzik railed on about his unfair income-tax conviction. He spoke bitterly of the hypocrisy of reformers and "certain judges and prosecutors," but offered a surprising appraisal of prosecutor George E. Q. Johnson.

"That guy sent me up for five years," Guzik said, his voice high-pitched and squeaky. "But he's a good, honest, sincere guy . . . a square shooter."

" 'Square shooting,' " O'Brien reflected, "plays a big part in gangster psychology."

After numerous meetings with Guzik, O'Brien—having been thoroughly checked out and sized up—was ushered into the Lexington. He found it an unlikely "gangster hangout," a hotel like countless others in many small cities. His eye immediately found the bulletin board, where a sign announced: KIWANIS CLUB MEETS EVERY THURSDAY, 2ND FLOOR.

But O'Brien couldn't ignore the "swarthy men" lazing about the lobby, hoodlum types "in pearl-gray spats and fawn-colored fedoras and tight-fitting jackets, with salmon-pink neckties and eyes like oysters." Reaching the fourth floor without incident, the journalist was given "one last bath of inquiry" by various watchdogs, but, surprisingly, no one searched him.

Capone's office might have been a bank president's—file cabinets, adding machines, thick carpeting, framed paintings. At the big desk in a bay window sat Joe Fusco, the youthful head of Capone's beer racket, his tall frame clad in brown tweed. With the entrance of Guzik and his guest, Fusco vacated the throne.

Guzik said a newspaper had referred to Capone as a "brothel-keeper," but Al didn't know what the word meant. "Then he looked it up and it made him kind of sore!"

Guzik also volunteered his opinion of the word "hoodlum."

"I don't know what they mean by that word. I've never been able to figure out where being a hoodlum stops and respectability begins. There's a lot of good square guys in this racket; and I know lawyers and bankers I wouldn't sit in the same room with without keeping my hands on my watch."

Soon, "like a gust of wind, Capone himself blew in."

The gangster cut an impressive figure, big but not fat, his movements "lithe and graceful." Typically well dressed in a double-breasted blue serge, he was brusquely affable, greeting his guest with a firm handshake, black hair thinning at the temples but wavy above his thick neck. His expression seemed "Mephistophelian and droll."

Behind his desk now, Capone ordered champagne from a waiter who seemed to materialize. Then a table was laid for supper, which at five o'clock was early for O'Brien, but the feast was hard to resist. Silver buckets of iced Piper-Heidsieck, 1915, began to appear, and then—"like something in the Arabian Nights"—came antipasto, platters of Parmesan-drenched spaghetti, squab, fennel, and more.

Capone went from gracious host to roaring beast, lambasting a waiter slow with service.

"It petrified me," O'Brien admitted. "I should not have been in the least surprised to see him rend the wretched creature into pieces."

Quickly Capone returned to smiles and hospitality, his mood swing reminding O'Brien of temperamental "artists and opera singers." Guzik had said Capone was unfailingly generous—"He doesn't spend two dollars a day on himself. He gives the rest away."

Their conversation stayed casual, not a formal interview, though O'Brien would regret not asking for Capone's advice to young men on "How to Succeed"—what wonderful guidance "this eminently successful young man might have given!"

Capone showed the journalist a letter offering $2 million for the ganglord's memoirs. He had no interest in taking the offer, but longed to answer the fabrications written about him. Maybe O'Brien was interested in writing his real story . . . ?

Apparently, the meetings with Guzik and the behind-the-scenes vetting had led to this. O'Brien was the man to write Capone's story—a "square guy."

Capone was called away—a senator was phoning from Washington, D.C.—leaving O'Brien to mull the possibility of such an exciting project. The autobiography of Al Capone, as told to Howard Vincent O'Brien! Such a book, he mused, might be "the most significant contribution to current history that could possibly be written."

Upon his return, Capone signed a document before two witnesses: "This will authorize you (Howard Vincent O'Brien) to act as my agent in the sale of the manuscript of my autobiography, which will be the only one I ever consented to write."

Capone made clear to his prospective coauthor how important family was to him. He gestured to Sonny's framed photo on the desk and said pointedly, "I don't want my boy to get mixed up in my business, either." As he talked to his wife on the phone, Capone referred to himself as a "kid," and when his mother came on the line, he spoke in Italian.

He truly seemed to want out of the rackets, yearning to be free of bodyguards and cops both bent and straight. He longed for a life of real family, not crime family, away from lawyers and courts and jail cells, with no reporters and photographers hounding him.

"Everybody seems to think I like Prohibition," Capone told O'Brien. "I don't. . . . It's a lousy racket for the retailer. He's got to work twenty hours a day and spend everything he makes to keep the cops off him. No, I'm against Prohibition."

The topic of murder came up—as a business practice.

Big corporations, O'Brien was told, forced out competitors till devastated men found a high window to crawl out of—that was murder, too.

The gangsters' code of ethics, their sacred "standards of right and wrong," fascinated O'Brien. A man was square or he wasn't—they did business with dishonest cops, judges, and reporters but detested them. That their own business was outside the law was to them irrelevant. But they made "a sharp distinction between the honest, forthright crook; and venal respectability."

More meetings followed, after O'Brien had a promising conference with the editor of *Collier's* about running the autobiography as a serial. The editor hedged, however, fearing Capone would want only to talk about his soup kitchen and how often he called his mother on the phone.

Sure enough, as O'Brien began to question his prospective coauthor, the response would inevitably be, "No, I couldn't say that. It wouldn't be fair to my people." This became Capone's standard refrain whenever O'Brien touched on a sensitive subject—such as the baseball bat banquet, for example.

O'Brien sensed he was learning more than was healthy. Capone said as much one day.

"You know," the gangster reflected, "sometimes I lose my temper and I say, 'Gee, I wish somebody would bump that guy off,' and then one of these young punks who wants to make a name for himself goes ahead and does it. And then I have to pick up the pieces."

An example would seem to be Mike "de Pike" Heitler, last seen April 29 playing cards with Capone mobsters Lawrence Mangano and Frankie Pope. The next morning, Heitler's charred remains were found near Itasca, Illinois, in a burned icehouse fifteen miles from a torched car belonging to the big-time pimp's longtime girlfriend. Unwisely, Mike de Pike had been in touch with Judge Lyle and State's Attorney Swanson. Heitler, loosely affiliated with Capone, had significant West Side vice holdings but resented the Outfit's cut.

Asked about Heitler, Capone said, "Well, you see, that fellow had a reputation of being a professional stool pigeon for many years."

Collier's interest in the autobiography eroded, and O'Brien abandoned the project as his welcome rapidly ran out. Important-looking hoodlums gave him disapproving stares from the sidelines. Occasionally a cold-eyed unknown would ask him a question with the authority of an executive. Their behavior made O'Brien wonder whether Capone was "merely a cog in the machine," constantly evading questions as much to protect himself as his "people."

For all his fame, Capone seemed not to be Public Enemy Number One, but somewhere "down the list"—in the Outfit, men were above him and perhaps above them, "shadowy figures whose names never appear in print." Perhaps Capone was "a symbol," and not "the potentate" he seemed to be—"titular head of a great corporation; but behind him is a board of directors; and behind them, stockholders."

The identities of those stockholders, O'Brien felt, would come as a shock to the public.

For a man contemplating his autobiography when much larger, pressing matters needed attending, Capone seemed to know publicity was doing him no favors. O'Brien sensed this "board of directors who sit in the shadows" disapproved of the grandiose myth his host had generated.

"Their sordid but profitable affairs do not thrive in the bright white light of publicity," O'Brien wrote. "In their own vernacular, Capone is providing too much 'heat.'" Would those incorruptible government men be investigating the Outfit's finances and knocking off their breweries if the papers had never heard of Scarface? A swaggering public figure like Capone was bad for business.

One day soon, O'Brien presciently wrote, Capone would disappear into private life, or prison, or perhaps the grave. The forces of public good would cheer, headlines announce a new day, arrests and deportations be made, but as Capone retreated into legend, the Outfit would roll on.

"And in faraway hideouts," O'Brien wrote, "thin-lipped men will sit quietly . . . counting up the profits."

The idea of a secret, shadowy collection of unidentified mobsters acting as Capone's puppet masters reflected a fundamental misunderstanding of how the Outfit worked. The press and popular culture tend to depict the gang as having the strict, top-down hierarchy of a legitimate corporation, with Capone at its head.

But the Outfit was never so neatly organized—instead, as criminal-justice historian Mark Haller observed, the Chicago mob was "a complex set of partnerships," a conglomeration of illegal businesses held together by a loose network of alliances.

By 1931, four men had emerged as "senior partners": Capone, his brother Ralph, Jack Guzik, and Frank Nitto.

"They shared more or less equally in their joint income and acted as equals in looking after their varied business interests," Haller writes. "The senior partners, in turn, formed partnerships with others to launch numerous bootlegging, gambling, and vice activities in the Chicago Loop, South Side, and several suburbs."

Acting as entrepreneurs, the partners benefited from their larger organization's resources—including political influence and protection from the police—while pursuing their own independent ventures.

These assorted enterprises, Haller writes, "were not controlled bureaucratically. Each, instead, was a separate enterprise on a small or relatively small scale." Taken together, they added up to a massive criminal organization, its leadership much more diffuse than most people realized, divided among scores of gangsters.

Outside observers, who had come to view Capone as Chicago's emperor of crime, were surprised to see him treat men like Guzik and Nitto as his equal—or possibly even superior. Capone's status in the Outfit depended entirely on his ability to make deals and forge alliances with other gangsters, building the organization piece by piece, racket by racket.

In any venture, Capone might have one or more coequal partners, men he had to deal with on an equal plane. He emerged as the city's leading racketeer because he had a stake in more operations than his partners.

Such wheeling and dealing had been easier in Capone's early years, when he could still operate with relative anonymity. Now he could no longer move about the city freely, thanks to necessary, rather elaborate security measures and the constant spotlight of publicity.

This could only have limited his ability to make deals and forge new alliances. That he spent more and more time away from Chicago also helped diminish his influence. He could run his rackets from afar, but only to a point, and his partners—most especially Nitto and Guzik—seem to have stepped in to fill the power vacuum back home. Their shared talent for staying out of public view gave them additional advantage over the increasingly notorious Capone.

"Because he lived chiefly at his Miami home after 1927 and spent much of 1929 in a Philadelphia prison . . . ," Haller writes, "Capone was perhaps the least important of the four partners." The media, meanwhile, painted him supreme.

Capone seemed increasingly willing to give up that mantle. He wanted to retire, he continually said; he was worn-out, exhausted.

"We don't want any trouble," he would say before offering a bribe or a favor, and the older he got, the more he seemed to believe it.

"He looks fifteen years older than his age," observed one Chicago journalist. "He is thirty-two years old but, as he himself frequently remarks, he 'has lived a thousand.'"

But then he'd issue grandiose statements to the press, as if to exonerate himself in the court of public opinion. This only served to further elevate his celebrity status, generating more notoriety—and the heat he claimed to abhor, further placing his organization in jeopardy. How long could Capone's partners put up with such behavior?

Gus Winkeler of the St. Valentine's Day Massacre hit squad found out. As his wife Georgette told the FBI, in 1931 her husband worked out a deal with an experienced fixer to ensure Capone's acquittal on the tax charges. The cost would be $100,000, barely a fraction of the Outfit's massive profits.

But as the FBI reported, "Winkeler went before the Board of Directors of the 'Syndicate' with the above proposition, but they refused to advance the money, or aid in any way, and, in conclusion they told Winkeler to mind his own business."

Winkeler told Georgette "that the boys," including Frank Nitto and Louis "Little New York" Campagna, "apparently were in favor of Capone going to jail in order that they could carry on the operation of the 'Syndicate' for their own profit."

This would have come as a surprise to the federal officials considering Nitto's application for parole in mid-1931. As part of his plea bargain, Nitto personally promised George Johnson "he would leave his gang connections and lead a useful, upright life."

Under the terms of the deal, Nitto would be eligible for parole as early as July, with time off for good behavior. And his behavior at Leavenworth was exceedingly good—he worked as a chauffeur and laundryman at a home outside the prison walls, his supervisor in an official report describing him in Boy Scout terms: "Trustworthy," "Friendly," "Pleasant," "Energetic," and "Faithful."

Still, Nitto kept up with events in Chicago. Shortly after arriving at Leavenworth, he met with his brother, William, a visit prison officials allowed before learning Nitto had no brother. After that they monitored his visitors more closely, preventing him from seeing "Tony Nitto," another alleged relation.

Yet they didn't stop their prisoner from corresponding with his fictitious sibling, and "William" sent him a stream of letters during his confinement, to which Nitto occasionally replied.

On March 8, Nitto received a pair of visitors from St. Louis, identified in the official register as Mr. Rogers and Mr. O'Hare—obviously reporter John Rogers and his pal E. J. O'Hare, both informers on Capone to the feds. Prison officials kept no record of what Nitto and his visitors discussed, other than "Business."

Perhaps they talked about Nitto and O'Hare's shared dog-racing ventures, or maybe gave Nitto an update on the Capone investigation. After all, Leslie Shumway, the gangland bookkeeper O'Hare handed over to the feds, had testified before the grand jury less than two weeks before.

On May 5, Nitto had what prison officials recorded as another "Business" meeting in the warden's office. This time he met with two tax investigators deeply involved in the Capone case: Frank Wilson and Nels Tessem. Again, no other record of the meeting made it into Nitto's prison file—whatever was discussed, the tax men kept it to themselves.

Armed with George Johnson's promise of an early release, Nitto applied for parole on June 18, 1931. He was to move to Kansas City, where a job waited for him at a dairy company, whose manager confirmed the position would pay $150 a month. Two character witnesses, fellow Italians claiming to be close family friends, also sent letters urging Nitto's release.

"During the past ten years or so that I have been acquainted with Frank," wrote one, "I have learned to know him as [an] honest trustworthy citizen, a man of his word at all times. He has always been one of the first and largest givers to all deserving charity campaigns."

The other writer hit precisely the same notes, claiming he had "never met a man, whom I consider more trustworthy and honorable than Mr. Frank Nitto. He has been at all times a liberal giver to all deserving charities. In other ways he has at all times been a good neighbor and a credit to the community in which he lived."

Nitto's best advocate was his wife, Anna, whom he'd married two days after the St. Valentine's Day Massacre. In a letter to the parole board, Anna said Nitto's incarceration marked "the first time he has been away from me" since their marriage—they "were the closest of companions."

She went on to stress his determination to turn his back on a criminal career.

"We both agreed," she wrote, "that to return to Chicago, where he is known and every one aware that he has been in the penitentiary, would be the wrong thing to do. . . . As soon as he is released I will join him at Kansas City, make him a home and keep him in the straight and narrow path in the future. . . . Please grant my prayer, and send my husband back to me."

All that remained was for Nitto to plead his case before the parole board at Leavenworth, which he did on July 3. The official questioner was apparently unaware of Nitto's connection to the Capone Outfit, and began by trying to figure out how much tax the prisoner had failed to pay.

With some reluctance, Nitto admitted to "something like $200,000." When asked how the government believed Nitto had made all that money, he replied, "Well, all they done was take the bank receipts."

What kind of business did they claim he'd been in?

"Well," Nitto replied, "they didn't exactly know the nature of the business. . . . They didn't go into details as to the losses and things like that."

Although Nitto was guilty of a major sin of omission, he had described Frank Wilson's work fairly accurately.

But the parole officer pressed: "What kind of business were you in?"

"Well, the last time there I was gambling and working around the racetrack."

"You weren't in the liquor business, beer business, or anything like that?"

"I handled some of that, too, sir."

But Nitto went on to deny having any leadership role.

"In fact," he said, "I wasn't working for myself. I was working for another person, which I have already told the authorities, and I just done all this banking business for this other person and from that I drawed [sic] a salary and also had a small interest in it. Naturally, the deposits were large, but it wasn't all mine."

"You have a pretty good idea about what your part was?" the parole official asked.

"Well," Nitto replied, "I made some money."

When asked exactly how much, Nitto put his take at "about $80,000 or $90,000." He said he would have been happy to pay whatever tax he owed, but the law "was so complicated, I didn't understand it myself."

Nitto told of his arrangement with George Johnson to plead guilty with consideration for parole; the prosecutor was supposed to file a report on the prisoner's behalf, recommending his release.

But Nitto was in for a shock.

"There is nothing in the file from the District Attorney at all that I can find," the parole official said.

"Well," Nitto replied, "I am just stating what they said."

"I wanted to let you understand if there was an understanding like that, there is no evidence of its having existed so far as the court record is concerned."

"I can't understand that," Nitto said. "It was promised to me."

The parole official advised him to consult his attorney.

"I would like to get a chance to start all over again," Nitto said, "and I don't want to go back to Chicago because there is nothing there for me. . . . I want to start over again and keep away from past associates and go straight."

But no letter from Johnson had come, and no record backed up the prisoner's story. Without the promised report, the official had no reason to approve Nitto's release.

"Defendant hasn't a bad court record and has maintained a good institutional record," he said, but the need to set an example to others who might defraud the government was important. The application was denied.

Because George Johnson hadn't kept up his end of the bargain, Frank Nitto wouldn't be going free anytime soon.

In May 1931, Fred Girton, editor of a Miami nightlife paper, visited Capone's Palm Island estate, keen to satisfy the curiosity of two pretty young girls in his company. A Capone pal since 1928, Girton—handsome, oval-faced, with swept-back widow's-peaked hair—had accompanied Al on the Bahamian boat trip that became an issue in the contempt-of-court trial. Now he used that friendship to get his female companions past the ten-foot concrete fence, recording his impressions for what would become a *Startling Detective Adventures* magazine article.

Capone's young brother Mimi answers the bell. Al's playing pinochle with the boys. Come on in!

Moving past a gleaming limousine, tropical plants on either side, Girton and the girls cross a porte cochere, past a growling police dog. Gladder to see them is young Sonny, who brags of a fish he's just nearly caught down at the pier.

Inside, they are greeted with smiles by Capone's mother and sister, and Al's wife, Mae, who usher them to the sun porch, where Capone is playing cards. Their host invites them to sit and have a drink.

Capone looks heavier—270 pounds, Girton estimates—but is his usual jovial self. He ends the card game, reminding his opponent, "You owe me twenty smackers for four games."

After introductions and small talk, Girton asks Capone how everything is going.

"Ah, not so good," Capone replies. "But they'll get better. We should be having a good season right now in Chicago, but there's so many politicians looking for something, that everything's gone wrong. But it'll come out all right."

A bunch of people, including Walter Winchell and Damon Runyon, are coming for dinner, and Al wants Girton and the girls to join the party.

"Haven't you a home in Chicago, Mr. Capone?" one girl asks.

"Yes, I have one there."

"Is it furnished as nicely as this one?"

Mae speaks up: "How does he know? He has only been in it once in three years." Her eyes go to her husband. "When are you coming up to see it again?"

"Where is it?" Capone asks with a grin.

Behind this gentle ribbing, Girton senses "a sort of sorrow permeating the Capone household," an attitude "of silent rebellion against what they claim is unwarranted persecution."

Under the watchful eyes of bodyguards, Capone walks his guests to the pool—"a sparkling affair of tile and glass"—to take in the new diving board off the bathhouse's second floor.

"My kid goes in every day," Al tells them. "But he can't get his head wet on account of some trouble he's had with his ears. That fat youngster over there is my brother Ralph's son. Isn't he a husky? Look, I've got this bathhouse fitted with showers on both sides. If you want to go swimming I've got plenty of suits."

A girl on Girton's arm points out a sleek yacht. Their host says they could go on board for fishing, if they like. Mae won't join them, he says, because she gets seasick.

Back in the house, Al takes a call from Chicago while the guests ooh and ahh over various treasures—a formidable carved mahogany table, a gold tableware set, gilt-edged china, goblets and glassware, "linens that the fingers of some French woman of Alsace must have spent many weeks in constructing."

Girton's girls are having a good time, no longer apprehensive about entering Capone's world, where they'd expected "to view a wild boogey man . . . who would carry one off on a mysterious ride from which there was no return."

"He isn't as bad as I thought he would be," one girl whispers, almost disappointed. "He acts just like a big kid."

"Stick around and make yourselves at home," Capone tells his guests. "I'm going up and get ready for dinner. Anything you want, just ask for it."

He crosses to the stairs quicker than a much lighter man.

"Snorkey's full of pep today," Mafalda says, then adds, "He's that way most of the time he's in Florida."

As a small army sets the horseshoe-shaped table—flowers, fancy glasses, golden knives/forks/spoons—Girton's girls seem to wonder: How much would a hock shop give for that loot?

Capone returns in a doeskin sportcoat, striped trousers, and silk shirt with fiery tie and emerald stickpin, a massive diamond on a massive hand. Guests are arriving and he greets them, a publisher here, an attorney there, here a Winchell, there a Runyon.

As more guests stream in, some arriving by car, others by boat, Capone supervises, moving among his guests to make sure they're getting what they want, as strangers get to know each other and those making return trips toss wisecracks. The host makes sure "more spaghetti, more squab, more steak, more vegetables," are served up by a gunman turned waiter.

"Frankie, hurry up, will you," Capone says genially, "or I'll cut your throat!"

A guest inquires of his green peppers and broccoli, "What's this stuff cooked in?"

"Pure imported olive oil," Capone answers. "You never hear of Italians having stomach trouble, do you? Why? Because they cook their foods in pure olive oil. It's the fats and lards and grease that cause so much sickness in this country."

And the macaroni is from Italy, not that lousy American stuff, and be sure to try the Italian peppers—don't be afraid. Why, their host crunches down two at a clip!

Meanwhile, Mother Capone is eating only the broccoli, while everything stops for Sonny to tell a joke about the reason the chicken crossed the road (a rooster was waiting). And Mae eats in silence, glancing at her guests, perhaps cataloging them, keeping her thoughts to herself.

Now comes coffee, cheese, strawberry shortcake, ice cream. Then cigars and cards for the men, a drawing room for the ladies to "engage in topics that appeal to feminine minds."

As the guests take their leave, their host says, "Come back any time. Bring some friends. See you tomorrow, okay?"

Girton and the girls thank Mr. Capone for the wonderful dinner. He's glad they liked it. "Come over any time, and bring some friends."

As handshakes are exchanged with the host's kin, Mae is subdued, Al's mother smiling, Mafalda off somewhere, Sonny offering one more riddle. In the dining room, Capone's gunman/waiter is counting the gold tableware.

Outside the gate, the girls pause for a last Lot's wife's look at the estate. "Gosh," one says, "I'd hate to be taken for a ride by Al Capone, but I'll go any time for another one of those meals!"

Girton had paid careful attention to what he and his young companions saw at Palm Island. Shortly after, he gave Frank Wilson of the Intelligence Unit a sworn statement "regarding the lavish mode of living by Al Capone at his Miami Beach home."

The editor spilled it all—how he'd been friendly with Capone since 1928, had visited Palm Island maybe thirty times, that meals seated fifteen to twenty, that parties averaged forty to sixty guests, the gold dinner service, the gourmet chef, the Cadillac limo, and more.

Startling Detective hadn't been the only market for his story.

Capone arriving at the Federal Building to plead guilty, June 16, 1931. *(Cleveland Public Library Photograph Collection)*

Twenty-Four

June–July 1931

After months of buildup in the press, George E. Q. Johnson turned his signature legal weapon on Al Capone.

On June 5, 1931, Johnson's office handed down a sixty-five-page indictment charging Capone with twenty-one counts of income tax evasion from 1925 to 1929. When combined with the earlier, secret indictment covering 1924, Capone faced a total of thirty-two years in prison and as much as $80,000 in fines.

Capone went to the Federal Building to post bond.

"Al was nattily garbed, as usual," said the *Herald and Examiner*, "wearing a grey [*sic*] suit, black shoes, a white shirt, a black tie and new straw hat, but, for the first time in his infrequent appearances in a courtroom, he had lost his smile and affable mood."

"Frowning, surly, and obviously worried," Capone ducked reporters' questions. Would he plead guilty?

"There's nothing to it," Capone shot back.

Federal officials were anything but tight-lipped. Unnamed "government men" told the *Herald and Examiner* they'd compiled an "overwhelming" and "airtight case" that "hits at the very inner circle of the Capone organization." After A. P. Madden spun the tale of the tax investigation for eager reporters, the *New York Times* rather generously compared their work to the exploits in "a dime novel."

George Johnson offered his own words of praise for the agents, but remained measured and reserved, unwilling to get ahead of himself. Like the defense, he assured the press Capone would not and could not seek a plea bargain.

"We don't expect him to try and plead guilty and secure a lighter sentence," Johnson said. "We want no compromise with Capone."

The indictments seemed impressive. They laid out in minute detail just how much the government alleged Capone had taken in—$1,038,654.84 from 1924 to 1929—and how much he owed in back taxes—$215,080.48. They even allowed him $1 in deductions per year, which made the whole business seem that much more official.

But for all this bureaucratic exactitude, the tax men's charges were little more than educated guesses based largely on the Capone lawyer's letter seeking a settlement. No one knew whether those figures were accurate, nor had attorney Mattingly claimed as much. And that was the only hard government evidence giving any hint of Capone's income.

The ganglord and three of his partners each received one-sixth of the Outfit's profits, Mattingly had written. From witness testimony, the tax men knew Capone's partners were his brother Ralph, Frank Nitto, and Jack Guzik. Though lacking any of Al's financial records, the feds had plenty of bank statements and canceled checks from those three.

To compute Capone's income for a given year, the government added up deposits made by Nitto, Guzik, and Ralph and assigned one-sixth of the total to Capone. This produced convincing-looking but essentially worthless figures—nothing showing any money deposited by Nitto, Guzik, and Ralph winding up in Capone's pocket.

Nor could the feds be sure the crucial letter could even be used at trial. Mattingly had made the government a confidential, good-faith offer to settle. Under standard rules of evidence, such "bona fide offers to compromise," made by an attorney on behalf of a client, were not admissible. The judge might well abide by precedent and throw the letter out.

And even if the judge allowed it, the jury might view the letter as an honest attempt to pay up, undermining the government's central charge that Capone willfully and deliberately avoided paying his taxes—a necessary element for charging him with a felony.

Frank Wilson managed to dig up a few other scraps of evidence, such as wire transfers made to Capone under various names. But most of what he and his agents had related to Capone's lavish purchases—$2,500 cash up front for thirty custom-made diamond belt buckles, $3,780 for more than twenty tailored suits (each with a specially lined pocket to hold a revolver), and $84 for seven pairs of underwear of "a knitted very fine silk similar to ladies gloves."

Still, Capone spending money didn't prove he'd received it from a taxable source. Although such testimony might make for compelling courtroom theater, and enrage a Depression-starved jury, a good lawyer could get it thrown out.

The government's best piece of hard evidence remained the Hawthorne Smoke Shop ledger; still, nothing in it proved Capone earned any income from the casino. Wilson had spoken with several employees and cobbled together an estimate of Capone's share of the profits; but their statements had been conflicting and unreliable.

At least one had recanted, in fierce loyalty to the boss, and all were too risky to call at trial.

Uncle Sam would have to settle for calling bookkeeper Leslie Shumway and a few others to say Capone behaved like he owned the place, and even claimed he did. If so, then presumably he made money from it. But that remained an assumption, a leap of faith for a jury.

Even worse, the ledger ended in April 1926, well outside the three-year statute of limitations. Wilson had worked under the assumption that a six-year statute applied to tax evasion, but the higher courts had yet to decide which rule applied. Even if prosecutor Johnson managed to eke out a conviction, Capone's attorneys could file for an arrest of judgment, putting the gangster's sentence on hold for a year or two, dashing Johnson's hopes of jailing Capone before the 1932 campaign and the World's Fair. And the Supreme Court might very well decide the three-year rule applied, wiping out most of the felony charges against Capone.

The tax case rested on quicksand and Johnson knew it, but had rushed it into court anyway. With the ledger about to expire and the Justice Department breathing down his neck, Johnson had little choice—otherwise, he'd lose his shot at Capone. But with so many holes in his case, he could see little chance of winning a speedy conviction, his best hope the one thing he'd refused to do in public—cut a deal with Capone.

Back in late April or early May, a Capone lawyer met with Johnson, surprising the prosecutor by revealing his client knew of the secret indictment handed down in March. Capone feared what would happen in court, believing press notoriety made a fair trial impossible. If Johnson would recommend "a satisfactory sentence," Capone would plead guilty.

Johnson brought the offer to Attorney General William Mitchell and his assistant, G. A. Youngquist. They gave him tacit approval to negotiate, but reserved the right to sign off on any plea bargain. Above all, this had to remain secret; the country wouldn't look kindly on the Justice Department bargaining with a notorious "public enemy."

For a few weeks, Johnson met repeatedly with Capone's lawyers, who said Capone would settle for eighteen months behind bars, as had Frank Nitto for his guilty plea. Johnson held firm at two and a half years. The defense came up to two years, and Johnson seemed ready to accept—the tax indictments had yet to come down, and Johnson considered shaving off some of the charges to make it seem as though he'd driven a harder bargain.

The Justice Department, as Youngquist wrote, cared less about the length of Capone's sentence "than the restoration of public confidence in law enforcement that would follow upon his actually being put behind the prison bars." Jailing Capone was about making a statement; the appearance mattered more than the legal realities.

But convicting Capone of tax evasion—on a guilty plea, no less—would send a mixed message to the public.

"It is not conducive to American pride," wrote the *Louisville Courier-Journal* after Capone's indictment, "that gangsters, guilty of every abomination from operating a chain of brothels to committing wholesale massacre, should be found guilty only of failing to pay taxes on their ill-gotten gains."

To put the best possible face on the deal, the feds couldn't just lock Capone up as a tax cheat; they needed something more. And the government still held the power to charge Capone with his signature crime: bootlegging. A Prohibition conviction would keep the president's promise to back up the Eighteenth Amendment, handing Herbert Hoover a major, and much-needed, symbolic victory.

During a visit to Chicago in May, Youngquist suggested Johnson dredge up an old liquor conspiracy indictment against Capone and roll it into the plea bargain. That might get the defense to agree to the two-and-a-half-year sentence and would certainly please the president.

"If the guilty plea to the liquor conspiracy case can be secured in addition to the plea in the tax case," Frank Wilson wrote Elmer Irey, "[the president] can tell the world that he has the biggest bootlegger and most notorious gangster in the country in jail. That ought to show the country he is doing his best for law enforcement and perhaps would result in considerable support in 1932," when Hoover faced reelection.

But Johnson didn't need the old indictment—he had the work of Eliot Ness and the Untouchables. During their first two raids, the team had seized important records and arrested key figures in the beer business. And pencil detective Lyle Chapman had strung together evidence from every raid on an Outfit-connected brewery since 1924, effectively tying Capone to the racket.

The case remained, at best, a work in progress—more raids would yield more evidence and a fuller picture of the gang's operations. Johnson already had enough for a sweeping indictment implicating Capone and several of his top aides in a vast, ongoing bootleg conspiracy.

As with the tax charges, the normally snail-paced Johnson would be pushing this case into court before its time. But that didn't matter, because he never expected to take it to trial anyway—Ness's work would be another bargaining chip in his negotiations with Capone's lawyers.

One week after the tax indictment, the grand jury charged Capone and sixty-eight others with five thousand counts of conspiracy to violate the Volstead Act. Each count represented either 1,500 gallons of beer seized in a brewery or a confiscated truckload of thirty barrels. That amounted to some 7.5 million gallons, with a total street value in excess of $2.7 billion.

Newspapers ate these figures up, running enormous headlines dwarfing those about tax charges.

5,000 CRIMES INDICT CAPONE, screamed the front page of the *Herald and Examiner*. INDICT CAPONE; 5,000 COUNTS, proclaimed the *Tribune*. News of the tax indictment had only made it to page four of the *New York Times*. The Prohibition indictment, on the other hand, landed squarely on page one.

Asked by reporters how he felt about his chances in court, Johnson smiled. "We never indict unless we have a good case," he said.

"This is the end of Scarface Al."

The next day, Ness led a squad of federal marshals out to round up all the defendants. Most big shots were expected to turn themselves in quietly, but asking around about some lesser-known names, the investigators got only belly laughs in response—at least ten named in the indictment did not exist, their names springing from the fertile imaginations of gangsters forced to testify before the grand jury. Federal officials threatened perjury indictments against the "belligerent Capone henchmen," as the *Daily Times* described them, who had pulled the stunt.

"At any rate," wrote the *Times,* "the false names do not affect the validity of the indictment."

Congratulatory messages flooded Johnson's office. But the prosecutor insisted the real credit belonged to the agents, heaping praise on Ness's special squad.

"They worked at the risk of death," wrote the *Tribune,* "and resisted the temptation of bribes several times as high as their salaries for a year, Mr. Johnson said."

Johnson also revealed the group's nickname, which first appeared in print in that evening's *Herald and Examiner.* An Associated Press writer included the name in his story, and the following morning Ness and his "Untouchables" made coast-to-coast headlines.

In praising Ness's team, Johnson went far above and beyond the pat on the back he'd given the tax men—playing up the peril of the Untouchables' work, stressing the huge payoffs they'd refused, and describing in detail the threats and intimidation they'd ignored. He led reporters to believe this was more than a ragtag band of misfits.

"The average age of these agents is 30 years," said the *Tribune,* "and the average salary $2,800. All are college graduates, and they are the picked men in the prohibition service from all parts of the country."

Really, their average age was closer to thirty-five, and apart from Ness, only Chapman had graduated from a four-year university. Claiming otherwise painted these men as something they weren't—clean-cut, fresh-faced feds, models of what the world would soon come to know as "G-men."

Johnson put the squad's best face forward, the one belonging to the college-educated, twenty-something Ness.

"Seven of the eight . . . remain anonymous for various reasons," reported the AP.

Only Ness's name made the papers. His photo, taken from his government credentials, went out on the AP wire, running everywhere from Washington, D.C., to Enid, Oklahoma.

Exploits having little to do with the current Capone case—such as Ness cheating death at the hands of a stiletto-wielding henchman in Chicago Heights—made it into the articles, helping make the plea deal seem a hard-won victory. Capone's story already had an engaging villain—Johnson merely supplied a hero.

And Ness willingly filled that role. The same day the story hit the papers in Chicago, Ness sat down for an interview with twenty-two-year-old Priscilla Higinbotham of the *Herald and Examiner*. Higinbotham moved in Ness's sphere, having studied under Goddard at the Northwestern crime lab. But she treated him less like a lawman than a celebrity—a charming, well-educated, engaging personality.

"Ness is only 28, but he has formed some very definite views," Higinbotham wrote. "While feeling that the Prohibition amendment, as a law, should be enforced, he has a greater interest, apparently, in wiping out the evils that the law has brought about."

She closed by noting Ness cut the interview short to go play a few rounds of tennis—"just a 'workout,' necessary to prepare him for more hours and hours of intensive work to ensure Alphonse Capone's ultimate sojourn behind the bars."

Yet Ness remained a bit player in crafting his own legend. From the moment it hit the papers, his story had a life of its own, spinning well outside anyone's control. Far-flung editorial boards, who knew next to nothing about Ness, sang his praises in lofty terms.

"No soldier on the battlefield ever performed more heroic work than has Eliot Ness performed," said the *Hollywood Daily Citizen* on June 17. "He should be honored as are the heroes of the battlefield honored."

Individual citizens sent Ness a string of fan letters.

"God bless you and the others for the good work you have done," wrote one Californian to Ness. "I knew that some day some one would appear and make an end of Al's terrible situation."

In a private letter to Ness, the editor of a Wisconsin newspaper offered his own endorsement.

"I am a 100-per cent wet, but I honor you for your bravery," he wrote. "The sooner you can put these boot-legger-drys where they can't vote for prohibition, the quicker we can get a repeal of the 18th amendment. I'm for you."

Thrust from obscurity into the limelight, Ness arrived at just the right time to become a cultural hero. Thanks to the onset of the Depression, the American infatuation with racketeers had turned to loathing.

"A well fed, busy, money-making America could forget a massacre and continue to wink at gangsters," *Liberty* magazine said that fall. "The glamour has been stripped from the gangsters. Even the most stupid of us see them now as they are, yellow louts, red-handed plunderers. . . . Hunger has made us see the truth."

Americans hungered for heroes, too, now that the clay-foot idols of the Roaring Twenties had begun to crumble. After overdosing on individualism, many warmed to the idea of a man who placed the country's needs before his own.

"One of the things that brought malignant power to Capone was a passion for owning things," said the *Birmingham Age-Herald*. "If one may judge the mind and spirit of young Ness by his first public service, his passion lies in making a better social state—a passion for clean and fine things, something quite apart from the acquisitive passion."

Capone and his breed represented the heartless, take-no-prisoners capitalism that drove the country into Depression. The story of the Untouchables offered a heroic alternative, a necessary corrective to a decadent decade.

Ness, of course, was far from the only figure embodying these virtues—George Johnson, Frank Wilson, and others who worked on the Capone case could lay similar claims. But none shared Ness's youth, good looks, or boyish charm, and none had taken the fight to Capone as directly as the Untouchables. In a nation reared on tales of frontier lawmen, Ness couldn't help but stand out. He became the symbol of everything the Justice Department hoped to prove with Capone's conviction—that law and order still reigned in the United States.

"This is an achievement that will go far towards strengthening the faith of our people in their government," an Oklahoma pastor wrote Ness. "We had begun to wonder whether criminals and their purchased lawyers were not our real rulers. The success of the government through the diligence and courage of men like yourself renews the courage of all of us."

Another Oklahoman drew inspiration from Ness's courage. Chester Gould had moved to Chicago in 1921, hoping to ply his trade as a cartoonist. But after ten years of turning out such strips as *Fillum Fables*, *The Radio Catts*, and *The Girl Friends*, a successful nationally syndicated strip remained beyond his grasp.

He began badgering Captain John Medill Patterson of the Tribune Syndicate with one idea after another. Patterson rejected them all.

"I'm capable and determined," Gould wrote Patterson in March 1930, "give me a chance. Won't you believe me when I say I know my stuff and can deliver the goods?"

Gould liked to think of himself as a newspaperman, with the front page as his competition, and he ripped his next idea right from Chicago's headlines. The big gangsters, who had been given a free pass by corrupt local cops, were being hounded now by a new breed of federal investigators.

In the summer of 1931, he began to envision a strip about a modern Sherlock Holmes. Instead of a deerstalker, this detective would wear a fedora; instead of an Inverness cape, a camel's-hair topcoat. Newspaper stories about Ness and the Untouchables gave Gould real-life models, crystalizing the character in his mind—a courageous, scientific crime fighter battling a modern Moriarty.

Gould worked up a week's worth of strips pitting a cigar-chomping, Capone-modeled gangster against a hook-nosed, square-jawed detective—*Plainclothes Tracy*. Grim and violent, with sneering, brutal villains speaking the argot of Chicago's streets, *Tracy* was like nothing that had ever appeared in America's funny pages, which was precisely what piqued Captain Patterson's interest.

YOUR PLAINCLOTHES TRACY HAS POSSIBILITIES, he wired Gould. WOULD LIKE TO SEE YOU WHEN I GO TO CHICAGO NEXT. The telegram left Gould trembling and dizzy. When Gould showed up for his meeting with Patterson, the captain began pacing the room.

"This name is too long," he said. "Charlie, Harry, Harry Tracy, Buck Tracy, Dick Tracy. Let's call this man Dick Tracy. They call cops Dicks."

"I was a little jealous that I didn't think of it myself," Gould recalled. "It was a brilliant idea. Dick Tracy. Tracy was a play on tracing, in my book."

The feature debuted the following October. Like the story of the Untouchables from which it drew, *Dick Tracy* offered everything Americans wanted in a lawman—a detective who shot first, asked questions later, and never let a bad guy get off with a plea bargain.

Shortly after the return of the Prohibition indictment, George Johnson met in private with Judge Wilkerson. Johnson had every reason to see the judge as an ally, considering the man's history with the Capones. But Wilkerson's fierce determination to go his own way made him a wild card.

The two had discussed the plea bargain before, with Johnson outlining the flaws in the tax case. Wilkerson had remained noncommittal, saying only the matter merited consideration, reserving his final decision.

Now, after reminding the judge of the risks in bringing Capone to trial, Johnson said the Justice Department and the defendant had come to an arrangement. As before, Wilkerson was careful not to promise to abide by the deal, but he didn't reject it outright, which was enough for the prosecutor. Johnson went back to Capone's attorneys and told them Wilkerson had approved the bargain.

To close the deal, Johnson compromised even further. The attorney general had reluctantly signed off on concurrent sentences of two years for bootlegging and two and a half for tax evasion, with the understanding that Capone would serve his full time. But Johnson agreed to only eighteen months on the Prohibition charges, and left Capone's lawyers with the option of appealing the tax conviction on statute-of-limitations grounds.

Capone surely viewed this as a victory. Prison would give him a respite from constant raids and other federal harassment—he'd walk out in 1934 still in his prime, his slate essentially wiped clean. The Depression might even be over by then. People would have the money to start drinking and gambling again; Capone could return to an organization healthier and more profitable than before.

If he fought the charges at trial and took his case to the Supreme Court, Capone might end up going to jail just as prosperity began to kick in. Better to take his lumps now.

On Tuesday, June 16, a few minutes before 2:00 P.M., Capone arrived at the Federal Building with bodyguard Phil D'Andrea. Onlookers thronged the streets, many more packing the halls inside, desperate to catch a glimpse of the great gangster. When Capone stepped from his car, ten police detectives surrounded him and cleared a path to Judge Wilkerson's crowded courtroom. A sea of spectators tried to force their way in, but guards kept doors sealed tight.

Capone took a seat alongside his attorneys, his camel's-hair suit—a tasteless bright yellow—offering a stark contrast to their sober attire. Journalists crowded in, bombarding him with questions. The *Evening*

American's correspondent made herself heard over the ruckus, asking about Capone's sunshine suit.

"Yeah, it is loud, isn't it?" Al said. "Well, I got to do something to give the crowds their thrill."

Capone crossed his legs, showing off red-white-and-blue silk socks. Everything about the defendant, from his eye-watering outfit to his self-satisfied smile, telegraphed his delight at getting away with murder.

Elmer Irey had come from Washington to witness the Intelligence Unit's signal victory. With him were the agents who'd dogged Capone for the past three years: Frank Wilson, A. P. Madden, Nels Tessem, and Clarence Converse.

Wilson studied the man who'd outfoxed him time and again.

"There's a bad streak in him," Wilson said, "but I can't help thinking that he's what could have been a good man gone to waste. . . . The abilities he undoubtedly has might have been turned into quite different channels."

Eliot Ness had also come to see Capone plead guilty. Perhaps that was when, according to one report, Al asked his lawyer to point out that meddlesome Prohibition agent. Ness, who had never laid eyes on Capone short of a newsreel, kept his impressions of the gangster largely to himself.

But the defendant's cool confidence didn't sit well with Eliot, whose calm demeanor masked boiling frustration at Capone's having managed to cheat the law.

When Wilkerson walked in, the spectators got to their feet like sports fans for the national anthem. Then they fell back in their seats, ready for the show. Capone, his attorneys, and the prosecution team approached the bench.

Standing alongside George Johnson were his two assistant prosecutors: Dwight H. Green, in charge of the tax case, and Victor E. LaRue, handling the Prohibition indictment. Green faced the defendant.

"Alphonse Capone," he declared, "in indictment No. 22852 you are charged with attempting to evade and defeat your individual income taxes for the year 1924. . . . How do you plead, guilty or not guilty?"

"I plead guilty," Capone said softly.

"In indictment No. 23232," Green said, "you are charged with attempting to evade and defeat your individual income taxes for the years 1925, 1926, 1927, 1928 and 1929, and with willful failure to file . . . individual income tax return[s] for 1928 and 1929. . . . How do you plead, guilty or not guilty?"

Capone murmured, "I plead guilty."

Now LaRue stepped forward. "And in indictment No. 23256," he said, "you are charged with conspiracy to violate the National Prohibition Act—how do you plead, guilty or not guilty?"

"I plead guilty."

With that, it was over, and the court moved on to another case.

Capone said he "hoped everybody was satisfied," sighed, and slipped out, a phalanx of police hurrying him into a freight elevator and away from the crowd. In the airy rotunda, gawkers lined the balconies like gargoyles, waiting for Al, already gone out a side door.

Asked for a comment by the *Tribune,* Johnson offered only a weary smile. He told the *Herald and Examiner:* "I'll be able to sleep easy for the first time in a long while tonight—I'll be able to relish a good meal, too."

The long-suffering Prohibition Bureau greeted the news with elation. "Personally," Dwight Avis wrote Johnson, "I do not believe that there could be any more distinct accomplishment that would tend to create public confidence in the proper enforcement of the National Prohibition Act."

The agency's internal newsletter, the *Bureau Bulletin,* ran a brief story listing the agents responsible for Capone's indictment—Ness, Joe Leeson, and Lyle Chapman getting the most credit. The piece also acknowledged the work of Maurice Seager, Warren Stutzman, Paul

Robsky, Marty Lahart, Barney Cloonan, Robert Sterling, and Marion King—the first and only time the names of all ten Untouchables would appear together in print during their lifetimes.

The tax men, too, were celebrating. "There seems to be a feeling in Washington, since Al Capone was forced to plead guilty in Chicago," said the *New York Times,* "that the Federal Government at last has an effective weapon with which to break the backbone of racketeering in the United States."

Irey pledged to clean up Manhattan by sending the same agents who had so effectively snared Capone. Meanwhile, Frank Wilson, his work seemingly finished, closed off a new but promising phase of the investigation.

Back in March, he'd sent two undercover agents, Michael Malone and James Sullivan, to investigate Capone's ties to brothels in Stickney. They'd rented rooms in the Lexington Hotel, posing as gangsters, hobnobbing with Outfit men. But the pair hadn't penetrated very deeply into the mob before Capone pleaded guilty and their work came to an abrupt end.

The day after Capone gave his pleas, Irey, Wilson, and Johnson went down to Springfield to see Herbert Hoover, in town to rededicate Abraham Lincoln's newly renovated tomb. Illinois Republicans packed the place; congratulations from officials and citizens alike greeted Johnson everywhere. Reporters hounded the prosecutor, asking if the president planned to congratulate him in person.

No, Hoover hadn't sent for him, Johnson said. "After all, I'm only the district attorney, and my boss is Attorney General Mitchell."

Johnson insisted he wasn't a gubernatorial candidate, adding, "I don't want to claim too much credit." He stressed the strength of the indictments, saying he could have won in open court had it been necessary.

"Capone," Johnson said, "must have been pretty well convinced we had an air-tight case."

At the ceremony in Oak Ridge Cemetery, the president received an unusually warm greeting, four hundred–some protesters having been nudged out of town before his arrival.

"There can be no man in our country," Hoover told those assembled, "who, either by his position or his influence, stands above the law."

In the crowd was Samuel Insull, chief financier of the Secret Six, his utilities empire not yet fallen.

Afterward, the president went over to his old friend Frank Wilson and congratulated him on "a fine job up in Chicago." For Wilson, this made the past year's work worthwhile. At the governor's mansion, Hoover gave George Johnson a few private moments.

"The president was very kind in what he said to me," Johnson told reporters, refusing to elaborate.

Almost as soon as Capone left the courtroom, word of the plea deal began to creep out.

"The most frequently heard report around the Federal building," wrote an AP correspondent, "was that [Capone] would be sentenced to two and a half years on each charge, the sentences to run concurrently, but Federal authorities refused to discuss the reports."

Other officials flatly denied Capone made any kind of bargain, claiming "the czar of rumdom had thrown himself wholly on the mercy of the court."

But within hours of the guilty plea, the *Evening American* printed the agreed-upon sentence as fact, as if all Judge Wilkerson had to do was rubber-stamp it. Capone might come up for parole in eight months, or get out in under two years with time off for good behavior. And it was all "the result of a compromise with the government." This came from the defendant himself, bragging to reporters about the "easy out" he'd finagled from the feds.

So accustomed had the city grown to gangsters buying their way out of prison, seeing one bargain his way in—however briefly—seemed an improvement. Yet Frank Loesch sensed "a very distinct undertone of dissatisfaction" among his fellow Chicagoans, who only reluctantly granted getting Capone in court was better than having him gunned down by fellow gangsters.

"I hope that someday," Loesch wrote the president, "you will allow me to tell the public how much you had to do with it and how much of the impetus was personally given by you."

"Some time when the gentleman you mention is safely tucked away, and engaged in very hard labor," Hoover responded in good humor, "you can tell all about it."

Hoover's attorney general felt less optimistic.

"It was, no doubt, a tactical mistake to receive the plea of guilty and then allow two or three weeks to elapse before sentence is imposed," William Mitchell wrote Johnson on June 25. The public was liable to develop "very exaggerated ideas" of how severe the sentence should be.

Having agreed "with some misgivings" to the two-and-a-half-year sentence, Mitchell was livid Johnson had offered further concessions behind his back. The attorney general was convinced if Capone didn't serve his full two and one-half years, "the reaction would be such that we would have been better off never to have commenced the effort to bring him to justice."

In late June, Judge Wilkerson delayed the sentencing hearing until the end of July, with Capone set to go to jail then. Johnson went on a brief vacation only to return to find that the judge expected the prosecutor and his team to present all their evidence.

But Capone had already admitted his guilt, eliminating the need for a trial. A confused Johnson met with Wilkerson to see what, exactly, the judge had in mind.

Wilkerson singled out the Prohibition indictment, saying he had just come to realize how tenuous the evidence was. The prosecutor found this surprising, since details of the case had been widely reported. That was precisely the problem—the judge showed Johnson letters and newspaper editorials, negative reactions to the plea bargain, demanding Capone receive a stiffer sentence.

By playing up the strength of their case against him, the government had overpromised. They couldn't accuse Capone of five thousand crimes, then send him away for two and a half years and expect the American people to applaud.

Wilkerson flatly accused the prosecutor of recommending too short a sentence. Johnson said he couldn't go back on his promise to Capone's attorneys—his sense of honor demanded he follow through. Anyway, the Treasury and Justice Departments had approved the deal. If Wilkerson wouldn't abide by it, Capone would have every right to change his plea to not guilty.

And that was the last thing Johnson wanted, because he knew they stood such a slim chance in court. The judge, seeming to soften, asked Johnson to get written approval of the bargain from both Treasury and Justice. If Wilkerson had such statements in hand before passing sentence, any backlash might be mitigated.

Johnson did so, but Wilkerson remained unsatisfied, calling the prosecutor a week before the hearing and demanding Capone plead guilty without condition.

Otherwise, Wilkerson would bring the tax case to trial, which he felt stood a better chance of success than the Prohibition charges. He leaned on judicial precedent, but also brought up public demands for a harsh sentence. Federal judges were supposed to be immune from outside pressure—they didn't need votes to stay in office—but Wilkerson took the political realities very seriously.

"A judge," he told Johnson, "would be a damned fool not to pay attention to that!"

This left Johnson, already celebrated as the man who got Capone, in a perilous position. His strategy of jailing gangsters on tax charges had become the model for fighting crime in other cities—having the deal exposed publicly, and then losing his battle in court, would destroy him.

Caught between a stubborn judge and his promises to the defense,

Johnson could only double down on the plea bargain. He prepared a lengthy statement for the sentencing hearing, reminding Willkerson of the hazards in each case and urging him to accept the two-and-a-half-year sentence.

But if he thought he could reason with this judge, Johnson was mistaken. By leaking the story, the arrogant Capone had sealed his own fate—and the prosecutor's, too.

Judge Wilkerson was not about to let a gangster tell him what to do.

Top: Judge Wilkerson's courtroom in 1931. Bottom: Editorial cartoon satirizing the federal government's inability to convict Capone, 1931. *(Top: Cleveland Public Library Photograph Collection. Bottom: Library of Congress.)*

Twenty-Five

Summer 1931

On the morning of July 30, 1931, Eliot Ness arrived in Judge Wilkerson's court before 10:00 A.M., moving through the latest mob of onlookers, his government credentials getting him past the guards.

Ness had come prepared to recite the evidence he and his Untouchables had gathered against Capone, as had Frank Wilson and A. P. Madden of the Intelligence Unit.

"I seethed inwardly," Ness recalled, "at what could easily become a shallow victory for the law and could put Capone back in circulation very soon."

Capone breezed in before ten, in a summery green-and-white ensemble with a straw boater. He'd spent the previous day at the Lexington Hotel, meeting with associates and getting his affairs in order, assuming he'd be off to jail as early as this evening but not dismayed in the least.

"A rumor being circulated among lawyers representing Capone hoodlums in the federal courts," said the *Tribune,* "is that the gang leader is confident he will have to serve only eleven months."

Taking his chair at the front of the crowded courtroom, Capone bantered with reporters, grinning as he chewed gum.

"No, boys," he said, "none of my family will be here. I am feeling fine, but I have nothing to say. Now let me alone for a few minutes, boys."

Almost immediately, Wilkerson went off script with a statement confirming prosecutor Johnson's worst fears.

"The United States Attorney," said the judge, "has stated that he wishes to offer suggestions with reference to the judgments to be entered in these cases. Pleas of guilty, I am advised, were entered upon his undertaking to make such recommendations."

The Court would receive these suggestions, Wilkerson said, giving them proper weight.

But, the judge went on, "in consenting to receive these suggestions, the Court does not bind itself to adopt them, or to enter judgments in conformity therewith. There can be no exception to this rule. The parties to a Criminal case may not stipulate as to the judgment to be entered. That duty rests on the Court, and no one may relieve the Court of that responsibility."

Capone's cool confidence evaporated. "The smiling underworld boss suddenly lost his affable mood and became obviously worried," wrote the *Herald and Examiner*.

The crowd leaned forward.

The judge was saying, "It is the duty of the Court to hear all of the facts, consider the suggestions of the parties, and then pronounce its judgment in accordance with the record as it is made, when the case is submitted for decision."

Then Wilkerson dropped a second bombshell—he insisted Capone take the stand in his own defense.

"If the defendant asks leniency of the Court," Wilkerson said, "he should be ready to answer all proper questions put by the Court, touching the matter which he has confessed by his plea."

Capone's right against self-incrimination had disappeared when he pleaded guilty. He must answer questions under oath about his business, without any guarantees of a reduced sentence. With that, Wilkerson continued the case until the afternoon.

A different Capone returned to the courtroom at three o'clock.

"The collar that had been white and fresh in the morning was wilted," wrote the *Tribune,* "and his greasy hair was disarranged by the nervous mopping of his brow during the colloquy at the bar."

Capone stood tapping the trial table, waiting for the session to begin. Asked if he'd switched to a not-guilty plea, Capone ignored the question.

Under the law, a defendant could rescind a guilty plea "only when it appears that the pleas of guilty were entered through ignorance or inadvertence," wrote the *Tribune,* "or through the holding out of some false hope or inducement." Without permission to change his plea, Capone could face thirty-four years in prison and $90,000 in fines.

Michael Ahern, Capone's attorney, had little choice but to argue George Johnson had falsely induced his client to plead guilty. Once Wilkerson resumed the bench, Ahern described his negotiations with the prosecutor, explaining the deal had been approved at the highest levels of government.

"We felt," Ahern said, "particularly after [Johnson] had obtained the approval of the Secretary of the Treasury, that his recommendation would be approved of by the Court." Otherwise, without this inducement, the defendant would never have pleaded guilty.

"You have not any doubt," the judge asked, "that I stated the law correctly this morning, have you, as to the duty of the Court in the imposition of the sentence, on a plea of guilty?"

"I—"

"Of course," the judge went on, "the Court is obliged to keep the record open until all the facts are disclosed to the Court."

"Well," Ahern said, "I draw—"

"And the Court can act only on the record after it has been presented."

"I draw a distinction, if it please the Court, between the act of a court in imposing penalties, and the act of a court in prejudging a case. . . . If the Court would follow the recommendation of the District Attorney as made, and if we could have the assurance of the Court—"

"Suppose the Court does not agree with that?"

The hearing was a disaster for both prosecution and defense, Ahern branding the prosecutor a liar and embarrassing both the Justice and Treasury Departments. The close quarters of the crowded court forced both sides together, heightening the tension.

To the *Tribune,* Johnson appeared "manifestly distressed . . . crushed against the bar with Capone and the other counsel in the only vacant space—six feet square—in the courtroom."

After lecturing Ahern on a judge's prerogative in sentencing, Wilkerson asked Johnson if he would accept Capone's motion for a change of plea.

It would be unfair, the prosecutor said, to have the government present its evidence before Capone switched his plea, thereby giving the defense a preview of their whole case.

"For that reason," Johnson went on, "we feel that the motion should be disposed of now . . . [and] to make a statement here of the facts that led up to the United States Attorney saying that he would make a recommendation in this case."

Johnson then described the negotiations in detail, with an eye toward protecting himself from blame. Capone's attorneys had come to him—he hadn't sought to make a deal. Elmer Irey had participated in the negotiations, with the Justice Department's full awareness.

At the judge's request, Johnson shared Attorney General Mitchell's confidential letter approving the plea deal.

Johnson explained "that it seemed very desirable on the part of the officers of the Government who are charged with this responsibility, if we could avoid the hazards of a trial, so that this defendant might at an early date be imprisoned in the penitentiary."

The prosecutor, his hands shaking, appeared as distressed as the defendant, perhaps more so.

Ahern pushed to have the Court grant his motion for a change of plea, but Wilkerson stubbornly refused. Nothing the prosecutor had done, he argued, constituted a false inducement under the law.

Johnson "is doing everything he told you he would do," Wilkerson said. "He has dealt with you openly and above board."

Capone was at the Court's mercy. The judge seized the moment to attack the true source of his frustration—"contemptuous" publications bringing into disrepute the administration of justice in the courts. Such publications had "undertaken to announce definitely, in advance, what the action of this Court would be."

Leaning forward, eyes blazing, Wilkerson said, "I do not know what weight this defendant attached to them, but it was high time that somebody bring to his attention, and bring to his attention forcibly, the fact that it is utterly impossible to bargain with the Federal Court with respect to the judgment to be entered in a criminal case."

Ahern said he agreed with the Court: "I think that many of the publications have been contemptuous."

"And they may have to be dealt with hereafter," said the judge.

But nothing Ahern said changed Wilkerson's mind—the guilty plea stood. The attorney only dug his client in deeper by suggesting the judge was "upset" over the case.

"Oh," Wilkerson shot back, "I am not upset about it."

"Well, over these publications, I mean."

"No, no, they do not disturb me," Wilkerson said, despite his earlier outburst. "Now, do not make any mistake about that."

Wilkerson asked Johnson if he would consent to the change of pleas. The ever-cautious prosecutor replied he would not object to it, then shifted responsibility for approving the motion onto his boss, the attorney general.

"Very well," Wilkerson said. "I will take this motion under advisement, and dispose of it tomorrow afternoon at two o'clock."

Capone turned to leave, but Wilkerson's next words froze him.

"In the meantime," said the judge, "the defendant is remanded to the custody of the marshal."

Capone glared at his lawyers as several deputy marshals blocked his path. Ahern asked that his client be allowed to go free—after all, Capone was out on bond.

"I thought I was doing something for the protection of the defendant here," the judge said. "He is being brought down to the building here every day under guard and I thought if that was true, he had better be here."

"He has a wife and child, and mother," Ahern said. "If somebody chooses to attach guards around him, may it please the Court, that is their business. I don't believe that the defendant is requesting those guards. He feels—"

"I will withdraw the order," Wilkerson cut in, "until tomorrow afternoon at two o'clock."

At that, wrote the *Herald and Examiner,* "Capone picked up his hat and walked hastily toward the door, forcing his way through the crowd as he went."

The judge had one more surprise in store for the defense. The next morning, Wilkerson summoned George Johnson and Capone's legal team to his courtroom at ten, where he agreed to let the defendant plead not guilty on the tax charges. But he put the Prohibition case on hold, suggesting Johnson had missed an opportunity to charge the gangster with more serious offenses. Several violations listed in the indictment, the judge noted, fell within the three-year statute of limitations for liquor crimes and carried "a much heavier penalty" than mere conspiracy.

Wilkerson sent the indictment back to the grand jury to consider charging Capone with direct violations, if the evidence warranted. Meanwhile, the Court would proceed with the tax case, which could go to trial as early as September.

Wilkerson's comments on the Prohibition charges made no legal sense. The indictment included only one charge against Capone within the statute of limitations: his meeting with Joe Fusco, Bert Delaney, and other top bootleggers in 1930. That, in and of itself, was a crime only when connected with violations committed by his partners, as proof of an ongoing conspiracy. Stripping that context away destroyed the entire case.

And that was precisely what Wilkerson wanted. He resented being given a trio of half-finished, shoddy indictments on the assumption he'd accept the government's bad deal. His ruling all but accused the prosecutor of cooking up the Prohibition case "merely for the purpose of creating the impression that this defendant had been a flagrant law breaker over a long period of time."

Wilkerson, facing a public clamor to give Capone a stiff sentence, knew the longest term he could impose on the Prohibition case was two years, six months shorter than the plea deal. The tax charges, however, carried a potential penalty of up to thirty-two years, a much more appropriate sentence for such a notorious gangster.

Wilkerson's intentions were clear to Capone's lawyers. "I would just as soon try a case before you as anybody," Ahern told the judge obsequiously. "I think your rulings are fair. But I know the attitude of the defendant and I think he thinks you are prejudiced."

"There is a method provided for you in such cases," Wilkerson replied. He meant that Capone and his attorneys could request a change of venue—a strategy they probably should have employed, but nothing indicates they ever tried.

The Justice Department had their own reasons for discontent—Wilkerson's ruling was a public embarrassment not only for the prosecutor, but his entire agency.

"A letter of praise to Mr. Johnson and his Chicago staff was ready to be sent out by the department," said the *Herald and Examiner,* "but Judge Wilkerson's refusal to fall in with the 'gentlemen's agreement' between officials and the gang leader upset all the neat plans."

One U.S. senator even proposed a congressional investigation, harshly criticizing the department for contemplating a deal with Capone. By exposing the bargain to the nation, Wilkerson alone in the justice system seemed courageous enough to stand up to Public Enemy Number One.

He'd also set the stage "for a real fight to the finish between disorganized law and organized crime," as one upstate New York paper put it. "A month ago the impregnable honesty of the half-dozen federal 'untouchables' seemed to have the Haughtiest Hoodlum well on the way to presiding behind a new kind of bars. Today the Best-Dressed Gangster bids fair to be, so far as the law is concerned, the most untouchable of them all."

Although pleased that Judge Wilkerson had thrown out the devil's bargain, Eliot Ness knew that when it came to bootlegging, Capone could be convicted only on conspiracy charges.

The next day, the *Tribune* cited unnamed Untouchables—likely including Ness—who explained the difficulty, if not impossibility, of "link[ing] Capone with any substantive offenses, such as manufacture, sale or transportation of beer, within the statute of limitations."

In early August, Ness and his Untouchables appeared before the grand jury, presenting their evidence in what seemed a vain attempt to secure new charges against Capone.

In the meantime, their most important work remained cutting off the Outfit's income wherever they could. And summer provided bootleggers with a much-needed cash infusion as roasting Chicagoans sought icy glasses of beer. Taking no joy in denying refreshment to the city's citizens, Ness and the Untouchables provided heat of their own, hoping to dry up an already weakened criminal organization.

As early as mid-May, Capone's men were fleecing speakeasy owners by underfilling beer barrels and forcing more product on them than they could use.

"Raids on Capone's breweries and his gambling dives," reported the *Tribune*, "as well as high bonds required of his gangsters in federal Court are reported to have hit [Capone] hard financially, probably accounting for the cheating."

Federal agents told the *New York Times* the Outfit was "virtually insolvent" from bailing out its members and replacing seized equipment. When the tax charges first came down, Capone barely had enough cash on hand to make his $50,000 bond.

The Untouchables kept up the pressure. Cruising around the South Side on June 20, Leeson and Robsky noticed the driver of an ice truck glancing around furtively, as if to spot a tail. They followed him to a large double garage at 2636 Calumet Avenue and stormed inside.

A trio of startled bootleggers lit out the back way. The agents flagged down a passing police car and leapt onto its running board as it sped after one of the fleeing men. A few warning shots brought the bootlegger skidding to a stop, ready to surrender.

He turned out to be James Calloway, an associate of Bert Delaney, Capone's brewery location spotter. The other two escaped, but back in the garage the Untouchables found more than 360 barrels of iced beer ready for delivery—some 12,000 gallons all told, worth $20,285. They also discovered another piece of evidence linking Capone to the racket—some barrels had been loaded onto a truck owned by the World Motor Service Company, a Capone front.

Less than a month later, as a thick, oppressive heat wave settled over the city, Ness got a tip liquor was stored in a garage at 3419 North Clark Street. He and the Untouchables quickly raided the place, but found nothing apart from some empty bottles and whiskey wrappers. Wilting from the weather and their failure, they had to admit defeat.

"Well, boys," Ness said. "It looks like we're dished again."

But then one of the Untouchables pulled a handkerchief from his pocket and a half-dollar coin fell out, rolling across the floor and dropping through a metal grating, landing with a soft clink. Ness walked over to the grate, raised it, and looked down into a secret chamber, twelve feet square, packed with more than one hundred cases of fine imported liquor, worth about $15,000.

The *Evening American* whined, "Prohibition agents, aided by police, today destroyed enough bourbon whisky, which, if mixed into mint juleps, poured into tall, thin frosted glasses and garnished with a sprig of mint—which would . . . Anyway, here's looking at you."

Ness still received regular tips from the Kid, his informant inside the Outfit, who said top gangsters met every Monday morning to discuss how to stop the Untouchables. The gang set up a special round-the-clock tip line to monitor the squad's activities—anyone with news of an impending raid got a $500 reward.

The Kid gave Ness the number, and the squad had it tapped. Looking over the transcripts, Ness could see "the gang was keeping a close check on someone"—right down to when and where he went to lunch, and the shows and sporting events he attended at night . . . reports precisely matching Ness's social calendar. The Kid, Ness realized, had been alerting the Outfit to his every move.

"This was a danger," Ness recalled, "and also an opportunity." The mob "knew I loved to raid and that raids were rarely made without my being present." Whenever the Untouchables planned a raid, Ness would tell the Kid he was taking the night off to enjoy a show or see a game. Then he'd "turn up seizing a beer truck or a brewery when they least expected it."

The Outfit paid the Kid well—"his automobiles," Ness said, "kept getting fancier"—but they weren't getting what they paid for. Sooner or later, they'd settle up in blood.

Ness called the Kid and reminded him of his emergency fund at the Postal Savings Bank. The time had come to draw down his balance "and take a quick but long trip." The Kid obliged and disappeared.

Had the undercover Kid achieved the goal of impressing his stripper wife? That remains a mystery.

While the Untouchables dismantled Capone's empire, the gangster kept working the media. In late August, he agreed to meet with *Liberty* magazine's Cornelius Vanderbilt Jr., thirty-three, rich man's son turned journalist.

Vanderbilt, having heard "strange things were known to happen to the gentlemen entertained by Al Capone," decided to take precautions. On his way to the 3:00 P.M. meeting, he left a letter for the manager of his hotel, to be opened at 6:30: "If I am not back by the time you read this note, please notify the police."

At the Lexington, Capone welcomed Vanderbilt as his equal, assuming an almost aristocratic attitude for himself. Sitting behind his desk and constantly relighting his cigar, Capone insisted that the rich must band together in these dark times, or else hand their country over to the Bolsheviks.

"Us fellas has gotta open our pocketbooks," Capone said, "and keep on keeping them open, if we want any of us to survive. We can't wait for Congress or Mr. Hoover or anyone else. We must keep tummies filled and bodies warm."

Capone complained about being blamed for things he hadn't done and getting no credit for the good he did.

"I guess I'm like you, Mr. Vanderbilt. . . . You'd think I had unlimited power and a swell pocketbook. Well, I guess I got the power all right; but the bank book suffers from these hard times as much as anyone else's."

That was perhaps as much from Eliot Ness as the Depression, but Al didn't get into that.

Capone said he expected the Eighteenth Amendment would soon be repealed. But that didn't bother him, because he'd branched out— the booze business now made up only about a third of his take. He also believed the dry law's end would help bring back family values.

"When the Prohibition law is repealed there'll be less desire for birth control," he said. "Without birth control, America can become as stalwart as Italy. With an American Mussolini, she could conquer the world."

The gangster decried the decline of American morals, saying— without apparent irony—that graft and payoffs were "undermining this country." He had harsh words for "crooked bankers," using Florida as a case in point.

"Do you think those bankers went to jail? No, sir. They're among

Florida's most representative citizens. They're just as bad as the crooked politicians! I ought to know . . . I've been feeding and clothing them long enough."

"You are very frank," Vanderbilt said.

"Why should I lie?"

As his reference to "an American Mussolini" suggested, Capone's politics leaned fascist. The way to cure America's ills, he said, was to "kick out state governments, jail all mayors and have the whole show run by the Federal people."

"Coming from a man about to encounter the U.S. Collector of Internal Revenue," Vanderbilt wrote, "it sounded quite courageous. I told him so."

"Oh, they are only trying to scare me," Capone said with a yawn. "They know very well there'd be hell in this city if they put me away."

"Mr. Capone," Vanderbilt asked, "there is one thing I would like to clear up before I go."

"What is it?"

"Do you have to kill many people?"

"Well, believe it or not, I personally never killed nor wounded a single person."

"And your men?"

"They kill only the rats and they do it on their own. I find out about it from the papers."

Capone closed by once again urging the wealthy to stand strong against the creep of Communism. "I think we both speak the same language," he told Vanderbilt, "and I think we're both patriots. We don't want to see them tear down the foundations of this great land."

Much of what Capone said seemed plucked from the mouths of the city's elite, comments traded over cigars and brandy in exclusive social clubs. But was this patrician posture all an act, another attempt at public relations in advance of the trial, or had Capone really come to see himself on a par with men like Vanderbilt and the tycoons who made up the Secret Six?

Gangland observer Edward Dean Sullivan believed the latter. Capone "merely regards himself as any other business executive," Sullivan wrote, "and keenly resents the efforts to hamper his activities, especially of a social nature."

"Prohibition is a business," Capone would say. "All I do is to supply a public demand. I do it in the best and least harmful way I can."

As he prepared, for the first time in his life, to go before a jury of his peers, Capone seemed to feel that his true peers sat elsewhere, outside the jury box. But even with all his money, he still couldn't buy respectability.

The barber's son and a rich man's son were hitting it off until a phone call brought the interview to an uncomfortable close.

"Police Headquarters," Capone grumbled. "They say I kidnapped you."

The note Vanderbilt had left at his hotel had caught up with him.

After Ness's team made their second appearance before the grand jury, the Prohibition Bureau began siphoning off Untouchables for duty in other cities. In late August, Marion King went back to Virginia; Marty Lahart was transferred to Minneapolis in mid-September. Lyle Chapman returned to Detroit, but Ness managed to keep his pencil detective on the Capone case, following up leads in Michigan, Indiana, and Ohio.

Other work fell to Ness himself. On September 5, driving W. E. Bennett, Chicago's special agent in charge, through the near North Side, Ness noticed a heavy Ford truck rumbling just ahead. Its driver was Frank Uva, a defendant in the Prohibition indictment, whom the Untouchables had arrested back in May. Just as Ness saw Uva, Uva saw Ness.

The truck surged forward and swerved onto Chicago Avenue, heading west. Ness sped after it, a convoy car of gangsters in hot pursuit. At Dearborn, Uva made a hard high-speed left, scattering other cars, sending frightened drivers up and over the curb. Ness managed to get ahead and tried to block the truck's way, but the convoy car zoomed, ready to crash headlong into him to let the truck escape. Ness had no choice but to back up and let the truck by, though he stayed tight on its tail, zigzagging through the Gold Coast for almost half an hour as Uva tried to shake him.

Finally, the men in the convoy car flashed a signal to Uva: *Give up the truck*. Uva and another man leapt from the moving vehicle moments before it collided with a light pole at 436 North Clark Street. Ness slammed on the brakes, jumped out of his car, and dashed after Uva, arresting him after a short pursuit.

Bennett searched the wrecked truck, finding seven barrels of beer—hardly a cargo worth such a chase. A few years earlier, Capone's men would have just pulled over, knowing they'd be out of jail in no time. But now, the gang's woeful financial straits left them desperate to protect every last drop of beer.

And with the conspiracy indictment hanging over them, Uva and others couldn't risk another arrest.

Three days later, Judge Wilkerson met in his chambers with Michael Ahern and assistant prosecutor Dwight Green, setting the start date for Capone's tax trial. Wilkerson allowed Ahern to quietly withdraw Capone's guilty plea on the Prohibition charges. The grand jury's work was winding down, their verdict largely a foregone conclusion. On September 10, they issued new indictments against several men and prepared a detailed report explaining why, legally, they could charge Capone only with conspiracy.

But Wilkerson didn't want to hear their excuses. "I am interested in indictments," he told assistant prosecutor Victor LaRue, "not reports."

Grand jury foreman S. J. Nelson shuffled around the Federal Building, office to office, the report in his pocket. Wilkerson wouldn't give him a hearing; no one else offered to read the document. Finally, Johnson pulled Nelson into conference.

After fifteen minutes, the foreman emerged, shamefaced and sullen. In full view of reporters, he withdrew the report and tore it to pieces.

"I have nothing to say," Nelson said. "I don't want to spoil Mr. Johnson's case. He has handled it well."

Asked by a reporter what he and Nelson had discussed, Johnson said the foreman had merely come in to say good-bye.

Ness's chances of getting his day in court with Capone dissolved the moment Nelson tore up his report, but Ness seemed not to know it. On September 20, he and the Untouchables raided a beer distribution plant at 222 East Twenty-Fifth Street.

This time they chose not to use their trademark truck. Ness, Leeson, Robsky, and another agent concealed themselves near the plant's front door and waited for a beer truck to arrive. When one did, they climbed in back and rode inside, then sprang out and collared four gangsters.

One was Frank Conti, a Capone lieutenant arrested at three previous brewery raids. Another was the manager, caught looking over a list of ninety-six speakeasies—each joint's name in code, but the addresses spelled out. Ness recognized "some very well-known places of business," including one owned by a Capone associate named in the Prohibition indictment.

Ice had been dumped all over the floor, turning the place into a giant refrigerator. Evidently the gang had just started to convert the plant into a distillery, installing a costly ventilator to funnel out fumes. The agents seized more than nine thousand gallons of cooled beer and $25,000 worth of equipment, but Ness decided to see if another delivery truck could be snared as well. His men locked the entrance and began to wait.

Before long, another truck rumbled up and its driver pounded on the front door. The Untouchables let him in and arrested him. His companion jumped from the truck and made a break for it, but didn't get far before two Untouchables ran him down. These agents knew the fleeing man all too well; he'd tried and failed to bribe them once before.

By now, federal officials estimated the Untouchables had cost Capone more than half a million dollars in seized vehicles, wrecked equipment, confiscated product, and legal fees. The stills and breweries they'd shut down represented an even greater loss of $2 million in annual income.

Apart from this economic damage, the squad's very existence had a chilling effect. The coverage given their exploits made this small, unruly band seem like a crack team of omnipresent crime fighters. Capone's drivers, fearing arrest, began abandoning beer trucks if they so much as got caught in traffic.

"The word that Ness's men are working automatically closes breweries and liquor depots owned by the syndicate," wrote the *Herald and Examiner*. "The menace of the 'untouchables,' gang members have admitted, has seriously curtailed the syndicate's revenues."

A *Chicago Daily News* reporter confided to the Bureau of Investigation "that members of the Capone syndicate had on various occasions made known the fact that [Ness] was the one Prohibition Agent that they were afraid of."

Ness cemented this reputation with perhaps his most audacious stunt. That fall, he received orders to move all the trucks and equipment his squad had confiscated to a warehouse across town. A handful of men could do the job in several shifts, but Marty Lahart suggested doing it all at once. Ness readily agreed, and had the trucks washed and polished until they practically gleamed.

Then he plotted out a route taking the motorcade well out of its way but right past Capone's Lexington Hotel headquarters. The Untouchables, heavily armed, sat scattered throughout the convoy, ostensibly to guard against hijackers but mainly as a show of force, wearing the pearl-gray hats favored by the Capone mob just to rub it in.

Shortly before the trucks set out, Ness placed a call into Capone's office at the Lexington. After months of listening in on the gang's wire-tapped conversations, Ness knew how to talk his way past the under lings and get to the "Big Fellow" himself—he used Capone's favored nickname, "Snorky."

Finally, a soft, breathy voice came on the line. Ness asked who was speaking; Capone identified himself. Ness said to look out the window "for something interesting" at eleven o'clock. Capone, growing impatient, asked what this was all about. Ness hung up, grinning.

When eleven o'clock arrived, the parade made its appearance on Michigan Avenue, truck after truck cruising under Capone's window, no faster than fifteen miles an hour. Many were brand-new, confiscated before the gang could make back the purchase price. Some bore the names of fake businesses, but their former owners recognized them easily enough.

Capone could see thousands of dollars sluicing past him like water from a broken pipe. And these trucks represented only a fraction of what the Untouchables had taken from him.

Ness sat in a parked car outside the Lexington and watched the windows as the parade rumbled by, searching for any sign of Capone. He never saw the gangster, but an informant said Capone had vowed to kill him, even if it meant murdering him right outside City Hall. William Connors, a Chicago Prohibition agent who'd joined the Untouchables on some raids, recalled hearing "Capone was so mad that he wanted to machine-gun Ness but was restrained by some of his men."

Nothing would come of these threats. Ness could make the gang bleed, but he couldn't steal its leader's freedom. This Capone surely knew, once his rage cooled. The parade of trucks gave Ness his one brief moment of reckoning with the man the press had already begun calling his "nemesis."

Then he had to step aside to let the tax men take over.

Capone leaving the Federal Building during his trial, October 1931. *(Library of Congress)*

Twenty-Six

October 1931

Several days before the trial, a list of one hundred potential jurors reached Al Capone—thanks to what Frank Wilson called "an underhand method and the payment of a large sum of money." Or, business as usual in Chicago.

Capone turned the list over to Outfit associates to start bribing and influencing potential jury members. A file of ten men who'd fallen prey to these efforts came to Wilson either from E. J. O'Hare or St. Louis newspaperman John Rogers. In his chambers, the judge looked expressionlessly at the ten names Wilson gave him.

Wilkerson said he didn't have the list of one hundred potential jurors yet, adding he couldn't request it now without raising suspicion. "We will sit tight and wait for it to come to me."

The next day, Wilson and George Johnson were called into Wilkerson's office, where the judge had the list—which included the ten tainted names, jurors 30 through 39.

But Wilkerson kept his intentions to himself, telling Johnson to go ahead with his case.

"Leave the rest to me," he said.

October 6, day one of the trial, the usual Capone-drawn crowd gathered, including several pickpockets who got themselves arrested. The defendant himself came in on Dearborn Street, a detective squad escorting him into an elevator. Just before 10:00 A.M., Capone was seated before the judge with a narrow aisle separating him from prosecutor Johnson, the adversaries trading appraising glances.

Johnson was a study in gray—gray flannel suit, gray hair, broken only by the gold of his wire-rimmed glasses, "lean and lawyerlike," the *Tribune* said.

No yellow suit for the defendant today, rather blue serge with a white breast-pocket handkerchief, white-and-brown tie, and diamond-studded gold chain. No knuckle-sized diamond ring, either, just a well-barbered gent whose scars were powdered into near oblivion.

A reporter asked, Was he worried?

A chuckling Capone said, "Well, who wouldn't be?"

Soon Wilkerson—in a suit, not judicial robes—was on the bench asking, "What is the plea?"

"Not guilty," Michael Ahern said.

"Is the defendant in court?"

Capone rose and faced the judge. All very perfunctory, until a few minutes into the proceedings, Wilkerson surprised the defendant and his attorneys with a seemingly matter-of-fact order to the bailiff.

"Take this entire venire to Judge [Barnes's] court," he said. "And bring his venire to me."

To the uninitiated, this might have seemed a routine request. Only the smug smile coprosecutor Dwight Green was giving Capone said otherwise. That, and Capone's scowl in response.

What Wilkerson had done was remove all one hundred tainted potential jurors, swapping them for a new, untainted bunch.

The fix was no longer in.

And lawyers Ahern and Albert Fink could do nothing about it. About now, Capone might be wishing he had his usual counsel, prime litigator Tommy Nash, whose absence from this trial has never been explained. Instead, Capone got stuck with Nash's bookish partner, Ahern, and assistant counsel Fink, a happy, scrappy warrior mostly on hand for his mastery of the new tax laws.

Behind Capone sat a natty individual in gold-frame glasses, body-guard Phil D'Andrea—violence at trials in Chicago courts had happened before, and Al would be ready.

Early on Ahern objected to the number of reporters in the chamber—more than thirty journalists hogging the spectator seats, including Damon Runyon, who'd traded covering the World Series for this better tournament.

The new panel of eighty potential jurors ambled in, bringing with them a "fragrant whiff of green fields and growing rutabagas and parsnips along with echoes of good old Main Street," Runyon wrote. Because this was a federal court, rather than a municipal one, the venire need not hail from Chicago or even Cook County. Most came from rural areas and Chicago's outlying suburbs, folks who "don't feel right without a hoe in their hand," as the *Herald and Examiner* put it. Where they came from, people tended to feel more sympathy for the dry law than big-city bootleggers.

Ahern used his ten challenges to remove jurors most likely to be hostile to his client, including several who'd already served on one or more federal juries. Four had been on the grand jury investigating Capone's brother Ralph, another on the one indicting Al himself.

"It seems to me more than a coincidence," the defense lawyer said. "The jurors themselves may be fair; but their selection certainly appears not to have been fair."

Ahern was suggesting the prosecution, or even Wilkerson himself, stacked the jury. Losing a fixed jury dealt Capone a serious blow; the sequestered jurors would be sheltered from bribes—probably.

To the jury, the judge emphasized Capone was on trial for tax evasion and nothing more. Only how the defendant handled his taxes was pertinent, and if any reasonable doubt existed of Capone's guilt, he should be acquitted.

Nonetheless, Capone was not going to get a fair and impartial trial by a jury of his peers. Some jurors already thought Capone should be convicted for being a gangster, while others disliked Italians and/or Catholics. Another said, "To hell with the evidence!"

Years later, juror Arthur O. Prochno reflected, "Like other newspaper readers, I had formed a pretty fair picture of Capone. I understood that he was a terrible man who did not hesitate to murder those who stood in his way." Prochno knew about the O'Banion, Aiello, and St. Valentine's Day murders. "To me, as to many others, [Capone] epitomized all that was evil."

The second day of the trial, defense lawyers Ahern and Fink seemed edgy and excitable, adamantly refusing to ignore (as the *Herald and Examiner* put it) "even the most minute technicality that might be made the basis of an appeal." They objected to a juror and got nowhere. They made objections and comments throughout Dwight Green's opening remarks. Then they waived their own right to an opening statement, and ignored the key issue—the statute of limitations on tax evasion.

After preliminary testimony establishing Capone never filed an income tax return for the years in question, the prosecution began trying to link him to a taxable source of revenue. Called to the stand was the pompous reverend Henry Hoover and several of his vigilante raiders, describing in detail the Hawthorne Smoke Shop raid of May 16, 1926. They swore Capone referred to himself as "the owner of this place," with behavior appearing to confirm it. Having thus established Capone's ownership, the government could enter the Hawthorne ledger as proof of income.

On cross-examination, Ahern revealed his lack of courtroom skills by asking raider Chester Bragg the wrong question.

"How do you have such a distinct recollection of this raid?"

"Well, if you had your face busted like I did you wouldn't forget it for a while."

Fink fared even worse, stupidly getting raider Frank Morgan to discuss being beaten by a blackjack and/or brass knuckles. Now Capone looked like the brutal thug he sometimes was.

The government remained focused on linking Capone to the casino. After Fink finished with Morgan, Dwight Green took redirect. "Mr. Morgan," he asked, "did this man . . . . have any marks on his face of any kind?"

"Yes, he had a scar on his face."

"Do you recall which side of his face?"

Fink cut in: "Now, don't look at him when you answer the question."

Addressing the jury, Morgan said, "The left side."

Green repeated it for emphasis: "The left side."

"As I recall it."

And all the jurors, and for that matter the spectators, sent their eyes to Capone to confirm the identification.

"That is all, Mr. Morgan," Green said.

"That is all," Fink added.

After lunch, the prosecution produced their star witness—Leslie Shumway, cashier/bookkeeper for Outfit gambling operations in both Cicero and Florida.

Anxious and gaunt, with spectacles perched on his beaky nose, Shumway seemed older than his fifty-three years—"a drab, bald-headed man of uncertain age," according to the *New York Times*. He avoided meeting Capone's gaze, and held a hanky or hand over his mouth throughout much of his testimony, nearly inaudible to all but the judge, questioner, and maybe the jury.

The witness handed over the loose-leaf, thirty-four-page Hawthorne Smoke Shop ledger with daily reports in his own hand and sometimes that of managers Pete Penovich and Frankie Pope. This was the next crucial link in the prosecution's chain of circumstantial evidence. The raiders placed Capone in the Smoke Shop, reporting his claims to be its owner. The ledger proved the place had turned a profit. Now they needed Shumway to link Capone with those profits by identifying him as the top man.

Coprosecutor Jacob Grossman questioned the witness: "Now you stated a little while ago that Mr. Penovich and Mr. Pope were the managers."

"Yes, sir."

"They were sort of bosses right over you?"

"Yes, sir."

"Who was the boss over them?"

From the defense table, Fink said, "If there was one."

Grossman amended, "If there was one."

"And if he knows," Fink put in. "That is really a conclusion, if your honor please."

The judge said, "It may or it may not be. It may be a fact, if he knows." Wilkerson asked the witness, "Do you know?"

"Well, from hearsay," Shumway said, "or what I was told."

Grossman asked the witness who had told him.

"Mr. Penovich."

"Anybody else tell you?"

"Yes, Frankie Pope."

"Well, who was the man that they mentioned?"

Several shouted defense objections were sustained. Wilkerson advised Grossman to try a different tack.

Grossman asked, "Just what part of the place did you occupy as an office?"

"I was right next to the cashier."

After getting Shumway to describe the office, Grossman asked, "Did you at any time see the defendant, Alphonse Capone, in that establishment?"

"Yes, sir, I have seen him in there."

"Where did you see him?"

"Well, it would be in the office because I would never be anywhere else."

Grossman then pressed Shumway on whether Capone had ever gambled in the place. The bookkeeper said Capone had placed some bets directly over the race wire, but never from the main floor like a normal patron—further suggesting the defendant enjoyed privileges of ownership.

Shumway described how he'd walked each day's profits to a safe in another building down the block. He usually traveled by himself, running the risk of robbery. Capone, he said, "asked me what I would do if I was stuck up, if I got stuck up, and I told him, I says, I would just let them take it, and he says, 'That's right.'"

In other words, Capone could give orders to the bookkeeper—strong circumstantial evidence Al owned the place.

But Grossman wouldn't leave it there. He kept trying to get Shumway to name Capone as the owner, and the defense kept objecting. Grossman sidestepped their objections with a fresh line of questioning.

"Did you ever see Jack Guzik around these gambling establishments?"

"Yes, sir."

"What if anything did he do around there?"

"Well, he never did do anything. Just, he would come around."

"Did Guzik ever look at your books?"

"No, sir, I don't know that he ever looked at the books. He has looked at the daily sheet that we kept on the wall there."

The prosecution planned to show Capone and Guzik were business partners. By linking Guzik to the Smoke Shop, Grossman had given the jury still more reason to see Capone as its owner.

But that wasn't the same as positive proof. Finally, Grossman asked who the "boss" was, which brought more heated defense objections.

Wilkerson closed the debate with a direct question: "Do you know who owned this place?"

"No, sir," Shumway said. "Hearsay—only from hearsay."

"With the explanations which all the counsel and the court have been making, can you say whether you know whose place this was? Can you answer that question yes or no?"

"From positive proof, I could not say."

Capone's attorneys had successfully stopped Shumway from implicating their client directly. But the prosecution had—effectively, if circumstantially—tied Capone to the casino's profits.

The defense chose not to grill Shumway on cross-examination. Instead, they asked where he lived (the Copeland Hotel) and whether he had a job. Shumway said he was unemployed, but had recently worked at a St. Louis racetrack—probably one associated with his old codefendant, E. J. O'Hare.

As Shumway left, Ahern called out, "Can we get in touch with you at the Copeland?"

Shumway said yes.

"You won't try to hide out on us, will you?"

Shumway said no.

The defense's threat to recall the bookkeeper was an empty one.

The next day the prosecution introduced the letter and other documentation from the meetings between Al, his lawyer Lawrence P. Mattingly, and four employees of the Bureau of Internal Revenue.

The *Tribune* referred to the settlement offer as a "confession letter," and even Fink admitted it was "most damning." The *Herald and Examiner* ran a seven-column banner headline screaming: CAPONE CONFESSION BARED!

Ahern objected: "Congress doesn't want to send people to jail. Congress wants people to pay their taxes. It wants them to come in and settle with their government before criminal or civil action is started so it won't have to be started."

Hadn't Capone done everything expected of a delinquent taxpayer?

"It is human nature to evade taxes," Ahern said. "We had our Boston tea party—"

"And what is this?" the judge asked. "Is this another Boston tea party?"

"No," Ahern said. "I don't know what it is."

Ahern recovered slightly by saying the letter established Capone's innocence.

"To prove an attempted crime," he said, "there must be an overt act. These communications show Capone had abandoned any attempt to evade tax and is therefore guiltless of the felony counts against him."

The jury was removed as Fink went over the letter with the judge, describing it as tantamount to a guilty plea. And no lawyer could plead a client guilty without consent.

"It is an effort to send a man to the penitentiary on his lawyer's confession," Fink said.

"It might well do that," the judge said, "ultimately."

Wilkerson clearly leaned toward admitting the letter, even as the defense tried frantically to change his mind. In the heat of the argument, they started referring to Capone as "Caponi," a faux pas the prosecutors never made. Fink repeatedly questioned Mattingly's competence, asking, "Was the man crazy?"

With every word, Capone's lawyers played up the letter's significance, when they should have done the opposite. Better to question its accuracy, suggesting Mattingly stretched the truth to win a settlement. Nor did they argue Mattingly's "without prejudice" meant the letter could only be used in negotiations with the Bureau of Internal Revenue—not in court.

Instead, they argued the letter announced their client's guilt.

But despite Fink and Ahern's obvious incompetence, they were right and Wilkerson was wrong—the Mattingly letter should not have been admitted. The standard rules of evidence did not allow the use of such "bona fide offers to compromise" as evidence in a criminal trial.

Of course, the revenue agents at the meeting had effectively informed Capone whatever he said could be used against him. From this, Wilkerson ruled transcripts of the discussion between Capone, Mattingly, and the Bureau admissible.

"When a man makes statements," Wilkerson said, "he does so at his own peril. He cannot bind the government not to prosecute him."

The judge also allowed the letter as evidence.

Fink's response was straight out of Lewis Carroll: "This is the last toe. They have got him nailed to the cross now. This is just putting the last toe on him. . . . Let the whole thing go in now, because there are some things in this letter that at least indicate the lawyer is crazy."

The next day began a long process to establish through expenditures and other means the defendant's substantial income.

Florida friend Parker Henderson talked of picking up Western Union money orders addressed to "Albert Costa" and cashing them for Capone, the money wired by Jack Guzik's brother and other Outfit guys. Henderson told how he'd helped Al buy his mansion in Mae's name. He recalled various renovations made to the Palm Island place—$4,000 swimming pool, $3,000 perimeter fence with iron gate, thousands in interior decoration and landscaping.

A clerk from the Metropole Hotel took the stand, going through a record of what Capone spent—$1,500 here, $1,633 there, all of it in cash. Ahern and Fink protested—the trial was to establish income, not expenditures. But Wilkerson said, "I presume that what he paid out he must have taken in."

The defense was right: expenditures made decidedly circumstantial evidence, entered because the government's case lacked actual documentation of Capone's income. Yet three trial days focused on Al Capone's spending, in a cavalcade of excess designed to impress the jury and tantalize the press.

The unsophisticated, Depression-era jurors listened in awe to tales of Capone's high living. Where their yearly phone bills were perhaps $36 (if they owned a phone at all), Capone had in 1929 spent $3,141.50. They literally gasped when they heard Capone spent $2 on collars and $25 on shirts. They took a special interest in the thirty custom belt buckles riddled with diamonds Capone gave out as Christmas presents.

Small businessmen, store clerks, and tailors trooped into court. A salesman from Marshall Field's described the four pairs of fine silk underwear Capone purchased for $12 each. Fink asked if they were warm.

"No," the salesman said, "it is just a nice suit of underwear."

Fink asked what they cost now. The salesman said the price had dropped two dollars. To Damon Runyon, the defense attorney seemed to be shopping for himself.

Other attempts at cross-examining these witnesses went nowhere. One workman said Mae Capone paid him $500—"She peeled the money off a roll that was big enough to choke an ox."

Fink asked acidly, "How big an ox would it choke?"

"Well, it was as big as your fist," came the unhelpful reply.

No better was Fink's questioning of a butcher who'd been paid $6,500 in weekly installments of $200 or $250.

"You don't think Al ate all this meat himself, do you?"

"One man couldn't eat all that. I didn't say that Al did eat it."

Fink objected to prosecutors introducing Capone's phone bills for 1930 and half of 1931, periods not covered under the indictment, asking what those years could possibly have to do with this case.

Coprosecutor Grossman said, "The bill payments show that money was available to pay taxes."

Wilkerson, not exactly impartial, jumped in: "And they used it to pay telephone bills with."

"We were trying to pay the taxes," Fink said with a smile, "and apparently the government wouldn't take them, and had us indicted."

Wilkerson smiled back at him. "Because you did not want to pay enough."

Between days in court, Capone had his tailor come around to the Lexington to make two lightweight summer suits for his next Florida trip. Bodyguard Frankie Rio saw this as detached from reality: "You don't need to be ordering fancy duds. You're going to prison; why don't you have a suit made with stripes on it?"

"The hell I am," Al said. "I'm going to Florida for a nice, long rest and I need some new clothes before I go."

Capone carried this confidence with him into court. He remained in a jovial mood, munching on peppermint candies as if watching a picture show, smiling at evidence he found amusing. To the *Tribune*, he seemed to be "enjoying himself immensely"—trading smiles with the Florida witnesses, "former workmen, contractors, butcher, baker and others."

He got annoyed only once, at the contractor who had built the Palm Island pier and boathouse—still owed $125 but nervous about collecting, frightened by Capone's associates. Capone seemed to take this as an insult, besmirching his reputation for always paying his debts.

Federal agents had been keeping an eye on sharply dressed, briefcase-carrying bodyguard D'Andrea—his gold-rimmed glasses didn't fool them. On October 11, tax unit man Mike Malone noticed the bulge of a probable shoulder-holstered weapon. At the noon recess, signaling Frank Wilson, Malone followed D'Andrea out. They grabbed the bodyguard and found a .38 under his arm.

Ahern, keen on keeping as much gangster stigma away from the defense as possible, claimed D'Andrea was armed because he was a deputy bailiff of the Municipal Court. *Was* was the correct word—his appointment had expired.

But Wilkerson had watched D'Andrea throughout the trial, seeing how the bodyguard intimidated witnesses with his sinister stare. At a later hearing, the judge found D'Andrea in contempt of court and had him locked up for six months—not so much for packing a gun as for trying to influence testimony.

"The pistol," Wilkerson said, "was far less serious than the perjury."

Bald beanpole Fred Ries—back from his Secret Six-funded South American vacation—took the stand on October 13, holding everyone's attention, particularly Capone's.

Ries had been the key witness at Jack Guzik's trial, his testimony linking the defendant to profits from three Cicero gambling joints. Ries said he'd worked as cashier in each establishment, converting the daily profits into cashier's checks, which he then turned over to Guzik's hirelings, Pete Penovich and Bobby Barton. Sometimes he'd given checks to Guzik directly. Intelligence Unit agents had located dozens of these checks on file at a Cicero bank, giving the government direct proof of Guzik's untaxed income.

At the earlier trial, Ries had identified his "bosses" as "Mr. Guzik, Al Brown, Frank Nitti and Ralph Brown. I have heard since that the name of Al Brown is Al Capone," he added, "and I know Ralph Brown by the name of Ralph Capone."

But Ries knew of Al Capone's role only through hearsay; he'd had direct dealings with Guzik and Ralph, never taking orders from, or giving any money to, Al. Once again, George Johnson and his assistants relied on circumstantial evidence to link Capone with these sources of income.

Grossman questioned the stoic witness, who betrayed no fear, his answers steady. Ries recalled one day in early 1927 when Ralph came in with Pete Penovich, announcing the place was under new management. Around the same time, Ries saw Capone speaking with Guzik in the joint's telegraph office.

"And was [this] a part of the main establishment where the public usually congregated?" Grossman asked.

"The telegraph office was right next to the main office," Ries replied. "The public didn't congregate at the telegraph office as a rule, no, nobody is supposed to be there, no outsiders."

"No outsiders," Grossman repeated. "Is that the first time you saw the defendant Capone at that place?"

"Yes sir."

The inference was clear—Guzik and the Capone brothers had muscled in on the joint, leaving them entitled to its profits. Grossman tried to make this explicit by having Ries recount a conversation with the casino's previous manager, who'd claimed "Al and his bunch declared themselves in today." But the defense objected to this secondhand testimony.

"Just what are they trying to prove?" Fink asked. "What is the purpose of this?"

"They are trying to prove . . . that Capone had an interest," replied the judge.

"And they are trying to do it by hearsay."

"By hearsay, yes."

Still, Wilkerson hesitated to throw the statement out, even though he seemed to know it was inadmissible. Grossman saved him the trouble by offering to withdraw it.

"It is too near the line," Wilkerson said.

"Very well," Grossman said, "I will withdraw it."

Grossman didn't need it anyway, because he had something much better. He presented the judge with forty-four cashier's checks (purchased by Ries with gambling profits) for admission into evidence. Most had already been used by the government as proof of Guzik's income, but would now be held against Capone, one defendant swapped for another.

"We," Grossman explained, "have been establishing here right along the business relationship of Jack Guzik and the defendant Capone. . . . We find Jack Guzik at the place Shumway testified about looking at the daily sheets. . . . We find Guzik at the Lexington, at the Metropole and we find him at this place with the defendant under circumstances when they weren't just outsiders. . . . And we show Guzik at some of the places from which this money was sent, such as the Metropole and Lexington."

The Mattingly letter, too, described Capone as having three partners. The government intended to show Guzik was among them.

Over defense objections, Wilkerson ruled the checks admissible. The lack of any direct proof against Capone, he said, forced the government to use "negative evidence," which showed "this defendant had undertaken to build around him a stone wall so that those who sought to learn his condition as to financial affairs would find him inaccessible."

The government was building "a chain of circumstances," Wilkerson said, adding, "I think it is proper evidence."

Ries described how he'd purchased these checks under various aliases, most frequently "J. C. Dunbar." Sometimes he'd endorsed them himself before giving them to Barton, Penovich, or Guzik. He couldn't say where the checks had gone after that.

"Of course," Fink said, "we object to them as incompetent and irrelevant."

"I think they are connected with the enterprises of the defendant," Wilkerson said. "They have some connection."

"The only evidence of any connection on the part of the defendant—"

Wilkerson cut him off: "His name appears on one of them."

"On one of these?" Ahern interjected.

"Yes."

At the defense table, Capone's head jerked up. He'd often insisted he
never signed checks, at least not in his own name. Yet for the first time,
the government had produced a document with Capone's surname—
let alone his signature—on it.

Fink gamely tried to recover. "Well," he asked the judge, "what does
that prove?"

Grossman gave the check to Fink. Purchased June 1, 1927, for
$2,500, it had been made out to Ries's favorite alias, J. C. Dunbar,
with Dunbar's endorsement. Whether Ries had signed Dunbar's name,
as he often did, or someone else, remained unclear.

Below Dunbar's signature, the name "Al Capone" had been written
in pencil. Stamps on the back showed the check had been deposited
into the account of the Laramie Kennel Club, another name for the
Hawthorne Kennel Club—the Cicero dog track where Capone was a
silent partner with Frank Nitto and E. J. O'Hare.

As damning as this seemed, the check raised several unanswered
questions. Why would a second signature from Capone be required, if
the payee—J. C. Dunbar—had already signed it? Under what circumstance would Capone—who at that time was at the height of his power,
surrounded by people keeping him insulated from illegal activities—
find himself depositing a check into a racetrack's account?

If Capone had deposited the check, why didn't he use one of his
aliases—Al Brown, Albert Costa? Why had he used the nickname "Al,"
when he typically used his full first name—Alphonse—on those rare occasions when he signed official documents? And why would he sign the
check in pencil instead of pen? Every teller's window surely had a pen.

But the defense largely ignored the check on cross-examination. Instead, Michael Ahern got Ries to admit he'd seen Capone only twice,

once each in two of three establishments. Then Ahern got creative, scrambling to find some reason why Capone would be allowed in the back office if he didn't own the place.

Suppose, Ahern said, a gambler like Capone made a very large bet on a single horse. If word got around, presumably people would think he had inside information. Wouldn't the owner let him make that bet in back, in private, to keep it secret from the other customers?

"Well," Ries said, "we didn't do it."

"It is sometimes done," Ahern pressed, "is it not?"

"We didn't do it out there."

"No one ever did it?"

"The bets were all over the counter."

Ahern then established Ries had taken no orders from the brothers Capone. But he hurt his own case by asking whether Guzik had told Ries "that no money was to be given to Alphonse Capone, or Penovich?"

"He didn't mention Alphonse Capone," Ries said. "He mentioned Al."

"He said 'Al'?"

"Yes sir."

"You did not know what Al he meant?"

"I didn't know what Al he meant."

"No."

Ahern had won a small victory, creating some shred of doubt about the identity of this "Al"—until, that is, Ries kept talking.

"But I figured who he meant."

"You thought he meant the defendant?"

"Yes sir."

More circumstantial evidence of the Capone-Guzik partnership, courtesy of the defense.

Finally, Ahern turned his attention to the signed check. Ries admitted he hadn't given the check to Capone; he couldn't remember *who* he'd given it to—maybe Barton or Penovich, but not Guzik. In the gambling joint, or at the bank? Ries couldn't recall.

Ahern asked, "Do you know how the name Al Capone got on the back here?"

"No sir."

"Well this check was deposited apparently to the credit of the Laramie Kennel Club, was it not, the same check I showed you before?"

"According to the stamp on it."

And Ahern moved on to another check.

The morning session closed with a prosecution handwriting expert comparing the signature on the check to one on a safety deposit box form. He found they matched.

After lunch, George E. Q. Johnson—silent throughout the trial thus far—stood and intoned, "Your honor, at this time the government rests its case."

Just like in the movies, reporters flew to their feet and ran to the telephones. Capone and his attorneys huddled as a murmuring shock wave rolled across the courtroom. Several name witnesses, including Johnny Torrio, would not be testifying after all.

The judge said to Fink and Ahern, "Are you ready to proceed?"

All the lawyers approached the bench; the jury was removed.

Fink, clearly caught flat-footed, said, "Well, if your honor please, this is a kind of a surprise. We would like a little time to get ready for our defense."

"We have a jury confined here," Wilkerson reminded Fink and Ahern. "I think the limit of the continuance will be until ten o'clock tomorrow morning."

"Give us a couple of days," Fink begged. "The government has been preparing this case since October 17, 1928. I put it to your sense of fairness."

Ahern said, "Your honor, there has been no proof of income established by the government."

"Well," the judge replied, "if you take that view, then the case is simple."

And he told them to prepare to present their defense at ten the next morning.

Top: Capone with attorney Michael Ahern. Bottom: Capone's jury, with Arthur Prochno standing (third from right). *(Top: Courtesy of the Boston Public Library, Leslie Jones Collection. Bottom: Library of Congress.)*

Twenty-Seven

October 1931

As the nation followed every twist and turn of Capone's trial, other gangsters quietly carried on his work.

On October 8, one of Capone's lieutenants—handsome thirty-five-year-old Nick Juffra—stepped out of his apartment building in placid Jackson Park, just up the block from where Torrio had been shot.

More than seven years earlier, Juffra had been arrested with Torrio in the Sieben Brewery raid, after Dean O'Banion double-crossed his Italian rival.

At the time, "Juffra was the most persistent offender of all the early beer runners," according to sociologist John Landesco. "He had been arrested twenty-four times between the advent of Prohibition and the Sieben Brewery case." On one of those busts, Juffra had been caught hauling beer with Joe Fusco and Bert Delaney, back before both men became heads of Capone's beer empire.

Since then, Juffra had managed to stay out of custody, and gave every appearance of having gone legit. But the *Tribune* later pegged him as "the head of Al Capone's beer delivery service," where he worked under his longtime compatriot, Joe Fusco. That, and the earlier arrest, earned Juffra the distinction of being named along with Capone in the massive Prohibition conspiracy indictment.

As Juffra exited his building, he ran into one of his neighbors—

Eliot Ness, a few blocks south of the Paxton Avenue apartment he shared with Edna. Ness had brought two Untouchables with him, and together they placed Juffra under arrest. They hauled the bootlegger back to the Federal Building and left him locked up despite his protests.

"What's the idea?" Juffra complained. "I've been going straight for the last eight years."

Ness knew better.

Eager to hit the mob however he could, Ness would lock up any Capone man crossing his path, all the better to put the gang on the spot and stretch its already thinning resources. This harassment would continue after Juffra's release, when the hood was arrested again and turned back over to the Untouchables. Federal officials considered deporting him to Italy.

To the *Tribune,* Ness gave a brief statement explaining Juffra's arrest, mentioning the bootlegger's partnership with Joe Fusco. But he failed to comment on events occurring elsewhere in the Federal Building, where the fate of his nemesis hung in the balance.

Whatever his thoughts on the court case, Ness kept them largely to himself; his memoir of the Capone investigation skips over the trial in a single sentence. And this silence speaks volumes for a man who, though often generous with giving credit to others, usually avoided criticizing anyone.

Relations between the Intelligence Unit and the Prohibition Bureau had long been strained, poisoned by years of mutual suspicion and jealousy.

"An intense bitterness developed between the two branches of the Treasury Department," wrote Assistant Attorney General Mabel Walker Willebrandt in 1929, "and it was not an uncommon thing for agents of the Intelligence Unit . . . to be 'shadowed' by agents of the Prohibition Unit and their friends."

After the dry force became part of the Justice Department, the Treasury men increasingly took offense at news coverage of their colleagues. Even before Ness's name made headlines, the tax men working the Capone case feared losing credit for their work to the Prohibition Bureau.

"By the way," wrote G. A. Youngquist to Attorney General William Mitchell even before the Untouchables began raiding, "some of the Special Agents of the Bureau of Internal Revenue who have been doing very effective work in Chicago are resentful over the appearance of newspaper statements to the effect that the work has been done by Special Agents of the Department of Justice. I told Mr. Irey that I was sure no such statement had been made by you and that it was merely an inference of the reporters."

The sudden fame of the Untouchables can only have added to this resentment, but Ness always made sure to give credit where credit was due. Although his team worked independently of the Intelligence Unit, both groups stayed in contact, and Ness knew Frank Wilson well enough to list him as a character reference on a future job application. The two men enjoyed a cordial relationship for years, as Ness praised Wilson's work while often downplaying his own.

A decade after the trial, Ness described Wilson as "the brains behind the successful drive on the Capone gang," while the former tax investigator complimented the Untouchable on his own "excellent" work, adding that it deserved its nationwide publicity.

Only later, after Ness became famous as a television icon, would Wilson claim the Untouchables had contributed nothing worthwhile to the Capone investigation.

Al Capone strongly discouraged his wife, sister, and mother from attending the trial. They sneaked in a few times anyway, sitting in back and slipping out fast at the end of sessions.

Mae abandoned Palm Island for Prairie Avenue, with Sonny along, though the boy would miss the start of school. They intended to make Chicago their home through any appeals and, if Al was convicted, see where he'd serve his sentence—if nearer Chicago than Florida, Sonny would go to school in the former, otherwise mother and son would return to the latter, making prison visits from Miami.

On October 14, a surprise visitor appeared in court: film star Edward G. Robinson, who lately made his living playing Capone clones onscreen. According to the *Herald and Examiner,* Robinson had come "to give Snorky a few pointers on how a gangster acts." He'd arrived on the first day of Capone's defense, as courtroom observers awaited whatever strategy Ahern and Fink had cooked up.

Earlier in the trial, the press intimated Capone's lawyers would demonstrate the government had targeted their client unfairly, while allowing other "well-known Chicagoans" to avoid prosecution by settling their tax debts.

"This argument," wrote the *Herald and Examiner,* "is based on the contention it is not the general practice of the Department of Internal Revenue to prosecute tax delinquents when there is a possibility of settlement without court action."

That, of course, had always been Elmer Irey's policy; the Bureau of Internal Revenue gave many wealthy tax cheats the opportunity to settle without being prosecuted. When Capone sought the same treatment, Ahern and Fink planned to show, this "statute was used virtually to effect an entrapment when his offers were rejected."

Yet for reasons that remain unclear, the defense chose not to pursue this shrewd strategy. Nor did they attack the prosecution's predominantly circumstantial evidence.

Instead, Ahern and Fink based their entire approach on claiming Capone lost most of his money gambling. This made little sense; gambling losses were only deductible from winnings—and only in states where gambling was legal. Capone, it seemed, could be taxed on income from other people's illicit bets, but couldn't claim deductions from any illicit bets he happened to make himself.

To have any chance of success, the defense team needed to produce betting slips or other concrete proof of each loss—evidence they did not have. So they relied instead on an array of witnesses, mainly bookies, to give ballpark estimates of how much Capone had lost over the years. As the testimony dragged on, Damon Runyon happily ceded his own blue ribbon for "world's worst horse player to Mr. Alphonse Capone."

The Mattingly letter asserted Capone earned no more than $3,900 in 1924, but bookie Milton Held estimated Al lost $8,000 to $10,000 to him that year alone. Another bookie put Al's losses at no less than $14,000 during that time. Subsequent years reported by various shady witnesses were all over the map, adding up to more than $200,000 all told.

Asked if he ran an Outfit club, a North Side bookmaker responded, "I am running the club for 'Bugs' Moran and his associates."

"Who," asked the prosecution, "are the associates?"

"I don't know," said the witness. "I guess they're all dead!"

A flurry of laughter, and defense objections, followed.

Coprosecutor Dwight Green wondered if these bookies had been called to the Lexington of late, to discuss their testimony with Capone and his legal team. Yes, they had. But that didn't mean they could keep their stories straight. These men functioned outside the law, betting slips destroyed, account books nonexistent. Their testimony was so much air—not even hot air, just foul.

"You said Capone lost between $20,000 and $30,000 in 1926," Green asked one bookie. "Could you make it $40,000?"

"Y-e-s," the witness said, "maybe $40,000."

"How about $50,000?" Green asked, as if this were an auction.

"Well," the witness said with a smile, "I guess not $50,000."

Wilkerson couldn't help interrupting: "Do you know what it is to remember anything?"

"I never kept no books," the bookie replied.

None of this served to exonerate Capone. If anything, it only drove home the prosecution's central argument—that the defendant was recklessly rich.

Midway through the morning session, the defense took a break from bookies and called Peter P. Penovich Jr., the much-mentioned Hawthorne Smoke Shop manager. He'd also been on the government's witness list but hadn't been called.

After Penovich was sworn in, Fink produced a handwritten document first introduced during Leslie Shumway's testimony, probably a page from the all-important ledger. He described it as "apparently a list of the owners of this gambling house . . . with amounts set opposite their respective names, from which it can be ascertained exactly, the percentages in which they owned the business." Penovich identified the handwriting on it as his own.

Much of the government's case depended on proving Capone's ownership of the Hawthorne Smoke Shop. If this list did not include Capone—and it almost certainly didn't, since his surname appeared nowhere in the ledger—doubt might be sown about the defendant receiving any income from there.

But Fink did not read the list into evidence. Instead, he began asking Penovich about his secret testimony before the grand jury. The prosecution immediately objected, on grounds such testimony was confidential.

"Is he trying to impeach his own witness?" asked assistant prosecutor Samuel Clawson.

"I don't know what the purpose of it is," the judge said.

Objection sustained.

Fink tried and failed to explain himself, then turned Penovich over for cross-examination. Clawson's questioning immediately zeroed in on another page from the ledger—the one first catching Wilson's eye with the tantalizing notation: "Frank paid $17,500 for Al."

That page also included a list of names and initials next to large dollar amounts, two entries marked "Paid." Under questioning from Clawson, Penovich admitted writing the list, but denied disbursing any of the money. Clawson pressed him on one item in particular: "J & A," apparently the recipient of $5,720.22. Capone watched intently. Although Penovich never said what "J & A" stood for, Clawson's inference was clear—"J" for Jack Guzik and "A" for Al Capone.

Clawson began asking questions about the Hawthorne Smoke Shop—how long it had existed, what Penovich's duties had been, to whom did he report.

"Frankie Pope was my boss," Penovich said, "and so was Ralph Capone."

How did Penovich know to take orders from Pope?

"Ralph told me that there would be a different disposition of the money," Penovich said, "and to go along, and that he would take care of me."

How had Penovich become connected with the Smoke Shop in the first place?

Penovich explained he'd previously had a gambling joint in "a bad location," and had gone to Ralph in search of a better arrangement.

"Why did you speak to Ralph?" Clawson asked.

"Because I understood Ralph was the boss," Penovich said, "and he could do the fixing for me."

Clawson made sure the jury got that: "You understood he was the boss?"

"Yes sir."

"And he could do the fixing?"

"In Cicero."

"Fixing with whom?"

"With the powers that might be in a position to let me go along and run without being molested."

"What powers?"

"Political powers, the police departments, anybody that might be in a position to stop me."

Penovich couldn't say why, exactly, he'd had such faith in Ralph. "Well," the witness said, "he seemed to be prosperous, and he was catered to."

"Catered to by whom?"

"Well, every place he went he was welcomed; he was pointed out . . . theaters, cafés, places of amusement."

Clawson asked whether "there was an organization or syndicate in control of Cicero at that time, and of its gambling activities."

Penovich said no.

Clawson asked if Penovich had cut a deal "with Al Capone to open up at the Smoke Shop because . . . you had to make certain arrangements for a cut with the organization or gang that had control of the gambling interests out in Cicero?"

Ahern objected, and Wilkerson, after some hesitation, sustained. Clawson had strayed from the rules of cross-examination. If the government wanted to question Penovich on these matters, he should have been called as a witness.

Penovich never directly implicated Al Capone. But by pinning so much on Ralph, the Smoke Shop manager only added to the pile of circumstantial evidence showing both Capone brothers involved in a profitable criminal enterprise. One lawyer would later call Penovich "a better witness for the government than any the government put on."

How did this help the defendant's case again . . . ?

The next day, October 15, the defense called one last bookie, whose testimony boosted Capone's gambling losses (and his apparent income) by at least a third. Then Fink questioned Elmer Irey, apparently trying to show Capone had attempted to pay his taxes immediately after leaving the Pennsylvania prison. But Irey said little that would help.

Finally, Fink put Dwight Green on the witness stand to demand he reveal Lawrence Mattingly's confidential grand jury testimony—something the prosecutor could not legally do.

"That is not a proper question," Wilkerson said.

"Then," Fink declared, "I ask your honor to direct the United States attorney to produce Mattingly's grand jury testimony."

Before the judge replied, he sent the jury out of the room so they wouldn't hear the rest of this farce.

"I have never heard of such a request," Wilkerson told the defense. "Why haven't you called Mattingly?"

Rather than explaining why they hadn't, Ahern asked the judge "to put Mattingly on the stand, so that we can cross-examine him."

Wilkerson refused.

Ahern then moved for a directed not-guilty verdict.

Motion denied.

Fink tried to have the indictment thrown out as unconstitutional, arguing the government had never proven an overt act of evasion on Capone's part.

"Well," Wilkerson said, "I think I will hold the act constitutional."

At long last, Ahern demanded all charges before 1928 be dismissed because they fell outside the three-year statute of limitations for income tax evasion. In response, coprosecutor Grossman cited rulings upholding the convictions of Ralph Capone and another defendant as proof the six-year rule applied.

Wilkerson sided with the prosecution. But Ahern was right and Grossman wrong. Ralph Capone was convicted of tax fraud, not just evasion, and the law specifically reserved the six-year limit for those who defrauded the government.

The other case awaited a final ruling from the Supreme Court.

That same afternoon, closing arguments began with prosecutor Grossman emphasizing Capone's high-roller behavior, which so resonated with the jury.

"Capone himself produced witnesses to show that he got revenue in these years," Grossman told the jury. "His defense witnesses said he lost large sums in race bets in four of those years. These losses totaled $217,000."

Where had Capone gotten all this money?

"At the start," Grossman continued, "we find a man living on a fine estate in Florida, spending money like a baron and with the lavishness of an Indian prince. We have heard of jewels and fine furnishings—everything bought with cash."

The defense witnesses, he claimed, had only proven the government's case.

"All through this testimony, gentlemen," the coprosecutor said, "you have heard certain names mentioned together—Al Capone, Jack Guzik, Charles Fischetti, Ralph Capone, and Pete Penovich. They all constitute one gang."

What did that have to do with Capone's income taxes?

"It means that when one embarks on a life of crime, one crime leads to another. The watchword of the gang was 'Sign nothing.' Conceal your name and conceal your income. . . . Gentlemen, I think the evidence has shown beyond all possibility of a doubt that this defendant had an enormous income. All that you can do is find him guilty."

The defense had their turn the next day.

Fink went first, praising Capone as beloved by his men, generous, and trustworthy (if you were a bookie).

"This does not fit in with the government picture of a miserly effort to evade income tax," Fink said. "A tin horn and a piker might try to defraud the government of such a tax, but not Capone."

The defense attorney spoke for nearly two and a half hours, drawing on his knowledge of tax law to carefully dissect the prosecution's case. He pointed out, for instance, that Capone could not be found guilty of evasion simply because he hadn't paid any taxes.

"If I were sick on the day my income tax was due," Fink said, "and failed to make a return, that would be no crime."

Nor, he argued, should all the evidence of lavish expenditures count as proof of taxable income.

"How do you know that the money spent wasn't borrowed?" he asked.

The defendant, Fink insisted, "like many other men," had believed illegal income was not taxable.

"Suppose he had been advised of that," Fink said, "and that just as soon as he discovered the contrary he went to Washington and hired an attorney and tried to pay what he owed. And why didn't they let him pay it instead of using the evidence to try to put him in jail?"

Fink insisted the defendant was not being prosecuted because he'd attempted to cheat the government, but merely "as a means to stow Al Capone away."

"If the latter," Fink said, arms flailing, "don't you be a party to it. You are our only bulwark that can resist oppression in a time of public excitement. Judges cannot do it."

Looking at a wall mural of the Founding Fathers forging the Constitution, Fink told the jurors, "The fathers of this country put this power in the hands of the people."

After lunch, Ahern picked up, pounding his fist on the jury rail as he said, "The government has sought by inference, by presumption and by circumstantial evidence to prove this defendant guilty. It has sought to free itself from the law, to convict him merely because his name is Alphonse Capone."

Why had the government gone to so much trouble to convict a man on such scant evidence?

"Because Capone has grown into a mythical Robin Hood," Ahern said, "whose name is bandied all over the nation."

That Capone was a spendthrift was all the government had proved.

"The government, too," the codefender insisted, "is guilty of profligacy by bringing these witnesses here to recite their inferences. It is spending thousands of dollars for that purpose, and in these depressed times this money could better be spent on soup kitchens."

The jury, Ahern said, was "the only barrier between this defendant and the encroachment of government." Did he imagine these Depression-era jurors would show any sympathy for the tax problems of rich people?

Ahern was more effective when addressing the evidence, pointing out that Fred Ries's cashier's checks had already been used against Guzik.

"How many defendants," Ahern cried, "will these checks convict?"

But he failed to challenge the check with Capone's name on it, letting that damning signature stand.

He could have explored how friendly to forgery a penciled signature might be, or perhaps traced the check's provenance as it passed through accounts connected to E. J. O'Hare and Frank Nitto, before reaching government agents intent on putting Capone away.

Strangely, neither Ahern nor anyone else would ever seriously question that one unusual signature written in lead—maybe not the Chicago typewriter variety, but destructive in its own way.

The next morning, the courtroom was packed for what everyone knew would be the last day of the trial. Impeccably groomed, jovial but anxious, Capone wore a new green suit as if taking to heart Ahern's Robin Hood comparison.

George E. Q. Johnson rose to give the final closing statement—his first remarks to any jury since becoming U.S. attorney. Capone made a show of ignoring him, pretending to read notes and documents handed him by his lawyers.

"Mr. Johnson was earnest," the *Tribune* reported, "so much so that he was almost evangelical at times, clenching his fist, shaking his gray head, clamping his lean jaws together as he bit into the evidence and tore into the defense theories of its meaning and lack of strength."

Johnson, in his pinched, reedy voice, preached the gospel of income tax. If the American people paid taxes only when the government came after them, the country would collapse—its military disbanding, institutions vanishing, and courts "swept aside."

"American civilization will fall," Johnson insisted, "and organized society will revert to the days of the jungle, where every man will be for himself."

Who was this creature about whom the defense had woven "a halo of mystery and romance," who lavishly wasted some half a million dollars?

Johnson wondered, "Is he the little boy . . . who succeeded in finding the pot of gold at the end of the rainbow, that he has been spending so lavishly, or maybe, as his counsel says, is he Robin Hood?"

Johnson indicated the plump man in green.

"You will remember how Robin Hood in the days of the barons took from the strong to feed the weak and the starving peasants. . . . But was it Robin Hood in this case who bought $8,000 worth of diamond belt buckles, to give to the unemployed? Was it Robin Hood in this case who bought a meat bill of $6,500? Did that go to the unemployed?"

No, it had gone to the house on Palm Island. Had he bought "$27 shirts to protect the shivering men who sleep under Wacker Drive at night? No."

Defense insinuations had Ralph Capone, not Al, present during Reverend Hoover's raid on the Hawthorne Smoke Shop. But, Johnson asked, "Could anyone forget the hulking form of this defendant with the flaming scars upon his cheek? If it was Ralph Capone, if there was any question about it, why was not Ralph Capone called as a witness?"

Johnson asked the jury to consider the case in its entirety.

"Take every fact and circumstance, and consider it, and see how it keys into the other, and then when you see that, you will find that every page of this record cries out the guilt of this defendant."

Every witness testimony for Capone, the prosecutor reminded them, came "from the lips of a man who is violating the laws of the State of Illinois . . . so shifty they could not look you in the eye."

Johnson asked the jury to remember the countless men and women paying taxes on hard-earned incomes of barely more than $1,500 a year. He compared these $1,500 men and women who helped their government in a "time of national deficit" to a defendant whose "extravagances" testified to the wealth he so selfishly hoarded to himself.

This case was, as the defense itself had indicated, historic. But people would not remember it, Johnson declared, because the defendant was Al Capone.

"They will remember it for a more important reason," he told the jury. It would establish "whether any man can be above the law, whether any man can so conduct his affairs that he can escape entirely the burdens of Government; and that is the record, gentlemen of the jury, that your verdict will write in this case."

He thanked the jury and took his seat.

Arthur Prochno and his fellow jurors found the various closing arguments thrilling, but Johnson's most of all, because it signaled the trial had reached its conclusion.

Almost the conclusion, as Wilkerson took an hour charging and instructing the jury.

"You are the judges of the weight which is to be given to the testimony of the witnesses who have appeared before you in this case," Wilkerson intoned. "You have had many witnesses here who have testified from the witness stand, men from all walks of life. You have had government agents, ministers of the gospel, business men and other classes of witnesses."

That last seemed a veiled slight at the defense, whose parade of bookies belonged in a class all its own.

Other parts of Wilkerson's statement favored the prosecution. He talked at length about how the lack of any concrete proof of Capone's income had forced the government to rely on circumstantial evidence. This reinforced the idea that Capone had something to hide, establishing the willful intent necessary to convict him of felony tax evasion.

"Now," Wilkerson said, "in this case . . . you may consider all the facts and circumstances which have been shown here in evidence. You may consider the evidence relative to the activities of the defendant in the places in Cicero. You may consider the evidence relating to the living by the defendant at the two hotels, the Metropole and the Lexington; the manner in which he there lived."

This included "moneys which were transmitted from Chicago to the defendant in Florida," and "expenditures of money by the defendant in Chicago and in Florida." Evidence of the possible business connection between Capone and Guzik was fair game, too.

"You must look at the evidence as a whole," the judge emphasized. "You must consider each fact in relation to all of the other facts, and so viewing the case arrive at a conclusion whether each one of the essential elements of these indictments . . . have been established to your satisfaction beyond a reasonable doubt."

When the judge had finished, the defense attorneys offered a few minor quibbles, but never seriously questioned his impartiality. One observer took this peaceful acceptance as "an unusual tribute which bespoke Judge Wilkerson's ability."

The jury proceeded into deliberation with various notions about the appropriate sentences for Capone's crimes. Other defendants had been jailed from two-and-a-half to five years for tax offenses. Although Capone faced a maximum of thirty-two years in prison, the jurors mistakenly believed they could send him away for up to seventy-two years. Some were ready, even eager, to "give him the limit"—nearly three-quarters of a century for not paying his taxes.

According to juror Prochno, who gave his story to the *Tribune* half a decade later, the twelve men sitting in judgment of Capone had soon broken down into two distinct factions—one intent on convicting Capone on all counts, regardless of what might be said in court; the other with no illusions about the defendant, but wanting to make at least some effort to weigh the evidence.

As one juror remarked, "A quick verdict would look bad for us. The public might think we framed and railroaded him."

Prochno said he became leader of this second faction. Once the jurors began deliberating, and the first two ballots revealed an even split between conviction and acquittal, those set on finding Capone guilty began lobbying Prochno to wrap things up.

"You're not dumb," one said. "You know Capone is a bad man. The papers for years have been full of his activities, and now that we have the chance, let's give him the limit. All you have to do is to give the word and it will all be over."

Another appealed to Prochno on grounds of shared ethnicity and class, suggesting Capone deserved harsh treatment because he was Italian and Catholic.

"After all," this juror said, "he's only a dago."

The twelve passed around exhibits and debated what they might mean. But the substance of their deliberations boiled down to a question Chicagoans—and so many Americans—had wrestled with throughout Capone's rise to infamous fortune: Was this man, this bootlegger, pimp, and killer, really all that bad?

"He's no good," one juror said. Hadn't the newspapers said he ran brothels and gambling joints? Another replied, "But he's done good things, such as supporting soup kitchens and helping the poor."

Hours passed, and the jurors grew hungry.

"We asked for sandwiches, but didn't get them," Prochno recalled. Some jurors resented being starved into a verdict—even soup kitchens provided sandwiches.

Their hunger only added to the growing sense of frustration and unease—they'd been sequestered for days, unable to see their families or go to church, their reading material strictly censored. No deliberations could be held on Sunday, so if they deadlocked tonight, they'd remain confined until Monday at the earliest.

"We wanted to get home," Prochno wrote.

They voted to acquit Capone on the first indictment, covering 1924, which Johnson had pushed through in secret to skirt the statute of limitations, because they all agreed the prosecutors had placed little emphasis on it. Jurors determined to convict used that vote as a bargaining chip, convincing the others to come around on the second indictment.

But the jury didn't vote to convict on all counts. Instead, Prochno said, "we agreed to take the first counts in each year and call it quits."

This produced a somewhat confusing verdict, convicting Capone of misdemeanors for failing to file a tax return in 1928 and 1929, but acquitting him of felony tax evasion for the same years. In their haste, the jurors kept making mistakes, their foreman filling out the verdict incorrectly and having to start over. Another juror belatedly realized they'd convicted Capone of two misdemeanors while acquitting him of several felonies.

"He'll only get ten or twelve years," the juror complained. "I want to give him more."

The others overruled him; they wanted to go home. Five years later, Prochno still seemed confused.

"I really believe the final intent was to convict Capone on two, not three, felony counts," he said, "and two misdemeanors."

But no matter—the jury had decided.

All the painstaking detective work, legal wrangling, and courtroom drama amounted to nothing—the jurors voted to convict essentially at random, giving more thought to the defendant's sordid reputation than the finer points of income tax law.

And if the Prohibition case had gone to trial instead of the tax one, the result would almost certainly have been the same, though the law mandated a much lighter punishment for those charges.

On the night of October 17, 1931, Al Capone was finally defeated at the hands of twelve tired, hungry men, who'd probably made up their minds before setting foot in Judge Wilkerson's court.

From the jury room, at 9:30 P.M., applause said the twelve had finally reached their decision.

Capone and attorney Fink were at the Lexington Hotel when news of a verdict came. A few minutes later, the defendant darted into a waiting limo, a reporter ready.

How was he feeling?

Capone smiled—the lengthy deliberation could mean good news. "I'm feeling fine," he said.

Any comment?

"Not a thing now," he said, climbing into the comfy backseat of the humming vehicle, about to head north on Michigan Avenue.

Within fifteen minutes, Capone had arrived. The defendant took his usual seat and sat mopping his brow with a silk handkerchief, but smiling. He and his attorneys chatted casually as the jurors filed in.

The twelve men looked weary, solemn. Capone watched, curious but restrained. The judge emerged from chambers and took the bench, getting right to it.

"Have you arrived at a verdict?"

The foreman nodded and handed a sheaf of papers to a bailiff, who passed them to the court clerk.

The clerk broke the pin-drop silence, clearing his throat. "We, the jury, find the defendant not guilty as charged in Indictment No. 22852 . . ."

Capone's big face split in a smile, for half a moment.

". . . and we find the defendant guilty on counts 1, 5, 9, 13, 18, and not guilty on 2, 3, 4, 6, 7, 8, 10, 11, 12, 14, 15, 16, 17, 19, 20, 21 and 22 in Indictment No. 23232."

Capone's grin turned sick, his gaze lowering. He spoke to his lawyers, who then got up and went to the bench. Capone's easy smile returned, his poise, too.

A reporter behind him asked, "How are you feeling?"

As he had outside the Lexington, before he'd made the ride to court, Capone said, "I'm feeling fine."

But he had nothing else to say—his attorneys would do his talking now. He was looking at a possible seventeen years behind bars—five years each for three felonies, one year for each misdemeanor, and $50,000 in fines. The final sentence, after a week of review, would be Wilkerson's.

George E. Q. Johnson wasn't in court, but when reached told the *Tribune*, "The verdict speaks for itself."

The federal prosecutors wanted Capone sent immediately to Leavenworth. His lawyers demanded bail while their client's appeals were in motion. According to the *Herald and Examiner*, courtroom observers predicted Capone would probably end up serving around five years in prison—no more than nine or ten.

But Johnson, and the civic leaders who had supported his antigangster campaign, might not get their wish to put Capone behind bars before the start of the 1933 World's Fair. Appeals could delay the start of his sentence for up to two years.

"Should this prove the case," said the *Herald and Examiner*, "the Capone gang is assured of adequate leadership. Al Capone himself will be able to keep the reins until Frank Nitti . . . is out of prison. Nitti will then be in a position to carry on for Al."

Meanwhile, the feds undertook a civil suit to seize Capone's assets for unpaid taxes. A $137,328 lien was put on his Chicago and Florida homes (though he legally owned neither).

"By the time the government finishes its collection," wrote the *Herald and Examiner,* "Al may be stripped of all his personal property."

On Saturday, October 24, an anxious Capone arrived at his sentencing hearing, all alone in a putrid purple suit. He sat slumped, waiting for Ahern and Fink, and his mood lightened when they showed. Shortly, Judge Wilkerson emerged from his chambers.

The tension in the courtroom was only heightened as the judge said flatly, "Let the defendant stand before the bar."

Capone rose and lumbered forward, his attorneys remaining seated. A U.S. marshal and the entire prosecution team met him at the bench. The *Herald and Examiner* found the once "fearless gangster" droop-shouldered and beaten-looking: "a picture of abject helplessness."

In a courtroom crowded but millpond still, Wilkerson read the income tax offenses and their maximum penalties. Capone glanced at Johnson and his other adversaries with a forced half smile, hands clasped behind him, a white bandage (as the *Trib* noted) "around a cut on his trigger finger."

"It is the judgment of the Court in this case," Wilkerson said, "that on count one of the indictment, the defendant is sentenced to imprisonment in the penitentiary . . . for a period of five years, and to pay a fine of ten thousand dollars, and to pay all costs of prosecution."

Capone took that stoically, as did his attorneys—five years was what they had expected, any other sentences probably running concurrently.

"On count five of the indictment," the judge said, "the defendant is sentenced to imprisonment in the penitentiary . . . for a period of five years, and to pay a fine of ten thousand dollars, and to pay the costs of the prosecution."

Wilkerson continued: "On count nine of said indictment, the defendant is sentenced to imprisonment in the penitentiary . . . for a period of five years, and to pay a fine of ten thousand dollars, and to pay the costs of prosecution."

Capone listened intently.

"On each of counts thirteen and eighteen of said indictment," Wilkerson continued, "the defendant is sentenced to imprisonment in the county jail . . . for a period of one year, and to pay a fine of ten thousand dollars, and to pay the costs of the prosecution."

The sentences on the first and fifth counts would run concurrently. But the rest would "be consecutive and cumulative."

Finally, Wilkerson said, "The result is, that the aggregate sentence of the defendant is eleven years in the penitentiary, and fines aggregating fifty thousand dollars."

Fink asked, "Eleven years, did you say?"

"Yes."

Capone wore a poleaxed expression—clearly he'd expected a lighter sentence. His attorneys seemed similarly stunned.

Ahern said, "Can't you have the misdemeanor counts run first, your honor?"

"No," the judge said. "The order will stand."

The judge refused a motion for bail, pending an appeal. "The defendant is remanded to the custody of the United States marshal."

Capone's attorneys argued with the judge—denying their client bail meant he'd be sent to Leavenworth immediately!

"You have not the power to hold this man," Fink insisted, "to deny bail when he is making his appeal. . . . This will mean the defendant will go to Leavenworth. Your honor might permit keeping this defendant here until Monday at least."

When Wilkerson refused, Ahern heatedly maintained the judge was not within his rights to do this, even suggesting the jurist go to his chambers and check his law books.

An angry Wilkerson said, "You cannot undertake to instruct this court—that is all."

Then the marshal gestured at Capone "to come along."

The prisoner went along.

In the corridor, reporters flocked for a quote.

"Well, I'll get a lot of time off for good behavior," Capone said, working to stay jovial.

Then came a deputy collector of Internal Revenue, who gave Capone a notice of the tax lien on everything he owned. An unhappy Capone, accompanied by deputy marshals and an Intelligence Unit agent, was hustled out.

"It's all my own fault," he told his captors, as they rode in a cab to the county jail. "I've nobody but myself to blame, I suppose. Publicity—that's what got me. Too much hollering about Capone."

When they reached the jail, reporters again swarmed Capone. By now he was not in a good mood.

"It was a blow below the belt," he said, "but what can you expect when the whole community is prejudiced against you? I've never heard of anyone getting more than five years for income tax trouble, but when they're prejudiced, what can you do even if you've got good lawyers?"

His fingerprints were taken and his pockets searched. After a compulsory bath, he was put in a cell. Among his cellmates was a down-and-outer who couldn't come up with a $100 fine. Al would try to get it paid.

Capone took in his surroundings with a frown. Someone called out a question: How was this compared to the Philadelphia pen?

"Well," Al admitted, "it's a little cleaner."

A radio began playing "All the World Is Waiting for the Sunrise."

A photographer, who had no doubt bribed his way onto the cellblock, asked Al to pose.

The prisoner's rage boiled over. "I'll knock your block off!" he yelled, and reached for a bucket to throw.

But the guards settled him, saying they'd move him to a more private cell in the hospital ward. They were in the process of doing that when even more photographers descended.

"Think of my family," Capone whimpered. "Please don't take my picture."

Paul Muni as Tony Camonte in *Scarface* (1932). *(Authors' Collection)*

Twenty-Eight

October 1931–January 1932

On the day Capone received his sentence, Robert Isham Randolph asked, "Now after Capone, what?"

Without "a militant drive that will free Chicago of the shackles of the syndicate," Randolph warned the *Chicago Evening American*, Capone's conviction would be meaningless.

"Knock over their breweries and stills," Randolph urged, "keep them on the run. . . . Now we must make sure that a new boss does not step into [Capone's] shoes and carry on the scheme of corruption. The syndicate must be smashed."

Eliot Ness seemed determined to keep up that fight, still hounding the gang as if Capone remained at large. Perhaps he knew, as George Johnson certainly did, that the tax conviction might be overturned at any time. If that happened, federal officials would need the Untouchables' case to keep Capone behind bars.

Or perhaps, as seems more likely, Ness agreed with Randolph, recognizing Capone's conviction as only the first step in a long process.

Ironically, the guilty verdict represented a greater threat to Ness's work than any gangster packing a pistol or a payoff. Would the public, and the politicians they elected, still care about cleaning up the Outfit with its most visible leader in jail?

"It is up to Chicago now to follow up the blow," Randolph said, "and follow up swiftly to get in the knockout punch."

Although the Prohibition indictment remained locked in legal limbo, Ness kept hunting for a handful of defendants not yet accounted for. The biggest figure still at large was George Howlett—"the Jekyll and Hyde playboy of the Capone mob," one newspaper called him, and the front man for renting breweries. After months without a lead, Ness connected Howlett to an unlisted telephone number, tracing it to an upscale residential hotel on the North Side.

In mid-November, Ness visited the place and made the manager an offer: help track down Howlett, and the press would never learn gangsters lived under his roof. The manager obliged, giving Ness descriptions of Howlett's three cars—an unimaginable extravagance in Depression days. Ness found Howlett's two Cadillacs, but the suspect's sixteen-cylinder roadster was missing.

So Ness placed a man near the entrance and they waited until Howlett drove up in the missing car.

"It was not difficult to identify him," Ness wrote. "He arrived with a lady companion who was one of the most beautiful women I have ever seen."

Before Howlett could reach the elevator, Ness and the other agent arrested him. The pinch made the papers, but Ness kept his word to the manager, telling reporters he'd caught Howlett after spotting him at a football game.

Ness's boss did not share the Untouchable's inexhaustible zeal. George E. Q. Johnson understood the need to keep hammering the gang, praising Randolph's "courageous statement" in the *Evening American*. But the Capone case seemed to have drained him of any desire to fight on.

"You remember the pace we all set in the Federal Building," Johnson wrote years later to Frank Wilson. "I was older than the rest of the men and I expect it took more out of me than I realized at the time."

The week after Capone's conviction, a *Kansas City Star* reporter found Johnson in court looking "worn out" and exhausted, "resting his chin wearily upon the palm of his right hand" and letting his assistant do all the talking. In an interview with the *Star,* Johnson focused on his past success, insisting Capone was just as bad as the press had painted him and well worth the effort of putting away.

"Why, then," the *Star* reporter asked, "did the government delay prosecution of the liquor charges and present first what seems to be the minor offense of evasion of the income tax?"

"There were many things to be considered," Johnson replied. "The first was that I believed we had an air-tight case in the income tax matters. We can get most conclusive evidence in income tax cases—it is far more difficult to obtain in liquor violations charges. When a man or a syndicate receives such vast sums of money as this Capone organization it is not easily hidden."

None of this was true.

Judge Wilkerson, not Johnson, chose the tax case. Framing the story this way, however, made it appear everything had gone according to Johnson's plan—turning Capone's conviction into the culmination of a hard-fought, well-thought-out campaign, not a messy, kitchen-sink strategy succeeding despite itself. Johnson glossed over his missteps and implied he'd achieved his end goal, leaving little reason to keep fighting.

"Industrial and civic leaders believe the most crucial battle in the long and frightful war against organized crime has been won," the *Star* proclaimed. "The gang syndicate's leader has been captured."

During his Chicago visit, the reporter also interviewed the leader of the Untouchables—or, as the *Star* put it, the "Incorruptibles." Johnson's office, thinking highly of Ness, permitted use of Eliot's name in print. In all probability, Johnson had encouraged it.

Like many journalists before and since, the writer marveled at how "boyish" and soft-spoken Ness was, not at all the hard-bitten fellow one might expect.

"He is an athletic, most presentable young man," the *Star* said. "Direct in speech, modest almost to the point of bashfulness."

Ness's utter dedication to his job made him a man of mystery straight out of a pulp novel.

"He has no office and very, very few persons even know where he lives," the *Star* claimed. "And naturally one doesn't ask too many questions about his home and family—if he has a family."

During the interview, another apparent member of the "Incorruptibles" let himself into the room.

"You left this on my desk," he said to Ness. "Thought you might want it."

And he handed Ness a large automatic pistol.

Ness casually stuffed the gun under his arm, thanked the agent, and went on talking.

The reporter asked, "Ever get in many jams where you need weapons?"

"Once in a while," Ness said, adding it paid to be careful.

Had the gun been left on the desk for the *Star*'s benefit? Eliot's puckish sense of humor, and general dislike for carrying a weapon, seemed to say it had.

With such a modest, courageous defender at its gates, Chicago could seemingly rest easy after a chaotic and bloody decade. The *Star* envisioned a glowing future for the city—"a busy winter of business readjustment, a year of progress, and then the world's fair in 1933."

Optimism was not uncalled for—Chicago had replaced the corrupt administration of Big Bill Thompson with Cermak and his promise of reform. In June 1931, the month of Capone's indictments, the city's crime rate fell to its lowest point in years. Of the Chicago Crime Commission's original twenty-eight "public enemies," nineteen had been removed from the streets, either by the law or the bullets of rivals. Among them were the biggest names in bootlegging: the Capones and Jack Guzik, among others. To the rest of the country, as the *New York Times* put it, Chicago seemed to have "exorcised her evil spirits."

But some demons, rum or otherwise, remained, or would soon return once their prison terms ran out. And with the Depression tightening its grip, Chicago's problems would only get worse—years of financial mismanagement and public apathy had left the city $300 million in debt. "Unless citizens put money in the till on a large scale," a civic group warned in 1930, "hospitals will shut, inmates of lunatic asylums will be left without food, heat and light, prisons will be unable to house their tenants, and the police and fire brigades will have to be disbanded."

Chicago's unemployment rate sat at 30 percent, well above the national average. Within a year, 750,000 Chicagoans would be out of work, as their city failed to pay its teachers, firemen, or cops. For gangsters, this fiscal chaos was a golden opportunity—they knew how to offer their own form of stability when public institutions failed.

"Citizens already paying heavy taxes to racketeers, who can deliver what they promise," one observer noted, "are refusing to pay taxes to a city government which cannot."

Judge John Lyle called 1931 "the summer of decision"—the moment when authorities missed their one real chance to break the back of the Outfit.

"If Chicago had persisted then in a relentless, untiring crackdown on organized crime," Lyle wrote in 1960, "we would have a minimum rather than a flood of racketeering today." Instead, the city and the nation focused on other problems, leaving Chicago's gangsters to survive and thrive.

And in some ways, the very public war on Capone made this inevitable. The feds had winnowed the herd, removing the most public of the "public enemies." Those who remained knew how to keep a low profile—running them out of business would be difficult, dirty, thankless work, without the public relations payoff of convicting Capone. The political will for such a fight simply didn't exist.

Herbert Hoover had already moved on, directing Elmer Irey and the Intelligence Unit to focus on New York. Chicago's top-flight gangsters had all been locked up (if temporarily), but Manhattan still had plenty of marquee mobsters for the tax men to pursue.

Then the president began doling out rewards for a job well done. In mid-December, he had a private White House lunch with James Wilkerson, urging the judge to run for Illinois governor. The land of Lincoln was reliably Republican, Hoover said; a man of Wilkerson's popularity would coast to victory. The judge said he'd prefer a seat on the Court of Appeals. Hoover promised to make it happen.

That evening, Wilkerson joined the president at the Gridiron Club dinner, a white-tie affair where Washington's newspapermen rubbed shoulders with politicians. Introduced as the judge who "found a home for Al Capone," Wilkerson got thunderous applause—"the greatest ovation" for a public figure at the event in a long time, one reporter said.

Three days later, the Republican Party announced it would hold its 1932 convention in Chicago. Atlantic City had been in the running, but the party selected Chicago in part because the president had taken an interest in the political situation there. Robert Isham Randolph assured delegates they'd made the right choice.

"We now have all the bad characters locked up," Randolph told the *Tribune,* making Chicago every bit as safe as Atlantic City.

Was it? Getting Capone had hardly changed Chicago's crime picture; it merely slapped on a fresh coat of paint. Less than two years earlier, Frank Loesch had prevailed upon the president to bring all his federal power to bear on cleaning up the town. Now, Loesch declared victory.

"Organized law enforcement has fought it out with organized crime and we have won," Loesch told the Associated Press in late December. "The gangster has been conquered."

Newspapers coast-to-coast quoted Loesch under such headlines as CHICAGO WINS WAR ON CRIME, while praising the city on their editorial pages.

After so much unfavorable publicity, wrote the *Charleston Daily Mail,* "the signs are sure that [Chicago] will be hailed as a model in crime suppression, and rise out of the muck a comparatively purified and exemplary community."

The message was clear: Chicago was open for business once more—just in time for the World's Fair.

As the city celebrated his defeat, Al Capone awaited the results of his appeal from the confines of the Cook County Jail. Judge Wilkerson had ruled the time Capone served in Chicago would not count toward his eleven-year sentence, but the gangster had good reasons for postponing his arrival at the penitentiary.

On December 2, Wilkerson received an anonymous telegram from someone claiming to work at the jail.

WISH TO INFORM YOU THAT AL CAPONE IS USING THE COUNTY JAIL FOR HIS LIQUOR BUSINESS, it read, AND TRANSACTS FROM THERE POSSIBLY AS MUCH IF NOT MORE THAN HE USED TO AT HIS OLD HEADQUARTERS AT THE LEXINGTON HOTEL . . . PLEASE INVESTIGATE.

Wilkerson passed the telegram on to the local office of J. Edgar Hoover's Bureau of Investigation, which arranged a meeting with George Johnson, Intelligence Unit agent Art Madden, and other federal officials at the prosecutor's office.

Johnson had received an identical telegram, and Madden also had word Capone enjoyed "special privileges" at the jail. Rather than occupying a cell like any other inmate, Capone resided in a spacious dormitory for convalescent prisoners, with a "soft mattress, clean linen and private shower bath," according to the *Herald and Examiner*.

A Bureau of Investigation agent reported rumors "that Capone is allowed to receive visitors, sometimes in large numbers, at almost any hour of the day or night, regardless of the regularly established rules for visiting."

Those visitors included local politicians and top Outfit figures, including Johnny Torrio, Joe Fusco, and George Howlett, as well as Capone's latest mistress. And if Capone couldn't meet with his associates in person, he had every opportunity to reach them by phone.

Another report said an Outfit associate had on occasion "escorted a number of women to Capone's quarters in the jail [where] these women put on an obscene performance for the entertainment of Capone's guests."

William Froelich, the special U.S attorney who'd overseen the work of the Untouchables, suggested prosecuting Capone for contempt of court if evidence supporting these claims could be found.

But Johnson opposed launching a full investigation. Doing so would almost certainly tip the newspapers to Capone's living conditions, and the prosecutor didn't want these rumors publicized. That would reveal his prosecution of Capone hadn't really done as much damage to the Outfit as the media claimed.

Instead, Johnson suggested the Bureau quietly discuss the rumors with jail officials.

Federal agents duly questioned David Moneypenny, the warden of the Cook County Jail, and his subordinates. To avoid the press, they held these meetings in the Bureau's Chicago office. Moneypenny and his men insisted the rumors were false, claiming Capone received no special privileges and lacked the freedom to run his business.

Capone, they said, received frequent visits from his family—his mother visited every day—but never from other women. The visitors' log did not include the names of any gang associates, merely anonymous "friends" and "cousins." Warden Moneypenny admitted he allowed Capone to live in the relative luxury of the convalescent ward—but only for the good of the other inmates.

"I didn't want him mingling with the other prisoners," Moneypenny said, "because I was afraid he'd have a bad influence on them."

In mid-December, W. A. McSwain, the special agent in charge of the Bureau's Chicago office, reported to George Johnson that nothing definitive had been turned up. They discussed whether to pursue a broader investigation.

"Mr. Johnson was of the opinion that an inquiry of this character would naturally result in considerable newspaper publicity," the agent said, "and in view of the facts to date, he did not believe such action warranted, and that further inquiry would be unnecessary at this time."

Johnson had already tried to solve the problem quietly, arranging with Warden Moneypenny not to let anyone see Capone "without a pass from the United States Marshal."

Despite Johnson's efforts to avoid publicity, the press soon got wind of the Bureau's efforts. On December 17, the *Chicago Daily News* reported federal agents were investigating claims "Capone has been receiving telephone, telegraph and secretarial service to enable him to carry on his rackets" while in custody.

Other papers followed suit. The *Herald and Examiner* said investigators "discovered that late at night expensive automobiles were parked within the jail shadows. Guarding them were men who had every appearance of hoodlums."

Unnamed officials told the newspaper they "had been unable to substantiate" the allegations, while Warden Moneypenny, who prided himself on running a "crack proof" jail, dismissed the claims as "a lot of poppycock."

"Capone's in a cell like any other hoodlum," Moneypenny said. "He's getting no special privileges and I'm not letting anyone see him unless I know who he is and what he wants."

Reporters found Capone in the convalescent ward, wearing a blue pinstriped suit and open-collared shirt as he played cards with an ailing inmate.

"I'm in jail . . . ," Capone remarked. "Aren't they satisfied? Anybody who wants this place is welcome to it. I don't see anything swell about this."

The next day, Special Agent McSwain met with Johnson to suggest a deeper probe. Though the investigation had already gone public, Johnson clung to stifling the coverage.

"Mr. Johnson expressed the opinion that he did not believe additional investigation warranted," McSwain wrote, "and accordingly, no further action need be taken."

On December 21, the *Chicago Daily Times* reported Warden Moneypenny had been driven to Springfield in a Cadillac registered to Mae Capone. The warden claimed he'd accepted a ride without knowing who owned the car.

Requests for passes to see Capone flooded into the U.S. marshal's office, many from "petty politicians" probably gathering passes for Outfit members. Another report claimed Torrio had brought a pair of rival New York mobsters, Lucky Luciano and Dutch Schultz, to see Capone. The foursome met in the room housing Cook County's electric chair, and Capone amused himself by sitting in the hot seat as he tried to broker a peace. But the rapacious Schultz refused to accept Capone's ruling, and the meeting ended badly.

"If I'd had him outside," Capone said, "I'd have shoved a gun against his guts."

But Torrio felt differently, and he went on to build a partnership with Schultz ending with the latter's murder, allegedly on Luciano's orders, in 1935.

As late as January 18, 1932, George Johnson told the Bureau he still opposed any further probe into Capone's jailhouse activities. But a week later, a Johnson assistant gave Special Agent McSwain "information to the effect that Capone had been allowed to have visitors other than those who possessed proper passes for such visits."

The warden, citing overcrowding, had placed other inmates in the convalescent ward, and those prisoners had reportedly been receiving Capone's visitors as their own, under such names as "Mr. Smith" and "Mr. Jones."

"I'll put a stop to that if I have to move him," the U.S. marshal told the *Tribune*. "I can understand now why we haven't had a lot of gangster-looking fellows coming to my office for passes."

Melvin Purvis, the new special agent in charge of the Chicago office, met with Moneypenny on January 26, finding him surprised by reports of Capone's conduct in prison.

"Mr. Moneypenny takes every opportunity," Purvis wrote, "to inform me of his sincere efforts to circumvent any action by which Al Capone might continue the supervision of his so-called business interests in Chicago."

Purvis also said Moneypenny had suggested to Johnson that Capone be moved to a military installation "and placed in the brig there, but that this suggestion had probably not met with a favorable reception."

In mid-February, federal officials placed a guard of U.S. marshals on Capone around the clock. Johnson lent his support, writing the attorney general on February 20 that confidential nongovernment sources had told him Capone was "in fact directing his illicit enterprises from the County Jail" with no record "of visitors or persons with whom he communicates."

One source said the defendant, if the judgment went against him, might seek to escape.

"With the influence this defendant seems to be able to exert," Johnson added, "such a thing is not impossible."

Two days before Christmas, Eliot Ness's father died at a hospital in Roseland, a few months shy of his eighty-second birthday.

Age had forced Peter Ness to retire from the bakery some years prior, a stroke leaving him partially paralyzed for his last few months. But the man who once urged his youngest son to continue his education had lived to see that advice bear fruit, as Eliot won a college degree and fame as a federal agent. After a lifetime spent carving out his family's place in America, Peter could take pride in that.

The elder Ness's unrelenting drive lived on in Eliot, who wasted little time in getting back to work. For weeks, the Untouchables had closed in on a trio of big breweries connected with the Capone syndicate. They hit the first, in a garage at 2271 South Lumber Street, on January 8. After crashing through several sets of heavy steel doors, Ness and his men found no one inside, but confiscated 140 barrels of beer and destroyed $75,000 worth of equipment.

The squad found more success a few days later, at a garage at 1712 North Kilbourn Avenue. To make sure this raid took prisoners, they waited until a truck drove inside before swooping in, arresting four bootleggers right away and two more who wandered in soon after.

The garage proved to be among the biggest breweries on Chicago's North Side, holding $250,000 worth of beer and eight large vats valued at $125,000. Ness told reporters its owner was George "Red" Barker, a rebellious West Side hood once allied with Capone, now vying to replace him. The raid inflamed an already tense situation; federal officials told the *Herald and Examiner* "rival gangs were oiling their guns for war of vengeance, blaming each other for 'tip-offs.'"

Barker died just over six months later, courtesy of machine-gun bullets and, one police official said, "too much ambition."

Ness's latest raid campaign climaxed on January 21, when the Untouchables captured a brewery hidden in a two-story brick structure at 2024 South State Street. They again smashed through the front door in their battering-ram truck—Ness's "customary calling card," said the *Chicago Daily News*—before arresting five men, seizing $75,000 worth of equipment, and destroying sixty-seven barrels of beer.

They also confiscated a familiar vehicle: the same truck that, months earlier, Bert Delaney used trying to recover Capone's property from the brewery at 3136 South Wabash, before the Untouchables sprang their trap and arrested him. The gang had bought the truck back at government auction, only to lose it once more to the feds.

The first two raids earned little coverage in the press, but this time Ness took pains to make headlines. He called up several papers, letting them know when and where the bust would take place. Reporters and photographers showed up on cue, along with a newsreel crew from Universal Studios. Flashbulbs popped and celluloid whirred as the federal men took axes to the barrels, dumped buckets of beer, and opened spigots on giant vats, flooding the place with froth.

Ness stayed in back of the cameras. Courting the press was part of his job—George Johnson and William Froelich urged him to pursue cases that would make good headlines—but he never seemed quite comfortable with the limelight. Unlike his brother-in-law, who often posed for pictures after raids, Ness avoided photo ops and showed no interest in cashing in on his newfound fame.

Shortly after Capone's indictments, Ness received a letter from an old classmate at the University of Chicago, now a public relations man, offering him the chance to write a few "short but very brisk articles" on the case.

"The proceeds should run well into the thousands," this PR man wrote, "and your end would be remitted by check to yourself or any fund you might care to designate." Ness passed up the offer, content with his $3,800 a year.

The more Ness's work made the papers, however, the more his colleagues resented it. Decades later, Untouchable Barney Cloonan would inaccurately depict Ness as "a publicity hound of the worst type," who never made a bust without reporters present. Prohibition agent William Connors recalled a nasty spirit of competition arising between the regular dry force and Ness's elite special agents. Both groups kept trying to outdo each other.

"At times," Connors said, "the situation wasn't too healthy."

And this attitude went some distance up the chain of command. W. E. Bennett, Chicago's special agent in charge, would complain of Ness's "egotism and publicity-seeking activities" in a Bureau of Investigation interview, claiming Ness's fame spread "dissension" throughout the office.

But Bennett had his own reasons to feel aggrieved. The Prohibition Bureau had chosen him over Ness as Alexander Jamie's replacement back in 1930, and since then the young Untouchable had constantly upstaged him. Although reporters usually referred to Ness as Bennett's "assistant" or "aide," anyone could see Eliot got far more ink than his supposed boss.

William Froelich later insisted any criticism of Ness as a press hound most likely stemmed from jealousy. The lead Untouchable did publicize his activities, Froelich said, but never without first getting Johnson's approval.

Johnson had, after all, constantly courted the media throughout the Capone investigation and, far more than Ness himself, created the legend of the Untouchables.

Nor was Ness the only Untouchable who faced pressure to grab headlines. Around this time, Maurice Seager got into an argument with Johnson and Froelich over whether or not to press bribery charges against a particular bootlegger. Seager saw the case as a waste of time, believing no Chicago jury would ever convict.

But Johnson and Froelich insisted on an indictment, simply for the sake of good press. Disgusted by this naked grab for "headline publicity," Seager left the squad and refused to do any more work on the Capone case.

Unlike Seager, Ness never objected to the public relations aspects of his work—from his mentor, August Vollmer, he'd learned law enforcement could and should use the press to reach out to the general public.

As police chief in Berkeley, Vollmer worked tirelessly to promote his own reforms, ingratiating himself with reporters and providing access to departmental files in exchange for favorable coverage.

Ness tried to follow Vollmer's example but struggled to connect with Chicago's hardboiled newsmen. They dismissed him as "not quite a phony but strictly small time," according to Tony Berardi, a photographer with the *Evening American*. In his fumbling attempts to win them over, Ness fell back on a time-honored Prohibition agent tactic— letting the press sample the evidence.

Berardi recalled Ness calling photographers to a government warehouse where they could fill their camera cases with seized liquor. They gladly took the booze, but didn't let it change their minds—everything about this fed, especially his quirky sense of humor and fancy college degree, rubbed them the wrong way.

Capone had come up through the school of hard knocks, like many a Chicago newsman. He spoke their language. Berardi told of Capone approaching him at a racetrack, offering a tip on a horse that couldn't lose. The cameraman didn't bite, but Capone had a winning ticket slipped into Berardi's pocket anyway.

Asked years later whose company he preferred—Ness's or Capone's—Berardi, after a half second's hesitation, chose Capone.

"Because I knew what Al Capone was," he said. Ness was just a publicity hound, "a messenger boy."

But as a proud Italian-American, Berardi was quick to say of the gangster, however newsworthy, "Personally, I hated his guts."

The Universal Newsreel featuring Ness's raid on South State Street debuted four days after the bust, jaunty music accompanying footage of agents demolishing the brewery as the quavering voice of a narrator bewailed the loss of so much beer. The whole piece had an air of comedy, as if the raid had been carried out purely for the cameras.

By early 1932, the Beer Wars had largely migrated from America's streets into the cool comfort of its movie theaters. The first great gangster film had appeared the year before: Warner Bros.' *Little Caesar*, based on W. R. Burnett's novel. The Ohio-born writer moved to Chicago in 1928, and soon after befriended a North Side hood who taught him the ins and outs of gangster psychology.

"I had the old-fashioned Ohio ideas about right and wrong," Burnett recalled, "remorse and all that stuff, which to him was utter nonsense. I'd ask him, after he'd kill guys, leave 'em on the street, how did he feel? And he said, 'How do soldiers feel?' To him it was a war."

On February 14, 1929, Burnett got to view casualties firsthand. A *Tribune* reporter took him to the site of the St. Valentine's Day Massacre while bodies still littered the floor and blood still spattered the walls. Burnett left sickened but inspired.

Published in June 1929, *Little Caesar* captured the public's imagination by presenting life from a gangster's point of view. In director Mervyn LeRoy's film version, Edward G. Robinson played Rico "Little

Caesar" Bandello, an ambitious small-time thug who rises up from the gutter only to return there in the final reel.

Though the film's "Big Boy" is more directly patterned on Capone, Rico dresses with gaudy ostentation and happily poses for photographs, delighted at seeing his picture in the newspapers. Robinson's fast-talking, sneering style defined the public's perception of a gangster, and they couldn't get enough. When *Little Caesar* premiered in New York, three thousand people fought their way in, smashing windows and overwhelming the box office.

Later that year, Warner's followed with director William A. Wellman's *The Public Enemy*, with James Cagney starring as Tom Powers, an amalgam of Dean O'Banion, Terry Druggan, Frankie Lake, and other Chicago hoods. Just as nasty as Rico Bandello, Powers kills a cop, roughs up a bartender who doesn't buy his beer, and famously smashes a grapefruit into his girlfriend's face.

But Cagney's all-American charm proved irresistible, disturbing moralists who saw in him a glorification of gangsters, despite Tom Powers winding up wrapped like a mummy and dropped off to his loving mother.

Violent and uncompromising, *The Public Enemy* styled itself as a study of slum life, offering a grimmer view of gangsters than *Little Caesar*. Yet its startling brutality paled in comparison to the bloodiest of the early gang films, the one most clearly patterned on Capone—1932's *Scarface*.

Millionaire Howard Hughes had bought the rights to the 1930 Armitage Trail novel and hired director Howard Hawks to make it into a film. W. R. Burnett wrote the first draft, but to polish it up Hawks hired Ben Hecht, former Chicago newspaperman whose script for *Underworld* won the first Academy Award for screenwriting in 1929. Hecht penned his draft of *Scarface* in eleven days, drawing less from the novel and more from actual history.

The murders of Big Jim Colosimo and Dean O'Banion, the tommy gun fusillade at the Hawthorne Hotel, the St. Valentine's Day

Massacre—all of it and more appeared, in one form or another, in *Scarface*. Capone was now Tony Camonte, Johnny Torrio had become Johnny Lovo, and various North Side leaders were combined into Gaffney, played by a pre-*Frankenstein* monster, Boris Karloff.

This fast-and-loose fidelity to the facts brought the film the wrong kind of attention. Before its release, two Capone men showed up at Hecht's hotel room late one night and demanded an explanation.

"They had a copy of my *Scarface* script in their hands," Hecht wrote. "Their dialogue belonged in it."

One gangster asked, "Is this stuff about Al Capone?"

"God, no," Hecht replied. He said he'd been acquainted with the late Colosimo and O'Banion, but left town before getting to know Capone.

"If this stuff ain't about Al Capone," one said, "why are you callin' it *Scarface*? Everybody'll think it's him."

"That's the reason," Hecht replied. "Al is one of the most famous and fascinating men of our time. If we call the movie *Scarface*, everybody will want to see it, figuring it's about Al. That's part of the racket we call showmanship."

Now he was speaking their language. The gangsters departed, convinced Hollywood meant their boss no harm. The censors would not be so easily won over.

"Under no circumstances is this film to be made," came word to Hughes from the industry censorship board. "If you should be foolhardy enough to make *Scarface*, this office will make certain it is never released."

Hughes made the movie anyway, but included a few cosmetic changes to appease the censors—for example, Camonte's mother, who loved her son unconditionally in Hecht's first draft, now rejected his evil deeds.

Paul Muni's Capone was a wild-eyed maniac, lacking the gangster's charm and sometime warmth. When Camonte first gets his hands on a tommy gun, it's love at first sight.

"Some little typewriter, eh?" Camonte asks his mentor. "I'm gonna write my name all over this town with it in big letters!"

Then he shoves the Torrio character aside and opens fire at the camera, giddy as a kid on Christmas morning. Hawks's film shared Camonte's evident delight in dealing out death, which left some viewers feeling sick.

"It should never have been made," wrote the trade publication *Film Daily,* fretting how it might damage the whole industry. But audiences didn't seem to mind; *Scarface* broke advance-booking records even before its release, and took in a whopping $90,000 in just two weeks at New York's Rialto Theatre alone, going on to outearn each film that house had shown in the past sixteen years.

As a contemporary observer noted, gangsters reflect "the here and now, with the vital reality of something that might be happening at the present moment in the next street. No wonder the pictures about them fascinate us, sometimes to the verge of terror and anger."

Burnett called his Little Caesar "a gutter Macbeth"; the *New York Times* saw Rico as "a figure out of Greek epic tragedy" transported to the modern era. The violent, degrading deaths of Rico Bandello, Tom Powers, and Tony Camonte gave viewers a much-needed catharsis. To many Americans, Capone's conviction was an empty victory, no matter how much the government tried to dress it up.

"The public wanted justice," wrote historian Richard Gid Powers, "not technical and legalistic justice, but a poetic justice that took into account moral, and not merely legal, guilt."

The movies gave them what real life could not. Censors imposed on *Scarface* a new ending replacing Camonte's bullet-ridden death with a sequence showing him tried, convicted, and hanged for murder. This made the film a triumph for the justice system, but its audience had grown tired of the legal niceties.

Soon Hughes restored the original ending—Camonte dying in the street, begging for his life under a lighted sign that mockingly declares:

THE WORLD IS YOURS. Tony gets it from the barrel of a gun—the way audiences wanted, and so many gangsters did.

No movie captured this thirst for vengeance better than director Gregory La Cava's *Gabriel over the White House*, produced by press baron William Randolph Hearst in 1933. The film tells of a corrupt, incompetent president who suffers a head injury, transforms into a benevolent dictator, and takes on Nick Diamond, a racketeer closely patterned on Capone. Diamond thinks he's untouchable—"I've paid my income tax," he sneeringly tells the president—and demonstrates his power with a drive-by shooting at the White House. The president responds by establishing a "Federal Police to Eliminate Gangsters"— heavily armed and wearing fascist-style uniforms, riding out in armored cars to subdue Diamond and his men.

Dragged before a court-martial where his smooth-talking lawyer can't save him, Diamond is convicted without benefit of a jury and executed by firing squad within sight of the Statue of Liberty. The film presents his demise not as a perversion of due process and rule of law, but as long-overdue justice. Like many Americans, Hearst saw gangsters as enemies of the state, an invading army to be subdued.

Hollywood, as it so often had, provided America with a more satisfying ending than the justice system was giving Al Capone.

Ness (top, far left; bottom, second from left) escorting Capone through Dearborn Station, in the only known photographs of both men together, May 3, 1932. *(Top: Cleveland Public Library Photograph Collection. Bottom: Michael Esslinger.)*

Twenty-Nine

February–May 1932

By early 1932, Eliot Ness had begun to show the strain of the Capone case.

The job had become his obsession, consuming much of his time and energy. Always on the hunt for another brewery or still, he grew distant from his wife and family, and he expected the same dedication from his men. Albert H. Wolff, a young investigator who joined the Chicago Prohibition office that January, observed in Ness a man under immense pressure.

"The niceties of the law no longer meant all that much to him," Wolff recalled. "He bent a few rules and even broke a few. . . . I will say this, though: any time Ness ignored the formalities or bent the rules, he had a darned good reason to do it."

Ness's disillusionment likely reflected his growing suspicion a touchable agent was on his squad. The team kept raiding empty spaces only recently vacated. Wolff felt sure someone was tipping off the mob.

"I don't say any of the Untouchables sold out," Wolff reflected. "But the leaks happened." The agent passed his hunch on to Ness, who placed several agents under surveillance.

Confirmation seemed to come in early February. While monitoring Capone gang wiretaps, Ness and another agent overheard a series of highly suggestive conversations.

The first involved "Hymie," a bootlegger who dispatched "Barney" to pick up something valuable, probably money, at a set location at noon. Three days later, two bootleggers discussed paying off a "long-time" Prohibition agent in the Chicago office, who "had helped them before."

Then, on February 15, the agents heard "Hymie" tell another boot-legger that "Barney"—described as "the guy who used to be downstairs and is upstairs now"—had accepted a $100 bribe.

Everything seemed to point to one man: Untouchable Bernard Cloonan. "Barney," as friends and family called him, had been a Pro-hibition agent for five years, enough to qualify as "long-time." After his promotion to special agent in January 1931, Cloonan had switched offices, moving from the fourth floor of the Transportation Building to the twelfth—from downstairs to upstairs.

Hardly absolute proof—the bootleggers never identified "Barney" Cloonan as the corrupt agent—but enough to warrant investigation. Yet no record of any such inquiry exists. Instead, Cloonan stayed in Chicago another eight months, then transferred to Colorado in October.

Ness remained silent about the affair, leaving no hints he ever sus-pected Cloonan, or any other Untouchable, of corruption. But years later, Paul Robsky insisted at least one squad member had indeed taken bribes for a brief period before being found out. Robsky claimed the touchable Untouchable confessed, and William Froelich quietly let him go without pressing charges.

The team's credibility depended on its spotless reputation—Froelich felt any hint of crookedness would ruin their image. Better to cover the whole thing up, he believed, than destroy the myth of the Untouch-ables.

Almost certainly, Ness would have agreed. He had an innate sensi-tivity to criticism, preferring to hide his missteps rather than open him-self up to attack. As the man charged with handpicking a supposedly incorruptible squad, he could never admit letting a grafter onto the team. The Untouchable image had become his own—he would spend the rest of his law enforcement career trying to live up to it.

After the Prohibition Bureau disbanded in 1933, Cloonan found himself without a job and returned to Chicago. The following year, he signed on with the Bureau's successor agency, the Alcoholic Beverage Unit. But when his superiors ran a background check on him, the damning wiretap transcripts resurfaced. This time the Justice Department launched a full investigation, diving deep into Cloonan's record and placing a tap on his home phone.

An unsubstantiated rumor—the kind dogging even the best Prohibition agents—accused Cloonan of shaking down speakeasy owners in the early 1930s. But no evidence of corruption turned up, and the agent was nearly broke. Had the elusive "Barney" been scared straight by the threat of exposure? Or had these supposed payoffs been a one-time thing, a lifeline to get his family through the darkest days of the Depression?

The investigator on the case felt certain Cloonan took bribes back in 1932 but couldn't prove it. "It seems that the proper time to have brought the matter to a conclusion," he wrote, "was immediately after the offenses were alleged to have been committed."

Rather than prying any further, the investigator recommended Cloonan be kept on the force but watched very closely. No further hints of graft surfaced.

Cloonan went on to serve with distinction for twenty-some years, retiring in 1960 with the agency's gratitude. At that time, he was one of the last known living Untouchables. Robert Stack, famous for playing Cloonan's old boss on TV, called to congratulate him on his retirement.

On February 27, an assistant warden entered the convalescent ward of Cook County Jail and found Al Capone on his cot, playing cards with other inmates. He took the gangster aside to say the Circuit Court of Appeals had just unanimously upheld Al's conviction.

With a silent shrug, Capone returned to playing cards. His lawyers would take the case all the way to the Supreme Court; for now, he wasn't going anywhere.

In the meantime, Capone kept working the media. He received a visit in late February from famed humorist Will Rogers, who marveled at Capone's notoriety.

"What's the matter with an age when our biggest gangster is our greatest national interest?" Rogers asked. "Part is the government's fault for not convicting him on some real crime."

With his trademark wit, Rogers scornfully dismissed the tax charges against Capone as "five counts of silk underwear."

That didn't mean the wry political commentator had any sympathy for Capone—far from it—and spending two hours with the man failed to change his mind. Realizing he couldn't write about Capone "and not make a hero out of him," Rogers chose not to mention the visit in his regular newspaper column. Few journalists had ever shown such restraint.

Within days of Rogers's visit, Capone found an even better shot at redemption. On the evening of March 1, the twenty-month-old son of aviator Charles Augustus Lindbergh was stolen away from the family home in New Jersey.

Lindbergh's celebrity rivaled Capone's—his 1927 solo flight across the Atlantic turned him into an American icon. Now the entire country reeled with shock, and Capone said he felt the family's pain.

"It's the most outrageous thing I ever heard of," Al raged. "I know how Mrs. Capone and I would feel if our son were kidnapped, and I sympathize with the Lindberghs."

Capone had always derided kidnapping as a dirty, nasty racket, perhaps because Mae lived in perpetual fear of someone trying to snatch Sonny. He offered a $10,000 reward for information leading to the Lindbergh baby's return.

But this was perhaps not the wisest move for a man whose finances remained under government scrutiny. The Bureau of Internal Revenue quickly promised to slap a lien on the reward money if and when Capone produced it.

Behind the scenes, Capone worked other leads. Georgette Winkeler, wife of Outfit hitman Gus Winkeler, said Capone ordered his lieutenants "to 'shoot' every angle in the underworld to find the baby and to learn who kidnapped him."

Even if Capone did sympathize with the Lindberghs, he had self-interest at heart. According to Georgette, "Capone believed that if his men could have found the baby, some consideration would have been given him" on shortening his prison sentence. Like Capone's soup kitchen, the investigation of Little Lindy's kidnapping was just another racket. Al figured if he did something good for the U.S.A., the U.S.A. would do something good for him.

Capone soon became convinced he'd found the kidnapper: Robert Carey, alias Bob Conroy, a member of the American Boys hit squad behind the St. Valentine's Day Massacre. Carey had once partnered in the "snatch racket" with Fred Burke before going to work for the Outfit. He'd recently had a falling out with Capone, after trying to blackmail a crony of Al's.

The effort netted Carey some cash but also a stern warning "to get out of Chicago and stay out." Georgette Winkeler said Carey left town promising to "pull a job that will set the world by the ears." She later "often wondered if the 'job' . . . was the Lindbergh baby kidnapping."

Capone apparently thought so.

But he wouldn't just *give* this lead away—he wanted his release to seek the perpetrator personally. While Frankie Rio and other Outfit members went looking for Carey, Capone met repeatedly with the local head of the Secret Service, asking him to serve as a chaperone on the hunt.

On March 10, Capone granted an interview to a columnist with the Hearst syndicate, insisting he could solve the crime if only the government would let him out of jail.

"I'm pretty positive a mob did it," Capone said. "I ought to be able to turn up something in the case. Well, I'm willing. Let's get going."

Capone offered to put up a quarter-of-a-million-dollar bond and leave his brother Mimi behind bars as collateral.

"You don't suppose anybody would suggest that I would double-cross my own brother and leave him here?" Capone asked. Should they fail, Al promised to "come back here, take my brother's place and let justice go on with her racket."

The interview served Capone's purposes in multiple ways. Newspapers ran his offer on front pages nationwide, helping him rehabilitate his image. And the article ranged well beyond the kidnapping, letting him complain of unfair treatment in court.

"How do they know anything about my income since they never proved that I ever received a dollar?" Capone asked. "They may have been able to prove that I spent some money, but that didn't prove that I have any income. What I have might have been given to me by admiring friends."

An Intelligence Unit memo said George E. Q. Johnson felt "quite disturbed" by all this positive press for his old adversary. The prosecutor had already failed to keep rumors of Capone's cushy life in the county jail out of the newspapers. Now Al had gone back to using the media to present himself as a hero.

Prominent lawyers urged a close friend of Lindbergh's to take Capone up on his offer. A senator from Connecticut took the opposing view, accusing Capone of planning the crime as a ploy to win his freedom. But Georgette Winkeler insisted "under no circumstances would [Capone] have harmed a woman or a child."

The interview reached its intended audience. Charles Lindbergh placed a call to the secretary of the Treasury, asking if there was any truth in what Capone had to say. The secretary ordered Elmer Irey to go to New Jersey and consult with Lindbergh.

Back in Chicago, Art Madden of the Intelligence Unit prepared a memo for Irey on what they knew about Capone's offer. Madden found it unlikely Capone would try to escape; rather, he believed the gangster hoped "to procure information that might result in leniency in the end."

But Madden doubted Capone could really deliver.

"It is my judgment," he wrote, "and it is the judgment of the United States Attorney . . . that Capone could only be useful if the kidnapping was perpetrated by underworld characters or characters having underworld connections." And Capone's influence had withered, Madden felt; other mobsters "would now pay no attention to instructions from him."

Irey went to New Jersey and advised Lindbergh to disregard Capone's offer. The aviator, according to Irey, confided he "wouldn't ask for Capone's release . . . even if it would save a life." Impressed by the Intelligence Unit chief, Lindbergh asked Irey to stay on the case. Irey agreed, even though his department had no kidnapping jurisdiction.

Although they never considered releasing Capone, the government took his lead seriously. Irey sent Madden and Frank Wilson to New York with orders to find Bob Carey. They had no luck until August, when the missing man and his girlfriend turned up dead in Manhattan, an apparent murder-suicide. The Intelligence Unit probed a possible connection to the Lindbergh kidnapping, noting the Chicago Outfit learned of Carey's death before it made the papers.

Another explanation surfaced years later, when a former North Side mob truck driver recalled running into Bugs Moran at a bar in 1932. The year before, Moran had left Chicago in exchange for a $25,000-a-year stipend from the Outfit. Now the mobster—still active in northern Illinois and Wisconsin—claimed to have recently "taken care of Bob Carey," apparently in belated payback for St. Valentine's Day.

In the end, Capone's offer did nothing to shorten his prison sentence, while handing the Intelligence Unit another high-profile victory. By asking Elmer Irey for help, Lindbergh had given the Unit their entree into the case, and Irey turned it over to the agents who had gathered the evidence against Capone.

Wilson and Madden supervised the preparation of the ransom money, pushing for the inclusion of highly noticeable gold certificates among the cash. They also recorded the serial numbers over Lindbergh's objections. Exactly who came up with the idea remains in dispute; Irey and Wilson both claim credit for it in their respective memoirs.

Either way, these precautions led directly to the capture of Bruno Richard Hauptmann in 1935 and his dubious conviction the following year. By then, the search was a murder investigation—in May 1932, a wooded area near the Lindbergh home gave up the baby's badly decomposed corpse. In a roundabout way Capone, having failed to return the child, brought the case to its conclusion.

The kidnapping and murder of Lindbergh's infant son provoked a period of national soul-searching. Many saw the child's death as an inevitable reckoning—as if, in the words of one newspaper, "the baby's blood is on the hands of the average American citizen because of his long complacency to crime."

The *New York World-Telegram* explicitly tied the kidnapping to Capone. "God knows why little Charles Lindbergh was murdered," the paper said, "but indirectly the wicked, wanton, causeless crime can be attributed to the wise-cracking, jazzed-up, hypocritical age in which we live—an age . . . that outlaws bootleggers, buys their goods at exorbitant prices, and then claps them in jail when they fail to pay income taxes on the profits they make."

Before the Lindbergh baby had even been found, Chester Gould's comic strip version of Eliot Ness, *Dick Tracy,* rushed into print with its own version of the kidnapping. Not only did Tracy rescue the missing child, the strip's Capone substitute, "Big Boy," masterminded the crime.

Just over a week after police found a decaying corpse and quickly identified it as the Lindbergh baby, Gould gave readers the slam-bang climax real life had denied them: Tracy saved the child and knocked Big Boy senseless. Cold comfort, perhaps, and tasteless to some degree, but the comic strip resolution appealed to a national hunger for black-

and-white battles between good and evil, where the guilty got punished in a way that anyone could understand.

Although he hadn't yet found a way out of jail, Capone could still take comfort in leaving his organization in good hands. His protracted stay in the Cook County Jail allowed him to oversee the Outfit till Frank Nitto got out of Leavenworth. If Nitto had won his parole on schedule, Capone might have begun serving his federal sentence sooner, rather than cooling his heels throughout the appeals process. But George Johnson's failure to confirm the Nitto plea bargain inadvertently delayed the transfer of power.

Since being denied parole in July, Nitto had kept fighting for release. "I have maintained a good conduct record here as I have not been reported for any infraction of the prison rules," Nitto informed the parole board that September. "My file will disclose an offer of a job in Kansas City, Missouri, where I intent [*sic*] to go if released on parole."

After weeks without another hearing, Nitto wrote again, warning he might face difficulty raising the money to pay his fine if he had to spend another "four or five months" behind bars.

George Johnson wrote the parole board as well, after finally submitting his promised report. He included a copy of the missing document with his letter, detailing the plea bargain and urging Nitto's parole. "I have a moral responsibility," Johnson wrote, "of seeing to [it] that a promise made by the United States Attorney is discharged."

Five days after Capone received his sentence, Elmer Irey called the parole board to say Nitto should be released, arranging to meet with the head of the board a few days later. No record of their conversation survives.

So far, Nitto maintained he wouldn't be able to pay his fine until after release. But when reminded the fine was a condition of the sentence and "should be paid without delay," Nitto's wife, Anna, quickly sent in the $10,000.

"I am sure that my husband in view of all that has happened in Chicago . . . has learned his lesson," she wrote, "and I am only standing by him because I know that I shall have no occasion to feel ashamed of anything that he will do in the future."

Her words failed to move the board, which formally denied Nitto's parole.

Anna Nitto responded by visiting George Johnson, insisting Frank would go to Kansas City as soon as he got out of prison and remain on the straight and narrow. Johnson sent three members of the Bureau of Investigation to relay her message to the parole board in a meeting on January 20. Elmer Irey also sat in on the meeting, presumably once again urging Nitto's release, though again no record of what he said survives.

Johnson's report, designed to recommend Nitto's parole, had convinced the board to keep him behind bars. That was the first they learned about Nitto's connection to the Chicago Outfit, and they weren't about to let one of Capone's men out ahead of schedule.

Their decision was final. Despite the head-scratching efforts of George Johnson and Elmer Irey to go to bat for him, Nitto served out his term. With a few months off for good behavior, he left Leavenworth on March 24, a free man.

Since the government had failed to keep its end of the bargain, Nitto saw no reason to do the same. His plans to go to Kansas City and begin an honest career remained indefinitely on hold—had those plans ever really existed.

Four days later, the Associated Press reported Nitto's return to Chicago might initiate "open warfare," with some Outfit members seeking to stop him "from taking charge of the syndicate" during Capone's incarceration.

Two days after Nitto's release, Eliot Ness prepared a report for George Johnson summarizing his activities over the past fifteen months.

The Untouchables, Ness wrote, seized six breweries, five beer distribution plants, four stills, twenty-five trucks, and two cars. Brewery losses cost Capone more than $9.1 million in annual revenue; seized equipment, vehicles, and product another $530,700.

Ness noted, with obvious pride, "the Capone organization felt the presence of this small United States Attorney's group more acutely than any other organization."

As proof, Ness cited growing desperation among Capone's men: "The attitude of the persons arrested has . . . changed from one of kind indulgence such as was shown in the beginning of 1931 to despair and violence . . . as these individuals realize that their backs are to the wall and that the United States Attorney plans to go through with the drastic seizures and arrests to its complete destruction."

For his work on the Capone case, Ness received a promotion to chief investigator of the city's regular Prohibition force. The new job freed him from having to deal with routine raids and busts, placing him in charge of all major liquor cases in Chicago.

By then, the Untouchables had collected some four thousand pages of evidence charting the beer racket's structure. Now they had enough to link Ralph Capone and several others to defendants named in the original Prohibition indictment. On June 10, a year after the first charges came down, federal prosecutors promised to seek a broader indictment wrapping up every known member of the bootleg conspiracy.

"When the bombshell breaks," said the *Chicago Daily News,* "the men at arms of the Capone syndicate, scores of crooked policemen and hungry prohibition agents will be starting out of Chicago with no plans for returning."

But reports of the Outfit's demise were sorely premature. Despite declaring, as late as April 1932, that he was definitely "going to try this case," George Johnson had no intention of actually going through with it. He saw the indictment solely as insurance, a tool to keep Capone behind bars.

With a conspiracy charge hanging over his head, Capone had little hope of winning parole. And if a higher court overturned his tax conviction, the government could use the Prohibition indictment to seize him right away and haul him back into court as a bootlegger.

Although Ness had provided an opening to break up the rest of Capone's gang, Johnson remained narrowly focused on his primary target—the Big Fellow.

The task of distilling all the squad's evidence into a final case report fell to Lyle Chapman, who had returned to Chicago earlier in the year. As usual, Chapman attacked the job with all the sluggishness and recalcitrance that give government employees a bad name.

Soon after receiving the assignment, Chapman asked Special Agent in Charge W. E. Bennett for permission to work at home, where he kept all the evidence—sensitive, irreplaceable documents. This surely horrified Bennett, who ordered Chapman to bring the records into the office at once and place them under lock and key. But Chapman kept dragging his feet.

"It is now approximately two months after you were supposed to start writing this report," Bennett wrote him on August 25, "and I have still to see any evidence of your progress."

Like an exasperated teacher, Bennett ordered Chapman to "conform to the working hours of this office" and to "perform your work . . . in this office," providing status updates every ten days.

Chapman blamed his slow pace on the "awful mass of evidence" the Untouchables had gathered. Records from Ness's earlier investigation of Ralph Capone, including the Montmartre wiretap, now had to be collated with information from more recent raids.

"I think the time is well spent in doing this job in thorough shape," Chapman wrote. "It will not only put everything in shape for the report, but it will be in just the shape the U.S. Attorney trying the case will want it, and the job would have to be done by somebody anyhow."

The Bureau had little choice but to wait. Few agents had Chapman's skills for synthesizing such data or his knowledge of the case.

Meanwhile, Chapman lived in scandalously high style. He'd recently married a woman almost twenty years his junior, and they liked to spend their evenings at the "notorious" Vanity Fair nightclub, where liquor was served openly—"probably a questionable place for government officers to be," Chapman admitted.

He claimed he stuck to ginger ale and ordered it only because everyone around him "was drinking something." But a companion, teenaged Viola Bourke, swore she saw him imbibe more than once. Eager to impress, Chapman would often bring her into the office, brag about his work on the Capone case, and show off pieces of the case file.

The Prohibition Bureau learned of this after Bourke's mother, concerned "her daughter was running around with a 'fast' crowd," complained. Chapman so desperately wanted to be seen as a "big shot," she said, he would display top secret Capone evidence to anyone who cared to see it. And his boasting only got worse when he was drunk.

Other complaints filtered in about the disturbing amount of debt Chapman had racked up. Beginning in early 1931, the Untouchables had received $150 in monthly hazard pay, which Chapman took as license to fill his closet on credit. He spent $400 at one clothing store, and purchased two custom suits from a Detroit tailor for $130.

But after Capone's indictment, the Bureau cut off Chapman's hazard pay, leaving him unable to handle his bills. He made his troubles known to the ever-trusting Ness, who said the Secret Six might tap into their slush fund to help him out. On the strength of Ness's word, Alexander Jamie secured Chapman a loan of $300, which he seems never to have paid back in full.

Bennett put up with Chapman's layabout ways for some time, hoping the Capone report would still materialize. By mid-December, with no report in sight, an exasperated Bennett took Chapman off the case and brought Maurice Seager in from Iowa to finish up. The following summer, in the culling of the force post-Prohibition, Chapman was among the first to go. He returned to California, and spent his later years finding new ways to handicap football teams.

The evidence Ness and the Untouchables gathered did eventually make it into a courtroom, but as part of a civil, not a criminal, proceeding. In September 1935, the city of Chicago sued Al and Ralph Capone, Joe Fusco, Bert Delaney, and several other defendants named in the conspiracy indictment for unpaid sales tax of $119,367 on 15,894.5 barrels of beer sold during Prohibition.

Demanding taxes on the sale of illicit products was bold, especially as these bootleggers had already paid taxes of a sort in the form of bribes to city officials. But some defendants, seeing just another payoff, settled up for a few thousand dollars or, at the very least, a $25 fine. For those who didn't pay, the case ended in July 1942 when the Court dismissed the charges with prejudice.

Though ordered to turn over all evidence, Chapman left the Bureau with one big souvenir: a duplicate of the entire 150-page case file. Three decades later, he showed it off to a reporter who'd come to find out if the Untouchables were anything like they seemed on TV.

"I often find myself looking it over," the seventy-two-year-old Chapman said. "It brings back exciting memories."

Even after all those years, Chapman still wanted to be seen as a big shot.

On May 2, 1932, the United States Supreme Court refused to hear Ca- pone's appeal. Federal officials in Chicago prepared to whisk him away to the federal pen.

Mother Capone was with her son at the county jail when he learned of the decision and flew into a rage, screaming about the plea bargain Wilkerson had refused to let him take.

"I'm still ready to fight if my lawyers say so," Capone said. "The Supreme Court should have reversed my case. The sentence was excessive. I was a victim of public clamor."

The month before, the Supreme Court had ruled the statute of limitations on income tax evasion ran out after three years instead of six. George Johnson had feared just such a ruling—the bulk of the case he and Frank Wilson had built fell outside the three-year limit. And the jury, in their rush to a verdict, had convicted Capone of misdemeanors instead of felonies for 1928 and 1929—the only years unaffected by the court's ruling.

This should have been a major victory for Capone, invalidating all his felony convictions and shaving a decade off his prison sentence. But Michael Ahern and Albert Fink again let their client down, never seriously raising the issue on appeal. And having missed that opportunity, Johnson said, "Capone could not recover it again."

A new set of Capone lawyers would attempt another appeal, arguing that from the moment Judge Wilkerson decided to proceed under the six-year rule "everything done thereafter was void." But the court decided the time Capone spent away from Illinois—whether in Florida or in a Pennsylvania prison—would not be counted toward the statute of limitations. On that absurd basis, Capone's eleven-year sentence stood.

"If the Capone defense had pleaded the statute of limitations in his behalf at the trial," observed the *Christian Science Monitor*, "he probably would have gone free."

Only then did Capone realize how badly Ahern and Fink had mishandled his case. Eventually, he would demand his money back. But the pair's incompetence had been obvious all along—they never sought a change of venue from a clearly biased judge; failed to challenge such key evidence as the Hawthorne Smoke Shop ledger, the Mattingly letter, and the signed check; and all but ignored the central issue: the statute of limitations.

Even worse, their half-baked defense played right into the prosecution's hands, providing evidence of Capone earning a large and taxable income. One lawyer who studied the case described Ahern and Fink as "really inept," their courtroom tactics "terrible."

But Ralph Capone had another explanation. According to his granddaughter, Bottles believed the Secret Six bribed Ahern and Fink to throw the case. Of course, the Six never proved themselves that effective, but a payoff from somewhere would explain the awful performance of two otherwise successful attorneys.

On May 3, Capone awoke at 8:00 A.M. A light rain dampened the city, gloomy skies a perfect match for Capone's mood. He ate little for breakfast, then packed the few items he needed for his trip: a toothbrush, a clean shirt, and a pair of socks. His hairbrushes went as a parting gift to his cellmate, a teenager accused of voter fraud.

"Here, kid," Capone said. "Go brush your hair."

Restless and surly, Capone paced his cell and played cards with his cellmate, who kept trying to cheer him up. But Capone's cocky confidence had dissolved.

Fink and Ahern arrived later that morning for a brief conference. Like doctors with a terminal patient, they could offer little hope.

"I don't know anything we can do for him now," Fink told reporters as he left the jail.

After all, hadn't they done enough?

At noon, U.S. Marshal Henry Laubenheimer received the court order sending Capone to the penitentiary. Most everyone, the prisoner included, assumed Capone would go to Leavenworth, where Jack Guzik was serving his own tax-evasion term.

But the Justice Department, seeking to isolate Capone from his allies, chose instead to send him to Atlanta, reputed to be the "toughest" federal prison in the country. The once-proud bootleg baron, rumor said, would soon be washing other prisoners' dirty laundry.

After lunch, which Capone chose not to eat, his family arrived to say good-bye. Mae, Sonny, Theresa, Mafalda, and Capone's younger brother Matthew crowded into the cell as a deputy warden, a deputy marshal, and a cop kept watch.

"For a while there was quiet weeping," reported the *Herald and Examiner*. "Whispered conversation. Impulsive embraces." Then the family left, eyes dry, bodies dragging.

Federal officials reserved a Pullman car on the southbound Dixie Flyer leaving Dearborn Station at 11:30 P.M. They hoped to keep their destination secret, but word of the last-minute switch leaked out almost immediately.

Capone heard the news that evening in his cell over the radio. Fearing the gang might attempt a rescue, or that someone would try to shoot Capone, the authorities gathered twenty men—police detectives, Prohibition agents, and deputy marshals—to guard him from all sides. Among those chosen was Eliot Ness, ready to see the work of the Untouchables to its conclusion.

Ness arrived at the county jail around 9:30 P.M., in a light fedora and a rain-flecked topcoat. Marshal Laubenheimer, fifty-eight, face as pinched as a Puritan preacher's, gave the clerk his warrant for "the bodies of one Alphonse Capone and one Vito Morici." The latter—a young car thief, handsome, slight—was headed to Florida for trial.

Capone left his cell wearing a topcoat over a custom-tailored $125 blue suit and his trademark pearl-gray fedora with matching ribbon, looking every bit the iconic gangster. When the marshals shackled him to Morici, Capone asked his handcuffs be kept out of sight. He didn't mind press photogs or onlookers as much as the newsreel cameramen—Al didn't want his moviegoing son seeing his father looking like a crook.

The prisoners walked out into the receiving yard ten minutes before ten, surrounded by Ness and the other guards. The group had to push its way past a throng of photographers. Camera flashes assaulted Capone's eyes; huge lamps, set up by the newsreel crews, bathed the whole scene in light. An occasional flare split the night sky.

Capone smiled around the cigar clamped between his teeth, doing nothing to hide his notorious scars. "You'd think Mussolini was passin' through," he said.

"You got a bum break, Al," someone shouted.

The marshals loaded the prisoners into Laubenheimer's car. Ness took his place inside the lead vehicle, peeling out the front gate just after 10:00 P.M. A crowd outside hoped for a glimpse of Capone, but the car carrying the gangster charged out of the jail, sending onlookers scattering.

"After that it was every driver for himself," reported the *New York Times.* "Fenders and bumpers clashed and pedestrians were trampled in the stampede to avoid being hit by the fast moving official motors."

The convoy of cars raced up California Avenue, then cut across Ogden to Jackson. Wailing sirens echoed through the Loop, alerting everyone to the passing procession.

"Police officials," said the *Times,* "described the ride . . . as the wildest and noisiest in their experience."

At Clark Street, a stoplight brought the parade to a halt. Capone found himself outside the great "granite octopus" of the Federal Building, the last place he'd entered as a free man. Then the cars whipped around the corner and screeched to a stop in front of Dearborn Station, its redbrick clock tower looking out over the Transportation Building half a block away.

More onlookers pressed in as the marshals struggled to get Capone out of the car, the handcuffs and his bulk making it difficult to maneuver. The prisoner couldn't hide his distress, looking like "a picture of misery," according to the *Times,* but he managed a few smiles for the cameras. Then, as the group moved into the station, Capone jerked at the handcuffs, temper flaring, pulling Morici along.

"Damn it, come on," he snapped.

The deputy marshals led the way, clearing a path into the train shed with police picking up the rear. Capone walked at the center of the thick knot of men, hands thrust deep into his pockets to hide the cuffs. Marshals strode on either side, Morici just behind. Ness marched at Capone's right, at times within arm's length of him. As they rounded a corner, straight into another snarl of press, Ness straightened his hat and tugged at the lapel of his coat, as if collecting himself for the cameras. His head jerked back and forth from the crowd to Capone. The gangster lumbered forward calmly, seemingly unfazed, with a faint, defiant sneer. A wire service photographer snapped their picture—the only known photo of both adversaries together.

Just before they reached the Pullman car, Capone spotted a few old friends among the crowd, including two of his younger brothers. They exchanged nonverbal good-byes. Then the marshals led Capone up and inside the train, securing him and Morici in the first compartment. Reporters crowded into the car, eager to snap a photo or snag a quote.

As the Dixie Flyer pulled away, Ness stood on the platform, watching it disappear into the night. This was the closest he'd ever get to Capone, his one chance to meet the man face-to-face. He'd been circling the gangster for almost four years—breaking up the Outfit's allies in Chicago Heights, listening in on Ralph's operations in Cicero, and finally with his raiders hounding "Snorky" to the gates of federal prison.

Seeing Capone depart filled Ness with immense relief, and the sense the Untouchables had served their purpose. Yet he felt a certain emptiness, too, after this final, fleeting brush with the nemesis he'd been denied taking head-on.

"We did our part, of course," Ness later told a reporter. "But the real work of sending Capone to prison was done by the tax investigators. Our job was more spectacular, that was all."

His modesty would not be contagious: the tax men would in future often neglect to mention Ness and the Untouchables, or play down their role shamefully.

Capone was thirty-three, Ness twenty-nine. Each had used up more than half his life, and neither would see the other again.

Frank Nitto in 1933. *(Abraham Lincoln Presidential Library & Museum [ALPLM])*

Thirty

1932–1934

Like Al Capone, Secret Six financier Samuel Insull spent the waning days of the Roaring Twenties defending his empire from greedy rivals, battling not with bullets but with stocks and bonds. After the stock market crash, Insull created holding companies to prop up his failing empire. High-pressure salesmen went out falsely inflating stock values, trading on the great man's good name, targeting "little people."

Insull took out massive illegal loans from Chicago's biggest banks, burdening his holding companies with catastrophic debt. As one judge observed, Insull's empire devolved into "nothing but a glorified gambling institution."

The collapse came in the spring of 1932. Chicagoans watched in horror as Insull's companies filed bankruptcy, igniting a panic culminating with forty-two bank failures, hundreds of millions of dollars gone, thousands of investors ruined.

Facing state and federal fraud and embezzlement charges, a confused Insull fled to Europe. "What have I done," he asked, "that every banker and business magnate has not done in the course of business?"

Not much—Senate hearings in early 1933 uncovered the roots of the stock market crash, exposing the heads of major financial institutions gambling recklessly with depositor savings, paying themselves huge bonuses, short-selling their own stock, and giving preferential loans to Insull and other insiders.

President Hoover, noting the unmasking of these corrupt bankers with disgust and dismay, told his attorney general, "If only part of the things brought out prove true, these men have done the American people more damage than . . . Al Capone."

They were not bankers, Hoover wrote, but "banksters who rob the poor, drive the innocent to poverty and suicide and do infinite injury to those who honestly work and strive."

The public wanted someone to pay for all the sins of the Roaring Twenties, and the government chose Insull. An extradited Insull arrived in federal court almost exactly three years after the Capone trial, to face lead prosecutor Dwight Green, a Johnson assistant on the Capone tax case. Green didn't have just one incriminating ledger, but enough financial records to dizzy a jury.

Insull's lawyer made the same argument as Capone's—the government indicted his client not because he'd done anything wrong, but because of what he'd come to symbolize.

Insull even faced the same judge as Capone: James H. Wilkerson.

Back in January 1932, Herbert Hoover had rewarded Wilkerson with a nomination to the Circuit Court of Appeals, a stepping-stone to the Supreme Court. But that stalled in the Senate over organized labor's objections to the judge's antiunion prejudice.

The confirmation hearings also turned up evidence of Wilkerson's unethical handling of bankruptcy cases, verging on outright corruption—"a pure and simple racket," according to congressional investigators. The judge's boosters played up his gangbuster record, slandering his critics as allies of organized crime. But the political winds had shifted—the nomination would never come up for a Senate vote.

Wilkerson's misconduct led to calls for impeachment, though he remained on the federal bench when Samuel Insull came before him. Perhaps because the two men had been friends for decades, Wilkerson's rulings heavily favored the defense, helping portray Insull as a victim of his own success, as much a casualty of the financial collapse as his investors.

The jury decided on acquittal in five minutes, but waited two hours to announce it, not wanting to look hasty.

Insull died in Paris in 1938, at least $14 million in debt but never convicted of any crime. Wilkerson retired from the bench three years later, his reputation for honesty overruling memories of his more questionable conduct—to say nothing of his narrow definition of running a racket.

The Secret Six, dealt a serious blow by the collapse of Insull's empire, struggled to stay afloat.

Alexander Jamie said he had some fifteen investigators on staff, though an agent with the Bureau of Investigation put the actual number at no more than five.

"I am inclined to believe," the agent reported, "that the Secret Six is gradually passing out of existence."

But the Six's public profile remained high. A 1931 film, *The Secret 6*, glorified the group as "the greatest force for law and order in the United States." Copycat crime commissions sprang up around the country.

Robert Isham Randolph became a national law enforcement authority, advocating Prohibition's repeal and a federal antikidnapping law. He bragged of driving around town with a gun in hand, "ready to shoot to kill," and openly defended police using the third degree.

Yet for all Randolph's talk, battling gangsters seems not to have been the Six's primary mission. Instead, they focused largely on crimes against the rich—extortion, kidnapping, and labor trouble. Their most shadowy work, according to the *New York Times*, didn't involve organized crime at all, but rather suppressing "political matters such as communism, which involves criminal activity only occasionally."

When Secret Six investigators searched for the sender of threatening letters to a steel company executive's daughter, they arrested a young

broker named William Kuhn. But after another poison-pen letter—
sent while Kuhn was in custody—cleared the broker, a $100,000 law-
suit was filed against Jamie and others for false arrest and malicious
prosecution, exposing the Six's shoddy detective work in the press.

The Six's most publicized success involved a $2.8 million bank heist
in Lincoln, Nebraska. Jamie cracked that case by having Gus Winkeler
charged with the crime—not because he believed the former American
Boy had anything to do with it, but because he hoped the killer could
lean on underworld contacts to get the bonds back. Winkeler did just
that, "thereby saving," Jamie wrote, "five banks from possible closing."

But not everyone approved of Jamie's methods. Nebraska's governor,
disgusted Jamie would bargain with such a notorious criminal, called
the deal "one of the blackest pages in the history of Nebraska." Other
investigations echoed the work Jamie had done for the Pullman Company, helping businessmen keep tabs on workers. In one case, a Secret Six
operative posed as a labor organizer to spy on Standard Oil employees.
He and Jamie gave their findings to the company for $5,000.

Such cases didn't make the papers, preserving the Six's antigangster
image. In truth, they'd become a private police force for the wealthy,
dangerously unregulated and hidden from public scrutiny. Tapping
phone lines and paying off informers, they amassed information ripe
for blackmail, even as Jamie staffed his group with castoff cops and
criminals.

Among them was Shirley Kub, a former snitch for the Chicago
P.D. now in her early forties. The stout, diminutive investigator was no
looker, her spine bent by a childhood tumble. Savvy or perhaps crazy,
she had a magnetic personality and a smooth tongue that, one police
official noted, made her "a dangerous person to have around."

Somehow Jamie fell under her spell. They made an odd pair—
drawling six-footer Jamie and glib four-footer Kub. She did most of the
talking, and he would light two cigarettes at a time for them. Although
privately resenting Jamie for bringing such a disreputable character into
the Six, Randolph stuck up for them in public.

"When digging in the mud," Randolph told the *Evening Post*, "you use mud-digging tools."

Kub won Jamie's confidence with an outlandish story custom-fit for his vanity and ambition. She described a nationwide "Crime Syndicate" taking orders from a shadowy organization—"The System"—made up of leaders in business and government. The System extorted money from The Syndicate, sending those who couldn't pay to prison.

Kub said The Syndicate, having resolved to expose The System, wanted Jamie—a man "absolutely clean and free from any double-crossing"—to do the job. Playing on his yen to return to the Bureau of Investigation, Kub hinted The System included the man who'd kicked him out—J. Edgar Hoover. Expose Hoover, Kub said, and Jamie would be first in line to take over.

Breaking up The System became Jamie's "crusade," even as Kub sold info from his files to the underworld. State's Attorney John Swanson—who'd inspired Randolph to establish the Six—suspected blackmail, and tapped Kub's office phone.

When Jamie found out, he and Randolph launched a mudslinging campaign to foil Swanson's reelection, damaging only the Six's reputation. George Johnson, once a backer of the Six, now considered it untrustworthy.

Jamie laid off half the Six's staff, claiming a lack of funds. Among those who lost their jobs was Jamie's stenographer, Edna Ness. Her abrupt dismissal, apparently on Kub's orders, drove a rift between Jamie and his onetime hero-worshiping brother-in-law, Eliot Ness.

The once-inseparable pair had chosen very different paths. Ness embraced the ethos he'd learned from August Vollmer—he might bend the rules to make a case, but he always saw himself as a servant of the public good.

Jamie let his ambition warp his judgment, his allegiance going to the rich men who paid his salary. As he let Kub take over his life, he seems to have grown apart from Ness.

William Froelich told the Bureau of Investigation in 1933 "that misunderstandings exist between [Ness] and his brother-in-law." Though Jamie's son Wallace remained close to Eliot, the in-laws were clearly on the outs—the two men seem not to have kept in touch after the early 1930s.

The Chicago Association of Commerce disbanded the Six in April 1933, replacing it with a "Co-ordinating Committee for Prevention of Crime and Civic Injustice." Fearing information gathered by the Six might be blackmail fodder, the new committee burned the group's records.

Jamie went into business as a private investigator, still working to expose The System and restore his good name. In 1935, wealthy residents of Minneapolis hired him to run a committee gathering dirt on local labor unions.

Once again, Jamie turned to Kub. She told him whom to hire as investigators, siphoning off anything they uncovered for blackmail fodder. Throughout, she kept Jamie hooked with the idea of toppling J. Edgar Hoover. But in early 1936, a former FBI agent exposed Kub's lies to Jamie.

"I had the utmost confidence in Mrs. Kub's sincerity . . . ," Jamie wrote, "and in spite of the loss of my position and two years of unpaid effort . . . the greatest disappointment is that I could have been so deceived."

He would later attempt a return to federal service, but the Treasury Department wanted nothing to do with him, his long history with Kub leaving his reputation in ruins.

In the months following Capone's departure, Eliot Ness and Prohibition Administrator Malachi Harney launched an aggressive effort to shut down every brewery, still, and speakeasy in Chicago. They mapped out the city's known watering holes—nearly two thousand—and promised to padlock them all. Their pledge prompted laughter from the city's seasoned reporters, but Harney remained undeterred.

"We'll close these places, positively, as fast as we can get around to it," he said, adding they'd shuttered thirty speakeasies just that past weekend.

The raids and arrests came at a bad time for the already weakened Outfit. The Depression had driven down prices, but Ness's raids forced the mob to keep charging $55 for a barrel of beer, squeezing their profit margin even further. With Capone in prison, Joe Fusco had stepped in to run the beer racket, but Ness kept shutting his breweries down.

By mid-July, Fusco and Bert Delaney had no choice but to slash wages. Truckers responded by going on strike.

"Matters became so desperate," reported the *Tribune*, "that Fusco and Delaney themselves, gallantly arrayed in white linen suits, buckskin shoes, and panamas, were forced to get out and hustle a few barrels of beer."

After that daylong indignity, they called another meeting. The drivers walked in to find a muscle-bound bruiser, "Mussolini," cracking a whip and flanked by two hoods. Work resumed the next day.

That fall, Ness's agents arrested two men delivering Capone beer to a South State Street speakeasy. The pair drove a Ford sedan converted into a camouflaged delivery vehicle. All the seats, save the driver's, had been removed and a pair of skids installed under the door, so beer barrels could be rolled into and out of the vehicle.

"We have seized so many of their trucks that the syndicate is running short on finances," Ness told the press. "Also, they probably thought they could fool the agents with these small automobiles."

What they drove didn't matter—the days of hauling contraband freely through Chicago's streets were long over.

As the last full year of national Prohibition drew to a close, the booze business had grown so quiet Ness and his raiders had to go outside the city for action. In early September, they raided a brewery concealed on a farm in Lake County, Illinois, arresting four people and confiscating ten thousand gallons of beer. The brewery belonged to Bugs Moran, who had taken over Lake County's gambling and liquor rackets since leaving Chicago, so well hidden the agents had to search for three weeks—by land and by air—to find it.

Then, on December 27, Ness's men smashed a still hidden on the upper level of a barn on a dairy farm near Dundee, Illinois. After making seven arrests, the agents found themselves in a predicament.

"For there were forty dairy cows on the place," reported the *Herald and Examiner*, "and neither Eliot Ness . . . nor any of his assistants was able to milk a cow."

Fortunately, the arrested men made bond, getting back to their barn in time to give the cows much-needed relief.

On January 9, police pulled in Bert Delaney, onetime head of Capone's $20 million-a-year beer business, who now insisted he was eking out a living as a trucker, hauling produce for eighty-five cents a barrel.

"Why pick me up?" Delaney complained. "Once I was in the bucks. Now the racket is done. Eliot Ness of the prohibition department put Capone out and everybody else has folded up. There's no more money in anything crooked."

Thanks in part to the deepening Depression, Ness's strategy of bankrupting the gang was proving remarkably effective. But that would only work as long as the Outfit depended on alcohol to stay in business—and as long as booze remained illegal.

Delaney would spend the next few years trying to make his way as a labor racketeer, but success eluded him. He died in October 1938, shot in the back.

Mayor Anton Cermak seemed to be fulfilling his pledge to voters to cleanse the city of crime, assuring rich backers he'd do so before the World's Fair opened. But to Frank Nitto and his associates, Cermak wasn't battling crime—he was targeting only the gangs who'd backed his opponent, Big Bill Thompson.

The new mayor didn't go after gangsters on his own West Side, or certain North Side gangs, either. Deals had been sealed and plans made to remove Nitto and take over Outfit bootlegging and gambling rackets, giving Cermak domain over vice citywide.

On December 19, Harry Lang and Harry Miller, bent cops assigned to the mayor as his "hoodlum squad," raided the offices of the Quality Flour Company, an Outfit front on the fifth floor of 221 North La Salle.

Stupidly taking along a cop unaware of their intentions—and who would expose them in court—the two Harrys rousted half a dozen mobsters, including Frank Nitto.

Lang shot the handcuffed Nitto three times. As Capone's successor fell, apparently mortally wounded, Lang gave himself a flesh wound and beat his victim to a doctor.

While Nitto clung to life in a hospital bed, Eliot Ness interrogated Louis Campagna and five other hoods arrested at the "flour company" offices. Campagna set the tone by remaining tight-lipped. The other gangsters followed his lead, refusing to give up any useful information. Before long, they all got out on bail.

Two months later, a Sicilian assassin fatally shot Mayor Cermak in Miami at a rally for President-elect Franklin Roosevelt. History records the shooting as a botched attempt on FDR's life, but Chicago gangland observers—including Frank Loesch and Judge John Lyle—always held that Giuseppe Zangara was on a suicide mission for the Outfit.

In late February 1933, Ness raided a major brewery occupying the top two floors of a South Side warehouse near the University of Chicago. With Ness in the lead, the raiders hurried up a fire escape and broke in through a window, discovering a $100,000 plant capable of turning out $10,000 worth of beer a day. The bust turned violent—two men inside assaulted a raider before their arrest.

Ness couldn't have known it, but he'd never raid another Capone brewery. The federal government, with the best of intentions, was about to take away his primary means of fighting the mob.

A few days later, Franklin Delano Roosevelt took his oath of office. During the campaign, Roosevelt had promised to legalize real beer "just as fast as the Lord will let us." His pledge had to wait amid the flurry of his first week in office, as he worked to pull the country out of an economic tailspin. Some of those measures required serious belt tightening, but the new president knew just how to win the public over.

On March 12, he told his aides: "It's time the country did something about beer."

Later that night, the president drafted a three-sentence amendment to the Volstead Act, redefining "intoxicating liquor" to exclude 3.2 percent beer. Cheers greeted the proposal at the Capitol; Congress passed it immediately. The Eighteenth Amendment remained in effect, but the beleaguered nation celebrated this as its symbolic end. A truck loaded with beer arrived at the White House under police escort, carrying a banner that proclaimed: PRESIDENT ROOSEVELT, THE FIRST BEER IS FOR YOU.

"Bars were opening overnight, with every other beer on the house!" Studs Terkel recalled. "In the midst of the Depression it was a note of hope that something would be better."

Robert Isham Randolph had long argued legalizing beer would deal a fatal blow to organized crime. Now the president put that thinking to the test, claiming the previous summer "that this is a way to divert $300 million or more by way of taxes from the pockets of the racketeers into the Treasury of the United States."

But the bootleggers had burrowed in so deeply, they naturally had a head start on legitimate competition. And with their illicit brewing operations in tatters, Chicago gangsters saw the return of legal beer as a much-needed source of new revenue.

In the spring of 1933, Ness told reporters the bootleg gangs would do whatever it took to control the beer business. Already federal officials had reports of gangsters telling Chicago retailers to buy Outfit beer "or else."

As Ness saw it, the government's best hope of beating back the mob lay in controlling who got licenses to open up legitimate breweries. Gangsters might use men with clean records as fronts, or take over brewing companies by buying up stock—the feds had to vigorously investigate possible mob ties, or else hand the industry back over to the gangs.

"Only a dictator for the breweries," Ness said, "can meet the problem."

That dictatorship fell to Ness's old boss, E. C. Yellowley, who promised to investigate applicants for brewing permits "from top to bottom." Once again, Yellowley's leadership left much to be desired. In 1934, he failed to stop Joe Fusco's distribution company, Gold Seal Liquors, from getting its own license. Yellowley later personally renewed the permit, citing evidence of Fusco's criminal activities as "not very strong."

Ness and the Untouchables had previously identified Fusco as a key Outfit leader, but the hood's role in the racket remained unproven, because George Johnson never brought their case to trial. Now this onetime "public enemy" claimed he'd gone legit, and no one could prove otherwise.

So had Nick Juffra, the onetime beer baron Ness arrested during Capone's trial, who soon found work with a liquor wholesaler.

Through such semilegitimate businessmen, organized crime infiltrated American commerce in the post-Prohibition era. Fusco and his associates locked up a sizable chunk of the midwestern beer and liquor market, enforcing their monopoly with pipe bombs. By the early 1950s, Fusco took in a reputed $30 million in gross annual sales.

As the head of the Chicago Crime Commission observed in 1952, "The repeal of Prohibition has not interfered with the lucrative nature of Chicago's liquor and beer industry insofar as some of Al Capone's friends are concerned."

By locking Capone up for income tax evasion, the feds proudly and publicly plucked the largest criminal weed in Chicago, but left the root structure intact.

Within days of legal beer's return, Michigan became the first state to ratify the Twenty-First Amendment to the Constitution, to repeal the Eighteenth. As the amendment raced toward ratification, its success a foregone conclusion, the Prohibition Bureau faced extinction; deep cuts whittled their agents down to a select few—mostly "elders."

Despite his youth, Ness managed to hang on. He kept working with his usual determination, in June raiding his biggest still yet. Concealed on the top floors of an iron company warehouse, this $250,000 "cooker in the sky" was reportedly the last major Outfit distillery, its demise marking the end of Ness's anti-Capone campaign.

The new attorney general, Homer Cummings, had plans for what remained of the Prohibition Bureau. He dreamed of creating a new federal law enforcement agency, an "American Scotland Yard" making war on organized crime. J. Edgar Hoover's Bureau of Investigation fit the bill, but remained small and largely unknown, employing just 326 agents.

Cummings needed more men, and the Prohibition Bureau had them to spare, even at reduced strength—1,200 agents who, unlike Hoover's, had experience carrying guns. On June 10, Roosevelt signed an executive order merging both bureaus into a new Division of Investigation. But Hoover bristled at the thought of so many corrupt and inept dry agents flooding his ranks.

"They would have swamped us," Hoover said, "and undone all the work we had done to make the Bureau honest, sound, and efficient."

Then on June 17, bandits opened fire on a group of law enforcement officers in Kansas City, killing one of Hoover's agents. This "Kansas City Massacre" galvanized the nation, spurring Cummings and Hoover to build their "super police force" without castoffs from the Prohibition Bureau. When Hoover became director of the new Division on August 10, he sequestered the dry agents into their own Alcoholic Beverage Unit.

Ness now reported, at least indirectly, to J. Edgar Hoover, but he abhorred the Prohibition ghetto and hoped to join the Division's elite special agents, the G-men doing battle with bandit gangs roaming the Midwest.

Hoover's agents, like Ness, were mostly college boys, typically with law degrees. But their book-learning didn't always translate into street smarts. Too many lacked Ness's law enforcement experience and ability to keep a cool head. In the coming months, they would shoot multiple innocent bystanders and repeatedly let suspects slip away.

With Hoover sorely needing competent men, Ness's background and temperament made him an ideal candidate. But in trying to win that job, he would compromise the one trait that always set him apart: his straight-arrow honesty.

After a miraculous recovery from his gunshot wounds, Frank Nitto went back to furthering Capone's plans to muscle in on legitimate industry by taking over labor unions. He displayed little of the Big Fellow's trademark charm and empathy; no newsmen ever wrote misty-eyed profiles of Nitto.

"If you don't do like I say," Nitto told one union official, "you'll get shot in the head. How would your old lady look in black?"

Through such strong-arm tactics, the Outfit came to control Chicago's bartenders' union, drumming up business for their legitimate breweries and distilleries.

"We've got the world by the tail with a downhill start," Nitto said in the summer of 1933.

Having seemingly learned from Capone's mistakes, Nitto kept a low profile—refining the organization, shaving off its rough edges to create the modern Syndicate. With the same cold ruthlessness marking the murders of Hymie Weiss and Joe Aiello, Nitto wiped out the gunslingers who had made the Beer Wars so bloody.

Gus Winkeler of the St. Valentine's hit squad bought it in October 1933, shot in the back on a North Side street. Another American Boy, Fred Goetz, died in a shotgun ambush a few months later. Winkeler's wife, Georgette, saw the killings as an attempt to stifle any and all opposition.

With the deaths of these "independent bastards," as one Outfit member called them, others rose to take their place, men more in Nitto's businessman mold—addicted to their work, scorning the spotlight, undistracted by the pleasures and passions leading to Capone's downfall. Their ranks included Louis Campagna, Joe Fusco, and up-and-comer Paul Ricca, who emerged as Nitto's protégé, as Nitto had once been Capone's. Above all, they avoided the kind of publicity that painted a target on Capone's back.

Racing remained a major source of Outfit revenue, thanks to the ever-resourceful E. J. O'Hare. After all his talk of separating himself from the mob, O'Hare only got in deeper following Capone's conviction.

As much of the country made Depression ends meet, O'Hare raked in millions. By 1939, he controlled dog- and horse-racing tracks in six states, with Nitto a silent partner in at least three. But Artful Eddie's ambition outstripped his judgment. On November 8, 1939, after trying to cheat Nitto out of his share, O'Hare was shot to death while driving home from his Cicero track.

Only then did the *Tribune* reveal O'Hare's role in the Capone investigation. O'Hare's motives, they said, were twofold: to save himself from prosecution on tax charges, and to protect the Outfit from damage caused by Capone's notoriety. Raids, arrests, and high bail bonds "put a serious crimp in the gang's revenue," said the *Trib*. "It is significant that O'Hare's real rise to power in the gang began with Capone's departure for prison."

Publisher Robert McCormick nonetheless found a way to repay O'Hare for his role in Capone's conviction, pushing in 1949 to name Chicago's international airport for another Ed O'Hare—son Butch, the first navy flier to receive the Medal of Honor in World War II.

The inquiry into the O'Hare murder uncovered a familiar name: Leslie Shumway. Investigators were shocked to discover the bookkeeper whose testimony landed Capone in jail had worked until recently as the pari-mutuel betting manager at Sportsman's Park, the Cicero racetrack run by O'Hare under the Outfit's aegis.

Unlike O'Hare, Shumway's role in Capone's downfall was no secret—he had testified before the gangster in open court. Yet here he was, less than ten years later, working amid underworld characters known for having very long and unforgiving memories. And he would continue to work in Outfit-affiliated tracks until at least 1950, when his employer claimed that Shumway's presence proved he had no gang-land ties.

"If I had any strings on Capone," the track owner said, "or he had on me, is it likely that Shumway would be working in that track?"

Likely or not, Shumway stayed in Miami, dying in 1964 at the ripe old age of eighty-six. His continued association with the Outfit reflected their approval of what he'd done in 1931—fingering Capone without touching other gangsters. The little bookkeeper had, after all, played a key role in a coup d'état, removing a mob boss whose notoriety and increasingly erratic leadership threatened the entire organization.

The men who took over the Outfit benefited from, and welcomed, Capone's departure. Although rumors would persist of Capone directing the gang from jail, in reality he was suddenly cut off after 1932—a surprising circumstance, given that prison bars had never stopped him from running his rackets before.

Instead, Frank Nitto slid quickly onto the throne, showing little further interest in his old boyhood friend from Brooklyn. When coupled with Shumway's otherwise inexplicable survival, Nitto's behavior during and after the investigation suggests a possibility never seriously considered by gangland observers—that he used the income tax case to get Capone out of the way.

As Frank Wilson told the story, O'Hare acted alone, informing on Capone out of love for his son. But O'Hare passed along information he couldn't have known on his own, and the *Tribune* referred to at least one other "gang associate" who informed along with him.

That Nitto, and perhaps other gangsters as well, also served as a conduit to the tax investigators seems obvious. Why else would Nitto meet with Wilson's two key informers, O'Hare and St. Louis reporter John Rogers, at Leavenworth in March 1931—less than two weeks after Shumway testified before the grand jury?

Equally telling is Nitto's refusal of Gus Winkeler's offer to fix Capone's trial. As Winkeler explained it, Nitto and his top aides wanted Capone gone so they could be in charge.

Nitto might have been in league with Johnny Torrio, perhaps doing the elder gangster's bidding. Torrio had long desired a peaceful, profitable, smoothly operating Outfit; after reclaiming certain powers from Capone at the Atlantic City conference, he'd surely seen how Chicago's gangsters got along while the Big Fellow was locked up elsewhere. Maybe that brief stay behind bars convinced Torrio that his former protégé had to go—for the good of the organization. And with Capone safely behind federal bars, Torrio finally got his wish.

In their single-minded determination to topple Scarface, George Johnson and the tax investigators had unwittingly facilitated the transfer of power from Capone to Nitto, allowing the Outfit to go underground and evolve into something far more insidious.

Whether Nitto informed on Capone directly, or hid behind O'Hare and Rogers, will likely never be known. But what *is* known is this: on May 5, 1931, one month before Capone's indictment on tax charges, Frank Wilson of the Intelligence Unit met with Nitto at Leavenworth. And five days after Capone was sentenced to prison, Wilson's boss, Elmer Irey, called the head of the parole board to urge Nitto's early release.

Perhaps Irey simply wanted to abide by the plea bargain Johnson had struck, believing Nitto sincerely intended to abandon his criminal career. Or perhaps his call was meant as a reward for services rendered.

In the summer of 1933, Eliot Ness made himself a presence around the office of flamboyant Illinois senator J. Hamilton Lewis, who shared the Bankers Building with the Chicago branch of the Division of Investigation.

Ness appears to have been trying, as Alexander Jamie had so often done, to make a political contact who could help him switch jobs. Democrat Lewis had long controlled federal patronage in Ness's home state, making him just the man to see about pulling strings with the Justice Department.

That August, Ness met frequently with Lewis's secretary, a man known to authorities only as Mr. Kemp. During one visit, Kemp introduced Ness to Walter Newton, a young Ninth Ward precinct captain who worked as a Bankers Building elevator operator. Newton hoped to help a constituent, Joe Kulak, a Polish immigrant who ran an illicit still.

After promising to get payoff-seeking cops off Kulak's back, Newton went to see Kemp, who agreed to arrange protection for a few hundred dollars a month. Days later, Newton came back to make sure the deal was squared away and was assured it was. Ness, sitting a few feet away, apparently took no notice of the conversation.

But when the police kept shaking Kulak down, Newton returned to the senator's office and once again found Kemp with Ness. When Newton asked why the still hadn't been protected, Kemp "patted Mr. Ness on the back and told him to give the boys a break." Then he wrote down Kulak's address and handed it to Ness, who slipped it inside his jacket and told Kemp "that it would be OK."

Newton went downstairs and waited for Ness to get off the elevator, then hit him up for more information. Although Ness had no authority over the cops harassing Kulak, he said (according to Newton) "that if the police bothered Joe, there will be no case on it."

This was a statement of fact—with the dry law limping toward its demise, Kulak faced a slim chance of prosecution. When Newton asked how many dry agents remained in Chicago, Ness replied "very few"—again, the obvious. Newton assumed Ness expected a bribe, and offered to "take care of him." But Ness "shook his head and didn't answer."

Ness had never much cared about busting small, lone operators like Kulak, who didn't make nearly enough money to contribute more than a trickle to the flood of Prohibition-era corruption. Better to go after the major players.

But Newton took his words as a promise, reporting back Ness had them covered. To make it official, Newton gave Kulak a handwritten note directing anyone who raided the still to see Kemp "or E. Ness."

Ness did nothing to shelter the still—six Prohibition agents raided it a few weeks later, placing Kulak under arrest. The agents found Newton's note on him, with its damning implication Ness was on the take.

The Unit launched a full investigation, interrogating both Newton and Kulak. Neither said anything suggesting Ness was corrupt, but Newton's statement indicated Ness at least knew of the still. The new Chicago Prohibition office chief, Robert Coyne, questioned Ness on August 28.

The two men had once been rivals—Coyne had dated Edna Stahle before she became Mrs. Ness. Now the new chief held her husband's federal fate in his hands. Although no report on their conversation survives, Ness never faced any formal disciplinary action—nor, apparently, was Kulak prosecuted.

But within a month, the Unit transferred Ness to the Cincinnati office, his first posting outside Chicago. This may well have been a penance—if Ness hadn't exactly crossed a line, he'd come dangerously close, led astray by his own ambition. In his determination to move up the federal ladder, Ness had stumbled, attempting the brand of Chicago politicking he'd always before rejected—only to have it backfire terribly.

The man who spurned Capone's offer of $2,000 a week still wouldn't accept a bribe to protect anyone. But he would, with reluctance, let slip a small-timer like Kulak, who was breaking a law soon to be defunct, if it meant staying in the good graces of a powerful friend.

The transfer came just as Ness's marriage was fraying. Edna felt her husband's extended family, the Jamies, thought Eliot had married beneath him—Edna might be good enough to be Alexander's secretary, but not his sister-in-law. Her firing from the Secret Six must have increased her resentment, with Eliot's closeness to Jamie's son, Wallace, an ongoing source of tension.

On weekends, Ness often spent his time with Wallace, not Edna; when she'd suggest an evening out, he'd be too tired, saying she didn't like spending time with his friends anyway. Feeling abandoned, Edna stayed in touch with Robert Coyne, her old beau, "a very dear friend."

Edna took to sitting around the Chicago Prohibition office where she'd once worked, waiting for Eliot. Her husband, she confided emotionally to another agent, "apparently preferred to associate with other people instead of being with her." Eliot arrived soon after, walking wordlessly by. Later, when he was transferred to Cincinnati, Edna stayed behind.

Ness seemed determined to get back home, arranging with a friend in the U.S. Attorney's office for temporary Chicago assignments. But his best chance at a permanent posting remained a transfer to the Division of Investigation, and he put in a formal application that fall.

He reached out for a recommendation from ex-prosecutor George Johnson, now a former judge. Herbert Hoover had promoted Johnson to the federal bench in 1932 as a reward for Capone's conviction. But with Hoover voted out, Senate Democrats refused to confirm Johnson.

Now in private practice, Johnson wrote J. Edgar Hoover, praising

Ness's intelligence and experience. The Untouchables, Johnson wrote, "did a splendid piece of work. [Ness's] integrity was never questioned and I recommend him to you without reservations."

The Director promised to review Ness's application personally, then ordered his Chicago office to run a full background check, giving it "preferred attention." The agents sifted through Ness's scholastic record and questioned former coworkers. Johnson, William Froelich, Dwight Green, and others gave glowing recommendations.

Ness felt certain he had the job—he'd driven the Capone gang to the brink of bankruptcy, as just about anyone in the know would attest. With his record and connections, how could Hoover turn him down?

On November 18, while speaking over the phone in the Chicago Prohibition office, Ness remarked he had it all sewn up. The Division would surely make him Chicago's special agent in charge, and he wouldn't accept anything less.

"Boss is using his influence," Ness said, apparently referring to George Johnson. But that indiscreet admission destroyed Ness's chances of ever becoming one of Hoover's G-men—word soon got back to the man whose job Ness expected to take: the current special agent in charge, Melvin Purvis.

Within the year, Purvis would become the Division's most celebrated agent, nationally known as the man who got John Dillinger. He and Eliot Ness would become the most famous real-life American detectives of the twentieth century.

But in late 1933, Purvis's leadership of the Chicago office was notable only for its incompetence, his men blundering from one fiasco into another—arresting the wrong men in two separate kidnappings, letting the notorious bandit "Machine Gun" Kelly slip through their fingers, and failing to turn up any leads on Dillinger.

Hoover had long shown a special fondness for Purvis, using Melvin's first name in official memoranda and kidding him about his good looks. But even the Director's patience had reached its limit. In June,

Hoover would bring in a more dependable man to take over the Dillinger case.

Purvis was a poor fit for the Chicago office, dangerously ignorant of the complex currents of the city's underworld. An aristocratic southerner, arrogant and entitled, he'd come to town with his own horse, chauffeured car, and black manservant.

Ness had crossed Purvis's path during one of the agent's botched investigations. As a native Chicagoan, knowledgeable of local gangs, Ness had every reason to believe he could do a better job.

But Purvis would not give up his post without a fight. On November 28, he sent a letter to Hoover saying Ness was pulling strings to become special agent in charge, attaching a file from Coyne on the Joe Kulak affair. Purvis claimed the file showed "a connection between Mr. Kemp and Mr. Ness in the obtaining of money for the purpose of allowing stills to operate without interference."

He also passed along second- and thirdhand gossip about Ness's marital woes, even attacking Ness's leadership of the Untouchables—Purvis said they had failed to make a case against Capone. At least three times, in letters and over the phone, Purvis reminded the Director that Ness was the brother-in-law of Alexander Jamie, a pariah due to his history with the Bureau and the newly collapsed Secret Six.

Meanwhile, Ness—unaware Purvis was working against him—sat for a job interview with the Division. Before making his final report, the interviewer consulted with Purvis, who claimed Ness was using "political influence" to become special agent in charge "after the removal of the present Director and Mr. Purvis."

Nothing Ness had said suggested he wanted Hoover out of the way; on the contrary, he would often express his respect, even admiration, for the Director's work.

But just that hint of treachery was enough to make the Division close ranks. Somewhat incredibly, the report on Ness's interview concluded the former leader of the Untouchables "does not appear to be resourceful nor to have executive ability; and is not likely to develop."

Ness was "primarily a politician"—something not even his worst enemies could claim with a straight face—and "temperamentally unfit for the position sought."

On December 4, Hoover scribbled a note at the bottom of one of Purvis's poison-pen letters about Ness: "I do not think we want this applicant."

That effectively closed the matter, the case wrapping up officially a month later. The next day, December 5, Utah became the last state to ratify the Twenty-First Amendment, bringing Prohibition to an immediate end.

On May 27, 1933, an orgasmic display of lights, music, and pyrotechnics marked the start of the Century of Progress Exhibition on Chicago's southern shore. Unlike the classically designed "White City" of the 1893 fair, this sleekly modern "Rainbow City" looked ahead to a wondrous and optimistic future. Exhibits extolling the progress of science and the cultures of many nations filled 477 neon-lit acres, which visitors could view from the popular Sky Ride gliding hundreds of feet above.

Or they might take in the fair's more titillating attractions, like exotic dancer Sally Rand, or Calvin Goddard's Crime House. The host of the latter—his job at the Northwestern Crime Lab terminated—showcased the latest in forensic science, but also depictions of torture, an electric chair, and "Chicago's most beautiful murderess." Goddard would soon find himself written out of the history of American forensics by the FBI, which welcomed his methods but not the man who pioneered their use.

The fair was held over another summer, hosting more than 48 million visitors, the local economy reaping the benefits. But the city fathers' goal—to "adorn Chicago's reputation with something more decorative than grafting politicians and murdering racketeers," as one observer put it—proved elusive. The organizers had hoped to showcase their city's cultural attainments, but Chicago's underworld heart kept beating just within earshot.

Once again, the job of defending Chicago's honor fell to Robert Isham Randolph, who served as the exposition's "director of public protection." On June 7, 1934, Randolph arranged for the arrests of Joe Fusco and Capone's younger brother Matthew, who made the mistake of dropping by the fairgrounds for a beer and a sandwich. Randolph couldn't tolerate the presence of a former public enemy and the brother of Public Enemy Number One, not at the Century of Progress.

Like so many arrests over the years, this was merely Chicago-style theater. The Outfit had been at the fair from the very beginning, skimming money from construction through local trade unions, controlling everything from alcohol to hot dogs, parking lots to hat checks.

"If a wheel turns on the fairgrounds, we get a cut of the grease on the axle," one Outfit member boasted. "We got the whole place sewed up."

Instead of reclaiming Chicago from the gangsters, the fair helped keep the mob afloat as its bootleg operations dried up. Many tourists ventured from the fair into the Outfit's saloons, casinos, and brothels, which ran around the clock both summers, filling the coffers that once belonged to Capone.

With another burst of fireworks, the Century of Progress came to a close on October 31, 1934, ten days shy of ten years after Dean O'Banion's murder touched off the Beer Wars. By then, most of the key combatants were either dead or in exile. Names that had made so many headlines over the past decade—O'Banion, Weiss, Drucci, Genna, Lingle—now adorned tombstones and mausoleums at Mount Carmel Cemetery on Chicago's far West Side. Others—McGurn, Nitto, Capone—would soon join them, lying alongside the men they'd put in the ground. Chicago would never see their kind again—gangsters so much larger than life they became icons in death—because their conflict created a different world, one in which they had no place.

The bloody battle for Chicago's soul had never been about the rule of law, or preservation of morality, or even good versus evil; but about commerce. As gangsters fought for control of illicit markets, the federal government stepped in to protect the men whose businesses remained, if sometimes only barely, within the bounds of the law. Shooting and killing were bad for everybody's bottom line, from Samuel Insull's to Al Capone's. Both sides needed a city that was a little less Wild West, a little more Midwest. For the White House and the Secret Six, saving Chicago meant stopping the violence—not, as Eliot Ness might have had it, destroying the Outfit.

"There's plenty for everyone," Johnny Torrio always said.

And once the guns stopped echoing and the legal beer began flowing, the businessmen of the upper and underworlds had little reason to battle on. The city fathers got their World's Fair, all right, but Frank Nitto controlled the concessions—and the Outfit. So long as he stayed in the shadows and kept the killing to a minimum, no one seemed too concerned.

The bantam Enforcer, hidden from history behind Capone's outsized personality, won the war for precisely the same reason Ness's efforts to smash the gang came up short. Chicago only wanted the *appearance* of having been cleaned up. Ness and the Untouchables served that purpose until Capone's conviction, their story legitimizing the federal drive to put Scarface away. But once Capone left the scene, Ness found himself all but alone, still fighting the mob while his onetime allies packed up and moved on.

Capone had paved the way for his own downfall. He knew the dangers of too much bloodshed.

"I told them we were making a shooting gallery of a great business," he said after the Hotel Sherman peace conference, "and that nobody profited by it."

To survive, Capone had to civilize the underworld—forging peace agreements and absorbing rival gangs, turning hardboiled hoods into disciplined workingmen, and replacing open gunfights with targeted assassinations. In short, he professionalized crime, placing himself at the head of a new kind of big business.

But Capone remained too big, too famous, and too associated with the old violent ways to stay on top. He had to be sacrificed so his organization could survive.

As the mob modernized, law enforcement had to do the same. Ness and his Untouchables were lawmen in transition, a bridge between the old-school cops and the new kind of federal agents. Rough-hewn, unpolished, and imperfect, they looked ahead to a professionalized future, the best of them transforming themselves into the forerunners of J. Edgar Hoover's G-men.

But they had no place among these new crime-fighters—Ness would not be the only Untouchable denied a career as an FBI agent. J. Edgar wanted fresh faces, men he could mold into American heroes. And he carefully kept them away from the corrupting influence of organized crime, preferring to fight battles he could win.

This meant targeting a different kind of "public enemy"—the bank-robbing bandits crisscrossing the country on the wings of powerful V8 engines. The FBI's battles with the likes of John Dillinger, "Pretty Boy" Floyd, and "Baby Face" Nelson were *Dick Tracy* adventures writ large in the real world, with attractive heroes, grotesque villains, and all the violent spectacle the Capone case had lacked. Yet they remained a kind of sideshow, a diversion from more substantive forms of criminality.

"The war on crime is no more furthered by the killing of a Dillinger than by the jailing of a Capone for income-tax evasion," wrote one observer in 1935. "There are a thousand Dillingers . . . and a thousand Capones who know better than to write checks. The Bureau of Investigation is designed to prune the criminal tree; the tree goes on flowering."

Too pure for Chicago, too tainted for the FBI, Ness found himself banished from the city of his birth, as much a victim of the federal government as his scar-faced nemesis.

Yet while Capone had lost his town—and would soon lose his mind—Ness's greatest triumphs, and tragedies, lay ahead.

Untouchable Tours guide Craig "Southside" Alton outside the Lexington Hotel before its demolition in 1995. *(Wikimedia Commons)*

Epilogue:
The Great American City

The summer of 1934 found Eliot Ness busting hillbilly stills in the "Moonshine Mountains" of Kentucky and Tennessee. Bootlegging remained chiefly a big-city business, however, and Uncle Sam still needed someone with Ness's unique talent for battling the illicit alcohol trade.

In August, Ness was transferred to Cleveland to head the local office of the newly renamed Alcohol Tax Unit. His exile at an end, Ness threw himself into another flurry of raids—busting, the *Plain Dealer* reported, "an average of one still a day."

His work caught the city's attention, and in December 1935 he became Cleveland's new director of public safety. Over the next six years, Ness would reform a corrupt, inefficient police department and lower Cleveland's horrific traffic death rate until the city was among the safest in America. Thanks to Ness, the Cleveland Police became a model for the nation. Along the way, the Untouchable battled gangsters and labor racketeers, and personally led raids against the gambling operations of Moe Dalitz's nationwide Cleveland Syndicate.

Drawing upon ideas he'd learned from August Vollmer, Ness made Cleveland's Safety Department among the most progressive in the country—modernizing the police, outfitting squad cars with the latest in radio and teletype technology, and urging cops to fix the deeper social problems that created crime. He made fighting juvenile delinquency a chief priority, establishing "Boystown" clubs and a "Dick Tracy Detective Squad"—never realizing he had been the template for Chester Gould's comic strip detective.

"Millions have been spent in efforts to cope with the problem of adult crime," Ness declared in 1939. "I think the time is at hand when police officials, teachers, and educators should join to prevent problem children from becoming criminals."

As Ness reached new heights, his nemesis fell farther than anyone could have predicted. On November 16, 1939, Al Capone emerged from federal prison after serving seven years, six months, and twelve days of his eleven-year sentence. Capone had spent more than half of that time at "the Rock," a new maximum-security prison on Alcatraz Island.

Model prisoner Capone posed little threat of escape, and tax evaders rarely merited such heightened security. Once again, the federal government had happily bent its own rules to make an example of Public Enemy Number One.

After years of harsh discipline, enforced silence, and attacks from other inmates, Capone's mind finally cracked. The syphilis lying latent within him caused a psychotic break that no doctor could repair. Although he left prison a free man, Capone would always be a mental prisoner—trapped in a childlike state, subject to mood swings and delusions, terrified of strangers, and lost in premature senility.

"He is nutty as a cuckoo," Jack Guzik said in 1946.

Capone's family brought him back to the Palm Island estate, where walls and guards hid his condition from outsiders. Sometimes he would dream of returning to Chicago and his old haunts in Cicero. Ralph, still engaged in shady business but pushed to the Outfit's margins, encouraged these fantasies, to the dismay of other family members, who preferred Al in his calmer moments, content to enjoy retirement as a quiet family man and forty-something geriatric.

Apart from a brief stopover at Prairie Avenue on his way to Wisconsin, Capone would return to Chicago only in his fractured mind. When his family took him to restaurants in Miami, he'd imagine himself back in a speakeasy. At Palm Island, he'd sit by the pool and carry on conversations with deceased gangsters whose passing he had bidden.

"He talked to dead people," his relatives recalled, "and told them why they had to die. Sometimes he gave away Outfit business. We couldn't take a chance that any of this would get out."

The men who'd replaced Capone in Chicago would never have to worry about him reclaiming his throne. They subsidized him in his final years, giving the family a $600 weekly pension, enough to live on—just.

When Capone's body came back to Chicago for burial in 1947, his Outfit successors all trooped dutifully to the cemetery to pay their respects.

Like Capone, Eliot Ness spent his final days reliving the battle for Chicago.

In the 1940s, Ness left law enforcement—his one true calling—first for business and then for politics, a washout in both. Broke by the 1950s, his taste for alcohol deepening, Ness found himself working for a failing paper company in the small Pennsylvania town of Coudersport, desperate to make a living for his third wife and their adopted son.

In 1956, the sportswriter friend of a business partner offered to collaborate with Ness on a book about the Capone squad. Ness reluctantly agreed, and shared with his coauthor what memories he could muster. Now dying from his childhood heart condition, Ness hoped the book might provide financial security for his family after he'd gone. But his inherent modesty made him uncomfortable with the manuscript.

"It makes me out to be too much of a hero," Ness said. "It was the whole team that did the work, not just me."

Ness also had doubts about *The Untouchables* as a title, fearing readers would mistake it for a book about India. He wouldn't live to see its publication, nor the television series and films it would inspire.

The gangster era had just begun to fade from America's cultural memory when *The Untouchables* debuted on TV in 1959. Thirty years after the St. Valentine's Day Massacre, Chicago seemed poised to shake the stigma of Capone. But the series, produced by Desilu, revived the struggle for the city's reputation, its backlot Beer Wars forever making gangsters synonymous with Chicago.

As the writer Thomas Dyja put it, "Whatever else the city was responsible for would be lost in a hail of bullets from Robert Stack's tommy gun."

In December 1942, physicist Enrico Fermi and his colleagues set off a nuclear chain reaction, the first ever created by human beings, in their laboratory beneath the bleachers of the University of Chicago's Stagg Field—where Eliot Ness had once watched football. Their discovery ushered in the Atomic Age, announcing Chicago's emergence as America's cultural and commercial heart.

After World War II, the city projected its brand of friendly, matter-of-fact capitalism onto the country as a whole. Immigrant Ludwig Mies van der Rohe envisioned a new kind of skyscraper—sleek, modern, and spare—which soon dominated Chicago's skyline and others coast-to-coast.

Up in the northern suburb of Des Plaines, Chicago salesman Ray Kroc built his first McDonald's, ushering in uniform cuisine, created quickly and consumed the same way. On the North Side, around the block from Dean O'Banion's old flower shop, the headquarters of Hugh Hefner's upstart magazine, *Playboy,* mass-produced sex like Kroc's hamburgers.

Businessmen like Kroc and Hefner were the true heirs of Al Capone—identifying the basest of human needs, from food to sex, and catering to them cleanly, efficiently, with self-interest as naked as

Playboy's centerfolds. They helped create America's new consumer culture, while the city blossomed around them—growing up from the days of speakeasies and stockyards into Mies's starkly modern steel and glass structures.

In 1955, with the election of Mayor Richard J. Daley, Chicago had a new boss, at least vaguely in the Capone mode. A Democrat out of Anton Cermak's political machine, Daley ran his city like a monarchy, with power far outdistancing Scarface's. Critics and supporters alike saw him as a throwback to the city's corrupt past. On the night of Daley's election, a gleeful alderman cried out, "Chicago ain't ready for reform!"

Despite Daley's innate pragmatism—a willingness to work with anybody, no matter how crooked—the new mayor was not just another grafter. One historian called him "Chicago personified," somehow managing to embody both the ruthlessness of Al Capone and the public-spiritedness of Eliot Ness.

"The old bosses were not interested in what was good for the public welfare," Daley said. "They were interested only in what was good for themselves."

Daley appropriated Big Bill Thompson's favored nickname— "the Builder"—repaving downtown streets, encircling the city with highways, and littering the landscape with huge office buildings and housing projects. Chicago saw the rise of its newest and most iconic skyscrapers, the John Hancock Center and the Sears Tower—the latter reigning as the world's tallest building for more than twenty years.

The new metropolis Daley built along the lakefront looked resolutely forward instead of backward. Just as Chicago had rebuilt itself after the fire, so this new city had to destroy its former self to exist.

To that end, Daley's administration oversaw the demolition of many brick-and-mortar reminders of the Prohibition era. Colosimo's Restaurant was among the first to go, replaced by a parking lot in 1958. Two years later, Holy Name Cathedral leveled the entire block that included O'Banion's flower shop, making space for parking and a playground.

The church covered the bullet damage to its cornerstone, but tourists still looked for the pockmarks. The Four Deuces came down around 1964, leaving a garbage-strewn lot in its place.

That same year saw the construction of a new Federal Building, a thirty-story modernist monolith. Designed by Mies, the black skyscraper rose directly in front of the original gray granite courthouse, dwarfing its squat, compact dome.

The cold inhumanity of Mies's new structure was no accident, according to Judge James Wilkerson's replacement on the federal bench. He derided the old building's "cracker box surroundings," insisting that "pure justice" was insufficiently impressive to the public. Like a certain tax evasion conviction, the new building went beyond "pure justice" to create the *appearance* of justice, the better to demonstrate the government's power.

Despite some calls to save the old Federal Building, the aging structure couldn't escape Daley's march toward progress. In 1965, the courtroom where Al Capone and Samuel Insull had stood trial fell to the wrecking ball, making way for a post office, where wanted posters would go on traditional display.

Like the elite men behind the Secret Six, Daley sought to make Chicago appear safe, approachable, and business friendly by scrubbing any memory of gangsterism from its streets. The city made this explicit when it destroyed perhaps the most notorious remnant of Capone's Chicago.

For years, the owner of the garage at 2122 North Clark Street endured tourists looking through her windows, trying to talk their way inside, or even forcing themselves in, to see the wall where seven North Siders were tommy-gunned.

By 1967—the same year Roger Corman re-created *The St. Valentine's Day Massacre* on film—she finally had enough, selling the building to the city for demolition.

"Generally we try to preserve buildings which are of historical significance to the city," one official told the *Tribune*. "But this is something we'd rather not remember."

Mayor Daley's office did allow a Canadian businessman to preserve the building's most important feature—its southern wall. The wrecking crew numbered the bricks, then shipped them to Vancouver, where the wall was rebuilt in a Roaring Twenties–themed nightclub. Covered by glass, the murder wall stood in the men's room, where customers could line up like Bugs Moran's boys and relieve themselves.

But it wasn't enough to keep the nightclub in business. Eventually, the wall made its way west, where it stands today, still behind glass, but sans urinals—in Las Vegas's Mob Museum.

Not all residents of Daley's "city that works" enjoyed its benefits.

Chicago's African-American population increased by the hundreds of thousands in the years after World War II, while a rigid system of de facto segregation squeezed blacks into vast swaths of slums and housing projects. The South Side—home of Al Capone, Eliot Ness, and Richard Daley—became the "Black Belt," given over by its city to poverty and neglect.

"On Lake Shore Drive, life in Chicago is lovely—for the few," said the *Saturday Evening Post* in 1960. "For the millions, life in Chicago is toil and ugliness . . . squalor and privation."

Capone's South Michigan Avenue headquarters, the Metropole Hotel, sat trapped within this "Second Ghetto." In January 1975, a *Tribune* reporter found the halls once patrolled by pearl-hatted gangsters gloomy and still—heat, water, and electricity all shut off—as the few remaining residents stood guard against vandals. Only a dozen renters still called the Metropole home—some too old and infirm to move, others too stubborn to go anywhere else.

Conversing by candlelight in the dining room, near the gas ovens cranked up against Chicago's typically brutal winter, one resident told the *Tribune* he'd grown "attached to the building," calling it "a good old lady."

When the city tore the Metropole down later that year, the media paid no heed. One concerned citizen wrote the *Tribune* months later, lamenting the loss of another landmark.

"How long will we let this wanton destruction of our heritage continue?" he asked.

Thirteen years later, Tim Samuelson of the Commission on Chicago Landmarks sought to preserve the Capone family home at 7244 South Prairie Avenue, asking the state to designate the building an official landmark—not to honor Capone, but to recognize his undeniable importance as "Chicago's most famous citizen."

"Chicago has vainly tried to close its eyes and run away from Capone's ghost," Samuelson said, "but he has remained in close pursuit, breathing down the city's neck and tugging at its coattails."

The proposal drew immediate protest. Other homeowners on South Prairie, already enduring regular visits from gangster-seekers, feared an even greater tourist invasion. And a local Italian-American group resented "this attempt to resurrect the fading memory of Al Capone," which would "stereotype all Italians." Why not honor, say, Enrico Fermi? Even if "the father of the atomic bomb" had far more blood on his hands than Capone.

"No doubt, Chicago is better known around the world for Al Capone than for its great and many humanitarians, artists, authors and scientists," admitted the *Chicago Sun-Times*. "And, if the city is pleased with this image, then we suppose Capone's South Side home ought to be declared a landmark."

Local officials leaned toward recognizing the home, but following the bitter outcry rejected Samuelson's proposal twice. One local amateur historian appealed to the Department of the Interior to place Capone's home on the National Register of Historic Places. But when residents and local Italian-American groups again objected, the man behind the appeal quickly withdrew his proposal.

Despite never receiving landmark designation, Capone's home has so far avoided the fate of many gangster landmarks. Put up for sale in 2014, its asking price dropped precipitously—from $300,000 to $179,000. The listing became an excuse for the curious to get inside and see where Capone slept. A headline in the *Tribune* wondered whether the building was "Untouchable."

Almost four years later, the Capone home remains unsold.

While Chicagoans battled over the future of the South Prairie house, the Lexington Hotel deteriorated along with its neighborhood—from hotel to brothel to flophouse. By the time a court order closed its doors in 1980, the once-grand structure had become a hazard.

"It's a monstrosity," the local alderman told the *Sun-Times*. "The bricks are falling off, and the roof is falling in."

A nonprofit foundation bought the shuttered Lexington, seeking to rehabilitate it. After workers came upon a walled-off space in the basement, television personality Geraldo Rivera agreed to host a two-hour live broadcast from the Lexington on April 21, 1986, for the opening of Al Capone's vaults.

"I was pretty sure we would find either guns or money or dead bodies," Rivera recalled.

The heavily promoted program confirmed Capone's lasting hold on the American imagination. During the broadcast, a "Capone safecracking party" filled the nearby Hyatt Regency with guests decked out Roaring Twenties style, while the IRS—still intent on collecting Capone's tax debt—waited to seize whatever money might be found. A crowd gathered outside the decaying hotel, harsh spotlights revealing its every crack and fissure.

"With no panes in the windows and with a huge hole in the sidewalk out front," reported the *Sun-Times*, "the Lexington looked like a battle casualty."

After exploring Capone's old office and test-firing a tommy gun, Geraldo dynamited the supposed vault, exposing nothing but dirt and discarded bottles. He wandered off-screen singing about "that toddling town," fully expecting he'd blown his career right along with the vault.

But some 30 million households tuned in, breaking records for a syndicated program. Rivera had not only turned his career around, he'd created a new genre: reality television.

The Lexington would never enjoy such redemption; various plans to restore and reopen it all failed. Within a decade, the building became "a stinking corpse," according to the *Sun-Times,* "fouling a Near South Side community that is struggling for life."

By then, the ownership of the Lexington had fallen into dispute. In November 1995, as both claimants battled in court, the city lost its patience and ordered the structure razed. As the Lexington fell to rubble, a local architect working for the city hoped to save Capone's bathroom tiles.

In 1960, after eight Chicago cops were revealed to be part-time burglars, Mayor Daley fired the police chief and replaced him with a disciple of August Vollmer. The new chief instituted a series of reforms that would have made his (and Eliot Ness's) mentor proud, cutting crime in Chicago by 15 percent.

Once again, however, these reforms were mostly for show. Daley knew wide-open police graft would delegitimize his whole administration, even as other forms of corruption persisted elsewhere. He "amputated an appendage to keep the body alive," as one historian put it.

As for the Outfit, Daley—ever the pragmatist—chose to let the rackets operate under the radar, rather than drive them out.

"Well, it's there," Daley said of the mob, "and you know you can't get rid of it, so you have to live with it."

Organized crime helped Daley get elected, and he wasted no time in repaying the favor. He hired Outfit comrades to official posts, giving criminals "another chance." In 1956, he closed down an elite task force gathering intelligence on Chicago gangsters.

"The police department," declared the Chicago Crime Commis-

sion, "is back where it was ten years ago as far as hoodlums are concerned."

Under Daley's benign neglect, the Outfit grew to new levels of
power and influence. As late as 1968, Chicago's gangsters still obeyed
the territorial divisions laid out in Capone's day. Their organization
increasingly behaved like a major corporation, extending its reach into
new markets and territories—from Florida to Hollywood and especially Las Vegas, with its legal gambling.

"There's money pouring in like there's no tomorrow," gangster
Johnny Rosselli said in 1960.

The Outfit reached its peak in the 1960s, when the Central Intelligence Agency, through Rosselli, sought their help in its failed attempts
to assassinate Cuban dictator Fidel Castro.

Yet even as one arm of the federal government briefly became the
Outfit's allies, others worked with increasing determination toward
their destruction. In 1957, after state and local police in Apalachin,
New York, raided a nationwide Mafia summit, J. Edgar Hoover could
no longer deny the reality of nationally organized crime, and the FBI
finally went into action on that front. Meanwhile, Robert F. Kennedy
and an Untouchables-like team battled corruption in the mobbed-up
Teamsters Union.

But the feds still faced the same problem Eliot Ness and his Untouchables had dealt with in 1931. Federal law remained largely concerned with criminals as individuals, giving prosecutors few tools to go
after crime syndicates as organizations. Thirteen years after the Apalachin conference, that changed with the passage of the Racketeer Influenced and Corrupt Organizations (RICO) Act of 1970.

The law's author, G. Robert Blakey, designed it to essentially outlaw
membership in any criminal group, with much harsher punishments
than old conspiracy statutes—no longer two years, but up to two decades in prison.

"You've got to go after the organization," Blakey said. "Individuals commit organized crime, but organizations make the organized crime possible. You're in it to destroy a family."

RICO codified the root-and-branch approach Ness and his Untouchables had pursued against the Outfit, echoing their strategy of proving Capone's role in the booze business by linking him to other members of the gang. Crime bosses could no longer hide behind underlings. Now every member of a criminal syndicate could be found equally guilty of any crime committed by that organization.

Blakey spent a decade urging law enforcement to adopt this new weapon, often by showing the Capone-inspired film *Little Caesar* to groups of FBI agents. Although he always refused to say whether the film's protagonist—Rico Bandello—inspired the name of his law, Blakey used the movie to demonstrate the foolishness of trying to fight organized crime by targeting marquee mobsters. While the film's flashiest, most press-hungry gangster dies in the end, his boss—the shadowy "Big Boy"—lives on after "The End."

"What about Big Boy?" Blakey would ask. "They forgot about Big Boy . . . nothing ever happens to him. He's still in charge. Oh sure, they got Rico. What's the use of that?"

Beginning in the 1980s, federal prosecutors started using RICO to break up criminal syndicates. The endgame for the Outfit came in 2007, when federal prosecutors in Chicago—led by Patrick Fitzgerald, known as "Eliot Ness with a Harvard degree"—won the convictions of four gang leaders and their coconspirator, a corrupt cop.

The case, Operation Family Secrets, had been in the works for almost ten years, after an imprisoned Outfit enforcer agreed to inform on his associates. His testimony and that of dozens of other witnesses linked the Outfit to eighteen murders and decades of racketeering. By sending the four bosses to prison for life, federal officials finally completed the work begun by Ness's Untouchables seventy-six years earlier.

Even before Family Secrets, the gang had become a shadow of its former self. Years of federal investigations and deaths of key leaders— whether by natural or highly unnatural causes—had whittled the ranks. Those who remained—"Mob Lite," one magazine called them—retreated to Cook County, ceding the rackets in other states to local criminals.

"The Outfit is a business," one criminal justice professor observed, "and they've learned that having a smaller core is good business."

Unlike their fictional counterparts in the *Godfather* films, the literal descendants of Capone, Nitto, and their associates had little trouble escaping the family business if they were so inclined. By the new millennium, the children of the Outfit had entered business after business along Michigan Avenue—and not by muscling in, but by making their way honestly.

Asked at the dawn of the 2000s what had happened to the Outfit, the current head of the Chicago Crime Commission laughed and said, "They're everywhere. They've become involved in every possible Chicago business."

Descendants of Italian and Jewish immigrants no longer found their paths to prosperity blocked by prejudice. The crime and violence some of their ancestors had used to steal a slice of the American Dream had migrated south, into the region once known as Chicago's Black Belt. Decades of predatory mortgage lending and deindustrialization have turned Eliot Ness's old South Side neighborhood into a war zone, where street gangs battle over personal slights while innocents get caught in the crossfire.

As Ness well understood, stopping such killing requires repairing the surrounding environment, fixing the social and systemic problems that lead people into lives of crime. Local leaders have pursued that goal for years—the Ness family's final home in Roseland stands within sight of the church where a young Barack Obama began his career as a community organizer.

In 2015, the governor of Illinois froze all funding to Operation CeaseFire, a crime prevention program designed to treat violence like a sickness, sending former gang members like antibodies into dangerous neighborhoods. Once funding stopped, Chicago saw a roughly 60 percent jump in homicides, with 762 murders in 2016—more than the 729 gang killings Cook County endured throughout Prohibition. The city's renewed murderous reputation prompted a presidential promise to "send in the Feds."

Yet that same year, Chicago broke its own tourism record with 54 million visitors, an increase of 15 million in six years. Most violence stayed concentrated in Roseland, Englewood, and other outlying neighborhoods, while the Loop remained what Robert Isham Randolph and the city fathers of his generation envisioned—a place where businessmen and tourists could walk without fear of catching a bullet.

So long as its most vulnerable residents are pushed to the margins, Chicago will remain "the murder capital," as Kanye West called it, "where they murder for capital."

In 1989, Chicago's second Mayor Daley—son Richard M.—traveled to London, England, to promote foreign trade. When the younger Daley appeared on a BBC talk show, the host began by bringing up Al Capone and Eliot Ness.

"Are there still fellows around with mustaches, funny hats and tommy guns?" he asked. "I'm not foolish. I know the reason you're here is to clean up Chicago's image."

Daley patiently reminded British viewers that Capone had left Chicago more than fifty years earlier.

"It's a very warm, friendly city," Daley said.

Five years later, Daley continued his father's crusade to rewrite Chicago's reputation by hosting the World Cup tournament. At the same time, Capone's familiar face could be seen around town on a brewing company's billboards, part of a series showcasing famous figures from the city's past. Protests came from Italian-American groups and the mayor's office, the brewery soon replacing Capone with Enrico Fermi.

Even so, Capone's presence still hovered over the World Cup. International visitors would have their pick of Capone T-shirts, coffee mugs, and other souvenirs in the city's many gift shops. Or they could visit "Capone's Chicago," a "Disney-like" museum on the North Side where guests saw an animatronic Capone—complete with cigar—sharing his life story. At Water Tower Place, an exhibit featured life-sized dummies of Capone, Ness, and the St. Valentine's Day victims.

"Capone's Chicago" would eventually close, as would the Water Tower Place exhibit, but Capone remains an undeniable presence downtown. Walk into any souvenir shop and you're likely to see his face on a T-shirt or hip flask. His stylized portrait hangs in Chicago's upscale Blackstone Hotel, where the baseball bat banquet was reenacted for the 1987 *Untouchables* film.

If Capone lost the battle for Chicago, his ghost won the war. That he remains the city's inescapable face is more fitting than either Mayor Daley might ever admit. Foremost, Al Capone wanted to be loved; wealth was always secondary. Chicago, too, desires both your adoration . . . and business.

"It cannot be denied," one Italian journalist observed, "that Chicago wants to be, and is, a lovable city."

Perhaps that explains the loud, predictable protests raised against every visible reminder of Scarface Al. Chicago's defenders still want to absolve their city of responsibility for Capone by branding him an outsider—an *other*, unreflective of their town.

As Chicago's director of tourism said, "Al Capone was a New Yorker. He only lived in Chicago for 12 years. This city has spent millions of dollars to change its image. We have more Nobel Prize winners than any other city. More medical centers, more beach than Rio de Janeiro, the greatest symphony in the world. What we don't need is the memory of Al Capone."

When the question of making the Prairie Avenue home a landmark came before the city, prosecutor George E. Q. Johnson's son wrote a letter to the *Sun-Times*, laying all the evils of Prohibition at Capone's feet.

"This fiend killed, robbed, stole, murdered, corrupted public officials in such a brazen manner as to ruin the reputation of our great city," he wrote.

Yet well before Capone arrived, Chicago was corrupt and violent, and it remained that way after he had gone. Pathologizing Capone—making of this opportunistic businessman a "fiend"—allows Chicago's boosters to sidestep the central question: What kind of city—what kind of country—would allow such a man to exist, much less turn him into an icon?

Henry Ford considered Prohibition both morally and "economically right," because sober workers were better workers.

"There can be no conflict between good economics and good morals," Ford insisted. "In fact the one cannot exist without the other."

By that logic, virtually every murder Capone committed was justified. The liquor ban offered wealth to those who couldn't get it any other way, but bootleggers who wanted to stay in business had to defend themselves and their territory any way they could. Violence was not only "good economics" but self-defense—a necessary evil along the fastest available road to the American ideal of affluence.

"I can't change conditions," Capone said. "I just meet them without backing up."

The same forces that created the assembly line also birthed the Cicero brothel whose cold, industrial efficiency so sickened Robert St. John. The laws of commerce, its system of incentives and rewards, guarantee every Henry Ford will create at least one Al Capone.

In 2007, as the Family Secrets trial coincided with a slew of local corruption scandals, the *Sun-Times* reflected on Chicago's morbid fascination with its own crookedness.

"It's not so much that we like our mobbed-up reputation," the editorial said, "although some of us treat it as entertainment and revel in our infamous history. . . . But until we are more outraged than entertained . . . Al Capone will remain our favored forefather and unofficial mascot."

Yet Chicago's attitude toward Eliot Ness is strangely harsher than its love-hate relationship with Al Capone. The Transportation Building still stands, as does nearby Dearborn Station, where Ness and Capone had their one fleeting encounter; but no plaque or marker memorializes either structure. Back when Tim Samuelson was working to get Capone's house designated a landmark, he considered registering Ness's home at the same time, as a compromise to win the city over. But he dropped the plan after discovering Ness shared a two-flat with his parents.

"The real Eliot Ness really wasn't that impressive a guy," Samuelson claimed decades later, in his role as Chicago's official cultural historian. "He gets his job through his brother-in-law. You rarely see his name in the newspapers of doing anything. He was kind of an underling."

Ness's true legacy and that of his Untouchables lives on in the Bureau of Alcohol, Tobacco, Firearms and Explosives (ATF), the successor agency to the Prohibition Bureau. In 2014, Illinois's senators—Democrat Dick Durbin and Republican Mark Kirk—cosponsored legislation to name the ATF headquarters in Washington after Ness. Democratic Senator Sherrod Brown of Ohio introduced the bill, in recognition of Ness's remarkable work in Cleveland.

"Chicago gangster Al Capone believed that every man had his price," Durbin said. "But for Eliot Ness and his legendary law enforcement team 'The Untouchables,' no amount of money could buy their loyalty or sway their dedication to . . . Chicago's safety. That steadfast commitment to public service is why it is so fitting that we remember Eliot Ness with this honor."

Official Chicago quickly spoke up in protest—this time in the form of "the city's most powerful alderman," Edward M. Burke. A self-described "old-school" political boss, Burke became known as "the City Council's resident historian" for his efforts to correct the record on Chicago's past.

In 2010, Burke—having already worked to exonerate Mrs. O'Leary's cow for allegedly causing the 1871 fire—convinced the Chicago police to reopen their investigation into the seventy-year-old slaying of E. J. O'Hare. But the alderman seemed unconcerned with actually solving the crime, telling reporters his real goal was recognizing the long-dead mob lawyer as the true hero of the Capone investigation instead of Eliot Ness.

"If nothing else," Burke said, "O'Hare's reputation ought to be rehabilitated and the truth ought to be known. . . . It was not 'The Untouchables' . . . that led to the conviction of Al Capone. . . . It's a fiction of Hollywood."

Four years later, Burke had lost none of his desire to write Ness out of the Capone story. After learning of the Senate proposal, Burke and another alderman immediately introduced what the *New York Times* called a "purely symbolic resolution" declaring Ness unworthy of such an honor.

"He's a Hollywood myth," Burke mistakenly claimed. "He probably never laid eyes on [Capone]."

Senator Kirk did his cause no favors by citing the 1987 film *The Untouchables* as his reason for honoring Ness.

"I think he did pretty well in that movie . . . ," Kirk said of Ness. "I'm going with the Eliott [sic] Ness that was in the movie."

At a City Council hearing over Burke's resolution, three federal tax investigators seized the opportunity to vent their agency's frustration with how Ness's posthumous fame had come to eclipse Frank Wilson's. One retired IRS official spoke of his relationship with Mike Malone, the undercover agent whose brief stint at the Lexington was spun into legend by Wilson's and Elmer Irey's embellished memoirs.

"Malone," this former agent said, "told me Eliot Ness was afraid of guns and didn't like leaving the office."

The *Sun-Times,* which had ridiculed Burke's earlier move to find O'Hare's killer as "a lousy stunt," now agreed with the alderman— Ness's name had no place in Washington.

The paper opined, "Much as we love the legend of Eliot Ness . . . we can't imagine why anybody would want to name a building for the real Eliot Ness, who just annoyed Capone."

Even though the *Sun-Times* wildly understated the Untouchables' effect on the Outfit, their editorial reflected a deeper truth about Chicago's relationship with Ness. Today's tourist will not find Ness's face alongside Capone's in the souvenir shops. If his memory survives in Chicago at all, thank Robert Stack's late fifties incarnation and Kevin Costner's portrayal in the *Untouchables* movie. While the 1959 two-part pilot film is, perhaps surprisingly, among the more accurate screen depictions, Brian De Palma's brash, swaggering retelling of the Capone investigation bears scant resemblance to actual history.

Costner's Ness defeats Capone only by adopting gangster methods, what Sean Connery's character calls "the Chicago way." Like Carl Sandburg's "City of the Big Shoulders," the phrase came to symbolize Chicago's self-image—proud, tough, and defiant—even as it misrepresents Eliot Ness.

The real man, the antithesis of the Chicago way, still seems like a foreigner in his own hometown, dismissed by Burke and others as a Hollywood invention.

The American public will always prefer the fictitious, gun-toting Nesses to their mild-mannered inspiration. Writer Rick Polito's sardonic summary of *The Untouchables*—"A federal agent in Chicago hampers the work of an enterprising American job creator"—suggests why.

Yet when the laws of commerce create a monster like Capone, Americans expect their government to ride to the rescue with a hero like Ness. They cheer the Dick Tracy–esque G-men who slay the most visible villains. But they don't want the feds to stick around too long. A crusader like the real Eliot Ness, with ideas of fighting crime by rewriting the social fabric, will inevitably wear out his welcome.

Burke's effort to kill the Senate proposal succeeded. Durbin, Kirk, and Brown abandoned it without further comment.

Though ATF headquarters remains nameless, the building displays a memorial to the Untouchables. Its central atrium, now named for Eliot Ness, greets visitors with his portrait. On an opposite wall are pictures of several real Untouchables, and an exhibit explains their importance to the history of federal law enforcement.

The symbolic battle for Chicago lives on in De Palma's *Untouchables*, which rewrites the city's geography right along with its history. Although many of the story's real-life locations remained standing when the movie was made, the filmmakers invariably chose to exchange those buildings for more elegant and elaborate landmarks.

Thus Roosevelt University stands in for the Lexington Hotel; the Rookery replaces the Transportation Building. Ness and the Untouchables appear on the streets outside the Board of Trade, as defenders of "all the concentrated wealth of Chicago," as one film critic put it.

The movie, while unmistakably set in Chicago, creates a fantasy landscape indulging in the myth that the Untouchables truly cleaned up the town. And as the physical reminders of Capone and Ness fade away, their very real conflict seems just another Hollywood myth.

The 1987 film inspired a television remake that ran for two seasons in the early 1990s. Christopher Crowe's script for the pilot episode imagines a scene of Capone and Torrio, in 1919, walking along a bridge over the Chicago River—probably the Michigan Avenue Bridge, whose dedicatory plaque still bears Big Bill Thompson's name.

Capone points out a skyscraper: the Wrigley Building, built by a man who made so much money selling chewing gum, he could afford to memorialize himself in steel.

"Johnny," Capone says, "people want booze more than they want gum. If we make the right moves—now—there can be a building over there with *our* name on it someday."

These lines didn't make it into the finished episode, just as Capone's fictitious dream failed to become a reality. If you stand on the Michigan Avenue Bridge today, the only name you're likely to see (apart from

Mayor Thompson's) is TRUMP, looming on the side of the blue-glass tower standing next to the Wrigley Building.

But walk along Wacker and over to State, up the stairs and onto the L. You may see a sign directing you to the airport, still bearing the surname of the lawyer who secretly worked to get rid of Capone, but don't follow it. Take the Green Line instead, past the former site of a stop—Randolph/Wabash—that shared half its name with the head of the Secret Six. The train will carry you through the thicket of Chicago's proud skyscrapers, leaving the Loop to head straight south. Get off at Cermak-McCormick Place, the stop named for the mayor who tried to have Frank Nitto assassinated and the publisher whose newspaper employed Jake Lingle and introduced the world to Dick Tracy.

Walk east along what was once Twenty-Second Street, but now bears the name of the martyred Mayor Cermak. You'll cross Wabash Avenue half a block from the site of Eliot Ness's first Capone raid, now an event space for weddings and other celebrations. Next door a gangster-themed dinner theater, Tommy Gun's Garage, offers the experience of a Roaring Twenties speakeasy, complete with police raid. The menu includes a lasagna named after Big Jim Colosimo, whose famed café once occupied the parking lot.

Go one more block and stop at the corner of Cermak Road and Michigan Avenue, former site of the Lexington Hotel. As recently as 2010, an official historical marker from the Chicago Department of Transportation identified this spot as the previous residence of "one of Chicago's most notorious citizens, Al Capone."

Even that may have been too much for Chicago. The only historical marker in sight now prefers to mention a nearby hospital and church and all the development brought to the area by the 1893 World's Fair, without referencing Capone.

"South Michigan Avenue," it awkwardly reads, "has also been home to the Metropole and Lexington hotels, Chess Records, Chicago Defender and to many major car manufacturer [*sic*] in the world. . . . People who want to be close to the downtown area have moved into lofted apartments and condominiums, reinventing the area as a neighborhood that is just as vibrant."

Where the Lexington once stood is a gleaming modernist skyscraper, all glass and sharp angles, the tallest south of the Loop. Built in 2010, this pet-friendly property offers more than three hundred spacious apartments, perfect for young professionals seeking their fortunes in Chicago.

Floor-to-ceiling windows provide the kind of sweeping, unobstructed views that Capone once enjoyed. If your window faces north, you may catch a glimpse of the Transportation Building, long since converted into condominiums, tucked away amid the jumble of the Loop. Only the top few floors are visible, including the one where Eliot Ness used to work.

Once or twice a day—and four times on Saturdays—a black bus full of tourists rumbles past. Photos of Capone, Torrio, O'Banion, and Moran look out from the windows as if taking a trip down memory lane, over huge white text: UNTOUCHABLE TOURS.

But when the bus is out of sight, you might look at the apartment building and never guess who lived there, more than eighty-five years ago. Not unless you notice, just above the door, the six letters making up the building's name.

THE LEX.

Acknowledgments:
A Tip of the Fedora

by A. Brad Schwartz

This project began with the goal of chronicling Capone and Ness from birth to death, with research retracing their paths through their lives—from the neighborhoods where they grew up to the homes where they died. Innumerable people and institutions gave of their time and expertise, sharing memories, documents, and other artifacts, helping us walk in the footsteps of legends. Every scrap of information, no matter how small, added brushstrokes to the portraits of these men, and our thanks go out to everyone who provided paint. Any errors, of course, are our own.

Very late in the process, we realized we had gathered more narrative than could comfortably fit between two covers. The "battle for Chicago" asserted itself, telling such a compelling and complete story that we decided to focus on it, limiting our acknowledgments to the research reflected here.

For their help in reconstructing the St. Valentine's Day Massacre, we are indebted to Lt. Mike Kline and departmental historian Chriss Lyon of the Berrien County Sheriff's Department in St. Joseph, Michigan; and James P. Sledge and Mary Marik of the Cook County Medical Examiner's Office in Chicago, Illinois. The Mob Museum in Las Vegas, Nevada, opened to us their collection of massacre-related documents and artifacts, and Jonathan Ullman, Carolyn Fisher, and Geoff Schumacher arranged a smooth and productive visit. A fedora tip goes to Lora Kalkman, special assistant to Mayor Carolyn Goodman, for paving the way.

The Federal Bureau of Investigation field office in Norfolk, Virginia, offered a tommy gun firing demonstration at the Chesapeake Police Department shooting range. William Gannaway of the Ballistics Research Facility at the FBI Academy in Quantico, Virginia, corrected several of our misconceptions about these iconic weapons.

Rebecca McFarland has worked diligently to preserve the memory of the real Eliot Ness, even down to seeing that the Untouchable—forty years after his death—received a proper funeral. She lent her full support here, sharing decades of research and making herself readily available. Max is particularly gratified that Rebecca—inspired to study the real Ness years ago by Max's novel *The Dark City*—could help bring our mutual fascination with the subject to fruition.

Scott Leeson Sroka, grandson of Untouchable Joe Leeson, made available his groundbreaking research into the lives of the other Untouchables, bringing these famed but blurry figures into focus. A tireless defender of Ness's reputation, Scott opened doors, making much of our research into the real Untouchables possible, and we look forward to his own upcoming book on Ness's men. Special thanks to Scott's wife, Marla, and son, Eliot, for their hospitality during one of Brad's many visits to D.C.

Barbara Osteika, historian for the Bureau of Alcohol, Tobacco, Firearms and Explosives, granted access to personnel files on every Untouchable as well as other Ness-related documents. She put faces to the names of several agents with their official ID photos. Thank you to Barbara and everyone at ATF headquarters in Washington, D.C.—especially Ginger Colbrun, Hilary Martinson, and Corey Ray.

Paul Heimel, Ness's first biographer, gave selflessly of his insight and research, from articles and documents to interviews with those no longer with us. If we've seen farther, as the old saying goes, it's because we had Paul's shoulders to stand on.

James B. Cloonan, son of Untouchable Barney Cloonan, supplied memories, photographs, and documents of his famous father, including his father's daybook—a precious piece of history giving a unique and personal window onto the lives of the Untouchables.

Marco Bruzzi, Monica Melotti, Emanuela Verlicchi Marazzi, and Francesca Balestrazzi of MB America furnished a tour of 93 Palm Island in Miami, which proved vital in picturing the house as it appeared in Capone's day. We thank them both for the visit and for ensuring the preservation of this historic property.

Vanya Scott arranged a visit to view the Ness collection at the National Law Enforcement Museum in Washington, D.C., making available amazing artifacts before their display in our nation's capital. The staff of Eastern State Penitentiary in Philadelphia made going to prison both fun and enlightening, and staff historian Annie Anderson shared key material regarding Capone's time behind bars. Ken Alder of Northwestern University disclosed documents illuminating Ness's relationships with the inventors of the lie detector. We're grateful to John Carson of the University of Michigan for making introductions (as well as training Brad to be a historian).

The resources of various branches of the National Archives and Records Administration were key to the writing of this book. We salute the archivists and staff in Chicago, College Park, San Bruno, and Washington, D.C., as well as at the Herbert Hoover Presidential Library in West Branch, Iowa. Special fedora tips to Adam Berenbak in D.C. for opening the files of the Kefauver Committee, Henry Mac in San Bruno for pulling Capone's prison records, and Gene Morris in College Park for helping with the Notorious Offenders files.

The Federal Bureau of Investigation gave access to a wealth of information by processing numerous Freedom of Information Act requests in a comprehensive and timely manner. The National Personnel Records Center in St. Louis, Missouri, quickly located personnel files for Eliot and Edna Ness and Alexander Jamie at long distance. The United States Secret Service delivered information on Giuseppe Zangara.

Crucial research was conducted at numerous archives in and around Chicago, including the Chicago History Museum, the Newberry Library, the South Suburban Genealogical and Historical Society, the Harold Washington Library Center of the Chicago Public Library (Special Collections and Microfilm divisions), and the University of Chicago archives. Librarians, archivists, and staff at each institution made every visit a privilege and a pleasure.

The Western Reserve Historical Society in Cleveland, Ohio, remains the first port of call for Ness research, and they offered vital help on this project as they have for Max's previous Ness-related works. The Cleveland Public Library and Cleveland State University Library yielded essential information. Special thanks to Brian Meggitt at the Cleveland Public Library for scanning loads of photos quickly and courteously, and Emily Vernon for opening the archives of the Cleveland Police Historical Society Museum.

In Coudersport, Pennsylvania, John Rigas and Natalie Phelps shared their memories of Eliot Ness, making the Untouchable come alive. Natalie's siblings, Linda and Joe Phelps, gave their own recollections of Ness in phone interviews. Doug Bretz of Coudersport presented his private collection of Nessiana. David Castano and Diane Caudell arranged a quick but valuable visit to the Potter County Historical Society. Special thanks to Matthew Pearl for making the trip to Coudersport happen, and sharing his own research.

Additional research was conducted among the collections of the Lilly Library at Indiana University in Bloomington, the American Heritage Center of the University of Wyoming in Laramie, the Bancroft Library of the University of California–Berkeley, the Miami-Dade Public Library, the University of Michigan Library, the Michigan State

University Library, the Wisconsin Historical Society Library at the University of Wisconsin–Madison, the Capital Area District Library, the Library of Michigan, and the Princeton University Library. We are indebted to the librarians and staff at each institution. At the main branch of the Pima County Library in Tucson, Arizona, Betsy and Victoria kindly tracked down a newspaper article about Eliot Ness.

For insights helping illuminate the life of Al Capone, we are indebted to Eleanor Benson, Art Bilek, Deirdre Capone, Jan Greco, and Peg Hagenauer. Suzanne Andrukaitis, Ron Lazer and Kathy Fitzsimmons, and Sue and Tom Stewart generously offered lodging on research trips.

Governor James J. Blanchard helped us understand Capone's time in Lansing, Michigan.

Ross Harris of the Stuart Krichevsky Literary Agency has been a tireless advocate for this project. Fedora tips to Ross, Stuart Krichevsky, Shana Cohen, Hannah Schwartz, and the entire SKLA team.

Few editors are more enthusiastic and encouraging than Peter Hubbard at William Morrow; we're grateful to him, Nick Amphlett, Maureen Cole, Kaitlin Harri, and everyone at HarperCollins for their support.

Max Allan Collins wishes to thank his wife, writer Barbara Collins, for her editorial assistance throughout, as well as his friend and agent, Dominick Abel, who offered a key piece of advice late in the process.

Finally, I will take the liberty of stepping out from behind third person to thank numerous friends and teachers who offered advice, encouragement, and ready sounding boards. At the University of Michigan, Jim Burnstein, Phil Hallman, and Matthew Solomon contributed to this project in ways large and small; Vincent Longo deserves special credit for submitting to more Nessiana than any friend should have to endure, including critiquing several draft chapters. At Princeton University, Jaime Sánchez Jr. offered insight as a keen student of Chicago and its politics. At Okemos High School, Matthew Morrison and Chris Smith let one of their students indulge his fascination with Eliot

Ness—and, in the process, kindled a lifelong love of American history. Anna Zielinski always made the road to Chicago worth taking.

Dennis and Nancy Austin Schwartz continue to be better parents than anyone could possibly deserve. This book is the culmination of countless acts, both large and small, that they performed over the years—among them introducing their son to *Dick Tracy* and *The Untouchables,* driving him around the South Side of Chicago late one night to view the scenes of Ness's raids, making repeated attempts to visit the Cleveland Police Historical Society Museum, and letting him drag them to Des Moines to see his hero portrayed onstage.

Most importantly, they made trip after trip to the Centuries & Sleuths Bookstore in Forest Park, Illinois, so their son could get to know his favorite author. They set this book in motion, and helped carry it over the finish line.

Note on Sources

Al Capone's credo is often summed up by his most famous quote: "You can get much further with a kind word and a gun than you can with a kind word alone."

But Capone never said this: "Professor" Irwin Corey did. As "Quote Investigator" Garson O'Toole has shown, Corey came up with the phrase in the 1950s and first attributed it to Capone—as a joke—in 1969.

But as soon as the gangster's name became attached to it, the line took on a life of its own. It eventually found its way into the *Yale Book of Quotations*—not to mention Robert De Niro's mouth, by way of David Mamet's screenplay for the 1987 film *The Untouchables*. Jonathan Eig accepts the quote as genuine in his 2010 book *Get Capone,* writing that Capone "best captured the essence of the gangster life" with this line he never used.

Much conventional wisdom about Al Capone and Eliot Ness has a similar pedigree—lies, errors, and half-truths repeated so often they became accepted as fact. Further muddying the record is a rising tide of revisionism from those authors "who," as the writer Loren D. Estleman once observed, "in their fanatical pursuit of Truth often gallop straight past the facts." Between these two conflicting trends, the real Capone and Ness have nearly been lost in the shuffle.

To find them, we returned to contemporary primary sources, synthesizing as many different accounts as we could and drawing upon multiple (and often conflicting) versions of events. We have listed the sources most useful in writing each chapter below, with the caveat that they sometimes disagree with each other, and with our own text. We often found it necessary to use a few credible details from one source while ignoring others contradicted elsewhere, or to break with the conventional wisdom if a reliable source told a more convincing story. Explaining each judgment call would take another volume, but some of the major ones are outlined in brief below.

Readers familiar with previous works on Capone and Ness will find ours differs from them frequently, and sometimes starkly. Time and again, we have uncovered evidence contradicting earlier books on basic matters of character and chronology. Halting the narrative to explain each disagreement would be undesirable and impractical. We believe the depth of our research, as outlined below, speaks for itself.

Abbreviations

ABBREVIATION	COMPLETE CITATION
ABS	A. Brad Schwartz (Personal Collection)
BOP-AP	Comprehensive Case Files of Inmates Incarcerated at U.S. Penitentiary, Alcatraz, ca. 1924–ca. 1988; Record Group 129 (Records of the Bureau of Prisons), National Archives and Records Administration, San Bruno, CA
CCF	Criminal Case Files 1892–; Record Group 21 (Records of the U.S. District Court, Northern District of Illinois, Chicago); National Archives and Records Administration, Chicago, IL
CDN	*Chicago Daily News*
CDT	*Chicago Daily Times*
CEA	*Chicago Evening American*
CEP	*Chicago Evening Post*
CHE	*Chicago Herald and Examiner*
CN	*Cleveland News*
CP	*Cleveland Press*
CPC	*Cleveland Press* Collection, Cleveland State University, Cleveland, OH
CPD	*Cleveland Plain Dealer*
CRCC	Calumet Region Community Collection, Harold Washington Library Center, Chicago Public Library, Chicago, IL

CT	*Chicago Tribune*
DMM	David Mamet manuscripts, Lilly Library Manuscripts Collection, Indiana University, Bloomington, IN
ENPS	MS3699 Eliot Ness Papers/Scrapbooks Collection No. 171, Western Reserve Historical Society, Cleveland, OH
FBI-AC	Federal Bureau of Investigation File on Al Capone, "FBI Records: The Vault," https://vault.fbi.gov/Al%20 Capone (accessed August 12, 2015)
FBI-AJ	Federal Bureau of Investigation file on Alexander Gleig Jamie, obtained by ABS through a Freedom of Information Act request, February 11, 2016
FBI-DA	Federal Bureau of Investigation file on Desi Arnaz, "FBI Records: The Vault," https://vault.fbi.gov/Desi%20 Arnaz (accessed February 22, 2017)
FBI-EN	Federal Bureau of Investigation File on Eliot Ness, "FBI Records: The Vault," https://vault.fbi.gov/Eliot%20 Ness (accessed August 12, 2015)
FBI-ENA	Federal Bureau of Investigation Applicant File on Eliot Ness, obtained by ABS through a Freedom of Information Act request, February 3, 2015
FBI-RIR	Federal Bureau of Investigation file on Robert Isham Randolph, obtained by ABS through a Freedom of Information Act request, March 22, 2016
FBI-SVDM	Federal Bureau of Investigation File on the St. Valentine's Day Massacre, "FBI Records: The Vault," https:// vault.fbi.gov/St.%20Valentines%20Day%20Massacre (accessed August 12, 2015)
FJW	Frank John Wilson Papers, Collection No. 8312, American Heritage Center, University of Wyoming, Laramie, WY

GEQJ   Donated Materials, Johnson Papers; National Archives
                     and Records Administration, Chicago, IL

GH   George Hagenauer

HHPL   Herbert Hoover Presidential Library, West Branch, IA

HVO   Howard Vincent O'Brien Papers, The Newberry Li-
                     brary, Chicago, IL

IRS-1   W. C. Hodgins, Jacque L. Westrich, and H. N. Clagett,
                     Memo "In re: Alphonse Capone, 7244 Prairie Avenue,
                     Chicago, Illinois," July 8, 1931, Internal Revenue Ser-
                     vice, "Historical Documents relating to Alphonse (Al)
                     Capone," http://www.irs.gov/pub/irs-utl/file-1-letter-
                     dated-07081931-in-re-alphonse-capone.pdf (accessed
                     August 8, 2015)

IRS-2   Frank J. Wilson, Summary Report "In re: Alphonse
                     Capone, Lexington Hotel, 2300 Michigan Boule-
                     vard, Chicago, Ill.," December 21, 1933, Internal
                     Revenue Service, "Historical Documents Relating
                     to Alphonse (Al) Capone," http://www.irs.gov/pub/
                     irs-utl/file-2-report-dated-12211933-in-re-alphonse-
                     capone-by-sa-frank-wilson.pdf (accessed August 8,
                     2015)

IRS-3   Frank J. Wilson to Elmer Irey, March 27, 1931, Inter-
                     nal Revenue Service, "Historical Documents Relating
                     to Alphonse (Al) Capone," http://www.irs.gov/pub/
                     irs-utl/file-3-letter-dated-03271931-to-chief-irey-from-
                     sa-wilson.pdf (accessed August 8, 2015)

IRS-4   Frank J. Wilson to Elmer Irey, April 8, 1931, Internal
                     Revenue Service, "Historical Documents Relating to
                     Alphonse (Al) Capone," http://www.irs.gov/pub/irs-
                     utl/file-4-letter-dated-04081931-to-chief-irey-from-sa-
                     wilson.pdf (accessed August 8, 2015)

JBC   James B. Cloonan (Personal Collection)

JIG   Jacob I. Grossman Collection on Al Capone, Chicago History Museum, Chicago, IL

KC   Records of the Senate Special Committee to Investigate Organized Crime in Interstate Commerce, 1950–51 (Kefauver Committee); Record Group 46 (Records of the U.S. Senate); Center for Legislative Archives, National Archives and Records Administration, Washington, D.C.

KDB   Karl & Doug Bretz (Personal Collection)

LAT   *Los Angeles Times*

MAC   Max Allan Collins

MM   Calvin Goddard Collection, Mob Museum, Las Vegas, NV

Ness MS.   Untitled manuscript by Eliot Ness, Roll 1, Folder 2, Eliot Ness Papers and Scrapbooks, Western Reserve Historical Society, Cleveland, OH

NLEM   Collection of the National Law Enforcement Museum, [2012.39.4], Washington, D.C.

NOF   Notorious Offenders Files, 1919–1975; Record Group 129 (Records of the Bureau of Prisons), National Archives and Records Administration, College Park, MD

NYT   *New York Times*

OPF   Official Personnel Folder, National Personnel Records Center, St. Louis, MO

OPF/ATF   Official Personnel Folders from the National Personnel Records Center (St. Louis), held by the Bureau of Alcohol, Tobacco, Firearms and Explosives, Washington, D.C.

PCF   Prohibition Case Files; Record Group 21 (Records of the U.S. District Court, Northern District of Illinois, Chicago); National Archives and Records Administration, Chicago, IL

PCHS	Potter County Historical Society, Coudersport, PA
PU	Records of the Prohibition Unit, Record Group 58 (Records of the Internal Revenue Service), National Archives and Records Administration, College Park, MD
PWH	Paul W. Heimel (Personal Collection)
RIR	Robert Isham Randolph Scrapbooks, Chicago History Museum, Chicago, IL
RM	Rebecca McFarland (Personal Collection)
RRPAC	Records Relating to the Prosecution of Alphonse Capone, 1930–1931; Record Group 118 (Records of U.S. Attorneys, 1821–1994), National Archives and Records Administration, Chicago, IL
SLS	Scott Leeson Sroka (Personal Collection)
SPD	Records of the Office of Community War Services, Social Protection Division General Records, 1941–1946; Record Group 215, National Archives and Records Administration, College Park, MD
SSGHS	South Suburban Genealogical and Historical Society, Chicago, IL
UC	Special Collections Research Center, University of Chicago Library, Chicago, IL
UCB	Courtesy of the Bancroft Library, University of California, Berkeley, Berkeley, CA
UCR	Lyle B. Chapman to Director of Prohibition, re: Case No. 122-B, June 13, 1932, examined by ABS at Heritage Auctions, New York, NY, October 11, 2018
USvAC	"U.S. v. Al Capone, non-record material received from Internal Revenue Service," National Archives and Records Administration, Chicago, IL
WP	*Washington Post*

Source Notes

Epigraph

Williams, *Mysterious Something*, p. 95 ("There is something").

Introduction ("Untouchable Truth")

THE UNTOUCHABLES: LAT, April 20, 1959. "The Surprised Mr. Stack," *TV Guide*, December 5, 1959, p. 10, in FBI-DA. For a detailed overview of the *Untouchables* TV film and series, see Tucker, *Eliot Ness and the Untouchables*, pp. 98–191.

NESS AND FRALEY: Oscar Fraley, "The Real Eliot Ness," *Coronet*, July 1961, pp. 26–27. William J. Ayers, "As I Knew Eliot Ness," *The Potter Enterprise Sportsmen's Special*, November 24, 1971, PCHS. Scott Martell, "'Untouchable' Memories," *News-Press*, December 7, 1994, PWH. "Bill Ayers," n.d., PWH. "Virginia Kallenborn Interview," March 25, 2000, PWH. Nickel, *Torso*, p. 204. John Rigas, personal interview with ABS, November 15, 2016.

As an example of attempts to debunk the Ness/Fraley *Untouchables*, Eig (*Get Capone*, p. 239) falsely claims that "almost nothing in Fraley's book checks out." Our own research (and the independent work of Scott Leeson Sroka, grandson of Untouchable Joe Leeson) reveals that the vast majority of incidents described in Ness's memoir are in one way or another verifiable.

HOOVER AND MA BARKER IN *THE UNTOUCHABLES*: Director, FBI to SAC, Los Angeles, October 16, 1959; M. A. Jones to Mr. DeLoach, Re: "'The Untouchables,' Television Program Produced by Desilu," October 23, 1959; SAC, Los Angeles to Director, FBI, October 20, 1959; J. Edgar Hoover to Redacted, October 27, 1959, all in FBI-DA.

EIG'S *GET CAPONE*: Eig (*Get Capone*, pp. 223–224) and Bair (*Al Capone*, pp. 149–151) both cite Burns's *One-Way Ride* (1931) and Murray's *Legacy of Al Capone* (1975) as the sources of the baseball bat story, even though at least two printed sources (*X Marks the Spot*, p. 55, in FBI-AC; and Pasley, *Al Capone*, pp. 329–332) predate Burns by a year. Eig's misguided theory of the St. Valentine's Day Massacre (*Get Capone*, pp. 250–253) is thoroughly debunked in Binder, *Al Capone's Beer Wars*, pp. 190–197. See also Allen Barra, "Getting Caponed," *Birmingham Weekly*, July 8, 2010, http://bhamweekly.com/birmingham/print-article-1663 -print.html (accessed July 10, 2010).

BAIR: Bair, *Al Capone*, p. 211 ("sure the press").

BURNS AND NOVICK: Esther Cepeda, "'Prohibition' Gives Lie to Era's Myths," *Chicago*

Sun-Times, September 26, 2011, http://www.suntimes.com/news/cepeda/7827740–417 /prohibition-gives-lie-to-eras-myths.html (accessed September 29, 2011) ("Eliot Ness had").

ALFORD: Nathaniel Popper, "The Tax Sleuth Who Took Down a Drug Lord," NYT, December 25, 2015, http://www.nytimes.com/2015/12/27/business/dealbook/the-unsung-tax-agent -who-put-a-face-on-the-silk-road.html (accessed May 28, 2016) ("They don't write").

WILSON AND *UNDERCOVER MAN:* Frank J. Wilson and Howard Whitman, "Undercover Man: He Trapped Capone," *Collier's,* April 26, 1947, pp. 14–15, 80–83. Joseph D. Brady to the William Morris Agency, July 28, 1947; Frank J. Wilson to Joseph Donald Brady, July 30, 1947; John Weber to Judge Lester Roth, August 5, 1947; Joseph D. Brady to Frank J. Wilson, August 5, 1947; Frank J. Wilson, undated memo; C. E. Erkel, memo to Lester Wm. Roth, Re: "Undercover Man—He Trapped Capone," August 7, 1947; Frank Wilson to Joseph Brady, August 15[, 1947]; Columbia Pictures Corporation Agreement, August 20, 1947; Memorandum of Agreement, July 11, 1947; Frank Wilson to Joseph Brady, September 23, 1947; Frank J. Wilson to Joseph D. Brady, September 30, 1947; Frank Wilson to Joseph D. Brady, October 18, 1947; Frank Wilson to Joseph D. Brady, October 20, 1947; Joseph D. Brady to Frank J. Wilson, October 22, 1947, all in Box 5, "Auctorial—Contract, The William Morris Agency 1947" Folder, FJW. Helen Alpert, "Uncle Sam's Tough Guy," *Miami News,* May 1, 1949, in Box 18, "Scrap Book #1—Secret Service Stories," FJW. *The Undercover Man* (1949), directed by Joseph E. Lewis, in *Glenn Ford: Undercover Crimes* (Culver City, CA: Sony Pictures Home Entertainment, 2013), DVD. Wilson and Day, *Special Agent,* pp. 28–56.

IREY AND *T-MEN:* Irey and Slocum, *Tax Dodgers,* pp. 25–65. *T-Men* (1947), directed by Anthony Mann (New York: Sony Wonder, 2005), DVD. Rappleye and Becker, *All-American Mafioso,* pp. 118–121.

Prologue

ST. VALENTINE'S DAY MASSACRE: CT, February 14–15, 1929 (February 15, "brains"). CHE, February 15–16, 1929 (February 15, "Nobody shot me"). Cook County Coroner's Office, Statement of Effects and Estate, February 14, 1929; Frank Gusenburg [*sic*] Autopsy Report, February 14, 1929; Statement of Mrs. Josephine Morin, February 14, 1929; Statement of Mrs. Max Landesman, February 14, 1929; Statement of Mr. Clair McAllister, February 14, 1929; Patrolmen Connelley and Devane, memo to Commanding Officer, 36th District, Re: "Murder of Peter Gusenberg, Frank Gusenberg, Albert Weinshenk [*sic*], John May, James Clark, Adam Heyer, J. Snyder, Alias Hayes," February 15, 1929; Statement of Sam Schneider, February 17, 1929; 36th District Police Report, March 28, 1929; Acting Deputy Commissioner of Detectives, memo to Commissioner of Police, February 1929 [?], all MM. Autopsy Reports for Frank Gusenberg, Peter Gusenberg, Albert Kachallek (Alias James Clark), John May, Reinhardt Schwimmer, and Albert Weinshank, February 1929, Cook County Medical Examiner's Office, Chicago, IL. Sullivan, *Rattling the Cup,* pp. 192–194. Calvin Goddard, "The Valentine Day Massacre: A Study in Ammunition-Tracing," *The American Journal of Police Science* 1 (January–February 1930), pp. 60, 73, 75. Pasley, *Al Capone,* pp. 118–119, 254. Burns, *One-Way Ride,* pp. 256–265. Charles DeLacy, "The Inside on Chicago's Notorious St. Valentine Massacre," pt. 1, *True Detective,* March 1931, pp. 53–55, 96–97. Kobler, *Capone,* pp. 250–253. Schoenberg, *Mr. Capone,* pp. 209, 212–214. Helmer and Bilek, *St. Valentine's*

Day Massacre, pp. 3–11, 99–100, 161, 232–233. Kyle and Doyle, *American Gun,* pp. 157, 175–176. Lt. Mike Kline, personal interview with ABS, October 2, 2013. William Gannaway, phone interview with ABS, November 24, 2015. James P. Sledge, personal interview with ABS, April 19, 2016.

The original St. Valentine's Day Massacre guns remain with the Berrien County Sheriff's Department in St. Joseph, Michigan, which seized them as evidence in 1929. Lt. Mike Kline, the keeper of these historic weapons, showed them to ABS in October 2013, and his vivid description of the crime was invaluable in writing this account. Lt. Kline's theory, based on the position of shell casings visible in photographs and his personal knowledge of the ins and outs of these weapons, is that the killers waited to use the second Thompson, equipped with the stick, until they first spent the one with the drum. Coroner Herbert N. Bundesen's report on the autopsies of the massacre victims (see Bergreen, *Capone,* p. 316) confirms the gunmen fired into the prostrate bodies of the men as they lay on the floor.

ABS gained vital insights into the Thompson submachine gun from a firing demonstration arranged by the Norfolk field office of the Federal Bureau of Investigation at the Chesapeake Police Department firing range on September 18, 2015.

In 2012, the dropped revolver was on display, with its original evidence envelope and alongside the bricks from the St. Valentine's Day Massacre wall, at the Mob Museum in Las Vegas, Nevada.

Eig (*Get Capone,* pp. 199, 250–253) largely bases his theory of the St. Valentine's Day Massacre on a statement the dying Gusenberg allegedly made to police: "Cops did it." From this, and other spurious information, Eig goes on to claim that the men wearing police uniforms really were cops. But he offers no source for Gusenberg's supposed statement, vaguely citing it (on p. 428) as "contained in some accounts of Tom Loftus's statement to police, February 14, 1929."

The police reports, articles, and books cited above agree Gusenberg said nothing about the men who killed him except how they were dressed. A few present differing versions of Gusenberg's last words to police, but none match Eig's account. Burns (*One-Way Ride,* pp. 265–266) offers a similar version, in which Gusenberg claims that "coppers done it." Eig appears to have based his account on Helmer and Bilek (*St. Valentine's Day Massacre,* p. 7), but they offer no source. See also Binder, *Al Capone's Beer Wars,* pp. 195–196.

REACTION TO MASSACRE: CHE, February 15, 1929 ("Chicago gangsters graduated"). CT, February 15, 1929; February 19, 1929. James O'Donnell Bennett, "Chicago Gangland: Golden Flood Makes Czars, Befouls City," CT, April 7, 1929 ("Only one gang"). Sullivan, *Rattling the Cup,* pp. 193–194. Pasley, *Al Capone,* pp. 124, 255. Burns, *One-Way Ride,* p. 30. DeLacy, "Inside on Chicago's," pt. 1, p. 53. Trohan, *Political Animals,* p. 25 ("I've got more"). Kobler, *Capone,* p. 253. Schoenberg, *Mr. Capone,* pp. 219–220. Bergreen, *Capone,* pp. 315–316. Helmer and Bilek, *St. Valentine's Day Massacre,* pp. 9–10 (10, "the circle of"), 95–98, 108–110, 133–134.

CAPONE DESCRIPTION: William G. Shepherd, "$119.25 Poison Money," *Collier's,* October 16, 1926, p. 27 ("The business pays"). Alva Johnston, "Gangs Á La Mode," *The New Yorker,* August 25, 1928, http://www.newyorker.com/magazine/1928/08/25/gangs-a-la-mode (accessed March 10, 2017). Pasley, *Al Capone,* pp. 9, 60 ("the most-shot-at"). W. R. Burnett,

"The Czar of Chicago," *The Saturday Review of Literature,* October 18, 1930, p. 240 ("Capone is no"). Burns, *One-Way Ride,* pp. 33 ("Everybody calls me"), 310–312 (312, "Once in the"). Mary Borden, "Chicago Revisited," *Harper's,* April 1931, pp. 541–542 ("No one is"). Alva Johnston, "Capone, King of Crime," *Vanity Fair,* May 1931, http://www.vanityfair.com/news/1931/05/al-capone-chicago-new-york-prohibition (accessed June 22, 2017). Katharine Fullerton Gerould, "Jessica and Al Capone," *Harper's,* June 1931, pp. 93–97 (93, "one of the"). IRS-2. Ross, *Trial of Al Capone,* pp. 64–65. Anonymous, "The Capone I Knew," *True Detective,* June 1947, pp. 45–47. Irey and Slocum, *Tax Dodgers,* p. 37. Allsop, *Bootleggers,* p. 285. Kobler, *Capone,* pp. 12–13, 285. Schoenberg, *Mr. Capone,* pp. 21, 177. Bergreen, *Capone,* pp. 49–50. Helmer, *Al Capone and His American Boys,* p. 182 ("had no regard"). Bair, *Al Capone,* pp. 61 ("go buy some"), 67–68, 77, 182, 208.

NESS DESCRIPTION: Ness MS., p. 22, in ENPS, Roll 1, Folder 2. Elisabeth Ness, "My Husband, Eliot Ness," *TV Guide,* March 11–17, 1961, p. 6. Peter Jedick, "Eliot Ness," *Cleveland,* April 1976, p. 52, RM. Abbie Jones, "The Real Eliot Ness," *Tucson Citizen,* July 17, 1987. Steven Nickel, "The Real Eliot Ness," *American History Illustrated,* October 1987, p. 44. Scott Martell, "'Untouchable' Memories," *News-Press,* December 7, 1994, PWH ("I have never," "extremely modest," "who could get"). Lew Wilkinson, interviewed in "Eliot Ness: Untouchable" (1997), *Biography,* directed by Michael Husain (New York: New Video, 2001), VHS. Heimel, *Eliot Ness,* p. 100 ("immediately strikes one").

CAPONE AND NESS'S FATHERS: Fraley, "Real Eliot Ness," p. 28 ("who never cheated"). Bair, *Al Capone,* pp. 5–7, 33.

Chapter One

CAPONE AS IMMIGRANT: CEA, October 13, 1926. Allsop, *Bootleggers,* p. 283 ("I'm no foreigner"). Bergreen, *Capone,* pp. 20–23. Bair, *Al Capone,* p. 10.

BROOKLYN: Riis, *How the Other Half Lives,* pp. 1–69, 137–165, 199–209. Julian Ralph, "The City of Brooklyn," in Ellen, Murphy, and Weld, *A Treasury of Brooklyn,* p. 53. Weld, *Brooklyn Is America,* pp. 138–143. Snyder-Grenier, *Brooklyn,* pp. 6–7, 16, 40–49, 66–69, 80. Hanson, *Monk Eastman,* pp. 17–25.

GABRIELE CAPONE / AL'S BIRTH AND EARLY LIFE: C. R. F. Beall, Neuro-Psychiatric Examination of Alphonse Capone, May 18, 1932, in Box 0202, "[Capone, Alphonse] Capone-Atlanta #1 [40886-A] [Folder 3 of 4]" Folder, BOP-AP. Joseph Mulvaney, "A Brooklyn Childhood," in Ellen, Murphy, and Weld, *A Treasury of Brooklyn,* pp. 99–104. Schoenberg, *Mr. Capone,* pp. 17–19. Bergreen, *Capone,* pp. 28–30, 32. Capone, *Uncle Al Capone,* pp. 17–25. McArthur, *Two Gun Hart,* pp. 17, 19. Bair, *Al Capone,* pp. 5–36. Lombroso, *Criminal Man,* pp. 1–41, 114–131.

NITTO IN BROOKLYN: Eghigian, *After Capone,* pp. 3–16.

VINCENZO CAPONE / JAMES HART: McArthur, *Two Gun Hart,* pp. 7–24. Bair, *Al Capone,* p. 14.

BOYS OF NAVY STREET: Daniel Fuchs, "Where Al Capone Grew Up," *The New Republic,* September 9, 1931, pp. 96–97. Bergreen, *Capone,* p. 35. Balsamo and Balsamo, *Young Al Capone,* pp. 1–9 (7, "We are the"). Bair, *Al Capone,* pp. 10–11.

TORRIO IN NEW YORK AND BROOKLYN: Allsop, *Bootleggers,* pp. 48–49. McPhaul,

Johnny Torrio, pp. 38–48. Kobler, *Capone*, pp. 25–26. Schoenberg, *Mr. Capone*, pp. 23–24, 27–28. Keefe, *Man Who Got Away*, pp. 73–75.

FRANKIE YALE: Meyer Berger, "Mom, Murder Ain't Polite," in Ellen, Murphy, and Weld, *A Treasury of Brooklyn*, p. 339. Kobler, *Capone*, pp. 35–36. Kobler, *Ardent Spirits*, pp. 249–250. Peterson, *The Mob*, pp. 149–152. Schoenberg, *Mr. Capone*, pp. 28–29. Critchley, *Origin of Organized Crime*, pp. 162–163.

CAPONE'S EARLY GANG ACTIVITIES / HITTING TEACHER: Fuchs, "Where Al Capone," pp. 95–97 (97, "as a training"). Kobler, *Capone*, p. 26. Schoenberg, *Mr. Capone*, pp. 21–23. Bergreen, *Capone*, pp. 35–40. Iorizzo, *Al Capone*, p. 27. Bair, *Al Capone*, pp. 10–11, 14–19.

HARVARD INN: Schoenberg, *Mr. Capone*, pp. 28–32.

CAPONE'S SCARRING AND SYPHILIS: Schoenberg, *Mr. Capone*, pp. 33–34 (33, "You got a"). Bergreen, *Capone*, pp. 44–46, 49. Balsamo and Balsamo, *Young Al Capone*, pp. 109–124.

MAE COURTSHIP AND MARRAIGE: Fuchs, "Where Al Capone," p. 97 ("something of a"). Bair, *Al Capone*, pp. 22–31 (29, "colored"), 72, 134.

SONNY'S BIRTH AND SYPHILIS: Bair, *Al Capone*, pp. 30–31, 35.

CHICAGO HISTORY: Keefe, *Man Who Got Away*, pp. 25–43.

TORRIO AND COLOSIMO: McPhaul, *Johnny Torrio*, pp. 85–86. Keefe, *Guns and Roses*, p. 107. Bilek, *First Vice Lord*, pp. 25–83, 98–100, 128–132, 151–158, 189–261. Lombardo, *Black Hand*, pp. 110–113.

PROHIBITION: *Baltimore American*, January 17, 1920 ("Heaven rejoices"). NYT, January 17, 1920. Pasley, *Al Capone*, pp. 92, 222. Kobler, *Capone*, p. 69. Schoenberg, *Mr. Capone*, p. 77. Behr, *Prohibition*, pp. 82–83. Lender and Martin, *Drinking in America*, pp. 68–80, 98–102, 109–110, 124–131. Okrent, *Last Call*, pp. 1–4, 7–114.

TORRIO AND PROHIBITION: Landesco, "Organized Crime," pp. 912–913. McPhaul, *Johnny Torrio*, pp. 121, 141–147, 156–160. Schoenberg, *Mr. Capone*, pp. 60–62. Bilek, *First Vice Lord*, pp. 218–219.

COLOSIMO DIVORCE AND MURDER: Kobler, *Capone*, pp. 64–65, 70–76. Schoenberg, *Mr. Capone*, pp. 62–65. Lindberg, *Return to the Scene*, pp. 369, 373. Bilek, *First Vice Lord*, pp. 17–24, 221–251, 264.

CAPONE'S MOVE TO CHICAGO AND GABRIEL'S DEATH: Kobler, *Capone*, pp. 36, 102–103. McPhaul, *Johnny Torrio*, pp. 121, 460. Schoenberg, *Mr. Capone*, pp. 35–36, 53, 67–68. Bergreen, *Capone*, pp. 36, 57–58. Bair, *Al Capone*, pp. 33, 37–38. Binder, *Al Capone's Beer Wars*, p. 121.

Biographer Bergreen (*Capone*, pp. 56–57) claims Capone worked as a bookkeeper in Baltimore between living in Brooklyn and moving to Chicago, apparently based on a single interview with the son of Capone's supposed employer. No other evidence supports Bergreen's claim. Capone didn't reference this job when giving his employment history upon arriving at prison in 1932, and his granddaughter, Diane, disputes the Baltimore story because Mae never mentioned it. (Mario Gomes, "Al Capone Myths," My Al Capone Museum, http://www.myalcaponemuseum.com/id213.htm (accessed June 23, 2017). Bair, *Al Capone*, p. 340.)

Biographer Bair largely accepts the bookkeeper story, even though Diane Capone (one of her major sources) disagrees. She also has Al Capone returning from Baltimore for his father's funeral in 1919, even though all the other biographies date Gabriel's death to November 1920 (as do both of his tombstones) and the U.S. Census still lists him as alive earlier that year. (Bair, *Al Capone*, pp. 31–37, 340. 1920 U.S. Census Record for Gabriel Capone.)

Both Bergreen and Bair use the story to similar effect, claiming Capone attempted to go straight in Baltimore and only chose the rackets after his father's death. This is consistent with the view of Capone as a victim of circumstance, held by his descendants and apologists. As Bair (*Al Capone*, pp. 327–328) puts it, "The family believes that he might have become the lifelong businessman he always claimed to be had it not been for his father's death and the need for him to become the main breadwinner for his extended family. If he was indeed working as a bookkeeper in his only honest job, and if his father had lived, they think there is every possibility that he might have risen through the ranks of accounting and financial affairs to the top of the legitimate corporate world." But the best evidence indicates that Capone had already chosen to join Torrio's operation in 1919, before Gabriel died. The decision to enter Chicago's rackets was his, and his father's death had nothing to do with it.

Chapter Two

NESS INTRODUCTION: *The Story of Eliot Ness: A Brief Biography* (campaign pamphlet, 1947), p. 5, NLEM ("the thrifty and"). Ness and Fraley, *The Untouchables*, pp. 6, 87. Heimel, *Eliot Ness*, p. 20 ("What I now").

PEDER/PETER NESS: "Peter Ness," *Album of Genealogy and Biography*, pp. 207–208, SSGHS. Christian H. Jevne, "A Norwegian Immigrant in Chicago in the 1860's," in Pierce and Norris, *As Others See Chicago*, p. 178 ("There are better"). Ness and Fraley, *The Untouchables*, pp. 86–87. Adelman, *Touring Pullman*, p. 14. Bjarne Jørmeland, "Gangsterjeger Fra Ålvundfjord," *Tidens Krav*, June 25, 2011, pp. 25–26, RM. "The Ness Family," *Where the Trails Cross*, vol. 44, no. 4 (Summer 2014), p. 83.

Ness and Fraley (*The Untouchables*, pp. 86–87) claim that Peder Ness arrived in America on the day President James Garfield was shot, but Jørmeland (p. 26) documents his arrival two months prior.

KENSINGTON, PULLMAN, AND ROSELAND: Richard T. Ely, "Pullman: A Social Study," *Harper's Magazine*, February 1885, pp. 455–465 (464, "the company care"). "Modern Methods in Bread Baking," *The Calumet Weekly Index*, April 30, 1910, in *Where the Trails Cross*, vol. 19, no. 3 (Spring 1989), p. 98 ("little more than"). Theophilus Schmid, "Business History of Roseland" (unpublished manuscript), May 1, 1931, pp. 1–3, 5, in Box 4, Folder 31, CRCC. Simon Dekker, *History of Roseland and Vicinity* (unpublished manuscript), p. 178, in Box 5, "11 Bakeries, pp. 177–186" Folder, CRCC. CT, March 28, 1948 ("Bumtown"). Buder, *Pullman*, pp. 41–44 (44, "elevated and refined," "strictly business proposition"), 53 ("busy season"), 63–64, 66–69, 83–84, 88–89, 119–123 (120, "Leave the well-paved"; 122, "raise hell"). Adelman, *Touring Pullman*, p. 2 ("discontent and desire," "evil influences"). Pacyga, *Chicago*, pp. 121–125. Papke, *The Pullman Case*, pp. 11–14.

NESS BAKERIES: "Peter Ness," *Album of Genealogy and Biography*, p. 208, SSGHS. Adelman, *Touring Pullman*, pp. 14, 38. "Modern Methods in Bread Baking," p. 98. Chicago City Directory 1892, p. 1103. *Lakeside Business Directory* 1892, p. 1661.

Chicago's streets were renumbered in 1909; prior to that time, the address of the first

Ness bakery was 2398 Kensington Avenue. (*Plan of Re-Numbering*, p. 83.) We use post-1909 addresses throughout to avoid confusion.

EMMA KING NESS, AND EFFIE, NORA, AND CHARLES NESS: 1900 U.S. Census Record for Peter Ness; 1910 U.S. Census Record for Eliot Ness. "Peter Ness," *Album of Genealogy and Biography*, pp. 207–208, SSGHS. Ness and Fraley, *The Untouchables*, p. 23. Jørmeland, p. 26. Tucker, *Eliot Ness and the Untouchables*, p. 13. "The Ness Family," p. 83. The *Album of Genealogy and Biography* gives the year for Peter's immigration as 1880, and the year of his marriage to Emma as 1885.

BAKERY FIRE: CT, January 15, 1893 ("The origin of").

PULLMAN STRIKE: "Peter Ness," *Album of Genealogy and Biography*, pp. 207–208 (207, "reputation for integrity"), SSGHS. Ness and Fraley, *The Untouchables*, p. 23. Buder, *Pullman*, pp. 148–158, 178–185, 200–210. Adelman, *Touring Pullman*, p. 38. Pacyga, *Chicago*, pp. 143–147. Papke, *The Pullman Case*, pp. 10, 21–23 (22, "the paternalism of Pullman"), 25–37, 84.

An investigation into Eliot Ness's background conducted in 1933 by the Bureau of Investigation (later known as the FBI) also documented Peter Ness's standing in the neighborhood. George E. Q. Johnson, who lived in Roseland in the early 1900s and went on to prosecute Capone, said he had known the Ness family "for approximately twenty-five years [since 1908] and that [Peter Ness] was well respected in the community." A childhood friend of Eliot's, R. E. Jones, told the BI investigator that Eliot "comes from a very good family," and that Peter "has an excellent reputation in the community." (W. S. Murphy, Report on Eliot Ness, November 15, 1933, pp. 5–6, FBI-ENA. See Also "Eliot Ness Is Appointed Chief Dry Investigator," *Calumet Index*, April 29, 1932, in ENPS, Roll 1, Scrapbook 1, p. 46.)

ELIOT NESS BIRTH: 1900 U.S. Census Record for Peter Ness. Chicago City Directory 1900, p. 1394. "Peter Ness," *Album of Genealogy and Biography*, p. 208, SSGHS. Paul Havens, "Personalities in Law Enforcement: Eliot Ness," *True Detective*, November 1939, p. 61 ("at least a"). "About Eliot Ness," CN, September 22, 1947, in "Ness, Eliot" (microfiche), CPC. Jedick, "Eliot Ness," p. 50. "The Ness Family" and "The King Family," *Where the Trails Cross*, vol. 44, no. 4 (Summer 2014), pp. 83–85.

NESS/CAPONE NEIGHBORHOODS: Robert E. Park, "The City: Suggestions for the Investigation of Human Behavior in the Urban Environment," in *The City*, ed. Park, Burgess, and McKenzie, pp. 40–41. Landesco, "Organized Crime," p. 1057 ("The good citizen"). Shaw and Myers, "The Juvenile Delinquent," pp. 650–661. Theophilus Schmid, "Business History of Roseland," May 1, 1931, pp. 3–7, 9, in Box 4, Folder 31, CRCC. Reckless, *Vice in Chicago*, pp. 281–285. Ronald G. Patterson, "The Historical Geography of 300 Block West on 110th Place, Roseland Community, Chicago, Illinois" (unpublished manuscript), Chicago Teachers College, March 1964, p. 8, in Box 5, Folder 36, CRCC. Robert Raffin and Roland Raffin, "Kensington and Pullman Historics," SSGHS. Buder, *Pullman*, pp. 122 ("pretty homes and"), 222–223. Adelman, *Touring Pullman*, p. 38. "The Parise Family," *Where the Trails Cross*, vol. 19, no. 3 (Spring 1989), p. 96.

NESS CHILDHOOD: William Townes, "As Boy in Chicago, Ness Was 'Just A Regular Guy,'" CP, February 23, 1937, in ENPS, Roll 1, Scrapbook 3 ("He was so," "a good listener," "a mind and"). "About Eliot Ness," CN, September 22, 1947, in "Ness, Eliot" (microfiche),

CPC. *Story of Eliot Ness*, pp. 4–5. Art Petacque, "Capone's Lawyer and His Wife—Ness' Schoolmate—Rip 'The Untouchables,'" *Star*, June 30, 1987, p. 23, PCHS ("Elegant Mess"). Heimel, *Eliot Ness*, pp. 20–22 (20, "never had a"; 22, "like he thought").

ALEXANDER JAMIE: "Application for Appointment to Position of Special Agent of the Department of Justice," August 4, 1918 ("in a precarious"); "Application for Appointment," November 10, 1923, both in FBI-AJ. Application for Position of Federal Prohibition Agent, November 28, 1925; Edward J. Brennan to E. C. Yellowley, November 28, 1925; E. C. Yellowley to L. C. Andrews, February 26, 1926; Alexander Jamie to John T. Doyle, July 5, 1927; H. M. Dengler to J. M. Doran, September 1928 (declassified), all in Alexander Jamie OPF. Record for Alexander Jamie and Clara Ness, *Cook County, Illinois, Marriages Index, 1871–1920*, Provo, UT: Ancestry.Com Operations, Inc., 2011. Record for Wallace Ness Jamie, Cook County, Illinois, Birth Certificates Index, 1871–1922. 1910 U.S. Census Record for Eliot Ness. Chicago City Directory 1900, p. 953. Chicago City Directory 1910, p. 969. "The Ness Family," p. 84. "Modern Methods in Bread Baking," pp. 98–99. Townes, "As Boy in Chicago."

NESS AS PROTECTOR: GH to ABS, personal email, July 11, 2014.

CHRISTIAN SCIENCE: Jones, "Real Eliot Ness." Robert A. Johnson, "Early History of Sixth Church of Christ, Scientist, Chicago," October 6, 1987, SSGHS. Peters, *When Prayer Fails*, pp. 89–97. Paul Vitello, "Christian Science Church Seeks Truce with Modern Medicine," NYT, March 23, 2010.

SCARLET FEVER: Selzer, *The Heart*, pp. 132–139, 197. Rusty Brown, "This Ness Family Rejects Other Mrs. Ness," CP, April 20, 1973, in "Ness, Robert Eliot" Folder, CPC. Jedick, "Eliot Ness," p. 55. Heimel, *Eliot Ness*, p. 269.

BAKERY SUCCESS AND FAILURE: "Police Called to Dekker's, the Baker's, Place," *Calumet Index*, May 4, 1917. "Dekker's, the Baker," *Calumet Index*, May 7, 1917. "Modern Methods in Bread Baking," pp. 98–99 ("Every morning and," "hustling young salesladies"). Alexander Jamie to John T. Doyle, July 5, 1927, Alexander Jamie OPF. City of Chicago Directory 1911, pp. 1003, 1519. City of Chicago Directory 1912, pp. 691, 1029, 1560. City of Chicago Directory 1913, pp. 993, 1501. Theophilus Schmid, "Business History of Roseland," May 1, 1931, pp. 7–9, in Box 4, Folder 31, CRCC. *Story of Eliot Ness*, p. 5. "About Eliot Ness," CN, September 22, 1947, in "Ness, Eliot" (microfiche), CPC. Buder, *Pullman*, pp. 222–223.

The Ness bakeries disappear from Chicago city directories in 1917, and Alexander Jamie stopped working for Peter that same year, suggesting the business collapsed around that time.

ELIOT NESS WORKING THROUGH HIGH SCHOOL: 1920 U.S. Census Record for Peter Ness. (Eliot is misidentified as a girl named "Ella," and Emma's age is incorrectly given as fifty.) *Story of Eliot Ness*, p. 5, NLEM. Townes, "As Boy in Chicago." U.S. Civil Service Commission Temporary Appointment, Transfer, Reinstatement, Or Promotion Form, April 1942, Eliot Ness OPF. J. Edgar Hoover, Memo, November 7, 1933; W. S. Murphy, Report on Eliot Ness, November 15, 1933, p. 2; Howard P. Locke, memo to J. Edgar Hoover, November 25, 1933, all in FBI-ENA. Jedick, "Eliot Ness," p. 55.

JAMIE WITH PULLMAN, APL, AND BOI: "Application for Appointment to Position of Special Agent of the Department of Justice," August 4, 1918 ("securing data as"); Edward

J. Brennan, memo to William J. Burns, January 20, 1922; "Application for Appointment," November 10, 1923, Royal N. Allen, Report on Alexander G. Jamie, September 16, 1918, all in FBI-AJ Application for Position of Federal Prohibition Agent, November 28, 1925; Alexander Jamie to John T. Doyle, July 5, 1927; Alexander Jamie to the U.S. Civil Service Commission, July 3, 1928, all in Alexander Jamie OPF. Potter, *War on Crime*, p. 34. Ackerman, *Young J. Edgar*, pp. 6–7, 27, 65, 380. Mills, *The League*, pp. 7–15, 17–39, 56–57, 61–77, 79–90, 108–109, 153–175.

NESS INSPIRED BY HOLMES AND JAMIE: Ness and Fraley, *The Untouchables*, p. 6. For Holmes as a crime-solving textbook, see Wagner, *Science of Sherlock Holmes*, passim.

NESS GRADUATING HIGH SCHOOL, GOING TO WORK, ENROLLING AT COLLEGE: "What We Notice in Our Classmates," *The Fenger Courier*, January 1920, p. 21; "June Class, 1920," *The Fenger Courier*, June 1920, p. 13 ("Although he has"), both SSGHS. Currey, *Chicago*, p. 345. "Application for Appointment," November 10, 1923; Royal N. Allen, Report on Alexander G. Jamie, September 16, 1918; James P. Rooney, General Estimate of A. G. Jamie, November 5, 1921, all in FBI-AJ. W. S. Murphy, Report on Eliot Ness, November 15, 1933, pp. 2, 7, in FBI-ENA. Townes, "As Boy in Chicago" ("One day") Ness and Fraley, *The Untouchables*, p. 86 ("set his own"). Heimel, *Eliot Ness*, p. 22 ("He said he hadn't").

PRAIRIE AVENUE: Pasley, *Al Capone*, pp. 88–89 (89, "a refuge to"). Tyre, *Chicago's Historic Prairie Avenue*, pp. 7–8 (7, "the richest half-dozen"). Dahleen Glanton, "Capone Home Languishes on the Market," CT, October 28, 2014, http://www.chicagotribune.com/classified /realestate/ct-al-capone-house-sale-met-20141028-story.html (accessed June 25, 2017).

Chapter Three

PRAIRIE AVENUE HOUSE AND NEIGHBORHOOD: Pasley, *Al Capone*, pp. 88–90. *Hearings Before the Special Committee to Investigate Organized Crime in Interstate Commerce*, pt. 5, pp. 1227, 1231. Kobler, *Capone*, pp. 103–104. Bergreen, *Capone*, pp. 94–95 Bair, *Al Capone*, pp. 42–44. GH, undated interviews with grandparents who were parishioners of St. Columbanus and knew the Capone family.

CAPONE AT FOUR DEUCES: Schoenberg, *Mr. Capone*, pp. 51, 53.

LEVEE: Kirk, *Map of Chicago*. Wendt and Kogan, *Lords of the Levee*, p. 8. *Historic City*, pp. 41–75. Mayer and Wade, *Chicago*, pp. 146, 150, 218–220, 224.

TORRIO'S VISION: Landesco, "Organized Crime," pp. 912–919, 923.

CAPONE'S FAMILY BUSINESS: Cornelius Vanderbilt Jr., "How Al Capone Would Run This Country," *Liberty*, October 17, 1931, p. 18 ("We had to"). St. John, *This Was My World*, p. 180 ("had a strong"). Kobler, *Capone*, pp. 103–104, 145 ("Bottles"). Bergreen, *Capone*, pp. 43, 98–99. Bair, *Al Capone*, pp. 9–10, 16–17, 20, 45–47.

BIG BILL THOMPSON: Nels Anderson, "Democracy in Chicago," *Century*, November 1927, pp. 71–78 (71, "Big Bill the Builder"; 78, "Winning the election"). Wendt and Kogan, *Big Bill of Chicago*, pp. 86–115 (103, "a mother"), 119–131, 163–171. Bukowski, *Big Bill Thompson*, pp. 5, 14–15, 19–36.

CAPONE ANTIQUES SHOP: CT, May 10, 1924. Pasley, *Al Capone*, p. 19. McPhaul, *Johnny Torrio*, pp. 121–122.

CAPONE'S EARLY RUN-INS WITH THE LAW: CT, January 21, 1921; August 31, 1922 (quotes). Helmer and Mattix, *Public Enemies*, pp. 73, 77. Binder, *Al Capone's Beer Wars*, p. 122.

TORRIO HIRES NITTO: Eghigian, *After Capone*, pp. 39, 73–74, 81–83.

O'BANION AND THE NORTH SIDERS: Sullivan, *Rattling the Cup*, pp. 8–12 (9–10, "I didn't know"), 15–17. Pasley, *Al Capone*, pp. 45–46 (45, "could twist a," "His round Irish"; 46, "We're big business," "like a man"). Burns, *One-Way Ride*, pp. 80–86. Lyle, *Dry and Lawless Years*, pp. 89–91. Kobler, *Capone*, pp. 80–88. Schoenberg, *Mr. Capone*, pp. 104–107. Helmer and Mattix, *Public Enemies*, pp. 21–22. Keefe, *Guns and Roses*, pp. 59–66.

GENNAS AND MCERLANE: James Crayhorn, "The End of Gangland's Mad Dog," *Master Detective*, September 1933, pp. 26–29, 59–63. Kobler, *Capone*, pp. 77–101.

POLICE CORRUPTION AND ENFORCEMENT PROBLEMS: Landesco, "Organized Crime," pp. 1061–1087. Pasley, *Al Capone*, pp. 43–47.

1923 ELECTION: Wendt and Kogan, *Big Bill of Chicago*, pp. 206–233. Douglas Bukowski, "William Dever and Prohibition," *Chicago History*, Summer 1978, pp. 109–118. Schmidt, *Mayor Who Cleaned*, pp. 65–68, 72, 76, 79–80, 83–89. Bukowski, *Big Bill Thompson*, pp. 133–153.

TORRIO INTO THE SUBURBS: Lyle, *Dry and Lawless Years*, p. 88 ("cash register mind"). Allsop, *Bootleggers*, p. 65.

FOREST VIEW: CT, May 31, 1926. James O'Donnell Bennett, "Chicago Gangland: Golden Flood Makes Czars, Befouls City," CT, April 7, 1929 ("Caponeville"). Kobler, *Capone*, pp. 123–125 (125, "It looked like," "I moved"). See also Schoenberg, *Mr. Capone*, p. 96.

CICERO: CT, September 2, 1926 ("brought an automobile," "Then Torrio made"). Pasley, *Al Capone*, pp. 12, 39–40, 62–63. Burns, *One-Way Ride*, pp. 38–40. St. John, *This Was My World*, pp. 165–166, 171, 173–174 (173, "Why don't you") (see also Bergreen, *Capone*, pp. 104–105). Allsop, *Bootleggers*, pp. 58–59. Kobler, *Capone*, pp. 111–112, 116. Schoenberg, *Mr. Capone*, pp. 95–97.

O'DONNELL WAR: Keefe, *Man Who Got Away*, pp. 105–106, 127–129.

WEST HAMMOND RAID: McPhaul, *Johnny Torrio*, pp. 174–180.

CICERO ELECTION AND FRANK CAPONE'S DEATH: CT, April 1–3, 1924; April 7, 1924. Schoenberg, *Mr. Capone*, pp. 97–99. Bergreen, *Capone*, pp. 104–112. Eig, *Get Capone*, pp. 28–29.

JOE HOWARD MURDER: CT, May 9–10, 1924 (May 9, "Hello, Al"). Pasley, *Al Capone*, pp. 25–29 (29, "I hear the," "Who, me"). Kobler, *Capone*, pp. 122–123 (122, "Go back to"). Schoenberg, *Mr. Capone*, pp. 102–103.

SIEBEN BREWERY: CT, May 20, 1924. Kobler, *Capone*, pp. 127–130. Keefe, *Man Who Got Away*, pp. 143–145. "Sieben's History," Sieben's Brewing, 2006, http://www.siebensbrewing.com/history.htm (accessed September 15, 2017).

O'BANION MURDER: Keefe, *Guns and Roses*, pp. xvi–xxi, 195–204.

CAPONE'S DOCTOR'S OFFICE: Pasley, *Al Capone*, pp. 69–70. Capone, *Kobler*, p. 121. Eghigian, *After Capone*, p. 102.

CAPONE'S CAR SHOT UP: CDN, January 12, 1925. CT, January 13, 1925. Pasley, *Al Capone*, p. 75 ("everything but the"). Schoenberg, *Mr. Capone*, pp. 123, 399. Helmer and Mattix, *Public Enemies*, p. 86. Keefe, *Man Who Got Away*, p. 167.

CAPONE UNDER GUARD: Johnston, "Gangs Á La Mode" ("For Al's protection"). James O'Donnell Bennett, "Chicago Gangland: Golden Flood Makes Czars, Befouls City," CT, April 7, 1929. Burns, *One Way Ride*, p. 31. Pasley, *Al Capone*, pp. 10, 78–79, 325 ("You fear death"). Schoenberg, *Mr. Capone*, p. 117. Bergreen, *Capone*, pp. 138–139, 172–173, 176–189. Bair, *Al Capone*, pp. 58–64, 85–89.

TORRIO SHOOTING: Pasley, *Al Capone*, pp. 75–78. William Mangil, "Torrio the Immune," *True Detective*, September 1940, pp. 52–55, 91–97. McPhaul, *Johnny Torrio*, pp. 213–223. Kobler, *Capone*, pp. 139–141. Schoenberg, *Mr. Capone*, pp. 123–127.

TRANSFER OF POWER: Burns, *One-Way Ride*, pp. 111–112. Asbury, *Gem of the Prairie*, p. 354. Schoenberg, *Mr. Capone*, p. 127.

Chapter Four

CICERO: CT, November 21, 1924 ("The Free Kingdom," "Nearly all the"). James O'Donnell Bennett, "Chicago Gangland: Death Stalks Booze Route to Affluence," CT, February 24, 1929. Burns, *One-Way Ride*, pp. 38–40 (39, "If you are"). Asbury, *Gem of the Prairie*, pp. 334–336. Schoenberg, *Mr. Capone*, p. 99.

ROBERT ST. JOHN: CHE, April 7, 1925. CT, April 7–8, 1925. James O'Donnell Bennett, "Chicago Gangland: Death Stalks Booze Route to Affluence," CT, February 24, 1929. Pasley, *Al Capone*, pp. 66–67. St. John, *This Was My World*, pp. 167–168 (167, "had great executive," "might have wound"; 168, "knew that [the press]"), 171, 174–175, 181–186 (185, "Here in this"), 188–196 (191, "He was rather"; 193, "I'm an all-right," "right on the"). Kobler, *Capone*, pp. 151–157. Schoenberg, *Mr. Capone*, pp. 99–101. Robert St. John, interviewed in *The Mystery of Al Capone's Vaults* video, 1:33:22, April 21, 1986, Geraldo, http://www.geraldo.com /page/al-capone-s-vault (accessed March 9, 2017) ("the biggest roll"). Robert St. John, interviewed in "The Road to Repeal," *Prohibition: Thirteen Years That Changed America*, written by Marius Brill, directed by Clive Maltby (New York: A&E Television Networks, 1997), DVD ("had a scar"); "Prohibition: Robert St. John—About His Personal Contact with Al Capone," video, 00:04:29, Onlinefootage.tv, http://www.onlinefootage.tv/stock -video-footage/7743/prohibition-robert-st-john-about-his-personal-contact-with-al-capone (accessed March 9, 2017). Douglas Martin, "Robert St. John, 100, Globe-Trotting Reporter and Author," NYT, February 8, 2003, http://www.nytimes.com/2003/02/08/us/robert-st -john-100-globe-trotting-reporter-and-author.html (accessed March 11, 2017).

NESS IN COLLEGE: *City of Chicago Directory 1923*, pp. 1262, 2108; *Polk's Chicago City Directory 1923*, p. 2852. *Cap and Gown* (University of Chicago Yearbook), 1924, p. 248; *Cap and Gown* (University of Chicago Yearbook), 1925, pp. 89, 210–211, UC. Willebrandt, *Inside of Prohibition*, p. 33. CHE, June 15, 1931 ("the monotony of"). Allen, *Only Yesterday*, pp. 88–122 (94, "the eat-drink"). W. S. Murphy, Report on Eliot Ness, November 15, 1933, p. 3, in FBI-ENA. Townes, "As Boy in Chicago" ("could always count"). Nell C. Henry to Harold H. Swift, October 26, 1939, in Box 156, Folder 7, Harold H. Swift Papers, UC. *Story of Eliot Ness*, pp. 5–6, NLEM. Ness and Fraley, *The Untouchables*, p. 6. Fraley, "Real Eliot Ness," pp. 28–29. Allsop, *Bootleggers*, pp. 32–33. Porter, *Cleveland*, p. 102. Fass, *Damned and the Beautiful*, pp. 134–136, 139, 157–167, 172–182, 201–202, 262–276, 281–285, 292–300, 310–324. Jones, "Real Eliot Ness" ("had the girls," "We used to," "almost priestly"). George

Condon, "The Last American Hero," *Cleveland*, August 1987, p. 139 ("Eliot had a," "He wasn't handsome"), RM. Bergreen, *Capone*, pp. 345, 598. Heimel, *Eliot Ness*, pp. 23–24. Alder, *Lie Detectors*, p. 76. Okrent, *Last Call*, pp. 205–215, 222–225. Tucker, *Eliot Ness and the Untouchables*, pp. 30, 42–43. McGirr, *War on Alcohol*, pp. 116–117. See also Perry, *Eliot Ness*, pp. 11–12.

Jonathan Eig (*Get Capone*, p. 237; see also Perry, *Eliot Ness*, p. 16) claims that Ness "was an undistinguished student, scraping by on a steady diet of Cs and C-minuses." But Eig grades Ness like a modern student, and doesn't take into account the "grade inflation" observed over the course of the twentieth century. According to *The Atlantic*, the average GPA at American colleges rose from a 2.3 (C+) in the 1930s to 3.3 or 3.0 (B+ or B) today, while academic performance has not (Aina Katsikas, "Same Performance, Better Grades," *The Atlantic*, January 13, 2015, http://www.theatlantic.com/education/archive/2015/01/same-performance-better-grades /384447/ [accessed January 23, 2015]).

W. S. Murphy, a Bureau of Investigation agent who ran a background check on Ness in 1933, reported that during his first two years at the University of Chicago Ness "received an average grade of C and the last two years his average grade was raised to a B." (W. S. Murphy, Report on Eliot Ness, November 15, 1933, p. 3, in FBI-ENA.) While not outstanding, Ness's grades rose from average to above average during his college career—a far cry from "scraping by."

NESS, ALCOHOL, AND CHRISTIAN SCIENCE: Bernice W. Carter, "Enforcing Prohibition," *The Christian Science Journal*, March 1921, pp. 680–682. "The Lectures," *Christian Science Sentinel*, June 29, 1918, p. 873. "The Chimes Rang Out," *Christian Science Sentinel*, April 20, 1918, p. 670. "Greenhorn," *American Magazine*, March 1936, in ENPS, Roll 1, Scrapbook 3. Wallace Ness Jamie, "Man Cannot Die," *Christian Science Sentinel*, February 10, 1945, pp. 201–203. Ness and Fraley, *The Untouchables*, p. 19. CPD, May 17, 1957, in ENPS, Roll 1, Folder 1. Jedick, "Eliot Ness," p. 55. Fass, *Damned and the Beautiful*, pp. 310–324 (318, "In order to"). Jones, "Real Eliot Ness" ("He didn't drink"). Okrent, *Last Call*, p. 222 ("girls simply won't"). Tucker, *Eliot Ness and the Untouchables*, p. 13. RM to ABS, personal interview and emails, December 4, 8, and 10, 2015. McGirr, *War on Alcohol*, p. 10. *Honolulu Advertiser*, January 29, 1961.

NESS TRAINING TO BE LAWMAN: Agent in Charge Hamlin to J. Edgar Hoover, November 25, 1924; James P. Rooney, Evaluation of A. G. Jamie, May 20, 1924; James P. Rooney to William J. Burns, March 8, 1922; T. B. White, "Inspection of the Chicago Office," April 28, 1925; J. Edgar Hoover to R. A. Darling, July 15, 1925; R. A. Darling to J. Edgar Hoover, July 1, 1925; J. Edgar Hoover to R. A. Darling, June 29, 1925; R. A. Darling to J. Edgar Hoover, June 25, 1925; Roy A. Darling to J. Edgar Hoover, July 17, 1925; Roy A. Darling to J. Edgar Hoover, September 22, 1925; Arthur M. Millard to Roy O. West, September 21, 1925, all in FBI-AJ. "Personal History," August 26, 1926, in Eliot Ness OPF. Conan Doyle, *Complete Sherlock Holmes*, pp. 386, 486 ("the Japanese system," "baritsu"). W. S. Murphy, Report on Eliot Ness, November 15, 1933, pp. 3–5, in FBI-ENA ("a bright, energetic," "regretted losing"). Havens, "Personalities in Law Enforcement," p. 61 ("skippers"). Ness MS., p. 1, in ENPS, Roll 1, Folder 2. Ness and Fraley, *The Untouchables*, pp. 6–7. William Adams Flinn, "History of Retail Credit Company: A Study in the Marketing of Information About

Individuals" (PhD diss., Ohio State University, 1959), pp. 236–253. Fraley, "The Real Eliot Ness," p. 29 ("I liked it"). Fraley, *4 Against the Mob*, p. 10. "Ness Called 'Mild, Quiet' in Real Life," n.p., February 11, 1962, and untitled clipping, n.p., December 9, 1976, both in "Newspaper Clippings (Photocopies) Circa. 1930–1970" Folder, DMM. Jones, "The Real Eliot Ness." Bergreen, *Capone*, p. 345. James D. Calder, "Eliot Ness (April 19, 1903–May 16, 1957): Gangbuster to Security Executive—A Meandering Career of Great Highs and Tragic Lows," *Journal of Applied Security Research*, vol. 6, no. 2 (2011), pp. 196–197. See also *Kansas City Star*, April 19, 1936, in ENPS, Roll 1, Scrapbook 2, p. 68; *Baltimore Sun*, May 17, 1936, in ENPS, Roll 1, Scrapbook 2, p. 80.

In a hearing before the Chicago City Council in 2014, former IRS special agent Robert Fuesel claimed that Alcohol Tax Unit agents who had served with Ness during the Untouchables days had told him that Ness "was afraid of guns and barely left the office." But this flies in the face of firsthand testimony from those who knew Ness personally, and probably reflects institutional jealousy (discussed in later chapters) of Ness's posthumous celebrity. Most likely, these agents mistook Ness's dislike of firearms for fear. As Armand Bollaert recalled, Ness "had no interest in guns; he was absolutely fearless." (John Byrne, "Chicago Aldermen: Eliot Ness Overhyped," CT, February 28, 2014, http://articles.chicagotribune.com/2014-02-28 /news/chi-chicago-aldermen-eliot-ness-overhyped-20140228_1_eliot-ness-the-untouchables -atf-hq [accessed October 24, 2015]; Jones, "The Real Eliot Ness.")

JAMIE AND HOOVER: A. G. Jamie, memo to "Mr. Darling," July 20, 1925; Darling, telegram to Director, September 16, 1925; Hoover, telegram to R. A. Darling, September 16, 1925; Darling, telegram to Director, September 16, 1925; J. Edgar Hoover to R. A. Darling, September 17, 1925; Alexander G. Jamie to Director, September 19, 1925; Roy A. Darling to Director, September 19, 1925; Arthur M. Millard to Roy O. West, September 21, 1925; Roy A. Darling to J. Edgar Hoover, September 22, 1925; Roy O. West to John Sargent, September 22, 1925; A. G. Jamie, telegram to Director ("certain influential friends"), September 24, 1925; Director to A. G. Jamie, September 24, 1925 ("a special assignment," "two months or"); Director, memo to "Mr. Marshall," September 24, 1925 ("efficiency and obedience"); Hoover, telegram to Darling, September 29, 1925; Darling, telegram to Director, September 29, 1925; Hoover, telegram to Darling, September 29, 1925; J. Edgar Hoover, memo to "Mr. Marshall," October 5, 1925 ("that there is"), all in FBI-AJ. Potter, *War on Crime*, pp. 32–33.

Ness apparently knew nothing of Jamie's conflict with Hoover. In his first draft manuscript for *The Untouchables*, Ness claims Jamie came into the Prohibition Bureau when it was transferred to the Department of Justice, which actually happened in 1930. Ness MS., p. 1, in ENPS, Roll 1, Folder 2.

PROHIBITION BUREAU: "Application for Position of Federal Prohibition Agent," November 28, 1925; Edward J. Brennan to E. C. Yellowley, November 28, 1925 ("absolutely honest, capable"); Oath of Office, December 23, 1926; E. C. Yellowley to J. T. Brereton, December 24, 1926; E. C. Yellowley to James E. Jones, December 15, 1928; D. H. Blair to Alexander Jamie, January 7, 1928; Oath of Office, January 18, 1926, all in Alexander Jamie OPF. Schmeckebier, *Bureau of Prohibition*, pp. 49–51, 53. *Law Observance*, ed. Durant, p. 34. J. A. Buchanan, "A National League to Educate," in *Law Observance*, ed. Durant, p. 99. G. L. Cleaver, "No More Joking," in *Law Observance*, ed. Durant, p. 139.

A. T. Cole, "Mr. and Mrs. Prominent Citizen," in *Law Observance*, ed. Durant, p. 155. Frederick C. Dezendorf, "Stop Supplies for Home Brew Forfeit 'Pre-Volstead' Cellars," in *Law Observance*, ed. Durant, p. 196. Sinclair, *Prohibition*, p. 184. Allsop, *Bootleggers*, pp. 36 ("twenty-three innocent"), 304–305. Kobler, *Ardent Spirits*, pp. 272–273. Calder, *Origins and Development*, pp. 55, 233n17. Behr, *Prohibition*, pp. 239 ("a corps of"), 241. Potter, *War on Crime*, pp. 13–20, 26. Nishi, *Prohibition*, p. 20. Helmer and Bilek, *St. Valentine's Day Massacre*, p. 57 ("Don't shoot"). Ackerman, *Young J. Edgar*, p. 65. Folsom, *Money Trail*, p. 29. Okrent, *Last Call*, pp. 221–222, 245. McGirr, *War on Alcohol*, pp. xviii, 59–102, 123, 144–153, 165–166, 172, 201–210.

NESS JOINS PROHIBITION BUREAU: Oath of Office, August 26, 1926, in Eliot Ness OPF. Fraley, "The Real Eliot Ness," p. 29 ("So many of," "Not me"). Porter, *Cleveland*, p. 106 ("I looked around"). Jedick, "Eliot Ness," p. 50 ("Someone has to").

NESS'S FIRST RAID: Jedick, "Eliot Ness," pp. 50–51. Heimel, *Eliot Ness*, p. 51 ("He couldn't wait," "I'll say this").

Chapter Five

CAPONE AND THE PRESS: CHE, January 24, 1927 ("gaudy pink apron"); March 9, 1927 (Capone quotes). Schoenberg, *Mr. Capone*, p. 95 ("You're a public"). Bergreen, *Capone*, pp. 148–149. Bair, *Al Capone*, p. 103.

HAWTHORNE SMOKE SHOP RAID: IRS-2, pp. 10–16 (quotes, our italics). Ross, *Trial of Al Capone*, pp. 43–46, 50–52. Kobler, *Capone*, pp. 154, 157–159. Bair, *Al Capone*, pp. 69–70.

WEISS AND O'DONNELL: Keefe, *Man Who Got Away*, pp. 175–176, 183.

GENNAS: Sullivan, *Rattling the Cup*, pp. 59–61 (59, "though they were," 61 "overdressed, boastful, reeking"). Burns, *One-Way Ride*, pp. 113 ("bloody Angelo"), 131. Asbury, *Gem of the Prairie*, pp. 346–347. Allsop, *Bootleggers*, pp. 76–79 (76, "the Terrible Gennas"). Kobler, *Capone*, pp. 33–34, 88–92, 162–163.

WEISS: Sullivan, *Rattling the Cup*, p. 35 ("the most energetic"). Keefe, *Man Who Got Away*, p. 163.

MCGURN: Shmelter, *Chicago Assassin*, pp. 20–40. Sifakis, *Mafia Encyclopedia*, p. 283.

ANGELO GENNA MURDER: CT, May 27, 1925. Burns, *One-Way Ride*, pp. 113–119. Schoenberg, *Mr. Capone*, pp. 129–131. Eghigian, *After Capone*, pp. 108–109.

SCALISE AND ANSELMI: Burns, *One-Way Ride*, p. 94 ("They were abnormal"). Asbury, *Gem of the Prairie*, p. 346. Kobler, *Capone*, pp. 89–90. Binder, *Al Capone's Beer Wars*, p. 103 ("Murder Twins").

MIKE GENNA MURDER: CT, June 14, 1925. Sullivan, *Rattling the Cup*, pp. 61–64. Schoenberg, *Mr. Capone*, pp. 131–132 (132, "resisted arrest"). Keefe, *Man Who Got Away*, pp. 177–179. Eghigian, *After Capone*, pp. 109–111.

ANTHONY GENNA AND THE UNIONE SICILIANA: Kobler, *Capone*, pp. 163–164. Shmelter, *Chicago Assassin*, pp. 65–67.

SONNY'S SURGERY AND ADONIS CLUB MASSACRE: NYT, December 27, 1925. CHE, March 9, 1927 (Capone quotes). Meyer Berger, "Mom, Murder Ain't Polite," in Ellen, Murphy, and Weld, *A Treasury of Brooklyn*, pp. 339–340. Kobler, *Capone*, pp. 167–169 (167,

"Merry Christmas and"). Schoenberg, *Mr. Capone*, pp. 141–144. Balsamo and Balsamo, *Young Al Capone*, pp. 245–259.

CAPONE CALLING HOME: Bair, *Al Capone*, pp. 69–70.

SYPHILIS: Bergreen, *Capone*, pp. 44–46. Kathleen Brewer-Smyth, "Neurological Correlates of High-Risk Behavior: A Case Study of Alphonse Capone," *Journal of Neuroscience Nursing*, vol. 38, no. 6 (December 2006), pp. 442–445. Eig, *Get Capone*, pp. 17, 375. Bair, *Al Capone*, pp. 71–72, 290–291. Dardoff, Jankovic, Mazziotta, and Pomeroy, *Bradley's Neurology in Clinical Practice*, p. 102.

THOMPSON SUBMACHINE GUN: Sullivan, *Rattling the Cup*, p. 37 ("That's the gun"). Harry T. Brundidge and Frank L. Thompson, "The Truth About Chicago," *Real Detective*, December 1930, pp. 17, 19. "Munitions: Chopper," *Time*, June 26, 1939, p. 67 ("the deadliest weapon"). Helmer, *Gun That Made the Twenties Roar*, pp. 26–27, 32, 74–79, 82. Kobler, *Capone*, p. 109. Schoenberg, *Mr. Capone*, pp. 140–141. Helmer and Mattix, *Public Enemies*, p. 96. Helmer and Bilek, *St. Valentine's Day Massacre*, pp. 21–23, 37. Kyle and Doyle, *American Gun*, pp. 175–176.

Binder (*Al Capone's Beer Wars*, pp. 293, 382n32) credits Frank McErlane with the first use of a Thompson in a gangster murder, but in that killing the weapon was fired semiautomatic (one bullet for each pull of the trigger) instead of full auto.

MCGURN'S VENGENACE: Shmelter, *Chicago Assassin*, pp. 75–77, 79–81.

MCSWIGGIN MURDER AND AFTERMATH: CT, April 28, 1926 ("We are going"); April 30, 1926; May 2, 1926 ("Scarface Al Brown," "was in a"); May 31, 1926 ("said no attempts"). James O'Donnell Bennett, "Chicago Gangland: Golden Flood Makes Czars, Befouls City," CT, April 7, 1929. CDN, April 28–30, 1926. CHE, April 28–30, 1926. Edgar Wolfe, "The Real Truth About Al Capone," *Master Detective*, September 1930, pp. 36–40. Pasley, *Al Capone*, pp. 128–131 ("Capone in person"), 214 ("Who killed McSwiggin?"). Stephen Hull, "Cicero Ambush," *True Detective*, July 1948, pp. 36–49, 58–59. Kobler, *Capone*, pp. 175–183. Schoenberg, *Mr. Capone*, pp. 148–152 (149, "Little Mac," "the Hanging Prosecutor"). Record for William Harold McSwiggin, *Illinois Deaths and Stillbirths Index, 1916–1947* (Provo, UT: Ancestry.com Operations, 2011).

CAPONE IN HIDING: CT, April 13, 1986. *Lansing State Journal*, June 9, 1987 ("He'd be out"). Bergreen, *Capone*, pp. 15–16 (16, "If you do"), 94, 172–189 (172, "all business," 178, "Capone was not"), 191–192, Bair, *Al Capone*, pp. 58–63, 85–89. Binder, *Al Capone's Beer Wars*, p. 152.

Bergreen quotes Capone's errand boy under a pseudonym, but that individual is almost certainly the same man referred to in the *Lansing State Journal* article.

Chapter Six

CAPONE'S RETURN: CT, July 28–29, 1926 (July 28, "I think the," "my friend McSwiggin"). CHE, July 28–29, 1926. Landesco, "Organized Crime," pp. 827–841 (829, "I liked the"). Kobler, *Capone*, pp. 182, 185–187 (186, "I paid him"). Schoenberg, *Mr. Capone*, pp. 154–155.

ANTHONY MCSWIGGIN: Pasley, *Al Capone*, pp. 133–134 ("If you think"). Schoenberg, *Mr. Capone*, pp. 155–156 (156, "was just too").

WEISS: Pasley, *Al Capone*, pp. 124–125 ("Weiss, the Pole").

CAPONE'S CHAUFFEUR MURDERED: Burns, *One-Way Ride*, pp. 185–186. Keefe, *Man Who Got Away*, p. 191.

WEISS/DRUCCI GUNFIGHTS: Pasley, *Al Capone*, pp. 121–123. Burns, *One-Way Ride*, p. 186. Keefe, *Man Who Got Away*, pp. 191–192. Kobler, *Capone*, pp. 189–190.

HAWTHORNE RESTAURANT SHOOTING: CT, September 21, 1926. James O'Donnell Bennett, "Chicago Gangland: Golden Flood Makes Czars, Befouls City," CT, April 7, 1929 ("The Big Fellow"). Pasley, *Al Capone*, pp. 113–120 (114, "It's a stall"). Burns, *One-Way Ride*, pp. 187–188. Kobler, *Capone*, pp. 190–192. Schoenberg, *Mr. Capone*, pp. 159–160 (160, "A machine gun"). Binder, *Al Capone's Beer Wars*, pp. 169–170.

PEACE PARLEY: CT, October 12, 1926. CEA, October 13, 1926. Pasley, *Al Capone*, p. 91 ("I wouldn't do"). Burns, *One-Way Ride*, pp. 188–189. Eghigian, *After Capone*, p. 123.

WEISS MURDER: CT, October 12, 1926. CEA, October 13, 1926. CHE, March 9, 1927. Burns, *One-Way Ride*, pp. 189–195. Keefe, *Man Who Got Away*, pp. 195–198. Eghigian, *After Capone*, pp. 123–125.

CAPONE PRESS CONFERENCE: CT, October 13, 1926 ("other notables," "I'm sorry Weiss," "He was supposed"). CEA, October 13, 1926 ("beer racket," "I have to," "I'll tell them"). NYT, October 13, 1926 ("tried since the," "I know that"). Pasley, *Al Capone*, pp. 126–127. Kobler, *Capone*, pp. 195–196.

WEISS FUNERAL: Allsop, *Bootleggers*, pp. 87, 116. Schoenberg, *Mr. Capone*, p. 165. Keefe, *Man Who Got Away*, pp. 62, 199.

PEACE TREATY: CHE, October 23, 1926 ("I believe it's," "I'm going home"). Pasley, *Al Capone*, pp. 139–144 (142, "Here they sat"; 144, "the John D."). Wendt and Kogan, *Big Bill of Chicago*, pp. 89, 133, 243. Kobler, *Capone*, pp. 197–200 (199, "feast of ghouls"). Schoenberg, *Mr. Capone*, pp. 166–168. Eghigian, *After Capone*, p. 125. Binder, *Al Capone's Beer Wars*, pp. 171–172.

VOLSTEAD ACT: Willebrandt, *Inside of Prohibition*, p. 17. Kobler, *Ardent Spirits*, pp. 213–214, 275. Behr, *Prohibition*, pp. 79–80, 83–84. Okrent, *Last Call*, pp. 108–114, 134–135.

PROHIBITION UNIT: Schmeckebier, *Bureau of Prohibition*, pp. 35, 43–53. Willebrandt, *Inside of Prohibition*, pp. 17, 94, 111–114 (113–114, "that hundreds of"), 132–149. Pasley, *Al Capone*, p. 40 ("When the cops"). Allen, *Only Yesterday*, pp. 249–250. Sullivan, *Chicago Surrenders*, p. 137 ("Gold badges look"). Irey and Slocum, *Tax Dodgers*, pp. ix–xv, 4–24 (4–5, "As I think"). Kobler, *Ardent Spirits*, pp. 271, 273–275, 277. Schoenberg, *Mr. Capone*, pp. 57–58. Behr, *Prohibition*, pp. 79–80, 83–84, 152–153. Potter, *War on Crime*, pp. 16–17, 26. Trespacz, *Trial of Gangster Al Capone*, p. 39. Fiorello H. La Guardia, "Prohibition Is Unenforceable," in Nishi, *Prohibition*, p. 96. Okrent, *Last Call*, pp. 108–118, 134–135, 137, 141–144, 232, 331. Folsom, *Money Trail*, pp. 15–30.

   Although initially called the Special Intelligence Unit and sometimes referred to as the SIU in accounts of the period, the unit had dropped *Special* from its name by the time of the Capone case. (See IRS-1; IRS-2; IRS-3; IRS-4; Messick, *Secret File*, p. 36.) We refer to it as the Intelligence Unit throughout to avoid confusion.

YELLOWLEY: Towne, *Rise and Fall of Prohibition*, p. 13 ("I drink as"). CT, November 7, 1926; September 5, 1927 ("rip snortin'"). Schmeckebier, *Bureau of Prohibition*, pp. 62, 65, 68. Pasley, *Al Capone*, pp. 40, 47–48, 92, 94–95, 163. Robert Isham Randolph, "How to Wreck

Capone's Gang," *Collier's*, March 7, 1931, pp. 8–9. Allsop, *Bootleggers*, pp. 34–35, 66. Schoenberg, *Mr. Capone*, p. 77. Vern Whaley, interviewed in *Al Capone: the Untouchable Legend*, written and directed by Rike Fochler (Langbein and Skalnik TV, 1990), DVD. Eghigian, *After Capone*, pp. 45–46. Helmer and Bilek, *St. Valentine's Day Massacre*, p. 107. Okrent, *Last Call*, p. 141. Folsom, *Money Trail*, p. 62. McGirr, *War on Alcohol*, pp. 55–56.

ROCHE INVESTIGATION: A. P. Madden to Chief, Intelligence Unit, June 7, 1927 ("You appear to"); G. J. Simons, Agent's Memorandum of Violation, June 8, 1927; G. J. Simons to E. C. Yellowley, June 11, 1927; Clarence Converse and Patrick Roche to Chief, Intelligence Unit, July 31, 1928 ("the 'Al Caponi'," "the brewery was," "of putting out"), all in Alexander Jamie OPF. CT, August 6, 1927. UCR, pp. 31–32.

BUREAU OF PROHIBITION: CT, March 1, 1927; January 17, 1928; July 28, 1929. Schmeckebier, *Bureau of Prohibition*, pp. 1, 19–21, 54–60, 62. Willebrandt, *Inside of Prohibition*, pp. 111, 114–115, 135–138. Kobler, *Ardent Spirits*, pp. 278–279. Behr, *Prohibition*, pp. 153–154. Potter, *War on Crime*, p. 26. McGirr, *War on Alcohol*, p. 208.

NESS AGE: Personal History, August 26, 1926, in Eliot Ness OPF. Announcement, "United States Civil Service Examination No. 122," c. May 1927, in Robert D. Sterling OPF/ATF. Oath of Office, December 23, 1926; E. C. Yellowley to J. T. Brereton, December 24, 1926; Charles S. Deneen to L. C. Andrews, June 13, 1927; H. H. White to Ismar Baruch, June 20, 1927; I. Baruch to H. H. White, June 22, 1927; Alexander G. Jamie to the United States Civil Service Commission, July 5, 1927; E. C. Yellowley to J. M. Doran, July 6, 1927; J. M. Doran to E. C. Yellowley, July 11, 1927; I. Baruch to H. H. White, August 5, 1927; Alf Oftedal to E. C. Yellowley, August 6, 1927, all in Alexander Jamie OPF. Murphy, Report on Ness, p. 10; P. T. Sowell, interview with William J. Froelich, November 21, 1933, both in FBI-ENA.

A letter in the official personnel folder of Prohibition agent Marion A. R. King—the only Untouchable younger, by a couple of months, than Ness—shows that he encountered the same problem. "Owing to the fact that at the time examinations were held for the position of Prohibition agent he was only twenty-four years of age," wrote Prohibition Commissioner J. M. Doran, "[King] was not eligible to compete in the examination, the minimum age being twenty-five years." King got around this problem by taking the Civil Service exam for the Bureau of Narcotics, which was open to anyone twenty-one years of age or older. The Civil Service Commission, however, stating "that the examinations for Anti-Narcotic agent and Prohibition agent are not of the same type," denied King's request for Civil Service status until he qualified under the new rules. (J. M. Doran to the Secretary of the Treasury, July 6, 1928; John T. Doyle to the Secretary of the Treasury, July 19, 1928, both in Marion A. R. King OPF/ATF.)

Perry (*Eliot Ness*, p. 27), citing Ness's personnel file, accepts 1902 as Ness's birth year, but the preponderance of other evidence—especially from sources that could have only come from Ness or his family—strongly suggests 1903. The 1910 and 1920 U.S. Censuses give ages consistent with 1903 (in the latter, Ness is misidentified as a girl named "Ella"). So do the record of his marriage to Evaline McAndrew in 1939 (Tucker, *Eliot Ness and the Untouchables*, p. 31) and the vast majority of newspaper articles, particularly from his Cleveland years. Ness's University of Chicago records give his birth year as 1903 (Murphy, Report on Ness, p. 3), as does his death certificate (*Pennsylvania Death Certificates, 1906–1963*, Provo, UT: Ancestry.

com Operations, 2014). After he left federal employment for good in 1942, Ness was particularly open about his age, giving it as forty-two in a *Fortune* magazine article published in January 1946 and giving his birth year as 1903 in the campaign literature from his 1947 run for mayor of Cleveland ("There Goes Eliot Ness," *Fortune*, January 1946, p. 196; *Story of Eliot Ness*, pp. 3–4, NLEM). The *Who's Who in America* c. 1951 also gives his birth year as 1903 ("*Who Was Who in America*," c. 1951–1960, p. 635, RM), as does his job application to join the Fidelity Check Corporation in 1955 (Application for Employment, December 28, 1955, KDB). Ness consistently reported his birth year as 1902 in his official personnel folder, and the 1930 Census gives an age consistent with that same year, but taken together these sources are outliers.

Less clear is how, when Ness joined the Prohibition Unit in 1926, he could have anticipated needing to add a year to his age. As stated above, the reform bill that Congress finally passed in 1927 had been proposed, in essentially the same form, more than once. Jamie or others in the unit could certainly have seen these reforms coming. It's also possible that Ness, thanks to Jamie's influence, was able to alter his file after the fact. On the personal history statement in his OPF—the only pre-1927 source, as far as is known, giving his birth year as 1902—Ness's birth year has been heavily written over and "(1902)," apparently in his handwriting, added just above it. It's not at all clear, however, that the document once read 1903; it could have initially read "'02" or something similar. Without access to the original, it is impossible to say.

Ness's birth certificate, which gives his birth year as 1902, would not be filed until January 1932 (Eliot Ness Certificate of Birth, No. 33469, Bureau of Vital Records, Cook County Clerk, Chicago, IL; Murphy, Report on Ness, pp. 1–3, in FBI-ENA).

NESS'S EARLY INVESTIGATIONS: CHE, April 22, 1927 ("You can't arrest"). CT, April 22, 1927; April 28, 1927 ("Kentucky colonels who"). *Rockford Republic*, April 28, 1927. CDT, June 13, 1931. CHE, June 15, 1931 ("there certainly is"). Murphy, Report on Ness, p. 11, in FBI-ENA. I. L. Kenen, "Ness' New Aide, Who Tried Out Raiding, Sees Chance to Realize Some Ideals," CN, February 4, 1937, in ENPS, Roll 1, Scrapbook 3.

The *Daily Times* article doesn't give an exact date for Ness's University of Illinois investigation, placing it only in 1926, but it must have been the fall, since Ness joined the Prohibition Unit in August and the school year probably began in September.

PROHIBITION AGENTS AND ALCOHOLISM: Willebrandt, *Inside of Prohibition*, p. 114 ("seven hundred glasses"). Personal History Statement, May 21, 1932, in Bernard V. Cloonan OPF/ATF ("making buys"). Dwight E. Avis to Special Agent in Charge Jacksonville, August 25, 1932, in Paul W. Robsky OPF/ATF.

Untouchable Barney Cloonan's daybook for the year 1929, shared with ABS by JBC, meticulously documents Cloonan's expenses, showing him purchasing several drinks at different speakeasies over the course of an investigation.

Of the Untouchables who struggled with alcohol later in life, William Gardner's alcoholism is documented in Benjey, *Doctors, Lawyers, Indian Chiefs*, pp. 131–132. Lyle Chapman admitted using alcohol "sparingly" when becoming a special agent in September 1927. In October 1932, Chapman was charged with "frequenting places where liquor is sold" and "consuming liquor not in line of duty." The charges, while never proven, led to his being furloughed from the Prohibition Bureau (Application for Position of Prohibition Agent, September 2, 1927; D. A. Sloan to the Director of Prohibition, April 24, 1932; Everett H. Kuebler, memo to A. V. Dalrymple, April 27, 1933; D. H. Reichgut, memo to Dwight Avis, June 9, 1933; A. V. Dalrymple to Lyle B. Chapman, June 27, 1933, all in Lyle B. Chapman OPF/ATF). Paul Robsky admitted to "limited" use of intoxicating beverages as early as 1932, prompting a rebuke from his superior. In 1951, Robsky was arrested for drunk driving in a misappropriated government car, which led to his resignation from federal service (Personal History Statement, May 21, 1932; Dwight E. Avis to Special Agent in Charge Jacksonville, August 25, 1932; R. E. Tuttle to Deputy Commissioner of the Alcohol Tax Unit, April 12, 1951; Statement of Paul Robsky, April 20, 1951; Statement of Roger B. Parker, April 11, 1951; Statement of George E. Baker, April 12, 1951; Statement of Arvell L. Perry, April 12, 1951; R. E. Tuttle to the Deputy Commissioner of the ATU, April 20, 1951, all in Paul W. Robsky OPF/ATF). Daniel R. Vaccarelli, who worked with Ness in the Chicago office of the Prohibition Bureau and may have been involved with the Capone case (see "Theft of Cars Seen As Plot to Halt Agents," n.p., n.d., in ENPS, Roll 1, Scrapbook 1, p. 31), resigned from the ATU in March 1935 after getting into a drunken brawl off duty (E. C. Yellowley to Arthur J. Mellott, May 13, 1935, in Daniel R. Vaccarelli OPF/ATF).

NESS AND ALCOHOL: Background check on Eliot Ness, February 23, 1928, in FBI-EN. Murphy, Report on Ness, pp. 11–13, in FBI-ENA. Bryce Nelson, "The Addictive Personality: Common Traits Are Found," NYT, January 18, 1983. Jones, "The Real Eliot Ness." *Honolulu Advertiser,* January 29, 1961. "Prohibition: Tony Berardi—About Eliot Ness and 'the Untouchables,'" Onlinefootage.tv, 08:42, http://www.onlinefootage.tv/stock-video-footage/7684/prohibition-tony-berardi-about-eliot-ness-and-the-untouchables (accessed August 26, 2015). David J. Linden, "Addictive Personality? You Might Be A Leader," NYT, July 23, 2011. Perry, *Eliot Ness,* p. 117.

Marjorie Mutersbaugh, a Ness family friend, insisted Ness never drank socially while Prohibition was in force, per RM to ABS, personal interview and emails, December 4, 8, and 10, 2015.

Perry (*Eliot Ness,* p. 33) claims Ness drank surreptitiously both as a college student and as a Prohibition agent, but this contradicts the available evidence. When the FBI conducted a background check on Ness in 1933, four of the ten people who gave personal testimony of his character stated Ness did not drink at all, including one who knew Ness from childhood (see Murphy and Jones, cited above). Perry offers no citations to back up his claims.

For more on Ness as a workaholic, see CN, December 11, 1935, in ENPS, Roll 1, Scrapbook 2, p. 4; CP, December 11, 1935, in ENPS, Roll 1, Scrapbook 2, p. 6; CPD [?], December 12, 1935, in ENPS, Roll 1, Scrapbook 2, p. 9.

NESS AND YELLOWLEY: Murphy, Report on Ness, p. 10, in FBI-ENA ("always on the"). Untitled clipping and photograph, n.p., August 6, 1927 [?], ATF.

Jamie's OPF makes clear Yellowley kept a right rein on how his agents interfaced with the press. Just a few days after being appointed assistant Prohibition administrator, Jamie sent a memo to Yellowley apologizing for being quoted at length in the *Chicago Daily News.* "I want you to understand that I fully realize that if any statements are to be given to the press that the administrator [Yellowley] is the person to give out such statements," Jamie wrote. "I did not anticipate that any remarks made by me were to be used for a newspaper article." Alexander G. Jamie, memo to E. C. Yellowley, December 30, 1926; CDN, December 29, 1926, both in Alexander Jamie OPF.

NESS'S FRUSTRATION: Indictment, *United States of America v. Joe Cohen*, May 17, 1928; Petition to suppress evidence and quash information, *United States of America v. Joe Cohen*, October 16, 1928, both in Box 4, "Criminal Case # 17506" folder, PCF. Indictment, *United States of America v. Joe Mealki*, July 24, 1928; Commitment of sentence, *United States v. Joe Mealki*, December 6, 1928; Petition in support of motion to quash search warrant, *United States of America v. Joe Melky* [*sic*], January 12, 1928, all in Box 1, "Criminal Case 17598" folder, PCF. Schmeckebier, *Bureau of Prohibition*, pp. 12, 66–67, 79–80. CHE, June 15, 1931. CPD, January 23, 1936. Ness MS., p. 22, in ENPS, Roll 1, Folder 2. "Illegal Breweries Sparked Capone's Downfall, Says Ness," *Potter Enterprise*, September 27, 1956, PCHS. Ness and Fraley, *The Untouchables*, pp. 7 ("white knight on"), 13–15, 17–19, 21, 25, 39. Kobler, *Ardent Spirits*, p. 283. Jones, "The Real Eliot Ness" ("But nevertheless, he"). Wilkinson, interviewed in "Eliot Ness: Untouchable" ("legislate against human"). Okrent, *Last Call*, pp. 252–255, 261, 264. McGirr, *War on Alcohol*, pp. 201–206.

Dating the incident where Ness gave liquor to his fraternity brothers is difficult, based on the vagaries of Bollaert's recollection. Perry (*Eliot Ness*, p. 37) claims it happened in late 1928, but conflates it with a different incident mentioned in the article that Bollaert specifically dates to 1932. He also implies Ness partook of the liquor, even though Bollaert stated clearly he did not.

GEORGE E. Q. JOHNSON: CT, December 21, 1930 ("crime with riches," "human in form," "I don't take," "which George E.," "If you are," "only with indictments"). "One-Man Drive in Chicago Has Gangs Quaking with Fear," *The Evening Star*, March 3, 1931, in FBI-AC (also in Box 1, Eig Boxes, National Archives and Records Administration, Chicago, IL). NYT, April 3, 1932. Murphy, Report on Ness, pp. 11–12, in FBI-ENA ("a very intelligent," "was that he"). *Christian Science Monitor*, November 7, 1934 ("one of the best"). George E. Q. Johnson, "Shoot Square!" CPD [?], May 30, 1937 [?], in ENPS, Roll 1, Scrapbook 4 (also in ENPS, Roll 2, Scrapbook 6, p. 21). George E. Q. Johnson, "The Enforcement of the Law," *Credit Craft*, n.d., 7–8, 25, in Box 1, "Articles—Gangbusting (3 of 9)" folder, GEQJ. Bergreen, *Capone*, pp. 274–276, 345. Eig, *Get Capone*, pp. 66–72, 85. "'They Can't Win', Declares U.S. Attorney Johnson, Prosecutor of Capone," *Fox Movietone News*, c. 1931, 05:25:49, http://www.historicfilms.com/tapes/9211_1530_1608 (accessed February 12, 2016).

Perry (*Eliot Ness*, p. 51) incorrectly claims that Johnson didn't know Ness before picking him to head the Untouchables squad. Johnson's law office was at 11110 South Michigan Avenue, close to the Ness bakery at 11290 South Michigan Avenue, and he mentioned his early acquaintance with Peter and Eliot Ness in an FBI interview. ("Professions: Geo. E. Q. Johnson," *Calumet Index*, January 5, 1917. "George E. Q. Johnson" Advertisement, *Elmis Budbärare*, May 1923, in Box 1, "Newspaper Clippings (2 of 9)" folder, GEQJ. Murphy, Report on Ness, pp. 11–12, in FBI-ENA.)

Chapter Seven

CAPONE AT PEACE / MOVE TO METROPOLE: CHE, January 21, 1927 ("I have merely," "I found that"), March 9, 1927 ("Just like the," "The reason I," "He's been sick"). James O'Donnell Bennett, "Chicago Gangland: Golden Flood Makes Czars, Befouls City," CT, April 7, 1929 ("I positively have," "I am out"). Pasley, *Al Capone*, pp. 68–69, 165. Allsop, *Bootleggers*, p. 346. Bergreen, *Capone*, pp. 147–148, 226. Lindberg, *Return to the Scene*, pp. 378–379.

1927 ELECTION: Anderson, "Democracy in Chicago," pp. 71–78 (71, "friend of the"; 72, "Yes, they lie"; 73, "Dever and decency," "Away with decency"; 74, "America First"). Wendt and Kogan, *Big Bill of Chicago*, pp. 243–274 (244, "The Dever administration," "When I'm elected"). Schmidt, *Mayor Who Cleaned*, pp. 78–79, 85–90, 140–141, 147–170. Bergreen, *Capone*, pp. 228–221. Bukowski, *Big Bill Thompson*, pp. 178–187.

DRUCCI DEATH: CT, October 15, 1926 ("the Devil"). Wendt and Kogan, *Big Bill of Chicago*, pp. 269–270. Keefe, *Man Who Got Away*, pp. 211–214.

THOMPSON'S INAUGURATION: Anderson, "Democracy in Chicago," pp. 76–78 (76, "The people were," "the kind of," "That is essentially"). Wendt and Kogan, *Big Bill of Chicago*, pp. 268, 274–276 (274, "They was trying"; 275, "give the old," "political blunderbuss," "indolent, ignorant of," "a striking example"; 276, "out in ninety"). Kobler, *Capone*, p. 206.

SCALISE AND ANSELMI ACQUITTED: Kobler, *Capone*, p. 209.

AIELLO: Pasley, *Al Capone*, pp. 171–172. Burns, *One-Way Ride*, pp. 225–226, 228. Enright, *Al Capone on the Spot*, p. 65. Kobler, *Capone*, pp. 209–210.

GUS WINKELER: Mrs. Gus Winkeler, "I'm on the Spot Facing Death," *Famous Detective Cases*, December 1935, pp. 65–66. Schoenberg, *Mr. Capone*, p. 201. Helmer and Bilek, *St. Valentine's Day Massacre*, pp. 80–81, 83–85, 233. Waugh, *Egan's Rats*, p. 239. Helmer, *Al Capone and His American Boys*, pp. 1–3, 10–12, 23–24, 52–55 (55, "Al Capone is," "bum"), 307, 345–346. Bair, *Al Capone*, pp. 156, 251.

CAPONE'S SENSE OF HONOR: James O'Donnell Bennett, "Chicago Gangland: Golden Flood Makes Czars, Befouls City," CT, April 7, 1929 ("a square shooter," "If he gives"). Lyle, *Dry and Lawless Years*, p. 115. Helmer, *Al Capone and His American Boys*, p. 55. Schoenberg, *Mr. Capone*, p. 175.

MCGURN VS. AIELLO: CT, May 26, 1927; May 29, 1927. Enright, *Al Capone on the Spot*, pp. 65–68. Shmelter, *Chicago Assassin*, pp. 112–119.

AIELLO ARREST: Pasley, *Al Capone*, pp. 174–175 (174, "You started this"). Allsop, *Bootleggers*, pp. 128–130 (129, "You're dead," "Give me fourteen"). Kobler, *Capone*, pp. 211–213 (213, "But I'm going"). Schoenberg, *Mr. Capone*, pp. 186–187. Eghigian, *After Capone*, pp. 119–120. Sifakis, *Mafia Encyclopedia*, pp. 76–77.

THOMPSON FOR PRESIDENT: Kobler, *Capone*, pp. 213–214. Schoenberg, *Mr. Capone*, p. 188.

MAE'S PLEA: CHE, December 15, 1927 ("Can't something be").

CAPONE PRESS CONFERENCE: CT, December 6, 1927 (Capone quotes). CHE, December 6, 1927. CEP, December 6, 1927. Kobler, *Capone*, pp. 214–215. Eghigian, *After Capone*, pp. 128–130, 141.

CAPONE IN LOS ANGELES: LAT, December 14, 1927 ("Why should everybody"). McPhaul, *Johnny Torrio*, p. 349. Bair, *Al Capone*, pp. 107–108.

CAPONE BACK IN ILLINOIS: CHE, December 16, 1927 ("Despite the cold"); December 17, 1927 ("It's pretty tough," "I'm going back," "into the arms," "You may want," "I am going"). "Capone Home; Foes Bombed," *Chicago Tribune*, December 17, 1927 ("You're Al Capone," "made too much," "When I come"); December 18, 1927 ("I wouldn't invade," "That doesn't worry," "Besides, I like").

THOMPSON'S TRAVELS: Wendt and Kogan, *Big Bill of Chicago*, pp. 281–283 (283, "America First"). Kobler, *Capone*, pp. 213, 217.

CAPONE RETURNS TO JOLIET: LAT, December 23, 1927 ("Please take that").

Chapter Eight

BEATTY SHOOTING: CT, March 30–April 1, 1928 (March 30, "shotguns, pistols, rifles"; March 31, "stick 'em up!").

GOLDING AND THE SPECIAL AGENTS: Application for Position of Prohibition Agent, April 20, 1927; George Golding to A. E. Bernsteen, August 29, 1927; George Golding to David H. Blair, May 27, 1927 ("The fact cannot"); George Golding to William B. Robinson, September 8, 1927; Michael F. Malone to Arthur A. Nichols, July 11, 1927; "A Fugitive Law Enforcer," n.p., August 2, 1929 ("His raids are spectacular"), all in George Golding OPF/ATF. CT, March 28, 1928; March 30–April 1, 1928; April 7, 1928; April 29, 1928 ("hard-boiled"). J. M. Doran to Samuel M. Seager, May 14, 1928, in Samuel Seager ATF/OPF. Schmeckebier, *Bureau of Prohibition*, p. 164. Irey and Slocum, *Tax Dodgers*, p. 20. Ness MS., p. 1, in ENPS, Roll 1, Folder 2. Richard D. Hyde, " 'Hard Boiled' Golding: Big-Time Racket Buster," *The Free Lance-Star*, April 11, 1977 ("a fighter").

BEATTY SHOOTING AFTERMATH: CT, March 30–April 1, 1928 (March 30, "men had to," "I don't care"; April 1, "If there is"); August 29–30, 1928; September 1, 1928; March 18, 1951. Pasley, *Al Capone*, pp. 202–203. Irey and Slocum, *Tax Dodgers*, p. 20.

NESS AND JAMIE BECOME SPECIAL AGENTS: Charles S. Deneen to L. C. Andrews, June 13, 1927; H. H. White to Ismar Baruch, June 20, 1927; I. Baruch to H. H. White, June 22, 1927; Alexander G. Jamie to the United States Civil Service Commission, July 5, 1927; E. C. Yellowley to J. M. Doran, July 6, 1927; J. M. Doran to E. C. Yellowley, July 11, 1927; I. Baruch to H. H. White, August 5, 1927; Alf Oftedal to E. C. Yellowley, August 6, 1927; George E. Q. Johnson to James Doran, March 5, 1928 ("I have been"); George E. Q. Johnson to Mabel Walker Willebrandt, March 5, 1928; Better Government Association to Seymour Lowman, March 12, 1928; J. M. Doran to the Secretary of the Treasury, May 11, 1928; E. C. Yellowley to Acting Prohibition Administrator, May 11, 1928; J. M. Doran to Acting Prohibition Administrator, May 11, 1928; G.C.B., Memorandum for the Personnel File of Alexander Jamie, May 11, 1928; J. M. Doran to Alexander G. Jamie, May 18, 1928; Alexander G. Jamie to James M. Doran, May 23, 1928, all in Alexander Jamie OPF. J. M. Doran to Samuel Seager, May 14, 1928, in Samuel Seager OPF/ATF. J. M. Doran to Eliot Ness, May 21, 1928, Eliot Ness OPF. George Golding to the Director of Prohibition, August 30, 1930, in George Golding OPF/ATF. Ness MS., p. 1, in ENPS, Roll 1, Folder 2.

Golding's letter, an unconvincing defense against charges of sexual harassment, is a problematic source, but Jamie's personnel file does corroborate Golding's basic claims about Jamie's transfer to the Special Agent Squad.

EDNA STAHLE: Percy Owen to James E. Jones, May 4, 1925; Personal History, May 25, 1925; Oath of Office, May 25, 1925; Edna M. Stahle to E. C. Yellowley, May 23, 1928; George Golding to Alf Oftedal, May 24, 1928, George E. Golding to the Commissioner of Prohibition, May 25, 1928; J. M. Doran to Edna M. Stahle, May 25, 1928; Oath of Office, June 1, 1928; Questions Respecting Personal History, March 2, 1929; Alexander G. Jamie, Personnel Classification Board Form No. 4, May 5, 1929, all in Edna S. Ness OPF. George Golding to the Director of Prohibition, August 30, 1930, in George Golding OPF/ATF. CT, December 23, 1986 ("were afraid to"). *St. Petersburg Times*, November 19, 1994. Heimel, *Eliot Ness*, p. 23. Record for Edna Margaret Stahle, *Cook County, Illinois, Birth Certificates Index, 1871–1922* (Provo, UT: Ancestry.com Operations, 2011). Perry, *Eliot Ness*, pp. 9–13.

Golding's letter is again a problematic source, especially when discussing the love life of a woman accusing him of sexual harassment. But the relationship between Stahle and her beau, Robert Coyne, appears to be borne out in Melvin Purvis to J. Edgar Hoover, November 28, 1933, in FBI-ENA.

MARTY LAHART: Edward C. Wilcox, memorandum for Mr. Jackson, May 12, 1928, in Samuel M. Seager OPF/ATF and Albert M. Nabers OPF/ATF. Alf Oftedal to Martin J. Lahart, May 21, 1928; Personal History, May 28, 1928; Oath of Office, May 28, 1928; Personal History, March 4, 1929; Isham Railey, Evaluation of Candidates for Placement, October 31, 1962 ("tiresome and repetitive talker"), all in Martin J. Lahart OPF/ATF. Ness MS., p. 6, in ENPS, Roll 1, Folder 2 ("tall, happy Irishman"). Ness and Fraley, *The Untouchables*, pp. 28–30, 32, 108–110, 144–145, 162. *Honolulu Advertiser*, January 29, 1961 ("as a kind"). Borroel, *Story of the Untouchables*, pp. 49–53.

POLICE STATION RAID: CT, July 26, 1928 ("Let us raid"). Ness and Fraley, *The Untouchables*, pp. 28–29. Richard D. Hyde, " 'Hard Boiled' Golding: Big-Time Racket Buster," *The Free Lance-Star*, April 11, 1977. Scott Martell, " 'Untouchable' Memories," *News-Press*, December 7, 1994, RM.

NESS'S FIRST MAJOR INVESTIGATION: Ness MS., p. 1, in ENPS, Roll 1, Folder 2 ("This is where").

FRANK BASILE: Record for Frank Basile, 1920 United States Census. CDN, December 12, 1928 ("Fat"). CHE, December 13, 1928. CT, December 13, 1928; June 21, 1930; April 3, 1932. WP, December 13, 1928 ("Fat"). *Chicago Heights Star*, December 14, 1928. Alf Oftedal to George E. Golding, December 19, 1928, in Box 4, "December 1928" folder, PU ("Burt"). NYT, April 3, 1932. Ralph Foster, "Blackhand War Rages in Chicago Heights," *Startling Detective Adventures*, December 1932, p. 53. Ness MS., p. 2, in ENPS, Roll 1, Folder 2 ("No door could"). Ness and Fraley, *The Untouchables*, pp. 47–49. Record for Francesco Basile, *Cook County, Illinois, Birth Certificates Index, 1871–1922* (Provo, UT: Ancestry.com Operations, 2011). Record for Frank Basile, *Illinois Deaths and Stillbirths Index, 1916–1947* (Provo, UT: Ancestry.com Operations, 2011).

Foster ("Blackhand War," p. 53) notes that Basile "posed among the Sicilians as non-Italian, 'just 'Merican.' " Perplexingly, Perry (*Eliot Ness*, p. 33) renders this quote as " 'just Mexican'—just a boozer."

LORENZO JULIANO: CT, October 15–16, 1927; April 4, 1928; January 7, 1929; June 21,

1930. Sullivan, *Chicago Surrenders*, p. 34. Foster, "Blackhand War," p. 58. Luzi, *Boys in Chicago Heights*, p. 37.

CHICAGO HEIGHTS LIQUOR RACKET: CT, January 7, 1929. Foster, "Blackhand War," pp. 52–53. *WPA Guide to Illinois*, pp. 399, 524. Bergreen, *Capone*, pp. 196–203. Eig, *Get Capone*, pp. 86–87. Luzi, *Boys in Chicago Heights*, pp. 13–37. Corsino, *Neighborhood Outfit*, pp. 17–24, 29–33, 101.

JULIANO AS ENFORCER: CT, October 15–16, 1927; April 4, 1928; January 7, 1929; June 21, 1930. Sullivan, *Chicago Surrenders*, p. 34.

BASILE TURNS ON JULIANO: Alf Oftedal to George Golding, December 19, 1928, Box 4, "December 1928" folder, PU. CDN, December 12, 1928. CHE, December 13, 1928. CT, April 3–4, 1928; December 13, 1928; June 21, 1930; April 3, 1932. WP, December 13, 1928. *Chicago Heights Star*, December 14, 1928. NYT, April 3, 1932. Ness MS., p. 2, in ENPS, Roll 1, Folder 2.

HEIGHTS INVESTIGATION BEGINS: CEP, November 28, 1928. CT, July 27, 1929. *U.S. v. Thomas D'Amico, et al.* Indictment, April 1929, in Box 1, "Criminal Case 19444 (Prohib. Chicago Heights)" folder, PCF. *U.S. v. Joe Martino and John Giannoni*, indictment, November 1928, pp. 1–3, in Box 607, "Criminal Case 18299" folder, CCF. Foster, "Blackhand War," p. 53. Ness MS., pp. 1–4, in ENPS, Roll 1, Folder 2 (1, "were immediately approached," "a diamond stickpin"; 2, "a rather short," "who was an").

   Most sources, following the Ness MS. (pp. 3–5, in ENPS, Roll 1, Folder 2) give Giannoni's name as "Giannini," though court documents and press coverage strongly suggest "Giannoni" is the correct spelling. The Ness MS. also misspells Kooken as "Koken" and Nabers as "Nabors."

   The Ness MS. is vague on the identity of who exactly approached Golding, giving the name "Gramini," but the narrative seems to suggest that this was Giannoni. The final version of the book, which corrects other errors in Ness's text, specifically identifies him as Giannoni (Ness and Fraley, *The Untouchables*, p. 48).

NESS AND NABERS JOIN INVESTIGATION: Record for Don L. Kooken, 1910 United States Census. Edward C. Wilcox, memorandum to Mr. Jackson, May 12, 1928; J. M. Doran to Albert M. Nabers, May 16, 1928; Alf Oftedal to Albert M. Nabers, May 21, 1928; Alf Oftedal to George E. Golding, May 21, 1928; Oath of Office, June 1, 1928; Personal History, June 1, 1928; George E. Golding to Commissioner of Prohibition, June 1, 1928; Personal History, March 2, 1929; *Savannah Morning News*, February 2, 1930; Roy H. Bryant to U.S. Treasury Department, February 2, 1943, all in Albert M. Nabers OPF/ATF. *U.S. v. Thomas D'Amico, et al.*, indictment, April 1929, in Box 1, "Criminal Case 19444 (Prohib. Chicago Heights)" folder, PCF. *U.S. v. Joe Martino and John Giannoni*, indictment, November 1928, in Box 607, "Criminal Case 18299" folder, CCF. Ness MS., pp. 2–4, in ENPS, Roll 1, Folder 2 (2, "Nine Toed").

COZY CORNER MEETING: *U.S. v. Joe Montana, et al.*, indictment, June 1928, in Box 583, "Criminal Case 17283" folder 1, CCF. CT, July 7, 1928. CEP, November 28, 1928. CT, December 1, 1928; July 27, 1929. *U.S. v. Joe Martino and John Giannoni*, indictment, November 1928, in Box 607, "Criminal Case 18299" folder, CCF. Foster, "Blackhand War," pp. 52–53. Ness MS., pp. 1–5, in ENPS, Roll 1, Folder 2 (1, "spotted with numerous"; 3, "They would leave"). Ness and Fraley, *The Untouchables*, pp. 48–54. Bergreen, *Capone*, pp. 199–202, 347. Luzi, *Boys in Chicago Heights*, pp. 26, 28–31, 37, 47.

In his manuscript, Ness claims only Giannoni took part in this meeting, but the indictment gives Martino's presence. Ness's manuscript gives the name of the saloon as "Cozy Corners," but Luzi (who gives it as "Cozy Corner") seems more credible here, considering Ness's faulty memory for names. Perry (*Eliot Ness*, pp. 33–35) falsely conflates the Cozy Corner meeting with another in East Chicago, while also giving the wrong amount for the bribe.

HEIGHTS INVESTIGATION CONTINUES: CEP, December 1, 1928. CT, December 1, 1928. *U.S. v. Thomas D'Amico, et al.*, indictment, April 1929, in Box 1, "Criminal Case 19444 (Prohib. Chicago Heights)" folder, PCF. NYT, June 18, 1931. Ness MS., pp. 2–5, in ENPS, Roll 1, Folder 2 (4, "We told him"). Foster, "Blackhand War," pp. 53–54; Ness and Fraley, *The Untouchables*, pp. 48–56.

The chronological location of the night searches is conjectural, though it does seem to fit best at this point in Foster's "Blackhand" narrative. Ness recalled it happening in the Heights, but seeking out the stills in secret makes little sense if they were trying to earn the gang's confidence, especially considering Martino's willingness to show them around. Instead, Ness probably misremembered an incident where the special agents sought out stills in Calumet City on the Syndicate's behalf, as described in NYT, June 18, 1931. The fact that the special agents later met with the still owners in East Chicago adds more credence to this conclusion, because East Chicago is just across the state line from Calumet City.

EAST CHICAGO MEETING: CHE, June 15, 1931. NYT, June 18, 1931. *Evening Star*, June 18, 1931, in ENPS, Roll 1, Scrapbook 1. "Hail Two South End Men for Overthrow of Alphonse Capone," n.p., n.d., in ENPS Roll 1, Scrapbook 1. Jack Dillard, "How the U.S. Gov't Caught Al Capone!" *The Master Detective*, February 1932, p. 56. Foster, "Blackhand War," pp. 53–54. Ness MS., pp. 4–5, in ENPS, Roll 1, Folder 2 (4, "the main objector"; 5, "If you don't," "The silk-shirted"). Ness and Fraley, *The Untouchables*, pp. 54–56. CPD, October 17, 1959 ("I felt young"). Fraley, "Real Eliot Ness," p. 28.

Ness, in his manuscript, gives a slightly different version of events, writing Martino showed up in place of the still owners, having met with them earlier and agreed to represent them. Ness also implies this was the first time he met Martino, though the indictment confirms Martino's presence at the earlier meeting. It's likely that Ness, nearly thirty years later, conflated these separate meetings in memory. The *Startling Detective* article, written closer to the event, mentions the still owners' presence, and it seems more credible here, particularly because other published accounts of the knife incident suggest more people were present than are mentioned in Ness's narrative.

Ness's manuscript also claims the gangsters made the $500 payoff, but there's nothing in the indictments to suggest this happened (unlike the Cozy Corner meeting, where the $300 bribe recorded in the indictment closely matches the $250 in Ness's manuscript and the $300 in Ness and Fraley's book). *Startling Detective* doesn't identify the man who called off the killer as Giannoni (that name, or any of its variations, doesn't appear in the article), but it's clear from Ness's recollections he's the person referred to as the bootleggers' "leader."

Chapter Nine

CAPONE IN HIS PRIME: CHE, April 19, 1927 ("if someone handed"). James O'Donnell
Bennett, "Chicago Gangland: Golden Flood Makes Czars, Befouls City," CT, April 7, 1929
("really a bigger," "Capone likes that," "big business"). Pasley, *Al Capone*, pp. 8, 60 ("No
accurate estimate"), 63–64 (63, "The winnings did"; 64, "a racket"), 177 ("In December
of"). Lyle, *Dry and Lawless Years*, pp. 141, 146 ("in the direct"). Waller and Calabrese, *Fats
Waller*, pp. 62–63 ("swung it so"). Schoenberg, *Mr. Capone*, pp. 178–179. Bergreen, *Capone*,
pp. 244–260. Lucille Zinman and Doc Cheatham, interviewed in "The Road to Repeal"
("Every nightclub you," "very much of"). Trespacz, *Trial of Gangster Al Capone*, p. 25. Moore,
Anything Goes, pp. 43–44. Brothers, *Louis Armstrong*, pp. 226–227 (226, "This is our night,"
"He had all"; 227, "nice little cute," "belonged," "Nigger, you better").

JOE E. LEWIS: CT, November 9, 1927 ("to take [Lewis]"). CHE, November 9, 1927. Cohn,
Joker Is Wild, pp. 3–25, 31–46, 61–69, 78, 89–92 (90, "Why the hell"). Kobler, *Capone*,
p. 148. Bergreen, *Capone*, pp. 251–254.

CAPONE AND CELEBRITIES: Richman and Gehman, *A Hell of A Life*, pp. 6–13 (8, "Richman, you're the"; 9, "It was hard"). Charles "Buddy" Rogers, interviewed in *Mystery of Al
Capone's Vaults*. Welles and Bogdanovich, *This Is Orson Welles*, pp. 311–312 ("Capone used
to"). McGilligan, *Young Orson*, pp. 149–150, 164.

CAPONE'S GENEROSITY, CHARM, AND WOMANIZING: Sullivan, *Rattling the Cup*,
pp. 44–45 ("Those who have"). CT, March 17, 1930. Pasley, *Al Capone*, pp. 11 ("a fervent
handshaker"), 67, 90. Borden, "Chicago Revisited," p. 543 ("Capone fans," "with tears in,"
"the hungry and," "with a catch," "the petted and"). Irey and Slocum, *Tax Dodgers*, p. 37. Kobler, *Capone*, pp. 320–321. Berle and Frankel, *Milton Berle*, pp. 168–169 (169, "I don't need").
Bergreen, *Capone*, p. 149. Doc Cheatham, interviewed in "Road to Repeal" ("Everybody was
making"). Bair, *Al Capone*, pp. 40–41, 66–67, 91.

CAPONE IN WISCONSIN AND MIAMI: *Miami Daily News*, January 10, 1928. NYT, January 22, 1928. Sullivan, *Rattling the Cup*, pp. 45–46. Pasley, *Al Capone*, pp. 84–85. Fred
Girton, "Al Capone Tells His Side of It," *Startling Detective Adventures*, September 1931,
pp. 20 ("very general and," "I wanted a," "They threaten to"), 70. IRS-2, pp. 36–38, 40–42,
49. Ross, *Trial of Al Capone*, pp. 66–68 (66, "Albert Costa"), 79. Kobler, *Capone*, pp. 220–
222 (221, "Let's lay the," "You can stay," "I'll stay as," "I've been hounded," "the garden of").
Schoenberg, *Mr. Capone*, pp. 193–195. Bergreen, *Capone*, pp. 268–272, 283, 286–288, 291–
292. Mario Gomes, "Al Capone's Tax Trial and Downfall," My Al Capone Museum, January
2010, http://www.myalcaponemuseum.com/id146.htm (accessed July 3, 2017) ("PH"). Bair,
Al Capone, pp. 43, 70 ("Your father broke"), 80–83, 110–119, 132–134, 156–157.

PINEAPPLE PRIMARY: CT, March 22, 1928. *Seattle Daily Times*, April 1, 1928 ("to protect
American"). Merriam, *Chicago*, pp. 268–299. Pasley, *Al Capone*, pp. 204–223 (216, "Ours is
a"; 219, "The political revolution"; 220, "the good city"). Burns, *One-Way Ride*, pp. 216–223.
Wendt and Kogan, *Big Bill of Chicago*, pp. 303–317 (312, "He drank constantly"). Lyle, *Dry
and Lawless Years*, pp. 185–186. Kobler, *Capone*, pp. 223–228. Schoenberg, *Mr. Capone*,
pp. 195–197. Bergreen, *Capone*, pp. 276–281. Hoffman, *Scarface Al*, pp. 34–35.

BURKE AND THE "AMERICAN BOYS": L. A. Foster, "High Lights of Burke's Crimson Career," *True Detective*, July 1931, pp. 12, 62–64. Helmer and Bilek, *St. Valentine's Day Massacre*, pp. 80, 84–85. Waugh, *Egan's Rats*, pp. 105–106, 120–121, 240–242. Shmelter, *Chicago Assassin*, p 174 Helmer, *Al Capone and His American Boys*, pp. 19–24, 307, 322–323, 346. Bair, *Al Capone*, p. 8 ("Americans").

YALE MURDER: NYT, July 2, 1928; August 1, 1928. CT, August 1, 1928. Winkeler, "I'm on the Spot," p. 67. Burns, *One-Way Ride*, pp. 225–228. Kobler, *Capone*, pp. 229–231. Schoenberg, *Mr. Capone*, pp. 201–203. Johnson and Sautter, *Wicked City*, p. 274. Helmer and Bilek, *St. Valentine's Day Massacre*, pp. 91–93. Shmelter, *Chicago Assassin*, pp. 150–154. Helmer, *Al Capone and His American Boys*, pp. 72–75, 361–362.

LOESCH AND THE FAIR: Cook, *Educational History of Illinois*, p. 646. *Year-Book of the Union League Club*, p. 24. CT, March 23, 1928 ("America's worst advertisement," "Well, I see," "heard evil remarks," "Judging from the"); August 1, 1944. Dawes, *Notes as Vice President*, pp. 144–146, 165–166. Allsop, *Bootleggers*, pp. 166–167, 188, 269. Schoenberg, *Mr. Capone*, pp. 176, 290–291. Hoffman, *Scarface Al*, pp. 8–10, 13–15, 31–32. Bergreen, *Capone*, p. 86. Boehm, *Popular Culture*, pp. 108–109. "Frank Joseph Loesch," Find a Grave, August 23, 2011, http://www.findagrave.com/cgi-bin/fg.cgi?page=gran damp;grid=75389266 (accessed April 12, 2016).

CAPONE MEETS LOESCH: CT, March 25, 1931 ("But they'll only," "I'll have the," "I can tell"); October 13, 1931. *Hearings . . . on the Nomination of James H. Wilkerson*, pp. 144–146 (145, "I am here," "I'll help"). Dobyns, *Underworld of American Politics*, pp. 1–3. Kobler, *Capone*, pp. 11–15. Schoenberg, *Mr. Capone*, pp. 203–204.

CAPONE GOLFING AND SHOOTING HIMSELF: CT, September 21, 1928 ("The bullet plowed"). Clinical Record: Family and Personal History, n.d., in Box 203, "[Capone, Alphonse] [40886-A]" folder, BOP-AP. Timothy Sullivan with John Kobler, "Caddying for a Man Who Never Shot Par," *Sports Illustrated*, November 6, 1972, pp. 72–78 (73, "Nobody had ever"; 75, "He could drive"; 78, "and carry a," "You might get"). Bergreen, *Capone*, p. 183. Eig, *Get Capone*, p. 179. Bair, *Al Capone*, pp. 95, 159.

Chapter Ten

GOLDING, JAMIE, AND YELLOWLEY: E. C. Yellowley to L. C. Andrews, November 25, 1926 ("a very fine"); E. C. Yellowley to James E. Jones, December 4, 1926; E. C. Yellowley to James Doran, July 5, 1927; John T. Doyle to the Secretary of the Treasury, May 23, 1928; G.C.B., memorandum, June 11, 1928; Alexander Jamie to Alf Oftedal, August 6, 1928; C. M. Cuneo, memorandum, August 10, 1928; Alf Oftedal to Alexander Jamie, August 11, 1928; George Golding, "Special Agent Alexander Jamie," August 31, 1928 ("lazy," "a sort of"); Alf Oftedal to the U.S. Civil Service Commission, September 5, 1928, all in Alexander Jamie OPF. Alf Oftedal to George Golding, May 16, 1928, Box 4, "April-May 1928" Folder, PU ("If you deal"). CT, June 23, 1938 ("little black book"); August 29–30, 1928; September 1, 1928 ("reign of terror"); September 11, 1928. CHE, December 1, 1928. George Golding to the Director of Prohibition, August 30, 1930, pp. 29, 31, George Golding OPF/ATF. W. S. Murphy, Report on Eliot Ness, November 15, 1933, p. 10, FBI-ENA.

ADAMS SHOOTING: CT, August 22–23, 1928 (August 22, "in a frenzy," "Get out"); August 25–26, 1928 (August 25, "the size of," "I got him," "grape juice salesman"; August 26, "in a frenzy," "Dumdums are often," "monstrous"). Record for Merle and Connie Adams, 1930 United States Census.

Perry (*Eliot Ness*, pp. 19, 301) claims Ness took part in this raid, apparently citing documents in Golding's OPF that, as far as we have been able to determine, do not exist. Given Perry's rather loose attitude when it comes to other sources, we are skeptical Ness was involved. The NYT later noted, "Ness never took part in any of the high-handed forays that made Golding unpopular." (NYT, June 18, 1931; see also *The Evening Star*, June 18, 1931, in ENPS, Roll 1, Scrapbook 1.)

GOLDING'S DISMISSAL AND JAMIE'S PROMOTION: CT, August 26, 1928; August 29–30, 1928; September 8, 1928; September 11–12, 1928; September 20, 1928; October 1, 1928; December 1, 1928. J. M. Doran to H. M. Dengler, September 13, 1928; H. M. Dengler to J. M. Doran, September 1928 ("a Chicago man"), all in Alexander Jamie OPF. CHE, December 1, 1928.

GOLDING'S DOWNFALL: George Golding to the Director of Prohibition, July 17, 1930; Myron M. Caffey to George Golding, July 17, 1930; L. V. Treglia to George Golding, July 17, 1930; Harry S. Webster to George Golding, July 17, 1930; Myron M. Caffey to George Golding, July 18, 1930; George Golding to Earle E. Koehler, July 18, 1930; Ireland H. Caffey, sworn statement, July 18, 1930; L. V. Treglia, memo, July 23, 1930; Myron H. Caffey, memo, July 23, 1930; Howard T. Jones to George E. Golding, August 13, 1930; George Golding to the Director of Prohibition, August 30, 1930 ("fight until the last"); Everett H. Kuebler, memo to Amos W. W. Woodcock, October 18, 1930 ("It is impossible"); A. W. W. Woodcock to George E. Golding, October 18, 1930; Thomas M. Lee and Leon B. Stayton to George Golding, n.d. ("succeeded in kissing"), all in George Golding OPF/ATF. CT, August 19, 1930.

NESS'S HEIGHTS INVESTIGATION: Alf Oftedal to Harry Dengler, November 19, 1928, in Box 4, "December 1928" folder, PU. CEP, December 1, 1928. CT, December 1, 1928 ("one of the"); January 8, 1929. Ness MS., pp. 5–6, in ENPS, Roll 1, Folder 2. Bergreen, *Capone*, p. 347 ("was on the").

Dating the still raids is difficult, because the internal chronology of Ness's manuscript is so scrambled, but it seems to make the most sense here.

Citing a pseudonymous interview with a former Heights bootlegger, Bergreen (*Capone*, p. 347) describes an incident where Ness and other agents supposedly assaulted the drivers of some liquor trucks around this time, refusing to let them pass until they received a bribe. Perry (*Eliot Ness*, p. 35) claims that Ness and Nabers were responsible for this attack, though Nabers's personnel file proves he wasn't in Chicago when this would have taken place. (Recommendation for Change in Designated Post of Duty, October 22, 1928; Alf Oftedal to Albert M. Nabers, October 26, 1928; Dwight E. Avis to the Commissioner of Prohibition, October 29, 1928; Alexander G. Jamie to the Commissioner of Prohibition, January 8, 1929; Alexander G. Jamie to Alf Oftedal, January 31, 1929, all in Albert M. Nabers OPF/ATF.)

It seems more likely, as Perry suggests in his endnotes (p. 303), this incident "was something mistakenly attributed to the legendary Eliot Ness long after the fact." The kind of brutality Bergreen describes fits Golding's other special agents, but not the resolutely nonviolent Ness. This is one of several instances in which Bergreen's book relies on anonymous or pseudonymous sources and offers scant verification for their claims. See *Kirkus*, August 1, 1994, https://www.kirkusreviews.com/book-reviews/laurence-bergreen/capone/ (accessed March 13, 2016).

MARTINO INDICTMENT AND ARREST: Bench Warrant for Joe Martino, November 27, 1928, in Box 607, "Criminal Case 18299" folder, CCF. CEP, November 28, 1928. CHE, December 1, 1928. CT, December 1, 1928. Ness MS., pp. 8–9, in ENPS, Roll 1, Folder 2. Ness and Fraley, *The Untouchables*, pp. 210–213.

Ness claims that Nabers went with him to arrest Martino, but Nabers was not in Chicago at the time, per his personnel file (see above).

MARTINO MURDER: *Chicago Heights Star*, November 30, 1928 ("lying on the"); December 4, 1928. CT, November 30, 1928; December 1, 1928. CHE, January 8, 1929. Daniel Anderson to George E. Q. Johnson, "Re: Killings of Defendants or Government Witnesses," March 26, 1932, in "Records Relating to Indictment and Sentencing (2 of 12)" folder, RRPAC. Ness MS., p. 9, in ENPS, Roll 1, Folder 2 ("That was the").

Ness's own manuscript and most other accounts (such as Perry, *Eliot Ness*, p. 37) accept the early press report that Martino died in a drive-by shooting (*Chicago Heights Star*, November 30, 1928; CT, December 1, 1928). But Martino's death certificate confirms the later report from the *Chicago Heights Star* (December 4, 1928) that he died at the hands of a revolver-wielding pedestrian. See death certificate for Joseph Martino, December 3, 1929, in Box 607, "Criminal Case 18299" folder, CCF.

GILBERT MURDER: *Chicago Heights Star*, December 7, 1928; December 11, 1928. CT, December 7–9, 1928. CEP, December 7, 1928. CHE, December 8, 1928; December 13, 1928. *St. Petersburg Times*, December 8, 1929.

Perry (*Eliot Ness*, pp. 26–27), apparently following Foster, "Blackhand War," p. 53, falsely gives Gilbert's first name as "Lester" and incorrectly places his death before the start of Ness's Heights investigation.

BASILE MURDER: Alf Oftedal to Alexander G. Jamie, December 5, 1928, in Box 4, "December 1928" folder, PU. CDN, December 12, 1928. CHE, December 13, 1928 ("The challenge to"). WP, December 13, 1928. *Chicago Heights Star*, December 14, 1928. Daniel Anderson to George E. Q. Johnson, "Re: Killings of Defendants or Government Witnesses," March 26, 1932, in "Records Relating to Indictment and Sentencing (2 of 12)" folder, RRPAC. CT, April 3, 1928. NYT, April 3, 1932. Ness MS., p. 6, in ENPS, Roll 1, Folder 2. Ness and Fraley, *The Untouchables*, pp. 191–194.

Ness's manuscript has Nabers present for the identification of Basile's body, though Nabers's personnel file (cited above) strongly suggests he wasn't in Chicago at the time. Ness and Fraley, on the other hand, say Ness visited the funeral home with Lahart, which seems an invention of Fraley's; they also place Basile's murder much later in the timeline than it actually occurred. Ness's manuscript also suggests the special agents viewed Basile's body in the police station, while Ness and Fraley revise it to say they went to Doty's Funeral Home next door. In this case, the book seems more credible, as that's the kind of detail that could have only come from Ness (and his sparsely written manuscript is ambiguous about such things). The funeral home building, like the police station, still stands on East 115th Street in Kensington. Now a church, the name "Doty" is still written above the door.

FELTRIN ARREST AND DEATH: CT, December 13, 1928; December 24, 1928; June 21, 1930. Sullivan, *Chicago Surrenders*, pp. 34–35. Hopkins, *Our Lawless Police*, pp. 15–27, 36–42, 45–60, 88–99, 167, 189–221, 264–287. Ness MS., pp. 6, 9, in ENPS, Roll 1, Folder 2. Record for Frank Basile, "Homicide in Chicago 1870–1930 Interactive Database," Northwestern University, http://homicide.northwestern.edu/data base/9163/?page=object%20 id%20#28 (accessed March 14, 2016). Record for Anthony Feltrin, *Illinois, Deaths and Stillbirths Index, 1916–1947* (Provo, UT: Ancestry.com Operations, 2011).

    A 1932 article by Robert Isham Randolph includes a probable reference to Feltrin's death ("the known murderer of a government agent hanged himself in his cell because he did not dare to tell who had hired him to do the job"). Randolph suggests the killer was more afraid of his fellow gangsters than the police, but hints police subjected him to the third degree while in custody, without getting him to crack. Robert Isham Randolph, "The 'Third Degree,'" *New York Herald Tribune Magazine*, August 7, 1932, p. 2.

COZY CORNER RAID: Ness MS., pp. 6–7, in ENPS, Roll 1, Folder 2 (6, "In Chicago Heights"; 7, "four revolvers and," "Look who's here").

    Dating this incident is difficult, but it must have occurred after December 9, 1928, when Lahart was transferred back to Chicago from St. Paul. (See "Recommendation for Change in Designation Post of Duty," December 5, 1928, Martin J. Lahart OPF/ATF.)

NESS CALM UNDER PRESSURE: Ness MS., pp. 6–7, in ENPS, Roll 1, Folder 2 (7, "We always traveled"). Murphy, Report on Eliot Ness, p. 11, in FBI-ENA. CT, March 1, 1970. Jedick, "Eliot Ness," p. 55.

MIKE PICCHI CHASE AND ARREST: CT, December 28, 1928; January 3, 1929; January 5, 1929. Petition of Mike Picchi, *U.S. v. Mike Picchi*, October 15, 1929, in Box 1, "Criminal Case 19444 (Prohib.—Chicago Heights)" folder, PCF. Indictment, *U.S. v. Thomas D'amico, et al.*, April 1929, in Box 1, "Criminal Case 19444 (Prohib.—Chicago Heights)" folder, PCF. "'Untouchables' Hazard Death in Campaign Against Capone," *The Evening Star*, June 18, 1931, in ENPS, Roll 1, Scrapbook 1. NYT, June 18, 1931. Ness MS., p. 7, in ENPS, Roll 1, Folder 2 (quotes).

    See also Foster, "Blackhand War," p. 54; Ness and Fraley, *The Untouchables*, pp. 175–177, both of which incorrectly name Basile as the driver. Perry (*Eliot Ness*, p. 40) incorrectly gives Ness's quote as: "This gun was obviously meant for me."

    Per Nabers's personnel file, Nabers returned to the Chicago area on December 19 to give testimony before the grand jury, bearing out Ness's recollection (and the CT article) that he helped arrest Mike Picchi. See Alexander G. Jamie to the Commissioner of Prohibition, January 8, 1929; Alexander G. Jamie to Alf Oftedal, January 31, 1929, both in Albert M. Nabers OPF/ATF.

NESS HOME AND PARENTS: *City of Chicago Directory 1928–1929*, p. 2260. Personal History, June 5, 1928; Personal History, April 12, 1929, both in Eliot Ness OPF. Murphy, Report on Eliot Ness, p. 9, in FBI-ENA. Ness and Fraley, *The Untouchables*, pp. 161, 169–170 (169, "killed by those"), 186–187. Adelman, *Touring Pullman*, p. 42.

    The Ness house still stands, but its street name has since changed. It can now be found at 11015 South Dr. Martin Luther King Jr. Drive.

NESS MEETS INFORMANT: Ness MS., pp. 7–8, in ENPS, Roll 1, Folder 2.

See also Ness and Fraley, *The Untouchables*, pp. 168–173, which places this call (more dramatically) *before* Ness arrests Picchi, rather than after (as in the Ness MS.). Here, again, is another instance where the information in the manuscript and book is corroborated by outside sources. The Nesses first show up at the 11015 South Park Avenue address in 1928 (see above), right around the time this event happened.

NESS MOVES OUT, STOPS SEEING EDNA: Alexander G. Jamie to Alf Oftedal, April 10, 1929; Alexander G. Jamie, Personnel Classification Board Form No. 4, May 5, 1929, both in Edna S. Ness OPF. Ness MS., p. 8, in ENPS, Roll 1, Folder 2. Ness and Fraley, *The Untouchables*, pp. 172–173, 186–187. Here, as elsewhere, the Ness-Fraley book replaces Edna's name with that of Ness's third wife, Betty.

JOHNSON PLANS HEIGHTS RAID: CHE, December 1, 1928; January 7–8, 1929 (January 7, "the strange distinction," "the municipal sanctuary"). CT, January 7, 1929 ("center of lawlessness," "May I have," "Twenty if you"). *Chicago Heights Star*, January 7, 1929 ("The good name," "the bad work"). CDN, January 7, 1929. CEP, January 7, 1929. *Pittsburgh Press*, January 7, 1929. Willebrandt, *Inside of Prohibition*, p. 155. Corsino, *Neighborhood Outfit*, p. 28.

HEIGHTS RAID: CHE, January 7, 1929. CT, January 7, 1929 ("Where are the," "We're running the," "Their silence smacks"). CEP, January 7, 1929. CDN, January 7, 1929 ("We'll need all," "We are anxious"); February 24, 1936. *Chicago Heights Star*, January 7, 1929. *Pittsburgh Press*, January 7, 1929. Foster, "Blackhand War," pp. 40–41, 54. Ness MS., pp. 8–9, in ENPS, Roll 1, Folder 2. Ness and Fraley, *The Untouchables*, pp. 193–194. CPD, October 17, 1959 ("There would be").

HEIGHTS INDICTMENTS: *U.S. v. Thomas D'amico, et al.*, indictment, April 1929, in Box 1, "Criminal Case 19444 (Prohib. Chicago Heights)" folder, PCF. CT, May 4, 1929. Dillard, "How the U.S. Gov't," p. 56. Foster, "Blackhand War," p. 55. CDN, February 24, 1936. Luzi, *Boys in Chicago Heights*, pp. 41–44. Corsino, *Neighborhood Outfit*, pp. 33–41.

GIANNONI ARREST: CT, July 27, 1929. Bench Warrant for John Giannoni, November 27, 1928; Bench Warrant for John Giannoni, July 26, 1929; Brief Statement of Motion, December 3, 1929, all in Box 607, "Criminal Case 18299" folder, CCF.

The Ness MS. asserts that Giannoni "is still a fugitive," suggesting that Ness was unaware of his arrest (Ness MS., p. 9, in ENPS, Roll 1, Folder 2). Perry (*Eliot Ness*, p. 38) claims that "an unidentified man" found shot to death in the Heights on December 9 was believed by police to be Giannoni. Nothing in the article he cites suggests this was the case. (CT, December 10, 1928.) In any event, a later *Tribune* report identified the victim as a laborer with no connection to the alcohol mob. (CT, December 11, 1929.)

JULIANO DEATH: CT, June 21, 1930. Sullivan, *Chicago Surrenders*, p. 35. Foster, "Blackhand War," p. 54.

Foster claims that the special agents arrested Juliano during the Heights raid, but Juliano lived in Blue Island (not the Heights), which makes this unlikely. His name doesn't show up in any of the articles listing prisoners arrested in those raids.

OLIVER ELLIS: CHE, January 7, 1929. CT, January 7–9, 1929 (January 8, "split five ways"). CEP, January 7–8, 1929. CDN, January 7–8, 1929; February 24, 1936. Willebrandt, *Inside of Prohibition*, pp. 151–152. Bergreen, *Capone*, pp. 302–303.

INCOME TAX EVASION: *Sullivan v. United States*, 15 F.2d 809 (4th Cir. 1926). Willebrandt,

Inside of Prohibition, pp. 247–249. Messick, *Secret File*, pp. 34–35. Schoenberg, *Mr. Capone*, pp. 231–232, 255–256. Bergreen, *Capone*, p. 273. Trespacz, *Trial of Gangster Al Capone*, pp. 46–49 (47, "lawful"), 56–59. Folsom, *Money Trail*, pp. 35, 63–64. Mappen, *Prohibition Gangsters*, pp. 128–129.

The difficulty of proving income tax evasion would decrease somewhat in 1954, when a Supreme Court decision affirmed the use of so-called net worth prosecutions. In such cases, the prosecution merely has to establish the defendant's net worth at a certain "starting point" and prove that he or she has since made more money than his or her tax returns show. But this remained a questionable practice in Capone's day. (Schoenberg, *Mr. Capone*, pp. 231–232; Spiering, *Man Who Got Capone*, pp. 67–68.)

RALPH CAPONE INVESTIGATION: Opening Argument of Counsel for Government, *United States of America v. Ralph J. Capone*, April 24, 1930, JIG. NYT, June 6, 1931. Social Record of Ralph Capone, December 14, 1931; Nels E. Tessem, memo to Chief, Intelligence Unit, Re: Ralph J. Capone, February 24, 1932, both in Box 13, "Capone, Ralph J. 9346-M Transferred From Leavenworth 12.10.1931 (3 of 3)" folder, NOF. IRS-2, pp. 44–45. Dillard, "How the U.S. Gov't," pp. 14–15. CDN, February 24–25, 1936. Irey and Slocum, *Tax Dodgers*, pp. 28–31. Schoenberg, *Mr. Capone*, pp. 230–232, 242–243. Eghigian, *After Capone*, pp. 152, 159–160, 163. Folsom, *Money Trail*, pp. 65–67.

CAPONE TAX INVESTIGATION BEGINS: Robert H. Lucas, memorandum for Assistant Secretary Hope, March 19, 1930, in Presidential Subject Series, Box 164, "Federal Bureau of Investigation—Capone Tax Case, 1930–1931" folder, HHPL. CT, October 10, 1931. "War on Chicago Gangs Not Over, Say U.S. Officials," n.p., n.d., in ENPS, Roll 1, Scrapbook 1. IRS-2, p. 4. Wilson and Whitman, "Undercover Man," pp. 14–15. Irey and Slocum, *Tax Dodgers*, pp. 27, 32–33. Folsom, *Money Trail*, pp. 80–82.

Biographer Bergreen (*Capone*, p. 302) admits the Heights "raid . . . permanently altered the face of the conflict between the racketeers and law enforcement agencies," but—in keeping with his consistent anti-Ness bias—he rearranges the chronology of his narrative in order to make Ness seem as ineffective as possible. In Bergreen's telling, Ness's "spurious success in Chicago Heights" (*ibid.*, p. 351) comes *after* the raid netting Ellis's evidence. This implies they were two separate incidents, rather than the same event. Bergeen also appears unaware the name Ness used for Basile in his manuscript, "Burt Napoli," is a pseudonym. (Bergreen, *Capone*, pp. 301–304, 348–351.)

Irey's later testimony (in CT, October 10, 1931) that Internal Revenue's Capone investigation began on October 18, 1928, has led some to conclude President Calvin Coolidge ordered the inquiry (see Hoffman, *Scarface Al*, pp. 24, 33). As Folsom notes (in *Money Trail*, p. 77), however, no evidence suggests Coolidge had any direct involvement.

Chapter Eleven

CAPONE'S INFLUENCE, LEXINGTON HOTEL: James O'Donnell Bennett, "Chicago Gangland: Golden Flood Makes Czars, Befouls City," CT, April 7, 1929. Pasley, *Al Capone*, pp. 82 ("round-the-world"), 349. Vanderbilt, "How Al Capone," pp. 20–21. Murray, *Legacy of Al Capone*, pp. 124–125 (124, "Does your newspaper"; 125, "The man was"). Kobler, *Capone*, pp. 12–14. CT, April 13, 1986. Schoenberg, *Mr. Capone*, p. 180. Bergreen, *Capone*, p. 148. Bair, *Al Capone*, pp. 77–78.

LABOR RACKETEERING: Landesco, "Organized Crime in Chicago," pp. 986–990 (988, "I have no"). CT, April 20–21, 1930. Pasley, *Al Capone*, pp. 247–251. Vanderbilt Jr., "How Al Capone," p. 20. Lyle, *Dry and Lawless Years*, pp. 187–189, 192. Murray, *Legacy of Al Capone*, pp. 85–88 (87, "The members will," "You either buy"), 94–98, 155–167. Kobler, *Capone*, pp. 241–243 (242, "in the cleaning"). Schoenberg, *Mr. Capone*, pp. 199–201. Bergreen, *Capone*, pp. 148–151. Helmer and Bilek, *St. Valentine's Day Massacre*, pp. 62–63. Okrent, *Last Call*, pp. 329–330.

UNIONE MURDERS: Pasley, *Al Capone*, pp. 229–232. Burns, *One-Way Ride*, pp. 229–232, 235–239. Murray, *Legacy of Al Capone*, pp. 125–127 (126, "Why kill a"). Schoenberg, *Mr. Capone*, pp. 205–206, 232–233. Helmer and Mattix, *Public Enemies*, pp. 114–117.

BUGS MORAN: Lyle, *Dry and Lawless Years*, pp. 199–203 (201, "beautiful diamond ring," "If it's snatched"; 202, "the Beast," "the Behemoth," "The Beast uses"; 203, "Any enemy of"), 226. Allsop, *Bootleggers*, p. 131. English, *Paddy Whacked*, pp. 148, 165–166. Keefe, *Man Who Got Away*, pp. 6, 8, 44, 55, 371 ("could go berserk"). Bair, *Al Capone*, p. 46.

PLANNING THE MASSACRE: James O'Donnell Bennett, "Chicago Gangland: Golden Flood Makes Czars, Befouls City," CT, April 7, 1929. Pasley, *Al Capone*, p. 255. A. P. Madden to Chief, Intelligence Unit, March 11, 1932, in Box 4, "Career-Capone Case-Correspondence, 1931–1940" folder, FJW. John Edgar Hoover, "Memorandum for Mr. Joseph B. Keenan, Acting Attorney General," August 27, 1936; Memorandum Re: "St. Valentine's Day Massacre," October 26, 1936, both in FBI-SVDM. Helmer and Bilek, *St. Valentine's Day Massacre*, pp. 10–11, 101–102, 129, 131–133, 136, 231–232, 234–235, 245, 250. Keefe, *Man Who Got Away*, p. 233.

NITTO AS ENFORCER: Helmer and Bilek, *St. Valentine's Day Massacre*, pp. 232–233. Eghigian, *After Capone*, pp. 123–124 (123, "What had [Nitto]"; 124, "gangland's most perfect"), 162 ("the Enforcer"). Schoenberg, *Mr. Capone*, pp. 245–246 ("always acted kind").

GEORGETTE SEES UNIFORMS: Helmer, *Al Capone and His American Boys*, pp. 80–81 (81, "Goetz enjoyed his," "too sick with").

THE MASSACRE: Pasley, *Al Capone*, pp. 254–255. Helmer and Bilek, *St. Valentine's Day Massacre*, pp. 10–11, 101–104, 131–133 (132, "board of directors"), 234–235, 250. Keefe, *Man Who Got Away*, pp. 233–237, 256–257. Binder, *Al Capone's Beer Wars*, pp. 197–198.

Intelligence Unit agent A. P. Madden identified the key participants in the massacre in a memo written three years after the event: "It is said that the now famous St. Valentine's day murder in Chicago . . . was perpetrated at the direction of Al Capone. The plan was to assassinate George, alias 'Bugs' Moran. . . . The four principals in the killing are said to have been Fred Burke . . . Gus Winkler [sic] . . . Robert Conroy and a man known as 'Crane Neck' Neugent [sic]." (A. P. Madden to Chief, Intelligence Unit, March 11, 1932, in Box 4, "Career-Capone Case-Correspondence, 1931–1940" folder, FJW.)

CAPONE AND NUGENT IN MIAMI: NYT, August 1, 1928. CT, August 1, 1928; February 15, 1929; October 10, 1931 ("I'm a gambler," "Besides gambling, you're," "No, I never," "You didn't receive," "all of it"). LAT, February 19, 1929 ("Capone entertained with," "something harried about," "anxious only to," "'Scarface' led the"). J. R. Burdge, Report on Alphonse Capone and Kenneth Phillips, March 23, 1929, in FBI-AC ("I am not"). CHE, October 10, 1931. A. P. Madden to Chief, Intelligence Unit, March 11, 1932, in Box 4, "Career-Capone Case-Correspondence, 1931–1940" folder, FJW. Ross, *Trial of Al Capone*, pp. 64–65. Kobler, *Capone*, pp. 230–231, 246–249. Schoenberg, *Mr. Capone*, p. 203. Helmer and Bilek, *St. Valentine's Day Massacre*, pp. 151, 201. Helmer, *Al Capone and His American Boys*, pp. 279, 294–295, 345–346. Bair, *Al Capone*, pp. 257–258.

MORAN AND CAPONE AFTER MASSACRE: CT, February 16, 1929 ("The Moriarties of," "The butchering of"). *Miami Daily News*, February 17–18, 1929 (February 17, "Capone mob"; February 18, "That fellow Moran"). *Austin Statesman*, February 18, 1929 ("If I were," "I think it"). CHE, February 16, 19, 1929 (February 19, "The mass murder"). Keefe, *Man Who Got Away*, pp. 159 ("Everything I have"), 238.

MASSACRE INVESTIGATION: CHE, February 22–23, 1929. CT, February 22–23, 1929 (February 22, "a little bit," "The murder car"); March 20, 1929 ("We may find"). Lyle, *Dry and Lawless Years*, p. 221 ("Blonde Alibi"). Helmer and Bilek, *St. Valentine's Day Massacre*, pp. 84, 101–108, 127–128, 134–137, 140–144, 147–150. Shmelter, *Chicago Assassin*, pp. 147–148, 178–189.

CAPONE SUBPOENA AND GRAND JURY TESTIMONY: Kenneth Phillips affidavit, March 5, 1929 ("has not fully"); George E. Q. Johnson to the Attorney General, March 18, 1929; Mabel Walker Willebrandt, memorandum for Mr. Hoover, March 21, 1929 ("As a personal"); J. Edgar Hoover, memorandum for Mrs. Willebrandt, March 21, 1929; J. Edgar Hoover to G. A. Campana, March 21, 1929; J. R. Burdge, Report on Alphonse Capone and Kenneth Phillips, March 23, 1929 ("beyond a doubt," "was wholly and"); Affidavit of J. M. Coroneas, March 23, 1929; Affidavit of W. R. Foster, March 23, 1929; Affidavit of C. E. Bebler, March 23, 1929; Affidavit of M. G. Wood, March 23, 1929; J. Edgar Hoover to George E. Q. Johnson, March 25, 1929; George E. Q. Johnson to the Attorney General, March 25, 1929 ("It may become"); J. J. Perkins to Director, Bureau of Investigation, March 25, 1929; Affidavit of William P. Tremblay, March 25, 1929; Affidavit of John William Cooper Jr., March 25, 1929; *Washington Daily News*, March 27, 1929 ("all right"); *Washington Herald*, March 28, 1929 ("This is a," "That's easy," "See you later"); George E. Q. Johnson to J. Edgar Hoover, March 27, 1929 ("Permit me to"); George E. Q. Johnson to J. Edgar Hoover, March 28, 1929; Director to George E. Q. Johnson, April 1, 1929 ("It has been"); J. J. Perkins, Report on Alphonse Capone and Kenneth Phillips, M.D., April 3, 1929; J. Edgar Hoover, memorandum, March 4, 1931, all in FBI-AC. CT, February 28, 1929; March 19–22, 1929 (March 20, "the four or," "like the hoodlum"); March 26–28, 1929 (March 26, "friends," "might be defined"). CHE, February 28, 1929; March 2, 1929 ("I am sick"); March 21, 1929 ("bankers and brokers," "certain racketeering," "It's a bum," "seemed entirely mended," "I ought to," "Down in Florida"). WP, March 28, 1929 ("something was up," "a feminine hand"). Ross, *Trial of Al Capone*, pp. 13–28 (14, "willfully, corruptly, knowingly," "untrue and false"; 16, "anybody by that," "Here I am"; 17, "a brown camel," "He was pleasant"; 26, "sitting with their"; 27, "not serious"). Bergreen, *Capone*, pp. 322–327. Eig, *Get Capone*, pp. 217–218. Bair, *Al Capone*, pp. 131, 135, 209, 353.

Chapter Twelve

HOOVER IN MIAMI: *Miami Daily News*, June 20, 1928 ("Summer White House"). CT, January 26, 1929; February 1, 1929; February 13, 1929. Hynd, *Giant Killers*, pp. 10, 24. Irey and Slocum, *Tax Dodgers*, pp. 25–26. George Murray, "Why Capone Served 11 Yrs.," *Chicago American*, July 23, 1956, in "Newspaper Clippings (2 of 9)" folder, GEQJ ("Go to hell"). Galbraith, *Great Crash 1929*, pp. 9–12 (9, "inordinate desire"; 12, "the conviction that"). Kobler, *Capone*, p. 237. McElvaine, *Great Depression*, pp. 53–56 (53, "We were in," "superman," "If some unprecedented"), 61, 65. Eig, *Get Capone*, pp. 180–181, 183, 193–194. Leuchtenburg, *Herbert Hoover*, pp. 1–50 (17, "If a man"), 63, 66–81 (79, "superman," "If some unprecedented"; 81, "We were in"), 139 ("sour, puckered face"). "Did Retailing Genius J.C. Penney Hoodwink Herbert Hoover into Hyping Belle Isle Real Estate?" Belle Isle Blog, April 5, 2011, https://belleisleblog.wordpress.com/2011/04/05/did-retailing-genius-j-c-penney-hoodwink -herbert-hoover-into-hyping-belle-isle-real-estate/ (accessed March 22, 2016).

In his embellished memoir, Elmer Irey (Irey and Slocum, *Tax Dodgers*, p. 26) claims Hoover personally told him he "never saw Capone in Florida." Murray's article appears to be the earliest reference to the Capone party anecdote, and it implies Hoover was a guest of Harvey Firestone, not J. C. Penney, further suggesting the story is a myth.

HOOVER AND CRIME: CT, March 5, 1929. Hoover, *Memoirs*, pp. 267–277. Allsop, *Bootleggers*, p. 97 ("shocking conditions"). *Public Papers 1929*, pp. 2–3 ("Justice must not"). Robinson and Bornet, *Herbert Hoover*, pp. 85–88. Calder, *Origins and Development*, pp. 5–6, 14–17, 28–38, 103–128. Hoffman, *Scarface Al*, pp. 24–27 (26, "a subversion of"; 27, "The rest of the country"). Leuchtenburg, *Herbert Hoover*, pp. 28, 80, 85. Folsom, *Money Trail*, pp. 43–45 (44, "supergovernment"). Eig, *Get Capone*, pp. 207–208. McGirr, *War on Alcohol*, pp. 189–193.

HOOVER AND PROHIBITION: John H. Lyle, "The Story Behind the St. Valentine's Day Massacre!" CT, February 21, 1954 ("They're not touching," "Who is Al Capone?"). Robinson and Bornet, *Herbert Hoover*, pp. 86, 88. *Public Papers 1930*, p. 649. Calder, *Origins and Development*, pp. 109–110 (109, "large operations in," "It seems obvious"; 110, "the ultimate transfer"); 132–133 ("special corps of"). Bergreen, *Capone*, pp. 322, 378. Okrent, *Last Call*, pp. 133–134, 140. See also Merriner, *Grafters and Goo-Goos*, p. 120.

Most accounts of the Capone investigation mistakenly claim Hoover gave his order to "get Capone" shortly after his inauguration, following a meeting with Frank Loesch and other prominent Chicagoans. Among those said to be present at the meeting was Walter Strong, publisher of the *Chicago Daily News*. The source for this misconception appears to be Hoover's memoirs, which date the meeting to March 1929 (Hoover, *Memoirs*, pp. 276–277). Historian Robert S. McElvaine (*Great Depression*, pp. 52–53), however, has noted that "Hoover's own *Memoirs* were done very carelessly and are chock-full of errors," especially with regard to dates, making the March 1929 date suspect.

Hoover's calendar (*Public Papers 1930*, pp. 637–649) shows no meetings in March 1929 with Loesch or anyone else supposedly present at his "get Capone" conference. James Calder (*Origins and Development*, p. 18) suggests Hoover's meeting with "Claudius H. Huston and Mr. Strong" on March 19 (*Public Papers 1930*, p. 641) is the meeting in question, but it's doubtful this Strong is the same as the publisher of the *Daily News*. The April 14 meeting with McCormick (described by Lyle, cited above) is the only such meeting confirmed on Hoover's calendar in early 1929.

Hoover *did* meet with Loesch on March 15, 1930 (*Public Papers 1930*, p. 723), however, three days before the first known memos from Hoover administration officials referring to the Capone tax case (Calder, *Origins and Development*, pp. 133–134). A memo on the case prepared for the assistant secretary of the Treasury specifically dates the order "to proceed vigorously with the investigation of Al Capone" to March 18, 1930 (Robert H. Lucas, memorandum for Assistant Secretary Hope, March 19, 1930, in Presidential Subject Series, Box 164, "Federal Bureau of Investigation—Capone Tax Case, 1930–1931" folder, HHPL). In a memo to Frank Wilson dated March 21, A. P. Madden of the Intelligence Unit wrote, with regards to the Capone investigation, "that the White House may be expressing a desire to see it brought to an early conclusion" (Calder, *Origins and Development*, p. 134). If, as Wilson and others later claimed, Hoover sent the word out to "get Capone" in 1929, it seems highly unlikely Madden wouldn't know for certain a year later.

A WP article written not long after Capone's conviction dates Hoover's "get Capone" order to April 1930, which is consistent with this general time frame. ("Capone to Be Tried as Tax Law Evader," WP, November 22, 1930, in FBI-AC.) The *Boston Globe* also dated the order to around the time of Capone's 1930 release from prison in Pennsylvania ("Hoover Himself Wars on Capone," *Boston Globe*, May 14, 1930).

Although various federal agencies had expressed some desire to incarcerate Capone before March 1930, we have seen nothing to suggest Hoover or his administration took any direct interest in their actions. Instead, the evidence strongly suggests that the president gave his "get Capone" order not in March 1929, but March 1930.

BUNDESEN AND MASSEE: CHE, February 16, 1929. CT, February 16, 1929; April 14, 1929; May 23, 1972. Coroner's Jury list, December 23, 1929, MM. Goddard, "Valentine Day Massacre," pp. 61–63. "Purpose of the Journal," *The American Journal of Police Science*, vol. 1, no. 1 (January–February 1930), p. 3. C. W. Muehlberger, "Col. Calvin Hooker Goddard 1895–1955," *Journal of Criminal Law and Criminology*, vol. 46, no. 1 (1955), pp. 103–104 (104, "Blue Ribbon"). Kobler, *Capone*, pp. 258–259. Hoffman, *Scarface Al*, pp. 15–16, 72–74, 76–77, 80. Helmer and Bilek, *St. Valentine's Day Massacre*, pp. 113–116. Alder, *Lie Detectors*, pp. 115–116.

GODDARD: CT, April 13–14, 1929 (April 14, "systematic application," "check the slaughter"). Calvin H. Goddard, "Scientific Identification of Firearms and Bullets," *Journal of Criminal Law and Criminology*, vol. 17, no. 2 (Summer 1926), pp. 254–260 (257, "that no two"; 258, "These irregularities leave"). Calvin H. Goddard, "Who Did the Shooting?" *Popular Science Monthly*, November 1927, pp. 21–22, 172 ("By such methods"). Goddard, "Valentine Day Massacre," pp. 63–76. Muehlberger, "Col. Calvin Hooker Goddard," pp. 103–104. Hoffman, *Scarface Al*, pp. 16, 81. Helmer and Bilek, *St. Valentine's Day Massacre*, pp. 159–161. Yount, *Forensic Science*, pp. 71–77.

CRIME LAB: CT, April 14, 1929. "Purpose of the Journal," pp. 3–4. Calvin Goddard, "Scientific Crime Detection Laboratories in Europe," *The American Journal of Police Science*, vol. 1, no. 1 (January–February 1930), pp. 13–37 (13, "We had no"; 22, "In general, Europeans"). Muehlberger, "Col. Calvin Hooker Goddard," p. 104. Hoffman, *Scarface Al*, pp. 82–84 (83, "The city needs"; 84, "at least sixty"). Alder, *Lie Detectors*, pp. 115–116 (116, "outside the pale").

UNIVERSITY OF CHICAGO: CT, May 16, 1929; May 18, 1929. Carte and Carte, *Police Reform*, pp. 63–64.

ELIOT AND EDNA: Alexander G. Jamie to Alf Oftedal, April 10, 1929; Alexander G. Jamie, Personnel Classification Board Form No. 4, May 5, 1929; Alexander G. Jamie to the Commissioner of Prohibition, September 5, 1929, all in Edna S. Ness OPF. W. S. Murphy, Report on Eliot Ness, November 15, 1933, p. 7, in FBI-ENA ("never discussed his"). John Larson, "Summary of Contacts with the Secret Six of Chiago [*sic*] and Elliott [*sic*] Ness," n.d., in Carton 4, Folder 25 ("Clippings About—1947–1961"), John Larson Papers, BANC MSS 78/160cz, UCB. Porter, *Cleveland*, p. 102. Condon, "Last American Hero," p. 139. Heimel, *Eliot Ness*, pp. 23, 82, 272. Lindberg, *Return Again*, pp. 308–313. Perry, *Eliot Ness*, p. 62.

NESS RETURNS TO SCHOOL: Pol. Sci. 344 Official Class List, in Carton 4, "Chicago. University" folder, August Vollmer Papers, BANC MSS C-B 403, UCB. Murphy, Report on Eliot Ness, p. 3. "Greenhorn," *American Magazine*, March 1936, in ENPS, Roll 1, Scrapbook 3. "Evening Courses in Business Subjects," n.p., n.d., ENPS, Roll 1, Folder 1. William Townes, "As Boy in Chicago, Ness Was 'Just a Regular Guy,'" CP, February 23, 1937, in ENPS, Roll 1, Scrapbook 3. "Biographical Sketch: Eliot Ness," n.d., in Box 2, "Biographies" folder, SPD. John Larson, "Summary of Contacts with the Secret Six of Chiago [*sic*] and Elliott [*sic*] Ness," n.d., in Carton 4, Folder 25 ("Clippings About—1947–1961"), John Larson Papers, BANC MSS 78/160cz, UCB.

Ness's personnel file doesn't mention a leave of absence to go back to school, but newspaper and magazine profiles of him written during his time in Cleveland note he took a hiatus from the Prohibition Bureau to take the University of Chicago course. (*Kansas City Star*, April 19, 1936, in ENPS, Roll 1, Scrapbook 2, p. 68. *Baltimore Sun*, May 17, 1936, in ENPS, Roll 1, Scrapbook 2, p. 80. *Kansas City Star*, March 28, 1938, in ENPS, Roll 2, Scrapbook 8, p. 10. Havens, "Personalities in Law Enforcement," p. 61.)

Lending further credence to the class requiring Ness's full-time attention is a CT article about a later session of Vollmer's class, which notes that ten police detectives were "relieved of routine duty" in order to attend. (CT, January 3, 1931.)

VOLLMER: CT, May 16, 1929; December 14, 1929 ("stupid," "no business being"); January 7, 1931. "National Affairs: Professor Added," *Time*, September 16, 1929, p. 13. "Police: Finest of the Finest," *Time*, February 18, 1966, p. 49. Carte and Carte, *Police Reform*, pp. 1–3, 15–16, 19–21, 24–30, 33, 41–53 (46, "strike any person"), 69–74 (72, "an admission of"; 73, "If the communists," "make martyrs out"; 74, "bunch of morons"), 99–103 ("The eradication of"). Potter, *War on Crime*, pp. 36, 43–44. Alder, *Lie Detectors*, pp. 17–23 (22, "college cops"), 28, 60–61, 73, 106.

NESS INSPIRED BY VOLLMER: August Vollmer, "Aims and Ideals of the Police," *Journal of the American Institute of Criminal Law and Criminology*, vol. 13, no. 1 (May 1922), pp. 253–254 ("Merely arresting the," "Common sense teaches"). "Police Work a Profession, Not a Job," CDN, August 19, 1916, in *Journal of Criminal Law and Criminology*, vol. 7, no. 4 (May 1916–March 1917), p. 622. John Larson to Eliot Ness, November 19, 1929; John A. Larson to John Favill, May 17, 1938, both in John Augustus Larson Papers, Personal Collection of Beulah Allen Graham (courtesy of Ken Alder). August Vollmer, "The Scientific Policeman,"

The American Journal of Police Science, vol. 1, no. 1 (January–February 1930), p. 9 ("out-Sherlocking the"). CT, January 7, 1931. Eliot Ness to August Vollmer, December 16, 1935, in Box 24, "Ness, Eliot" folder, August Vollmer Papers, BANC MSS C-B 403, UCB ("I feel, and"). Ness MS., pp. 16, 20, in ENPS, Roll 1, Folder 2. Ness and Fraley, *The Untouchables*, pp. 134–136. Carte and Carte, *Police Reform*, pp. 33–36, 69–70, 84–86, 92–93. Alder, *Lie Detectors*, pp. xiii–xiv, 23–24, 55–61, 75–85, 90, 113, 115, 119–138, 147–148, 155–162. Perry, *Eliot Ness*, pp. 76–77 (76, "always smiling, but").

JAMIE, JOHNSON, AND YELLOWLEY: CT, September 20–21, 1929 (September 20, "intensive," "warn the enemy"; September 21, "harmonious," "A greater effort"). "Debate Plan for Arid Rule in Chicago," n.p., n.d.; "Johnson Is Given U.S. Orders to Dry Up Chicago," n.p., n.d.; "Jamie Hastens to See Doran; Purpose Is Secret," n.p., n.d., all in ENPS, Roll 1, Scrapbook 1. Calder, *Origins and Development*, pp. 124, 137.

TAX INVESTIGATION: "War on Chicago Gangs Not Over, Say U.S. Officials," n.p., n.d., in ENPS, Roll 1, Scrapbook 1, p. 36. Paul Ward, "The Man Who Got Al Capone," *Baltimore Sun Magazine*, March 20, 1932, p. 7. Irey and Slocum, *Tax Dodgers*, p. 32. Kobler, *Capone*, p. 279. Schoenberg, *Mr. Capone*, pp. 255–256. Calder, *Origins and Development*, pp. 19, 226n78. Bergreen, *Capone*, p. 304. Eghigian, *After Capone*, pp. 159, 163.

RALPH CAPONE ARREST AND QUESTIONING: CT, October 9, 1929; December 21, 1930 ("Well, you don't," "Only enough to"). Dillard, "How the U.S. Gov't," pp. 14–15. Irey and Slocum, *Tax Dodgers*, pp. 33–34. Schoenberg, *Mr. Capone*, p. 244.

Chapter Thirteen

SCALISE, ANSELMI, GIUNTA MURDER: CHE, May 9–11, 1929; May 20, 1929. CT, May 8–9, 1929 (May 9, "from Sicilian sources"). NYT, May 9, 1929. *X Marks the Spot*, p. 55, in FBI-AC. Pasley, *Al Capone*, pp. 329–332 (330, "Hop Toad"; 331, "This is the"). Vanderbilt Jr., "How Al Capone," p. 20 ("Those who work"). Edward Doherty, "The Twilight of the Gangster: How Much Longer Are We Going to Put Up with Him?" *Liberty*, October 24, 1931, p. 8. Enright, *Al Capone on the Spot*, pp. 10, 77. Burns, *One-Way Ride*, pp. 274–281 (281, "I am the"). Foster, "Blackhand War," pp. 41–43. Asbury, *Gem of the Prairie*, pp. 359–360. Anonymous, "Capone I Knew," p. 80 ("The word spread"). Lyle, *Dry and Lawless Years*, p. 222. Allsop, *Bootleggers*, pp. 140–141. Kobler, *Capone*, pp. 264–265. Schoenberg, *Mr. Capone*, pp. 233–234 (234, "I was in," "You're gonna know," "We frisked everyone," "Capone got so"). Capone, *Uncle Al Capone*, pp. 55–56 ("They were going").

ATLANTIC CITY CONFERENCE: CHE, May 9, 1929 ("Capone is not"); May 18–20, 1929. NYT, May 9, 1929 ("an average of," "a serious attempt"); May 18, 1929 ("co-operation in the," "sumptuous quarters," "We all agreed," "I want peace"). CT, May 18, 1929 ("have made it," "the idea of"); May 20, 1929 ("peace conference broke"). "Philadelphia Justice for Chicago's Al Capone," *The Literary Digest*, June 15, 1929, pp. 32, 34, 39 ("Big Four," "an executive committee"). Burns, *One-Way Ride*, p. 307. Powell, *Ninety Times Guilty*, pp. 64–65, 68. Thompson and Raymond, *Gang Rule in New York*, pp. 356–357. Herbert Asbury, "America's No. 1 Mystery Man," *Collier's*, April 19, 1947, p. 34. James A. Bell, "Frank Costello: Statesman of the Underworld," *The American Mercury*, August 1950, p. 132. Smith, *Syndicate City*, p. 81. Wolf and DiMona, *Frank Costello*, pp. 84–92. Murray, *Legacy of Al Capone*, pp. 137–

138 (137, "a good many," "the safest place"). Nelli, *Business of Crime*, pp. 212–216. Sloat, *1929*, pp. 81–83. Fox, *Blood and Power*, pp. 51, 66–67. Helmer and Mattix, *Public Enemies*, pp. 33, 122–123. Keefe, *Man Who Got Away*, pp. 238, 244–245. Critchley, *Origin of Organized Crime*, pp. 140–143. Mappen, *Prohibition Gangsters*, pp. 32, 79–104. Bair, *Al Capone*, pp. 152–156, 168, 188, 354, 358. Binder, *Al Capone's Beer Wars*, pp. 199–201, 227–228.

Most books on Capone describe the Atlantic City conference as a meeting of mobsters from all over the country, discussing plans for a nationwide Mafia commission. The guest list has grown in the retelling to include virtually every major gangster in America at that time, with dozens of attendees. Typical is Eig's *Get Capone* (pp. 226–227), which describes the conference as "the first meeting of the nation's top crime lords," whose "roster of attendees reads like an encyclopedia of crime," details for which Eig offers no citations. (See also Kobler, *Capone*, pp. 265–266. Schoenberg, *Mr. Capone*, pp. 234–235. Bergreen, *Capone*, pp. 331–336. Bair, *Al Capone*, pp. 151–155.)

Historian Marc Mappen, in his *Prohibition Gangsters* (pp. 79–96), offers a distinctly different and more convincing interpretation. Drawing on the work of David Critchley (*Origin of Organized Crime*, pp. 140–143), Mappen contrasts the "big conference" claim favored by Eig and others with a "small conference" theory—that the meeting was concerned with making peace between warring Chicago gangs, not the establishment of a nationwide crime syndicate. Mappen notes contemporary sources only mention the presence of Chicago gang figures at the Atlantic City conference, and the peace treaty only covered Chicago matters. The "big conference" narrative first showed up in print decades after the event, with a spate of dubious true-crime books adding their own embellishments from the 1970s on.

Our own research confirms Critchley and Mappen's interpretation. The books and articles cited above strongly suggest that the consensus view, from 1929 to the 1950s, was that Frank Costello called the conference with the goal of making peace in Chicago. Some New York gangsters attended, but they were not the focus of negotiations. Although more interstate cooperation may have come about as a result of the conference, it seems not to have been the primary goal.

The "big conference" theory first appears, in slightly humbler form, in a 1947 article by Herbert Asbury ("America's No. 1 Mystery Man," p. 34). Asbury writes that the conference included "gang captains from all over the East and Middle West," who "agreed to abandon internecine warfare and to arrange a suitable division of territory. A group known as the Big Mob was appointed to supervise the rackets and the liquor business from Chicago to the Atlantic Coast." This began the process of pushing the Chicago aspect of the conference into the background and frontloading its national consequences.

It took another twelve years for the "big conference" theory to become fully formed in Frederic Sondern Jr.'s *Brotherhood of Evil: The Mafia*, excerpted in *Reader's Digest* that May. Sondern claims Capone organized the conference himself, for the purpose of unveiling "a project on which he had been working for three years—a nation-wide organization or syndicate for gambling, prostitution, labor racketeering, extortion and, of course, bootlegging . . . The delegates were impressed, and within a few days [Capone] had put together a number of formidable and friendly combines to form a national syndicate." Sondern thus gives Capone credit for "the fundamental design and unwritten constitution of the modern American

Mafia." (Frederic Sondern Jr., "Brotherhood of Evil: the Mafia," *Reader's Digest*, May 1959, pp. 70–71.)

Sondern's claims are directly contradicted by the more reliable accounts of the conference cited above, which make clear that, far from being a victory for Capone, the conference severely limited his power. Other elements of Sondern's narrative are even less believable. For instance, Sondern claims that Capone received his famous scars from a Brooklyn barber who refused to give him a special haircut reserved for Mafia members. "Young Al Capone intensely admired the Mafia . . . and wanted his hair cut in the traditional *Mafioso* style," Sondern writes, "but he was not a Sicilian . . . and the barber, a Mafia man himself, considered such a request from a Neapolitan a sacrilege." (Sondern, "Brotherhood of Evil," p. 67.) Sondern's account of the Atlantic City conference is likely as fanciful as his ideas about Capone's scars. Yet his book seems to be the seed for the "big conference" theory, which later crime writers would plant in their own work.

CAPONE ARRESTED AND CONVICTED: CHE, May 18, 1929; March 17, 1930. CT, May 18–19, 1929 (May 18, "You're 'Scarface' Capone," "My name's Al," "quietly and in," "the boys," "most interesting talk," "a serious man," "I've been trying," "I've been in"). NYT, May 18, 1929 ("Give me a," "Listen, boy," "Worth about $50,000," "You made a," "All right"). *Philadelphia Evening Bulletin*, May 20, 1929 ("It's the breaks"). "Philadelphia Justice," pp. 32–42. Pasley, *Al Capone*, pp. 325–329, 332 ("Al figured on"). Murray, *Legacy of Al Capone*, pp. 137–138. Schoenberg, *Mr. Capone*, pp. 175–176, 235–238. Bergreen, *Capone*, pp. 336–338. Mappen, *Prohibition Gangsters*, pp. 107–111. Bair, *Al Capone*, pp. 155–156.

CAPONE IN PRISON: CHE, May 19–20, 1929; March 17, 1930. *Philadelphia Evening Bulletin*, June 4, 1929 ("a sinister figure," "The stories that," "the less I," "You see, I"); June 6, 1929 ("I've got a"); June 26, 1929; June 29, 1929. CT, June 5, 1929; August 20, 1929 ("very comfortable," "cheery and homelike," "soft colors and," "tasteful paintings"). *Philadelphia Record*, June 16, 1929 ("'star' pitcher"); June 27, 1929; August 21, 1929 ("I'm glad," "It is by," "This man, called," "silver-rimmed spectacles," "great little guy," "That shouldn't be," "Why can't I," "That is funny"); September 22, 1929. *Philadelphia Public Ledger*, August 10, 1929. NYT, August 9, 1929 ("an atmosphere of," "the threats and," "Perhaps Capone will"); December 11, 1929. *Philadelphia Evening Public Ledger*, November 25, 1929 ("Jail seems a," "If it takes," "The trouble with"). Pasley, *Al Capone*, pp. 332–336. Burns, *One-Way Ride*, p. 33 ("I'll have to"). "Baked to Death," *New Masses*, September 6, 1938, p. 14. Allsop, *Bootleggers*, p. 296. Kobler, *Capone*, pp. 269–270. Schoenberg, *Mr. Capone*, pp. 239–240, 243–244, 413. Dolan, *Eastern State Penitentiary*, pp. 21–23, 58 ("hardboiled"). Annie Anderson, "Al Capone: Approved Source for Tour Content," May 2013, pp. 2–9. Mappen, *Prohibition Gangsters*, pp. 111–115. Bair, *Al Capone*, pp. 160–161. Matthew Christopher, "Holmesburg Prison," Abandoned America, https://www.abandonedamerica.us/holmesburg-prison (accessed July 6, 2017). ABS visit to Eastern State Penitentiary, October 27, 2017.

STOCK MARKET CRASH: CT, October 25, 1929 ("If this goes"). NYT, October 25, 1929 ("The total losses"). *Philadelphia Evening Public Ledger*, November 25, 1929 ("Listen, Ben, if"). Allen, *Since Yesterday*, pp. 22–26. Hynd, *Giant Killers*, p. 10 ("blue-sky, big"). Galbraith, *Great Crash 1929*, pp. 21–22 (21, "the growing tide," "There are crimes"). Schoenberg, *Mr. Capone*, p. 245. Leuchtenberg, *Herbert Hoover*, p. 103. "Golder, Benjamin Martin (1891–

1946)," *Biographical Directory of the United States Congress*, http://bioguide.congress.gov/scripts/biodisplay.pl?index=g000259 (accessed October 28, 2017).

Chapter Fourteen

BURKE ON THE RUN: *Michigan*, p. 205. Helmer and Bilek, *St. Valentine's Day Massacre*, pp. 130–136, 154–155, 177–181. Helmer, *Al Capone and His American Boys*, pp. 91, 98–100 (98, "Killer"), 103, 114 ("was a victim"), 118. Lyon, *A Killing*, pp. 22–28, 56–63, 97–100, 104–124, 132.

GODDARD TRACES BULLETS: CT, December 24, 1929. Goddard, "Valentine Day Massacre," pp. 70, 77–78 (77, "The very presence," "I made long"). Pasley, *Al Capone*, pp. 262–263. Helmer and Bilek, *St. Valentine's Day Massacre*, pp. 179–180. Lyon, *A Killing*, pp. 176–178, 193 ("the turning point"). Helmer, *Al Capone and His American Boys*, pp. 91–92, 305.

BURKE ARREST AND CONVICTION: Helmer and Bilek, *St. Valentine's Day Massacre*, pp. 188–190. Helmer, *Al Capone and His American Boys*, pp. 114 ("imbecilic," "insipid"), 118–123. Lyon, *A Killing*, pp. 191–193, 210–212, 217–223 (221, "What are you"), 226 ("Get a spiritualist"), 230–233, 249–251, 255, 330–331.

CHICAGO'S REPUTATION THREATENED: *Kansas City Star*, November 1, 1931, in ENPS, Roll 1, Scrapbook 1. *Riverside News*, February 20, 1930, in RIR Scrapbook I, p. 89. Robert Isham Randolph, "Chicago—Enough of Her History to Explain Her Reputation," *Chicago Commerce*, February 22, 1930, in RIR Scrapbook I, p. 92. *Toronto Daily Star*, April 10, 1930, in RIR Scrapbook II. *Daily Mail*, March 5, 1930 ("CHICAGO IS NOT," "City of dreadful," "To the law-abiding"). CT, April 15, 1930; May 21, 1930; July 14, 1930. *Chicago American*, July 14, 1930; CEP, July 14, 1930; *Daily Mirror*, October 9, 1930, all in RIR Scrapbook II. Robert Isham Randolph, "Secret Six," *The Clevelander*, vol. 6, no. 12 (April 1932), p. 30, in RIR Scrapbook III. Dawes, *Notes as Vice President*, pp. 144–146, 165–166. Lyle, *Dry and Lawless Years*, pp. 85 ("A real Goddamned"), 122, 187–189, 192–194, 196. Allsop, *Bootleggers*, pp. 186, 188. Hoffman, *Scarface Al*, pp. 8–10, 31–32. Boehm, *Popular Culture*, pp. 75–76, 108–110 (109, "Unless gang rule").

MEAGHER SHOOTING AND AFTERMATH: Robert Isham Randolph with Forrest Crissey, "Business Fights Crime in Chicago," *The Saturday Evening Post*, August 16, 1930, p. 12, in RIR Scrapbook II, p. 72. CT, February 6, 1930. Unlabeled clipping, February 13, 1930, RIR Scrapbook I. *Kansas City Star*, November 1, 1931, in ENPS, Roll 1, Scrapbook 1. WP, August 21, 1932, in RIR Scrapbook III, pp. 120–121. Grant, *Fight for A City*, p. 234.

ROBERT ISHAM RANDOLPH: "Robert Isham Randolph Nominated to Head Association in 1930," *Chicago Commerce*, January 11, 1930, in RIR Scrapbook I, p. 39. "Engineer Heads Commercial Organization," *Professional Engineer*, February 1930, p. 14, in RIR Scrapbook I. CDN, February 7, 1930, in RIR Scrapbook I, p. 57 ("a war on crime")."Business to Start War on Gangs Today," CHE [?], February 7, 1930, in RIR Scrapbook I, p. 64. CDN, February 10, 1930, in RIR Scrapbook I. *The Sun*, February 10, 1930, in RIR Scrapbook I. Unlabeled clipping, February 13, 1930, in RIR Scrapbook I. *Toronto Daily Star*, April 10, 1930, in RIR Scrapbook II. Norman Paul Stoughton, "Chicagoans: Colonel Robert Isham Randolph—Challenger," *The Chicagoan*, April 12, 1930, in RIR Scrapbook II, p. 22. *Lancaster Post*, February 24, 1930, in RIR Scrapbook I, p. 95. *Yale Daily News*, January 9, 1931, in RIR Scrapbook II, p. 135. *Buffalo Times*, February 16, 1931, in RIR Scrapbook II, p. 163. Robert I. Randolph, "The Secret Six," *Police "13–13,"* December 1931, pp. 5, 13, in RIR Scrapbook III, p. 70 ("a real secret service"). Robert Isham Randolph, "Secret Six," *The Clevelander*, vol. 6, no. 12 (April 1932), pp. 3–4. CT, October 27, 1932. WP, August 21, 1932, in RIR Scrapbook III, pp. 120–121 ("Bob," "Colonel"). *St. Louis Times Star*, November 22, 1932, in RIR Scrapbook IV, p. 17. Daniels, *Randolphs of Virginia*, p. 327. Hoffman, *Scarface Al*, pp. 20–21.

BIRTH OF SECRET SIX / INSULL: *Toronto Daily Star*, April 10, 1930, in RIR Scrapbook II. Robert Isham Randolph, with Forrest Crissey, "Business Fights Crime in Chicago," *The Saturday Evening Post*, August 16, 1930, p. 13, in RIR Scrapbook II, p. 73. "Randolph Picks 'Courageous 6' to Study Gangs," n.d., in RIR Scrapbook I, p. 64 ("If our information"). *Yale Daily News*, January 9, 1931, in RIR Scrapbook II, p. 135. *Kansas City Star*, November 1, 1931, in ENPS, Roll 1, Scrapbook 1 ("Oh, the situation," "There may be"). Randolph, "Secret Six," pp. 3–4, in RIR Scrapbook III (3, "Citizens' Committee for"; 4, "bad enough," "you can put"). Allen, *Since Yesterday*, pp. 12–13, 75–76. Hynd, *Giant Killers*, p. 19. *WPA Guide to Illinois*, pp. 142, 190 ("tallest opera building"), 204, 219. *Miami Daily News*, January 29, 1940, in RIR Scrapbook V, p. 45. "'Secret Six' Described," [Unclear] *Tribune*, March 16, 1943, in RIR Scrapbook V, p. 60. Lyle, *Dry and Lawless Years*, pp. 194, 197. Allsop, *Bootleggers*, pp. 240, 244–245. Kael, "Raising Kane," p. 97. Bergreen, *Capone*, pp. 225–226, 367. Merriner, *Grafters and Goo-Goos*, pp. 125–126. Vickers, *Panic in the Loop*, pp. 1, 4–14, 47–61.

SECRET SIX MEMBERSHIP, BUDGET, PREJUDICES: CT, May 21, 1918; April 16, 1930. Randolph, *Randolphs of Virginia*, pp. 5, 112, 222, 371. "Robert Isham Randolph Nominated to Head Association in 1930," *Chicago Commerce*, January 11, 1930, in RIR Scrapbook I, p. 39. *Lancaster Post*, February 24, 1930, in RIR Scrapbook I, p. 95. "Business Men Act for War on Racketeers," *Journal of Commerce*, February 21, 1930, in RIR Scrapbook I, p. 86 ("If the needed"). *Toronto Daily Star*, April 10, 1930, in RIR Scrapbook II ("a little 'Red' wop"). "Al Capone's Just a Dago Bootlegger, Club Hears," n.d., in RIR Scrapbook II, p. 23 ("dago bootlegger"); *Yale Daily News*, January 9, 1931, in RIR Scrapbook II, p. 135. *New Orleans States*, January 12, 1931, in RIR Scrapbook II, pp. 136, 139 ("dirty, vicious killer"). *Philadelphia Public Ledger*, May 28, 1931, in RIR Scrapbook III ("He doesn't belong"). CDN, January 20, 1932, in RIR Scrapbook III, p. 73. LAT, January 21, 1932; NYT, January 21, 1932; and *Pittsburgh Post Gazette*, January 21, 1932, in RIR Scrapbook III. W. A. McSwain to J. Edgar Hoover, September 12, 1932, in FBI-RIR. *Japan Advertiser*, March 3, 1934, in RIR Scrapbook IV, p. 64. C. L. Rice to R. E. Wood, July 5, 1938, in Alexander Jamie Treasury OPF. CT, November 18, 1938. NYT, April 27, 1939, in RIR Scrapbook V, p. 39. *Memphis Press-Scimitar*, n.d., in RIR Scrapbook IV, p. 94. *Miami Daily News*, January 29, 1940, in RIR Scrapbook V, p. 45. "'Secret Six' Described," [Unclear] *Tribune*, March 16, 1943, in RIR Scrapbook V, p. 60. Grant, *Fight for a City*, p. 234. Fox, *Blood and Power*, pp. 133–134 ("The real Americans"). Schoenberg, *Mr. Capone*, p. 204 ("a xenophobic bigot"). Hoffman, *Scarface Al*, pp. 20–21, 164. Merriner, *Grafters and Goo-Goos*, p. 125.

SECRET SIX METHODS AND PRACTICES: *Chicago American*, February 8, 1930, in RIR Scrapbook I, p. 65. Unlabeled clipping, February 13, 1930, RIR Scrapbook I. CDN, February 27, 1930, in RIR Scrapbook I, p. 96. CT, March 4, 1930 ("We didn't choose"); April 15,

1930. "Chicago Not Crime Hub, Randolph Says," *Journal of Commerce*, March 4, 1930, in RIR Scrapbook I, p. 98. "Chicago Turns on the Gunman," *The Literary Digest*, March 8, 1930, in RIR Scrapbook II, p. 3. CT, April 4, 1930, in RIR Scrapbook II. *Toronto Daily Star*, April 10, 1930, in RIR Scrapbook II. Edwin Balmer, "The Chicago Battlefront," *The Register* [?], June 16, 1930, in RIR Scrapbook II, p. 46. *New Orleans States*, January 12, 1931, in RIR Scrapbook II, pp. 136, 139 ("Even now, it"). *Detroit Free Press*, January 31, 1931, in RIR Scrapbook II, p. 157. *Detroit News*, January 31, 1931, in RIR Scrapbook II, p. 157. *Buffalo Times*, February 16, 1931, in RIR Scrapbook II, p. 163. NYT, April 17, 1932 ("all sorts of," "forced to fight"). *St. Louis Times Star*, November 22, 1932, in RIR Scrapbook IV, p. 17 ("We wasted a"). "Chicago Crusader Urges Pittsburgh 'Secret Six,'" n.p., February 2, 1932, in RIR Scrapbook III. Randolph, "Secret Six," p. 32, in RIR Scrapbook III ("Give us the"). WP, August 21, 1932, in RIR Scrapbook III, pp. 120–121. *Japan Advertiser*, March 3, 1934, in RIR Scrapbook IV, p. 64. *Memphis Press-Scimitar*, n.d., in RIR Scrapbook IV, p. 94. Alexander Jamie to Henry Morgenthau Jr., September 1, 1938, in Alexander Jamie OPF. NYT, April 27, 1939, in RIR Scrapbook V, p. 39. *Miami Daily News*, January 29, 1940, in RIR Scrapbook V, p. 45. "'Secret Six' Described," [Unclear] *Tribune*, March 16, 1943, in RIR Scrapbook V, p. 60. Merriner, *Grafters and Goo-Goos*, p. 126.

RALPH CAPONE INVESTIGATION: CT, April 16, 1930; May 9, 1930; December 21, 1930 ("Take their money"). IRS-2, p. 26. "About Eliot Ness," CN, September 23, 1947, in FBI-ENA. Kobler, *Capone*, pp. 145, 269. Schoenberg, *Mr. Capone*, pp. 198, 244. Calder, *Origins and Development*, p. 226n77. Bergreen, *Capone*, p. 340. Haller, *Illegal Enterprise*, pp. 230–231.

LAHART AND SEAGER: *U.S. v. Joe Martino and John Giannoni*, indictment, November 1928, in Box 607, "Criminal Case 18299" folder, CCF. Edward C. Wilcox, memorandum for the personnel file of Samuel M. Seager, April 16, 1928; Edward C. Wilcox, memorandum to Mr. Jackson, May 12, 1928; J. M. Doran to Samuel M. Seager, May 14, 1928; Samuel M. Seager to the Treasury Department, May 18, 1928; J. M. Doran to Samuel M. Seager, May 22, 1928; Alf Oftedal to Samuel M. Seager, May 28, 1928; Oath of Office, June 8, 1928; Personal History, June 8, 1928; George E. Golding to Commissioner of Prohibition, June 8, 1928; Harry M. Dengler, Report on Probationary Employee U.S. Prohibition Service, November 14, 1928; Alexander Jamie to Alf Oftedal, February 23, 1929; Alf Oftedal to Alexander Jamie, February 27, 1929; Personal History, March 4, 1929; A. J. Jamie, Efficiency Report, n.d.; Personal History, January 22, 1931; Personal History Statement, May 28, 1932; Elmer L. Irey to the Commissioner of Internal Revenue, January 5, 1934, all in Samuel Seager OPF/ATF. Melvin Purvis to J. Edgar Hoover, November 28, 1933, in FBI-ENA. Ness and Fraley, *The Untouchables*, pp. 30–31, 64–65, 145. Mackenzie, *History of the 307th Field Artillery*, pp. 27–31, 44–47, 221. Borroel, *Story of the Untouchables*, pp. 57–60, 189–194.

RALPH CAPONE'S CLUBS: *Lawrence Journal-World*, May 8, 1930. *Pittsburgh Press*, May 8, 1930. *Spokane Daily Chronicle*, May 8, 1930. *DeKalb Daily Chronicle*, May 9, 1930. CT, May 29, 1930. Bergreen, *Capone*, pp. 98–99 (99, "whoopee"), 244, 246, 248 ("Ralph was always"). Bruck, *When Hollywood*, p. 22 ("boys patrolling the," "Is this a"). Capone, *Uncle Al Capone*, p. 23.

The Greyhound tap is specifically identified on the transcript dated April 12, 1930 (in

"Wire Taps (1 of 12)" folder, RRPAC). The existence of a tap on the Cotton Club is conjectural but seems likely, given the taps on the other two and the later raids by Jamie and Ness.

WIRETAPPING: Willebrandt, *Inside of Prohibition*, pp. 231–237. Okrent, *Last Call*, pp. 274–286. McGirr, *War on Alcohol*, pp. 199–200.

MONTMARTRE CAFÉ WIRETAP: Ness MS., pp. 17–18, in ENPS, Roll 1, Folder 2 (Ness quotes). Ness and Fraley, *The Untouchables*, pp. 107–125. Collins and Hagenauer, *Chicago Mob Wars*, no. 17 ("DINE" and "DANCE"). Tucker, *Eliot Ness and the Untouchables*, pp. 18–20. Date is conjectural, based on the dates of the transcripts in "Wire Taps (1 of 12)" folder, RRPAC.

The original source for the Montmartre Café wiretap incident is Ness's first draft manuscript for *The Untouchables* (Ness MS., pp. 17–18, in ENPS, Roll 1, Folder 2). Ness's account is light on details and doesn't name the man who went up the pole to put in the tap. Nor does it give a clear date for the incident, merely inserting it, along with many of Ness's other scattered memories, into the general timeline of the Untouchables investigation.

In the finished book (Ness and Fraley, *The Untouchables*, pp. 107–117), Fraley expands Ness's anecdote into a lengthy sequence. Unlike in Ness's manuscript, which describes an unnamed secretary placing a call to the Montmartre, Fraley's version has two Untouchables (Lahart and Thomas Friel) infiltrate the café undercover and place a call to one of Ness's other agents. Perhaps in an attempt at humor, Fraley has the agent making the call, Lahart, pretend to be speaking to his girlfriend, to the embarrassment of the agent on the receiving end. Fraley identifies the agent up the pole as Paul Robsky, who is described elsewhere in the book as "a telephone expert" from New Jersey (p. 34). Fraley dates the incident to mid- or late 1929, during Capone's incarceration in Pennsylvania, and describes it as an Untouchables operation.

Apart from the obvious dramatic embellishments (such as the undercover element), Fraley's description of the incident is problematic, particularly his identification of Robsky as the lineman. Robsky was born in Illinois and served as a Prohibition agent in South Carolina; he would later do temporary duty in Newark, New Jersey, but not until 1935 (Paul W. Robsky, Personal History, December 1, 1928; Oath of Office, December 1, 1928; R. Q. Merrick to the Commissioner of Prohibition, April 15, 1929; Recommendation for Change in Designated Post of Duty, July 20, 1935, all in Paul W. Robsky OPF/ATF). His personnel file also reveals that he didn't arrive in Chicago for Untouchables duty until April 1931 (J. L. Acuff to Paul W. Robsky, March 31, 1931; J. L. Acuff to Eliot Ness, March 31, 1931; Paul W. Robsky to M. L. Harney, April 26, 1932, all in Paul W. Robsky OPF/ATF).

Nor is there anything in Robsky's personnel file to suggest he was the "telephone expert" Fraley describes. Two efficiency reports from 1935 describe Robsky as having no "electrical, telephone or radio experience" (Efficiency Report, March 25, 1935; Efficiency Report, September 11, 1935, both in Paul W. Robsky OPF/ATF). Other efficiency reports from 1935, 1936, and 1937 describe him as having "some telephone experience" (Efficiency Report, October 5, 1935; Efficiency Report, March 19, 1936; Efficiency Report, September 22, 1936; Efficiency Report, March 15, 1937, all in Paul W. Robsky OPF/ATF).

By contrast, the personnel file of Untouchable Joe Leeson, who became a wiretapping expert following the Capone investigation, is littered with references to his telephone skills (see, for example, Efficiency Report, September 26, 1935, in Joseph D. Leeson OPF/ATF). While absence of evidence does not equal evidence of absence, it's difficult to explain Robsky's file being silent on his wiretapping prowess if he was truly the "telephone expert" Fraley describes.

In 1962, Robsky published his own account of the Capone case, written primarily or exclusively by Fraley (Fraley and Robsky, *Last of the Untouchables*, pp. 59–67). Although Robsky provided some authentic details, the book is heavily fictionalized, even more so than *The Untouchables*—a fact Robsky openly admitted (*Miami News*, March 27, 1966). The book presents its own version of the Montmartre wiretap incident, agreeing with *The Untouchables* in some basic details, but altering others to conform to Robsky's actual biography. In this version, Robsky is no longer an expert wiretapper, but is trained on the fly—a risky and improbable move for such a high-stakes operation. As in *The Untouchables*, Fraley here has Lahart undercover in the café placing a call to someone on the outside. But this time it isn't a fellow Untouchable but a woman referred to by the agents with the pseudonym "Edna."

Perry (*Eliot Ness*, pp. 72–75, 305) attempts to make Fraley's versions of the incident conform with the known facts by dating the wiretap to April 1931, after Robsky arrived in Chicago. Although Perry admits Robsky's book "generally is not a reliable document," he nevertheless uses it for Robsky's perspective on the incident. He also cites "official Prohibition Bureau records" and "official memoranda" describing the wiretap, apparently from Robsky's personnel file. We have been unable to locate these documents, despite having viewed the same copies of these files that he did.

Other evidence suggests Perry's dating of the incident is incorrect. A letter written by Ness notes that his squad had already "secure[d] telephone taps covering the various headquarters' [*sic*] spots of the Capone gang" by January 20, 1931 (Eliot Ness to the Director of Prohibition, January 20, 1931, in William J. Gardner OPF/ATF). By April, the Untouchables were already into the raiding phase of their investigation, and Ralph was already facing a prison term for tax evasion. Bringing Robsky in at that late date just to tap Ralph's headquarters makes little sense. (Incidentally, Perry misidentifies the name of the street where the agents rented their listening post apartment as "Cermak Road," a name it wouldn't receive until after the death of Mayor Anton Cermak in 1933.)

Nor are we convinced Robsky's use of the name "Edna" proves (or even suggests) that Edna Ness, as Perry claims, "was probably" the secretary who placed the call into the Montmartre. The fanciful details in Robsky's book strongly suggest the use of that name, which he describes as a pseudonym, is coincidental. (In Phil Karlson's *The Untouchables* 1959 telefilm, Eliot's girlfriend "Betty" makes the call, possibly starting all of this nonsense.) If anything, the most likely candidate for the woman who placed the call is Ione Nugent, a Prohibition Bureau secretary who later worked for the Secret Six. An FBI memo from 1932 notes Nugent "has been used for the purpose of contacting individuals whose telephone wires had been tapped so as to identify the voices of the persons conversing over the telephone." (W. A. McSwain to J. Edgar Hoover, August 6, 1932, in FBI-RIR.)

Fraley's books appear to be the only primary sources placing Robsky on the pole behind the Montmartre Café. We've located several interviews with Robsky, including two before the publication of his book and one in which he claims not to have read *The Untouchables*. He tells a few consistent anecdotes in those interviews, versions of which are included in *The Last of the Untouchables*, but the Montmartre wiretap is not one of them. (*Miami News*, April 20,

1959; March 27, 1966; October 9, 1973. *Milwaukee Journal*, January 10, 1961.) Given the lack of corroborating evidence outside Fraley's own work and Fraley's record of embellishment, it seems highly likely he misidentified Robsky as the man on the pole.

The Untouchables describes the background details of several members of Ness's squad quite accurately, typically men Ness served with for a long time, such as Lahart and Seager. Others—often men who served only briefly on the team—are characterized lightly if at all, with details contradicted or uncorroborated by other sources. Fraley had a list of names in Ness's scrapbook to work with, and when Ness couldn't flesh out the men on his team Fraley apparently filled in the gaps himself. This seems to be the case with Robsky. He came to the squad late, and his description in *The Untouchables* does not fit the known facts, suggesting his character is a product of Fraley's imagination. Later, when Fraley wrote *The Last of the Untouchables*, he corrected what *The Untouchables* got wrong about Robsky's background and character, but preserved the one scene from that book in which Robsky plays a major role— the Montmartre wiretap—even though it seems Robsky had nothing to do with it.

After removing Robsky from the equation, the remaining evidence clearly suggests the Montmartre wiretap happened in early 1930. Various news clippings indicate that Ness and Alexander Jamie investigated Ralph Capone in the first half of 1930 before Ness went after Bottles's brother. (CT, May 9, 1930; May 29, 1930; July 11, 1930. "Capone's Club Raided Again; Manager Held," n.p., n.d., in ENPS, Roll 1, Scrapbook 1, p. 122. *Reading Eagle*, May 10, 1930. CN, September 23, 1947, in FBI-ENA.) A 1932 memo from Untouchable Lyle Chapman explains the investigations of Ralph's Montmartre Café and Cotton Club were separate from and happened previously to the Untouchables' investigation into Al Capone, sometime between 1928 and 1930 (Lyle B. Chapman, memo to W. E. Bennett, September 7, 1932, in Lyle B. Chapman OPF/ATF).

But easily the strongest pieces of evidence placing the Montmartre wiretap in early 1930 are the wiretap transcripts preserved among George E. Q. Johnson's papers at the National Archives (in "Wire Taps (1 of 12)" folder, RRPAC). These transcripts are dated from February to April 1930, and several record conversations involving or concerning Ralph Capone. The locations aren't given (though at least one apparently came from a wiretap on the Greyhound Inn), but if Ralph's other clubs were under surveillance then, the Montmartre certainly was as well. The agents monitoring these taps were Ness, Lahart, and Seager—all future Untouchables. That would make it easy for Ness to misremember this tap as part of the later Capone investigation.

Given all this circumstantial evidence, it seems almost certain that with the Montmartre incident, as with the Chicago Heights raids, Fraley took an incident occurring before the Untouchables were formed and falsely made it part of the Al Capone investigation. Later writers have mistakenly taken him at his word.

NITTO TAX INVESTIGATION: Pasley, *Al Capone*, p. 352. IRS-2, p. 48. Irey and Slocum, *Tax Dodgers*, pp. 45–46. Eghigian, *After Capone*, pp. 159, 163–164, 166.

MEDICINE BALL CABINET: NYT, November 29, 1931. "The House: Hoover's Next-to-Worst," *Time*, November 10, 1930, p. 18 ("Medicine Ball Cabinet"). Irey and Slocum, *Tax Dodgers*, pp. 35–36. Eig, *Get Capone*, pp. 219–220.

GREAT DEPRESSION: NYT, November 12, 1930 ("a sort of," "at the corner," "Building construction may"). Hoover, *Memoirs*, p. 195 ("left their jobs"). Robinson and Bornet, *Herbert Hoover*, p. 133 ("that the worst"). Liebovich, *Bylines in Despair*, p. 116 ("I am sure"). McElvaine, *Great Depression*, pp. 58–62 (62, "Gentlemen, you have"). Leuchtenburg, *Herbert Hoover*, pp. 104–111 (104, "The fundamental business"; 107, "Gentlemen, you have"), 113–114 (113, "Hoovervilles," "Hoover Pullmans"), 130–131. Eig, *Get Capone*, p. 334.

HOOVER MEETS LOESCH, TARGETS CAPONE: *Boston Globe*, May 14, 1930. CEA, June 15, 1931. CHE, June 17, 1931 ("Have you got"). Dillard, "How the U.S. Gov't," p. 55. Irey and Slocum, *Tax Dodgers*, p. 36. Hoover, *Memoirs*, pp. 276–277 (276, "much more than"). *Public Papers 1929*, pp. 101–106 (106, "the very essence"). *Public Papers 1930*, p. 723. Calder, *Origins and Development*, pp. 5–12, 14–19, 28–38, 77–85, 100. Eig, *Get Capone*, pp. 210, 220–221.

Chapter Fifteen

CAPONE LEAVES PRISON: CHE, March 17–18, 1930 (March 17, "Each one cost"). CT, March 18, 1930 ("You get the"). "Coming Out Party," *Time*, March 24, 1930, p. 15. Pasley, *Al Capone*, pp. 333–335 (334, "the lights going"; 335, "I cannot estimate," "He had peace"). Sullivan, *Chicago Surrenders*, pp. 26–27. Ness and Fraley, *The Untouchables*, pp. 128–131. Schoenberg, *Mr. Capone*, p. 249. Lindberg, *Return to the Scene*, p. 332. Annie Anderson, "Al Capone: Approved Source for Tour Content," May 2013, p. 7.

CAPONE MEETS STEGE: CT, March 22, 1930 ("Did you pay," Capone, Stege, and Ditchburne quotes).

HERRICK INTERVIEWS CAPONE: CT, March 22, 1930 (quotes).

CAPONE TAX INVESTIGATION: "The Cabinet: Dry Hope," *Time*, November 11, 1929, pp. 11–12. Robert H. Lucas, memorandum for Assistant Secretary Hope, March 19, 1930 ("to proceed vigorously," "a desire to"); A. P. Madden to Chief, Intelligence Unit, April 28, 1930, both in Presidential Subject Series, Box 164, "Federal Bureau of Investigation—Capone Tax Case, 1930–1931" folder, HHPL. *Boston Globe*, May 14, 1930. IRS-2, p. 1. Irey and Slocum, *Tax Dodgers*, pp. 32 ("Treasury's prime function," "custom, not law"), 36–38. Schoenberg, *Mr. Capone*, pp. 255–256. Calder, *Origins and Development*, pp. 133–135 (134, "The difficulty"; 135, "prepared himself for," "is the type").

CAPONE INTERNAL REVENUE INTERVIEW: Testimony of Louis H. Wilson, n.d., pp. 11–15, 18, in Box 1, "Transcripts From U.S. v. Al Capone (Various Witnesses) [1 of 2]" folder, USvAC (quotes). CHE, October 9, 1931. Schoenberg, *Mr. Capone*, pp. 257–258.

CAPONE AS TOURIST ATTRACTION / *TIME* MAGAZINE COVER: CT, March 22, 1930 ("Where can I"). "Coming Out Party," *Time*, March 24, 1930, pp. 15–16 (15, "No desperado of"). Pasley, *Al Capone*, p. 62. Allsop, *Bootleggers*, p. 64.

CAPONE IN MIAMI: *Miami Daily News*, March 11, 1930 ("Our people have"). CT, March 20–21, 1930; March 23, 1930; March 25, 1930 ("He may for"); April 21, 1930 ("I have no"); April 23, 1930 ("the scene of"); April 27, 1930 ("It is no"); May 11, 1930; May 13, 1930; May 17, 1930 ("reign of terror"); May 19–20, 1930 (May 19, "The lawns were"); May 24, 1930 ("having some visible"); May 28, 1930; May 30, 1930; June 11–15, 1930 (June 13, "Why not," "It wouldn't do"); July 11–13, 1930. NYT, March 20–21, 1930 (March 20, "Arrest [Capone] promptly"); March 23, 1930; March 25, 1930; April 23, 1930; April 26, 1930;

April 27, 1930 ("Capone is charged"); May 9–11, 1930 (May 9, "I was in"); May 14–15, 1930; May 25, 1930; June 12–13, 1930 (June 12, "He harbors people"); June 15, 1930. Alphonse Capone Witness Transcript, *State of Florida v. S. D. Mccreary, et al.*, May 27, 1930, in Box 1, "Court Filings From Related Cases" folder, USvAC (4, "in the shit"; 5, "I asked him," "I wonder how"). Pasley, *Al Capone*, p. 335 ("And all I've"). Girton, "Al Capone Tells," pp. 70–71 (70, "the invasion of," "Al Capone's the"; 71, "I like Florida"). IRS-2, p. 43. Kobler, *Capone*, pp. 291–293. Schoenberg, *Mr. Capone*, pp. 254, 261–273. Bergreen, *Capone*, pp. 359, 369–373. Eghigian, *After Capone*, p. 325. Shmelter, *Chicago Assassin*, p. 207. Bair, *Al Capone*, pp. 195–196.

"PUBLIC ENEMIES": CEP, December 6, 1927. CHE, April 24–25, 1930 (April 24, "The purpose is," "constant observation," "law abiding citizens," "dealing with those," "Gangsters must be"). CT, April 24, 1930; January 22, 1931 ("the No. 1 public enemy"); February 28, 1931 ("the chief public enemy"); June 13, 1931. NYT, April 24–25, 1930. Pasley, *Al Capone*, pp. 349–350 (350, "I never heard"). *Hearings . . . on the Nomination of James H. Wilkerson*, p. 148 ("a list of"). Asbury, *Gem of the Prairie*, pp. 371–372 (371, "The phrase 'public'"). Hoffman, *Scarface Al*, pp. 110–115 (113, "Public Enemy Number One"; 114, "Capone is the"). Helmer and Bilek, *St. Valentine's Day Massacre*, pp. 186–187, 286–287. "Crime Commission in Chicago," British Movietone, 2:06, https://www.youtube.com/watch?v=z4g0nrfiemo (accessed March 31, 2017).

Chapter Sixteen

OUTFIT BUSINESS SUFFERS: *Atlanta Constitution*, March 16, 1930 ("Beer deliveries have," "Capone will return").

WIRETAPS: S. M. Seager, Wiretap Transcript 14, February 14, 1930; E. Ness, Wiretap Transcript 34, February 14, 1930; S. M. Seager, Wiretap Transcript 72, February 16, 1930 ("help their man"); S. M. Seager, Wiretap Transcript 155, February 20, 1930 ("Say, Dutch" exchange); S. M. Seager, Wiretap Transcript 191, February 22, 1930 ("bum stuff"); S. M. Seager, Wiretap Transcript 204, February 24, 1930 ("Have you got" exchange); E. Ness, Wiretap Transcript 215, February 24, 1930 ("I'm in a" exchange); M. J. Lahart, Wiretap Transcript 250, February 26, 1930; S. M. Seager, Wiretap Transcript 267, February 27, 1930 ("good stuff"); M. J. Lahart, Wiretap Transcripts 291 and 295, March 1, 1930; M. J. Lahart, Wiretap Transcript 71, March 11, 1930 ("Say, I'm out" exchange); M. J. Lahart, Wiretap Transcript 73, March 12, 1930 ("raising hell"); M. J. Lahart, Wiretap Transcript 72, March 11, 1930 ("Say, I was" exchange); M. J. Lahart, Wiretap Transcript (unnumbered), April 12, 1930 ("The state's attorney"), all in "Wire Taps (1 of 12)" folder, RRPAC. CPD, January 23, 1936. *Buffalo Courier-Express*, March 2, 1937, in ENPS, Roll 1, Scrapbook 5, p. 174 ("Well, we settled," "The criminal, you"). Ness and Fraley, *The Untouchables*, pp. 120–123. Calder, *Origins and Development*, p. 136.

Eig (*Get Capone*, pp. 257–258) quotes Transcript 215, but given the reference to one of the speakers as "Vic," it seems doubtful this was Jack McGurn, as Eig claims. Nor, given the harried nature of "Dutch" and the lack of any evidence Ralph Capone used that nickname, is Eig's identification of the other caller as Ralph likely.

Though the CPD article describing Ness learning about the two politicians working with

Capone doesn't name the candidates, they were probably Big Bill Thompson (the Capone candidate) and Anton Cermak (the supposed reformer). Cermak beat Thompson in the mayoral election of 1931 by pledging to end gang rule, with sub rosa help from Capone forces (Lyle, *Dry and Lawless Years*, pp. 258–262; Bergreen, *Capone*, pp. 416–417, 423–424).

This would further support the Montmartre wiretap going in before Paul Robsky arrived in Chicago. The mayoral election in 1931 was held in April, around the time Robsky joined the Untouchables, but only the February primary was truly contested. In the primary, Thompson faced off against Judge John Lyle, a true reform candidate. Supporting Thompson and Cermak, the latter in secret, kept the mob's bases covered. If Ness heard the gangsters discussing that election, it was almost certainly well before April 1931.

RALPH CAPONE TRIAL: M. J. Lahart, Wiretap Transcript 4, March 10, 1930 ("fix up"); S. M. Seager, Wiretap Transcript 999, April 9, 1930 ("This is Jim" exchange), both in "Wire Taps (1 of 12)" folder, RRPAC. CHE, April 9, 1930; April 11, 1930 ("What are those," "More records"). CT, April 10, 1930; April 16, 1930 ("poor race horse"); April 26, 1930. IRS-1, p. 8. Irey and Slocum, *Tax Dodgers*, p. 35. Bergreen, *Capone*, p. 363.

FEDS TARGET CAPONE: "Telephone Message from Mr. Youngquist of Dept of Justice," March 31, 1930; A. P. Madden to Chief, Intelligence Unit, April 28, 1930; "Mr. Youngquist of Justice Telephoned," May 12, 1930 ("I impressed upon"), all in Presidential Subject Series, Box 164, "Federal Bureau of Investigation—Capone Tax Case, 1930–1931" folder, HHPL. *Boston Globe*, May 14, 1930. "Crime: Capone's Week," *Time*, May 19, 1930, p. 13 ("reach"). Calder, *Origins and Development*, pp. 136–137 (137, "The enclosed," "many lengthy cases"), 257n38–39.

RALPH CAPONE BOOTLEGGING INVESTIGATION: *Lawrence Journal-World*, May 8, 1930. *Pittsburgh Press*, May 8, 1930. CT, May 9–10, 1930; May 29, 1930. *De Kalb Daily Chronicle*, May 9, 1930. "Capone's Club Raided Again; Manager Held," n.p., n.d., in ENPS, Roll 1, Scrapbook 1. *Reading Eagle*, May 10, 1930. CHE, May 11, 1930; May 29, 1930. Indictment, *U.S. v. Ralph Capone, et al.*, May 1930, in Box 690, Criminal Case 21504, CCF. Indictment, *U.S. v. Ralph Capone, et al.*, May 1930, in Box 690, Criminal Case 21505, CCF.

RALPH CAPONE SENTENCING: CT, June 17, 1930 ("I don't understand"). CEP, June 16, 1930. Irey and Slocum, *Tax Dodgers*, p. 35.

HAWTHORNE KENNEL CLUB INVESTIGATION: A. P. Madden to Chief, Intelligence Unit, April 28, 1930, in Presidential Subject Series, Box 164, "Federal Bureau of Investigation—Capone Tax Case, 1930–1931" folder, HHPL ("There is nothing," "As a matter," "the head of," "already been before," "a more determined").

E. J. O'HARE: Willebrandt, *Inside of Prohibition*, pp. 98–100. T. D. Metz, "Mystery of Eddie O'Hare's Mile-a-Minute Murder," *True Detective Mysteries*, July 1941, pp. 46 ("Artful Eddie"), 49, 87 (87, "If I can't"). Lyle, *Dry and Lawless Years*, p. 147. Kobler, *Capone*, pp. 243–245 (244, "You can make"). Spiering, *Man Who Got Capone*, pp. 81–82. Schoenberg, *Mr. Capone*, p. 295. Calder, *Origins and Development*, pp. 138–139. Ewing and Lundstrom, *Fateful Rendezvous*, pp. 3–4, 27–31, 34–35, 85–86 (85, "I have never"). Eghigian, *After Capone*, pp. 131–133. Cook, *King of the Bootleggers*, pp. 25–26 (25, "for medicinal purposes"), 78–79, 104–107, 114, 195–196. Okrent, *Last Call*, pp. 198–199. Eig, *Get Capone*, p. 162 ("Fast Eddie").

Most sources give O'Hare's first name as "Edward," which he apparently used officially when not using his preferred nickname, "E. J." But Ewing and Lundstrom's biography of O'Hare's son (*Fateful Rendezvous*, pp. 3–4), produced with the family's cooperation, reports his true first name as "Edgar."

The family's input left that book with a sanitized portrayal of O'Hare. For instance, Ewing and Lundstrom (*ibid.*, p. 85) stress O'Hare's defense in his 1926 bootlegging trial, involving his refusal "to reveal information on the grounds of attorney-client privilege." They also date Edward O'Hare's acquisition of the nickname "Butch" to the spring of 1936 (*ibid.*, p. 58), suggesting the younger O'Hare wasn't known by that name during this period.

FRANK WILSON: Frank J. Wilson Diary for 1930, April 5–18, April 29, May 15–16, June 2–7, in Box 1, "Personal Papers—Diaries—Frank J. Wilson, Judith Wilson, Mae Wilson, 1904–1906," FJW. 1930 U.S. Census Record for Frank John Wilson. 1940 U.S. Census Record for Frank John Wilson. IRS-1, p. 2. IRS-2, pp. 1, 53. Ward, "Man Who Got Al Capone," pp. 7, 9 ("investigating some politicians"). Richard Hirsch and Boyd Mayer, "Behind the Scenes with the United States Secret Service," *True Detective*, December 1938, p. 15. Wilson and Whitman, "Undercover Man," pp. 14–15 (14, "There are some"). Hynd, *Giant Killers*, p. 31. Irey and Slocum, *Tax Dodgers*, pp. 36 ("Wilson fears nothing"), 54. Wilson and Day, *Special Agent*, pp. 7–9 (7, "regulation forty-five"), 12–25, 29–31, 71 ("A year—ten"), 228. Spiering, *Man Who Got Capone*, pp. 46–62 (47, "Wilson would investigate," "sweats ice water"), 65–66, 83–84. Calder, *Origins and Development*, pp. 139, 258n49. Folsom, *Money Trail*, p. 78. Wilson can be heard speaking in *Doubtful Dollars* (Affiliated Aetna Life Companies, 1945), 15:55, Prelinger Archives, https://archive.org/details/doubtful_dollars (accessed July 22, 2016).

Like Ness and Irey, Frank Wilson would later publish his own embellished account of the Capone investigation. Unlike the other two, Wilson published multiple versions of the same story, which sometimes don't agree in the details. Revisionist historians who dismiss Ness's account of the Capone case tend to take Wilson's at face value, even though it plays fast and loose with the truth in ways that make him seem more central to the investigation than he was.

Typical is the date for Wilson's arrival in Chicago. Virtually all accounts accept Wilson's claim of taking charge of the Capone investigation in about 1928 (see Eig, *Get Capone*, p. 240). But IRS records are clear that Wilson's involvement in the investigation began in May 1930 (IRS-1, p. 2; IRS-2, p. 1). He had been in Chicago in 1928 or 1929 to investigate Terry Druggan and Frankie Lake, which might be the source of his claim that he joined the Capone case that early, but his work on the Capone case began in earnest the following year (Ward, "Man Who Got Al Capone," p. 9).

Wilson's own writings contradict the 1928 or 1929 date. In his *Collier's* article (Wilson and Whitman, "Undercover Man," p. 14), Wilson claims he got the Capone assignment because of his work on Druggan and Lake, both of whom were indicted in October 1929 (CT, October 12, 1931). In his memoir (Wilson and Day, *Special Agent*, pp. 29–30), Wilson gives the date of his arrival as 1928, but claims he was sent to Chicago *after* the St. Valentine's Day Massacre and Herbert Hoover's inauguration, both of which happened in 1929.

The best evidence for Wilson's arrival in Chicago is in his diary (cited above). The diary ends in early June but proves Wilson was based in Baltimore before May 1930, working primarily on other cases. His visit to Chicago in mid-April appears to have been primarily concerned with Druggan and Lake, although he did some work on the Ralph Capone case and sat in on a meeting with Mattingly at A. P. Madden's request. The entries for May 13 and 16, 1930, record Wilson's meetings with Irey and other top officials in Washington to discuss the "Chicago cases," after which Wilson "arranged to Be in Chgo. on May 26th, 1930." These were almost certainly the meetings where Irey assigned Wilson to the Capone case full time.

Wilson's accounts of the Capone case also stretch the truth about his plans to meet with Lingle. His summary account of the Capone case gives the date of his *Tribune* meeting as June 1, and states that Lingle "was murdered before they were able to fix the date of the interview with me" (IRS-2, p. 54). But in his *Collier's* article, Wilson claimed Lingle died just "twenty-four hours before" their scheduled meeting (Wilson and Whitman, "Undercover Man," p. 15), and in his memoir, the two men were set to meet within forty-eight hours (Wilson and Day, *Special Agent*, p. 31). Nothing in Wilson's summary report supports his claim (in both the *Collier's* article and in *Special Agent*) that the editor he met with was Robert McCormick. Wilson's diary is blank on June 1, the date given in IRS-2 for his meeting at the *Tribune*, but June 2 notes a visit to an "H. Ellis," apparently an attorney, at the *Tribune*.

Chapter Seventeen

LINGLE MURDER: CHE, June 10–11, 1930 (June 10, "Play Hy Schneider," "I've got him," "REPORTER KILLED BY"; June 11, "a new high," "This city is"). CT, June 10–11, 1930 (June 11, "The meaning of," "There will be"); June 13–14, 1930; June 30, 1930 ("Alfred Lingle now," "undreamed of," "That he is"). Pasley, *Al Capone*, pp. 267–308 (267, "A prize specimen," "unofficial chief of"; 268, "A Christmas present"; 270, "He knew all"; 271, "that nether stratum"; 280, "A *Tribune* man"; 285, "fixed the price," "Lingle's multifarious activities"). Edward Dean Sullivan, "Who Killed Jake Lingle?" *True Detective*, December 1930, pp. 20–25 (22, "Catch him!"), 104–108, 112. Boettiger, *Jake Lingle*, pp. 15–124. Enright, *Al Capone on the Spot*, pp. 81–95. Burns, *One-Way Ride*, pp. 283–298 (285, "Just a happy"; 289, "I am being"). Sullivan, *Chicago Surrenders*, pp. 3–12 (6, "Jake's like a"; 9, "a major power"), 21–29. Kobler, *Capone*, pp. 290–299 (295, "a $65-a-week"), 308. Scott Miller, "The Assassination of Jake Lingle," *Chicago Reader*, March 20, 1981, pp. 1, 20–24, 29–32. Schoenberg, *Mr. Capone*, pp. 274–279 (275, "a $65-a-week"). Hecht and Macarthur, *The Front Page*, p. 86 ("a cross between").

LINGLE FUNERAL / SOUTH WABASH RAID AND WIRETAP: CEP, June 12, 1930. CDN, June 12, 1930. CT, June 12–13, 1930; June 13, 1931. CHE, June 13, 1930; June 13, 1931. *U.S. v. Alphonse Capone, et al.*, indictment, June 1931, p. 7, Case No. 23256, in "Fusco, Joseph C. (Joe)" folder, Box 86, KC. Dillard, "How the U.S. Gov't," p. 56. Elsie L. Warnock, "Terms of Approbation and Eulogy in American Dialect Speech," *Dialect Notes*, vol. 4, pt. 1 (New Haven, CT: Tuttle, Morehouse and Taylor, 1913), p. 22 ("stylish," "up-to-date"). Schoenberg, *Mr. Capone*, p. 176.

The raid on 2108 South Wabash bears strong similarities to the raid on 2271 Lumber Street described in Ness and Fraley, *The Untouchables*, pp. 70–73. Both accounts have the agents surprised to find heavy steel doors barring the entrance to the brewery, which keep them from entering quickly. But the actual raid on the Lumber Street brewery occurred much later (CDN, January 8, 1932; CT, January 9, 1932).

Almost certainly, Fraley took Ness's memories of the Wabash raid and applied them to newspaper clippings (in Ness's scrapbooks) describing the later raid on Lumber Street. It's also likely the detail in *The Untouchables* of Ness using his .38 Colt revolver to shoot open the lock on the steel door (p. 72) is an embellishment of Fraley's. Tests carried out on the Discovery Channel show *Mythbusters* prove a handgun of that caliber would not be powerful enough to spring a lock, and that shooting a lock at close range would send dangerous shrapnel flying at anyone standing nearby. (*Mythbusters*, "Mega Movie Myths: Shootin' Locks," Discovery Channel, video, 5:49, September 13, 2006, http://www.discovery.com/tv-shows /mythbusters/videos/mega-movie-myths-shootin-locks/ [accessed April 22, 2016].)

LINGLE BALLISTICS EVIDENCE: CDN, July 1, 1930 ("This town is"). Sullivan, *Chicago Surrenders*, pp. 15–17. Kobler, *Capone*, pp. 301–302. Hoffman, *Scarface Al*, p. 97. Keefe, *Man Who Got Away*, p. 186.

NESS AND FOSTER'S GUN: Ness MS., pp. 18, 20 ("one of the"), in ENPS, Roll 1, Folder 2. See also Ness and Fraley, *The Untouchables*, pp. 132–136, 151–157.

The *Daily News* (CDN, July 1, 1930) claimed Jamie confiscated the gun from Foster, but they may have been generalizing, referring to members of Jamie's squad (Ness and Lahart) and not Jamie personally.

FOSTER'S ARREST AND RELEASE: Sullivan, *Chicago Surrenders*, pp. 17–18, 28–29. Burns, *One-Way Ride*, p. 296. Kobler, *Capone*, p. 302. Schoenberg, *Mr. Capone*, pp. 279–280. Hoffman, *Scarface Al*, pp. 97–98. Keefe, *Man Who Got Away*, pp. 267, 270–271, 279.

LINGLE MURDER INVESTIGATION: Boettiger, *Jake Lingle*, pp. 15–124. Eghigian, *After Capone*, pp. 167, 469.

ZUTA: CT, July 1–2, 1930; July 24, 1930. Pasley, *Al Capone*, pp. 299 ("brains"), 301–305 (301, "a shrewder mind"; 305, "If we can"). Sullivan, "Who Killed," pp. 108–109. Burns, *One-Way Ride*, pp. 293–295, 298–301 (298, "a noisome, slime-bred," "spill his guts"; 300, "Here they come"; 301, "I'll bet I"). Boettiger, *Jake Lingle*, p. 105 ("safe spot"). Sullivan, *Chicago Surrenders*, pp. 50–54 (51–52, "I'll be killed"). Kobler, *Capone*, pp. 303–305. Schoenberg, *Mr. Capone*, pp. 280–281. Keefe, *Man Who Got Away*, p. 193.

BRUNDIDGE INTERVIEWS CAPONE: CT, July 13, 1930; July 19–20, 1930 (July 19, quotes).

ZUTA MURDER AND AFTERMATH: Pasley, *Al Capone*, pp. 305–310. Sullivan, "Who Killed," pp. 109–110, 112. Boettiger, *Jake Lingle*, pp. 107–124. Burns, *One-Way Ride*, pp. 302–305. Sullivan, *Chicago Surrenders*, pp. 54–60, 64–66. Kobler, *Capone*, pp. 305–306.

Chapter Eighteen

WILSON AND O'HARE: Ward, "Man Who Got," p. 7 ("Every witness we"). IRS-2, p. 51. "The Press: Reporter Rogers," *Time*, March 15, 1937, p. 49 ("The whores"). CT, November 16, 1939. Frank J. Wilson, *Inside the Secret Service*, pp. 25-A–25-B, 32–38, in Box 12, "Manuscripts—Inside the Secret Service By Frank J. Wilson" folder, FJW (35–36, "He didn't then"; 38, "I saw my," "Eddie said here's"). Wilson and Day, *Special Agent*, pp. 31–32, 39–40. Spiering, *Man Who Got Capone*, pp. 77, 79–84 (83, "received a big," "unreported income of"). Calder, *Origins and Development*, pp. 138–139 (139, "knocked off"), 257–258. Ewing and Lundstrom, *Fateful Rendezvous*, pp. 8–9, 33–38 (38, "If we have"). Cook, *King of the Bootleggers*, pp. 105–107.

Wilson's unpublished memoir, like the published versions "Undercover Man" and *Special Agent*, omits any reference to tracing profits from the Hawthorne Kennel Club, instead claiming Rogers arranged for O'Hare to meet Wilson to satisfy O'Hare's desire to help out on the Capone case. But the version presented by Calder, and substantiated by the documents Calder cites, seems much more credible.

Many sources, following Wilson's version of events (cited above), claim or imply O'Hare sought some sort of deal to win a place for his son at the U.S. Naval Academy at Annapolis, Maryland, in exchange for O'Hare informing on Capone. Ewing and Lundstrom (*Fateful Rendezvous*, pp. 33–37) debunk this at length, though their theorizing about O'Hare's true motives for informing (drawing upon the rosy recollections of his relatives) are less convincing.

Perry (*Eliot Ness*, p. 97) lists O'Hare (along with Leslie Shumway and Parker Henderson) as one of the witnesses who testified against Capone in open court during his tax trial, apparently unaware O'Hare's role in the investigation was kept confidential.

GUZIK INVESTIGATION / FRED RIES: CT, November 20, 1930; November 16, 1931. IRS-1, pp. 5, 7. CHE, October 14, 1931. IRS-2, pp. 4–5, 17–24 (17, "When we questioned"), 36. CDN, February 26, 1936. Howard R. Marsh, "Untold Tales of the Secret Service," *Liberty*, January 16, 1937, pp. 14–15. Wilson and Whitman, "Undercover Man," p. 82. Irey and Slocum, *Tax Dodgers*, pp. 46–48. Wilson and Day, *Special Agent*, pp. 46–48. Spiering, *Man Who Got Capone*, pp. 140–141. Schoenberg, *Mr. Capone*, p. 256. Eghigian, *After Capone*, pp. 129, 145, 168.

Wilson and Whitman ("Undercover Man," p. 82) don't explain how the Intelligence Unit linked "Dunbar" and Ries. Marsh ("Untold Tales," p. 14) credits Leslie Shumway, but this is impossible, as Wilson hadn't yet found him. Wilson and Day (*Special Agent*, pp. 46–47) credit a bank teller with giving them a description of the "Fred" who purchased the checks, and telling Wilson about Ries's supposed fear of insects, but this seems too neat. Spiering (*Man Who Got Capone*, pp. 140–141) credits O'Hare with tipping Wilson off to Dunbar's identity, as does CT, November 16, 1939.

Irey and Slocum (*Tax Dodgers*, p. 47) give a slightly different account of Ries's capture, with Wilson learning of Ries's location after encountering a "hoodlum" who had just been in St. Louis, but this seems too coincidental. The CT article also differs, claiming John Rogers and the local authorities induced Ries to cross into Illinois, though it doesn't explain why federal officials would need him to cross state lines (CT, November 16, 1939).

Years later, Wilson would claim it took more than simple persuasion to get Ries to talk. Knowing the cashier had a crippling fear of insects, Wilson supposedly arranged to lock him in a cell swarming with bugs until he cracked (Wilson and Whitman, "Undercover Man," p. 82; Wilson and Day, *Special Agent*, pp. 48–49). But Wilson's habit of stretching the truth casts doubt. There's no contemporary evidence any of this happened; another report had it that the Intelligence Unit moved Ries around between several jails until he gave in (CT, November 16, 1939). Irey and Slocum (*Tax Dodgers*, pp. 47–48) make no mention of the infested cell. Neither does Marsh ("Untold Tales," p. 14), though he describes the jail as hot, "uncomfortable," and infested with rats.

If the story of the roach-ridden cell is in any way true, it could have undermined the government's whole case. Such psychological torture is tantamount to coercion, no less than if Wilson had beaten Ries until he talked. Any statement obtained under duress couldn't be trusted; a good lawyer could get such testimony thrown out of court. And without Ries's word, the Dunbar checks proved nothing.

When the American Bar Association held a mock retrial of the Al Capone tax case in 1990, the defense made Wilson's coercion of Ries a central part of their argument. This destroyed the jury's faith in Ries's testimony and contributed to their verdict of not guilty. But Thomas R. Mulroy Jr., who played a prosecutor at the mock trial, later explained evidence of coercion wouldn't have meant as much to a jury in 1931 as in 1990. During Jack Guzik's tax trial in 1930, the defense tried to attack Ries's credibility on similar grounds, but apparently got nowhere with the jury. (CT, November 20, 1930; August 6, 1990. Schoenberg, *Mr. Capone*, pp. 257, 324.)

WILSON FINDS LEDGER: Ward, "Man Who Got," p. 7 ("By midnight I," "As I was," "As soon as"). IRS-2, pp. 4–5, 35 ("town," "Ralph," "Pete," "Frank paid $17,500"). CDN, February 27, 1936. Marsh, "Untold Tales," pp. 13–14. Hirsch and Mayer, "Behind the Scenes," p. 15. CT, November 16, 1939. Metz, "Mystery of Eddie," p. 91. Hynd, *Giant Killers*, p. 56. Wilson and Whitman, "Undercover Man," p. 15. Irey and Slocum, *Tax Dodgers*, pp. 52–53. *Hearings Before the Special Committee to Investigate Organized Crime in Interstate Commerce*, pt. 2, p. 169. Wilson and Day, *Special Agent*, pp. 36–37.

The date that Wilson found the ledger is conjectural. Wilson later noted the "investigation had proceeded for several months" since May 1930 before he found the ledger (IRS-2, p. 5), and after they identified Shumway's handwriting, they searched "four months" before finding him in Miami the following February (*ibid.*, p. 6). In an interview, Wilson said the Intelligence Unit "worked another month" to identify the handwriting as Shumway's (Ward, "Man Who Got," p. 7). Therefore, if they began searching for Shumway circa October 1930, September is the most likely month for Wilson's discovery of the ledger. It certainly wasn't "a bitter cold night in the winter of 1929," as Marsh (p. 13) claims.

Wilson's accounts offer slightly differing versions of how he learned Shumway's name. Both "Undercover Man" and *Special Agent* suggest he learned of Shumway through handwriting comparisons alone, but in the *Baltimore Sun* interview (his earliest known narrative of the case) Wilson clearly states he somehow knew Shumway had filled out the ledger, even though the handwriting didn't match. The CT article, on the other hand, states O'Hare told Wilson about Shumway, and the *True Detective* article implies it. The *True Detective* article claims "government men were looking for Shumway for a long time before they . . . finally located him . . . on an anonymous tip," which investigators later suspected came from O'Hare. "Undercover Man" and *Special Agent* both refer to an unnamed "tipster" who gave Wilson a description of Shumway and suggested he might be found in Miami; this might also be a reference to O'Hare. O'Hare's prior history with Shumway seems to bear this supposition out. Furthermore, O'Hare's involvement solves the apparent contradiction in Wilson's narratives; Shumway kept books for Capone, Wilson knew, but needed the handwriting sample to prove it.

NITTO ARREST AND CONVICTION: CT, October 31, 1930. Boettiger, *Jake Lingle*, pp. 186–188. Dillard, "How the U.S. Gov't," p. 54. IRS-2, p. 49. CDN, February 25, 1936.

Irey and Slocum, *Tax Dodgers*, pp. 48–50. Wilson and Day, *Special Agent*, p. 41. Eghigian, *After Capone*, pp. 168–173, 177–182 (178, "a velvet glove," "no suggestion of"; 180, "useful life"; 181, "I have never")

GUZIK CONVICTED / RIES IN HIDING: CT, November 20, 1930. Ward, "Man Who Got," p. 7 ("When the witnesses"). Robert Isham Randolph, "Secret Six," *The Clevelander*, vol. 6, no. 12 (April 1932), p. 29, in RIR Scrapbook III. *Detroit Saturday Night*, February 13, 1932, in RIR Scrapbook III. IRS-2, p. 18. *Japan Advertiser*, March 3, 1934, in RIR Scrapbook IV, p. 64. CDN, February 26, 1936. Marsh, "Untold Tales," p. 15. Robert Isham Randolph to Frank J. Wilson, November 17, 1946, in Box 5, "Auctorial—Correspondence, 1946" folder, FJW. Wilson and Whitman, "Undercover Man," p. 82. Irey and Slocum, *Tax Dodgers*, p. 48. Wilson and Day, *Special Agent*, p. 49.

MATTINGLY LETTER / CAPONE TRIES TO SETTLE: Pasley, *Al Capone*, p. 87 ("sources of income"). David Burnet, memorandum to Walter E. Hope, December 18, 1930, in Presidential Subject Series, Box 164, "Federal Bureau of Investigation—Capone Tax Case, 1930–1931" folder, HHPL ("at least $3,500,000," "I have been"). Louis H. Wilson Witness Transcript, pp. 19–20, in Box 1, "Transcripts From U.S. v. Al Capone (Various Witnesses) (1 of 2)" folder, USvAC ("Mr. Mattingly . . . said"). IRS-2, pp. 25–26. Ross, *Trial of Al Capone*, pp. 58–61 (61, "taxable income for"). Schoenberg, *Mr. Capone*, pp. 259–260. Trespacz, *Trial of Gangster Al Capone*, pp. 56–59, 65–66. Eig, *Get Capone*, pp. 298–299.

ROCHE'S RAIDS: Boettiger, *Jake Lingle*, pp. 125–135, 147–188. Kobler, *Capone*, p. 307.

LYLE'S VAGRANCY WARRANTS: CT, September 17, 1930 ("Public Enemies"); October 5, 1930 ("There's Al Capone"); December 19, 1930 ("reptile"). Lyle, *Dry and Lawless Years*, pp. 232–238 (233, "I had within"). Schoenberg, *Mr. Capone*, pp. 300–301. Hoffman, *Scarface Al*, pp. 118–122 (118, "lawfully provid[ing] for," "houses of ill"), 125–129 (129, "It sought to").

CAPONE OFFERS LINGLE'S KILLER: John Boettiger, "The First Story of Al Capone in Lingle Inquiry," CT, April 20, 1931 (quotes). Boettiger, *Jake Lingle*, pp. 177–188. Binder, *Al Capone's Beer Wars*, pp. 232–233.

AIELLO MURDER: CT, October 24, 1930. Enright, *Al Capone on the Spot*, pp. 64–68. Burns, *One-Way Ride*, pp. 305–306. " 'Red' Barker, the Racketeer, Assassinated," n.p., n.d., in Box 0202, "[Capone, Alphonse] Capone-Atlanta #1 [40886-A] [Folder 4 of 4]" folder, BOP-AP. Eghigian, *After Capone*, pp. 123–124, 173–175.

Chapter Nineteen

SOUP KITCHEN: CEP, November 14, 1930 ("keen-eyed, silent men," "FREE SOUP, COFFEE," "Today it became," "out of the," "Nobody else was," "at a cost"). CT, December 25, 1930; April 29, 1932; May 7, 1932; February 14, 1980 ("At that time"). CHE, April 29, 1932. Borden, "Chicago Revisited," p. 542 ("a connection between"). Vanderbilt, "How Al Capone," p. 18 ("If machines are"). James Doherty, "How Capone Captured Hinky Dink!" CT Magazine, July 20, 1952. Lyle, *Dry and Lawless Years*, p. 41. Allsop, *Bootleggers*, pp. 241, 280–281. Murray, *Legacy of Al Capone*, pp. 22, 145–146, 163–167 (163, "You gotta have," "Do you guys"). Kobler, *Capone*, p. 315 ("My brother is"). Schoenberg, *Mr. Capone*, p. 179. Bergreen, *Capone*, pp. 400–403. Russo, *Outfit*, pp. 78–81. "Capone's Soup Kitchen—221178–17,"

Footage Farm, August 11, 2016, 02:24, https://youtu.be/yCMEzxJpQTs (accessed April 4, 2017) ("first real meal," "It wasn't for," "Look at what"). Paula Mejia, "The Capones' Foray Into the Dairy Business," Atlas Obscura, February 9, 2018, https://www.atlasobscura.com /articles/al-ralph-capone-dairy-industry-milk-cheese (accessed February 9, 2018).

CAPONE'S OFFER TO LYLE: Lyle, *Dry and Lawless Years*, pp. 250–253 (251, "straight from the," "Then he'll make").

LINGLE INVESTIGATION / LEO BROTHERS: CT, April 3–4, 1931. John Boettiger, "Reveal Capone Plot to Kill 4 Public Figures," CT, April 21, 1931 ("Al wants to," "You can tell"). Alan Hynd, "The Inside on the Lingle Murder Capture," *True Detective*, April 1931, pp. 20–27, 81–86. Boettiger, *Jake Lingle*, pp. 201–335. Kobler, *Capone*, pp. 309–311. Schoenberg, *Mr. Capone*, pp. 284–285. Helmer and Mattix, *Public Enemies*, p. 238. Eghigian, *After Capone*, pp. 167, 469n.

ALLEGED PLOT TO MURDER JOHNSON, WILSON, ET AL.: CT, December 1, 1930; November 16, 1939 ("gang associate," "You tell Capone," "The men have"). John Boettiger, "Reveal Capone Plot to Kill 4 Public Figures," CT, April 21, 1931 ("It seemed too," "a carload of," "to kill some," "They're tough birds"). Dillard, "How the U.S. Gov't," pp. 55–56. IRS-2, pp. 52–53. John H. Lyle and John J. McPhaul, "How Chicago's Crime Barons Were Smashed," Part 1, *True Detective*, August 1937, pp. 46–49, 120. John H. Lyle and John J. McPhaul, "How Chicago's Crime Barons Were Smashed," Part 3, *True Detective*, October 1937, pp. 90–91. Wilson and Whitman, "Undercover Man," pp. 15, 80. Frank J. Wilson, *Inside the Secret Service*, pp. 62–62-A, in Box 12, "Manuscripts—Inside the Secret Service by Frank J. Wilson" folder, FJW (62-A, "shoot him on," "that a posse"). Lyle, *Dry and Lawless Years*, pp. 20, 249. Wilson and Day, *Special Agent*, p. 45 ("No. It's best"). Kobler, *Capone*, p. 326. Spiering, *Man Who Got Capone*, p. 138 ("much disgusted," "By that breach"). "Prohibition: George E. Q. Johnson—About His Father, Who Successfully Won Tax Evasion Convictions of Al Capone," Onlinefootage.tv, 00:52, 1999, http://www.onlinefootage.tv/stock-video-footage/7634 /prohibition-george-e-q-johnson-about-his-father-who-successfully-won-tax-evasion-convicti ons-of-al-capone (accessed April 25, 2016).

Wilson later claimed O'Hare told him directly of the plot (Wilson and Whitman, "Undercover Man," p. 15; Wilson and Day, *Special Agent*, p. 44). His summary memo of the Capone case mentions he spoke with "a very confidential source," which could be a reference to Rogers or O'Hare (IRS-2, pp. 51–52). Although it's possible O'Hare contacted Wilson in person, the CT's version, with Rogers getting the tip, seems more credible, given Wilson's tendency to falsely place himself at the center of the action (see, for example, Eig, *Get Capone*, p. 275). John Lyle (in Lyle and McPhaul, "How Chicago's Crime Barons," pt. 3, pp. 90–91) describes Madden as the recipient of the tip, which is consistent with the CT article.

Irey's account of the Capone case places the murder plot after Capone's indictment in June 1931, and claims he, Wilson, and Madden were the only targets (Irey and Slocum, *Tax Dodgers*, p. 57). The former is demonstrably false, and no reliable evidence suggests the latter is true (see Schoenberg, *Mr. Capone*, p. 296).

Some sources, apparently seeking to synthesize Wilson's accounts of the Capone case (in which he learns of the plot directly from O'Hare) and Irey's (in which Wilson learns of the plot from an undercover Treasury agent), suggest Wilson received corroboration of the plot from Intelligence Unit special agent Michael Malone, who had penetrated the Capone outfit while posing as a gangster (Spiering, *Man Who Got Capone*, pp. 135–136; Eig, *Get Capone*, pp. 300–301). The best evidence suggests, however, Malone was not yet working undercover in November 1930. Wilson's summary report of the Capone case mentions he summoned Malone to Chicago in October 1930 to help locate Frank Nitto (IRS-2, p. 49). Even an undercover agent of Malone's legendary skill would have a hard time working his way into the Outfit to such a degree that they would let him in on such a sensitive matter as the murder of government officials—in under a month. And no matter how long Malone stayed undercover, the Outfit would hardly let an outsider ever hear of such a plot (see Schoenberg, *Mr. Capone*, pp. 296–297).

Wilson's memo and other IRS documents strongly suggest Malone's undercover work began in late March 1931 and concerned Capone-connected brothels in Stickney, further indicating he wasn't in a position to hear of the plot in November 1930 (IRS-1, p. 8; IRS-2, pp. 27–28; IRS-3). This resolves a chronological problem in Irey's account of the case, which strains credulity by having Malone (or "Pat O'Rourke," as Irey and Slocum refer to him) risk blowing his cover by slipping out of his gangster disguise to help track down Frank Nitto (Irey and Slocum, *Tax Dodgers*, pp. 48–50). That Malone was not yet undercover in October 1930 is much more likely.

Wilson also gives a different, and somewhat more flattering, version of how his wife, Judith, learned the truth about his work in Wilson and Whitman, "Undercover Man," p. 80. Wilson has the wife of the other agent buy up all copies of the *Tribune* at the local newsstand to keep Judith from seeing them. But he eventually breaks down and tells her the truth, which Judith accepts "with amazing calm." This appears designed to make him seem more sympathetic. The difference in these two accounts further shows Wilson's slippery relationship with the truth.

UNANSWERED QUESTIONS ABOUT MURDER PLOT: CT, November 19, 1930; November 16, 1939 ("A theory held"). Pasley, *Al Capone*, pp. 234–236. William G. Shepherd, "Can Capone Beat Washington, Too?" *Collier's*, October 10, 1931, p. 44. Lyle and McPhaul, "How Chicago's Crime Barons," pt. 3, p. 91. Lyle, *Dry and Lawless Years*, pp. 20, 249. Allsop, *Bootleggers*, pp. 127–128, 168. Schoenberg, *Mr. Capone*, pp. 296–297.

Schoenberg suggests the Outfit fed the false story of the murder plot to undercover Intelligence Unit agent Michael Malone to "get the opposition chasing phantoms and their tails" (*Mr. Capone*, p. 297). But the best evidence suggests the story came first from E. J. O'Hare, with Malone not yet undercover, rendering Schoenberg's theory moot. His analysis of the improbability of the plot, however—and the unlikelihood that anyone in the Outfit would have leaked it except on purpose—seems spot-on.

FRUSTRATION WITH JOHNSON / MITCHELL SENDS FROELICH: Personal History, April 11, 1929; John Marshall to William Froelich, April 11, 1929, both in William J. Froelich OPF/ATF. WP, November 22, 1930, in FBI-AC. CT, November 21, 1930; December 21, 1930 ("Yes, George E.Q."); June 13, 1931. CHE, June 13, 1931. Dillard, "How the U.S. Gov't," pp. 54–55. IRS-2, p. 51. Calder, *Origins and Development*, pp. 139–141, 143, 249n41 ("I think it"), 260n77 ("a chance appears," "A Florida jury"). Eig, *Get Capone*, pp. 294–295.

JAMIE JOINS SECRET SIX: Robert Isham Randolph to James M. Doran, June 17, 1930;

George E. Q. Johnson to the Attorney General, July 26, 1930; Howard T. Jones to Alexander G. Jamie, October 29, 1930, all in Alexander Jamie Justice Dept. OPF. Alexander G. Jamie to Henry Morgenthau Jr., January 4, 1936 [actually 1937]; C. L. Rice to R. E. Wood, July 5, 1938; Robert Isham Randolph to Robert E. Wood, July 7, 1938 ("Thousand dollar bills"); Alexander G. Jamie to Henry Morgenthau Jr., September 1, 1938, all in Alexander Jamie Treasury Dept. OPF. Resignation Form for Use of Field Service, November 6, 1930, in Edna S. Ness OPF. *Kansas City Star*, November 1, 1931, in ENPS, Roll 1, Scrapbook 1. Louis D. Nichols, memo to John B. Little, n.d.; John B. Little, memorandum for the Director, September 7, 1933, both in FBI-RIR. Calder, *Origins and Development*, pp. 140, 143.

NESS MADE HEAD OF CAPONE SQUAD: Alexander G. Jamie to the Director of Prohibition, October 22, 1930, in Alexander Jamie Justice Dept. OPF ("Mr. Ness is"). CT, November 11, 1930. P. T. Sowell, interview with William J. Froelich, November 21, 1933; Melvin Purvis to J. Edgar Hoover, November 28, 1933, both in FBI-ENA. CDN, January 2, 1936, in ENPS, Roll 1, Scrapbook 2, p. 19. *South End News*, January 9, 1936, in ENPS, Roll 1, Scrapbook 2, p. 20. Service record card, n.d., in Eliot Ness OPF. Ness MS., p. 9, in ENPS, Roll 1, Folder 2. Ness and Fraley, *The Untouchables*, pp. 17–25.

A letter from Johnson to the director of Prohibition refers to the director's "letter of November 29, 1930 requesting the names of the agents desired to do special work under my direction in Chicago." This suggests the plan got under way in late November (George E. Q. Johnson to Amos W. W. Woodcock, December 8, 1930, in William J. Gardner OPF/ATF). Bergreen (*Capone*, p. 408), citing a summary memo from Ness to Johnson, dates the founding of the Untouchables to November 1930.

Ness and Fraley (*The Untouchables*, pp. 17–18) credit Ness with coming up with the idea of the flying squad, though his original manuscript (and the historical record) make clear the plan originated higher up. The book also presents Johnson as a stranger to Ness, even though other evidence (see notes to Chapters Six and Eight) makes clear the two men knew each other before 1930. Ness and Fraley's account of Jamie lobbying Johnson and Randolph, however, while not in the manuscript, carries the ring of truth, tallying with Jamie's habit of pulling strings, and with details (such as Randolph reaching out to Herbert Hoover) confirmed elsewhere.

Most sources, following Ness and Fraley, claim that Ness got the Untouchables job after meeting directly with Johnson (see Eig, *Get Capone*, p. 239; Perry, *Eliot Ness*, pp. 51–52). Ness's manuscript is clear, however, that Ness got the job in a conference with Froelich. Paul Robsky's account of the Capone investigation, which (though largely fanciful) contains some authentic details, correctly depicts Froelich as the squad's immediate supervisor. (Fraley and Robsky, *Last of the Untouchables*, pp. 17–19.) Bizarrely, Perry (*Eliot Ness*, pp. 51, 304) cites a quote from the Ness-Fraley book ("coolness, aggressiveness, and fearlessness in raids," p. 23) in Ness's personnel file at ATF.

Chapter Twenty

UNTOUCHABLES BEGIN: George E. Q. Johnson to Amos W. W. Woodcock, December 8, 1930, in Joseph D. Leeson OPF/ATF (also in William J. Gardner OPF/ATF) ("special employee"). W. E. Bennett to the Director of Prohibition, December 8, 1930, in Samuel

Maurice Seager OPF/ATF. Randolph, "How to Wreck," p. 8. Ness MS., p. 10, in ENPS, Roll 1, Folder 2 ("If this group"). Ness and Fraley, *The Untouchables*, pp. 26–27. Perry, *Eliot Ness*, pp. 52–53.

Pinning down the number of men on Ness's squad at any one time is difficult, because its membership was fluid. Johnson's letter (cited above) includes the names of seven men: (1) Chapman, (2) Berard, (3) Leeson, (4) Gardner, (5) Seager, (6) Moore, and (7) a special agent "Neww," which is almost certainly a typo for "Ness." (George Golding makes the exact same mistake in his fifty-nine-page memo defending himself against sexual harassment charges [see George Golding to the Director of Prohibition, August 30, 1930, in George Golding OPF/ATF].)

Several sources agree with Johnson that the team initially numbered six, not counting Ness. Lyle Chapman stated more than once that "he was selected as one of a group of six as an investigator on the Capone case . . . under the immediate supervision of Eliot Ness," and some news accounts also give the number of men as six. (D. A. Sloan to the Director of Prohibition, April 24, 1933, p. 8, in Lyle B. Chapman OPF/ATF; see also LAT, November 5, 1957; CHE, June 13, 1931; *Evening Star*, June 18, 1931, in ENPS Roll 1, Scrapbook 1). Additionally, a biographical sketch of Ness from the 1940s, apparently prepared with his help, refers to his leadership of "the seven Untouchables," though it seems to imply Ness was not one of the seven. ("Biographical Sketch: Eliot Ness," n.d., in Box 2, "Biographies" folder, SPD.)

Perry (*Eliot Ness*, pp. 52–53) doubts Ness selected the members of the Untouchables himself, crediting George E. Q. Johnson and William Froelich instead. As proof, Perry cites the fact "that Albert Nabers didn't even make the short list for consideration [as] another indication that Eliot had little or nothing to do with choosing the unit's team." But the fact that Ness staffed the unit is certain; Johnson later testified that Ness "selected the squad." (CT, April 3, 1932.)

A more obvious explanation for Nabers's absence is his recent transfer to New Orleans, "for the reason that I believe my chances for advancement will be better there, and for the further reason that I have a younger brother and his family there who need my help and advice." Nabers would be busy chasing rumrunners from Belize while the Untouchables did their work in Chicago. A. M. Nabers to the Director of Prohibition, August 16, 1930 ("for the reason"); W. D. Hearington to the Director of Prohibition, August 16, 1930; W. K. Bruner to the Director of Prohibition, August 18, 1930; A. W. W. Woodcock to W. D. Hearington, August 19, 1930; A. W. W. Woodcock to A. M. Nabers, August 19, 1930; Recommendation for Change in Designated Post of Duty, September 15, 1930; W. K. Bruner to the Director of Prohibition, May 13, 1931; R. E. Herrick, memo to W. K. Bruner, May 13, 1931, all in Albert M. Nabers OPF/ATF.

JOE LEESON: Personal History, December 17, 1928; Personal History Statement, December 17, 1928 [?]; Oath of Office, December 17, 1928; Thos. E. Stone to the Commissioner of Prohibition, June 5, 1929; N. B. Miller, Efficiency Rating, April 11, 1930; N. B. Miller to the Commissioner of Prohibition, May 20, 1930; Wm. N. Woodruff to the Director of Prohibition, November 6, 1930; Thomas H. Brennan to William N. Woodruff, December 19, 1930 ("Mr. Leeson has"); Personal History, December 16, 1931; C. W. Hitsman to Chief, Intelligence Unit, "in Re: Joseph D. Leeson," September 18, 1934; W. K. Bruner, "Leeson, Joseph

D.," October 8, 1935; W. K. Bruner to Deputy Commissioner, Alcohol Tax Unit, August 10, 1936; *Cincinnati Times-Star*, January 12, 1940; Statement of Joseph D. Leeson, May 15, 1940, all in Joseph D. Leeson OPF/ATF. Ness and Fraley, *The Untouchables*, pp. 33–34. Perry, *Eliot Ness*, p. 53. SLS, personal interview with ABS, November 17, 2017.

LYLE CHAPMAN: Lyle B. Chapman to Lincoln C. Andrews, July 2, 1925; Application for Position of Prohibition Agent, January 26, 1927; Personal History, February 14, 1927; Personal History, September 10, 1927; Alf Oftedal to Harry D. Smith, April 26, 1928 ("He is inclined"); Personal History, March 8, 1929; J. M. Doran to Acuff, September 18, 1929; J. M. Doran to Dwight E. Avis, September 19, 1929; Recommendation for Change in Designated Post of Duty, February 3, 1930; B. F. Hargrove Jr. to Dwight Avis, March 29, 1930 ("out of his," "somebody is always"); Dwight Avis to Lyle Chapman, March 31, 1930; Dwight Avis to the Commissioner of Prohibition, April 3, 1930; J. L. Acuff to W. L. Ray, February 12, 1931; W. L. Ray to J. L. Acuff, February 17, 1931 ("It goes without"); Dwight Avis to W. L. Ray, February 20, 1931; E. P. Guinane to Director, United States Bureau of Investigation, October 6, 1932, all in Lyle B. Chapman OPF/ATF. LAT, June 30, 1931 ("a veritable registry"); November 5, 1957; September 23, 1962 ("hits you like"). Ness MS., pp. 13, 15, in ENPS, Roll 1, Folder 2 (15, "pencil detective"). Ness and Fraley, *The Untouchables*, pp. 31–32. "Lyle Chapman," Colgate Football Memorabilia Collection, http://www.colgatefootballcol lection.com/lyle-chapman.html (accessed May 3, 2016).

WILLIAM GARDNER: CT, November 24, 1907; March 30, 1928. 1920 U.S. Census Record for William J. Gardner. R. H. Allen to Frank T. Hines, March 24, 1926; Application for Position of Prohibition Agent, July 2, 1926; Oath of Office, July 29, 1926; A. J. Hanlon to Alf Oftedal, September 21, 1927; Alf Oftedal to Gerald P. Nye, October 1, 1927 ("investigative turn of"); Alf Oftedal to Thomas E. Stone, November 20, 1927; J. M. Doran to William J. Gardner, November 21, 1927; Alf Oftedal to Thomas E. Stone, November 30, 1927 ("quite lacking in"); Maurice Campbell to Alf Oftedal, January 21, 1928; Alf Oftedal to Mr. Billard, March 15, 1928; J. M. Doran to Charles Curtis, March 16, 1928; Alf Oftedal to William J. Gardner, March 16, 1928; Alf Oftedal to George Golding, March 16, 1928; William J. Gardner to J. L. Acuff, April 16, 1928 ("We are quite"); George E. Golding to the Commissioner of Prohibition, May 4, 1928; Application for Position of Prohibition Agent, May 14, 1928; W. J. Gardner, Resignation Form for Use of Field Service, June 16, 1928; George E. Golding to the Commissioner of Prohibition, June 18, 1928; Oath of Office, October 22, 1928; J. M. Doran to the U.S. Civil Service Commission, October 23, 1928; Alexander Jamie to Andrew McCampbell, June 7, 1930; Efficiency Report, January 17, 1931; W. J. Gardner to A. W. W. Woodcock, May 2, 1931; Dwight E. Avis to Mr. Jones, May 7, 1931; Howard T. Jones to Prohibition Administrator, San Francisco, May 20, 1931; Personal History Statement, June 3, 1932; "Educational, Military, Business Record of W. J. Gardner," n.d., all in William J. Gardner OPF/ATF. Knute K. Rockne, "What Thrills A Coach," *Collier's*, December 6, 1930, p. 21 ("down-the-field"). Glenn S. Warner, "The Indian Massacres," *Collier's*, October 17, 1931, p. 62. Ness MS., p. 13, in ENPS, Roll 1, Folder 2. Ness and Fraley, *The Untouchables*, pp. 34–37. Jenkins, *Real All Americans*, pp. 1–6, 74–81, 231–246. Benjey, *Doctors, Lawyers, Indian Chiefs*, pp. 5–6 ("Kill the Indian"), 12–13, 123–131 (126, "his leg wrenched"; 130, "one 'Hellacious' fight").

The dating of the Gardners' "Hellacious" fight is conjectural. Benjey dates it to right before Gardner's joining the Untouchables, but this seems unlikely as evidence suggests he and his wife were already separated by then. Gardner's return to the Prohibition Bureau in October 1928 seems more likely.

UNTOUCHABLES ASSEMBLE: Rowe to the Director of Prohibition, December 12, 1930; Woodcock to Rowe, December 15, 1930; Thos. H. Brennan to Wm. N. Woodruff, December 19, 1930; Ernest Rowe to the Director of Prohibition, December 22, 1930; Ernest Rowe to the Director of Prohibition, January 23, 1931; Dwight E. Avis to Eliott [sic] Ness, November 18, 1931, all in Joseph D. Leeson OPF/ATF. Amos W. W. Woodcock to George E. Q. Johnson, December 13, 1930; Recommendation for Change in Designated Post of Duty, December 15, 1930, both in Lyle B. Chapman OPF/ATF. Andrew McCampbell to the Director of Prohibition, January 6, 1931, in William J. Gardner OPF/ATF. Maurice Seager to "Phil + Belle," December 28, 1930, SLS ("ready to go," "share of blood," "relieve the monotony"). Ness and Fraley, *The Untouchables*, p. 25. LAT, September 23, 1962 ("I remember my").

Though the documentary record on the early days of the Untouchables is scant, what evidence survives suggests Seager had a leadership role. His letter home refers to men serving under him (Maurice Seager to "Phil + Belle," December 28, 1930, SLS). In late January, Ness wrote to Washington about the work of "Mr. Seager and myself," suggesting they were partners of some kind (Eliot Ness to the Director of Prohibition, January 20, 1931, in William J. Gardner OPF/ATF). That Seager was, along with Ness, the first special agent assigned to the case may also indicate a major role.

CONSPIRACY CASE STRATEGY: Schmekebier, *Bureau of Prohibition*, pp. 80–81. Willebrandt, *Inside of Prohibition*, pp. 258–259. *U.S. v. Alphonse Capone, et al.*, indictment, June 1931, Case No. 23256, in "Fusco, Joseph C. (Joe)" folder, Box 86, KC. CT, June 13, 1931; June 16, 1931; November 15–16, 1931. CHE, June 13, 1931. IRS-1, p. 7. William D. Mitchell to George E. Q. Johnson, July 24, 1931, Box 1, "Records Relating to Indictment and Sentencing (2 of 12)" folder, RRPAC. Shepherd, "Can Capone," p. 42. "Rich Business Man Called Capone's 'Brains,'" n.p., n.d., in ENPS, Roll 1, Scrapbook 1. "Hunt 'Playboy' of Capone Gang As Beer Ring Aid," n.p., n.d., in ENPS, Roll 1, Folder 1. Alexander Jamie, "Lifting the Curtain on the Crime Trust: How Organized Gang Lawlessness Has Become America's Newest Big Business," NEA Service, March 15, 1932, in RIR Scrapbook III ("Shrinking Violet"). Ness MS., p. 21, in ENPS, Roll 1, Folder 2.

The dates of various raids, liquor seizures, and other overt acts mentioned in the indictment conflict with those given in newspaper reports. Some articles, for instance, give the date of the Lexington Hotel meeting as June 12, 1928, even though the indictment dates it to 1930. Most confusing is the timeline of Capone-purchased trucks also tied to transporting liquor. News reports state that one truck was seized carrying beer on July 29, 1923, following its purchase by Capone on June 5, 1923 (CT, June 13, 1931). But the indictment states this truck was seized on July 24, 1922—*before* Capone is alleged to have bought it. Since the case never went to trial and the evidence was never presented in court, exactly which dates are accurate is impossible to determine, as is what the feds believed about the relationship between these acts.

WIRETAPPING, RAIDING SUGAR BUILDING: Eliot Ness to the Director of Prohibition,

January 20, 1931, in William J. Gardner OPF/ATF ("After experiencing great," "At the present"). CT, June 13, 1931. Dillard, "How the U.S. Gov't," p. 56. Ness MS., pp. 16–17, in ENPS, Roll 1, Folder 2 (17, "I, of course," "In a short"). Ness and Fraley, *The Untouchables*, pp. 102–105. John Larson, "Summary of Contacts with the Secret Six of Chiago [*sic*] and Elliott [*sic*] Ness," n.d., in Carton 4, Folder 25 ("Clippings About—1947–1961"), John Larson Papers, BANC MSS 78/160cz, UCB (Ness-Larson-Jim Exchange, "an underground 'death'"). Jedick, "Eliot Ness," p. 55. Jedick, *Cleveland*, p. 41 ("They won't be"). Bergreen, *Capone*, p. 345. Alder, *Lie Detectors*, pp. 90–102, 119–121.

Dating the sugar building incident is difficult, but it seems to have occurred after Larson's return to Chicago in the spring of 1930. Similarly, the incident where Ness got the Outfit to move their sales office is impossible to date with any degree of certainty—especially since he recalls the involvement of one informer who probably didn't contact him until later. Ness's January 20, 1931, memo (cited above), however, strongly suggests the team had finished putting their wiretaps in place by mid-January. Ness, in his scattered recollections, may have confused one informer with another. What's certain is it happened; the chronology can only be guessed at.

SQUAD FALLING APART: Eliot Ness to the Director of Prohibition, January 20, 1931 ("Mr. Seager and," "Mr. Gardner recently"); Dwight E. Avis to Eliot Ness, January 22, 1931 ("I am also"); Dwight E. Avis to the Prohibition Administrator, New York, NY, January 22, 1931; Andrew McCampbell to the Director of Prohibition, January 28, 1931; D. H. Reichgut to Everett H. Kuebler, February 5, 1931; Everett H. Kuebler to D. H. Reichgut, February 5, 1931; William J. Gardner to Amos W. W. Woodcock, May 2, 1931, all in William J. Gardner OPF/ATF. E. A. Moore OPF/ATF.

Berard's sparse personnel file (Ulric H. Berard OPF/ATF) offers no indications of when he left the Untouchables, though he must not have been with the squad long. He also went on to a long career with the Prohibition Bureau's successor agency, the Alcohol Tax Unit, and later worked with Ness on an investigation in Akron, Ohio, so the split must have been amicable. (See A. W. W. Woodcock, Chief, Coordination and Special Agency Division, February 28, 1931, in Samuel M. Seager OPF/ATF; L. B. Connell to District Supervisor, September 20, 1935, in Joseph D. Leeson OPF/ATF. *Akron Beacon Journal*, June 26, 1935, in ENPS, Roll 1, Scrapbook 1. 1940 U.S. Census Record for Ulric H. Berard.)

WARREN STUTZMAN: Application for Position of Federal Prohibition Agent, October 17, 1920; Personal History, January 22, 1926; Ambrose Hunsberger to the Director of Prohibition, May 8, 1926; Herbert E. Lucas to Arthur A. Nichols, February 15, 1927; Stewart Wilson to William J. Calhoun, February 8, 1929; Samuel W. Gearhart to Alf Oftedal, February 13, 1929; Alf Oftedal to George E. Golding, February 15, 1929; George E. Golding to the Commissioner of Prohibition, April 15, 1929 ("not lacking in"); J. M. Doran to W. N. Woodruff, May 2, 1929; W. N. Woodruff to J. M. Doran, May 7, 1929; Charles L. Hurlbut, Memo to William N. Woodruff, October 4, 1929; J. L. Acuff to William N. Woodruff, December 16, 1930; J. L. Acuff to "Mr. Jones," December 26, 1930; Questions Respecting Personal History, February 2, 1931; Personal History, February 2, 1931; W. E. Bennett to Chief, Coordination and Special Agency Division, February 4, 1931; Statement of Sylvan R. White, July 19, 1932, pp. 2–3 ("an untrained hunting," "invariably would go"); W. B. Disney to the Director of

Prohibition, August 9, 1932; Thomas M. Lee, memo to Chief, Intelligence Unit, "In Re: Warren E. Stutzman," February 11, 1935, pp. 2–3; D. S. Bliss to George J. Schoeneman, May 15, 1935, H. J. Anslinger, memo to "Mr. Harper," February 10, 1940 ("because of the"); V. B. Ferguson, memo to E. R. Ballinger, July 25, 1940 ("a youthful drunken"), all in Warren E. Stutzman OPF/ATF.

CHAPMAN TRIES TO LEAVE: E. E. Stone to Samuel M. Shortridge, February 10, 1931; Lyle B. Chapman to Dwight Avis, February 12, 1931; G. E. Chapman to W. E. Evans, February 12, 1931; Samuel M. Shortridge to Amos W. Woodcock, February 20, 1931; Dwight E. Avis to W. L. Ray, February 20, 1931 ("Climatic conditions on"); W. E. Evans to Amos W. W. Woodcock, with note to Dwight Avis by Woodcock, February 20, 1931 ("to use political"); A. W. W. Woodcock to Samuel M. Shortridge, February 27, 1931, all in Lyle B. Chapman OPF/ATF.

CLOONAN, FRIEL, LAHART: Application for Position of Prohibition Agent, December 6, 1928; Questions Respecting Personal History, January 5, 1931; Personal History, January 5, 1931; Oath of Office, January 5, 1931, all in Bernard V. Cloonan OPF/ATF. Employee's Record, n.d.; Application and Personal History Statement, August 21, 1941; Employee's Agreement and Record, n.d., Temporary Appointment, Transfer, Reinstatement, or Promotion, Etc., May 28, 1942; Employment Record, n.d., all in Thomas J. Friel OPF/ATF. Ness and Fraley, *The Untouchables*, pp. 31–32.

Lahart's personnel file (Martin J. Lahart OPF/ATF) offers no indications of when he joined the squad, but Ness's memoir lists him as one of the first agents onboard (Ness and Fraley, *The Untouchables*, pp. 28–30). The same is true of Friel, though his sparse personnel file doesn't make clear whether he was even serving in Chicago during the Untouchables period. Ness almost certainly worked with Friel when they both served under Alexander Jamie, and Ness may have misremembered him as an Untouchable years after the fact. The details Ness gives about Friel in his memoir (Ness and Fraley, *The Untouchables*, p. 31) match with the documents in Friel's OPF, specifically his service as a Pennsylvania state trooper and his apparent difficulties with women (the file contains no evidence Friel ever married).

GARDNER'S RETURN: Eliot Ness to Lowell R. Smith, February 13, 1931; Andrew McCampbell to the Director of Prohibition, February 19, 1931; George S. Taylor to Everett H. Kuebler, February 27, 1931; J. L. Acuff, "Memorandum to Mr. Reichgut," March 3, 1931; Eliot Ness to Chief, Coordination and Special Agency Division, March 3, 1931; William J. Gardner to Amos W. W. Woodcock, May 2, 1931; Dwight E. Avis, Memo to "Mr. Jones," May 7, 1931; William J. Gardner to Webster Spates, May 15, 1931; Eliot Ness to Dwight E. Avis, May 16, 1931; Oath of Office, June 19, 1931; A. W. W. Woodcock to Prohibition Administrator, July 1, 1932; D. H. Reichgut to Prohibition Administrator, July 5, 1932, all in William J. Gardner OPF/ATF. Benjey, *Doctors, Lawyers, Indian Chiefs*, pp. 131–132. Tucker, *Eliot Ness and the Untouchables*, pp. 98–99.

Perry (*Eliot Ness*, p. 81) claims Gardner was an alcoholic during the Untouchables period, and his frequent breaks with the service "were almost certainly drunken benders." While Gardner clearly became an alcoholic in later life, nothing in his personnel file suggests he was a drinker while a Prohibition agent. Such behavior would hardly have slipped the service's notice, especially because other agents (such as Lyle Chapman) got caught for even moderate drinking.

NESS LEARNING TO LEAD: CPD, February 27, 1937 ("Capone was a"); October 17, 1959. SLS, personal interview with ABS, November 17, 2017.

WILSON FINDS SHUMWAY: George E. Q. Johnson to G. A. Youngquist, Memo "In Re: Alphonse Capone," December 31, 1931, Box 1, "Correspondence (3 of 12)" folder, RRPAC. Ward, "Man Who Got," p. 7 ("underground channels," "White Steel Company," "Once we had," "It took some"). IRS-2, pp. 6–7 (7, "the only other"), 57. Hynd, *Giant Killers*, p. 21. Wilson and Whitman, "Undercover Man," pp. 80, 82. Irey and Slocum, *Tax Dodgers*, pp. 53–54. *Miami News*, May 1, 1949, in Box 18, "Scrap Book #1—Secret Service Stories," FJW. Frank J. Wilson, *Inside the Secret Service*, pp. 42–43, in Box 12, "Manuscripts—Inside the Secret Service By Frank J. Wilson" folder, FJW. Frank J. Wilson, "#5 Shumway Insert," n.d., in Box 7, "Manuscript—Capone Case (F. 255)" Folder, FJW. Wilson and Day, *Special Agent*, pp. 37–38.

Wilson later credited undercover agent Michael Malone with locating Shumway in Miami (Frank J. Wilson, "Women Kept No Secrets From Mysterious Mike," CT, April 3, 1961), but this is likely another of Wilson's embellishments. As outlined in the notes to Chapter Nineteen, Malone probably didn't go undercover until March 1931, and how he could have learned of Shumway's location while working in Chicago is unclear. O'Hare seems the safer bet.

SECRET INDICTMENT / RACING AGAINST TIME: IRS-3. IRS-4. George E. Q. Johnson to G. A. Youngquist, Memo "In Re: Alphonse Capone," December 31, 1931, in Box 1, "Correspondence (3 of 12)" folder, RRPAC. Wilson and Whitman, "Undercover Man," p. 82. Irey and Slocum, *Tax Dodgers*, pp. 54–55. Wilson and Day, *Special Agent*, p. 39. Calder, *Origins and Development*, p. 151 ("not because there").

Chapter Twenty-One

MAFALDA WEDDING: CT, November 19, 1930 ("I've hardly seen"); December 15, 1930 ("the elect of," "untoward event"). Schoenberg, *Mr. Capone*, pp. 301–302. Bair, *Al Capone*, pp. 205–206 (205, "Who would dare").

PATTERSON INTERVIEW: CHE, January 18, 1931 (all quotes except "favor," in Schoenberg, *Mr. Capone*, p. 304). Kobler, *Capone*, pp. 242–243. Schoenberg, *Mr. Capone*, pp. 303–304. Bair, *Al Capone*, p. 156.

WINCHELL: *Richmond Times-Dispatch*, October 31, 1931 (quotes). Gabler, *Winchell*, p. 120.

Bergreen (*Capone*, pp. 328–329) misdates the interview to 1929 or earlier; not only does Gabler provide evidence placing Winchell in Miami in early 1931, but the content of the story—specifically the references to Capone's upcoming contempt trial—fix it firmly around that time.

MAYORAL PRIMARY / CERMAK: CT, February 22, 1931; February 25, 1931 ("The majority of," "The chance of"). NYT, February 22, 1931 ("The real issue"). CHE, February 25, 1931 ("take the city"). Wendt and Kogan, *Big Bill of Chicago*, pp. 318–333 ("For Chicago"). Lyle, *Dry and Lawless Years*, pp. 259–265. Gottfried, *Boss Cermak*, pp. 3, 11–13, 15, 17, 48–50, 115, 137, 142–145, 199–287. Murray, *Legacy of Al Capone*, pp. 169–174. Johnson and Sautter, *Wicked City*, p. 348. Bukowski, *Big Bill Thompson*, pp. 233–237. Eghigian, *After Capone*, pp. 187–192.

WILKERSON: CHE, February 25, 1931. Shepherd, "Can Capone," p. 16 ("righteous wrath").

CT, October 1, 1948. Schoenberg, *Mr. Capone*, p. 311. Cahan, *Court That Shaped America*, pp. 81, 85–86. Eig, *Get Capone*, pp. 325–327.

CAPONE CONTEMPT TRIAL: CHE, February 25–28, 1931 (February 26, "dog-eared and," "Confined to bed"; February 27, "not serious," "I didn't want," "When you used," "I didn't mean," "But when you"; February 28, "with an attitude," "Capone-y," "Capone leaned nervously," "have to do"). CT, February 26–28, 1931 (February 26, "the complacency of," "A platinum watch," "We don't want"; February 27, "girl reporter," "I wanted to," "I wanted to," "Why, I think"; February 28, "a flashy brown," "If the judge," "income tax investigators," "If Mr. Johnson"). J. R. Burdge, Report on Alphonse Capone and Kenneth Phillips, March 23, 1929 ("for six weeks"); CEA, February 16–25, 1931 (February 25, "spent thousands of," "Get your hat"); CDN, February 25–26, 1931 (February 25, "people who had," "being trodden underfoot," "white marble walls," "It's on the," "Oh, I just," "tried to make," "I've been asked," "I don't belong," "Can you fancy"); *Evening Star*, March 3, 1931; J. Edgar Hoover, undated memo ("Well of all"); R. C. Harvey to Director, Bureau of Investigation, February 27, 1931 ("The U.S. Attorney's"); James H. Wilkerson, Opinion in *United States v. Capone*, February 27, 1931 ("glaringly false," "it is to," "Upon the record"), all in FBI-AC. Ross, *Trial of Al Capone*, pp. 13–34 (18, "to be in"). Bair, *Al Capone*, pp. 208–209.

CAPONE VAGRANCY HEARING: NYT, April 4, 1931 ("Couldn't you find"). CT, April 4, 1931. Schoenberg, *Mr. Capone*, p. 307.

CAPONE MEETS RANDOLPH: *St. Louis Times Star*, November 22, 1932, in RIR Scrapbook IV, p. 17 (Randolph-Capone exchange). CT, May 5, 1932 ("I laid my"). *Richmond Times-Dispatch*, July 1, 1931, in RIR Scrapbook III. "'Secret 6' Head Urges Repeal of Dry Law," n.p. ["Pittsburgh"], February 2, 1932, in RIR Scrapbook III. CP, March 8, 1932, in RIR Scrapbook III, p. 79.

Chapter Twenty-Two

CAPONE'S BEER BUSINESS: CT, February 27, 1931 ("Of course, that's"). Randolph, "How to Wreck," pp. 8–9. *New Orleans States*, January 12, 1931, in RIR Scrapbook II, pp. 136, 139. *Detroit Free Press*, January 31, 1931, in RIR Scrapbook II, p. 157. *Rochester Evening Journal*, October 14, 1931, in RIR Scrapbook III. *Kansas City Star*, November 1, 1931, in ENPS, Roll 1, Scrapbook 1. *Cincinnati Times Star*, November 15, 1932, in RIR Scrapbook IV, p. 16. *St. Louis Times Star*, November 22, 1932, in RIR Scrapbook IV, p. 17. "Chicago Crusader Urges Pittsburgh 'Secret Six,'" n.p., February 2, 1932, in RIR Scrapbook III. *Cincinnati Times Star*, March 22, 1932, in RIR Scrapbook III, p. 100. *Potter Enterprise*, September 27, 1956, PCHS. Ness and Fraley, *The Untouchables*, p. 65. Kobler, *Capone*, p. 246. Schoenberg, *Mr. Capone*, p. 73. Okrent, *Last Call*, p. 322 ("lousy").

NESS'S STRATEGY: Randolph, "How to Wreck," p. 9 ("slush fund"). NYT, June 18, 1931 ("We had to"). Dillard, "How the U.S. Gov't," p. 56. Alexander Jamie, "Jamie Tells How Voting Public Can Wreck Gang's 'Big Business,'" NEA Service, March 19, 1932, in RIR Scrapbook III ("Kill the revenue"). Ness MS., p. 10, in ENPS, Roll 1, Folder 2. Ness and Fraley, *The Untouchables*, pp. 17, 59, 65, 72–73.

SEARCHING FOR BREWERIES / BARREL-CLEANING PLANT: CEA, March 25, 1931. Dillard, "How the U.S. Gov't," p. 56. Ness MS., pp. 10–12, in ENPS, Roll 1, Folder 2 (11,

"We, of course," "a souped-up"). Untitled clipping, n.p., n.d., in ENPS, Roll 1, Scrapbook 1. *Potter Enterprise*, September 27, 1956, PCHS. Ness and Fraley, *The Untouchables*, pp. 66–68, 74–77.

The Ness MS. claims the two agents assigned to follow the barrels were Leeson and "Jim Seeley." In the finished book, Seeley is never mentioned, and his role in the investigation is given to Seager (Ness and Fraley, *The Untouchables*, p. 67). Some sources (such as Perry, *Eliot Ness*, pp. 62–63) follow the manuscript's lead in listing Seeley as an Untouchable, even though no evidence suggests he even existed. Seeley is not mentioned in any known documents or newspaper articles related to the Capone case; Scott Leeson Sroka and Barbara Osteika made a search for his official personnel folder and came up empty. Given this lack of corroborating evidence, and given the Ness MS. frequently gets the spelling of names and other such details wrong (Seager's first name, for instance, is given as "Ernest" [p. 13]), we believe that "Seeley" is an error on Ness's part, which he and/or Fraley corrected in the final book.

CICERO AVE RAID: CEA, March 25, 1931 ("an amber flood"). CDN, March 25, 1931. CDT, March 25, 1931 ("genuine Capone beer"). CEP, March 25, 1931 ("false face"). CT, March 26, 1931. CHE, June 15, 1931 ("It's funny, I"). *Kansas City Star*, November 1, 1931, in ENPS, Roll 1, Scrapbook 1. Dillard, "How the U.S. Gov't," p. 57. Ness MS., pp. 11–15 (13, "The doors fell"; 14, "What did you," "If the job"), in ENPS, Roll 1, Folder 2. Ness and Fraley, *The Untouchables*, pp. 76–84, 89. *Chicago American*, February 20, 1960, in "Newspaper Clippings (Photocopies) Circa. 1930–1970" folder, DMM. UCR, pp. 16–17, 35.

Ness and Fraley (*The Untouchables*, pp. 79–80) give the time of the raid as 5:00 A.M., while the Ness MS. doesn't specify. Press accounts make clear, however, that the raid took place at dawn, which occurred at 5:15 A.M. that day in Chicago (CT, March 25, 1931), validating Ness and Fraley's claim.

Most sources (see Perry, *Eliot Ness*, p. 68), following Ness's manuscript and the Ness-Fraley book, describe the raiders driving headfirst into the brewery doors with a specially equipped battering ram affixed to the head of their truck. But the CEP and CEA accounts of the raid (cited above) make clear the raiders decided to use the truck on the spot, and *backed* it into the doors. Apparently, Ness had the truck outfitted with a battering ram only after first seeing the vehicle in action during the Cicero Avenue raid.

Various spellings of Swoboda's name exist; Ness's manuscript, and many sources following from it, spell it "Svoboda." We've elected to go with the spelling given in court documents. See *U.S. v. Alphonse Capone, et al.*, indictment, June 1931, Case No. 23256; *U.S. v. Alphonse Capone, et al.*, civil complaint, September 3, 1941, Case No. 3375, both in "Fusco, Joseph C. (Joe)" folder, Box 86, KC.

ROBERT STERLING: Oath of Office, October 18, 1920; F. R. McReynolds to James E. Jones, February 8, 1927; Robert D. Sterling to James E. Jones, April 16, 1927; Robert D. Sterling to J. M. Doran, August 13, 1927; Personal History, September 1, 1927; W. L. Ray to James M. Doran, May 6, 1930; Robert D. Sterling to the U.S. Civil Service Commission, May 26, 1930; Dwight Avis to the Director of Prohibition, July 16, 1930; J. L. Acuff to W. L. Ray, February 13, 1931; W. L. Ray to J. L. Acuff, February 16, 1931; J. L. Acuff to Robert D. Sterling, March 31, 1931; Dwight Avis to Eliot Ness, April 18, 1931; Amos W. W. Woodcock to Prohibition Administrator, San Francisco, June 8, 1931; W. G. Walker to Amos W. W. Woodcock,

June 15, 1931; J. F. J. Herbert to the Director of Prohibition, June 26, 1931; Dwight E. Avis, Memo to "Mr. Reichgut," June 24, 1932 ("He is not"); Amos W. W. Woodcock to Robert D. Sterling, June 20, 1932, Robert D. Sterling to Amos W. W. Woodcock, July 1, 1932; Carl Jackson to A. W. W. Woodcock, July 21, 1932; D. H. Blair to Amos W. W. Woodcock, February 23, 1933, all in Robert D. Sterling OPF/ATF.

PAUL ROBSKY: Personal History, December 1, 1928; Oath of Office, December 1, 1928; R. Q. Merrick to Dwight E. Avis, October 15, 1930; Questions Respecting Personal History, December 4, 1930; Eliot Ness to Dwight E. Avis, January 20, 1931; Dwight E. Avis to Eliot Ness, January 22, 1931; Howard T. Jones to Paul W. Robsky, March 18, 1931; J. L. Acuff to Paul W. Robsky, March 31, 1931 ("a temporary detail"); J. L. Acuff to Eliot Ness, March 31, 1931; Recommendation for Change in Designated Post of Duty, April 20, 1931; Dwight E. Avis to Paul W. Robsky, April 22, 1931; Paul W. Robsky to M. L. Harney, April 26, 1932; M. L. Harney to the Director of Prohibition, April 26, 1932; Service Record Card, n.d., all in Paul W. Robsky, OPF/ATF. Ness and Fraley, *The Untouchables*, p. 34. *Miami News,* April 20, 1959. *Milwaukee Journal,* January 10, 1961 ("nervous and tense"). Fraley and Robsky, *Last of the Untouchables*, pp. 8–16 (12, "it might be"). *Miami News*, March 27, 1966 ("was never right"). *Leader-Post*, November 6, 1973.

MARION KING: Application for Position of Federal Prohibition Agent, September 13, 1924; Personal History, December 17, 1924; J. M. Doran to the Secretary of the Treasury, July 6, 1928; J. M. Doran to the Secretary of the Treasury, February 25, 1930 ("He is young"); J. M. Doran to the Secretary of the Treasury, March 14, 1930; Efficiency Report, January 15, 1931; Efficiency Report, June 1, 1931; Efficiency Report, December 8, 1931; Efficiency Report, June 1, 1932; Efficiency Report, December 1, 1932; Efficiency Report, September 30, 1950; Service Record Card, n.d., all in Marion A. R. King OPF/ATF.

Ness and Fraley (*The Untouchables*, pp. 34, 119) give King's first name as "Mike." Whether he actually used this nickname is unclear, though the portrait Ness and Fraley paint of him does seem to match his federal file. Special thanks to Scott Leeson Sroka and Barbara Osteika for figuring out "Mike King" was actually Marion King.

UNTOUCHABLES TRUCK: Personal History Statement, December 17, 1928; Questions Respecting Personal History, December 16, 1931; Personal History Statement, December 16, 1931; Personal History Statement, May 23, 1932, all in Joseph D. Leeson OPF/ATF. Ness MS., p. 13, in ENPS, Roll 1, Folder 2. Ness and Fraley, *The Untouchables*, p. 74. *Chicago American*, February 20, 1960, in "Newspaper Clippings (Photocopies) Circa. 1930–1970" folder, DMM. LAT, September 23, 1962. Nickel, *Torso*, p. 38. SLS, personal interview with ABS, November 17, 2017.

Weight of truck variously given as five tons (CHE, May 2, 1931; CN, December 11, 1935, in ENPS, Roll 1, Scrapbook 2, p. 4; CDN, January 2, 1936, in ENPS, Roll 1, Scrapbook 2, p. 19; CDN, June 4, 1936, in ENPS, Roll 1, Scrapbook 2, p. 87) and ten tons (CHE, April 12, 1930; Ness and Fraley, *The Untouchables*, p. 74).

Perry (*Eliot Ness*, p. 68) claims that the agents added "a huge, snowplow-like battering ram, shaped almost like an arrowhead," to their truck. This is how the vehicle appears in the 1959 TV adaptation of *The Untouchables* and the 1987 film, but the best evidence suggests that the actual battering ram didn't look anything like a snowplow. Many news articles refer to the Untouchables using a truck to break down brewery doors, but most don't mention the truck being modified in any way. This suggests the alterations may not have been especially noticeable.

Those sources mentioning modifications describe the truck as being "specially reinforced" (CDN, June 4, 1936, in ENPS, Roll 1, Scrapbook 2, p. 87) or "equipped with a piece of heavy steel like a bumper" (untitled clipping, n.p., n.d., in ENPS, Roll 1, Scrapbook 1). In his own manuscript, Ness refers to "a truck with a hugh [sic] steel bumper on the front of it" (Ness MS., p. 13, in ENPS, Roll 1, Folder 2). The Ness-Fraley book follows his lead, describing "a special steel bumper covering the whole radiator" (Ness and Fraley, *The Untouchables*, p. 74). No photos of the truck are known to exist, but newspaper illustrations of it show nothing resembling a snowplow (CEA, March 25, 1931; *Kansas City Star*, November 1, 1931, in RIR Scrapbook III [also in ENPS, Roll 1, Scrapbook 1]; Charles W. Lawrence, "Putting the Heat on Ohio's Bootleggers," n.p., n.d., in ENPS, Roll 1, Scrapbook 1).

SOUTH WABASH SURVEILLANCE AND RAID: CDT, April 11, 1931. CEA, April 11, 1931. *San Diego Evening Tribune*, April 11, 1931. CHE, April 12, 1931. CT, April 12, 1931; June 13, 1931. "U.S. Drys Raid Big Brewery of Capone; Nab 5," n.p., n.d.; untitled clipping, n.p., n.d., both in ENPS, Roll 1, Scrapbook 1. "U.S. Trap Nabs Brewery Chief of Capone Gang," n.p., April13, 1931; "5,000 Violations of Dry Law Cited in Bill," n.p., n.d., both in ENPS, Roll 1, Folder 1. Dillard, "How the U.S. Gov't," p. 57 ("No?"). Ness MS., pp. 13–15, in ENPS, Roll 1, Folder 2 ("were on the"). Ness and Fraley, *The Untouchables*, pp. 81–82, 88–91. Jedick, "Eliot Ness," p. 51. Nickel, *Torso*, p. 41 ("How much you," "All right," "You haven't got"). UCR, pp. 35–37.

In his manuscript, Ness describes arresting Swoboda, Conti, and the other three men during the team's first raid. But the details he gives match the Wabash brewery, not the one on South Cicero Avenue. Ness likely conflated the Untouchables' first two raids in his memory; these details, which he ascribed to the first, actually belonged to the second.

Conti's name is variously spelled "Conta" in the Ness MS. and the newspaper articles about this raid (cited above), "Conti" in newspaper articles about a later raid ("Agents Raid Capone Plant; Six Arrested," n.p., September 22, 1931, in ENPS, Roll 1, Folder 1. CEA, September 22, 1931; CEP, September 22, 1931, both in ENPS, Roll 1, Scrapbook 1), and "Contie" in the Prohibition indictment (*U.S. v. Alphonse Capone, et al.*, indictment, June 1931, Case No. 23256, in Box 86, "Fusco, Joseph C. (Joe)" folder, KC).

RETURN TO CHICAGO HEIGHTS: "Agents on Way to Two Plants Sniff Another," n.p., April 17, 1931; "Nab Five in Raid on Capone Stills; Alky Stock Seized," n.p., April 18 [?], 1931, in ENPS, Roll 1, Scrapbook 1 ("We secured convictions," "I can't understand," "I'll be back"); CDN, April 20, 1931; *Chicago Heights Star*, April 21, 1931, all in ENPS, Roll 1, Scrapbook 1.

"THE KID" / NESS REFUSES BRIBE: Service Record Card, in Eliot Ness OPF. Allen, *Since Yesterday*, pp. 57–65 (64, "a crowd of"). Ness MS., pp. 15–16, 19, in ENPS, Roll 1, Folder 2 (16, "I told him," "that the Government," "I couldn't understand," "the job would"; 19, "This was a," "The offer, of"). Ness and Fraley, *The Untouchables*, pp. 97–102, 140–141. McElvaine, *Great Depression*, p. 75.

Dating Ness's first meeting with the Kid is conjectural, though based on later news reports (see CT, June 14, 1931) it must have occurred after the Untouchables began raiding and before the indictments in June 1931.

UNTOUCHABLES REFUSE BRIBES: Ness MS., pp. 18–19, in ENPS, Roll 1, Folder 2. Ness and Fraley, *The Untouchables*, pp. 142–143. *Miami News*, April 20, 1959 ("two of us," "They told us"). *Milwaukee Journal*, January 10, 1961. LAT, September 23, 1962 ("Oh, we'd take," "hoods were outside"). *New Orleans Times-Picayune*, May 19, 1963. Drew McKillips, "Honolulu T-Man Was Ness Hero," n.p., n.d., SLS ("barrel wash," "We were about"). Lindberg, *To Serve and Collect*, pp. xi–xix. SLS, personal interview with ABS, November 17, 2017 ("They're working guys").

Chapman's quote from the LAT article says that the woman he and Ness went to save was "Penny (Chapman's wife)," but Chapman was unmarried at the time. He would marry Vesta Beck on July 16, 1931 (Personal History Statement, February 3, 1931; Affidavit of Vesta Beck Chapman, April 24, 1933, p. 1; Affidavit of Lyle B. Chapman, March 31, 1933, p. 1, all in Lyle B. Chapman OPF/ATF). It seems likely that, as Ness would do in his own recollections, Chapman replaced the name of his then-current girlfriend with that of his future wife.

OUTFIT HARASSES UNTOUCHABLES: Dillard, "How the U.S. Gov't," p. 56. CT, June 14, 1931 ("They have information"). "$2,000 A Year Drys Break Up Rich Beer Ring," n.p., n.d., in ENPS, Roll 1, Scrapbook 1. W. S. Murphy, Report on Eliot Ness, November 15, 1933, p. 6, in FBI-ENA. Ness and Fraley, *The Untouchables*, pp. 101, 105–106, 178. *Des Moines Register*, October 29, 1961 ("time to time").

TRUCK CHASE: CT, May 12, 1931; June 13, 1931. Untitled clipping, n.p., n.d., in ENPS, Roll 1, Scrapbook 1 ("suspicious looking automobiles").

CAR THEFTS / BREAK-INS AND WIRETAPPING / BANK VAULT: CHE, June 4, 1931 ("thieves were stealing"). CT, June 13, 1931; August 12, 1931. "Thefts of Cars Seen As Plot to Halt Agents," n.p., n.d., in ENPS, Roll 1, Scrapbook 1. Dillard, "How the U.S. Gov't," p. 56. *Baltimore Sun*, May 17, 1936, in ENPS, Roll 1, Scrapbook 2, p. 80. Ness MS., pp. 19–21, in ENPS, Roll 1, Folder 2 (21, "a large safety"). Ness and Fraley, *The Untouchables*, pp. 94–95, 141–142. "First National Bank of Chicago IV," Chicagology, https://chicagology.com/golde nage/goldenage116/ (accessed May 11, 2016).

BUILDING CAPONE CASE: *U.S. v. Alphonse Capone, et al.*, indictment, June 1931, Case No. 23256, in "Fusco, Joseph C. (Joe)" folder, Box 86, KC. CHE, June 13, 1931. CT, June 13, 1931. IRS-1, p. 7. Dillard, "How the U.S. Gov't," p. 56. UCR, pp. 25–26, 36–37.

NESS'S TEAM BECOMES "UNTOUCHABLES": Pratt, *India and Its Faiths*, pp. 125–126, 171–172. NYT, November 30, 1930; June 18, 1931. LAT, June 30, 1931. CPD, October 26, 1941. *Honolulu Advertiser*, January 29, 1961 ("I remember telling"). *Arizona Daily Star*, June 29, 1987. George E. Q. Johnson Jr., interviewed in "The Road to Repeal." "Prohibition: George E. Q. Johnson—About Eliot Ness and 'The Untouchables,'" Onlinefootage.tv, 1:12, 1999, http:// www.onlinefootage.tv/stock-video-footage/7733/prohibition-george-e-q-johnson-about-eliot -ness-and-the-untouchables (accessed May 11, 2016). "Untouchable," *Encyclopædia Britannica Online*, February 24, 2010, https://www.britannica.com/topic/untouchable (accessed January 10, 2017).

Several different explanations exist for where the "Untouchables" name came from. The most famous is in the Ness-Fraley book, which describes a reporter coming up with the name after Ness gives a press conference announcing his men cannot be bribed (Ness and Fraley, *The Untouchables*, pp. 146–147). No record of any such press conference exists.

The two most credible versions of the tale are a NYT article about Ness and a CPD story on Ness's return to Washington, D.C., in 1941, where he visited with Charles Schwarz and Frank Wilson (both cited above). The NYT claims Ness came up with the name, while the CPD credits it to Schwarz. Both sources agree, however, the name referred to the untouchables of India and not, at least initially, to the squad's purported incorruptibility.

Although the CDN does not appear to have used the "Untouchables" name any earlier than other Chicago papers (which first began using it in June 1931), we have concluded that the CPD's attribution of the name to Schwarz is likely correct. The CPD article is more detailed than the NYT piece, and at least some of the information in it came from Ness.

Ness may have wrongly taken credit for the idea in his interview with the NYT, the reporter may have misheard him, or the NYT may have oversimplified what he said; the article doesn't directly quote him on this point. But this kind of clever joke doesn't seem like something Ness would have come up with on his own. Whatever his other virtues, he wasn't much of a wordsmith. And Ness did not take credit for the name in his book, instead attributing it to an unnamed journalist.

Perry (in *Eliot Ness*, p. 88) twists the NYT article, which describes Ness finding humor in the "Untouchables" name, to claim the opposite of what's actually in the piece: "In one of his first interviews after the indictments, [Ness] showed off his fancy college education by saying he didn't approve of the nickname the press had given the team, because 'Untouchable' was the name for members of India's lowest caste."

Many secondary sources claim or imply the "Untouchables" name originated with newspaper articles (see Schoenberg, *Mr. Capone*, p. 252; Perry, *Eliot Ness*, pp. 87–88). This probably follows the fanciful version of the team's naming given in Ness and Fraley, *The Untouchables*, p. 147. But the contemporary press coverage and recollections of George E. Q. Johnson's son cited above make clear that Johnson used the name before it wound up in the papers. The fact that the press first printed it lowercase and in quotes, in articles drawing mainly on information given them by Johnson, further suggests he was its source.

Chapter Twenty-Three

CAPONE AND CROOKED COPS: Sullivan, *Rattling the Cup*, p. 99 ("A crook is"). Murray, *Legacy of Al Capone*, pp. 126–127 ("I got nothing").

CAPONE AND THE MEDIA: CT, December 6, 1927 ("Even over there"). CDT, May 1, 1931 ("So now I'm"). *Variety*, June 30, 1931 ("It's foolish to," "the flock of"). Parsons, *Gay Illiterate*, pp. 107–111 (108, "It has always").

HOWARD VINCENT O'BRIEN / HEITLER MURDER: Alphonse Capone to Howard Vincent O'Brien, March 4, 1931, in Box 1, Folder 20a ("This will authorize"); William Chenery to Howard Vincent O'Brien, May 4, 1931, in Box 1, Folder 27; Howard Vincent O'Brien, "The Best Known American," undated MSS., in Box 3, Folder 168 (all quotes unless otherwise noted), all HVO. CT, September 17, 1931 ("Well, you see"); October 1, 1947. O'Brien, *All Things Considered*, pp. 59–66 (60, "square guy"; 62, "the most significant,"

"No, I couldn't"; 64, "You know, sometimes"). John H. Lyle, " 'Mike De Pike' Heitler—He Betrayed Capone and Died," CT Magazine, March 14, 1954. Kobler, *Capone*, pp. 311–312. Schoenberg, *Mr. Capone*, pp. 308–309. "Jacob Guzik Testifies Before the Kefauver Committee Hearing HD Stock Footage," CriticalPast, 4:41, June 9, 2014, https://youtu.be/rNNtI SoBR-4 (accessed July 10, 2017).

    O'Brien was hardly the only observer who saw Capone as a figurehead. One young man who knew Capone in Lansing, Michigan, would later insist the gangster took orders from Frank LaPorte, a major figure in the Chicago Heights mob. According to this individual, LaPorte acted as a kind of clearinghouse between Chicago and various out-of-town rackets, and used his position to exert great influence over Capone. Outfit associate George Meyer recalled being shocked to see Nitto almost ordering Capone around. And Judge John Lyle later expressed the belief "that in some respects [Capone] was a straw man. I am convinced that certain men, never identified, composed a brains trust that guided Capone." (Lyle, *Dry and Lawless Years*, pp. 40–41 [41, "that in some"]. Schoenberg, *Mr. Capone*, pp. 245–246. Bergreen, *Capone*, pp. 181, 406, 499, 517, 591, 615. Eghigian, *After Capone*, p. 146.)

CAPONE AND THE OUTFIT POWER STRUCTURE: Sullivan, *Rattling the Cup*, pp. 105–106 ("We don't want"; 106, "He looks fifteen"). CHE, May 20, 1929. Helmer, *Al Capone and His American Boys*, pp. 286–288 (287, "Winkeler went before," "that the boys"), 298–299. Haller, *Illegal Enterprise*, pp. 63–65, 71, 76–77 (77, "Because he lived"), 230–234 (230, "a complex set," "senior partners"; 230–231, "They shared more"; 233, "were not controlled"). Bair, *Al Capone*, pp. 182–183.

NITTO PAROLE APPLICATION: Visitors' Register, January 22, 1931 ("Business"); Frank Nitto, Application for Parole and Biographical Sketch, June 18, 1931; Fred Genaearo [?] to the United States Board of Parole, June 29, 1931; James P. Marzano to the United States Board of Parole, n.d. ("During the past"); Joseph Dire to the United States Board of Parole, June 29, 1931 ("never met a"); W. J. Ryan, Confidential Work Report to Board of Parole, June 30, 1931 ("Trustworthy," "Friendly," "Pleasant"); Anna Nitto to "Gentlemen," n.d. ("the first time," "were the closest," "We both agreed"); E. L. Elsberry, Transcript of Frank Nitto's Hearing Before Irvin B. Tucker of the Board of Parole, July 3, 1931 (parole hearing quotes); George E. Q. Johnson, Parole Report by United States Attorney, September 14, 1931 ("he would leave"), all in Box 71, "Nitto, Frank (1 of 1)" folder, NOF. See also Eghigian, *After Capone*, pp. 184–187, 193–199.

FRED GIRTON: Girton, "Al Capone Tells," pp. 20–23, 68–71 (all quotes unless otherwise noted). J. J. Perkins to Director, Bureau of Investigation, March 25, 1929, in FBI-AC. IRS-2, pp. 43–44 (43, "regarding the lavish").

Chapter Twenty-Four

CAPONE TAX INDICTMENTS: CHE, June 6–7, 1931 (June 6, "Al was nattily," "Frowning, surly, and," "There's nothing," "government men," "airtight case," "overwhelming," "hits at the"; June 7, "We don't expect"). NYT, June 6, 1931 ("a dime novel"). CT, June 6, 1931. *Rockford Morning Star*, June 7, 1931. William D. Mitchell to George E. Q. Johnson, June 25, 1931, in Box 1, "Records Relating to Indictment and Sentencing (2 of 12)" folder, RRPAC. George E. Q. Johnson to G. A. Youngquist, Memo "in Re: Alphonse Capone," December 31, 1931, in Box 1, "Correspondence (3 of 12)" folder, RRPAC. "Summary of Indictments in the Case of United States vs. Alphonse Capone, for Violation of the Income Tax Laws," n.d., in Box 1, "Records Relating to Indictment and Sentencing (2 of 12)" folder, RRPAC. IRS-1, pp. 6–8. IRS-2, pp. 2–3, 6–17, 24–26, 30–31, 33–37, 42, 45–46 (45, "a knitted very"), 57. Ross, *Trial of Al Capone*, p. 59. *Christian Science Monitor*, November 7, 1934. Spiering, *Man Who Got Capone*, pp. 125–127. Schoenberg, *Mr. Capone*, pp. 317–319 (319, "bona fide offers"). Trespacz, *Trial of Gangster Al Capone*, pp. 57–58, 66, 73–77. See also Eig, *Get Capone*, p. 330.

JOHNSON NEGOTIATES PLEA BARGAIN: *Rockford Morning Star*, June 7, 1931 ("a satisfactory sentence"). CHE, June 18, 1931. "Uncle Sam Taking Capone for A Ride," *The Literary Digest*, June 27, 1931, p. 10 ("It is not conducive"). Untitled statement ("This is statement I had Prepared if plea of Guilty had not been withdrawn"), n.d. [c. July 1931], in Box 1, "Pre-Trial Notes and Argument (8 of 12)" folder, RRPAC. George E. Q. Johnson to G. A. Young-quist, Memo "in Re: Alphonse Capone," December 31, 1931, in Box 1, "Correspondence (3 of 12)" folder, RRPAC. Busch, *Enemies of the State*, p. 229. Kobler, *Capone*, pp. 336–337. Powers, *G-Men*, p. 8. Calder, *Origins and Development*, p. 152 ("than the restoration"). Schoenberg, *Mr. Capone*, pp. 310–311. Trespacz, *Trial of Gangster Al Capone*, p. 71.

PROHIBITION INDICTMENT: CHE, June 13, 1931 ("5,000 CRIMES INDICT"). CT, June 13, 1931 ("INDICT CAPONE; 5,000"). NYT, June 13, 1931. "5,000 Violations of Dry Law Cited in Bill," n.p., n.d., in ENPS, Roll 1, Scrapbook 1. "Crime: U.S. v. Capone," *Time*, June 22, 1931, p. 17 ("We never indict"). Spiering, *Man Who Got Capone*, pp. 150–152 (151–152, "If the guilty").

ROUNDING UP DEFENDANTS: CDT, June 20, 1931 ("belligerent Capone henchmen," "At any rate"). "U.S. Brings 'Chief Foe' to Bar Upon Two Charges," n.p., n.d., in ENPS, Roll 1, Scrapbook 1.

JOHNSON PRAISES UNTOUCHABLES: CHE, June 13, 1931. CT, June 14, 1931 ("They worked at," "The average age"). WP, June 15, 1931 ("Untouchables," "Seven of the"). "$2,000 A Year Drys Break Up Rich Beer Ring," n.p., n.d., in ENPS, Roll 1, Scrapbook 1. See also "Capone 'Landed' After Difficult Work By U.S.," n.p., n.d.; "Capone's Power Is Destroyed by Fearless Eight," n.p., n.d.; "Hail Two South End Men for Overthrow of Alphonse Capone," n.p., n.d.; "Eight Dry Agents in Chicago Inquiry Receive 'Rewards,'" *The Herald*, n.d.; *The Evening Star*, June 15, 1931, all in ENPS, Roll 1, Scrapbook 1.

Regarding the ages and educations of the Untouchables, Robert Sterling had a business degree and Maurice Seager had gone to chiropractor school. The rest ranged from one year at college (Paul Robsky) to a fifth-grade education (Warren Stutzman). (Questions Respecting Personal History, January 5, 1931, in Bernard V. Cloonan OPF/ATF. Application for Position of Prohibition Agent, January 26, 1927, in Lyle B. Chapman OPF/ATF. Application for Position of Federal Prohibition Agent, September 13, 1924, in Marion A. R. King OPF/ATF. Personal History, May 28, 1928, in Martin J. Lahart OPF/ATF. Questions Respecting Personal History, December 16, 1931, in Joseph D. Leeson OPF/ATF. Personal History, December 1, 1928, in Paul W. Robsky OPF/ATF. Personal History, June 8, 1928, in Samuel M. Seager OPF/ATF. Application for Position of Federal Prohibition Agent, July 9, 1920, in Robert D. Sterling OPF/ATF. Application for Position of Federal Prohibition Agent, October 17, 1920; George E. Golding to the Commissioner of Prohibition, April 15, 1929, both in Warren E. Stutzman OPF/ATF. See also Perry, *Eliot Ness*, p. 87.)

NESS BECOMES FAMOUS: 1920 U.S. Census Record for Priscilla Higinbotham; 1930 U.S. Census Record for Priscilla Higinbotham. "The First Class in Scientific Crime Detection Held in Chicago," *The American Journal of Police Science*, vol. 2, no. 2 (March–April 1931), p. 180. CHE, June 15, 1931 ("Ness is only," "just a 'workout'"). *The Evening Star*, June 15, 1931; William E. Jayce to Eliot Ness, June 16, 1931; *Boston Traveler*, June 16, 1931; *Hollywood Daily Citizen*, June 17, 1931 ("No soldier on"); Derwin H. Clark to Eliot Ness, June 17, 1931; *Birmingham Age-Herald*, June 17, 1931 ("One of the"); George H. Parkinson to Eliot Ness, June 17, 1913 [1931] ("This is an"); *Miami Daily News*, June 18, 1931; A. W. Becker to Eliot Ness, June 18, 1931 ("God bless you"); Halbert Louis Hoard to Eliot Ness, June 24, 1931 ("I am a"), all in ENPS, Roll 1, Scrapbook 1. NYT, June 19, 1931. Doherty, "Twilight of the Gangster," pp. 5–9 (6, "A well fed"). Potter, *War on Crime*, p. 138. Mappen, *Prohibition Gangsters*, pp. 119–121. "Priscilla Higinbotham (1909–1952)," Find a Grave, January 25, 2010, http://www.findagrave.com/cgi-bin/fg.cgi?page=grandamp;grid=47181477andamp;ref=a com (accessed May 25, 2016).

CHESTER GOULD AND DICK TRACY: Chester Gould told MAC that Ness served as his inspiration for Dick Tracy in a private conversation c. September 1980. Manchester, *Glory and the Dream*, p. 113. Powers, *G-Men*, p. 29. Maeder, *Dick Tracy*, pp. 7–16 (9, "I'm capable and," "YOUR PLAINCLOTHES TRACY"). Bergreen, *Capone*, p. 529. Smith, *The Colonel*, p. 247 ("This name is"). Collins and Masterson, "Chester Gould Speaks." Collins, introduction to *Complete Chester Gould's Dick Tracy*. Collins and Masterson, "Chester Gould Speaks, Part II" ("I was a"). Collins, "Shoot First."

No evidence supports author Ted Schwarz's claim (*Cleveland Curiosities*, pp. 8, 10–12) Ness knew he'd been the model for Dick Tracy. Ness was almost certainly unaware of this fact.

JOHNSON MEETS WILKERSON, FINALIZES DEAL: William D. Mitchell to George E. Q. Johnson, June 25, 1931, in Box 1, "Records Relating to Indictment and Sentencing (2 of 12)" folder, RRPAC. George E. Q. Johnson to G. A. Youngquist, Memo "in Re: Alphonse Capone," December 31, 1931, in Box 1, "Correspondence (3 of 12)" folder, RRPAC. CT, June 17, 1931. NYT, June 17, 1931. Calder, *Origins and Development*, pp. 150–152.

CAPONE PLEADS GUILTY: "United States of America vs. Alphonse Capone," June 16, 1931, JIG (Green-Capone-Larue exchange). CEA, June 16, 1931 ("Yeah, it is"). CHE, June 17, 1931 ("I'll be able"). CT, June 17, 1931. NYT, June 17, 1931 ("hoped everybody was"). WP, June 17, 1931 ("hoped everybody was"). Ward, "Man Who Got," p. 9 ("There's a bad"). Ness and Fraley, *The Untouchables*, pp. 246–247. Lindberg, *Return to the Scene*, p. 383. Merriner, *Grafters and Goo-Goos*, p. 120.

Precisely dating the incident described in Lindberg and Merriner, when Capone asked to see Ness among the crowd, is impossible, though this seems the most likely occasion because Capone and Ness would not have been together in court very often.

FEDS CELEBRATE: Dwight E. Avis to George E. Q. Johnson, June 17, 1931, in Box 1, "Correspondence (3 of 12)" folder, RRPAC ("Personally, I do not"). NYT, June 17–18, 1931 (June 18, "There seems to"). "A Gangster King Surrenders," *The Bureau Bulletin*, vol. 1, no. 10 (June 20, 1931); "Capone 'in Bag', U.S. Turns Guns on N.Y. Gangs," n.p., n.d., both in ENPS, Roll 1, Scrapbook 1. IRS-1, p. 8. IRS-2, pp. 1, 27–28, 51. IRS-3. CDN, February

27, 1936. Irey and Slocum, *Tax Dodgers*, pp. 16–17, 35–42. Frank J. Wilson, "Mysterious Mike Malone," CT Magazine, March 26, 1961, pp. 13, 15. Wilson and Day, *Special Agent*, pp. 33–35. Schoenberg, *Mr. Capone*, pp. 295–297. Eig, *Get Capone*, p. 300.

Wilson, Irey, and other sources have greatly embellished the length, depth, and extent of Michael Malone's undercover work on the Capone case, as well as its importance to the outcome of the trial. Irey attributes to Malone (or "Pat O'Rourke," as Irey refers to him) many actions more likely taken by E. J. O'Hare. IRS memos (see notes to Chapter Nineteen) make clear Malone's undercover work began in March 1931 and wrapped up in June. Wilson notes in IRS-2 (p. 51): "Considerable of [*sic*] the work in locating witnesses was performed at night in and around the hang-outs of the Capone organization by special agents Tessem, Malone, Converse and Sullivan and the agents were facing danger in the event their identity was discovered by the gangsters." This seems to have been Malone's primary contribution to the tax case.

JOHNSON, WILSON, AND HOOVER IN SPRINGFIELD: CT, June 15, 1931; June 18, 1931. CHE, June 18, 1931 ("After all, I'm," "I don't want," "Capone must have"). NYT, June 18, 1931 ("The president was"). Wilson and Day, *Special Agent*, p. 19 ("a fine job"). *Public Papers 1931*, pp. 315–318 (317, "There can be").

PLEA DEAL UNRAVELS: CEA, June 16, 1931 ("the result of"). WP, June 17, 1931 ("The most frequently"). CHE, June 18, 1931. "U.S. Plans to Wipe Out Gangs," n.p., n.d., in ENPS, Roll 1, Scrapbook 1 ("the czar of"). William D. Mitchell to George E. Q. Johnson, June 25, 1931, in Box 1, "Records Relating to Indictment and Sentencing (2 of 12)" folder, RRPAC ("It was, no," "very exaggerated ideas," "with some misgivings," "the reaction would"). Frank J. Loesch to Herbert Hoover, June 29, 1931 ("a very distinct," "I hope that"); Herbert Hoover to Frank J. Loesch, July 1, 1931 ("Some time when"), both in Presidential Personal Series, Box 169, "Loesch, Judge Frank J.—1931–32" folder, HHPL. Untitled statement ("This is statement I had Prepared if plea of Guilty had not been withdrawn"), n.d. [c. July 1931], in Box 1, "Pre-Trial Notes and Argument (8 of 12)" folder, RRPAC. Undated memo, in Box 1, "Correspondence (4 of 12)" folder, RRPAC. Shepherd, "Can Capone," pp. 16–17, 44 ("easy out"). George E. Q. Johnson to G. A. Youngquist, memo "In Re: Alphonse Capone," December 31, 1931, in Box 1, "Correspondence (3 of 12)" folder, RRPAC. Irey and Slocum, *Tax Dodgers*, p. 61. Schoenberg, *Mr. Capone*, p. 311. Calder, *Origins and Development*, pp. 152–153 (153, "A judge would").

Chapter Twenty-Five

SENTENCING HEARING: CT, July 30–31, 1931 (July 30, "A rumor being"; July 31, "The collar that," "only when it," "manifestly distressed"). CHE, July 30–31, 1931 (July 31, "No, boys, none," "The smiling underworld," "Capone picked up"). Transcript of hearings in *United States of America vs. Alphonse Capone*, July 30, 1931, in Box 1, "Trial Records (7 of 12)" folder, RRPAC (Wilkerson, Ahern, and Johnson quotes). Ness and Fraley, *The Untouchables*, pp. 246–247 (246, "I seethed inwardly").

WILKERSON DISMISSES PROHIBITION CASE: CHE, June 6, 1931; June 13, 1931; August 1, 1931 ("A letter of"). CT, August 1, 1931 ("a much heavier," "merely for the," "I would just," "There is a"). *North Tonawanda Evening News*, August 7 [?], 1931, ATF ("for a real"). Calder, *Origins and Development*, p. 153.

NESS BEFORE GRAND JURY: CT, August 1, 1931 ("link[ing] Capone with"). "Capone Liquor Deals Bared to Grand Jury," n.p., n.d.; "Grand Jury Gets [1]0-Year Story of Capone Rum," n.p., n.d., both in ENPS, Roll 1, Scrapbook 1. Ness and Fraley, *The Untouchables*, pp. 247–249.

CT cites "special Prohibition agents who developed the conspiracy case," which can only mean the Untouchables.

UNTOUCHABLES KEEP RAIDING: CT, May 15, 1931 ("Raids on Capone's"); June 21, 1931; March 31, 1932. NYT, June 13, 1931 ("virtually insolvent"). "Missing 'Clink' of Coin Bares Liquor Cache," n.p., n.d.; CEA, July 17, 1931 ("Prohibition agents, aided"), both in ENPS, Roll 1, Folder 1. "12,000 Gallons of Iced Beer Seized in Raid," n.p., n.d.; "Dry Flips A Half Dollar; Uncovers $15,000 Rum!" n.p., n.d. ("Well, boys"), both in ENPS, Roll 1, Scrapbook 1. UCR, pp. 37–40. CPD, September 19, 1934. Ness and Fraley, *The Untouchables*, pp. 233–237.

THE KID FINISHED: Ness MS., pp. 15, 19–20, in ENPS, Roll 1, Folder 2 (19, "the gang was," "This was a," "turn up seizing," "his automobiles kept"; 20, "and take a"). See also Ness and Fraley, *The Untouchables*, pp. 138–139, 154–155, 163–167.

Ness's manuscript remains silent on the Kid's fate, while the book (probably in one of Fraley's embellishments) suggests that the Kid and his wife lived happily ever after.

VANDERBILT INTERVIEW: Sullivan, *Chicago Surrenders*, pp. 204–205 (204, "merely regards himself"; 205, "Prohibition is a"). CT, August 27, 1931. Vanderbilt, "How Al Capone," pp. 18, 20–21 (18, "Us fellas has"; 20, "I guess I'm"; 21, "crooked bankers," "Do you think," "undermining this country," "When the prohibition," "I think we"). Vanderbilt, *Farewell to Fifth Avenue*, pp. 168–175 (169, "If I am," "strange things were"; 173, "You are very," "Why should I," "kick out state," "Coming from a," "Oh, they are," "Mr. Capone, there," "What is it," "Do you have," "Well, believe it," "And your men"; 174, "They kill only," "Police Headquarters"). NYT, July 8, 1974.

UNTOUCHABLES BEGIN TO BREAK UP: Service Record Card, n.d., in Marion A. R. King OPF/ATF. Service Record Card, n.d., in Martin J. Lahart OPF/ATF. Eliot Ness to J. Leland Acuff, August 29, 1931, in Lyle B. Chapman OPF/ATF.

NESS/UVA CHASE: CEA, September 5, 1931, in "Newspaper Clippings (Photocopies) Circa. 1930–1970" folder, DMM. CT, September 6, 1931. "Nab Frank Uva in Chase; Capone Truck Wrecked," n.p., September 8 [?], 1931, in ENPS, Roll 1, Folder 1.

WILKERSON REJECTS REPORT: CT, September 6, 1931; September 11, 1931. CHE, September 11, 1931 ("I am interested," "I have nothing").

E 25TH ST RAID: CEA, September 22, 1931; CEP, September 22, 1931, both in ENPS, Roll 1, Scrapbook 1. "Agents Raid Capone Plant; Six Arrested," n.p., September 22, 1931, in ENPS, Roll 1, Folder 1 ("some very well-known"). Ness and Fraley, *The Untouchables*, pp. 92–93.

IMPACT OF UNTOUCHABLES' RAIDS: CHE, September 26, 1931 ("The word that"); "College Men Help U.S. in Capone Ruin," n.p., n.d.; "Rah, Rah Prohis Hit 'Scarface,'" n.p., n.d.; "Capone Nemesis Costs Fortune," n.p., n.d., all in ENPS, Roll 1, Scrapbook 1. NYT, September 28, 1931. LAT, September 28, 1931. WP, September 28, 1931. Untitled clipping, in ENPS, Roll 1, Scrapbook 1. W. S. Murphy, Report on Eliot Ness, November 15, 1933, p. 6, in FBI-ENA ("that members of").

PARADE OF TRUCKS: "Capone's Nemesis Costs Fortune," n.p., October 1, 1931, in ENPS, Roll 1, Scrapbook 1 ("nemesis"). Parsons, *Gay Illiterate*, p. 108. *Potter Enterprise*, September 27, 1956, PCHS ("for something interesting"). Ness and Fraley, *The Untouchables*, pp. 200–209. "Ness Called 'Mild, Quiet' in Real Life," n.p., February 11, 1962, in "Newspaper Clippings (Photocopies) Circa. 1930–1970" folder, DMM ("Capone was so"). SLS, personal interview with ABS, September 13, 2016.

Dating this incident with any precision is impossible, though the fall of 1931 (around the time of Capone's tax trial) is easily the best bet. Enough trucks must have been seized to make a spectacle, while the parade could have happened no later than Capone's incarceration in October 1931.

Because the truck parade apparently failed to make the papers at the time, some sources doubt it happened (see Tucker, *Eliot Ness and the Untouchables*, p. 22). Scott Sroka has spoken with the daughter of Marty Lahart, however, who confirms she heard the story from her father before Ness's book was published. Lahart told his daughter he came up with the idea and the men wore pearl-gray hats to further the joke.

A 1960s interview with Prohibition agent William Connors also corroborates the basic details of the incident, though Connors misremembered the Lexington as the Metropole ("Ness Called 'Mild, Quiet' in Real Life," n.p., February 11, 1962, in "Newspaper Clippings (Photocopies) Circa. 1930–1970" folder, DMM).

Additional confirmation comes from Chris Kauffmann, the grandson of Albert Mayer, a former *Tribune* photographer who worked throughout Illinois in the 1930s. Kauffmann recalls watching the two-part *Untouchables* pilot with his grandfather when it first aired on TV, and hearing Mayer remark that although much of the show had been embellished, "the thing with the trucks going past Al Capone's hotel . . . that really happened, that one's true. . . . That was a good one." (Chris Kauffmann, telephone interview with ABS, February 11, 2016.)

Ness's third wife, Elisabeth, referred to the truck parade in a 1959 interview, and claimed it "was Eliot'[s] idea." But it's unclear from her comments whether he told her about it, or whether she referenced the Ness-Fraley book. (CPD, October 17, 1959.)

Chapter Twenty-Six

JURY-FIXING PLOT AND SWITCHING JURIES: CT, October 7, 1931 ("lean and lawyer-like," "What is the," "Not guilty," "Is the defendant"). NYT, October 7, 1931 ("Well, who wouldn't"). "Crime: Who Wouldn't Be Worried?" *Time*, October 19, 1931, pp. 12–13. *Sacramento Bee*, December 8, 1931. *Washington Star*, December 8, 1931, in FBI-AC. *Hearings . . . on the Nomination of James H. Wilkerson*, p. 252. IRS-2, pp. 55–56 ("an underhand method"). Arthur O. Prochno, "I Was a Capone Juror," CT Magazine, May 10, 1936. Wilson and Whitman, "Undercover Man," pp. 82–83 (82, "We will sit"; 83, "Leave the rest"). Casey and Douglas, *Midwesterner*, pp. 153–154 (154, "Take this entire"), gives the other judge's name as "Woodward," but Dwight Green (in *Sacramento Bee*, December 8, 1931) and juror Arthur Prochno (in CT cited above) both gave the judge's name as Barnes, and we have modified the quote accordingly.

As usual, Wilson told this story multiple times in multiple ways, once claiming an undercover agent (probably Michael Malone, though Wilson used a different name) gave him the list of jurors. (Frank J. Wilson, "#7 Re Capone Efforts to Reach Jury," n.d., in Box 7, "Manuscript—Capone Case (F. 255)" folder, FJW.) Given that Malone's undercover work had apparently wrapped up by this time (see above), O'Hare passing along the information is much more likely.

CAPONE'S LAWYERS / JURY SELECTION: CHE, October 7, 1931 ("don't feel right," "It seems to"). CT, October 7, 1931. "Crime: Who Wouldn't Be Worried?" *Time*, October 19, 1931, pp. 12–13. Prochno, "I Was a Capone Juror" ("To hell with," "Like other newspaper," "the limit"). Runyon, *Trials and Other Tribulations*, pp. 226–229 (226, "fragrant whiff of"). Busch, *Enemies of the State*, pp. 200–202. Schoenberg, *Mr. Capone*, p. 318. Okrent, *Last Call*, pp. 118, 240–241. Bair, *Al Capone*, pp. 233–234.

DAY TWO: CHE, October 8, 1931 ("even the most," Grossman-Shumway-Fink-Wilkerson exchange beginning "Now you stated"). CT, October 8, 1931 ("the owner of," Ahern-Bragg exchange). NYT, October 8, 1931 ("a drab, bald-headed"). David Morgan witness transcript, n.d., in Box 1, "Transcripts From U.S. v. Al Capone (Various Witnesses) (2 of 2)" folder, USvAC (7, Green-Morgan-Fink exchange). Ross, *Trial of Al Capone*, pp. 42–52. Busch, *Enemies of the State*, pp. 203–207. Schoenberg, *Mr. Capone*, p. 317. Record for Leslie Shumway, *U.S., Social Security Death Index, 1935–2014* (Provo, UT: Ancestry.com Operations, 2011).

DAY THREE: CHE, October 9, 1931 ("CAPONE CONFESSION BARED!," "Congress doesn't want," "To prove an," "When a man makes"). CT, October 9, 1931 ("confession letter," "most damning," "It is human," "And what is," "No, I don't," "It is an," "It might well," "Was the man," "This is the"). Ross, *Trial of Al Capone*, pp. 53–62. Runyon, *Trials and Other Tribulations*, pp. 229–232. Busch, *Enemies of the State*, pp. 207–210. Schoenberg, *Mr. Capone*, pp. 318–319 (318, "without prejudice," "bona fide offers"). Trespacz, *Trial of Gangster Al Capone*, p. 73.

CAPONE'S EXPENDITURES: CHE, October 10–11, 1931 (October 10, "I presume that"; October 11, "She peeled the," "How big an," "Well, it was"); October 13, 1931. CT, October 10–11, 1931 (October 11, "You don't think," "One man couldn't," "The bill payments," "And they used," "We were trying," "Because you did"); October 13, 1931. J. Pankan witness transcript (Capone Trial), n.d., in Box 1, "Transcripts From U.S. v. Al Capone (Various Witnesses) (1 of 2)" folder, USvAC (2, "No, it is"). IRS-2, pp. 36–48. Ross, *Trial of Al Capone*, pp. 63–80. Prochno, "I Was a Capone Juror." Runyon, *Trials and Other Tribulations*, pp. 232–240. Busch, *Enemies of the State*, pp. 210–216. Trespacz, *Trial of Gangster Al Capone*, p. 74.

CAPONE'S OVERCONFIDENCE: CHE, October 7, 1931. CT, October 8, 1931 ("enjoying himself immensely"); October 11, 1931 ("former workmen, contractors"). *Charlotte Observer*, October 19, 1931 ("You don't need," "The hell I"). Kobler, *Capone*, p. 343.

D'ANDREA ARREST: CHE, October 11, 1931; October 28–29, 1931. CT, October 11, 1931; October 14, 1931; October 28–29, 1931. *United States vs. Philip D'Andrea*, Disposition of Rule to Show Cause, October 28, 1931 ("The pistol was"), in Box 1, "Court Filings from Related Cases" folder, USvAC.

FRED RIES / PROSECUTION RESTS: CHE, October 14, 1931 ("Your honor, there," "Well, if you"). CT, October 14, 1931 ("Your honor, at," "Are you ready," "Well, if your," "We have a," "Give us a"). Fred Ries witness transcript (Guzik trial), n.d., in Box 1, "Court Filings from Related Cases" folder, USvAC (14, "Mr. Guzik, Al"; 15, "bosses"). Fred Ries witness transcript (Capone trial), n.d., in Box 1, "Transcripts From U.S. v. Al Capone (Various Witnesses) (2 of 2)" folder, USvAC (3, "And was [this]," "The telegraph office," "No outsiders. Is," "Yes sir"; 12, "We have been," "Of course we," "I think they," "The only evidence," "His name appears," "On one of," "Yes," "Well, what does"; 14, "We find Jack"; 16, "negative evidence"; 18, "Al and his"; 22, "Just what are," "they are trying," "And they are," "By hearsay, yes," "It is too," "Very well, I"; 29, "Well, we didn't," "It is sometimes," "We didn't do," "No one ever," "The bets were"; 31, "that no money," "He didn't mention," "He said 'Al,'" "Yes sir"; 32, "You did not," "I didn't know," "No," "But I figured," "You thought he," "Yes sir"; 33, "Do you know," "No sir," "Well this check," "According to the"). IRS-2, pp. 23–24. Ross, *Trial of Al Capone*, pp. 80–83. Runyon, *Trials and Other Tribulations*, pp. 240–242. Busch, *Enemies of the State*, pp. 217–219. Eghigian, *After Capone*, p. 133. Mario Gomes, "The Truth About Al Capone's Signature," My Al Capone Museum, March 2006, http://www.myalcaponemuseum.com /id76.htm (accessed July 21, 2017).

Chapter Twenty-Seven

JUFFRA ARREST: Landesco, "Organized Crime," pp. 914, 916 ("Juffra was the"), 1075. *U.S. v. Alphonse Capone, et al.*, indictment, June 1931, Case No. 23256, in "Fusco, Joseph C. (Joe)" folder, Box 86, KC. CT, October 9, 1931 ("What's the idea"); November 8, 1931; February 9, 1936; June 26–27 (June 27, "the head of"), 1936; August 13–14, 1936. Keefe, *Man Who Got Away*, p. 168. "Nick Juffra," Find a Grave, June 22, 2017, https://www.findagrave.com /memorial/180625663/nick-juffra (accessed November 21, 2017).

NESS AND WILSON: Willebrandt, *Inside of Prohibition*, pp. 234–235 ("An intense bitterness"). G. A. Youngquist, memorandum for the Attorney General, March 24, 1931, in Box 1, Eig Boxes, National Archives and Records Administration, Chicago, IL ("By the way"). CPD, September 19, 1934. Frank J. Wilson to George E. Q. Johnson, June 1, 1937, in Box 2, "Career—General—Correspondence, 1930–1939" folder; Frank J. Wilson, "Insert At X on Page 60," n.d., in Box 11, "Manuscripts—Crime Prevention Programs—TV Programs Contaminate Children (F. 295)" folder; Frank J. Wilson, untitled manuscript, n.d., in Box 7, "Manuscript—Capone Case (F. 261)" folder; Frank J. Wilson, "Untouchables Re Bad Effects of Television Programs," n.d., in Box 12, "Manuscripts—'Untouchables' Bad Effects of Television Programs (F. 472)" folder, all FJW. Frank J. Wilson, "Mysterious Mike Malone," CT Sunday Magazine, March 26, 1961. Wilson and Day, *Special Agent*, p. 6. CPD, October 26, 1941 ("the brains behind," "excellent"). Application for Employment in the Federal Security Agency, April 3, 1942, in Eliot Ness OPF. Ness MS., p. 9, in ENPS, Roll 1, Folder 2. Ness and Fraley, *The Untouchables*, pp. 24, 249.

CAPONE'S FAMILY / EDWARD G. ROBINSON: CHE, October 15, 1931 ("to give Snorky"). Bair, *Al Capone*, p. 245.

CAPONE'S DEFENSE: CHE, October 12, 1931 ("well-known Chicagoans," "This argument is," "statute was used"); October 15–16, 1931 (October 15, Green-witness exchange beginning "You said Capone," "I am running," "Who are the," "I don't know"). CT, October 15–

16, 1931 (October 15, "Do you know," "I never kept"; October 16, "That is not," "Then I ask," "I have never," "to put Mattingly," "Well, I think"). Peter P. Penovich Jr., witness transcript, October 14, 1931, in Box 1, "Transcripts From U.S. v. Al Capone (Various Witnesses) (2 of 2)" folder, USvAC (2, "Is he trying," "I don't know"; 3, "apparently a list"; 6, "Frankie Pope was," "Ralph told me"; 9, "a bad location," "Why did you," "Because I understood," "You understood he," "Yes sir"; 10, "And he could," "In Cicero," "Fixing with whom," "With the powers," "What powers," "Political powers, the"; 11, "Well, he seemed," "Catered to by," "Well, every place"; 12, "there was an"; 21, "with Al Capone"). IRS-2, p. 35 ("Frank paid $17,500," "Paid," "J & A"). Ross, *Trial of Al Capone*, pp. 59, 83–94. Runyon, *Trials and Other Tribulations*, pp. 242–244 (242, "world's worst horse"). Busch, *Enemies of the State*, pp. 219–221. Schoenberg, *Mr. Capone*, pp. 321–322 (322, "a better witness"). Trespacz, *Trial of Gangster Al Capone*, pp. 75–76.

CLOSING STATEMENTS: CHE, October 16–18, 1931 (October 17, "the only barrier," "How many defendants"). CT, October 16–18, 1931 (October 16, "Capone himself produced," "At the start," "All through this," "It means that"; October 17, "This does not," "like many other," "Suppose he had," "as a means," "If the latter," "The fathers of," "The government has," "Because Capone has," "The government, too"; October 18, "Mr. Johnson was"). "Closing Argument by Mr. Johnson on Behalf of the United States," n.d., in Box 1, "Closing Argument (11 of 12)" folder, RRPAC ("swept aside," "American civilization will," "a halo of," "Is he the," "You will remember," "$27 shirts to," "Could anyone forget," "Take every fact," "from the lips," "time of national," "extravagances," "They will remember"). James H. Wilkerson, Court's Charge to the Jury, October 17, 1931, in Box 1, "Closing Argument (12 of 12)" folder, RRPAC (20, "Now in this," "moneys which were," "expenditures of money"; 22, "You must look"; 32, "You are the"). Ross, *Trial of Al Capone*, pp. 94–106. Prochno, "I Was a Capone Juror." Runyon, *Trials and Other Tribulations*, pp. 244–249. Busch, *Enemies of the State*, pp. 221–228 (223, "If I were"; 224, "How do you"; 228, "an unusual tribute"). "'They Can't Win', Declares U.S. Attorney Johnson, Prosecutor of Capone."

JURY DELIBERATION: CT, October 18, 1931 ("I'm feeling fine," "Not a thing"). CHE, October 18–19, 1931. Prochno, "I Was a Capone Juror" ("give him the limit," "A quick verdict," "You're not dumb," "After all, he's," "He's no good," "But he's done," "We asked for," "We wanted to," "we agreed to," "He'll only get," "I really believe").

THE VERDICT: CHE, October 18–25, 1931 (October 19, "Should this prove"; October 20, "By the time"). CT, October 18–21, 1931 (October 18, "Have you arrived," "How are you," "I'm feeling fine," "The verdict speaks"); October 23, 1931. Partial transcript of evidence taken before Judge James H. Wilkerson on October 17, 1931, https://catalog.archives.gov /id/55312156 (accessed April 15, 2017) ("We, the jury," "and we find"). Ross, *Trial of Al Capone*, pp. 106–108. Schoenberg, *Mr. Capone*, p. 324.

SENTENCING AND JAIL: Signed Statement of Proceedings, September 25 and 29 and October 24, 1931, https://catalog.archives.gov/id/55311944 (accessed April 15, 2017) ("It is the," "On count five," "On count nine," "On each of," "be consecutive and," "The result is," "Eleven years, did," "Yes"). CHE, October 25, 1931 ("Let the defendant," "fearless gangster," "a picture of," "Can't you have," "No. The order," "The defendant is," "You have not," "You cannot undertake," "to come along," "It's all my," "Well, it's a," "I'll knock your"). CT, October 25, 1931 ("around a cut," "Well, I'll get," "It was a," "Think of my"). Ross, *Trial of Al Capone*, pp. 108–112. Trespacz, *Trial of Gangster Al Capone*, pp. 78–79.

Chapter Twenty-Eight

RANDOLPH AND NESS STILL FIGHTING: CEA, October 24, 1931, in RIR Scrapbook III, p. 50 ("Now after Capone," "a militant drive," "Knock over their," "It is up"). CT, March 8, 1932; September 26, 1932.

HOWLETT: *U.S. v. Alphonse Capone, et al.*, indictment, June 1931, Case No. 23256, in "Fusco, Joseph C. (Joe)" folder, Box 86, KC. CT, November 15, 1931. "Hunt 'Playboy' of Capone Gang as Beer Ring Aid," n.p., n.d. ("the Jekyll and"); "Howlett, Capone Aid, in Line at Police Showup," n.p., November 16, 1931, both in ENPS, Roll 1, Folder 1. Ness MS., pp. 21–22, in ENPS, Roll 1, Folder 2 (21, "It was not"). Ness and Fraley, *The Untouchables*, pp. 244–245.

The accounts of Howlett's arrest in the Ness MS. and contemporary newspapers are almost entirely different, but certain similar details (the description of Howlett's sixteen-cylinder car, and Ness's recollection that he tracked Howlett down on a Saturday) suggest that they both describe the same event. *The Untouchables* offers nothing to square both versions, but the version presented in the Ness MS. has enough details to seem more credible, while the press version seems too good to be true.

The Ness MS. describes Marty Lahart taking part in Howlett's arrest, but Lahart had already left for Minneapolis. Service Record Card, n.d., Martin J. Lahart OPF/ATF.

JOHNSON EXHAUSTED: George E. Q. Johnson to Robert Isham Randolph, October 24, 1931, in RIR Scrapbook III, p. 50 ("courageous statement"). *Kansas City Star*, November 1, 1931, in ENPS, Roll 1, Scrapbook 1 ("resting his chin," "worn out," "Why, then, did," "There were many," "Industrial and civic," "Incorruptibles," "boyish," "He is an," "He has no," "You left this," "Ever get in," "Once in a"). George E. Q. Johnson to Frank J. Wilson, May 10, 1945, in Box 2, "Career—General—Correspondence, 1940–1948" folder, FJW ("You remember the").

PREMATURE OPTIMISM: Untitled memo, March 16, 1931, in Presidential Subject Series, Box 164, "Federal Bureau of Investigation—Capone Tax Case, 1930–1931" folder, HHPL. NYT, June 18, 1931; December 21–22, 1931 (December 21, "Organized law enforcement"; December 22, "exorcised her evil"). *Kansas City Star*, November 1, 1931, in ENPS, Roll 1, Scrapbook 1 ("a busy winter"). Hopkins, *Our Lawless Police*, p. 170. CT, December 15–16, 1931 (December 15, "found a home," "the greatest ovation"; December 16, "We now have"). LAT, December 20, 1931 ("CHICAGO WINS WAR"); December 22, 1931. "Capone 'in Bag,' U.S. Turns Guns on N.Y. Gangs," n.p., n.d.; "U.S. Plans to Wipe Out Gangs," n.p., n.d., both in ENPS, Roll 1, Scrapbook 1. "Chicago's Victory Over Gangdom," *The Literary Digest*, January 9, 1932, pp. 21–22 ("the signs are"). Lyle, *Dry and Lawless Years*, pp. 270–271 (270, "the summer of," "If Chicago had"). Allsop, *Bootleggers*, p. 189 ("Unless citizens," "Citizens already paying"). Calder, *Origins and Development*, p. 146. Hoffman, *Scarface Al*, pp. 165–166. Pacyga, *Chicago*, pp. 253–256, 259–260.

CAPONE IN COOK COUNTY JAIL: Anonymous to George E. Q. Johnson, December 2, 1931, in Box 1, "Correspondence (3 of 12)" folder, RRPAC ("WISH TO INFORM").

W. A. McSwain, Report on "David T. Moneypenny, Superintendent; George Gibson, Assistant Superintendent; Cook County Jail," December 17, 1931, in Box 1, "Contempt of Court Report (6 of 12)" folder, RRPAC (also in FBI-AC) ("special privileges," "that Capone is," "escorted a number," "Mr. Johnson was," "without a pass"). W. A. McSwain to Director, Bureau of Investigation, December 7, 1931; V. W. Hughes, Memorandum for the Director, December 16, 1931; CDN, December 17, 1931 ("Capone has been"); CDT, December 18, 1931; CHE, December 18, 1931 ("discovered that late," "had been unable," "petty politicians"); *Kansas City Journal-Post*, December 18, 1931 ("crack proof," "a lot of," "Capone's in a"); CHE, December 19, 1931 ("soft mattress, clean," "I didn't want"); W. A. McSwain to Director, Bureau of Investigation, December 19, 1931 ("Mr. Johnson expressed"); CDT, December 21, 1931; W. A. McSwain, Report on "David T. Moneypenny, Superintendent; George Gibson, Assistant Superintendent; Cook County Jail," January 22, 1932; M. H. Purvis to Director, Bureau of Investigation, January 26, 1932 ("information to the"); CT, January 26, 1932 ("Mr. Smith," "Mr. Jones," "I'll put a"); CHE, January 27, 1932; M. H. Purvis to Director, Bureau of Investigation, February 1, 1932 ("Mr. Moneypenny takes," "and placed in"); CHE, February 26, 1932, all in FBI-AC. CT, December 18, 1931 ("I'm in jail"). George E. Q. Johnson to William D. Mitchell, February 20, 1932, in Box 1, "Correspondence (4 of 12)" folder, RRPAC ("in fact directing," "With the influence"). Kobler, *Capone*, pp. 352 ("If I'd had"), 359, 379. Helmer and Mattix, *Public Enemies*, p. 43.

PETER NESS DEATH: CT, December 24, 1931. "Hail Two South End Men for Overthrow of Alphonse Capone," n.p., n.d., in ENPS, Roll 1, Scrapbook 1. Heimel, *Eliot Ness*, pp. 134–135.

JANUARY 1932 RAIDS: CDT, January 8, 1932; January 21, 1932 ("customary calling card"). CT, January 9, 1932; January 22, 1932. CHE, January 14, 1932 ("rival gangs were"); "A $375,000 Dent in the Traffic," *The Bureau Bulletin*, January 23, 1932; "U.S. Raids Big Brewery; Six Men Arrested," n.p., n.d.; CEA, January 21, 1932; "5 Capone Hoodlums Seized By Drys in $75,000 Beer Raid," n.p., n.d., all in ENPS, Roll 1, Scrapbook 1. Eghigian, *After Capone*, pp. 134, 214–216 (216, "too much ambition"). Ness and Fraley, *The Untouchables*, pp. 91–92. "Federal Agents Demolish a Brewery and Puncture Beer Barrels in Chicago, Illinois During Prohibition," Critical Past, 00:46, January 25, 1932, http://www.criticalpast .com/video/65675023921_raiders-in-brewery_barrels-punctured_beer-flushed-on-streets _brewing-containers (accessed June 14, 2016). CEA, February 20, 1960, in "Newspaper Clippings (Photocopies) Circa. 1930–1970" folder, DMM. Tony Berardi, interviewed in *The Mystery of Al Capone's Vaults*. Tony Berardi, interviewed in "Eliot Ness," *The Real Untouchables*, written and directed by John Fothergill (Thousand Oaks, CA: Goldhil DVD, 2001), DVD. Kobler, *Capone*, p. 278. UCR (pp. 41–42) gives address as adjacent 7 Cullerton Street.

Ness and Fraley (*The Untouchables*, pp. 106–109) falsely list the Lumber Street raid as the Untouchables' first. Perry (*Eliot Ness*, p. 76) incorrectly dates it to April 1931. Ness calling up reporters in advance of the South State Street raid is conjectural, but based on comments cited above and the press coverage given this bust, it's all but certain he did.

NESS AND PUBLICITY: CT, November 7, 1926; September 18, 1927; January 7, 1929; March 26, 1931 ("assistant"). CDN, March 25, 1931 ("aid"). CEA, February 20, 1960 ("a publicity hound"); "Ness Called 'Mild, Quiet' in Real Life," n.p., February 11, 1962 ("At times the"), all in "Newspaper Clippings (Photocopies) Circa. 1930–1970" folder, DMM.

P. T. Sowell, interview with William J. Froelich, November 21, 1933; M. H. Purvis to J. Edgar Hoover, November 28, 1933 ("headline publicity"); H. B. Myerson, interview with W. E. Bennett, December 26, 1933 ("egotism and publicity," "dissension"), all in FBI-ENA. Raymond M. Schwartz to Eliot Ness, June 17, 1931 ("short but very," "The proceeds should"), in ENPS, Roll 1, Scrapbook 1. Carte and Carte, *Police Reform*, pp. 24–25, 50–53. Tony Berardi, interviewed in *The Mystery of Al Capone's Vaults* ("Because I knew," "a messenger boy," "Personally, I hated"). Schoenberg, *Mr. Capone*, pp. 89, 178. Bergreen, *Capone*, pp. 148–151, 433 ("not quite a"). Tony Berardi, interviewed in "The Road to Repeal." "Prohibition: Tony Berardi—About Eliot Ness and 'the Untouchables,'" Onlinefootage.tv, 08:42, http://www.onlinefootage.tv/stock-video-footage/7684/prohibition-tony-berardi-about-eliot-ness-and-the-untouchables (accessed August 26, 2015).

　　Purvis's letter describes a conversation special agent L. D. Nichols had with a member of Ness's squad named "Morris Seeger," who can only be (Samuel) Maurice Seager.

LITTLE CAESAR AND *THE PUBLIC ENEMY*: Powers, *G-Men*, pp. 13–16. McGilligan, *Backstory*, pp. 56–58 (56, "I had the"). Black, *Hollywood Censored*, pp. 111–121. Bergreen, *Capone*, pp. 524–526. Richard Maltby, "The Public Enemy," Senses of Cinema, December 2003, http://sensesofcinema.com/2003/cteq/public_enemy/ (accessed June 16, 2016).

SCARFACE: *Scarface* (1932), directed by Howard Hawks (Universal City, CA: Universal Studios, 2003), DVD ("Some little typewriter"). *The Film Daily*, March 25, 1932; April 5, 1932; April 13–14, 1932 (April 14, "It should never"); June 5, 1932; June 30, 1932. Hecht, *Child of the Century*, pp. 125, 129, 131–132, 486–487 (486, "They had a," "Is this stuff," "God, no"; 487, "If this stuff," "That's the reason"). Barlett and Steele, *Howard Hughes*, pp. 73–74. Powers, *G-Men*, p. 43. McGilligan, *Backstory*, p. 60. MacAdams, *Ben Hecht*, pp. 6–7, 101–102, 124–126, 149. Nollen, *Boris Karloff*, pp. 216–217. Bergreen, *Capone*, p. 527. Black, *Hollywood Censored*, pp. 124–130 (126, "Under no circumstances"), 132.

　　Nollen (*Boris Karloff*, p. 216) notes that *Scarface* "was shot in mid-1931, before Karloff began work on *Frankenstein*," even though the latter was released first.

PUBLIC NEED FOR CATHARSIS/VENGEANCE: NYT, January 10, 1931 ("a figure out"). *Scarface* ("THE WORLD IS"). *Gabriel over the White House* (1933), directed by Gregory La Cava (Burbank, CA: Warner Home Video, 2009, DVD ("I've paid my," "Federal Police to"). Busch, *Enemies of the State*, p. 229. Barlett and Steele, *Howard Hughes*, p. 74. Powers, *G-Men*, pp. 4–9 (8, "The public wanted"), 12–25, 29, 31. McGilligan, *Backstory*, p. 57 ("a gutter Macbeth"). MacAdams, *Ben Hecht*, p. 131. Black, *Hollywood Censored*, p. 121 ("the here and"), 129–130, 137–144. Potter, *War on Crime*, p. 138. Pizzitola, *Hearst over Hollywood*, pp. 294–300. Mappen, *Prohibition Gangsters*, pp. 122–124. Maltby, "The Public Enemy."

Chapter Twenty-Nine

NESS'S DISILLUSIONMENT: Personal History Statement, April 18, 1931; Recommendation for Change in Designated Post of Duty, December 19, 1931, both in Albert H. Wolff OPF/ATF. Ness and Fraley, *The Untouchables*, p. 86. *Akron Beacon-Journal*, June 1, 1987. *Lexington Herald-Leader*, June 1, 1987. Tiede, *American Tapestry*, p. 133 ("I don't say"). Heimel, *Eliot Ness*, pp. 81, 97–98 ("The niceties of").

　　Wolff must be quoted with caution, as many of the claims he made in later years seem embellished at best and outright fabrications at worst. But he did serve under Ness in the Chicago Prohibition office, and his assessment of Ness's character here rings true, especially given Ness's extralegal activities later on in Cleveland.

CLOONAN: Oath of Office, January 5, 1931; Recommendation for Change in Designated Post of Duty, October 26, 1932; A. V. Dalrymple to Bernard V. Cloonan, June 27, 1933; Oath of Office, February 24, 1934; Sam H. Scott to the Assistant Director, Alcoholic Beverage Unit, May 3, 1934 ("Hymie," "Barney," "long-time," "had helped them," "the guy who," "It seems that"); Hugo Keller to E. C. Yellowley, September 19, 1935; E. C. Yellowley to the Deputy Commissioner of the Alcohol Tax Unit, February 18, 1938; V. V. Sugg to E. C. Yellowley, October 21, 1939; E. C. Yellowley to the Deputy Commissioner of the Alcohol Tax Unit, April 2, 1940; Performance Review, November 27, 1940; V. V. Sugg to E. C. Yellowley, June 3, 1941; Report of Efficiency Rating, March 31, 1942; Report of Efficiency Rating, March 31, 1943; Report of Efficiency Rating, March 31, 1944; Report of Efficiency Rating, March 31, 1945; Report of Efficiency Rating, March 31, 1946; Report of Efficiency Rating, March 31, 1947; Report of Efficiency Rating, September 30, 1948; Report of Efficiency Rating, September 30, 1949; Report of Efficiency Rating, September 30, 1950; Efficiency Report, September 30, 1952; W. A. Collawn to Bernard V. Cloonan, July 31, 1960, all in Bernard V. Cloonan OPF/ATF. CT, July 17, 1960. *Milwaukee Journal*, January 10, 1961. Fraley and Robsky, *Last of the Untouchables*, pp. 35–39, 67–72. Jedick, "Eliot Ness," pp. 54, 91.

Robsky and Fraley's heavily fictionalized book describes two corrupt Untouchables, "George Steelman" and "Arnold Grant," who are both exposed after demanding bribes over tapped phone lines. Although the details seem largely fanciful, the use of wiretaps to expose the agents echoes the Cloonan case, and strongly suggests that was where Robsky and Fraley found their inspiration.

CAPONE'S APPEAL / WILL ROGERS: CT, February 28, 1932. White, *Will Rogers*, pp. 149 ("five counts of"), 219 ("What's the matter," "and not make").

LINDBERGH KIDNAPPING: Vanderbilt, "How Al Capone," p. 18. CT, March 6, 1932; March 11, 1932; November 17, 1946. *Miami Herald*, March 11, 1932 ("You don't suppose," "come back here," "How do they know"). A. P. Madden to Chief, Intelligence Unit, March 11, 1932, in Box 4, "Career-Capone Case-Correspondence, 1931–1940" folder, FJW ("quite disturbed," "to procure information," "It is my," "would now pay"). NYT, March 12, 1932. *St. Louis Post Dispatch*, February 17, 1935; *New York American*, April 15, 1937; Charles E. Fisher, "$14,600 in Ransom Cash Carried About in Court: Wilentz Tosses It to Witness for Identification," *The Bulletin*, n.d., all in Box 3, "Career—Lindbergh Case—Subject File, 1932–1935" folder, FJW. Irey and Slocum, *Tax Dodgers*, pp. 66–69 (68, "wouldn't ask for"), 71, 75–76. Waller, *Kidnap*, p. 18 ("It's the most"), 22–23. Wilson and Day, *Special Agent*, pp. 60–61. Messick, *Secret File*, pp. 73–77, 81. Fischer, *Lindbergh Case*, pp. 36–37 (36, "I'm pretty positive"). Kobler, *Capone*, p. 353. Spiering, *Man Who Got Capone*, pp. 215–219. Powers, *G-Men*, pp. 9–12 (11, "the baby's blood"; 12, "God knows why"). Maeder, *Dick Tracy*, pp. 22, 24–25. Bergreen, *Capone*, pp. 503–505. Berg, *Lindbergh*, p. 253. Keefe, *Man Who Got Away*, pp. 257–258. Gould, *Complete Chester Gould's Dick Tracy*, vol. 1, April 12, 1932–May 21, 1932. Helmer, *Al Capone and His American Boys*, pp. 55, 104–105 (105, "to get out," "pull a job," "often wondered if"), 151–152 (151, "under no circumstances"), 283 ("to 'shoot' every," "Capone believed that"), 307–308 (307, "snatch racket"; 308, "taken care of"). Bair, *Al Capone*, pp. 251–252. Binder, *Al Capone's Beer Wars*, pp. 233–234.

NITTO'S RELEASE: George E. Q. Johnson, Parole Report by United States Attorney, September 14, 1931; N. R. Timmons to H. C. Heckman, September 15, 1931; Frank R. Nitto to H. C. Heckman, September 19, 1931 ("I have maintained"); Frank Nitto to Arthur Wood, September 20, 1931; Frank Nitto to Arthur D. Wood, October 15, 1931 ("four or five"); N. R. Timmons to George E. Q. Johnson, October 15, 1931; George E. Q. Johnson to the United States Board of Parole, October 21, 1931 ("I have a"); untitled note, October 29, 1931; Arthur D. Wood to Frank Nitto, October 30, 1931 ("should be paid"); Anna Nitto to Arthur Wood, n.d. ("I am sure"); Charles M. Bates and Fred W. Scherer, receipt, November 20, 1931; Arthur B. Wood, Irvin B. Tucker, and Amy N. Standard, "Parole Having Been Denied, Reopened and Denied," November 30, 1931; George E. Q. Johnson to H. C. Heckman, November 30, 1931; H. C. Heckman to the Warden, U.S. Penitentiary, Leavenworth, December 2, 1931; Untitled note, January 20, 1932; "Memorandum for the File of Frank Nitti" [*sic*], January 20, 1932; "Capone Gang Revolt for Leadership Seen," undated AP clipping ("open warfare," "from taking charge"), all in Box 71, "Nitto, Frank (1 of 1)" folder, NOF. Murray, *Legacy of Al Capone*, p. 154. Eghigian, *After Capone*, pp. 201–203, 205–208.

END OF UNTOUCHABLES: CT, March 8, 1932; April 3, 1932 ("going to try"); April 24, 1932; June 11, 1932; September 26, 1932. NYT, April 25, 1932. *Calumet Index*, April 29, 1932; "U.S. Plans to Wipe Out Entire Capone Syndicate with One New True Bill," n.p. [CDN?], June 11, 1932 ("When the bombshell"); "Capone and 79 Followers in New U.S. Net," CEA, n.d.; "New Rum Indictments for Capones, 67 Others, to Be Sought by U.S.," n.p., June 11, 1932, all in ENPS, Roll 1, Scrapbook 1. Bergreen, *Capone*, p. 411 ("the Capone organization," "The attitude of").

CHAPMAN AND CAPONE CASE FILE: Lyle B. Chapman to Dwight E. Avis, December 16, 1931; W. E. Bennett, memo to Lyle B. Chapman, August 25, 1932 ("It is now," "conform to the," "perform your work"); L. B. Chapman, "Memorandum for Mr. Bennett," September 7, 1932 ("awful mass of," "I think the"); E. P. Guinane to Director, United States Bureau of Investigation, October 6, 1932 ("her daughter was"); Everett H. Kuebler to David A. Sloan, October 27, 1932; W. H. Huss to D. E. Avis, December 7, 1932; W. E. Bennett to Lyle B. Chapman, December 14, 1932; W. E. Bennett to Lyle B. Chapman, December 15, 1932; Dwight E. Avis to Special Agent in Charge, December 23, 1932; Unsigned [Lyle B. Chapman] to W. H. Huss and Company, January 3, 1933; Affidavit of Viola Bourke, February 23, 1933; Affidavit of Lyle B. Chapman, March 31, 1933; Affidavit of Vesta Beck Chapman, April 24, 1933; D. A. Sloan, Report on Special Agent Lyle B. Chapman, April 24, 1933 ("notorious," "probably a questionable," "was drinking something," "big shot"); Everett H. Kuebler, Memo to A. V. Dalrymple, April 27, 1933; Everett H. Kuebler, memo to D. H. Reichgut, May 26, 1933; A. V. Dalrymple to Lyle B. Chapman, June 27, 1933; John S. Hurley to Lyle B. Chapman, August 9, 1933, all in Lyle B. Chapman OPF/ATF. *United States of America vs. Alphonse Capone, Ralph Capone, Bert Delaney, August Dold, Joseph Fusco, Jack Guzik, George A. Howlett, Albert Johnson, Frank Juffra, Nicholas Juffra, Hyman Levine, Michael Lopristi, Charles Fuehrmeyer, John H. Nolan, and Steve Swoboda*, Civil Complaint No. 3375, n.d.; Memo, "SUBJECT: Testimony of Joseph C. Fusco," October 4, 1950, both in Box 86, "Fusco, Joseph

C. (Joe)" folder, KC. CT, October 22, 1938. CDN, March 24, 1948. *Hearings Before the Special Committee to Investigate Organized Crime in Interstate Commerce*, pt. 5, pp. 565–567. Ness MS., p. 21, in FNPS, Roll 1, Folder 2. LAT, September 23, 1962 ("I often find").

SUPREME COURT APPEAL / AHERN AND FINK: CHE, May 3, 1932 ("I'm still ready"). Ross, *Trial of Al Capone*, pp. 118–123 (122, "everything done thereafter was"). *Christian Science Monitor*, November 7, 1934 ("Capone could not," "If the Capone"). Schoenberg, *Mr. Capone*, pp. 317 ("really inept," "terrible"), 330–331. Bergreen, *Capone*, p. 516. Capone, *Uncle Al Capone*, p. 60.

TAKING CAPONE TO PRISON TRAIN: G. A. Youngquist to George E. Q. Johnson, Memo "In Re: United States v. Alphonse Capone," April 28, 1932, in Box 1, "Correspondence (4 of 12)" folder, RRPAC. CHE, May 4, 1932 ("Here, kid," "I don't know," "toughest," "For a while"). CT, May 3–5, 1932 (May 4, "the bodies of," "You'd think Mussolini," "You got a," "Damn it, come"). NYT, May 4, 1932 ("toughest," "You'd think Mussolini," "You got a," "After that it," "Police officials described," "a picture of"). CPD, September 19, 1934 ("We did our"). Ness and Fraley, *The Untouchables*, pp. 249–254. "Eliot Ness: Untouchable." Cahan, *Court That Shaped America*, p. 46 ("granite octopus"). "Prohibition: Tony Berardi—About Al Capone's Lifestyle," Onlinefootage.tv, video, 02:04, http://www.onlinefootage.tv/stock-video-footage/7660/prohibition-tony-berardi-about-al-capone-s-lifestyle (accessed June 30, 2016). "Al Capone Passes to His Long Rest," British Movietone, YouTube, video, 01:02, https://www.youtube.com/watch?v=KsPWP79w82g (accessed July 1, 2016). "Capone to Atlanta Prison—221529–01," Footage Farm, YouTube, video, 00:45, https://www.youtube.com/watch?v=5HjF1q7IrO0 (accessed September 8, 2016).

Lew Wilkinson, a friend of Ness's in his later years, confirmed in an interview that Ness said this was the only time he ever got close to Capone. Some of Wilkinson's other comments in the interview are unreliable (such as his claim Ness said he never went on raids, when there is ample evidence to the contrary), but Ness's presence at Dearborn Station that day is certain. See Lew Wilkinson, interviewed in "Eliot Ness," *The Real Untouchables*.

Eig (*Get Capone*, p. 373) contends Ness and Capone "never met" that day, even as he admits newspapers place Ness among the guards taking Capone to the station. Photographs and film footage also clearly show Ness taking Capone through the train shed at Dearborn Station.

The Ness-Fraley book (cited above) presents a short scene in which Ness and Capone exchange words in the Pullman car before Ness gets out and the train takes off. Capone's dialogue is adapted from his quotes in the CT story about his departure, while Ness's is likely invented. Fraley obviously based his account of the trip to Dearborn Station largely on the CT article and twisted Capone's quotes into an exchange with Ness, in keeping with Fraley's method throughout the book. No independent evidence suggests the other Untouchables joined Ness on the trip to Dearborn Station, as Fraley paints it in the book. News articles refer to unnamed Prohibition agents taking the journey with Ness, and some were likely members of the squad. But they didn't take the lead in guarding Capone in the way the book describes; that duty fell to the U.S. marshals.

Chapter Thirty

INSULL AND WILKERSON: CT, February 12, 1932; February 23, 1932; March 13, 1932; March 18–19, 1932; May 8, 1932; October 1, 1948. CHE, May 7, 1932. "Big Bankers' Gambling Mania," *The Literary Digest*, March 11, 1933, pp. 11–12. Paul Y. Anderson, "The Darrow Report," *The Nation*, May 30, 1934, pp. 611–612 (612, "a pure and"). Kenneth C. Cole, "Judicial Affairs: The Role of the Senate in the Confirmation of Judicial Nominations," *The American Political Science Review*, vol. 28, no. 5 (October 1934), pp. 882–883, 885–886. Allen, *Since Yesterday*, pp. 75–76, 100–101. Casey and Douglas, *Midwesterner*, pp. 96–99, 110, 161–191. Busch, *Guilty or Not Guilty?*, pp. 128–194 (138, "little people"). Galbraith, *Great Crash 1929*, pp. 153–156. Allsop, *Bootleggers*, pp. 244–245. *Public Papers 1932–1933*, pp. 20, 840–841, 1049 ("If only part," "banksters who rob"). Hoffman, *Scarface Al*, pp. 166–167, 169–170. Cahan, *Court That Shaped America*, pp. 101, 104–106. Merriner, *Grafters and Goo-Goos*, p. 126. McElvaine, *Great Depression*, pp. 136–137 (136, "What have I"). Eig, *Get Capone*, p. 326. Bradley, *Edison to Enron*, pp. 182–213, 216. Vickers, *Panic in the Loop*, pp. ix, 47–79 (59, "nothing but a"), 154–155, 240–243. "Biographical Directory of Federal Judges: Wilkerson, James Herbert," Federal Judiciary Center, http://www.fjc.gov/servlet/ngetinfo?jid=2580 (accessed June 7, 2016).

SECRET SIX COLLAPSING: CT, April 27, 1930; June 7, 1930; December 1, 1930; December 10, 1930; December 26–28, 1930; January 6, 1931; January 22–23, 1931; March 13, 1931; April 11, 1931; September 14, 1931; September 17, 1931; November 7–10, 1931; November 14–15, 1931; November 18, 1931; December 25, 1931; January 6–7, 1932 (January 7, "one of the"); January 29, 1932; February 26, 1932 ("ready to shoot"); April 16–17, 1932; May 4, 1932; May 8, 1932; May 10, 1932; June 6, 1932; August 24, 1932; November 17, 1932; November 23–24, 1932; December 2–3, 1932; December 5, 1932; January 5, 1933; January 11, 1933; January 14, 1933; January 18, 1933; January 16, 1934. CHE, June 6, 1930, in RIR Scrapbook II, p. 65. LAT, March 13, 1931; April 13, 1931; November 11, 1931. CDN, September 14, 1931, in ENPS, Roll 1, Folder 1 (also in RIR Scrapbook III, p. 37). *Atlanta Constitution*, September 14, 1931. WP, September 14, 1931. NYT, September 20, 1931 ("political matters such"); November 12, 1931; January 30, 1932. *The Secret 6* (1931), directed by George Hill (Burbank, CA: Warner Archive Collection, 2012), DVD ("the greatest force"). "Nebraska Governor Praises 'Secret Six,'" n.d., in ENPS, Roll 1, Folder 1. CDN, January 20, 1932; LAT, January 21, 1932; NYT, January 21, 1932; *Pittsburgh Post Gazette*, January 21, 1932; *Washington Herald*, February 26, 1932, all in RIR Scrapbook III. W. A. McSwain to J. Edgar Hoover, August 6, 1932; W. A. McSwain to J. Edgar Hoover, September 1, 1932 ("I am inclined"); W. A. McSwain to J. Edgar Hoover, September 12, 1932, all in FBI-RIR. Robert Isham Randolph, "The 'Third Degree,'" *New York Herald Tribune Magazine*, August 7, 1932, pp. 1–2. Melvin Purvis to J. Edgar Hoover, September 20, 1933; H. Nathan to J. Edgar Hoover, October 25, 1933; John J. Fox to J. Edgar Hoover, November 2, 1933, all in FBI-AJ. Robert Isham Randolph to Robert E. Wood, July 7, 1938; Alexander Jamie to Henry Morgenthau, September 1, 1938 ("thereby saving five"), in Alexander G. Jamie OPF. George Wilson, "Gangland Crime Arrives in Lincoln: The Lincoln National Bank and Trust Company Robbery of 1930," *Nebraska History*, no. 73 (Spring 1992), pp. 25–31. Hoffman, *Scarface Al*, p. 170. Potter, *War on Crime*, pp. 110–118. Pizzitola, *Hearst over Hollywood*, pp. 285–286.

Merriner, *Grafters and Goo-Goos*, p. 127. Helmer and Bilek, *St. Valentine's Day Massacre*, pp. 275–276. Helmer, *Al Capone and His American Boys*, pp. 140–148.
JAMIE AND KUB: CDN, August 31, 1932; CEP, September 1, 1932 ("When digging In"), both in RIR Scrapbook III, p. 124. CEA, September 1, 1932, in RIR Scrapbook III, p. 125. WP, September 1, 1932. CT, September 1–2, 1932; October 27–29, 1932; November 9, 1932; December 5, 1932; February 21, 1933; March 17, 1933. CDN, October 25, 1932, in RIR Scrapbook III, p. 131. CEP, October 25, 1932, in RIR Scrapbook III, p. 130. CHE, October 26, 1932, in RIR Scrapbook III, p. 132. "'Secret 6' Calls Swanson Unfit, Backs Courtney," n.p., October 25, 1932, in RIR Scrapbook III, p. 130. CHE, November 4, 1932, in RIR Scrapbook IV, p. 8. M. H. Purvis to J. E. Hoover, February 3, 1932; W. A. Smith, Memo for Melvin Purvis "Re: Shirley Kub," August 11, 1933 ("a dangerous person"); W. A. McSwain to J. Edgar Hoover, October 28, 1932; John B. Little, memorandum for the Director, September 7, 1933; L. D. Nichols, memo to J. B. Little, n.d., all in FBI-RIR. P. T. Sowell, interview with William J. Froelich, November 21, 1933, in FBI-ENA ("that misunderstandings exist"). Melvin Purvis to J. Edgar Hoover, March 20, 1934; Name Redacted to J. Edgar Hoover, April 7, 1937; D. M. Ladd, memo to J. Edgar Hoover, April 28, 1937 ("I had the utmost"); Name Redacted, Sworn Statement, May 25, 1937; W. S. Hardy, Report Re: Shirley Kub, June 4, 1937 ("Crime Syndicate," "the System," "absolutely clean and," "crusade"); D. M. Ladd to J. Edgar Hoover, June 10, 1937; R. N. Pranke, Report Re: Shirley Kub, September 14, 1938; J. Waldman, Report Re: Shirley Kub, October 24, 1938; R. N. Pranke, Report Re: Shirley Kub, December 10, 1938; R. N. Pranke, Report Re: Shirley Kub, March 22, 1939; R. N. Pranke, Report Re: Shirley Kub, May 24, 1939, all in FBI-AJ. Alexander Jamie to Henry Morgenthau, January 4, 193[7]; R. E. Wood to Henry Morgenthau, June 3, 1938; Henry Morgenthau to R. E. Wood, June 22, 1938; C. L. Rice to R. E. Wood, July 5, 1938; Robert Isham Randolph to Robert E. Wood, July 7, 1938; R. E. Wood to Henry Morgenthau, July 9, 1938; William H. McReynolds to R. E. Wood, July 15, 1938; "Memorandum for Mr. Thompson," September 12, 1938; Alexander Jamie to Henry Morgenthau, September 1, 1938; W. N. Thompson to Alexander Jamie, n.d.; Henry Morgenthau to R. E. Wood, September 27, 1938, all in Alexander G. Jamie OPF. Grant, *Fight for a City*, pp. 234–236 (235, "Co-ordinating Committee for"). Barnhart and Schlickman, *Kerner*, pp. 247–249. Hoffman, *Scarface Al*, pp. 170–171. Merriner, *Grafters and Goo-Goos*, p. 127.

The FBI memos refer to the fired stenographer as "Jamie's sister-in-law," and this can only be Edna Ness. Her resignation from the Prohibition Bureau states that she left "to accept a position with the Chicago Association of Commerce," the organization behind the Secret Six. (Resignation Form for Use of Field Service, November 6, 1930, in Edna S. Ness OPF.)

Decades later, the elderly Kub would win over another federal man, IRS special agent Jack Walsh, with essentially the same story, which she then referred to as Chicago's "true syndicate." Fascinated by what he learned, Walsh founded a special unit in the Chicago IRS office known as CRIMP (for "Conspiracy, Racketeer, Immunity, Money, Politicians") to explore connections between politics and organized crime. Walsh and CRIMP eventually discovered evidence linking then-Illinois governor Otto Kerner to corruption in the horse-racing industry, which began the investigation leading to Kerner's incarceration. Meanwhile, the IRS charged Kub with income tax evasion on payoffs she'd received from politicians, apparently to force her cooperation on other investigations. Despite being too ill to attend trial, she fought the case for six years until she lost her final appeal in 1977, when she was in her nineties. (Barnhart and Schlickman, *Kerner*, pp. 256–274.)

NESS RAIDS CRIPPLING BEER BUSINESS: CT, May 29, 1932; July 14, 1932 ("Matters became so," "Mussolini"); August 3, 1932; September 3, 1932; September 17, 1932; September 20, 1932; October 5, 1932; January 10, 1933 ("Why pick me"); October 22, 1938. "Big Buying Wave Brewing," n.p., n.d., in ENPS, Roll 1, Scrapbook 1, p. 42. CHE, July 7, 1932, in ENPS, Roll 1, Scrapbook 1, p. 48. "3 Held in Beer Raid Near Loop," n.p., n.d., in ENPS, Roll 1, Scrapbook 1, p. 49. "New Gang Chief May Be Elected by Machine Guns," n.p., n.d., in ENPS, Roll 1, Scrapbook 1, p. 46. "Cost of Living May Be Cut, But Beer's Still Up," n.p., n.d., in ENPS, Roll 1, Scrapbook 1. CDN, September 12, 1932, in ENPS, Roll 1, Scrapbook 1, p. 52 ("We have seized"). "Drys' Score Is 2,700 to 10,000 in 'Pin Game,'" n.p., September 17, 1932, in "Newspaper Clippings (Photocopies) Circa 1930–1970" folder, DMM. CEA, September 19, 1932, in ENPS, Roll 1, Scrapbook 1, p. 49 ("We'll close these"). CHE, December 28, 1932 ("For there were"); CEA, December 28, 1932, both in ENPS, Roll 1, Scrapbook 1, p. 52. Ness and Fraley, *The Untouchables*, pp. 237, 240. Keefe, *Man Who Got Away*, pp. 276–278, 304.

NITTO AND CERMAK SHOOTINGS: CT, December 21, 1932. LAT, December 21, 1932. Lyle, *Dry and Lawless Years*, pp. 254, 258–268. Gottfried, *Boss Cermak*, pp. 318–324, 424–425. Allsop, *Bootleggers*, pp. 169–170. Murray, *Legacy of Al Capone*, pp. 175–179. Lindberg, *To Serve and Collect*, pp. 233–236 (235, "hoodlum squad"). Eghigian, *After Capone*, pp. 216–234, 246–252.

NESS, FUSCO, AND THE END OF PROHIBITION: "$100,000 Capone Brewery Raided; Two Men Arrested," n.p., n.d.; "$100,000 Beer Plant Raided By U.S. Drys," n.p., n.d., both in ENPS, Roll 1, Scrapbook 1, p. 54. CT, March 29, 1933; August 13, 1936; June 3, 1941; October 19, 1950; October 24, 1961; December 6, 1976. "Brewers Told Hoodlums Are Periling Trade," n.p., n.d., in ENPS, Roll 1, Scrapbook 1, p. 55 ("or else"). "Ness Proposes Beer Dictator to Bar Gangs," n.p., n.d., in ENPS, Roll 1, Scrapbook 1, p. 56 ("Only a dictator"). CDN, March 23–24, 1948. W. D. Amis, Memo Re: "Joe Fusco Gold Seal Liquor, Inc.," October 3, 1950; W. D. Amis, Memo Re: "Joe Fusco Gold Seal Liquor, Inc.—Conclusion and Comments," October 3, 1950; Memo, "SUBJECT: Testimony of Joseph C. Fusco," October 4, 1950 ("not very strong"), all in Box 86, "Fusco, Joseph C. (Joe)" folder, KC. "Mr. McCain," Memo Re: "Joe Fusco," October 17, 1950; "Chicago Crime Commission Letter, September 25, 1950—Bloom," both in Box 88, "Gold Seal Liquors" folder, KC. *Hearings Before the Special Committee to Investigate Organized Crime in Interstate Commerce*, pt. 5, pp. 558–569, 593–622. Peterson, *Barbarians in Our Midst*, pp. 299–303 (303, "The repeal of"). Virgil Peterson, "The Mob Goes Legit," CT Magazine, November 11, 1956, p. 44. Behr, *Prohibition*, pp. 234–236. "The Road to Repeal" ("just as fast," "that this is"). Eghigian, *After Capone*, pp. 229, 238, 291, 293–294, 354. Alter, *Defining Moment*, p. 277 ("PRESIDENT ROOSEVELT," "Bars were opening"). Skilnik, *Beer*, pp. 173–178 (175, "from top to"), 193–195, 217–218. Haller, *Illegal Enterprise*, pp. 203–207. McGirr, *War on Alcohol*, pp. xiii–xiv (xiii, "It's time the"), 243, 246.

PROHIBITION BUREAU AND DIVISION OF INVESTIGATION: CT, April 8, 1933; April 11, 1933; June 23–24, 1933; August 7, 1933 ("elders"). "Raid Largest Capone Still," n.p., n.d., in ENPS, Roll 2, Scrapbook 1, p. 56. Ness and Fraley, *The Untouchables*, pp. 220–228 ("cooker in the sky"). De Toledano, *J. Edgar Hoover*, pp. 100–101 (101, "They would have"). Powers, *Secrecy and Power*, pp. 102–105 (103, "super police force"; 185, "American Scotland Yard"). "The Road to Repeal." Potter, *War on Crime*, pp. 29, 118–125. Burrough, *Public Enemies*, pp. 9–15, 48–53, 58–59, 308–315, 323–325, 367–371. Folsom, *Money Trail*, pp. 221, 223. Erick Trickey, "Eliot Ness vs. J. Edgar Hoover," *Smithsonian*, October 2014, p. 81. McGirr, *War on Alcohol*, p. 233.

NITTO TAKES OVER: Anonymous to J. Edgar Hoover, November 30, 1936, in FBI-AC. CDN, February 14, 1939, in FBI-SVDM. Murray, *Legacy of Al Capone*, pp. 181–205 (183, "We've got the"; 185, "If you don't"), 275. Helmer and Mattix, *Public Enemies*, pp. 21, 28–29. Russo, *Outfit*, pp. 135–148, 158–163. Eghigian, *After Capone*, pp. 239–240 ("independent bastards"), 252–259, 261–272, 289–297, 300–304, 336–337. Helmer, *Al Capone and His American Boys*, pp. 206–254, 272, 321–323, 345.

O'HARE LATER LIFE AND MURDER: CT, November 16, 1939 ("put a serious"); October 23, 1955. Metz, "Mystery of Eddie," pp. 44–49, 87–92. Ewing and Lundstrom, *Fateful Rendezvous*, pp. 76–80, 85–86, 303, 313. Eghigian, *After Capone*, pp. 325–329. Helmer, *Al Capone and His American Boys*, p. 285.

SHUMWAY COUP THEORY: Visitors' Register, January 22, 1931; untitled note, October 29, 1931, both in Box 71, "Nitto, Frank (1 of 1)" folder, NOF. CT, November 16, 1939 ("gang associate"). *Miami Herald*, November 13, 1935; December 30, 1935; January 12, 1936; November 16, 1936; December 11, 1936; December 27, 1936; December 11, 1938; December 25, 1938; December 10, 1939; December 27, 1939; December 19, 1943; December 4, 1949; February 26, 1950; August 11, 1950; January 17, 1964. Metz, "Mystery of Eddie," p. 91. *Hearings Before the Special Committee to Investigate Organized Crime in Interstate Commerce*, pt. 1, pp. 616–632 (628, "If I had"). *Hearings Before the Special Committee to Investigate Organized Crime in Interstate Commerce*, pt. 5, pp. 1295–1297. Eghigian, *After Capone*, pp. 193–194, 205. Helmer, *Al Capone and His American Boys*, p. 287. Record for Leslie Shumway, *U.S. Social Security Death Index, 1935–2014* (Provo, UT: Ancestry.com Operations, 2011).

Shumway's working at an Outfit-affiliated racetrack fits the pattern of how the gang rewarded other people who took risks for them—such as Leo Brothers, who took the fall for Jake Lingle's murder and received comfortable jobs in mob-run businesses once he got out of prison. (See Schoenberg, *Mr. Capone*, p. 285.)

NESS AND KULAK: George Golding to the Director of Prohibition, August 30, 1930, pp. 30–31, George Golding OPF/ATF. "Coyne Is Made New Prohibition Chief," n.p., n.d., in ENPS, Roll 1, Scrapbook 1, p. 46. "Robert W. Coyne Made Dry Czar in Chicago Area," n.p., August 19, 1933, in ENPS, Roll 1, Scrapbook 1, p. 47. W. A. S. Douglas, "Kindling-Wood Peddler," *The American Mercury*, July 1933, p. 341. Statement of Walter B. Newton, August 26, 1933 ("patted Mr. Ness," "that it would," "that if the," "very few," "take care of," "shook his head"); Statement of Joseph Kulak Jr., August 26, 1933; J. J. Keating, memorandum for Special Agent in Charge M. H. Purvis, November 27, 1933; M. H. Purvis to J. E. Hoover, November 28, 1933; Undated notes ("or E. Ness"), all in FBI-ENA. Service record card, Eliot Ness OPF. Burrough, *Public Enemies*, p. 147. Sagalyn, *A Promise Fulfilled*, p. 49. See also Trickey, "Eliot Ness vs. J. Edgar Hoover," pp. 80, 82.

NESS'S MARITAL PROBLEMS: M. H. Purvis to J. E. Hoover, November 28, 1933, in FBI-ENA ("apparently preferred to," "a very dear"). Heimel, *Eliot Ness*, p. 145.

NESS TRIES TO JOIN FBI: CT, August 10, 1932; December 8, 1932; July 22, 1933; September 21, 1949. George E. Q. Johnson to J. Edgar Hoover, October 30, 1933 ("did a splendid"); J. Edgar Hoover to George E. Q. Johnson, November 3, 1933; J. Edgar Hoover to Special Agent in Charge, November 7, 1933 ("preferred attention"); J. Edgar Hoover to Eliot Ness, November 7, 1933; W. S. Murphy, Report on Eliot Ness, November 15, 1933; P. T. Sowell, Report on Eliot Ness, November 21, 1933; Howard P. Locke, memorandum for the Director, November 25, 1933; M. H. Purvis to J. E. Hoover, November 28, 1933 ("a connection between"); M. H. Purvis to J. E. Hoover, November 28, 1933; Memorandum, December 1, 1933; M. H. Purvis to J. E. Hoover, December 1, 1933 ("Boss is using"); J. Edgar Hoover, notation on M. H. Purvis to J. E. Hoover, December 1, 1933 ("I do not"); Howard P. Locke, memorandum for the Director, December 13, 1933 ("political influence," "after the removal," "does not appear," "primarily a politician," "temperamentally unfit for"); M. H. Purvis to J. E. Hoover, January 5, 1934, all in FBI-ENA. George E. Q. Johnson to J. Edgar Hoover, October 30, 1933; Eliot Ness to George E. Q. Johnson, November 6, 1933, both in ENPS, Roll 1, Scrapbook 1. W. H. D. Lester to J. Edgar Hoover, May 28, 1936, in FBI-EN. Lender and Martin, *Drinking in America*, pp. 134–136. Bergreen, *Capone*, pp. 420–421, 594–595. Heimel, *Eliot Ness*, p. 188. Cahan, *Court That Shaped America*, p. 96. Burrough, *Public Enemies*, pp. 65–68, 147, 247–249, 369–373, 411–412. Eig, *Get Capone*, pp. 387–388. See also Trickey, "Eliot Ness," pp. 80–81.

Much of the gossip Purvis forwarded to Hoover came from L. D. Nichols, the Prohibition agent who'd lent Edna Ness a sympathetic ear. Now he seemed determined to sully her husband's reputation however he could. He related to Purvis a story that Maurice Seager (identified in the letter as "Morris Seeger") had told him about "a drunken party" supposedly held by several Untouchables. After learning of the incident from an alleged witness, George Johnson put the men up for charges, but Seager rushed to their defense. He was the only Untouchable the witness knew by sight, and he could prove he hadn't been at any party that night. As soon as Seager demanded a hearing, Johnson dropped the charges against the others. Nichols couldn't say whether Ness had attended the party, or whether the party had even happened, but he assailed Ness's character shamelessly. "Mr. Nichols," Purvis wrote, "states that it is the opinion of various persons who have come in contact with Mr. Eliot Ness . . . that Mr. Ness is an undermining sort of an individual and that he creates dissensions wherever he goes." Nichols's evident dislike of Ness suggests this statement, at least, carried some truth. (M. H. Purvis to J. E. Hoover, November 28, 1933, in FBI-ENA.)

1933 WORLD'S FAIR: CT, May 28, 1933; November 1, 1934. Norman F. Baker to August Vollmer, November 29, 1933, in Box 2, "Baker, Norman Freese, 1898–1941" folder; Leonarde Keeler to August Vollmer, March 19, 1934, in Box 17, "Keeler, Leonarde" folder ("Chicago's most beautiful"), both in August Vollmer Papers, BANC MSS C-B 403, UCB. CHE, June 8, 1934 ("director of public"); CEA, June 8, 1934, both in RIR Scrapbook IV. Calvin Goddard, "A History of Firearm Identification," n.d., p. 17, MM. Murray, *Legacy of Al Capone*, pp. 181–182 (182, "If a wheel"). Hoffman, *Scarface Al*, pp. 167–168. Russo, *Outfit*, pp. 97–99. Boehm, *Popular Culture*, pp. 107–125 (107, "adorn Chicago's reputation"). Eghigian, *After*

Capone, pp. 237–238. Alder, *Lie Detectors*, p. 137. Pacyga, *Chicago*, pp. 140–141, 143 ("White City"), 264–265 (264, "Rainbow City"). Kim Waggoner, "The FBI Laboratory: 75 Years of Forensic Science Service," *Forensic Science Communications*, vol. 9, no. 4 (October 2007), https://archives.fbi.gov/archives/about-us/lab/forensic-science-communications/fsc/oct 2007/research (accessed August 8, 2016).

CONCLUSION: Sullivan, *Rattling the Cup*, p. 57 ("I told them"). M. A. Jones to Mr. Nease, January 1959, in FBI-ENA. Milton S. Mayer, "Myth of the 'G Men,' " *The Forum*, September 1935, p. 148 ("The war on"). Powers, *G-Men*, pp. xi–xix, 24–25, 33–50, 74–93, 102–109, 139–160. Schoenberg, *Mr. Capone*, p. 24 ("There's plenty for"). Potter, *War on Crime*, pp. 5, 29, 57–74, 118, 121–139, 141, 198. Burrough, *Public Enemies*, p. 154. "The View From Mt. Carmel," CT, September 28, 2007, http://articles.chicagotribune.com/2007–09–28 /news/0709270652_1_mt-mob-family-secrets (accessed November 25, 2017). Cheryl Honigford, "Morbid Detour—the Celebrities of Mt. Carmel," July 28, 2017, http://cherylhonig ford.com/index.php/2017/07/28/morbid-detour-the-celebrities-of-mt-carmel/ (accessed November 25, 2017).

Epilogue

NESS'S SECOND CAREER: Transfer Order, March 10, 1934; Arthur J. Mellott to Eliot Ness, August 7, 1934; Service Record Card, n.d., all in Eliot Ness OPF. "Liquor Office Lost to Cincinnati," n.p., n.d.; "Alcohol Tax Unit to Be Abolished," n.p., n.d., both in ENPS, Roll 1, Scrapbook 1. CPD, September 19, 1934 ("an average of"); January 11, 1936. Eliot Ness to August Vollmer, December 16, 1935; Eliot Ness to August Vollmer, January 4, 1936, both in Box 24, "Ness, Eliot" folder, August Vollmer Papers, BANC MSS C-B 403, UCB. August Vollmer to Eliot Ness, December 26, 1935, in Box 44, "Letters Written By Vollmer, Dec. 1935" folder, August Vollmer Papers, BANC MSS C-B 403, UCB. August Vollmer to Eliot Ness, January 17, 1936; August Vollmer to Mrs. Herman Matzen, January 23, 1936, both in Box 44, "Letters Written By Vollmer Jan.–Feb. 1936" folder, August Vollmer Papers, BANC MSS C-B 403, UCB. CN, April 4, 1936, in ENPS, Roll 1, Scrapbook 2, p. 62 ("Dick Tracy Detective"). CPD, February 21, 1937, in ENPS, Roll 1, Scrapbook 5, p. 142. CP, August 4, 1937, in ENPS, Roll 2, Scrapbook 6, p. 39. CPD, December 10, 1937, in ENPS, Roll 2, Scrapbook 10, p. 12. CPD, December 16, 1937, in ENPS, Roll 2, Scrapbook 10, p. 16. Elliot H. [*sic*] Ness, "Public Safety and the Three E's: Enforcement—Engineering—Education," *The Clevelander*, March 1938, pp. 4, 21, in ENPS, Roll 2, Scrapbook 10, pp. 135–136. *Buffalo Courier-Express*, February 2, 1938, in ENPS, Roll 2, Scrapbook 10, pp. 80–81. *Buffalo Courier-Express*, February 6, 1938, in ENPS, Roll 2, Scrapbook 10, p. 81. CT, July 21, 1939 ("Millions have been"). Eliot Ness, "Radio-Directed Mobile Police," *The American City*, November 1939, pp. 35–36. Eliot Ness, "The Participation of Boys," *The Phi Delta Kappan*, March 1940, pp. 337–344. CPD, March 31, 1939, in ENPS, Roll 2, Scrapbook 8, p. 133. CN, March 29, 1940, in ENPS, Roll 2, Scrapbook 7, p. 104. Eliot Ness, "Streamlining Protection," *Real Detective*, October 1941, pp. 4, 92. Ness and Fraley, *The Untouchables*, pp. 255–256 (255, "Moonshine Mountains"). Messick, *Silent Syndicate*, pp. 10, 29, 85, 89–125, 132–133, 138–140, 174–175. Messick, *Secret File*, pp. 26–27. Porter, *Cleveland*, pp. 97–103. Jedick, "Eliot Ness," pp. 49–57. Van Tassel and Grabowski, *Encyclopedia of Cleveland History*, p. 122. Scott Leeson Sroka,

"Revisionist Theory," CT, October 16, 2011, http://www.chicagotribune.com/news/opinion /ct-perspec-1016-untouchables-20111016,0,3602318,print.story (accessed October 16, 2011).

CAPONE'S LATER YEARS: Alphonse Capone Identification Card, in Box 0202, "[Capone, Alphonse] Capone-Atlanta #1 [40886-A] [Folder 1 of 4]" folder, BOP-AP. Sanford Bates, "To the Warden of the U.S. Penitentiary, Atlanta, Georgia or His Duly Authorized Representative; and to the Warden of the U.S. Penitentiary, Alcatraz Island, California," August 15, 1934, in Box 0202, "[Capone, Alphonse] Capone-Atlanta #1 [40886-A] [Folder 2 of 4]" folder, BOP-AP. "Capone, Alphonse, Case History," October 23, 1939, in Box 0205, "[Capone, Alphonse] 1–19 [397-CAL]" folder, BOP-AP. Schoenberg, *Mr. Capone*, pp. 330–355 (353, "He is nutty as"). Bair, *Al Capone*, pp. 255–297 (285, "He talked to").

NESS'S LATER YEARS AND *THE UNTOUCHABLES*: Fraley, "Real Eliot Ness," pp. 26–30. William J. Ayers, "As I Knew Eliot Ness," *The Potter Enterprise Sportsmen's Special*, November 24, 1971, PCHS. Jedick, "Eliot Ness," pp. 92–94. Scott Martell, "'Untouchable' Memories," *News-Press*, December 7, 1994, PCHS. "Bill Ayers," n.d., PWH. "Virginia Kallenborn Interview," March 25, 2000, PWH ("It makes me"). Paul Heimel, "Coudersport's Most Famous Citizen," *Potter Leader-Enterprise*, April 16, 2003 (http://www.tiogapublishing.com /potter_leader_enterprise/coudersport-s-most-famous-citizen/article_cb0189bf-8079-5abd -873d-cd6cdf3eaff4.html [accessed December 6, 2017]). Dyja, *Third Coast*, p. 385 ("Whatever else the").

CHICAGO'S REVIVAL AND DALEY: Spinney, *City of Big Shoulders*, pp. 213–240 (214, "Chicago personified"; 216, "The old bosses"; 219, "the Builder"). Pacyga, *Chicago*, pp. 288–290, 324–327 (325, "Chicago ain't ready"), 342, 347. Dyja, *Third Coast*, pp. xxi–xxxiv, 66, 260–264, 296–301, 304, 328–343, 396–397, and *passim*. "History and Facts," Willis Tower, http://www.willistower.com/history-and-facts (accessed December 10, 2017).

GANGSTER BUILDINGS DEMOLISHED: CT, April 9, 1967; November 1, 1967 ("Generally we try"); February 17, 1972; August 2, 1978; February 11, 1979; December 23, 1979; February 13, 1987. LAT, October 17, 1988. *Chicago Sun-Times*, October 16, 1988; December 4, 1988; May 22, 1992. Lindberg, *Return to the Scene*, pp. xii–xiii, 101–102, 366–373, 379–381. Bilek, *First Vice Lord*, p. 264. Mario Gomes, "The Four Deuces," My Al Capone Museum, May 2009, http://www.myalcaponemuseum.com/id152.htm (accessed November 14, 2017). Pacyga, *Chicago*, p. 327. Edward McClelland, "It's Time to Embrace Al Capone," NBC Chicago, April 21, 2011, https://www.nbcchicago.com/blogs/ward-room/its-time -to-embrace-al-capone-120363329.html (accessed November 14, 2017). Cahan, *Court That Shaped America*, pp. 107–108, 140–142, 154–159 (156, "cracker box surroundings," "pure justice"). "St. Valentine's Day Massacre Wall," The Mob Museum, https://themobmuseum .org/exhibits/st-valentines-day-massacre-wall/ (accessed December 6, 2017).

SOUTH SIDE SLUMS AND METROPOLE: CT, January 31, 1975 ("attached to the," "a good old"); January 11, 1976 ("How long will"). Spinney, *City of Big Shoulders*, pp. 220, 227–228 (227, "Black Belt"), 231, 240 ("city that works"). Pacyga, *Chicago*, pp. 292–293 (293, "Second Ghetto"), 300, 307. Dyja, *Third Coast*, pp. xxvi, 393 ("On Lake Shore").

PRAIRIE AVENUE LANDMARK FIGHT: NYT, November 29, 1954 ("the father of"); March 22, 1989; April 21, 1989. *Chicago Sun-Times*, October 16, 1988 ("Chicago's most famous"); October 18, 1988 ("No doubt, Chicago"); October 28, 1988 ("Chicago has vainly," "this attempt to," "stereotype all Italians"); October 30, 1988; April 14, 1989; April 17, 1989; April 20, 1989; May 30, 1989. CT, April 14, 1989; October 29, 2014 ("Untouchable"). AJ Latrace, "Al Capone's First Chicago Home Returns with Big Price Chop," Curbed Chicago, February 4, 2016, https://chicago.curbed.com/2016/2/4/10941846/al-capones-house -returns (accessed November 29, 2017). 7244 S Prairie Ave, Zillow, https://www.zillow.com /homedetails/7244-s-prairie-ave-chicago-il-60619/2140426578_zpid/ (accessed November 29, 2017).

LEXINGTON HOTEL: *Chicago Sun-Times*, April 21, 1986; April 22, 1986 ("Capone safe-cracking," "With no panes"); August 23, 1989; September 30, 1989; August 17, 1995 ("It's a monstrosity"); August 20, 1995 ("a stinking corpse"); November 12, 1995; November 29, 1995. *The Mystery of Al Capone's Vaults* ("that toddling town"). David Bock, "Geraldo Rivera's Failure Launches His Career," *Entertainment Weekly*, April 22, 1994, http://ew.com/article /1994/04/22/geraldo-riveras-failure-launches-his-career/ (accessed November 29, 2017). Jake Rossen, "Oral History: 30 Years Ago, Geraldo Rivera Opened Al Capone's Vault," Mental Floss, April 21, 2016, http://mentalfloss.com/article/78842/oral-history-30-years-ago -geraldo-rivera-opened-al-capones-vault (accessed November 29, 2017) ("I was pretty"). Noel Murray, "When Geraldo Rivera Opened Al Capone's Vault, He Turned Nothing Into Ratings," The A.V. Club, October 25, 2016, https://tv.avclub.com/when-geraldo-rivera-opened -al-capone-s-vault-he-turned-1798253506 (accessed November 29, 2017).

DALEY, POLICE, AND THE MOB: Allsop, *Bootleggers*, pp. xi–xv. Spinney, *City of Big Shoulders*, pp. 217 ("amputated an appendage"), 224–226. Russo, *Outfit*, pp. 303–306 (304, "The police department"; 305, "another chance"; 306, "Well, it's there"). Alder, *Lie Detectors*, p. 245. Pacyga, *Chicago*, pp. 343–344. Dyja, *Third Coast*, pp. 226–228, 281, 332, 334.

OUTFIT'S RISE AND FALL / RICO: Russo, *Outfit*, pp. 327–504 (383, "There's money pouring"; 474, "Mob Lite," "The Outfit is"; 477, "They're everywhere"). Gregory J. Wallace, "Outgunning the Mob," *ABA Journal*, March 1994, pp. 60–65 (63, "You've got to"; 65, "What about Big"), 109–115. Mark Gordon, "Ideas Shoot Bullets: How the RICO Act Became a Potent Weapon in the War Against Organized Crime," *Concept*, vol. 26 (2003), https://concept .journals.villanova.edu/article/view/312/275 (accessed December 2, 2017). CT, April 26, 2005; March 7, 2007 ("Eliot Ness with"); September 26, 2017 (http://www.chicagotribune .com/news/data/ct-homicide-spikes-comparison-htmlstory.html [accessed December 4, 2017]). Simon Tisdall, "CIA Conspired with Mafia to Kill Castro," *The Guardian*, June 27, 2007, https://www.theguardian.com/world/2007/jun/27/usa.cuba (accessed November 30, 2017). "Family Secrets of the Murderous Kind," Federal Bureau of Investigation, October 1, 2007, https://archives.fbi.gov/archives/news/stories/2007/october/famsecrets_100107 (accessed December 2, 2017). *Wall Street Journal*, January 20, 2011, http://www.wsj.com/articles /sb10001424052748704881304576094110829882704 (accessed December 2, 2017). Scott Burnstein, "Ten Years Ago, Epic 'Family Secrets' Trial Crippled the Chicago Outfit," The Mob Museum, July 13, 2017, https://themobmuseum.org/blog/epic-family-secrets-trial -crippled-chicago-outfit/ (accessed December 2, 2017).

SOUTH SIDE VIOLENCE: *The Trentonian*, September 10, 2013, http://www.trentonian.com /article/tt/20130910/news04/130909760 (accessed December 2, 2017). NYT, March 22, 2014, https://www.nytimes.com/2014/03/23/us/the-catholic-roots-of-obamas-activism.html

(accessed November 11, 2017). CT, October 9, 2015, http://www.chicagotribune.com/news
/ct-ceasefire-funds-frozen-as-chicago-shootings-climb-20151009-story.html (accessed December 6, 2017); December 30, 2016, http://www.chicagotribune.com/news/opinion/page
/ct-chicago-murders-gun-violence-gary-slutkin-ceasefire-perspec-0101-jm-20161230-story
.html (accessed December 6, 2017); September 26, 2017, http://www.chicagotribune.com
/news/data/ct-homicide-spikes-comparison-htmlstory.html (accessed December 6, 2017).
Josh Saul, "Why 2016 Has Been Chicago's Bloodiest Year in Almost Two Decades," *News-
week*, December 15, 2016, http://www.newsweek.com/2016/12/23/chicago-gangs-violence
-murder-rate-532034.html (accessed December 6, 2017). Garrow, *Rising Star*, pp. 1–7, 24–29,
208–209. Binder, *Al Capone's Beer Wars*, pp. 271–275. Josh Sanburn and David Johnson,
"See Chicago's Deadly Year in 3 Charts," *Time*, January 17, 2017, http://time.com/4635049
/chicago-murder-rate-homicides/ (accessed December 6, 2017). Eliott C. McLaughlin, "With
Chicago, It's All Murder, Murder, Murder . . . But Why?" CNN, March 6, 2017, http://
www.cnn.com/2017/03/06/us/chicago-murder-rate-not-highest/index.html (accessed December 5, 2017) ("the murder capital"). Rafael Mangual, "Sub-Chicago and America's Real
Crime Rate," *City Journal*, Summer 2017, https://www.city-journal.org/html/sub-chicago
-and-americas-real-crime-rate-15341.html (accessed December 5, 2017). J. Weston Phippen,
"Trump Says He's Sending the Feds into Chicago," *The Atlantic*, June 30, 2017, https://www
.theatlantic.com/news/archive/2017/06/trump-chicago-gun-task-force/532410/ (accessed
November 30, 2017) ("send in the"). "Chicago Accounted for 22% of a Nationwide Increase
in Murders Last Year," *The Economist*, September 26, 2017, https://www.economist.com
/blogs/democracyinamerica/2017/09/neighbourhood-watch (accessed December 6, 2017).
"2016 Stats," Heyjackass!, 2017, http://heyjackass.com/category/2016-stats/ (accessed December 6, 2017).

CAPONE AND CHICAGO'S IMAGE: Ford and Crowther, *Moving Forward*, p. 280 ("economically right," "There can be"). Sullivan, *Chicago Surrenders*, p. 204 ("I can't change"). Lerner,
America as a Civilization, pp. 663–666. *Chicago Sun-Times*, October 28, 1988 ("This fiend
killed"); September 17, 1989 ("Are there still," "It's a very"); January 27, 1991 ("Disney-like,"
"Al Capone was"); May 22, 1992; June 25, 1993; June 7–8 1994; June 15, 1994; February 16,
2010. D'Eramo, *Pig and the Skyscraper*, pp. 3, 7–9 (9, "It cannot be"). Edward McClelland,
"It's Time to Embrace Al Capone," NBC Chicago, April 21, 2011, https://www.nbcchicago
.com/blogs/ward-room/its-time-to-embrace-al-capone-120363329.html (accessed November
14, 2017). Melanie Nayer, "From Prohibition to Playmates: Blackstone Hotel Showcases Chicago's Past," Boston.com, December 12, 2011, http://archive.boston.com/travel/explorene/
blogs/packup/2011/12/blackstone_hotel_showcases_chicagos_past.html (accessed December 6, 2017). Harris, *World Film Locations*, p. 62.

NESS'S CHICAGO LEGACY / ATF BUILDING: *The Untouchables* (1987), directed by Brian
De Palma (Hollywood: Paramount Pictures, 2004), DVD ("the Chicago way"). Spinney,
City of Big Shoulders, p. 3 ("City of the"). NYT, March 22, 1989; December 18, 2010, http://
www.nytimes.com/2010/12/19/us/19cncbrightonpark.html (accessed December 2, 2017)
("old-school"); March 5, 2014 ("purely symbolic resolution"). *Chicago Sun-Times*, July 23,
2007 ("It's not so"); May 25, 2009 ("the city's most"); January 13, 2010 ("the City Council's,"
"If nothing else," "a lousy stunt"); January 16, 2014 ("Malone told me"); February 28, 2014;

March 9, 2014 ("Much as we"); March 11, 2014. Eliot Ness ATF Building Designation Act, S. 1914, 113th Cong. (2014). Dick Durbin, "Durbin, Brown, and Kirk Introduce Bipartisan Resolution to Honor Famed Prohibition Agent Eliot Ness," press release, January 10, 2014, https://www.durbin.senate.gov/newsroom/press-releases/durbin-brown-and-kirk-introduce -bipartisan-resolution-to-honor-famed-prohibition-agent-eliot-ness (accessed December 2, 2017) ("Chicago gangster Al"). Peter Bella, "Eliot Ness, the Myth, the Legend, the Lie," Chicago Now, January 12, 2014, http://www.chicagonow.com/interesting-chicago/2014/01 /eliot-ness-the-myth-the-legend-the-lie/ (accessed December 2, 2017). "Argument Contin- ues over Naming ATF Building After Eliott [sic] Ness," 89 WLS, January 21, 2014, http:// www.wlsam.com/common/page.php?pt=argument+continues+over+naming+atf+build ing+after+eliott+nessandid=82334andis_corp-0 (accessed January 24, 2014) ("I think he"). CT, January 24, 2014. "The Eliot Ness Monstrosity," *The Weekly Standard*, February 3, 2014, http://www.weeklystandard.com/eliot-ness-monstrosity/article/775319 (accessed Decem- ber 2, 2017). LAT, March 2, 2014 ("He's a Hollywood"). Richard Horgan, "How Reddit Stole a Colorado Journalist's Wizard of Oz Thunder," Adweek, November 5, 2012, http://www.ad week.com/digital/rick-polito-lee-winfrey-jay-leno-reddit-george-takei-wizard-oz/#/ (accessed December 2, 2017) ("A federal agent"). Sean O'Neal and Ignatiy Vishnevetsky, "*The Un- touchables* mythologized a city the Chicago way," The A.V. Club, June 2, 2017, https://film .avclub.com/the-untouchables-mythologized-a-city-the-chicago-way-1798163914 (accessed November 11, 2017) ("the real Eliot"). ABS visit to ATF headquarters, September 13, 2016.
CONCLUSION: Christopher Crowe, *The Untouchables*, "Pilot (Working Draft)," July 28, 1992, p. 50 ("Johnny, people want"), ABS. CT, November 15, 1998. James D. McMahon, "Plaque Commemorating Opening of Michigan Avenue Bridge," *Encyclopedia of Chicago*, 2005, http:// www.encyclopedia.chicagohistory.org/pages/10481.html (accessed December 2, 2017). Kend- all, "Colosimo's Cafe," The Chicago Crime Scenes Project, August 30, 2008, http://chicago crimescenes.blogspot.com/2008/08/colosimos-cafe.html (accessed November 26, 2017). "Tommy Gun's Garage," https://www.tommygunsgarage.com (accessed November 14, 2017). *Chicago Sun-Times*. July 28, 2006 February 16, 2010 ("one of Chicago's"). Joe Zekas, "The LEX Apartments, 2138 S Indiana Ave, South Loop," YoChicago, December 2, 2013, http:// yochicago.com/the-lex-apartments-2138-s-indiana-st-south-loop/32815/ (accessed November 14, 2017). ABS visit to Chicago, May 14, 2015 ("South Michigan Avenue"). O'Neal and Vish- nevetsky, "*The Untouchables* mythologized" ("all the concentrated"). "Gangster Tour," Farehar- bor Support, YouTube, 2:30, June 15, 2017, https://youtu.be/biP_j_h1V1g (accessed November 14, 2017).

Note on Sources

Estleman, "Stuart Lake: Frontier Mythmaker," p. xi ("who in their"). Shapiro, *Yale Book of Quo- tations,* p. 130 ("You can get"). Eig, *Get Capone,* p. 81 ("best captured the"). O'Toole, *Hem- ingway Didn't Say That,* pp. 216–219.

Bibliography

Books

Ackerman, Kenneth D. *Young J. Edgar: Hoover, the Red Scare, and the Assault on Civil Liberties*. New York: Carroll and Graf, 2007.

Adelman, William. *Touring Pullman: A Study in Company Paternalism*. 2nd ed. Chicago: Illinois Labor Historical Society, 1977.

Album of Genealogy and Biography, Cook County, Illinois. Chicago: Calumet Book and Engraving, 1896.

Alder, Ken. *The Lie Detectors: The History of an American Obsession*. New York: Free Press, 2007.

Allen, Frederick Lewis. *Only Yesterday: An Informal History of the Nineteen-Twenties*. New York: Harper and Brothers, 1931.

———. *Since Yesterday: The Nineteen-Thirties in America, September 3, 1929–September 3, 1939*. New York: Harper and Brothers, 1940.

Allsop, Kenneth. *The Bootleggers: The Story of Chicago's Prohibition Era*. London: Hutchinson, 1968.

Alter, Jonathan. *The Defining Moment: FDR's Hundred Days and the Triumph of Hope*. New York: Simon and Schuster, 2006.

Asbury, Herbert. *Gem of the Prairie: An Informal History of the Chicago Underworld*. New York: Alfred A. Knopf, 1940.

Bair, Deirdre. *Al Capone: His Life, Legacy, and Legend*. New York: Nan A. Talese, 2016.

Balsamo, William, and John Balsamo. *Young Al Capone: The Untold Story of Scarface in New York, 1899–1925*. New York: Skyhorse Publishing, 2011.

Barlett, Donald L., and James B. Steele. *Howard Hughes: His Life and Madness*. New York: W. W. Norton, 1979.

Barnhart, Bill, and Gene Schlickman. *Kerner: The Conflict of Intangible Rights*. Urbana: University of Illinois Press, 1999.

Behr, Edward. *Prohibition: Thirteen Years That Changed America*. New York: Arcade Publishing, 1996.

Benjey, Tom. *Doctors, Lawyers, Indian Chiefs: Jim Thorpe and Pop Warner's Carlisle Indian School football immortals tackle socialites, bootleggers, students, moguls, prejudice, the government, ghouls, tooth decay and rum*. Carlisle, PA: Tuxedo Press, 2008.

Berg, A. Scott. *Lindbergh*. New York: G. P. Putnam's Sons, 1998.

Bergreen, Laurence. *Capone: The Man and the Era*. New York: Simon and Schuster, 1994.

Berle, Milton, with Haskel Frankel. *Milton Berle: An Autobiography*. New York: Delacorte Press, 1974.

Bilek, Arthur J. *The First Vice Lord: Big Jim Colosimo and the Ladies of the Levee*. Nashville, TN: Cumberland House, 2008.

Binder, John J. *Al Capone's Beer Wars: A Complete History of Organized Crime in Chicago During Prohibition*. Amherst, NY: Prometheus Books, 2017.

Black, Gregory D. *Hollywood Censored: Morality Codes, Catholics, and the Movies*. Cambridge: Cambridge University Press, 1994.

Boehm, Lisa Krissoff. *Popular Culture and the Enduring Myth of Chicago, 1871–1968*. New York: Routledge, 2004.

Boettiger, John. *Jake Lingle: Or Chicago on the Spot*. New York: E. P. Dutton, 1931.

Borroel, Roger. *The Story of the Untouchables as Told by Eliot Ness*. 2nd ed. East Chicago, IN: La Villita Publications, 2012.

Bradley, Robert L., Jr. *Edison to Enron: Energy Markets and Political Strategies*. Salem, MA: Scrivener Publishing, 2011.

Brothers, Thomas. *Louis Armstrong: Master of Modernism*. New York: W. W. Norton, 2014.

Bruck, Connie. *When Hollywood Had a King: The Reign of Lew Wasserman, Who Leveraged Talent into Power and Influence*. New York: Random House, 2003.

Buder, Stanley. *Pullman: An Experiment in Industrial Order and Community Planning 1880–1930*. New York: Oxford University Press, 1967.

Bukowski, Douglas. *Big Bill Thompson, Chicago, and the Politics of Image*. Urbana: University of Illinois Press, 1998.

Burns, Walter Noble. *The One-Way Ride: The Red Trail of Chicago Gangland from Prohibition to Jake Lingle*. Garden City, NY: Doubleday, Doran, 1931.

Burrough, Bryan. *Public Enemies: America's Greatest Crime Wave and the Birth of the FBI, 1933– 1934*. New York: Penguin Press, 2004.

Busch, Francis X. *Enemies of the State*. Indianapolis, IN: Bobbs-Merrill, 1954.

———. *Guilty or Not Guilty?* Indianapolis, IN: Bobbs-Merrill, 1952.

Cahan, Richard. *A Court That Shaped America: Chicago's Federal District Court From Abe Lincoln to Abbie Hoffmann*. Evanston, IL: Northwestern University Press, 2002.

Calder, James D. *The Origins and Development of Federal Crime Control Policy: Herbert Hoover's Initiatives*. Westport, CT: Prager, 1993.

Capone, Deirdre Marie. *Uncle Al Capone: The Untold Story from Inside His Family*. Bonita Springs, FL: Recap Publishing, 2012.

Carte, Gene E., and Elaine H. Carte. *Police Reform in the United States: The Era of August Vollmer: 1905–1932*. Berkeley: University of California Press, 1975.

Casey, Robert J., and W. A. S. Douglas. *The Midwesterner: The Story of Dwight H. Green*. Chicago: Wilcox and Follett, 1948.

Cohn, Art. *The Joker Is Wild: The Story of Joe E. Lewis*. New York: Random House, 1955.

Collins, Max Allan. Introduction to *The Complete Chester Gould's Dick Tracy*. Vol. 1, *1931–1933*. San Diego: IDW Publishing, 2009.

———. "Shoot First." Introduction to *The Complete Chester Gould's Dick Tracy*. Vol. 2, *1933– 1935*. San Diego: IDW Publishing, 2009.

Collins, Max Allan, and George Hagenauer. *Chicago Mob Wars: Eliot Ness vs. Al Capone*. Northampton, MA: Kitchen Sink Press, 1993.

Collins, Max Allan, and Matt Masterson. "Chester Gould Speaks." In *The Complete Chester Gould's Dick Tracy*. Vol. 1, *1931–1933*. San Diego, CA: IDW Publishing, 2009.

———. "Chester Gould Speaks, Part II." In *The Complete Chester Gould's Dick Tracy*. Vol. 2, *1933–1935*. San Diego, CA: IDW Publishing, 2009.

Conan Doyle, Arthur. *The Complete Sherlock Holmes*. New York: Doubleday, 1930.

Cook, John William. *Educational History of Illinois: Growth and Progress in Educational Affairs of the State from the Earliest Day to the Present, with Portraits and Biographies*. Chicago: Henry O. Shepard, 1912.

Cook, William A. *King of the Bootleggers: A Biography of George Remus*. Jefferson, NC: McFarland, 2008.

Corsino, Louis. *The Neighborhood Outfit: Organized Crime in Chicago Heights*. Urbana: University of Illinois Press, 2014.

Critchley, David. *The Origin of Organized Crime in America: The New York City Mafia, 1891–1931*. New York: Routledge, 2009.

Currey, Seymour. *Chicago: Its History and Its Builders*. Vol. 4. Chicago: S. J. Clarke Publishing, 1918.

Daniels, Jonathan. *The Randolphs of Virginia*. Garden City, NY: Doubleday, 1972.

Dardoff, Robert B., Joseph Jankovic, John C. Mazziotta, and Scott L. Pomeroy. *Bradley's Neurology in Clinical Practice*. 7th ed. Vol. 1. London: Elsevier, 2016.

Dawes, Charles G. *Notes as Vice President: 1928–1929*. Boston: Little, Brown, 1935.

d'Eramo, Marco. *The Pig and the Skyscraper—Chicago: A History of Our Future*. Translated by Graeme Thomson. London: Verso, 2002.

De Toledano, Ralph. *J. Edgar Hoover: The Man in His Time*. New Rochelle, NY: Arlington House, 1973.

Dobyns, Fletcher. *The Underworld of American Politics*. New York: Fletcher Dobyns, 1932.

Dolan, Francis X. *Eastern State Penitentiary*. Images of America. Charleston, SC: Arcadia Publishing, 2007.

Durant, W. C., ed. *Law Observance: Shall the People of the United States Uphold the Constitution*. New York: Durant Award Office, 1929.

Dyja, Thomas. *The Third Coast: When Chicago Built the American Dream*. New York: Penguin Press, 2013.

Eghigian, Mars, Jr. *After Capone: The Life and World of Chicago Mob Boss Frank "The Enforcer" Nitti*. Nashville, TN: Cumberland House, 2006.

Eig, Jonathan. *Get Capone: The Secret Plot That Captured America's Most Wanted Gangster*. New York: Simon and Schuster, 2010.

Ellen, Mary, Mark Murphy, and Ralph Foster Weld. *A Treasury of Brooklyn*. New York: William Sloane Associates, 1949.

English, T. J. *Paddy Whacked: The Untold Story of the Irish American Gangster*. New York: Regan-Books, 2005.

Enright, Richard T. *Al Capone on the Spot: The Inside Story of Chicago's Master Criminal*. [Chicago?]: Graphic Arts, 1931.

Estleman, Loren D. "Stuart Lake: Frontier Mythmaker." Introduction to *Wyatt Earp: Frontier Marshal* by Stuart N. Lake. New York: Pocket Books, 1994.

Ewing, Steve, and John B. Lundstrom. *Fateful Rendezvous: The Life of Butch O'Hare*. Annapolis, MD: Naval Institute Press, 1997.

Fass, Paula S. *The Damned and the Beautiful: American Youth in the 1920s*. New York: Oxford University Press, 1977.

Fischer, Jim. *The Lindbergh Case*. New Brunswick, NJ: Rutgers University Press, 1987.

Folsom, Robert G. *The Money Trail: How Elmer Irey and His T-Men Brought Down America's Criminal Elite*. Washington, D.C.: Potomac Books, 2010.

Ford, Henry, and Samuel Crowther. *Moving Forward*. Garden City, NY: Doubleday, Doran, 1930.

Fox, Stephen. *Blood and Power: Organized Crime in Twentieth-Century America*. New York: William Morrow, 1989.

Fraley, Oscar. *4 Against the Mob*. New York: Popular Library, 1961.

Fraley, Oscar, with Paul Robsky. *The Last of the Untouchables*. New York: Popular Library, 1962.

Gabler, Neal. *Winchell: Gossip, Power and the Culture of Celebrity*. New York: Vintage, 1994.

Galbraith, John Kenneth. *The Great Crash 1929*. New York: Time, 1962.

Garrow, David J. *Rising Star: The Making of Barack Obama*. New York: William Morrow, 2017.

Gottfried, Alex. *Boss Cermak of Chicago: A Study of Political Leadership*. Seattle: University of Washington Press, 1962.

Gould, Chester. *The Complete Chester Gould's Dick Tracy*. Vol. 1, *1931–1933*. San Diego, CA: IDW Publishing, 2009.

Grant, Bruce. *Fight for a City: The Story of the Union League Club of Chicago and Its Times, 1880–1955*. Chicago: Rand McNally, 1955.

Haller, Mark H. *Illegal Enterprise: The Work of Historian Mark Haller*. Edited by Matthew G. Yeager. Latham, MD: University Press of America, 2013.

Hanson, Neil. *Monk Eastman: The Gangster Who Became a War Hero*. New York: Knopf, 2010.

Harris, Scott Jordan, ed. *World Film Locations: Chicago*. Chicago: Intellect Books, 2013.

Hearings Before a Subcommittee of the Committee on the Judiciary, United States Senate, Seventy-Second Congress, First Session, on the Nomination of James H. Wilkerson to be United States Circuit Judge, Seventh Circuit, January 21, 22, February 9, 10, and 12, 1932. Washington, D.C.: United States Government Printing Office, 1932.

Hearings Before the Special Committee to Investigate Organized Crime in Interstate Commerce, United States Senate, Eighty-First Congress, Second Session. Part 1, *Florida*. Washington, D.C.: United States Government Printing Office, 1950.

Hearings Before the Special Committee to Investigate Organized Crime in Interstate Commerce, United States Senate, Eighty-First Congress, Second Session. Part 2. Washington, D.C.: United States Government Printing Office, 1950.

Hearings Before the Special Committee to Investigate Organized Crime in Interstate Commerce, United States Senate, Eighty-First Congress, Second Session. Part 5, *Illinois*. Washington, D.C.: United States Government Printing Office, 1951.

Hecht, Ben. *A Child of the Century*. New York: Simon and Schuster, 1954.

Hecht, Ben, and Charles MacArthur. *The Front Page: From Theater to Reality*. Edited by George W. Hilton. Hanover, NH: Smith and Kraus, 2002.

Heimel, Paul W. *Eliot Ness: The Real Story*. 2nd ed. Nashville, TN: Cumberland House, 2000.

Helmer, William J. *Al Capone and His American Boys: Memoirs of a Mobster's Wife*. Bloomington: Indiana University Press, 2011.

———. *The Gun That Made the Twenties Roar*. London: Macmillan, 1969.

Helmer, William J., and Arthur J. Bilek. *The St. Valentine's Day Massacre: The Untold Story of the Gangland Bloodbath That Brought Down Al Capone*. Nashville, TN: Cumberland House, 2004.

Helmer, William, with Rick Mattix. *Public Enemies: America's Criminal Past, 1919–1940*. New York: Checkmark Books, 1998.

Historic City: The Settlement of Chicago. Chicago: Department of Development and Planning, 1976.

Hoffman, Dennis E. *Scarface Al and the Crime Crusaders: Chicago's Private War Against Capone*. Carbondale: Southern Illinois University Press, 1993.

Hoover, Herbert. *The Memoirs of Herbert Hoover*. Vol. 2, *The Cabinet and the Presidency: 1920–1933*. New York: Macmillan, 1952.

Hopkins, Ernest Jerome. *Our Lawless Police: A Study of the Unlawful Enforcement of the Law*. New York: Viking Press, 1931.

Hynd, Alan. *The Giant Killers*. New York: Robert M. McBride, 1945.

Iorizzo, Luciano. *Al Capone: A Biography*. Westport, CT: Greenwood Press, 2003.

Irey, Elmer, and William J. Slocum. *The Tax Dodgers: The Inside Story of the T-Men's War with America's Political and Underworld Hoodlums*. Garden City, NY: Garden City Publishing, 1948.

Jedick, Peter. *Cleveland: Where the East Coast Meets the Midwest*. Cleveland, OH: Fine Line Litho, 1994.

Jenkins, Sally. *The Real All Americans: The Team That Changed a Game, a People, a Nation*. New York: Doubleday, 2007.

Johnson, Curt, with R. Craig Sautter. *The Wicked City: Chicago from Kenna to Capone*. New York: Da Capo Press, 1998.

Kael, Pauline. "Raising Kane." In *The Citizen Kane Book*. New York: Bantam Books, 1974.

Keefe, Rose. *Guns and Roses: The Untold Story of Dean O'Banion, Chicago's Big Shot Before Al Capone*. Nashville, TN: Cumberland House, 2003.

———. *The Man Who Got Away: The Bugs Moran Story*. Nashville, TN: Cumberland House, 2005.

Kirk, Fred W. *Kirk's Map of Chicago and Suburbs*. Chicago: Fred W. Kirk, 1917.

Kobler, John. *Ardent Spirits: The Rise and Fall of Prohibition*. New York: G. P. Putnam's Sons, 1973.

———. *Capone: The Life and World of Al Capone*. New York: G. P. Putnam's Sons, 1971.

Kyle, Chris, with William Doyle. *American Gun: A History of the U.S. in Ten Firearms*. New York: William Morrow, 2013.

Landesco, John. "Organized Crime in Chicago." In *The Illinois Crime Survey*. Chicago: Illinois Association for Criminal Justice, 1929.

Lender, Mark Edward, and James Kirby Martin. *Drinking in America: A History*. Rev. ed. New York: The Free Press, 1987.

Lerner, Max. *America as a Civilization: Life and Thought in the United States Today.* New York: Simon and Schuster, 1957.

Leuchtenburg, William E. *Herbert Hoover.* The American Presidents. New York: Times Books, 2009.

Liebovich, Louis W. *Bylines in Despair: Herbert Hoover, the Great Depression, and the U.S. News Media.* Westport, CT: Praeger, 1994.

Lindberg, Richard. *Return Again to the Scene of the Crime: A Guide to Even More Infamous Places in Chicago.* Nashville, TN: Cumberland House, 2001.

———. *Return to the Scene of the Crime: A Guide to Infamous Places in Chicago.* Nashville, TN: Cumberland House, 1999.

———. *To Serve and Collect: Chicago Politics and Police Corruption from the Lager Beer Riot to the Summerdale Scandal, 1855–1960.* Carbondale: Southern Illinois University Press, 2008.

Lombardo, Robert M. *The Black Hand: Terror by Letter in Chicago.* Urbana: University of Illinois Press, 2010.

Lombroso, Cesare. *Criminal Man.* Translated by Mary Gibson and Nicole Hahn Rafter. Durham, NC: Duke University Press, 2006.

Luzi, Matthew J. *The Boys in Chicago Heights: The Forgotten Crew of the Chicago Outfit.* Charleston, SC: The History Press, 2012.

Lyle, John H. *The Dry and Lawless Years.* Englewood Cliffs, NJ: Prentice-Hall, 1960.

Lyon, Chriss. *A Killing in Capone's Playground: The True Story of the Hunt for the Most Dangerous Man Alive.* Holland, MI: In-Depth Editions, 2014.

MacAdams, William. *Ben Hecht: The Man Behind the Legend.* New York: Charles Scribner's Sons, 1990.

Mackenzie, James Cameron, ed. *History of the 307th Field Artillery: September 6, 1917–May 16, 1919.* N.p., n.d.

Maeder, Jay. *Dick Tracy: The Official Biography.* New York: Plume, 1990.

Manchester, William. *The Glory and the Dream: A Narrative History of America, 1932–1972.* Vol. 1. Boston: Little, Brown, 1974.

Mappen, Marc. *Prohibition Gangsters: The Rise and Fall of a Bad Generation.* New Brunswick, NJ: Rutgers University Press, 2013.

Mayer, Harold M., and Richard C. Wade. *Chicago: Growth of a Metropolis.* Chicago: University of Chicago Press, 1969.

McArthur, Jeff. *Two Gun Hart: Lawman, Cowboy, and Long-Lost Brother of Al Capone.* Burbank, CA: Bandwagon Books, 2013.

McElvaine, Robert S. *The Great Depression: America, 1929–1941.* 25th Anniversary ed. New York: Three Rivers Press, 2008.

McGilligan, Patrick, ed. *Backstory: Interviews with Screenwriters of Hollywood's Golden Age.* Berkeley: University of California Press, 1986.

———. *Young Orson: The Years of Luck and Genius on the Path to Citizen Kane.* New York: Harper, 2015.

McGirr, Lisa. *The War on Alcohol: Prohibition and the Rise of the American State.* New York: W. W. Norton, 2016.

McPhaul, Jack. *Johnny Torrio: First of the Gang Lords.* New Rochelle, NY: Arlington House, 1970.

Merriam, Charles Edward. *Chicago: A More Intimate View of Urban Politics*. New York: Macmillan, 1929.

Merriner, James L. *Grafters and Goo-Goos: Corruption and Reform in Chicago, 1833–2003*. Carbondale: Southern Illinois University Press, 2004.

Messick, Hank. *Secret File*. New York: G. P. Putnam's Sons, 1969.

———. *The Silent Syndicate*. New York: Macmillan, 1967.

Michigan: A Guide to the Wolverine State. New York: Oxford University Press, 1941.

Mills, Bill. *The League: The True Story of Average Americans on the Hunt for WWI Spies*. New York: Skyhorse Publishing, 2013.

Moore, Lucy. *Anything Goes: A Biography of the Roaring Twenties*. New York: Overlook Press, 2010.

Murray, George. *The Legacy of Al Capone: Portraits and Annals of Chicago's Public Enemies*. New York: G. P. Putnam's Sons, 1975.

Nelli, Humbert S. *The Business of Crime: Italians and Syndicate Crime in the United States*. New York: Oxford University Press, 1976.

Ness, Eliot, with Oscar Fraley. *The Untouchables*. New York: Julian Messner, 1957.

Nickel, Steven. *Torso: The Story of Eliot Ness and the Search for a Psychopathic Killer*. Winston-Salem, NC: John F. Blair, 1989.

Nishi, Dennis, ed. *Prohibition*. Farmington Hills, MI: Greenhaven Press, 2003.

Nollen, Scott Allen. *Boris Karloff: A Critical Account of His Screen, Stage, Radio, Television and Recording Work*. Jefferson, NC: McFarland, 1991.

O'Brien, Howard Vincent. *All Things Considered: Memories, Experiences and Observations of a Chicagoan*. Indianapolis, IN: Bobbs-Merrill, 1948.

Okrent, Daniel. *Last Call: The Rise and Fall of Prohibition*. New York: Scribner, 2010.

O'Toole, Garson. *Hemingway Didn't Say That: The Truth Behind Familiar Quotations*. New York: Little A, 2017.

Pacyga, Dominic A. *Chicago: A Biography*. Chicago: University of Chicago Press, 2009.

Papke, David Ray. *The Pullman Case: The Clash of Labor and Capital in Industrial America*. Lawrence: University Press of Kansas, 1999.

Park, Robert E., Ernest W. Burgess, and Roderick D. McKenzie, eds. *The City*. Chicago: University of Chicago Press, 1925.

Parsons, Louella O. *The Gay Illiterate*. Garden City, NY: Doubleday, Doran, 1944.

Pasley, Fred D. *Al Capone: The Biography of a Self-Made Man*. Garden City, NY: Garden City Publishing Company, 1930.

Perry, Douglas. *Eliot Ness: The Rise and Fall of an American Hero*. New York: Viking, 2014.

Peters, Shawn Francis. *When Prayer Fails: Faith Healing, Children, and the Law*. New York: Oxford University Press, 2008.

Peterson, Virgil W. *Barbarians in Our Midst: A History of Chicago Crime and Politics*. Boston: Little, Brown, 1952.

———. *The Mob: 200 Years of Organized Crime in New York*. Ottawa: Green Hill Publishers, 1983.

Pierce, Bessie Louise, and Joe L. Norris, eds. *As Others See Chicago: Impressions of Visitors, 1673–1933*. Chicago: University of Chicago Press, 1933.

Pizzitola, Louis. *Hearst over Hollywood: Power, Passion and Propaganda in the Movies.* New York: Columbia University Press, 2002.

Plan of Re-Numbering: City of Chicago. Chicago: Chicago Directory, 1909.

Porter, Philip W. *Cleveland: Confused City on a Seesaw.* Columbus: Ohio State University Press, 1976.

Potter, Claire Bond. *War on Crime: Bandits, G-Men, and the Politics of Mass Culture.* New Brunswick, NJ: Rutgers University Press, 1998.

Powell, Hickman. *Ninety Times Guilty.* New York: Harcourt, Brace, 1939.

Powers, Richard Gid. *G-Men: Hoover's FBI in American Popular Culture.* Carbondale: Southern Illinois University Press, 1983.

———. *Secrecy and Power: The Life of J. Edgar Hoover.* New York: The Free Press, 1987.

Pratt, James Bissett. *India and Its Faiths: A Traveler's Record.* Boston: Houghton Mifflin, 1915.

Public Papers of the Presidents of the United States: Herbert Hoover—Containing the Public Messages, Speeches, and Statements of the President, March 4 to December 31, 1929. Washington, D.C.: United States Government Printing Office, 1974.

Public Papers of the Presidents of the United States: Herbert Hoover—Containing the Public Messages, Speeches, and Statements of the President, January 1 to December 31, 1930. Washington, D.C.: United States Government Printing Office, 1976.

Public Papers of the Presidents of the United States: Herbert Hoover—Containing the Public Messages, Speeches, and Statements of the President, January 1 to December 31, 1931. Washington, D.C.: United States Government Printing Office, 1976.

Public Papers of the Presidents of the United States: Herbert Hoover—Containing the Public Messages, Speeches, and Statements of the President, January 1, 1932 to March 4, 1933. Washington, D.C.: United States Government Printing Office, 1977.

Randolph, Robert Isham. *The Randolphs of Virginia: A Compilation of the Descendants of William Randolph of Turkey Island and his wife Mary Isham of Bermuda Hundred.* N.p., n.d.

Rappleye, Charles, and Ed Becker. *All-American Mafioso: The Johnny Rosselli Story.* New York: Doubleday, 1991.

Reckless, Walter C. *Vice in Chicago.* Chicago: University of Chicago Press, 1933.

Richman, Harry, with Richard Gehman. *A Hell of a Life.* New York: Duell, Sloan and Pearce, 1966.

Riis, Jacob. *How the Other Half Lives.* New York: Dover Books, 1971 (1901).

Robinson, Edgar Eugene, and Vaughn Davis Bornet. *Herbert Hoover: President of the United States.* Stanford, CA: Hoover Institution Press, 1975.

Ross, Robert. *The Trial of Al Capone.* Chicago: Robert Ross, 1933.

Runyon, Damon. *Trials and Other Tribulations.* Philadelphia: J. B. Lippincott, 1947.

Russo, Gus. *The Outfit: The Role of Chicago's Underworld in the Shaping of Modern America.* New York: Bloomsbury, 2001.

Sagalyn, Arnold. *A Promise Fulfilled: The Memoir of Arnold Sagalyn.* Burtonsville, MD: House of Printing, 2010.

Schmeckebier, Laurence F. *The Bureau of Prohibition: Its History, Activities, and Organizations.* Institute for Government Research: Service Monographs of the United States Government, No. 57. Washington, D.C.: Brookings Institution, 1929.

Schmidt, John R. *"The Mayor Who Cleaned Up Chicago": A Political Biography of William E. Dever*. DeKalb: Northern Illinois University Press, 1989.

Schoenberg, Robert J. *Mr. Capone: The Real—and Complete—Story of Al Capone*. New York: Quill, 1992.

Schwarz, Ted. *Cleveland Curiosities: Eliot Ness and His Blundering Raid, A Busker's Promise, the Richest Heiress Who Never Lived, and More*. Charleston, SC: The History Press, 2010.

Selzer, Arthur. *The Heart: Its Function in Health and Disease*. Berkeley: University of California Press, 1966.

Shapiro, Fred R., ed. *The Yale Book of Quotations*. New Haven, CT: Yale University Press, 2006.

Shaw Clifford R., and Earl D. Myers. "The Juvenile Delinquent." In *The Illinois Crime Survey*. Chicago: Illinois Association for Criminal Justice, 1929.

Shmelter, Richard J. *Chicago Assassin: The Life and Legend of "Machine Gun" Jack McGurn and the Chicago Beer Wars of the Roaring Twenties*. Nashville, TN: Cumberland House, 2008.

Sifakis, Carl. *The Mafia Encyclopedia*. 3rd ed. New York: Facts on File, 2005.

Sinclair, Andrew. *Prohibition: The Era of Excess*. Boston: Little, Brown, 1962.

Skilnik, Bob. *Beer: A History of Brewing in Chicago*. Fort Lee, NJ: Barricade Books, 2006.

Sloat, Warren. *1929: America Before the Crash*. New York: Macmillan, 1979.

Smith, Alison J. *Syndicate City: The Chicago Crime Cartel and What to Do About It*. Chicago: Henry Regnery, 1954.

Smith, Richard Norton. *The Colonel: The Life and Legend of Robert R. McCormick, 1880–1955*. Boston: Houghton Mifflin, 1997.

Snyder-Grenier, Ellen M. *Brooklyn!: An Illustrated History*. Philadelphia: Temple University Press, 1996.

Spiering, Frank. *The Man Who Got Capone*. Indianapolis, IN: Bobbs-Merrill, 1976.

Spinney, Robert G. *City of Big Shoulders: A History of Chicago*. DeKalb: Northern Illinois University Press, 2000.

St. John, Robert. *This Was My World*. Garden City, NY: Doubleday, 1953.

Sullivan, Edward Dean. *Chicago Surrenders*. New York: Vanguard Press, 1930.

———. *Rattling the Cup on Chicago Crime*. New York: Vanguard Press, 1929.

Thompson, Craig, and Allen Raymond. *Gang Rule in New York: The Story of a Lawless Era*. New York: Dial Press, 1940.

Tiede, Tom. *American Tapestry: Eyewitness Accounts of the Twentieth Century*. New York: Pharos Books, 1988.

Towne, Charles Hanson. *The Rise and Fall of Prohibition*. New York: Macmillan, 1923.

Trespacz, Karen L. *The Trial of Gangster Al Capone: A Headline Court Case*. Berkeley Heights, NJ: Enslow Publishers, 2001.

Trohan, Walter. *Political Animals: Memoirs of a Sentimental Cynic*. Garden City, NY: Doubleday, 1975.

Tucker, Kenneth. *Eliot Ness and the Untouchables: The Historical Reality and the Film and Television Depictions*. 2nd ed. Jefferson, NC: McFarland, 2012.

Tyre, William H. *Chicago's Historic Prairie Avenue*. Images of America. Charleston, SC: Arcadia Publishing, 2008.

Vanderbilt, Cornelius, Jr. *Farewell to Fifth Avenue*. New York: Simon and Schuster, 1935.

Van Tassel, David D., and John J. Grabowski, eds. *The Encyclopedia of Cleveland History*. Bloomington: Indiana University Press, 1996.

Vickers, Raymond B. *Panic in the Loop: Chicago's Banking Crisis of 1932*. Lanham, MD: Lexington Books, 2011.

Wagner, E. J. *The Science of Sherlock Holmes: From Baskerville Hall to the Valley of Fear, the Real Forensics Behind the Great Detective's Greatest Cases*. Hoboken, NJ: John Wiley and Sons, 2006.

Waller, George. *Kidnap: The Story of the Lindbergh Case*. New York: Dial Press, 1961.

Waller, Maurice, and Anthony Calabrese. *Fats Waller*. New York: Schirmer Books, 1977.

Waugh, Daniel. *Egan's Rats: The Untold Story of the Prohibition-Era Gang That Ruled St. Louis*. Nashville, TN: Cumberland House, 2007.

Weld, Ralph Foster. *Brooklyn Is America*. New York: Columbia University Press, 1950.

Welles, Orson, and Peter Bogdanovich. *This Is Orson Welles*. Edited by Jonathan Rosenbaum. New York: Da Capo Press, 1998.

Wendt, Lloyd, and Herman Kogan. *Big Bill of Chicago*. Indianapolis, IN: Bobbs-Merrill, 1953.

——. *Lords of the Levee: The Story of Bathhouse John and Hinky Dink*. Indianapolis, IN: Bobbs-Merrill, 1943.

White, Richard D., Jr. *Will Rogers: A Political Life*. Lubbock: Texas Tech University Press, 2011.

Willebrandt, Mabel Walker. *The Inside of Prohibition*. Indianapolis, IN: Bobbs-Merrill, 1929.

Williams, Tom. *A Mysterious Something in the Light: The Life of Raymond Chandler*. London: Aurum Press, 2012.

Wilson, Frank J., and Beth Day. *Special Agent: A Quarter Century with the Treasury Department and the Secret Service*. New York: Holt, Rinehart and Winston, 1965.

Wolf, George, with Joseph DiMona. *Frank Costello: Prime Minister of the Underworld*. New York: William Morrow, 1974.

The WPA Guide to Illinois. New York: Pantheon Books, 1983 (1939).

X Marks the Spot: Chicago Gang Wars in Pictures. Spot Publishing, 1930, FBI-AC.

Year-Book of the Union League Club of Chicago. Chicago: Union League Club, 1921.

Yount, Lisa. *Forensic Science: From Fibers to Fingerprints*. Milestones in Discovery and Invention. New York: Chelsea House, 2007.

Selected Articles

Anderson, Nels. "Democracy in Chicago: Big Bill Thompson, Friend of the Plain People." *Century*, November 1927, 71–78.

Anderson, Paul Y. "The Darrow Report." *Nation*, May 30, 1934, 611–612.

Anonymous. "The Capone I Knew." *True Detective*, June 1947, 45–47, 79–81.

Asbury, Herbert. "America's No. 1 Mystery Man." *Collier's*, April 19, 1947, 33–44.

"Baked to Death." *The New Masses*, September 6, 1938, 14.

Bell, James A. "Frank Costello: Statesman of the Underworld." *American Mercury*, August 1950, 131–139.

"Big Bankers' Gambling Mania." *Literary Digest*, March 11, 1933, 11–12.

Borden, Mary. "Chicago Revisited." *Harper's*, April 1931, 541–547.

Brewer-Smyth, Kathleen. "Neurological Correlates of High-Risk Behavior: A Case Study of Alphonse Capone." *Journal of Neuroscience Nursing,* vol. 38, no. 6 (December 2006), 442–446.

Brundidge, Harry T., and Frank L. Thompson. "The Truth About Chicago." *Real Detective,* December 1930, 12–21, 83–87.

Bukowski, Douglas. "William Dever and Prohibition: The Mayoral Elections of 1923 and 1927." *Chicago History,* Summer 1978, 109–118.

Burnett, W. R. "The Czar of Chicago." *Saturday Review of Literature,* October 18, 1930, 240.

"The Cabinet: Dry Hope." *Time,* November 11, 1929, 11–12.

Calder, James D. "Eliot Ness (April 19, 1903–May 16, 1957): Gangbuster to Security Executive—A Meandering Career of Great Highs and Tragic Lows." *Journal of Applied Security Research,* vol. 6, no. 2 (2011), 196–208.

Cole, Kenneth C. "Judicial Affairs: The Role of the Senate in the Confirmation of Judicial Nominations." *American Political Science Review,* vol. 28, no. 5 (October 1934), 875–894.

"Coming Out Party." *Time,* March 24, 1930, 15–16.

Condon, George. "The Last American Hero." *Cleveland,* August 1987, 88–91, 138–142, RM.

Crayhorn, James. "The End of Gangland's Mad Dog." *Master Detective,* September 1933, 26–29, 59–63.

"Crime: Capone's Week." *Time,* May 19, 1930, 13.

"Crime: U.S. v. Capone." *Time,* June 22, 1931, 17.

"Crime: Who Wouldn't Be Worried?" *Time,* October 19, 1931, 12–13.

DeLacy, Charles. "The Inside on Chicago's Notorious St. Valentine Massacre." Part 1. *True Detective,* March 1931, 50–55, 95–100.

Dillard, Jack. "How the U.S. Gov't Caught Al Capone!" *Master Detective,* February 1932, 10–17, 54–58.

Doherty, Edward. "The Twilight of the Gangster: How Much Longer Are We Going to Put Up with Him?" *Liberty,* October 24, 1931, 5–9.

Douglas, W. A. S. "Kindling-Wood Peddler." *American Mercury,* July 1933, 341–347.

Ely, Richard T. "Pullman: A Social Study." *Harper's,* February 1885, 452–466.

"The First Class in Scientific Crime Detection Held in Chicago." *American Journal of Police Science,* vol. 2, no. 2 (March–April 1931), 179–182.

Foster, L. A. "High Lights of Burke's Crimson Career." *True Detective,* July 1931, 12, 62–65.

Foster, Ralph. "Blackhand War Rages in Chicago Heights." *Startling Detective Adventures,* December 1932, 36–43, 52–54.

Fraley, Oscar. "The Real Eliot Ness." *Coronet,* July 1961, 25–30.

Fuchs, Daniel. "Where Al Capone Grew Up." *New Republic,* September 9, 1931, 95–97.

Gerould, Katharine Fullerton. "Jessica and Al Capone." *Harper's,* June 1931, 93–97.

Girton, Fred. "Al Capone Tells His Side of It." *Startling Detective Adventures,* September 1931, 21–23, 68–71.

Goddard, Calvin H. "Scientific Identification of Firearms and Bullets." *Journal of Criminal Law and Criminology,* vol. 17, no. 2 (Summer 1926), 254–263.

———. "The Valentine Day Massacre: A Study in Ammunition-Tracing." *The American Journal of Police Science,* vol. 1, no. 1 (January–February 1930), 60–78.

———, "Who Did the Shooting?" *Popular Science Monthly*, November 1927, 21–22, 171–172.

Gordon, Mark. "Ideas Shoot Bullets: How the RICO Act Became a Potent Weapon in the War Against Organized Crime." *Concept*, vol. 26 (2003), https://concept.journals.villanova.edu /article/view/312/275 (accessed December 2, 2017).

Havens, Paul. "Personalities in Law Enforcement: Eliot Ness." *True Detective*, November 1939, 61, 117–118.

Hirsch, Richard, and Boyd Mayer. "Behind the Scenes with the United States Secret Service." *True Detective*, December 1938, 12–15, 127–128.

"The House: Hoover's Next-to-Worst." *Time*, November 10, 1930, 18.

Hull, Stephen. "Cicero Ambush." *True Detective*, July 1948, 36–39, 58–59.

Hynd, Alan. "The Inside on the Lingle Murder Capture." *True Detective*, April 1931, 20–27, 81–86.

Jedick, Peter. "Eliot Ness." *Cleveland*, April 1976, 48–57, 91–94, RM.

Johnston, Alva. "Capone, King of Crime." *Vanity Fair*, May 1931, http://www.vanityfair.com /news/1931/05/al-capone-chicago-new-york-prohibition (accessed June 22, 2017).

———, "Gangs Á La Mode." *New Yorker*, August 25, 1928, http://www.newyorker.com/maga zine/1928/08/25/gangs-a-la-mode (accessed March 10, 2017).

Jørmeland, Bjarne. "Gangsterjeger fra Ålvundfjord." *Tidens Krav*, June 25, 2011, 23–27, RM.

Lyle, John H., and John J. McPhaul. "How Chicago's Crime Barons Were Smashed," Part 1. *True Detective*, August 1937, 46–49, 120–122.

———, "How Chicago's Crime Barons Were Smashed," Part 3. *True Detective*, October 1937, 64–68, 89–92.

Maltby, Richard. "The Public Enemy." Senses of Cinema, December 2003, http://sensesofcin ema.com/2003/cteq/public_enemy/ (accessed June 16, 2016).

Mangil, William. "Torrio the Immune." *True Detective*, September 1940, 52–55, 91–97.

Marsh, Howard R. "Untold Tales of the Secret Service." *Liberty*, January 16, 1937, 11–15.

Mayer, Milton S. "Myth of the 'G Men.'" *Forum*, September 1935, 144–148.

Metz, T. D. "Mystery of Eddie O'Hare's Mile-A-Minute Murder." *True Detective*, July 1941, 44–49, 87–92.

Miller, Scott. "The Assassination of Jake Lingle." *Chicago Reader*, March 20, 1981, 1, 20–24, 29–34.

"Modern Methods in Bread Baking." *The Calumet Weekly Index*, April 30, 1910. In *Where the Trails Cross*, vol. 19, no. 3 (Spring 1989), 98–99.

Muehlberger, C. W. "Col. Calvin Hooker Goddard 1895–1955." *Journal of Criminal Law and Criminology*, vol. 46, no. 1 (1955), 103–104.

"National Affairs: Professor Added." *Time*, September 16, 1929, 13.

Ness, Eliot. "The Participation of Boys." *Phi Delta Kappan*, March 1940, 337–344.

———, "Radio-Directed Mobile Police." *American City*, November 1939, 35–36.

———, "Streamlining Protection." *Real Detective*, October 1941, 4, 92.

Ness, Elisabeth. "My Husband, Eliot Ness." *TV Guide*, March 11–17, 1961, 5–7.

"The Ness Family" and "The King Family." *Where the Trails Cross*, vol. 44, no. 4 (Summer 2014), 83–85.

Nickel, Steven. "The Real Eliot Ness." *American History Illustrated*, October 1987, 42–52.

"The Parise Family." *Where the Trails Cross*, vol. 19, no. 3 (Spring 1989), 96–97.

"Philadelphia Justice for Chicago's Al Capone." *Literary Digest*, June 15, 1929, 32, 34, 39.

"Police: Finest of the Finest." *Time*, February 18, 1966, 49.

"Police Work a Profession, Not a Job." *Chicago Daily News*, August 19, 1916. In *Journal of Criminal Law and Criminology*, vol. 7, no. 4 (May 1916–March 1917), 622–624.

"The Press: Reporter Rogers." *Time*, March 15, 1937, 49.

"Purpose of the Journal." *American Journal of Police Science*, vol. 1, no. 1 (January–February 1930), 1–7.

Randolph, Robert Isham. "How to Wreck Capone's Gang." *Collier's*, March 7, 1931, 7–9.

———. "The 'Third Degree.'" *New York Herald Tribune Magazine*, August 7, 1932, 1–2.

Rockne, Knute K. "What Thrills a Coach." *Collier's*, December 6, 1930, 20–21, 36, 38.

Shepherd, William G. "Can Capone Beat Washington, Too?" *Collier's*, October 10, 1931, 16–17, 42, 44.

———. "$119.25 Poison Money." *Collier's*, October 16, 1926, 10, 27.

Sondern, Frederic, Jr. "Brotherhood of Evil: The Mafia." *Reader's Digest*, May 1959, 66–71, 283–312.

Sullivan, Edward Dean. "Who Killed Jake Lingle?" *True Detective*, December 1930, 20–25, 104–108, 112.

Sullivan, Timothy, with John Kobler. "Caddying for a Man Who Never Shot Par." *Sports Illustrated*, November 6, 1972, 72–78, 83–84.

"There Goes Eliot Ness." *Fortune*, January 1946, 196.

Trickey, Erick. "Eliot Ness vs. J. Edgar Hoover." *Smithsonian*, October 2014, 78–85, 104, 107.

Vanderbilt, Cornelius, Jr. "How Al Capone Would Run This Country." *Liberty*, October 17, 1931, 18, 20–21.

Vollmer, August. "Aims and Ideals of the Police." *Journal of the American Institute of Criminal Law and Criminology*, vol. 13, no. 1 (May 1922), 251–257.

———. "The Scientific Policeman." *American Journal of Police Science*, vol. 1, no. 1 (January–February 1930), 8–12.

Waggoner, Kim. "The FBI Laboratory: 75 Years of Forensic Science Service." *Forensic Science Communications*, vol. 9, no. 4 (October 2007), https://archives.fbi.gov/archives/about-us/lab/forensic-science-communications/fsc/oct2007/research (accessed August 8, 2016).

Wallace, Gregory J. "Outgunning the Mob." *ABA Journal*, March 1994, 60–65, 109–115.

Warner, Glenn S. "The Indian Massacres." *Collier's*, October 17, 1931, 7–8, 61–63.

Warnock, Elsie L. "Terms of Approbation and Eulogy in American Dialect Speech." In *Dialect Notes*, vol. 4, pt. 1. New Haven, CT: Tuttle, Morehouse and Taylor, 1913, 13–25.

Wilson, Frank J., and Howard Whitman. "Undercover Man: He Trapped Capone." *Collier's*, April 26, 1947, 14–15, 80–83.

Wilson, George. "Gangland Crime Arrives in Lincoln: The Lincoln National Bank and Trust Company Robbery of 1930." *Nebraska History*, Spring 1992, 25–31.

Winkeler, Mrs. Gus. "I'm on the Spot Facing Death." *Famous Detective Cases*, December 1935, 4–9, 60–67.

Films

Al Capone: The Untouchable Legend. Written and directed by Rike Fochler. Langbein and Skalnik TV, 1998. DVD.

Doubtful Dollars. Affiliated Aetna Life Companies, 1945. 15:55. Prelinger Archives, https://archive.org/details/doubtful_dollars (accessed July 22, 2016).

"Eliot Ness." *The Real Untouchables.* Written and directed by John Fothergill. Thousand Oaks, CA: Goldhil DVD, 2001. DVD.

Eliot Ness: An Untouchable Life (2006). Written and directed by Max Allan Collins. Tulsa, OK: VCI Entertainment, 2007. DVD.

"Eliot Ness: Untouchable" (1997). *Biography.* Directed by Michael Husain. New York: New Video, 2001. VHS.

Gabriel over the White House (1933). Directed by Gregory La Cava. Burbank, CA: Warner Home Video, 2009. DVD.

Little Caesar (1930). Directed by Mervyn LeRoy. Burbank, CA: Warner Home Video, 2010. DVD.

The Mystery of Al Capone's Vaults, April 21, 1986. 1:33:22. Geraldo, http://www.geraldo.com/page/al-capone-s-vault (accessed March 9, 2017).

The Public Enemy (1931). Directed by William A. Wellman. Burbank, CA: Warner Home Video, 2010. DVD.

"The Road to Repeal." *Prohibition: Thirteen Years That Changed America.* Written by Marius Brill, directed by Clive Maltby. New York: A&E Television Networks, 1997. DVD.

Scarface (1932). Directed by Howard Hawks. Universal City, CA: Universal Studios, 2003. DVD.

The Secret 6 (1931). Directed by George Hill. Burbank, CA: Warner Archive Collection, 2012. DVD.

T-Men (1947). Directed by Anthony Mann. New York: Sony Wonder, 2005. DVD.

The Undercover Man (1949). Directed by Joseph H. Lewis. In *Glenn Ford: Undercover Crimes.* Culver City, CA: Sony Pictures Home Entertainment, 2013. DVD.

The Untouchables: Season 1, Volume 1 (1959–1960). Directed by various. Hollywood: Paramount Pictures, 2007. DVD.

The Untouchables: Season 2, Volume 1 (1960–1961). Directed by various. Hollywood: Paramount Pictures, 2007. DVD.

The Untouchables (1987). Directed by Brian De Palma. Hollywood: Paramount Pictures, 2004. DVD.

The Untouchables: The Complete Collection (1993–1994). Directed by various. Toronto: Visual Entertainment Inc., 2017. DVD.

Rogues' Gallery Credits

All Rogues' Gallery images are from the author's collection, except:

Cleveland Public Library: Mary Josephine "Mae" Capone; Dr. Kenneth Phillips
National Archives: Alphonse "Scarface Al" Capone; Ralph "Bottles" Capone;
Frank "The Enforcer" Nitto; Jack "Greasy Thumb" Guzik; Arthur P. Madden
Wikimedia Commons: Samuel Insull
Library of Congress: John Torrio; Fred Goetz; Mayor William Hale "Big Bill"
Thompson; Mayor Anton J. Cermak; Robert E. Crowe; E. C. Yellowley; George E.
Q. Johnson; Attorney General William D. Mitchell; J. Edgar Hoover; Melvin Purvis;
Julius Rosenwald; Frank Wilson; President Herbert Hoover; August Vollmer;
Mabel Walker Willebrandt; Elmer Irey
University of Illinois Urbana-Champagne: Vincent "Schemer" Drucci
Bureau of Alcohol, Tobacco, Firearms, and Explosives: Albert M. Nabers; Lyle B.
Chapman; William J. Gardner; Martin J. Lahart; Joseph D. Leeson; Paul W. Robsky;
S. Maurice Seager; Robert D. Sterling; Warren E. Stutzman
Cleveland Press Collection, Cleveland State University: Edna Stahle Ness
James B. Cloonan; Bernard V. "Barney" Cloonan

Index

Italic page numbers indicate photos.

About the authors

Read on

Insights,
Interviews
& More . . .

Meet Max Allan Collins and A. Brad Schwartz

MAX ALLAN COLLINS is a recipient of the Mystery Writers of America "Grand Master" Edgar. He is author of the Shamus Award–winning Nathan Heller historical thrillers (*Better Dead*), and his graphic novel *Road to Perdition* became the basis of the Academy Award–winning film. His innovative Quarry novels led to a Cinemax TV series, and he is coauthor with his wife, Barbara, of the award-winning Trash 'n' Treasures mystery series (*Antiques Wanted*, Barbara Allan). He has completed a dozen posthumous Mickey Spillane mysteries, and has directed and/or written two feature-length documentaries and six features.

A. BRAD SCHWARTZ is the author of *Broadcast Hysteria: Orson Welles's War of the Worlds and the Art of Fake News*. In 2013, he cowrote a documentary about the *War of the Worlds* broadcast for the PBS series *American Experience*, based in part on research from his senior thesis at the University of Michigan in Ann Arbor. As part of the university's selective screenwriting program, he wrote *Open House*, a murder-mystery/comedy short film that premiered at the Traverse City Film Festival. He is currently a doctoral student in American history at Princeton University.

© Barbara Collins

Excerpts from the Untouchable Case Report

Read on

*The following are excerpts from a working draft of
the final summary report of the investigation into the
Capone Outfit for conspiracy to violate the National
Prohibition Act (Prohibition Bureau Case No. 122-B).
Untouchable Lyle B. Chapman prepared this fifty-
five-page document, dated June 13, 1932, as well as a
longer, more detailed case file referenced in the text
that seems not to have survived. Although Chapman's
supervisor in the Chicago Prohibition office ordered
him to surrender "all official data and memoranda
relative to the case, now in your possession" when
taking him off the case in December 1932, Chapman
apparently kept two copies of this document—the
only ones currently known to exist—along with other
papers relating to his government service, which were
sold at auction in 2018. This report not only testifies
to the extent and sophistication of the Untouchables'
work; it shows that Ness and his agents worked
under the assumption that these indictments would
be prosecuted rather than solely seeking to cut off
Capone's income, as is widely reported and wrongly
assumed. Comparing this document to Treasury
agent Frank Wilson's own summary report finds the
Untouchables' work no less complex or innovative
than the Intelligence Unit's—and resulting in an
arguably stronger case.*

This conspiracy is alleged against a large number
of individuals and groups of individuals under
certain firm names . . . known as the CAPONE
SYNDICATE. ▶

Excerpts from the Untouchable Case Report *(continued)*

This conspiracy is alleged to have had its inception on January 6, 1921, with the organization of the World Motor Service Company. From this nucleus of a few individuals is alleged to have grown an immense syndicate which controlled and operated its own breweries; cooperage plants; a fleet of beer trucks; tank trucks for hauling wort; and small trucks for deliveries, with many men on its payroll, each having specific duties to perform in this illicit enterprise. As thus organized, this conspiracy is declared to have continued throughout a period of more than eleven years, and to be still in existence.

The investigation on this case was initiated by George E. Q. Johnson, United States Attorney for the Northern Judicial District of Illinois, Eastern Division, about November 1, 1930. Through his efforts, a small group of investigators was organized by the assignment to Chicago of designated Special Agents and Prohibition Agents from various districts. This group was placed under the leadership of Eliot Ness, Assistant Special Agent in Charge of the Chicago office of the Special Agents Division, of which W. E. Bennett was Special Agent in Charge. The special group, so organized, operated from the latter office, but functioned as an independent unit under the close supervision of the United States Attorney, in order to coordinate this work with that of similar groups who were at the same time investigating members of the Capone syndicate as to income tax violations, etc., and William J. Froelich, Special Assistant to the Attorney General, was assigned to Chicago to assist the United States Attorney at Chicago, to render legal advice to the special groups, and to keep constantly in touch with these investigations by daily reports of the investigators. This plan was followed until about May 1, 1932, when the conspiracy, though not ended, was, for the purpose of this case, deemed to have closed, in order to complete the investigation and prepare the case for trial. . . . Numerous seizures of breweries, beer trucks, distributing points, etc., were made by the group from January 1, 1931, to May 1, 1932. All leads and clues were investigated at the time, and the seizures connected with the conspiracy. In addition, the whole life of the Capone Syndicate, prior to January 1, 1931, was thoroughly investigated, and many breweries, truck seizures, and events, several of which had received no prosecution for lack of information, were clearly connected to make a continuous chain of evidence from January, 1921, up to the present time. . . .

All of the above activity was conducted in the metropolitan area of Chicago, Illinois, during the period mentioned. . . . Investigation was also made at Chicago, Illinois; Springfield, Illinois; Aurora, Illinois; Elgin, Illinois; Hammond, Indiana; Michigan City, Indiana; Elkhart, Indiana; Connersville, Indiana; Kokomo, Indiana; South Bend, Indiana; Lake Geneva, Wisconsin; Milwaukee, Wisconsin; Detroit, Michigan; Grand Beach, Michigan; Springfield, Ohio; New York City; Philadelphia, Pennsylvania; and Miami, Florida, on November 1, 1930, and subsequent dates. . . .

The following list includes the names of agents and others who participated in the investigation of this case, together with the designation when assigned to the case and approximate number of months so engaged:

Eliot Ness, Assistant Special Agent in Charge, Chicago, Illinois
    (Now Chief Investigator, Prohibition Dept., Chicago)
    From November 1, 1930, to May 1, 1932...........18
Lyle B. Chapman, Special Agent, Detroit, Michigan
    (Now Special Agent, Chicago)
    From January 1, 1931, to date (Still assigned) 17
Joseph D. Leeson, Prohibition Agent, Detroit, Michigan
    (Now Special Agent, Detroit)
    From February 1, 1931, to May 1, 1932..........15
Paul W. Robsky, Special Agent, Richmond, Virginia
    (Now Special Agent, Jacksonville, Florida)
    From April 1, 1931, to May 1, 1932.............13
LeRoy W. Seney, Prohibition Agent, Detroit, Michigan
    From August 1, 1931, to May 1, 1932............9
Homer A. Goddard, Special Agent, Chicago, Illinois
    From December 1, 1931, to June 1, 1932..........6

Excerpts from the Untouchable Case Report *(continued)*

Samuel M. Seager, Special Agent, Chicago, Illinois
    From November 1, 1930, to April 1, 1931.........5
Marion A. King, Special Agent, Richmond, Virginia
    From April 1, 1931, to July 1, 1931.............3
Warren E. Stutzman, Special Agent, Chicago, Illinois
    From January 1, 1931, to March 1, 1931..........2
Martin J. Lahart, Special Agent, Chicago, Illinois
    Early in 1931......................................½
F. E. Christner, Prohibition Agent, Rochester, New York
    Early in 1931......................................½
Robert D. Sterling, Special Agent, Detroit, Michigan
    Early in 1931......................................½
Bernard V. Cloonan, Special Agent, Chicago, Illinois; Thomas J. Friel,
    Special Agent, Chicago (Now Special Agent, Philadelphia,
    Pennsylvania); Willard G. Malsie, Special Agent, Chicago, Illinois
    (Now Assistant Special Agent in Charge, Chicago); and William J.
    Gardner, Prohibition Agent, Buffalo, New York (Now Los Angeles,
    California) assisted at various times in investigation. . . .
Agents of Intelligence Unit, Chicago, Illinois; Agents of the Committee
    on Prevention and Punishment of Crime, Chicago Association of
    Commerce (Secret Six); and Officers under Chief of Detectives
    William Shoemaker [*sic*] of the Chicago Police Department,
    rendered valuable assistance and ready cooperation. . . .

While it was not the original intention of the group to make
seizures, as they were primarily interested in securing evidence,
it became apparent early in the investigation that probably the best
way to secure evidence was to make large-scale seizures, since this
syndicate was a going organization at the time of the investigation
and a persistent violator. . . .
Observation by agents shows that the system of beer distribution
employed by the Capone Syndicate is as follows: Saloon keepers
and other users would be supplied with beer from a beer drop or
distribution point, where barreled beer from the brewery remained

under ice for several hours. After consumption of the beer, the empty barrels would be picked up by syndicate trucks and brought to a cooperage plant operated by the syndicate, where they would be washed and coopered, if necessary. Trucks collecting these empty containers were always convoyed by at least one car. . . .

These men in their fast small cars would maneuver about the truck over a radius of about six blocks in each direction to make sure that agents were not following. To defeat this system, agents of the special group early devised the plan of "following" the trucks by preceding them, watching the movements of the truck from the rear-view mirror, and thus avoiding entirely the convoy cars. By this plan the location of six breweries was ascertained in 1931 and 1932. . . .

The activities of the various members of the syndicate in all stages of the operations described above were observed on a great number of occasions and accurate notes made, and the evidence thus secured made a part of this case.

In addition to the above operations, the syndicate also maintained a chain of district offices, a telephone switchboard through which by secret passwords members could communicate with other members, a bookkeeper, a messenger service, etc. These district offices collected from saloons in their districts, and rendered weekly reports to the main office, showing income from sales of beer and expenditures including regular payments to certain individuals for protection. Agents apprehended and copied one of these reports and it is available as evidence.

In connection with beer deliveries there is available as evidence a score or more of seized delivery slips, showing lists of saloons and other users to which beer was to be delivered, together with the number of barrels or half barrels of beer they were to get. Each of these slips was marked with a nickname of the particular driver assigned to make this delivery. . . .

As the syndicate failed to bribe the agents working on this case, so they failed in their other plan of safe movement of trucks, namely, the convoy system. Probably seventy-five small cars, mostly Ford ▶

7

Excerpts from the Untouchable Case Report *(continued)*

Coupes because of convenience in handling and their quick "get-away", are incorporated in this case, having been observed many times and ownership and registration investigated. Approximately four hundred certified copies of State of Illinois license applications are in evidence, as well as a large number of City of Chicago license applications. . . . These have been examined by a handwriting expert . . . and identified. . . .

The case gained its impetus by revelations shown by the investigation of two large breweries seized early in 1931. With the addition of four more following these, all connected to the syndicate, the investigation made good headway. . . .

In the files of evidence are photostatic copies of leases for the premises; applications for light and power; telephone and bank accounts. All handwritings have been examined and in a large number of instances are identified as having been written by defendants. . . .

In this connection more than one thousand separate specimens of handwritings have been carded and classified and submitted to the handwriting expert, who has already identified a large part of them and is still pursuing this part of the investigation, aided by the agents. . . .

Also, investigation at the Lincoln State Bank . . . developed the fact that this bank was during the same period the financial headquarters of this syndicate. More than thirty accounts were found under many aliases and fictitious names, most of which have been connected with defendants in this case. Signature cards, ledger sheets, receipts for canceled checks, canceled checks, deposit slips, and cashier's checks were found, and in several instances the actual rent checks for breweries were found and handwriting identified as that of defendants. Also the accounts of the cooperage companies were located in this bank, as well as accounts of two alleged cartage companies operated by defendants [Joe] Fusco and Nick and Frank Juffra to care for and maintain a fleet of syndicate trucks.

Also at this bank, cashier's checks were found from the account of defendant Ralph Capone at another bank deposited in the account of defendant Fusco. . . . Cashier's checks were also found purchased by Fusco and cashed by defendant Jack Guzik in large amounts. . . .

Although discretion was used in the tapping of telephone lines, several important telephones were tapped during this investigation with much success. At one time the syndicate established a central office on the second floor of the Coliseum Garage. Over this telephone defendants Fusco, [Bert] Delaney, [George] Howlett, and others transacted syndicate business for a month or more. Records of all conversations were made and filed with the Association of Commerce [the Secret Six], through whose cooperation this work was carried on by reason of their special equipment and facilities. These are, however, available for evidence and leave no doubt as to the connection of the defendants with the conspiracy, and were the basis of many important clues, leads, and useful information. Other conversations were from time to time overheard over important telephones used by the syndicate with equally valuable results. For instance, on one occasion several conversations were noted between defendants in this case, which indicated that a meeting of the important syndicate members with Alphonse Capone, to discuss ways and means of successfully carrying on the beer business, would be held at the Lexington Hotel on March 21, 1930. Also, in the same manner it was learned that a similar meeting was held on January 5, 1931. . . .

On March 7, 10, and 11, 1931, agents of the group were observing the Shields Cooperage and saw a large truck emerge at different times. This truck was followed to a garage at 4534 Cottage Grove Avenue where in 1930 a large brewery had been seized but which was now being used as a breaking-point. On March 12 this truck was again observed and followed. It was being convoyed by five cars, among which were two driven by defendants Frank Russo and John Miller. These men saw the agents and stopped in an alley, cutting off the agents' car, and then jumped up and confronted the agents, asking, "Who the hell are you guys?" The agents identified themselves and asked the identity of their questioners, who were then not known but later identified. For answer, Russo grabbed Agent Leeson and a physical combat ensued, in which the agents came out well enough to continue to follow the truck. They followed it to a garage at Shields Avenue and ▶

Read on

Excerpts from the Untouchable Case Report *(continued)*

29th Street, where it entered. About this time five cars came up, all with license plates removed, and surrounded the agents. . . . In the excitement the agents left a pistol on the seat of their car and Russo made an attempt to get it, but was restrained by Agent Leeson. By this time all the men . . . had alighted and surrounded the agents. One of them said, "You don't think you can take us all, do you?" The agents replied, "We are willing to try." A murmur went through the crowd as if contemplating an advance on the agents, when defendant Delaney stepped forward, waved his hand at the men, and said, "Cut it out." He then called the agents each by name and said, "Can't we get together? You fellows know whose trucks you are following around. We won't go into that." He then made an appointment to meet the agents at 4534 Cottage Grove Avenue at 11:00 A.M. the same day. The agents entered into this by prearrangement with the United States Attorney and William J. Froelich, Assistant to the Attorney General, who had instructed them to follow any such plan, if suggested by the more prominent syndicate members.

The appointment was kept and Delaney appeared and said, "What is it going to cost us to have you fellows lay off these trucks?" The agents stated that they did not know him and could only deal with someone they knew and who was in authority. Delaney then asked them to mention the names of some they knew with whom they would deal, and the agents mentioned, "Joe", meaning Fusco, to which Delaney said he would have Joe meet them at the same place the next day if they would agree not to make any seizures. This was reported to Mr. Ness and Mr. Froelich, who advised them to keep the appointment. This was done but nobody appeared and the agents proceeded to the garage at 29th and Shields, only to find that the truck was gone and the garage had been emptied. . . .

[T]he special group . . . was dissolved about May 1, 1932. The investigation is still in progress, however, especially with regard to recent events. There are a large number of witnesses to be interviewed, some of whom are expected to add large chapters to this story. Much work is yet to be done on the investigation of trucks which involves new handwritings and will undoubtedly link many unconnected pieces of information with definite defendants in this case. . . .

At present the witnesses in this case would make a list of well over six hundred names and more are continually being added. . . .

[F]or a number of years members of the syndicate enjoyed a large income. However, they have suffered greatly in the last fifteen months on account of attorneys' fees, bonds for arrested members, loss of breweries, trucks, and equipment. A recent report was published that the so-called "Untouchables", a name applied to the special group, had cost the syndicate a half million dollars in six months. While listening on a tapped telephone, an agent overheard Fusco tell that he was $50,000.00 in debt for the month of February, 1932, and was unable to operate his business. While it is not to be assumed that the syndicate is "broke" or that they are not still deriving a large income from beer, it is known that their power and financial affluence have been greatly curtailed and that, where formerly they absolutely controlled every district of Chicago and suburbs, they are now forced to allow rival operators to control certain districts, contenting themselves with a working agreement and nominal control under sort of a truce to keep peace. . . .

It is anticipated that the facts . . . here outlined will be presented to the Federal Grand Jury in the next two or three weeks for reindictment and that trial will be commenced in the Fall term of Court. It is recommended that investigation be continued until that time. Supplemental reports will be made as important developments transpire.

For more from the Untouchables' case report, visit maxallancollins.com and abradschwartz.com ᔐ

Read on

A Sneak Peek at Max Allan Collins and A. Brad Schwartz's Next Book
The Untouchable and the Butcher

For Eliot Ness, Al Capone was only the beginning. In their next book,
The Untouchable and the Butcher, *Max Allan Collins and A. Brad
Schwartz chronicle Ness's thrilling second act—an American tragedy
classic in structure, epic in scope. After becoming the crime-busting civic
savior of Cleveland, Ohio, Ness battled gangsters and racketeers with all
the verve of his Chicago days, only to be faced with a criminal he could
never understand—a monster littering the city with nameless, headless,
and dismembered bodies, taunting his pursuers like a latter-day Jack
the Ripper. The terror sown by this early American serial killer—known
variously as the "Torso Murderer" and the "Mad Butcher of Kingsbury
Run"—gripped the city, overshadowing the remarkable work done by
the youngest public safety director in the nation: Eliot Ness.*

The Untouchable and the Butcher *recounts in newly uncovered
depth and vivid detail the underestimated last great case of the famed
Untouchable, showing how Ness revolutionized the Cleveland Police
Department while laying the groundwork for how serial killing is
investigated to this day. Read an exclusive excerpt below.*

Emil Fronek couldn't remember when exactly he encountered the
doctor.

He was pretty sure it was in the latter part of 1934. In years past,
a strapping stevedore like Fronek could easily have found work in
Cleveland, Ohio, where the bustling lakefront always needed strong
men. But after the Great Depression robbed Fronek of his livelihood,
he fell into the tramp's life, roaming streets and shantytowns, scraping
by as best he could.

Fronek was at the mercy of a city wounded by the stock market crash
and the ensuing economic collapse—Cleveland had ridden high in the
1920s, rising to a level of prosperity it would never see again. Its prime

location on the shores of Lake Erie, between New York and Chicago, helped make it an industrial epicenter. Factories and steel mills—along the banks of the Cuyahoga, the greasy, snaky river slicing its way through the center of the city—thrummed day and night, giant blast furnaces filling the sky with smoke and fire. Workers swarmed in from all over, swelling Cleveland to America's fifth largest city—third, if you included the suburbs. Civic leaders wrote their optimism into the landscape with stone and steel, erecting a series of monumental public buildings along the grassy mall near the lakefront. In 1923, they broke ground for Cleveland's massive train station complex, overseen by the town's first skyscraper. Planned for twenty-five stories, neo-Gothic Terminal Tower rose to fifty-two, its 708 feet perched on a ridge overlooking the Cuyahoga and the industrial valley that spawned it—the tallest building in the world outside New York.

But when this $150 million monument opened in 1930, Cleveland had already begun to slide into despair and decay. One in seven Clevelanders were out of work in April 1930 and, within nine months, the jobless rate had risen to one-third. A legion of unemployed and underemployed sought refuge among factories in "the Flats," the low-lying region near the Cuyahoga. Amid the smokestacks and naked wrought-iron bridges, they built cities of their own—clusters of shanties, cobbled from whatever was at hand, offering poor protection from Cleveland's bitter, brutal winters. Other down-and-outers disappeared into the disease-ridden warren of East Side slums—the "Roaring Third" police precinct, where crime flourished as cops looked the other way.

One evening, Fronek wandered up Broadway, a major thoroughfare cutting through Cleveland's industrial center, in search of a pair of shoes. The working-class neighborhood of mostly Central European immigrants might include a countryman who'd take pity on Fronek's aching feet. But the man who answered his knock at the back door of a two-story house, somewhere between East 50th and East 55th Streets, was neither a fellow immigrant nor of the working class.

This middle-aged, smooth-faced host, with sandy hair going gray ▶

A Sneak Peek at Max Allan Collins and A. Brad Schwartz's Next Book
The Untouchable and the Butcher (continued)

at the temples, had strange, almost colorless eyes, which he trained on Fronek, escorting him upstairs into what seemed to be a doctor's office.

"He said he would give me some shoes," Fronek recalled. "He told me first he would give me something to eat." The apparent doctor stepped into another room and returned soon after with a large steak, French fries, coleslaw, and coffee. Desperately hungry, Fronek didn't stop to question so generous a handout, much less how such a meal had been whipped up. He just dove in, as the doctor watched.

When Fronek grew sick to his stomach, and told his host, the doctor stepped out again, promising to get him some whiskey. But the nausea kept building, and so did dizziness—Fronek knew the food had been drugged!

"All I could see was the door," he recalled, "and I jumped up and ran out. The doctor said: 'Wait a minute, wait a minute, let's have some more to drink.' But I kept going until I found an empty boxcar on some railroad tracks near there and I crawled in and went to sleep."

He came to three days later, after some tramps roused him, thinking he was drunk. When he'd come to his senses, an enraged Fronek set out to settle with the "doctor" who'd poisoned him. But by day, the street looked different, and Fronek couldn't pick out the house he'd wandered into. He cut his losses and jumped a train.

Fronek told his story to another man riding the rails. His listener said he'd "almost got cut up in that house, too."

The fellow traveler told his own tale of meeting the doctor, of being welcomed into his home and given a meal. After that, the man's memory was blank till he woke up in what appeared to be a "private hospital" with slashes in his chest and abdomen. He'd panicked and fled, vaulting over a fence to get away. And then the man displayed the scars on his chest.

Not that Fronek needed convincing—he'd already resolved to give Cleveland a wide berth, where a visit to a certain doctor could kill you.

* * *

Others weren't so lucky.

In August 1934, when Eliot Ness first arrived in Cleveland as an agent of the Alcohol Tax Unit, pieces of a woman's body began littering the Lake Erie shore—first her ribs, then part of her backbone, thirty miles east of town. On September 5, the lower half of her torso, its rotted flesh looking barely human, turned up at Euclid Beach on Cleveland's East Side. The woman's spine had been sliced as if by a butcher knife, her legs severed at the knees with surgical precision. When this discovery made the papers, other reports came in of body parts floating in the lake. One fourteen-year-old girl said she'd stumbled over two legs, five or six weeks earlier. Another claimed a hand waved at her from underwater, four weeks after that. Her father had seen it, too.

"I'm sure it was a human hand," he told the *Cleveland Press*.

But police only ever found the upper arm, not nearly enough to identify the woman's body. Denied a face and a name, she became "the Lady of the Lake."

Cuyahoga County Coroner Arthur J. Pearse placed her at around forty and estimated she had died back in March. She'd been cut up by someone with a fair amount of anatomical knowledge, who expertly separated her spine and unhooked her knees. In removing her right arm, however, the killer had slipped up or gotten careless—sawing it off instead of making a clean slice. This, Pearse believed, ruled out surgeons as potential suspects.

"No surgeon ever would have used a saw," Pearse insisted. "He would have known how to manipulate a knife around the joint."

A chemical preservative appeared to have been applied to the body, reddening and toughening its skin. But why would the killer keep his corpus delicti around, and not get rid of it as soon as possible? Had he slipped up again, mistaking slacked lime, which preserved the corpse, for quicklime, which would've destroyed it? No one could say for sure. ▶

Read on

A Sneak Peek at Max Allan Collins and A. Brad Schwartz's Next Book *The Untouchable and the Butcher* (continued)

Lake Erie's unpredictable currents might have carried the pieces from just about anywhere in Cleveland, or even from as far away as Canada. With no identity to go on, and no solid leads or suspects, police found themselves stymied.

Asked whether this was a perfect crime, the lead detective on the case claimed it was not, but added it was "so close to being perfect that we don't know what to do next." ∼

Discover great authors, exclusive offers, and more at hc.com.

CPSIA information can be obtained
at www.ICGtesting.com
Printed in the USA
LVHW091118230323
742375LV00005B/542

9 780062 441959